Bloomsbury Professional
Tax Guide 2016/17

Bloomsbury Professional Tax Guide 2016/17

The TACS Partnership

Bloomsbury Professional

Bloomsbury Professional Ltd, Maxwelton House, 41–43 Boltro Road, Haywards Heath, West Sussex, RH16 1BJ

© Bloomsbury Professional Ltd 2016

Bloomsbury Professional is an imprint of Bloomsbury Publishing Plc

A CIP Catalogue record for this book is available from the British Library.

ISBN: 978 1 78451 388 7

Typeset by Compuscript Ltd, Shannon

Printed and bound by CPI Group (UK) Ltd, Croydon, CR0 4YY

Preface

The latest edition of the Bloomsbury Professional Tax Guide continues the quest to produce an updated guide to UK taxation that is comprehensive and accessible.

This year has seen momentous changes to the political landscape with a new Prime Minister and a new Chancellor of the Exchequer no doubt wanting to put their own mark on the financial direction of the nation,

Above all the vote to leave the EU promises a background of uncertainty to financial and fiscal issues for the next few years. As in all divorces, the changes that occur are difficult to foresee, particularly when the separation has been announced but the lawyers have yet to battle through who gets what from the split.

Whilst 'Brexit might mean Brexit' how our tax rules will be impacted by the changes to come will be closely monitored over the coming years.

In the interim, we still have the challenge of the ever-changing tax legislation to contend with, as the government battles to square the circle of financing the public services required to preserve a civilised society whilst allowing sufficient funds to remain in the hands of those who drive forward an entrepreneurial economy.

We will be looking with interest at whether the government maintains the stated commitment of its previous leaders to produce a 'low tax' environment supported by a strong enforcement regime that identifies and punishes those who break the rules. It has been a long-held belief of this author that a vigorous anti-avoidance culture is welcome, but only if it is applied consistently and proportionately.

Whether it is the pressure of limited resources available to HMRC, or the existence of a culture of maximising yield by focussing on those who are less able to defend themselves, too often the approach of the tax authorities can seem akin to the playground bully who targets members of the chess club rather than taking on the school rugby team.

There can be a mismatch between policy statements from HMRC and the practical experience of dealing with the taxman 'on the ground'. Perhaps it would be helpful for HMRC to remember the words of Theodore Roosevelt when he said: 'Knowing what's right doesn't mean much unless you do what's right.'

In the book, we provide an overview of all major UK taxes, in one convenient volume, giving sufficient detail to help both the interested taxpayer and the non-tax specialist practitioner understand the complexities of the tax rules and how they are applied.

As in previous years we have adopted a 'practical' approach to explaining the topics covered, identifying, outlining and illustrating the key tax issues that will most often be encountered when dealing with UK taxation. We do not pretend to address the full technical complexities which are expertly covered elsewhere in the specialist Bloomsbury Professional tax publications, but we hope this volume may provide a helpful guide that will allow readers to identify and understand the majority of the tax issues they encounter.

The book is written by the team at The TACS Partnership, an independent tax advisory firm of highly experienced tax professionals with backgrounds in major UK accounting firms and HMRC. A list of the team who have contributed to the book is shown on the following pages, together with some brief biographical details.

We would once again like to thank Gwen Bennett, our office manager for keeping us sane; Mark McLaughlin for his guidance and support in planning the book; Linda Manson at our friends Ellis Chapman & Associates for her invaluable input into the VAT issues covered in this edition; and the team at Bloomsbury Professional for their support throughout the process. We would particularly like to thank Susan Butler and David Reynolds at TACS for their dedication in helping produce the book.

We hope that the book meets our quest to explain often complex matters in a straightforward way, and if any unintended errors have crept into the publication then we can only beg the reader's forgiveness.

We hope you once again find this Tax Guide an informative, readable and accessible source of help in dealing with UK tax issues.

The TACS Partnership
October 2016

Contributors

Stephen Willcox BSc (Hons), FCA, CTA – Stephen has specialised in corporate and capital gains tax planning, company reconstructions, acquisition and disposals. He was a leading tax partner in a major international firm of chartered accountants before becoming one of the founding partners of TACS. He is also an expert witness in litigation matters.

David Blake BSc (Hons), FCA, CTA – David is a specialist in corporation tax, capital gains tax and company reconstructions, as well as inheritance tax and trust issues. David became a partner in the TACS partnership following a career which included a number of years as a senior tax manager with a major international firm.

Ian Roberts BA (Hons) – Ian has extensive experience in both tax investigation and employment taxation issues, as well as being a share scheme specialist. A former Inspector of Taxes, Ian has worked in practice for many years. He was NW head of employment tax at a major accountancy firm before joining TACS and becoming a partner.

Susan Butler BSc (Hons), FCA, CTA – Susan is a corporation and capital gains tax specialist with significant experience in corporate reconstructions and share valuations. She was a senior manager with a major international accountancy practice before joining TACS.

James Darmon BA, ACA – James is a specialist in capital gains tax and property taxation with specialist knowledge of the capital allowance regime. With over 25 years' tax experience, James spent nine years as a tax advisor with a well-known property company, and also spent ten years as a senior tax manager with Group A firms before joining TACS.

Alix Hill CTA, ATT – Alix had many years' experience in a commercial environment developing a particular expertise in computerised accounts systems before joining TACS. She specialises in personal tax issues for both employees and the self-employed and has great experience of PAYE and NIC law and practice.

Anne Schilizzi BA (Hons), ACA, CTA – Anne qualified with an international accounting firm and spent several years working on a mixed tax portfolio as a tax manager before joining TACS. She has expertise in both personal and corporate tax and has experience of high level tax investigation support work.

Steve Taylor MEng, ACA, CTA – Steve specialises in corporate tax issues and has experience in implementing employee share schemes. Steve trained with a 'Big Four' accountancy firm before spending five years with a major financial institution as a manager in their in-house tax team before joining TACS.

David Reynolds, FCA, CTA – David specialises in corporate tax and capital gains tax with a wealth of experience in advising owner managed businesses. He has significant experience advising on corporate transactions and reconstructions. Prior to joining TACS, David worked both within major international accountancy firms (including time in tax technical specialist roles) and also for a large independent professional practice.

Contents

Contents

Contents

Contents

Part 5 Trusts and Estates

Contents

Contents

Contents

Table of Statutes

All references are to paragraph number

Table of Statutory Instruments

All references are to paragraph number

Table of Cases

All references are to paragraph number

Table of Examples

Table of Examples

Table of Examples

Part 1
Income Tax

1

Income tax – outline

SIGNPOSTS

- **Scope** – Individuals, trustees and personal representatives of a deceased individual are liable to income tax on taxable income which is worldwide income for a UK resident, subject to certain income which is exempt (see **1.1–1.5**).

- **Notifying HMRC** – Liability to income tax is reportable to HMRC by 5 October following the end of the tax year in which the income (or gain) arose (see **1.6–1.9**).

- **Filing deadlines** – Tax Returns must be filed by 31 October, if on paper, and by 31 January, if in electronic form, following the end of the tax year to avoid penalties (see **1.10–1.12**).

- **How tax is charged** – Tax is charged on taxable income at progressive rates of tax (see **1.13–1.18**).

- **Payment deadlines** – Tax due under self-assessment is primarily paid by 31 January following the end of the tax year; the self-employed may have to make payments on account (see **1.19–1.22**).

- **Collection of tax** – Most tax is collected at source, through the PAYE system. Tax due under self-assessment and student loan repayments may also be collected through PAYE (see **1.23–1.24**).

- **Tax refunds** – If tax has been overpaid, there are procedures in place to obtain a refund, depending on whether the person files returns under the self-assessment system or not and whether the claim relates to the current and previous tax year or earlier years (see **1.29–1.34**).

- **Record keeping** – All persons have a legal obligation to keep records relating to their tax liabilities for the required length of time (see **1.35–1.37**).

- **Appendix: Key tax dates** – A summary of key tax dates is included at the end of this chapter (see **1.38**).

INTRODUCTION

Who is liable?

1.1   The following are liable to income tax:

- individuals;
- trustees; and
- personal representatives of deceased individuals.

'Individuals' includes a child under the age of 18, although it will be the parents or guardian who will be obliged to give notice of the chargeability to HMRC and who may be held responsible for any tax chargeable.

Income received by a child that derives from capital given by the parents may be treated as the parent's income if the total income arising from such sources is more than £100 per parent in any one tax year (*ITTOIA 2005, s 629(3)*; *R v Newmarket Income Tax Commrs, ex parte Huxley* CA 1916, 7 TC 49). The exception to this rule is that parents can fund a Junior ISA for their children and such income which would normally fall to be assessed on them will be exempt (*ITTOIA 2005, s 694(1A)*). The child must not have received a Child Trust Fund Account and be UK resident in order to qualify (*Individual Savings Accounts Regulations 2011, SI 2011/1780*).

Companies, although they generally pay corporation tax on their profits and gains (see **Chapter 17**), may find income tax has been deducted at source, for example on investment income, and may have to account for income tax on certain payments.

What is chargeable?

1.2   Broadly speaking, income tax is charged on the worldwide income of UK residents although there are certain exceptions to this rule for individuals who are not domiciled in the UK (see **Chapter 56**). Where income is taxed twice, in the country where it arose and also in the UK, there is generally relief available under double taxation agreements (see **Chapter 58**).

The tax chargeable is based on the income arising in a tax year.

Focus

A tax year runs from 6 April to 5 April the following year. Thus the tax year for 2016/17 is from 6 April 2016 to 5 April 2017.

Exempt income

1.3   Certain income is specifically exempt from income tax and includes:

- compensation for loss of office (up to £30,000) (see **Chapter 2**, termination payments);

- income from certain investments (see **Chapter 7**), such as ISAs (Individual Savings Accounts);

- premium bond prizes;

- casual winnings from betting and competitions;

- certain social security payments eg income support and attendance allowance (but others are taxable such as jobseeker's allowance);

- damages and compensation for personal injury, including any interest thereon;

- scholarship income paid to a person in full-time education (*ITTOIA 2205, s 776* and see *SP 4/86*);

- certain types of pensions (such as wound and disability pensions paid to members of the armed forces);

- benefits payable under certain sickness and unemployment policies (but if sickness premiums have been claimed against business income, then the benefits would be taxable);

- housing grants.

ITTOIA 2005, Part 6, ss 690–783 contain the provisions for most of these types of income.

Capital receipts, as opposed to revenue receipts, are not chargeable to income tax but fall within the capital gains tax regime. However, there are occasions when what appears to be capital may be treated as income for tax purposes.

What are the charging provisions?

1.4   The major statutes which govern income tax law are:

- the *Income and Corporation Taxes Act 1988* (*ICTA 1988*);

- the *Income Tax (Earnings and Pensions Act) 2003* (*ITEPA 2003*);

- the *Income Tax (Trading and Other Income) 2005* (*ITTOIA 2005*); and

- the *Income Tax Act 2007* (*ITA 2007*).

Much of the legislation within *ICTA 1988* has been re–written as part of the Tax Law Re–write Project and the income tax provisions included in the other acts listed above.

Finance Acts are enacted every year (usually in July) and are the legislative machinery for imposing income tax. Amendments are also made to the existing statutes by way of the *Finance Acts*.

The *Taxes Management Act 1970* (*TMA 1970*) provides the legal framework for regulating HMRC in their administration of the tax system.

Information on the HMRC website

1.5   In considering how the law is applied by HMRC it can be helpful to look at the HMRC Manuals, which are available on their website (see www.gov.uk/government/collections/hmrc-manuals). The list of manuals is extensive and includes:

- Self-Assessment;
- Employment Income;
- Business Income;
- Capital Allowances;
- Savings and Investments;
- Property Income.

The HMRC website also lists help sheets available, providing further information on specific topics.

A further resource on the HMRC website is the provision of 'toolkits'. These information guides are aimed at tax agents and advisers. They highlight the most common errors made on returns, suggest ways of mitigating those errors, as well as outlining the tax treatment, and include cross-references to other guidance notes on the HMRC website. There are currently 20 toolkits available covering a variety of topics, ranging from directors' loan accounts and employment benefits and expenses to business profits and inheritance tax (see www.gov.uk/government/collections/tax-agents-toolkits).

NOTIFYING HMRC

Who needs to notify?

1.6   It is the legal responsibility of all individuals to notify HMRC of any chargeability to income (or capital gains) tax, If the individual is already registered for self-assessment, then the income (or gains) must be reported in their personal tax return which is filed annually. The tax return is the form issued by HMRC on which an individual records all income and gains received in the tax year. Not all individuals will be required to complete a tax return (see exceptions below) but if HMRC have issued a notice to make a return, then the individual is legally obliged to do so. it is important for an individual who has not received a notice to file a return to advise HMRC of any chargeability to tax.

If an individual does not currently file tax returns and needs to report a new source of income (or gains) or there is now tax arising on income received due to a change in the tax legislation, then they will need to notify HMRC so the tax can be collected. Depending on the nature and amount of the income and the circumstances of the individual concerned, this will be done either:

- by registering for self-assessment and filing a tax return or

- by contacting HMRC and reporting the income by phone, by post or online;

The HMRC website gives detailed guidance on how to report taxable income or gains. It lists the occasions when an individual is required to register for self-assessment and file a return and provides a tool "check if you need a tax return" which gives instructions as to how to notify HMRC in the situations when a tax return is not required but tax is still payable (see www.gov.uk/self-assessment-tax-returns/who-must-send-a-tax-return). The cases when a taxpayer must register for self-assessment include:

- receipt of untaxed income in excess of £2,500 (such as rental or savings income);

- receipt of savings or investment income in excess of £10,000 before tax;

- receipt of child benefit and the individual's income (or the individual's partner's income) in excess of £50,000. (See **Chapter 6** for more details);

- receipt of dividends from shares and the individual is a higher or additional rate taxpayer;

- a profit is made on the sale of shares or other assets (such as a second home) and capital gains tax is due (see **Chapter 12**);

- income over £100,000

- you are a company director.

Where there is chargeable income but it is below the limits stipulated above, HMRC can be notified to arrange for the tax to be collected either by phoning 0300 200 3300, by post or by asking for the PAYE code to be amended by submitting the online 2016–17 PAYE Coding Notice Query form; for example, where any taxpayer receives dividend income over £5.000 (the dividend allowance) as dividends no longer carry a tax credit from 6 April 2016.

Focus

If you have savings or dividend income, you may be liable to pay tax if the amounts exceed the personal savings and dividend allowances. Since 6 April 2016 most savings income is paid gross and dividends no longer carry a tax credit.

Exceptions

1.7 Generally speaking, an individual will not need to notify HMRC if his pension or employment income is already taxed under the PAYE system, his dividend income is £5,000 or less and his savings income is less than the personal savings allowance (£1,000 for basic rate taxpayers and £500 for higher rate taxpayers, see **7.4**). (*TMA 1970, s 7(3)–(7)*)

Time limits

1.8 The time limit for notification is by 5 October following the end of the tax year in which the income (or gains) arose (*TMA 1970, s 7(1)*).

Example 1.1 – Notifying HMRC

An individual who received rent from letting out a property between May and December 2016 would need to notify HMRC by 5 October 2017.

Failure to notify HMRC by the deadline stipulated will result in a penalty (see **Part 9**).

How to notify

1.9 It is necessary to register for self-assessment with HMRC in order to obtain a Unique Tax Reference number (UTR). To register online, the link is www.gov.uk/register-for-self-assessment. It is important to allow enough time to complete the registration process so that the 31 January deadline for submitting the return can be met.

There are two different options to follow online depending on whether the taxpayer is self-employed or not. The registration process takes 10 working days for the self-employed and 20 working days for other individuals.

Even if the taxpayer would prefer to file a paper return, it is still necessary to register online.

Focus

An individual must notify HMRC of any chargeability to tax for new sources of income by 5 October following the end of the tax year in which it arises (unless he has already received a notice to complete a tax return for that year).

FILING TAX RETURNS

Tax returns

1.10   The tax return (SA100) consists of a six-page core return plus supplementary pages which are used to report other types of income and gains such as income from employment, self-employment, partnerships, property, overseas, trusts and estates and additional information pages (SA101) for less common types of income, deductions and tax reliefs. There is a supplementary page for capital gains and for non-residence.

These supplementary pages can be downloaded from the HMRC website or can be obtained upon request from HMRC. Alternatively, if the return is filed online using the HMRC online return service, most of the pages are accessible, but not all of them. It is therefore recommended to check well before the filing date for paper returns, which is 31 October (see time limits below, **1.11**) to see if any additional supplementary pages are needed that are not provided online. If this is the case, the taxpayer can then decide whether to file the return on paper or to obtain the appropriate tax software, either directly or through an accountant, and file online. HMRC have issued a list of 'Self-Assessment Individual Exclusions for online filing – 2015/16' which contains very specific occasions when it is not possible to file online and which provide a reasonable excuse, allowing for a paper return to be submitted by the later deadline of 31 January.

The return is issued with guidance notes (SA150) on how to complete the basic return. Further guidance notes can be obtained from HMRC (on paper or online) on how to complete the supplementary pages. There is also an HMRC Helpline to provide further assistance.

If the individual's affairs are fairly straightforward, a short tax return may be issued (SA200) which currently consists of four pages.

What are the deadlines for filing tax returns?

1.11   An individual who has received a notice from HMRC to complete a personal tax return must do so by the statutory deadlines in order to avoid penalties (*TMA 1970, s 8*). The dates for submission depend on whether the return is filed in paper form or electronically.

- Paper returns need to be filed on or before 31 October following the year of assessment.

- Electronic returns need to be filed on or before 31 January following the year of assessment.

There are times when a later filing date may be applied, for example if the HMRC notice to make a return is issued after 31 July, then there is less than three months for a taxpayer to meet the paper return deadline and the deadline becomes three months from the date of the notice. Similar rules apply for notices issued after 31 October whereby the online filing date is correspondingly extended.

The penalty for late filing is £100 and there are additional penalties, on an escalating scale, if the return is still not returned within three months of the deadline or more (see **Chapter 53**.)

Focus

Tax returns must generally be submitted by 31 October following the end of the tax year if filed on paper and by the following 31 January next if filed online in order to avoid penalties.

Launch of digital tax accounts

1.12   In March 2015, HMRC announced plans to introduce secure digital 'personal tax accounts' for UK taxpayers, which is part of the "Making Tax Digital" (MTD) project. By the time the project is completed, which is estimated to be in 2020, the requirement to file self-assessment tax returns will be removed for virtually all individuals and small businesses. Other significant changes to the administration of the taxes systems are also envisaged.

On 16 December 2015, HMRC issued a further document (www.gov.uk/government/publications/making-tax-digital), which included a timetable rolling out the various stages between then and 2020. The full consultation process was delayed due to the EU referendum, with a raft of consultation documents being issued in August 2016. At the time of writing, the closing date for these consultations has just passed and HMRC is still to publish the documents summarising the responses.

The key elements to the digital tax accounts are:

1. The accounts are pre-populated with information HMRC already hold, such as employment and pension income, bank and building society interest received. HMRC are going to consult on where it might obtain information directly from third parties.

2. They bring together in one place all information that is relevant for an individual's personal tax affairs, their liabilities and entitlements. They will be able to see and understand their tax liability.

3. A taxpayer will be able to register, file, pay and update tax information at any time.

4. Businesses will be required to file quarterly returns, so reporting their income in 'real time'. They will be obliged to keep their records using digital tools. This applies to the self-employed and landlords when it is their main source of income (for those in receipt of employment or pension income this requirement only applies if their secondary source of income is more than £10,000). The timetable proposed is:

    a. By April 2018, all non-VAT registered businesses will be required to file online quarterly returns.

    b. By April 2020, all businesses will be required to file online quarterly returns.

5. Pay as you go tax payments will be an option for businesses filing quarterly returns, enabling them to choose payment patterns that suit them and better manage their cash flow. Instead of making a number of tax payments across different taxes, they will be able to make one. The government will consult in 2016 on how best to implement a pay-as-you-go system, as well as on simplifying the payment of tax and whether to align the payment dates.

6. Agents will be able to have access to their client's tax accounts and manage them if they so wish.

HMRC's intention to complete this project by 2020 is considered by some to be rather ambitious, particularly given the complexity of the tax legislation and the need to link the new system with agent authorisation. Concerns have been expressed that a large number of small businesses do not use digital software and so the quarterly reporting obligation will be a major challenge, both in terms of time and costs.

Personal Tax accounts

1.13   In 2016, personal tax accounts were implemented with 5 million individuals registered and over 2 million small businesses using them by June 2016. On 17 June 2016, HMRC's updated website showed that:

"You can use your personal tax account to:

- check your Income Tax estimate and tax code

- fill in, send and view a personal tax return

- claim a tax refund

- check and manage your tax credits

- check your State Pension

- track tax forms that you've submitted online

- check or update your Marriage Allowance

- tell HMRC about a change of address

- check or update benefits you get from work, eg company car details and medical insurance

More services will be added in the future".

Focus

Registering to access a personal tax account is very simple and provides useful information for taxpayers. Individuals are advised to keep their accountants informed of changes to their details as access for agents has not yet been provided. Small businesses in particular should take care to keep abreast of changes as they may need to consider investing in digital accounting well before the proposed deadlines for compulsory quarterly returns.

HOW IS THE TAX CHARGE CALCULATED?

Computing taxable income

1.14   The income tax charge is levied on an individual's taxable income that is allocated to a tax year. The tax year runs from 6 April to 5 April the following year.

The computation of taxable income broadly involves the following steps:

- taxable amounts from all sources of income are added together to give total income;

- various reliefs (such as trade losses and interest payments) may then be claimed to arrive at 'net income' (see **Chapters 3** and **9**);

- the personal allowance (including blind person's allowance if applicable) is deducted (see **Chapter 9**) to give the amount chargeable to income tax.

Taxable income falls under the following headings and is dealt with in separate chapters:

- income from employment, including pensions;

- income from self-employment;

- savings and investment income, including UK interest and dividends;

- foreign income;

- property income;

- miscellaneous income.

Certain income is exempt (see **1.3** above).

Rates of tax

1.15   The annual *Finance Act* imposes the charge to income tax and sets the main income tax rates (the basic rate, the higher rate and the additional rate.) The *Finance (No 2) Act 2015* set the final rates for 2016/17 and the *Finance Act 2016* set the rates for 2017/18 by amendment to the two earlier *Finance Acts of 2015*.

Rates of tax applicable (excluding special rates for dividend income)

	2014/15	2015/16	2016/17
	£	£	£
Starting rate for savings: 10% to 14/15 then 0% from 15/16	0 – 2,880	0 – 5,000	0 – 5,000
Basic rate: 20%	0 – 31,865	0 – 31,785	0 – 32,000
Higher rate: 40%	31,866 – 150,000	31,786 – 150,000	32,001 – 150,000
Additional rate: 45%	>150,000	>150,000	>150,000
Savings nil rate on PSA:	–	–	

for basic rate **taxpayers**	–	–	0–1,000
For higher rate **taxpayers**	–	–	0–500
For Additional rate **taxpayers**	–	–	N/A

*   The 10%/0% starting rate applies to savings only and only when non-savings income is less than the limit. See **1.18** for more details and **Example 1.3** below for how it is applied in practice.

The basic rate band for 2017/18 is £33,500 with the higher rate limit of £150,000 and the tax rates remaining unchanged from previous years. The personal allowance is £11,000 in 2016/17 and £11,500 in 2017/18.

Rates of tax on dividend income

1.16   Dividend income is taxed at its own special rates. Dividend income falls to be taxed as the highest slice of income.

Finance Act 2016 introduced significant changes to the taxation of dividends, which took effect from 6 April 2016. Dividends no longer carry a tax credit (*ITTOIA 2005 ss 382–393* as amended by *Finance Act 2016, Schedule 1*). Taxpayers are entitled to a dividend allowance of £5,000, which applies a 0% tax rate to the first £5,000 of dividend income (see **7.8** for an example of how this works in practice). The dividend tax rates have been amended as follows (*ITA 2007, s 8* amended by *Finance Act 2016, s 5(3)*):

- **7.5%** (previously 10% on gross dividends with a 10% tax credit) to be applied to the basic rate band (known as the ordinary rate);

- **32.5%** (previously 32.5% on gross dividends with a 10% tax credit) to be applied to the higher rate band (dividend upper rate);

- **38.1%** (previously 37.5% on gross dividends with a 10% tax credit) to be applied to the additional rate band (dividend additional rate).

See **Chapter 7** for more details of the effect of the recent changes

Computing the tax liability

1.17   *The Income Tax Act 2007, Parts 2–8*, give detailed provisions setting out how a person's income tax liability is calculated (*Part 2*), the allowances and tax reductions available (*Part 3*) and various reliefs available (*Parts 4–8*).

The calculation of the income tax liability for a tax year is broadly based upon the following steps (*ITA 2007, s 23*):

1   Total all taxable income (from all sources, including all taxable benefits and excluding all allowable deductions specific to that income).

To arrive at total income

2   Deduct any available reliefs (*ITA 2007, s 24* gives a full list of the potential deductions at this stage).

To arrive at net income

3   Deduct personal allowances

At Steps 2 and 3, *ITA 2007, s 25* provides for the reliefs and allowances to be deducted in the way that will give the greatest reduction in computing the income tax liability.

To arrive at taxable income

4   Allocate the income to the tax bands and then apply the appropriate tax rates (*ITA 2007, Ch 2*).

    (a)   Income and gains are allocated to the bands by treating the top slice of income in the following order:

- gains;
- life insurance policy gains;
- lump sum termination payments from employment;
- dividends;
- other savings income;
- all other income and profits.

    (b)   If gift aid donations have been made (*ITA, s 414(2)*) or pension contributions paid out of taxed income (*FA 2004, s 192(4)*) then the basic rate band (and higher rate band) is extended by the gross payments.

    (c)   'Top–slicing relief' may be available if income has been received from an investment bond whereby the income has been built up over a number of years and if it were to be taxed all in one year would be taxed at the higher rates. Note that such receipts, although described as gains, are subject to income tax.

5   Add together all tax liabilities for each band.

6   Deduct any eligible allowances or reliefs given as a tax reduction (*ITA 2007, s 26*) such as Enterprise Investment Scheme relief or married

couples allowance. These are deducted in the order which gives the maximum reduction in the income tax liability (*ITA 2007, s 27(2)*).

7   Where relevant, add any other additional tax liabilities that may be payable (*ITA 2007, s 30*) such as tax payable under the gift aid rules if the tax liability as calculated above is insufficient to meet the tax treated as deducted at source from the donation (*ITA 2007, s 424*) or tax payable under the pension payment provisions if an annual allowance charge is due (*FA 2004, s 227*).

To arrive at the income tax liability for the year

Arriving at total tax due to HMRC

1.18   Once the income tax liability has been calculated, this must be matched against any tax already paid over to HMRC for this tax year. The steps to be taken in arriving at the net amount payable are:

1   Deduct amounts already settled, being:

(a)   any notional tax charged (such as on life insurance policy bonds);

(b)   tax credits on dividends (only up to 5 April 2016);

(c)   all tax payments made, including:

- PAYE (note that an adjustment may need to be made to exclude from the amount of tax paid under PAYE any amount that has been collected for an underpayment from a previous tax year),

- tax deducted from savings income (although this will be less common from 6 April 2016),

- foreign tax paid that is eligible for relief.

2   Deduct any payments made on account.

This gives the outstanding tax liability to be paid over to HMRC.

Example 1.2 – Tax calculation

In the tax year 2016/17, Florence, is employed and receives a salary of £70,000 plus employment benefits of £2,500. She pays net pension contributions of £2,200 a year out of taxed income on which the pension fund managers claim the basic rate tax. She also lets out a property and receives a rental income of £6,800 and incurs allowable expenses of £900, giving a net profit of £5,900. She has two building society accounts on which she receives interest of £400. She also owns shares and receives dividends of £6,800.

	£	£	£
Income:			
Employment		72,500	
Property		5,900	
Other income:			
UK interest		400	
Dividends		6,800	
Total income		85,600	
Less personal allowance		(11,000)	
Taxable income		74,600	
Income tax due			
On non-savings income:	£34,750 at 20%		6,950
	£32,650 at 40%		13,060
UK interest	£400 at 0%		-
UK dividends	£5,000 at 0%		-
	£1,800 at 32.5%		585
	Income tax liability		20,595
	PAYE (as shown on the P60)		(18,200)
	Florence's total tax due		**2,395**

Points to note

1   The basic rate band for 2016/17 is 0–£32,000. It has been extended by the pension contributions paid, grossed up by the basic rate tax, giving an additional allocation of £2,750.

2   Florence has a Personal Savings Allowance of £500 as her income is taxed at the higher rate. So no tax is payable on the £400 savings income as the rate is 0%.

3   The way the tax due of £2,395 has arisen is:

(a)	Property income received gross is taxed at 40%	2,360
(b)	Higher dividend upper rate of 32.5% on £1,800 (being excess over dividend allowance of £5,000)	585
		2,945

Less:

(d)   Overpayment of tax on employment income
        (suggests no relief given for higher rate relief on
        pension contributions)

$$\underline{(550)}$$
$$\underline{\underline{2,395}}$$

4   PAYE deducted:

(a)   The P60 (a copy of which is provided to all
        employees by the employer) shows the total PAYE
        deducted and also the tax code applied.

(b)   The P11D records the taxable benefits, a copy of
        which is also provided to all employees.

(c)   As there is no further tax due on the benefits,
        this suggests that the coding notice had correctly
        estimated the benefits for the year. The taxpayer
        may have informed HMRC of the actual estimated
        benefits, such as health insurance.

(d)   As no relief appears to have been given on the
        pension contributions, this suggests that they had not
        been included in the Coding Notice. The taxpayer
        could contact HMRC to ask for the higher rate relief
        to be included for the current tax year, though this may
        be done following receipt of the tax return in
        any event.

4   Methods of payment of tax due:

(a)   The tax would normally be due for payment by
        31 January 2018.

(b)   As the tax due is less than £3,000, it will be
        collected by adjusting the PAYE Code to be applied
        in 2018/19, provided that the tax return for 2016/17
        is filed by 31 December and the taxpayer does not
        elect to pay the liability directly.

Chapter 9 provides further information on personal allowances, including
their withdrawal for taxpayers whose income exceeds £100,000 and the
mechanism for reducing age-related allowances. **Chapter 9** also deals with
relief for qualifying interest and charitable donations.

Effect of the starting rate of tax for savings

1.19 Since 6 April 2015, the starting rate of tax applicable to savings reduced from 10% to 0% and the maximum amount of taxable savings income that can be eligible for this starting rate increased to £5,000. Together with the introduction of the personal savings allowance from 6 April 2016 (see **7.4**) this means that an individual whose total taxable income is £17,000 or less, will not pay tax on their savings income.

The starting rate only applies to savings and it only applies if the individual's non-savings income does not exceed the limit. Thus, an individual whose taxable income comprises a pension of £25,000 and savings income of £4,500 would not be eligible as his non-savings income (after deducting the personal allowance of £11,000 in 2016/17) is £14,000 and this is more than the limit of £5,000.

Non-savings income includes state and other pensions, employment income and taxable benefits, property income and profits from a trade.

Savings income includes interest from a bank or building society account or other providers, interest distributions from authorised unit trusts and open-ended investment companies, gains from certain contracts for life insurance and most purchased life annuity payments.

Example 1.3 – Tax calculation illustrating the starting rate for savings

In the tax year 2016/17, Frederick is 79 and receives a state pension of £8,094. He also receives net savings income from a purchased life annuity of £8,500. His personal allowance is £11,000.

His non-savings income is £8,094 which is all covered by his personal allowance. This leaves £2,906 of his personal allowance to be offset against his savings income of £8,500; giving taxable income of £5,594 which is all savings income. The first £5,000 is taxed at the starting rate for savings at 0%. With the introduction of the Personal Savings Allowance (PSA), as none of his income is taxable at the higher rate, he is entitled to the £1,000 allowance taxable at the nil savings rate and so the balance of £594 is taxed at the savings nil rate of 0%. (Note that if his savings income were to exceed the £5,000 limit and his personal savings allowance, then the excess would be taxed at the basic rate of 20%, assuming his taxable income did not exceed the basic rate band of £32,000).

So Frederick has no tax liability for 2016/17.

Note that an individual's income sources are taxed in the following order: non-savings income, savings income and dividend income. See **7.4** for further details on savings income and its taxation.

PAYING TAX

How is tax collected?

1.20 Most income tax is collected and paid over to HMRC not by the taxpayer directly but by a third party, such as the employer or pension provider. Before 5 April 2016, banks or building societies deducted basic rate tax from interest paid but it is now paid gross in most cases. If the taxpayer is in receipt of income not already taxed which was previously received net of basic rate tax (such as dividends and savings pre-April 2016) or their taxable income was liable to be taxed at the higher rates of tax, then the tax will need to be paid over directly to HMRC through self-assessment.

- *Employment and pensions income*:

  For the majority of taxpayers who are in receipt of employment income or occupational and personal pensions, the tax payable on this income is deducted from the salary or pension payment by the employer or pension provider and is paid over directly to HMRC. This is done through the Pay As You Earn (PAYE) system (see **Chapter 2**).

- *Savings income*:

  o The tax due on most savings income, such as bank interest, was deducted at source at the basic rate until April 2016 but it is now paid gross in most circumstances. Thus a taxpayer whose total taxable income in 2015/16 and prior years is all charged at the basic rate would not need to report this savings income or be liable for further tax. From April 2016, all taxpayers will need to consider whether their savings income is covered by the personal savings allowance – see **Chapter 7** for more details.

  o Income from non-qualifying life insurance investments is taxable; the income is treated as having suffered basic rate tax so an additional tax liability only arises if the recipient is a higher rate taxpayer.

- *Dividend income:*

  For the tax years 2015/16 and prior, a shareholder whose total taxable income does not exceed the basic rate and who receives UK dividends (and other distributions) paid by companies has no additional tax to pay. This is because the dividend carried a tax credit of 1/9 of the amount distributed (being 10% of the gross payment).

For 2016/17 onwards, dividend income no longer carries a tax credit (*Finance Act 2016, Schedule 1 amends ITTOIA 2005, chapters 3 & 4*)). **Chapter 7** explains the changes made to the taxation of dividends, including the new dividend allowance of £5,000 on which the rate of tax is 0%.

- *All other income including business and property income*:

  Tax is paid over directly by the taxpayer to HMRC for tax liabilities arising from all other income. This is collected through self-assessment.

  If the taxpayer has the majority of income taxed through PAYE as well as other income taxed by direct assessment, it is possible that the tax on the other income (which includes rental and savings income but not business income) is being collected by an adjustment to the coding notice. This means that the tax will be paid over as a deduction from the salary or pension payments. If the taxpayer prefers to make direct payments to HMRC in line with the normal self-assessment payment dates, then a request can be made to remove these adjustments from the coding notice by contacting HMRC. The taxpayer also has the facility to indicate in box 3 of page 6 of his tax return that he does not want his PAYE code to include adjustments to collect tax on other income.

- *Collecting debts*

  From April 2015, HMRC have the power to collect debts of less than £17,000 from taxpayers who are in PAYE employment or receive a UK-based pension by adjustment to their PAYE code issued at the start of the tax year. There is a graduated scale linked to PAYE earnings so that the maximum of £17,000 only applies for earnings over £90,000 and the previous maximum amount that could be coded out of £3,000 still applies if earnings are £30,000 or less. The taxpayer's consent is not required. This applies to both tax debts and tax credit overpayments. The taxpayer will have already have been given a final chance to pay the debts in full or to contact HMRC to discuss other payment options before the tax code adjustment is made. The usual safeguards on the amount of tax that can be collected through PAYE still apply – see **1.24** below.

Self-assessment – when is the tax paid?

1.21   On receipt of the tax return, the tax liability (including any NIC Class 4 liability) for the tax year is calculated and must normally be paid over by 31 January following the end of the tax year in question. In other words, the tax due for the year 2016/17 must be paid by 31 January 2018.

Focus

Any outstanding tax liability must be paid over in full by 31 January following the end of the tax year in order to avoid interest and penalties. It may be possible for the liability to be collected through PAYE if certain criteria are met.

For those taxpayers for whom most of their income is received before any tax is deducted, such as the self-employed, payments on account will also have to be made.

Payments on account

1.22   Payments on account of income tax are payable in two equal instalments:

- The first payment on account is due by 31 January in the tax year.

- The second payment on account is due by 31 July following the end of the tax year.

The criteria for payments on account being due are based on the tax liability that was outstanding at the end of the previous tax year. The tax outstanding is the amount of tax that needs to be paid over directly to HMRC. This figure is arrived at by taking the total tax charge for the year and deducting the tax that has already been paid at source.

- If the outstanding tax liability is less than £1,000 there is no requirement to make payments on account.

- If the outstanding tax liability is more than £1,000 but less than 20% of the total tax charge for the year then there is no requirement to make payments on account.

- If the outstanding tax liability is more than £1,000 and is 20% or more of the total tax charge for that year, then payments on account need to be made.

The amount of each payment on account is half of the outstanding tax liability for the previous tax year (*TMA 1970, s 59A*).

Example 1.4 – Payments on account

In 2016/17, Joel trades online and anticipates a net profit from his e-trading business of £40,000 for the year ending 5 April 2017. He also has a part-time job and receives a salary of £13,000 on which PAYE of £400 is being deducted.

His taxable income for the year was £42,000, after deducting the single personal allowance. His total income tax liability was £10,400, of which £400 was paid at source. His Class 4 NIC liability was £2,874. This gives a total tax and NIC charge of £13,274, leaving an amount outstanding of £12,874.

As the liability is £12,874, which is more than 20% of the total charge of £13,274, payments on account (POA) for 2017/18 will need to be made as follows:

> By 31 January 2018: First payment on account of £6,437.

> By 31 July 2018: Second payment on account of £6,437.

This means that the total payment that will need to be made by 31 January 2018 will be £19,311 in total (the balancing payment for 2016/17 of £12,874 and the first POA of £6,437).

Claim to reduce payments on account

1.23   A claim can be made to reduce the payments on account at any time up to 31 January following the end of the tax year. This can be done at the time the tax return is submitted, as part of the return or by contacting HMRC directly. If the taxpayer is registered to use self-assessment online, the request to reduce can be done online by logging into the service and choosing 'Customer Services' or if not, the taxpayer can complete Form SA303 either online or by post.

It is necessary to provide a valid reason why the claim is being made, such as reduced business activity or further reliefs being available. It should be noted that if the final payments due on account are more than the reduced amounts, interest will be chargeable. In order to cancel a claim to reduce and reinstate the tax payable on account, it is necessary to contact HMRC directly as there is no facility on the government website to do this online. Penalties will be incurred if false information is provided when the claim to reduce is made.

When can the tax be collected through PAYE income?

1.24   For those taxpayers who are in receipt of employment or pension income that is taxed through PAYE and also have other income, the tax outstanding may be collected by adjustments to their notice of coding. In this way, the tax is collected by deduction from the salary or pension payments. There are restrictions on the amount of tax that can be collected in this way:

- If the amount of tax outstanding exceeds the maximum of £2,999.99 then it will need to be paid over directly to HMRC.

- The amount of gross income that the taxpayer receives on which PAYE is deducted must be sufficient to cover the tax liability. Moreover, the tax being collected through the PAYE system can never exceed 50% of the pay or pension. Nor can the tax being deducted be twice the usual monthly deduction before the adjustment for the underpayment was made.

HMRC will automatically try and collect the tax due through the coding notice unless the taxpayer has specifically put an X in the box on his tax return asking them not to do so. The return must be submitted by 31 October if a paper return or by 31 December if online if the taxpayer wishes to have the tax collected in this way so that HMRC have time to amend the coding notice for the following tax year.

For more information see the government website (www.gov.uk/pay-self-assessment-tax-bill/through-your-tax-code).

> **Focus**
>
> If the amount of tax outstanding is £3,000 or more, then it must be paid over directly to HMRC.

Student loan repayments

1.25   Although it is the Student Loan Company that provides loans to students in higher education, it is HMRC who collects the payments. Thus, although student loan repayments are not a tax, they do fall within the tax system as these loans are income-contingent repayment loans; the repayments depend upon the income of the borrower.

- From 6 April 2016, the income threshold is £17,495 for loans taken out to finance courses started before 1 September 2012 (known as Income Contingent Plan 1 loans).

- The income threshold is £21,000 for loans taken out to finance courses started after 1 September 2012 (known as Income Contingent Plan 2 loans).

- The rate of repayment is 9% on income over these limits.

● Repayments are only collected in the April after the course has finished: for a course finishing in June 2016, repayments will commence in April 2017 provided sufficient income is being earned.

For borrowers who are employed, it is the responsibility of the employer to deduct loan repayments when the income exceeds £1,457 a month (£336 a week) for those to whom the £17,495 threshold applies (£1,750 a month or £403 a week for those to whom the £21,000 threshold applies). The amounts are collected through the PAYE scheme and are handed over by HMRC to the Student Loan Company at the end of the tax year. The borrower should keep all payslips as a record of the deductions that have been made.

For borrowers who submit tax returns, any additional loan repayments are collected through self-assessment and are payable by 31 January following the end of the tax year. These are paid over as part of the balancing payment for tax liabilities due. The amount of any deductions for loan repayments that have been made by an employer over the year need to be entered on the return and will be taken in account when calculating the additional loan repayments to be made.

The income threshold includes all earned income plus savings income in excess of £2,000.

Focus

Student loan repayments may be due for payment by 31 January, through self-assessment, if the borrower's income has exceeded the income threshold and that income has not had repayments deducted at source through PAYE. All payslips and P60s (or P45s) should be retained as evidence of any repayments already made.

Problems in paying

1.26 It may be possible to come to an arrangement with HMRC if the taxpayer is genuinely unable to pay the full amount of tax on time. HMRC will need to be sure that the taxpayer has exhausted all avenues of obtaining the funds needed to meet their statutory obligation to pay their tax liability on time (such as borrowing or restructuring their business or personal affairs) before such an arrangement would be considered. A typical arrangement would be for the tax to be postponed and a direct debit plan set up giving the taxpayer a few extra months to pay.

Taxpayers are strongly advised to contact HMRC as soon as it appears likely that there will be difficulties in making the full payment and before a demand is received. This is to avoid a possible penalty or a surcharge or even direct recovery of the debt from their bank account (see **1.27**).

It is the Business Payment Support Service's Helpline on 0300 200 3835 which deals with taxpayers who have not yet received a demand for payment. If a demand has already been received then the contact details will be on the demand itself. The government website gives further details at: www.gov.uk/ difficulties-paying-hmrc .

HMRC's recovery proceedings for collecting unpaid tax is covered in **52.10–52.14**.

Direct recovery of debt

1.27   Under the *Finance (No 2) Act 2015*, HMRC have the power to instruct banks and building societies to deduct amounts to settle a person's tax debts directly from their accounts. It applies not only to individuals but to all types of taxpayers, such as companies, trustees and personal representatives. It also includes all types of taxes, including VAT, National Insurance contributions and tax credits. For further details see **50.9**.

How to pay

1.28   The HMRC website gives details on how to pay and the relevant link is www.gov.uk/pay-self-assessment-tax-bill.

- HMRC prefers payments to be made online; either directly or by debit or credit card or by direct debit. To make payments by direct debit, it is necessary to have registered for self-assessment online.
- Payment by cheque can still be made, either at a bank, a post office or by post as long as the payslip HMRC provided is used. Cheques are made payable to 'HM Revenue & Customs only' and the payslip reference number added directly afterwards.

An advantage of registering with the HMRC online self-assessment service is that the taxpayer can view his account at any time in order to see what the current liabilities are and the dates payments have been made.

Interest and penalties

1.29   Interest is charged on tax paid late. The rate of interest (last amended 23 August 2016) is 2.7%. No deductions can be claimed against income for interest charged by HMRC.

There are also penalties where tax is paid late (which apply to amounts owing for student loan repayments and Class 4 NIC as well). The initial charge for liabilities that remain unpaid 30 days after the due date is 5% of the tax unpaid at that date. These areas are covered in detail in **Chapter 53**.

CLAIMING A TAX REFUND

Tax overpaid in earlier years

1.30   The procedures for making claims are laid down in *TMA 1970, s 42*. Different procedures apply depending upon whether the person is required to submit a tax return or not. Claims requiring a deduction or repayment under PAYE are governed by the PAYE regulations (*TMA 1970, s 42(3)*).

Dividends paid prior to 5 April 2016 carried a tax credit but no tax could be claimed back for tax credits on these dividends even if the person was a non-taxpayer. Nor can the notional tax charge suffered on gains from life insurance policy bonds be reclaimed.

The error or mistake provisions (*TMA 1970, s 33*) were amended under *Finance Act 2009, s 100, Sch 52* and replaced with *TMA 1970, Sch 1AB (Recovery of Overpaid Tax, etc)* which applies for all claims made on or after 1 April 2010.

Advice on how to claim a refund for current and earlier years can be found at www.gov.uk/claim-tax-refund on the government website.

A taxpayer who has registered for his personal tax account (see **1.13**) can claim a tax refund by logging into his account and following the appropriate instructions: this applies for both individuals who have registered for self-assessment and those who have not. It will depend on individual circumstances whether this route or the steps outlined below are applicable.

If an individual wishes to claim tax relief for donations made under the gift aid scheme or for private pension contributions for a higher or additional rate taxpayer or if the scheme is not set up for automatic tax relief or for employment expenses exceeding £2,500, then this must be done by registering for self-assessment and completing a tax return.

Claim by a person who is taxed through self-assessment

1.31   Important points to note include:

● If a person has paid too much tax and files tax returns each year, then the repayment due will be made after the annual return has been filed through self-assessment. This will be done by repayment directly to the taxpayer's bank account, provided the details were entered on the tax return.

- If the overpayment was made in the previous tax year, then an amendment may be made to the tax return for that year. Amendments can normally be made up to 12 months from 31 January after the end of the tax year; so a tax return for 2015/16 can be changed by an amendment at any time until 31 January 2018.

- It may be necessary to request the refund, for example, if it has arisen from overpaying the tax due or because payments on account are no longer necessary due to a change in circumstances. For those who filed their returns online, the refund can be made by logging into their online account and selecting the option for 'request a repayment'. For those who filed a paper return, a letter should be sent to HMRC.

- If the overpayment is for earlier years, a letter must be sent to HMRC explaining why the taxpayer believes the overpayment has arisen and providing supporting documents as evidence of the claim, including evidence of the tax paid. The claim can only be made within four years of the end of the tax year in question. See **Example 1.5** below on the application of the time limits.

Claim by a taxpayer outside the system of self-assessment for earlier years

1.32   If a taxpayer does not need to submit returns but has overpaid tax in earlier years, then HMRC may need to be contacted directly. The steps to be taken depend on the circumstances of the individual claimant and how the overpayment of tax has arisen. Broadly, these are:

Tax overpaid through PAYE (either from an employment or from a pension provider):

- If the overpayment has arisen in the previous year, HMRC normally post out a P800 tax calculation towards the end of July showing how the overpayment has arisen. A cheque is then sent out 14 days later. It would be advisable for the taxpayer to check the income and tax deducted on the P800 with his or her own records.

- If the refund is for earlier years, relates to claims for further deductions or the taxpayer has not yet received a P800 and wants the refund earlier, HMRC should be contacted directly. It may be possible to do this online or the taxpayer can phone or send a letter by post. See the government website for further guidance at www.gov.uk/claim-tax-refund/ too-much-tax-taken-from-your-pay.

Tax overpaid through deduction from savings income:

- Until 5 April 2016, tax was deducted at source from most savings income at a rate of 20%. However, since that date the requirement for banks and building societies to do so has been removed and most interest is paid gross.

- A Form R40 needs to be completed and sent into HMRC to claim a refund of tax deducted. The government website gives the address at www.gov.uk/government/organisations/hm-revenue-customs/contact/r40-where-to-send-repayment-claim-forms.

- The reasons why a refund is due could be that the interest received (or part of it) was covered by the taxpayer's personal allowances or there is an entitlement to the 0% starting rate band being applied to the savings income (see **1.14**).

Time limits for claiming

1.33   The time limits for making a claim are that it must be made within four years after the end of the relevant tax year.

Example 1.5 – Claims for earlier tax years

In September 2016, Georgina, a higher rate taxpayer, realises she has not claimed higher rate relief for regular donations made under the gift aid scheme.

Georgina can make a claim going back four years. So she is still in time to claim for the tax year 2012/13 which ended on 5 April 2013 as it is still four years from when it ended. She must claim by 5 April 2017.

If a claim is made and the person subsequently realises an error was made (whether in a return or otherwise), the claim must be corrected by submitting a supplementary claim within the time limits applying to the original claim (*TMA 1970, s 42(9)*).

Focus

If a person believes he has overpaid tax, a claim must be submitted to HMRC within four years of the end of the tax year in question in order to obtain a refund.

Claim for repayment of PAYE in current tax year

1.34   It may be possible to arrange for a repayment of tax without having to wait until the end of the tax year. More details can be found on the HMRC website, particularly the facility to make a claim for the refund online, see www.gov.uk/claim-tax-refund/too-much-tax-taken-from-your-pay on the government website.

The following are a few examples when a repayment during the tax year can be made. More details can be found on the HMRC website:

- If the person is an employee or in receipt of a personal or occupational pension, an overpayment may arise if an incorrect coding notice is being applied, for example employment benefits or other untaxed income have been overestimated. It is important to understand the PAYE Coding Notice, which is usually issued to those taxpayers whose code is *not* based simply on the personal allowance and is sent out before the start of the tax year. To illustrate the position for 2016/17:

  - A taxpayer who has no other income included in the code nor any taxable employment benefits nor any claims for deductions (such as pension contributions) will have a code of 1100L, based on the personal allowance of £11,000 in 2016/17.

  - A taxpayer who has property income of £1,000 included in his code and whose employer provides private health insurance of £1,500 would have a code of 850L, based on the personal allowance of £11,000 in 2016/17 less deductions of £2,500.

  The refund would be included in the wages or pension payment. Conversely, if the code being applied is collecting too little tax, for example if employment benefits have been underestimated, then HMRC should be told so that it can be corrected. This can be done by completing the online 2016–17 PAYE Coding Notice Query form, found on the government website.

- If the person has stopped working part way through the tax year, such as:

  - a student who only worked in the holidays,

  - an employee who has retired and does not yet receive a pension from the employer, or

  - a person who has been unemployed for at least four weeks and is not receiving any taxable state benefits, such as jobseekers' allowance or taxable employment and support allowance,

  the refund can be claimed by filling in Form P50. This can be done by posting it to HMRC together with Parts 2 and 3 of Form P45 to the address shown on the form or by completing and submitting the form online. For online submissions, it is necessary to have registered for the personal tax account as the taxpayer is asked to sign in with User ID and password unless the taxpayer is registered under self-assessment in which case they will need to login using their self-assessment account.

> **Focus**
>
> If too much tax has been collected from salary or pension payments in the current or previous year, HMRC may be able to correct the situation if an online claim is submitted or by phone and arrange a refund of the overpayment made.

Interest on overpaid tax

1.35   Interest on tax overpaid is known as repayment supplement and is tax free (*ITTOIA 2005, s 749*). The current rate payable is 0.5% and this rate has applied since September 2009. The government website gives the rates used for earlier years.

The interest is normally payable from (*ICTA 1988, s 824*):

- the date of payment (or for income deducted at source, 31 January following the end of the tax year), to

- the date the repayment order was issued.

Income tax deducted at source includes PAYE but excludes amounts of PAYE collected for previous tax years.

KEEPING RECORDS

Statutory requirements for all taxpayers

1.36   It is a statutory requirement for any person (individual, trustee or partner) who may be required to submit a tax return to keep records and for a specified length of time (*TMA 1970, s 12B*). Thus all taxpayers need to keep records relating to their tax liability. These will include: certificates supplied by their employers or pension providers (P60, P45, P11D and P9D, as applicable), a note of any tips or benefits received in connection with their employment not identified by their employer, certificates of interest received and tax deducted, dividend vouchers or records of state pension or taxable state benefits.

It is also necessary to keep records verifying any claims for reliefs or allowances made (*TMA 1970, Sch 1A, s 2A*).

31

Under self-assessment, it is the legal responsibility of the taxpayer to be able to demonstrate how the figures entered on the return have been arrived at. If adequate records have not been kept, a penalty of up to £3,000 may be imposed (*TMA 1970, s 12B(5)*). More importantly, if upon enquiry from HMRC, evidence cannot be supplied substantiating the figures, then it is possible that alternative estimates may be suggested by the Inspector of Taxes which may not be in the taxpayer's favour.

This is covered in more detail in **Chapter 55.**

Additional record keeping requirements for those in business

1.37   Where the person is carrying on a trade, profession or business, the legislation sets out the basic requirements of the documents that need to be included in a business's records, including supporting documents (*TMA 1970, s 12B (3)*).

This is dealt with in more detail in **Chapter 55.**

The type of documents kept will depend upon the complexity of the taxpayer's affairs but need to be sufficient to enable the person to make a complete and accurate return for the year or period. The HMRC guidelines stress the importance of keeping good records as poorly kept records may result in sales or allowable expenditure being omitted and consequently the level of profits or losses may be incorrect. To help small businesses with record keeping, the government website includes a list of simple record keeping applications for mobile phones, which at the most basic level can record the date, amount and description of all business transactions (see www.gov.uk/government/publications/record-keeping-and-simpler-income-tax-applicationssoftware).

Focus

Every person has a legal responsibility to maintain records of their tax affairs and to keep them for the allotted time. Failure to take reasonable care to meet this obligation may lead to an inaccurate return or claim being submitted and penalties being charged.

Length of time records need to be kept

1.38   Individuals, trustees and partners need to retain the records that support the return submitted until a specified day (known as the relevant day), as laid down by statute (*TMA 1970, s 12B(2)*). The length of time that records need to be kept depends on whether a business is being carried out or not.

The detailed rules are set out in **Chapter 55.**

APPENDIX: KEY TAX DATES

1.39

Monthly

- 19th – Non-electronic payments of PAYE, Class 1 NIC and CIS deductions for the period ended 5th of the month should reach HMRC's Accounts Office by this date (*SI 2003/2682, reg 69(1)(b); SI 2005/2045, reg 7(1)(b); SI 2001/1004, Sch 4, reg 10(1)*). If an Employer Payment Summary (EPS) is required for the tax month ending on 5th of the month, it must reach HMRC by this date.

- 22nd – Electronic payments of PAYE, Class 1 NIC and CIS deductions for the period ended 5th of the month should clear into HMRC's bank account by this date (*SI 2003/2682, reg 69(1)(a); SI 2001/1004, Sch 4, reg 10(1); SI 2005/2045, reg 7(1)(a)*).

5 October 2016

- Any person chargeable to income tax or CGT for 2015/16 who has not received a notice to file a self-assessment return must notify HMRC by this date that they are so chargeable (*TMA 1970, s 7(1)*).

18 October 2016

- Employer non-electronic payments of income tax in respect of PAYE settlement agreements (PSAs) for 2015/16 should reach HMRC Accounts Office (*SI 2003/2682, reg 109(2)*) (the due date is extended to 22 October 2016 for payments made by an approved electronic payment method). This is also the normal due date for payment of Class 1B NIC liabilities in respect of PSAs for 2015/16 (or 22 October 2016 for electronic payments) (*SI 2001/1004, Sch 4, reg 13(1)*).

31 October 2016

- Paper (non-electronic) income tax self-assessment returns for 2015/16 must generally be filed. This applies to individuals (*TMA 1970, s 8(1D)– (1F)*), trustees (*TMA 1970, s 8A(1B)–(1D)*) and partnerships which include one or more individuals (*TMA 1970, s 12AA(4A)–(4D)*).

- If HMRC do not issue a notice to file a 2015/16 self-assessment income tax return until after 31 October 2016, the return must be filed within three months from the date of the notice, whether the return is electronic or paper (*TMA 1970, ss 8(1G), 8A(1E), 12AA(4E)*).

- An employed taxpayer who submits a paper self-assessment return for 2015/16 must do so by 31 October 2016 if he wishes HMRC to collect a tax underpayment of less than £3,000 by adjustment to his future PAYE code where possible (*ITEPA 2003, s 684(3A); SI 2003/2682, reg 186(4)*).

2 November 2016

- Employers must submit Form P46 (Car) if appropriate to report changes affecting car benefits during the quarter to 5 October 2016.

30 December 2016

- An employed taxpayer who submits an electronic self-assessment return for 2015/16 must do so by 30 December 2016 if he wishes HMRC to collect a tax underpayment of less than £3,000 by adjustment to his future PAYE code where possible (*ITEPA 2003, s 684(3A); SI 2003/2682, reg 186(4)*).

31 January 2017

- Electronic income tax self-assessment returns for 2015/16 must normally be filed by this date, and any balancing payment of tax due for that year received by HMRC. However, if the notice to file was issued after 31 October 2016, the deadline for filing the return (whether electronically or on paper) is extended to three months from the date of issue of that notice (*TMA 1970, ss 8(1D)(b), (1G); 8A(1B)(b), (1E); 12AA(4B), (4E)*).

- Any balancing payment of self-assessment income tax (and Class 4 NIC, if applicable) for 2015/16 plus any capital gains tax for that year is normally payable by 31 January 2017. However, for 2015/16 tax returns where HMRC was notified of chargeability to tax by 5 October 2016 and the notice to file was issued after 31 October 2016, the payable date is extended to three months after the date on which the notice to file was issued (*TMA 1970, s 59B(3), (4)*).

- If a first payment on account is required for the tax year 2016/17, the payment of tax (and Class 4 NIC, if applicable) must reach HMRC by 31 January 2017 (*TMA 1970, s 59A(2)(a)*).

1 February 2017

- Most individual taxpayers who have not paid their remaining tax liabilities (and Class 4 NIC, if appropriate) for 2014/15 by this date face a further 5% penalty, in addition to the 5% penalties suffered on amounts outstanding at 1 March 2016 and 1 August 2016 (*FA 2009, Sch 56, para 3; SI 2011/702, art 3*).

2 February 2017

- Employers must submit Form P46 (Car) if appropriate to report changes affecting car benefits during the quarter to 5 January 2017.

1 March 2017

- Most individual taxpayers who have not paid their tax liabilities (and Class 4 NIC, if appropriate) for 2015/16 by this date face a 5% penalty (*FA 2009, Sch 56, para 3; SI 2011/702, art 3*).

5 April 2017

- The end of tax year 2016/17, and a crucial day for deciding whether to take particular action either before or after 5 April 2017 (eg utilising personal allowances, the CGT and IHT annual exemptions, etc).

3 May 2017

- Employers must submit Form P46 (Car) if appropriate to report changes affecting car benefits during the quarter to 5 April 2017.

19 May 2017

- Employers within RTI for 2016/17 must submit the final FPS for 2016/17 to HMRC (*SI 2003/2682, reg 67B*).

31 May 2017

- Employers must provide a 2016/17 Form P60 to each employee who worked for them at 5 April 2017, and from whom the employer was required to deduct tax from relevant payments at any time during the tax year (*SI 2003/2682, reg 67*).

5 July 2017

- PAYE Settlement Agreements (PSAs) for 2016/17 must be agreed with HMRC (*SI 2003/2682, reg 112*).

6 July 2017

- Employers to submit returns of benefits and expenses (Forms P11D and P9D) to HMRC for 2016/17 (*SI 2003/2682, reg 85*).

- Returns of Class 1A NICs (Form P11D(b)) for 2016/17 must reach HMRC (*SI 2001/1004, reg 80*).

- Employers must supply relevant employees with P11D(b), P11D and P9D information for 2016/17 (*SI 2003/2682, reg 94*).

- Annual returns for share schemes, Forms 34, 35, 39, 40, and Form 42 (or equivalent) for reporting events relating to employment-related securities and options for the year to 5 April 2017 must reach HMRC (*ITEPA 2003, s 421J*).

19 July 2017

- Employer non-electronic payments of Class 1A NICs for 2016/17 on benefits returned on a declaration of expenses and benefits (Form P11D(b)) must reach HMRC. The due date is 22 July for payments made by an approved electronic payment method (*SI 2001/1004, reg 71*).

31 July 2017

- The second payment on account of self-assessment income tax (and Class 4 NIC) by individuals for 2016/17 must reach HMRC to avoid late payment interest charges (*TMA 1970, s 59A(2)*).

1 August 2017

- Individual taxpayers who have not paid their remaining tax liabilities for 2015/16 face a further 5% penalty, in addition to the 5% penalty suffered on amounts outstanding at 1 March 2017 (*FA 2009, Sch 56, para 3; SI 2011/702, art 3*).

2 August 2017

- Employers must submit Form P46 (Car) if appropriate to report changes affecting car benefits during the quarter to 5 July 2017.

31 August 2017

- If HMRC have not issued a 2016/17 income tax self-assessment notice to file until by now, the normal submission deadline of 31 October 2017 is extended to two months after the date on which the notice to file the tax return is issued (*TMA 1970, s 9(2)(b)*).

Note

The above list is for general information purposes only and is not exhaustive.

2

Employment taxation

SIGNPOSTS

- **Scope** – The employment tax rules cover earnings from an 'office or employment' including benefits-in-kind (see **2.1–2.3**).

- **Earnings** – The definition of 'earnings' is wide, and earnings can therefore take several forms, including bonuses, commissions and tips (see **2.4–2.6**).

- **PAYE** – Income tax is collected through the PAYE system and employers are required to report details of payments made and tax and NIC deducted to HMRC electronically as part of the Real Time Information system (see **2.7–2.13**).

- **Benefits-in-kind**, etc – Non-cash earnings have separate tax rules, although some expenses provided to an employee will not be taxable if certain conditions are satisfied (see **2.14–2.20**).

- **Living accommodation** – Special rules apply to tax living accommodation provided for an employee subject to potential exceptions from the benefit-in-kind charge (see **2.21–2.31**).

- **Cars, vans, fuel**, etc – Cars or vans and related fuel provided for employees are taxed under a complicated series of rules (see **2.32–2.54**).

- **Beneficial loans** – A benefit-in-kind charge can arise for an employee who is provided with a 'cheap' loan, subject to certain exceptions (see **2.55–2.58**).

- **Reporting requirements** – the provision of benefits-in-kind must be reported to HMRC on a Form P11D, by payrolling the benefit or under a PAYE settlement agreement (see **2.59–2.63**).

- **Leaving the employment** – Special rules apply where payments are made on the termination of employment, including an exemption for the first £30,000 in some cases (see **2.63–2.77**).

- **Anti-avoidance** – There are complex 'disguised remuneration' rules to catch certain indirect payments to employees (see **2.78**).

- **Appendix: Company car benefit charges** – See table at the end of the chapter (see **2.79**).

EMPLOYMENT INCOME

2.1   If a person receives income as the 'holder of an office or employment' this is charged to tax as 'employment income' (*ITEPA 2003, s 7*).

What is an 'office' or 'employment'?

2.2   'Office' and 'employment' are not defined in tax legislation but the meaning of these words has been considered in numerous tax cases. Several key tests have been established when considering if someone is employed or self-employed. These key tests are:

- Who is providing the work?

    - If an individual can provide services personally, but may also sub-contract work (or bring in outside assistance) then this indicates self-employment (but someone with a unique or special skill might have to do the work personally but may still be self-employed).

    - If an individual always provides services personally then this indicates employment.

- Is there a 'mutuality of obligation'?

    - If an individual has the right to refuse work if he wishes then this indicates self-employment.

    - If the individual is obliged to do work if he is instructed then this indicates employment.

- Who controls the work?

    - If an individual can decide on how a job is done, the resources needed, when and where the job is done then this is likely to indicate self-employment.

    - If the individual must do what he is told, when he is told and how he is told, that indicates employment (but note that more flexibility and freedom can come in highly skilled jobs).

- Who provides the equipment?

  ○ If an individual normally sources and supplies all equipment for the job then this is likely to indicate self-employment.

  ○ Employees will typically only provide small tools or equipment (at most).

- Who carries the financial risk?

  ○ If an individual gives a price for a job, risking losses if costs are higher than estimated, and having to put right (at his own time and/or expense) any matters that have gone wrong, this indicates self-employment.

  ○ An employee will seldom if ever carry these risks (other than the loss of potential reward through any bonus/commission scheme).

- Can extra profits be made?

  ○ If an individual makes more money if work is performed efficiently then this indicates self-employment.

  ○ If an individual is paid no more, however efficiently the work is done, this may indicate employment (but an employee might benefit from a bonus scheme etc).

- How long is the contract?

  ○ A fixed-term or short-term contract is normally, but not always, an indication of self-employment.

  ○ An employment contract will normally, but not always, have no automatic end date.

- What role is played in the business?

  ○ If an individual has no 'management' role in the business, has no part in appraisal systems and is not embedded in the structure of the business, this is an indication of self-employment.

- What 'perks' are available?

  ○ A self-employed individual is unlikely to be entitled to any 'employee' benefits such as company cars, loans, phones, etc.

- Can the engagement be terminated?

  ○ A self-employed contract will often be of a fixed term with the right to terminate the agreement if either party breaches the terms of the contract.

  ○ An employment contract will normally contain defined periods of notice.

HMRC provide further details of these tests and the tax cases dealing with these issues within their employment status manual. This can be found on their website along with an employment status indicator (ESI) tool (see www.gov.uk/guidance/employment-status-indicator).

The ESI asks a series of questions about the working relationship between the worker and the engager and provides an indication of the worker's employment status. If the answers to the questions accurately reflect the working relationship the result may be relied upon by the engager and the 14 digit ESI reference number should be carefully saved.

Focus

The tests relating to employment status should not be used in a 'mechanical' way. This is not a case where a majority of 'ticks' against the test items decides the case. They are guidelines which should be used in the context of the work relationship being considered. In all cases, it is important to consider what actually happens rather than just how any contract may define the relationships between the parties.

The area of employment status is complex and The Office of Tax Simplification undertook a review back in March 2015 to consider the dividing line between employment and self-employment and whether it was drawn in the right place and in the right way. Their report included a number of recommendations in this area, although these are yet to be acted upon.

How is employment income taxed?

2.3   Employment income will be classified as either:

- 'general earnings' (*ITEPA 2003, s 7(3)*), or

- 'specific employment income' (*ITEPA 2003, s 7(4)*).

General earnings includes 'earnings' from an office or employment (see **2.4**) and items treated as earnings under the benefits code (see **2.14**) or any other provisions within the legislation, such as:

- Income of agency workers (*ITEPA 2003, ss 44–47*)

- Workers providing services through intermediaries ('IR35' provisions) (*ITEPA 2003, ss 48–61*)

- Income received through managed service companies (*ITEPA 2003, ss 61A–61J*)

- Sick pay and injury pay (*ITEPA 2003, s 221*)

- Payments by employers on account of tax where deduction not possible (*ITEPA 2003, s 222*)

- Payment of director's tax (*ITEPA 2003, s 223*)

- Payments for restrictive undertakings (*ITEPA 2003, ss 225, 226*)

- Deemed payments for employee shareholder shares (*ITEPA 2003, ss 226A–226D*)

- Capital allowance balancing charges (*CAA 2001, s 262*).

An individual who is resident and domiciled in the United Kingdom is taxed on the full amount of their general earnings for the tax year (*ITEPA 2003, s 15*) while special rules apply to individuals who are neither resident nor domiciled in the United Kingdom (*ITEPA 2003, Pt 2, Ch 5*).

Specific employment income includes items deemed by the Act to be taxed as employment income (for Relevant benefits provided under employer-finance retirement benefit (or 'EFRB') schemes this purpose, irrespective of the individual's residence and domicile status) and include:

- (*ITEPA, Pt 6, Ch 1*)

- Termination payments and benefits (*ITEPA, Pt 6, Ch 3*);

- Employment related securities income (*ITEPA, Pt 7*)

- Disguised remuneration (*ITEPA, Pt 7A*).

WHAT ARE EARNINGS?

2.4   Earnings are defined as:

- any salary, wages or fee;

- any gratuity or other profit or incidental benefit of any kind obtained by the employee, if it is 'money or money's worth';

- anything else that constitutes an emolument of the employment.

(*ITEPA 2003, ss 7(3)(a), 62*)

This is a deliberately wide definition which includes all payments such as bonuses, commissions, tips, etc.

It should be noted that the National Insurance contributions (NICs) rules define earnings differently and whilst in many cases payments will be earnings under both definitions the NIC rules must be considered (see **43.7**).

Earnings from an employment

2.5   To be taxable, earnings have to arise from the employment. Current legislation follows its predecessor legislation in simply stating that a payment will be earnings for this purpose as long as it is 'anything that constitutes an emolument of the employment' (*ITEPA 2003, s 62 (2)*).

To establish what this means in practice we have to look again to case law. This can include apparent statements of the obvious:

'Did this profit arise from the employment? The answer will be no if it arose from something else.' Lord Reid in *Laidler v Perry* HL 1965, 42 TC 351;

statements which help to clarify:

'For my part I think that their meaning is adequately conveyed by saying that, while it is not sufficient to render a payment assessable that an employee would not have received it unless he had been an employee, it is assessable if it has been paid to him in return for acting as or being an employee.' Lord Radcliffe in *Hochstrasser v Mayes* HL 1959, 38 TC 673;

and statements which may appear contradictory. For example contrast:

A profit from an employment 'must be in the nature of a reward for services past, present or future.' Upjohn J in *Hochstrasser v Mayes*;

with the finding in *Hamblett v Godfrey* CA 1986, 59 TC 694, where a payment which was clearly not a reward for service (but rather for the change in employment rights) was held to be chargeable:

'The rights had been enjoyed within the employer/employee relationship. The removal of the rights involved changes in the conditions of service. The payment was in recognition of the changes in service ... It was referable to the employment and to nothing else.' Neill LJ.

Perhaps it is more accurate to say that the cases show the development of thinking in this area. It is important to ensure that this historical development of the case law is considered when these issues are being addressed.

Certain key principles emerge from these cases. These include:

●   Wages salaries, etc are clearly earnings from employment.

- Payments made because of changes to employment conditions are caught.

- Payments to encourage people to sign an employment contract are caught.

- Payments which don't come from the employer directly can be caught.

- Payments under the terms of an employment contract are caught.

- Certain voluntary payments (eg tips) are caught.

- Payments that are 'customary' to be made in a particular employment are caught even if there is no explicit contractual obligation for the payment to be made.

- Payments to encourage an employee to remain in employment are caught.

- Payments that 'replace' one form of remuneration with another are caught.

Focus

Where there is an employment relationship between the parties it is highly unusual for a payment to escape the employment tax legislation.

Payments in kind rather than cash

2.6   Before considering the earnings legislation which applies to non-cash items it is important to remember that here we are looking at the earnings code *not* the separate benefits code legislation that might tax such items. In most cases the benefits code will apply *only* if the general earnings rule does not capture tax on the benefit provided. In a few cases the benefit rules will be applied ahead of the earnings rules, these being:

- non-cash vouchers;

- credit tokens;

- living accommodation provided; and

- cars made available.

If non-cash items fall to be taxed under the earnings rule they are charged on the 'money's worth' value of the item. This is defined as:

- something that is of direct monetary value to the employee; or

- something that is capable of being converted into money.

2.7 *Employment taxation*

This covers items such as the second hand value of an asset given to an employee, cash vouchers (such as a cheque), shares transferred to an employee for a payment less than they are worth, the payment of an employee's personal liability, etc (*ITEPA 2003, s 62(3)*).

The principles which underlie these treatments have been confirmed in numerous tax cases, including:

● *Wilkins v Rogerson* CA 1960, 39 TC 344

● *Weight v Salmon* HL 1935, 19 TC 174

● *Ede v Wilson* KB 1945, 26 TC 381

● *Hartland v Diggines* HL 1926, 10 TC 247

● *Nicoll v Austin* KB 1935, 19 TC 531

● *Richardson v Worrall* ChD 1985, 58 TC 642

● *Heaton v Bell* HL 1969, 46 TC 211.

These rules set out the framework under which the main rewards of employment are to be taxed. They are supplemented by specific legislation that applies to certain benefits in kind (see **2.14**), but before moving onto those rules we need to consider how tax on mainstream earnings is captured through the PAYE system.

THE PAYE SYSTEM

2.7   Pay As You Earn (PAYE) is the system used to collect income tax and NICs from employees' (including directors') pay as they earn it.

Employers have a legal obligation to operate PAYE and deduct tax on payments to employees if their earnings reach the PAYE threshold, which is defined in terms of 1/52 of the personal allowance for a weekly and 1/12 for a monthly paid individual. Separate provisions, with lower starting rates, apply for NIC purposes.

Employers have to deduct tax and employees' NICs from pay each 'pay period' and also pay to HMRC employer's Class 1 NICs on earnings above a certain threshold. These sums have to reach HMRC by the 19th of the month following the pay period or by the 22nd if electronic payments are used. Where the average monthly payments are likely to be less than £1,500 it may be possible to agree quarterly payments.

Employers calculate the tax due under the PAYE rules by using the employee's tax code and national insurance category letter to work out how much income tax and NICs to deduct from pay and how much employer's Class 1 NICs to account for on earnings.

The introduction of the Real Time Information (RTI) system has imposed strict requirements on employers to report information electronically to HMRC (see **2.10**).

(*Income Tax (PAYE) Regulations 2003, SI 2003/2682*)

What payments does PAYE apply to?

2.8   PAYE is applied to earnings including:

- salary and wages;

- overtime, shift pay;

- tips – unless these are paid directly to an employee by a third party or they come out of an independent 'tronc';

- bonuses and commission;

- certain expenses allowances paid in cash;

- Statutory Sick Pay;

- Statutory Maternity, Paternity or Adoption Pay;

- lump sum and compensation payments unless they are exempt from tax;

- certain non-cash items like vouchers, quoted shares or premium bonds – where PAYE applies to the cash value of such items.

The PAYE system is also used to deduct other items, such as:

- student loan repayments;

- employees' pension contributions;

- payments under an attachment of earnings order;

- repayment of a loan from the employer to an employee.

How does an employer get started with PAYE?

2.9   Assuming an employer establishes that an employee will be paid earnings which should be subject to PAYE, the employer must register with HMRC (see www.gov.uk/register-employer) following which, HMRC will issue a letter containing an employer PAYE reference.

Registration must be done before the first pay date, although it is not possible to register more than two months in advance.

Running a PAYE system

2.10 The introduction of the real time information system (RTI) in 2013 significantly changed the reporting of PAYE with a regular transfer of data to HMRC at each pay date rather than the mere submission of annual returns.

In most cases, employers' payroll software will automatically collect and submit the required information to HMRC and there is a wide choice of software (both free and paid-for) available. HMRC offer some free basic payroll software and also test commercial software to ensure that it can make the required RTI online reports – further details can be found here www.gov. uk/payroll-software/overview.

The payroll software must be populated with accurate details of all individuals to ensure that the correct amounts are deducted from their pay and that the correct information is provided to HMRC, this includes the individual's:

- start date;
- first two forenames and surname;
- NI number;
- tax code;
- date of birth;
- works or payroll number, if applicable;
- gender; and
- whether the employee has a student loan.

For new employees, this information should come from the Form P45 or failing that, a starter checklist can be completed to collate this (www.gov.uk/government/publications/paye-starter-checklist).

All payments to employees (see **2.8**), whether or not they exceed the lower earnings limit, along with details of all deductions (including income tax, NIC, student loan repayments, pension contributions, payroll giving and attachment of earnings) should be maintained by the software, and this will form the basis of the data reported to HMRC under RTI.

Employers need to make a full payment submission (FPS) to HMRC in respect of each payday. This must be made on or before the payday and will include details of:

- the amount an employer pays to an employee;

- the deductions made from these payments, such as income tax and NIC; and

- commencement dates of any new employees (starters) and termination dates of any departing employee (leavers).

An employer payment summary (EPS) will also need to be submitted in respect of each tax month, on or before the 19th day of the following month in certain cases, for example, where the employer is:

- reclaiming statutory maternity, paternity or adoption payments;

- claiming the employment allowances (see **43.30**);

- reclaiming a construction industry scheme deduction.

If no payments are made within a tax month, an EPS will be sent instead of an FPS.

Since the move to RTI, there is no need for the completion and submission of year end returns (formerly Form P14 and Form P35), instead, the final FPS for the tax year is marked as such on submission.

Focus

Increasingly, HMRC are looking at employers who fail to accurately and comprehensively adhere to the PAYE system as a target for penalty action.

Leavers are dealt with through the FPS and, although a P45 does not need to be sent to HMRC, it still needs to be given to the employee (see **2.11**).

Further guidance on running a payroll can be found here www.gov.uk/running-payroll/overview.

Information the employee must be given

2.11   Employees must be given a pay statement – or payslip – (either on paper or electronically) at or before the time they receive their pay. It must show certain items, including:

- the employee's gross pay (before any deductions are made);

- all deductions and the purposes for which they are made; and

- the net amount payable after the deductions have been made.

Employers must give each employee who was working for them at 5 April that year (and whose earnings reached the national insurance lower earnings limit during the tax year) a summary of their pay and deductions on a Form P60 by 31 May following the end of the tax year.

In addition, on leaving employment, the employee must be provided with a P45 by their employer.

Tax codes

2.12   The tax code system enables an employer to establish the amount of income tax to deduct from an employee's pay. A tax code is based on an individual's tax-free income for a year which is calculated by:

- adding up an individual's allowances; and

- deducting from this any income that has not been taxed along with any taxable benefits;

The tax-free income for the year is then divided by ten and a letter added which relates to the personal circumstances of the taxpayer. The letter varies dependent upon the circumstances of the taxpayer and the common codes are as follows:

Code	Description
L	For those eligible for the basic personal allowance.
M	For people who have received a transfer of 10% of a partner's personal allowance.
N	For people who have transferred 10% of their personal allowances to a partner.
S	For those subject to the Scottish rate of income tax
Y	For people born before 6 April 1938 (for the tax year 2015/16 and earlier only).
T	Where items may need to be reviewed in the tax code, (for example the income-related reduction to the personal allowance).
0T	Where allowances have been used up or reduced to nil.
K	When total allowances are less than total deductions.
BR	Where all income from a source is to be taxed at the basic rate.
D0	Where all income from a source is to be taxed at the higher rate.
D1	Where all income from a source is to be taxed at the additional rate.
NT	Where no tax is to be taken from income.

The PAYE system works to calculate the cumulative income tax due on the individual's cumulative income to date, allowing relief for a pro rata share of their tax-free income. In most cases, assuming the correct tax code has been calculated and applied, this ensures that by the end of the tax year the correct amount of income tax will have been deducted.

An 'emergency tax code' will sometimes be used where there is a change to the individual's circumstances, for example, if they move to a new job. This will reflect the basic personal allowance for the tax year, will end in the letter L and will generally be followed by 'W1' or 'M1' (meaning 'week 1' or 'month 1'). The effect of this is that the income tax will be calculated for each period in isolation as opposed to the standard cumulative basis. The tax code will usually revert to a cumulative code once the individual provides their new employer with a Form P45 or completes a new starter checklist.

Where an individual has more than one source of income subject to PAYE (for example, more than one employment or receives a personal pension while employed) they will be issued with a tax code in respect of each source of income with the intention of collecting the correct amount of tax in the year from all sources.

End of year procedures

2.13   A number of tasks must be completed at the end of the tax year (by certain dates) the key ones being:

19 April	Final PAYE tax and Class 1 NICs for the year must be received by HMRC if paying by post.
22 April	Final PAYE tax and Class 1 NICs for the year must be received by HMRC if paying electronically.
31 May	Form P60 must be given to each employee (see **2.11**).
6 July	Expenses and benefits annual return forms (P11D, P9D and P11D(b)) must be filed and copies given to employees.
19 July	Class 1A NICs must be received by HMRC if paying by post.
22 July	Class 1A NICs must be received by HMRC if paying electronically.

BENEFITS IN KIND

2.14   Where employment income is not chargeable under the general earnings rule it may be caught by the benefits code (*ITEPA 2003, s 63(1)*).

The benefits code is covered in *ITEPA 2003, Pt 3, Chs 3–7* and *10* as follows:

Chapter 3	Expense payments (see **2.17**)
Chapter 4	Vouchers and credit cards (see **2.20**)
Chapter 5	Provision of living accommodation (see **2.21**)
Chapter 6	Cars, vans and related benefits (see **2.32**)
Chapter 7	Loans (see **2.55**)
Chapter 10	Residual liability to charge for benefits generally.

Before 6 April 2016 an individual who was in 'lower-paid employment' was exempt from a charge to tax on any benefit arising under Chapters 3, 6, 7 and 10 (*ITEPA 2003, s 63(4)*). For this purpose, 'lower-paid employment' was defined as an employment where earnings were less than £8,500 a year (*ITEPA 2003, s 217(1)*) although for directors, certain additional requirements needed to be met for this exemption to apply (*ITEPA 2003, s 216(3)*).

This general exemption was repealed with effect from 6 April 2016 being replaced in part by targeted exemptions for lower-paid ministers of religion (*ITEPA 2003, ss 290C–290G*) and certain home care workers (*ITEPA 2003, s 306A*).

The exemption for lower-paid ministers of religion is structured in the same way as the original general exemption and provides the same scope of exemption to them. The exemption for home care workers is more focussed and only excludes a charge under Chapter 10 in respect of the provision of board or lodgings to an individual who is employed as a home care worker, so long as the board or lodgings is reasonable and at the home of the person receiving the care.

2.15 The general rule has always been that all benefits are taxable, irrespective of how small or insignificant they may have been. However, HRMC allowed certain benefits to be excluded by concession, where they were not as a reward for services and were trivial in nature (for example, a gift of flowers to an employee who was unwell) although strictly these needed to be agreed with HMRC.

With effect from 6 April 2016, a statutory exemption for trivial benefits provided by employers has been introduced (*ITEPA 2003, s 323A–323C*) to reduce the burden and administrative cost of both employers and HRMC. This exemption only applies where each of the following conditions is met:

• The benefit is not in the form of cash or cash vouchers;

• The cost of the benefit does not exceed £50;

- The benefit is not provided by way of a 'relevant salary sacrifice arrangement', being an arrangement whereby the employee agrees to give up the right to receive an amount of general earnings or specific employment income; and

- The benefit is not provided in recognition of particular services performed in the course of their employment, for example, gifts as a reward for hitting performance targets.

For most employees the exemption is applied to each trivial benefit rather than to each employee, so for example, an employee may receive several trivial benefits through the tax year and they will all fall within this exemption so long as they each (in their own right) meet the relevant criteria.

Where the trivial benefit is provided to a director of a close company, or any other member of their family or household, there is a cap of £300 per tax year on the aggregate value of such benefits which can benefit from the exemption. This is aimed at preventing the abuse of this exemption by employees who have the ability to influence the benefits provided.

2.16 Expenses paid to directors and employees will be taxed under the benefits code unless:

- They are otherwise chargeable to income tax – a charge to income tax as 'earnings' takes priority to any charge under the benefits code. There will only be a charge under the benefits code to the extent that the amount that would be subject to income tax under the benefits code exceeds the amount charged to earnings (*ITEPA 2003, s 64*);

- They are exempt from the charge – for example, certain benefits provided to lower-paid ministers or religion and home care workers (see **2.14**) or where the benefit is a 'trivial benefit' (see **2.15**);

- They would otherwise be deductible from the employee's earnings (see **2.17**).

- They are expenses incurred in connection with a van or car to which a van or car benefit applies – the charge under Chapter 6 already takes account of such expenses (see **2.32**);

Expenses chargeable under the benefits code include:

- payments made to an employee to meet specific expenses;

- reimbursement of expenses met from the employee's own pocket;

- allowances paid relating to specific expenses (for example payments in excess of the approved mileage allowance payments – see below); and

- advance payments for future specific expenses.

But they do *not* include round sum expense allowances which will be charged to tax under the general earnings rule. This is important as PAYE will be applicable to such round sum allowances but not to expenses payments charged under the benefits code *(ITEPA 2003, ss 70(1), 72(1))*.

If a payment is made to settle a pecuniary liability (ie a personal liability of the employee) it is considered to be of direct monetary value to the employee and will be charged under the general earnings code as the receipt of money's worth *(ITEPA 2003, s 62(3)(a))*.

Following on from the developments of the *Apollo Fuels* case (see **2.32**) the *Finance Act 2016* introduced changes to ensure that a benefit code still applies in cases where there is a 'fair bargain' between the employee and the employer (ie where the employee receives goods or services from their employer at exactly the same cost and under exact the same terms and conditions as any other member of the public who was transacting with the employer on an arms-length basis). Before this change, no benefit would arise on a fair bargain. With effect from 6 April 2016, the benefits code of *Chapters 5–7* (ie living accommodation, cars and vans, and beneficial loans) will apply even where the provision of a benefit constitutes a fair bargain. This removes the ability for arranging the provision of benefits in a way to avoid a charge under the benefits code, as successfully achieved in *Apollo Fuels*.

The reason for restricting this change to these three chapters is that HMRC do not consider that there are any circumstances under which the fair bargain provisions could apply to the remaining chapters of the benefits code.

Amounts otherwise be deductible from the employee's earnings

2.17 Payments which would otherwise be deductible from the employee's earnings are covered in *Ch 2 and Ch 5, Part 5 of ITEPA 2003* and include for example:

- certain expenses incurred wholly, exclusively and necessarily in the performance of an employee's duties (see **2.18**);

- travel expenses necessarily incurred in performance of an employee's duties (see **2.19**); and

- certain professional membership fees and annual subscriptions to certain professional bodies *(ITEPA 2003, ss 343–345)*.

Before 6 April 2016 an employer was generally required to report all such benefits provided on the employees' Form P11D with the individual then making a separate claim for income tax relief in respect of them. These expenses were not subject to Class 1 NIC and therefore this resulted in no more than a paper exercise.

To avoid the administrative burden of this, employers were able to apply to HMRC for a dispensation to exclude the reporting of such benefits. This would only be granted if HMRC were satisfied that the employer has sufficient procedures in place to monitor the process (*ITEPA 2003, ss 65 and 96*).

With effect from 6 April 2016, the dispensation regime has been repealed and is replaced with a statutory exemption for paid or reimbursed expenses (*ITEPA 2003, ss 289A–289E*).

This exemption applies to any payment or reimbursement which would otherwise fall within Chapter 2 or Chapter 5 of Part 5 so long as the payment or reimbursement is not made pursuant to 'relevant salary sacrifice arrangements', being an arrangement whereby:

- the employee agrees to give up the right to receive an amount of general earnings or specific employment income in return for the payment or reimbursement; or

- the employee's general earnings or specific employment income is dependent upon the amount of the payment or reimbursement.

Where the employer operates a flat rate scheme of reimbursing expenses (for example, they reimburse a set amount per night in respect of working away from home rather than the actual amount incurred by the employee), whether in accordance with agreed published limits or limits separately negotiated with HMRC, the exemption can only apply where there is a system in place to ensure that the employee is actually incurring expenses of the nature being reimbursed and it is not known or suspected (nor would it be unreasonable to know or suspect) that the employee is not incurring such expenditure.

Wholly, exclusively and necessarily in performance of duties

2.18 Expenses paid to an employee will not be subject to tax if they fall within the definitions of *ITEPA 2003, s 336*. This is a tightly drafted and narrow piece of legislation and all tests within it must be passed before the expense qualifies for a deduction. The expense actually has to be incurred. For example, a payment for an overnight stay in a hotel whilst working away on business will be deductible only if the employee actually stays at that hotel and incurs that hotel expense.

Travel expenses are dealt with separately under *ITEPA, ss 337–342* (see **2.19**).

The *s 336* tests are set out in the HMRC Manuals at EIM31630 *et seq*. The tests are:

- *The expense must be one that each and every holder of that employment would have to incur.* The test looks at the requirements of the job itself rather than the circumstances or preferences of any particular individual doing it.

- *The expense must be necessarily incurred.* A deductible expense must also be one that is 'necessarily' imposed on the holder of the employment by the duties of that employment. This will depend on what tasks have to be undertaken in order to carry out the duties of the job. The test relates to the nature of the expense and not to the amount.

- *The expense must be incurred in the performance of the duties of the employment.* The expense must be incurred in actually carrying out the duties of the job. It is not enough for the expense to be relevant to the job, or to be incurred in connection with the duties of the job. Nor is it enough if the expense only puts the employee in a position to start work or keeps the employee qualified to do the work. Expenses that are incurred in preparation to carry out the duties of the employment or as training to carry out the duties of the employment are not deductible.

- *The expense must be incurred and paid.* Relief can only be claimed for the amount actually incurred and any amount deductible under *s 336* can only be deducted against employment income arising from the same source as which the expense was incurred and it cannot create an employment loss available against general income (*ITA 2007, s 128*).

- *The expense must be wholly and exclusively incurred in the performance of the duties of the employment.* No deduction will be given for expenditure that serves a dual purpose; that is both a business purpose and a non-business purpose (but note that the wholly and exclusively rule does not apply to travel expenses at **2.19**).

Example 2.1 – Each and every office holder must have to incur the expense

Jenny works in a garage and is supplied with protective overalls by her employer. However, they are uncomfortable so she buys, with agreement from her employer, her own overalls.

No deduction is due for the cost. Protective clothing is necessary for the job and is supplied by the employer. She has bought her own protective clothing because of her personal preference and this is not an expense that each and every employee in his employment would need to incur.

Example 2.2 – Expenses must be necessarily incurred

Colin is an in-house IT expert for a finance company. He is asked to attend an away 'bonding' weekend with other IT experts from the group. Colin lives alone but has a dog which he has to put into kennels whilst he is on the away weekend.

No deduction will be due for the costs of the kennels as the expense is not one which every employee would have to meet – not all employees have a dog.

Example 2.3 – Expenses must be incurred in the performance of the duties

Basil is a salesman for a local firm offering replacement windows and doors. His income depends on how well he sells and to try to improve his success rate he books himself onto a 'self-improvement' course which promises that by 'knowing yourself you will know your customers'.

The cost of this course is not deductible. The course may help him know himself but the expense of the course is not incurred in performance of his duties of selling.

Example 2.4 – Expenses must be incurred and paid

Sophie is an employee of a soft furnishing business which books a hotel room for her on an overnight trip. Instead of using that room she stays with a friend.

No deduction is due in respect of the cost of the unused hotel room.

Example 2.5 – Expenses must be wholly and exclusively in the performance of the duties

Jamilla is a receptionist at a law firm who run an 'employee of the month' scheme. In order to increase her chances of winning the award Jamilla buys herself a bespoke business suit which is commented on by both her colleagues and visiting clients. This helps her win the award for 'making sure the first impression clients get of our firm is of smart professionalism'.

No deduction is due for the cost of this suit as it does not only achieve the desired work benefit but also provides warmth, comfort and decency for Jamilla both at work and when she travels to and from home.

Travel expenses in performance of duties

2.19   The general rule is that travel expenses (together with any subsistence cost incurred in making that journey) paid to an employee will not be subject to tax if the employee is obliged to incur and pay them as holder of that employment and the expenses are either:

- necessarily incurred on travelling in the performance of their duties of that employment (*ITEPA 2003, s 337*); or

- attributable to the employee's necessary attendance at any place in the performance of the duties of their employment and the journey does not relate to 'ordinary commuting' or 'private travel' (*ITEPA 2003, s 338*).

The difference between these two tests is the necessity of the travel – for *s 337* to apply the travel must be necessary for the performance of duties while for *s 338* it must be for necessary attendance at a place to perform those duties. The test at *s 337* is therefore very restrictive, but it can still have its application where the conditions of *s 338* are not satisfied, due to the additional exclusion of 'ordinary commuting' and 'private travel'.

In order to consider *s 338* there are numerous definitions to take account of:

- Ordinary commuting – travel between an employee's home or place which is not a 'workplace' and his 'permanent workplace'. In most cases will be the home to office 'commute'.

- Private travel – travel between an employee's home and a place that is not a workplace or travel between two places neither of which are workplaces.

- Workplace – where an employee's attendance is necessary for the performance of their duties.

- Permanent workplace – where an employee attends regularly for the performance of the duties of their employment and which is not a 'temporary workplace'. An employee can have more than one permanent workplace, if work is done there regularly or frequently.

- Temporary workplace – where an employee goes only to perform a task of limited duration or for a temporary purpose.

Limited duration is a period of continuous work that lasts, or is likely to last, no more than 24 months, with continuous work normally being taken by HMRC as taking up 40% or more of an employee's working time. But if someone works regularly at a location each week (for example at a branch office each Friday) then such work will not be taken as of a limited duration.

Temporary purpose covers cases where the visits may break the limited duration test but each visit is itself self-contained, and not part of some larger on-going project.

An employee may undertake work from their home and this raises the question whether that forms a workplace. In these cases, particular consideration needs to be given the reason they work from home – if it is a personal choice rather than a requirement, then it is unlikely to be considered as a workplace and so travel from their home to another permanent workplace would be considered as ordinary commuting.

It is also possible that an employee may have no permanent workplace, for example the engineer who sets off from home each day and attends various appointments. In these cases, the travel from their home to each of the appointments will usually be considered as being in the performance of their duties of employment under *s 337*. This will not always be the case though, where for example the engineer works in a particular area located away from their home – the travel from their home to the boundary of that area will generally be considered as ordinary commuting.

Furthermore, where an employee regularly attends a place which forms a base of that employment or where tasks are allocated (for example, an office where the sales manager goes to at the start of each day for a short time before they head out on the road or a depot where the day's jobs are set and relevant equipment is collected) then this will be considered as a permanent workplace and travel from home to that place will be considered as ordinary commuting (*ITEPA 2003, s 339(4)*).

Changes were also introduced in the *Finance Act 2016* to restrict the relief available for travel expenses in the case of workers engaged through an employment intermediary (including recruitment agency, umbrella company, personal service company or other similar structure). Previously, it was possible for such workers to claim that they were under an over-arching contract of employment with the intermediary, each assignment they undertook was a temporary assignment and the travel from their home to the locations where they undertook their work was therefore not ordinary commuting. The result being that they could benefit from relief for all of their travel costs.

The restriction takes effect from 6 April 2016 to bring the treatment of such workers more in line with other employees and deems each assignment to be a separate employment. The effect of this is that the place of work for each assignment will be a permanent workplace and any travel from their home to those workplaces will be ordinary commuting, preventing any relief for the associated travel costs (*ITEPA 2003, s 339A*).

Example 2.6 – Secondment for less than 24 months

Sally works as an accountant for ABC Shipping Ltd in Hull. She is 'office based' and works standard hours of 9.00am to 5.30pm each day at the company head office. ABC Shipping has another office in Grimsby, which looks after the group's insurance arm. The accountant at the Grimsby office has to take some time off to recover from a broken arm and Sally agrees to work in the Grimsby office for six months to cover his absence.

Travel from her home to Grimsby is fully deductible as Grimsby is a temporary workplace.

Example 2.7 – Secondment for more than 24 months

Amir works in the Northampton warehouse of a major internet-based mail order firm. The firm opens up a depot in Nottingham and asks Amir to work from that depot to train up and supervise staff at that new location for a three-year period, with the intention of returning to Northampton after this period.

No deduction is due for Amir's travel to Nottingham as the new depot is not a temporary workplace, because he has breached the 24-month rule.

Example 2.8 – Changes to arrangements

Harry works for Shinebright Cleaners, a contract cleaning company in Liverpool, where he is based. He is asked to work at the company's Chester office for an 18-month period to help build up the company's business in that area.

His travel to Chester is deductible as it is a temporary workplace. However, after 12 months it becomes clear that the Chester business is booming and Harry agrees that he will stay on for another two years at Chester. At the point the decision is made to extend his stay at the Chester site to a total of more than 24 months, Chester loses its temporary workplace status for Harry and from the date of that decision no deduction will be due for his travel.

Example 2.9 – Fixed term contracts

Jenny lives in Croydon. She takes up a fixed term contract for 18 months to work in a care home in Brighton.

Whilst the period she is at the care home is less than 24 months, it covers the whole of the contract and therefore Brighton is her permanent workplace. She gets no deduction for her travel.

Example 2.10 – Working regularly at another location – not for a temporary purpose

Burt is employed by a large regional chain of estate agents. He works in their Barking office from Tuesday to Friday but spends every Saturday at their Chelmsford branch. This regular pattern means that his work at Chelmsford is not of a limited duration and the work he does there is not for a temporary purpose.

He gets no deduction for his travel.

Example 2.11 – Working regularly at another location – for a temporary purpose

Raheema is a company director of a structural engineering business. She is based in Leeds but once a month attends a strategy meeting in Manchester where one-off projects and ideas are considered.

Despite the fact that the regularity of these visits mean they are not of a limited duration, as each visit is for a temporary purpose her travel costs will be deductible.

Focus

The benefit and expense systems of an employer should be supported by comprehensive guidelines which should demonstrate that the system adopted is robust and 'thought through'. This will prove to be very useful if the systems are interrogated by HMRC in any review.

Vouchers and credit cards

2.20   This legislation applies to replace the 'second hand value' measurement of a benefit that would be charged under the earnings code and is applicable to non-cash vouchers and tokens, defined very widely to include:

- high street retail vouchers;

- childcare vouchers – although these are subject to a limited exemption;

- cheques;

- transport vouchers;

and any other 'voucher, stamp or similar document or token' whether in the form of paper (including letters), plastic disc or any other form of 'token' (*ITEPA 2003, ss 75, 84, 92*).

A tax charge will arise where a non-cash voucher is provided for an employee or a member of his family by reason of the employment. The tax charge will be based on the expense incurred by the employer (or third party) specifically for the purpose of providing:

- the voucher itself; and

- the money, goods or services for which the voucher can be exchanged;

less any part of the expense made good to the provider by the employee (*ITEPA 2003, ss 87, 94*).

Living accommodation

2.21   If an employer simply pays an employee some extra money to meet the costs of housing (eg to meet rent or mortgage payments) then such a payment will be taxed as earnings (see **2.4**). But where, alternatively, living accommodation itself is provided to an employee, separate legislation applies to bring the value of that accommodation into charge (*ITEPA 2003, Pt 3, Ch 5*).

Living accommodation is given its normal meaning and covers houses, flats, villas, apartments, etc.

In certain circumstances even though accommodation is provided no tax charge will arise. These circumstances are where the living accommodation is provided:

- for the proper performance of the duties of the employment (*ITEPA 2003, s 99(1)*);

- for the better performance of the duties of the employment and it is customary in employments of that sort for such accommodation to be provided (*ITEPA 2003, s 99(2)*); or

- where special security issues exist (*ITEPA 2003, s 100*).

Directors do not automatically qualify for either of the 'performance-based' exemptions above (*ITEPA 2003, s 99(3)*). To be considered for either exemption they must have no material interest in the company (which for this purpose means having less than a 5% interest in the company) and either:

- the director is a full-time working director of the company (usually taken as working at least 75% of the time for that employer); or

- the company is non-profit making (that is neither trading nor set up to hold investment or property) or is established for charitable purposes only.

The proper performance test

2.22   This test is very restrictive, requiring that the employee must show that occupation of the property in question is essential to the *proper* performance of the duties of the employment. He must show that he could not do his job unless he lives in that house and no other.

It is not enough to show that an employer requires the employee to live in a particular property. It is the nature of the work undertaken in the employment that is key, not the 'in house' rules of the specific employer. Nor is it enough to show that the personal circumstances of the employee dictate where he must live (eg that he could not afford to live elsewhere).

HMRC accept the following workers as potentially qualifying for this relief:

- agricultural workers who live on farms or agricultural estates;

- lock-gate and level-crossing gate keepers;

- caretakers living on the premises;

- stewards and green keepers living on the premises;

- wardens of sheltered housing schemes living on the premises, but only where they are on call outside normal working hours.

The better performance and customary test

2.23   This test falls into two parts, both of which must apply for the relief to be due. Living in the house must be shown to help the job to be done better and the sort of job must be one where it is normal for an employer to provide accommodation (*ITEPA 2003, s 99(2)*).

The 'better' requirement

2.24   The employee must show that the job is done better because of where he lives. This does not mean that simple 'convenience' of where the house is located, making a commute easy or short, is enough. A job does not normally begin until the employee arrives at work so ease of getting to the place of work is not relevant.

But where the nature of the job (rather than the convenience of the employee or employer) means that being quickly available is crucial to being able to do the job, then relief may be due.

HMRC identify the following situations where this might apply:

- the employee is required to be on call outside normal hours; and
- the employee is in fact frequently called out; and
- the accommodation is provided so that the employee may have quick access to the place of employment or other place to which the employee is called.

The 'customary' requirement

2.25   There is no statutory definition of this term, but in practice it is taken as referring to a job where it is normal to provide accommodation and not to provide accommodation would be a rare exception.

The test applies to the nature of the job across the 'sector' or 'industry', not the practice of a particular employer.

HMRC identifies the following categories of employees who are accepted as meeting the better and customary test:

- police officers;
- Ministry of Defence police;
- prison governors, officers and chaplains;
- clergymen and ministers of religion unless engaged on purely administrative duties;
- members of HM Forces;
- members of the Diplomatic Service;
- managers of newsagent shops that have paper rounds (but not those that do not);

- managers of public houses living on the premises;

- managers of traditional off-licence shops, that is those with opening hours broadly equivalent to those of a public house, but not those only open from 9am until 5pm or similar;

- in boarding schools (which includes schools where only some of the pupils are boarders) where certain staff are provided with accommodation on or near the school premises, including:

    o head teacher;

    o other teachers with pastoral or other irregular contractual responsibilities outside normal school hours (for example house masters);

    o bursar;

    o matron, nurse and doctor;

- stable staff of racehorse trainers who live on the premises and certain key workers who live close to the stables.

Calculating the benefit

2.26   Where a benefit arises, it is the 'cash equivalent' of providing the living accommodation which is treated as earnings and this depends upon whether the cost of providing the living accommodation is more than £75,000 (*ITEPA 2003, ss 103*).

Cost for this purpose is defined at *ITEPA 2003, s 104* by way of a formula:

$$A + I - P$$

Where:

- A is the amount spent to acquire the living accommodation (ie the cost of the freehold or leasehold of the property)

- I is the amount spent on improving it prior to the tax year in question

- P is any amount the employee pays to reimburse either A or I, or for the grant of a tenancy.

The cost will normally be met by the employer but the rules also cover accommodation provided by a third party as long as the accommodation is provided by reason of the individual's employment (*ITEPA 2003, s 112*).

Cost of providing accommodation is £75,000 or less

2.27   If the cost of providing the accommodation is £75,000 or less then the tax charge is based on the greater of:

- the 'annual value' of the accommodation provided; or

- the rent paid by the employer.

This is reduced by the amount of any rent paid by the employee for the period to arrive at the amount brought into charge (*ITEPA 2003, s 105*).

Annual value is defined in the legislation (*ITEPA 2003, s 110*) as the rent which might reasonably be expected to be obtained on a letting from year to year if:

- the tenant undertook to pay all taxes, rates and charges usually paid by a tenant, and

- the landlord undertook to bear the costs of the repairs and insurance and the other expenses (if any) necessary for maintaining the property in a state to command that rent.

In practice this means the gross rating value. For houses in England this is the 1973 value, for Northern Ireland this is the 1976 value and for Scotland the value is the 1985 value multiplied by 100/270 (effectively to ignore the uplift in values arising on that valuation, as the revaluation exercise of 1985 was not conducted across the whole of the UK).

Cost of providing accommodation more than £75,000

2.28   If the cost of providing the accommodation is more than £75,000 then the first step is to check if the actual cost should be replaced by a 'market value' figure (*ITEPA 2003, s 107*) for the purpose of calculating the amount brought into charge. This will apply only if:

- the employee first occupied the accommodation after 30 March 1983; and

- the employer (or third party providing the accommodation because of the employment) had an interest in the property throughout the six years preceding the date the employee first occupied the property.

You should note that even when these conditions are met, the market value of the property is never used in the calculation at *s 104* to determine whether the cost of providing the accommodation is more than or £75,000 – it is only for the calculation of the amount to be brought into charge once that has been determined (*ITEPA 2003, s 107(1)*).

The amount to be brought into charge is calculated by adding together:

- the basic charge as calculated as if the property had cost less than £75,000 (see **2.26**); and

- the 'additional yearly rent' – this is calculated by multiplying the official rate of interest by either:

    o where cost should be used – the cost of providing the accommodation by reference to the formula at *s 104* (see **2.26**); or

    o where market value should be used – the amount calculated by the formula set at *s 104* where the market value (MV) of the accommodation at the time the employee first occupied the property is substituted for 'A' (ie the resulting formula being MV+ I – P).

    o Where the employee pays any rent in respect of the accommodation and this exceeds the basic charge under *s 105*, then such excess will be allowed as a deduction in calculating the additional yearly rent.

Example 2.12 – Property worth less than £75,000 – the calculation (1)

Fred works as a shift supervisor for a logistics company. The company bought a house for £70,000 close to their factory and Fred rents that house from them at a low rent of £30 per month.

The gross rating value for the property is £900. No improvements have been made to the property.

Fred's benefit in kind is:

	£
Annual value	900
Less: rent paid £30 × 12	(360)
Benefit	540

Example 2.13 – Property worth less than £75,000 – the calculation (2)

Anita is an electrician employed by the same company. She also lives in a house provided by the employer but the house she occupies is actually rented by the company for £400 per month. The gross rating value of the property is £1,500. She pays a discounted rent of £100 per month.

Anita's benefit in kind is:

	£
The greater of	(i) annual value (£1,500); or
	(ii) rent paid by employer (£400 × 12 = £4,800)
Therefore	4,800
Less: rent paid £100 × 12 =	(1,200)
Benefit	3,600

Example 2.14 – Property worth more than £75,000 – the calculation

Greg works for a law firm as their internal accountant. He lives in a property bought by the firm for £200,000 in 1998. Greg has lived in that house since 2001 and pays a notional rent of £100 per month. The gross rating value is £1,700.

Greg's benefit in kind is:

The basic charge	£
Gross rating value	1,700
Less: rent paid £100 × 12	1,200
Basic (*s 105*) benefit	500

Plus

Additional yearly rent

	£
Cost of providing the accommodation	200,000
Less:	(75,000)
	125,000
At 3.0% (official rate of interest) =	3,750
So benefit is £3,750 + £500 =	4,250

Following a review of his reward package, the company renegotiates the rental agreement with Greg and starts to charge him a rent of £200 per month. The benefit is re-calculated as follows:

The basic charge	£
Gross rating value	1,700
Less rent paid £200 × 12	2,400
Basic (*s 105*) benefit	nil
Excess rent (£2,400 – £1,700)	700

Plus

Additional yearly rent

	£
Cost of providing the accommodation	200,000
Less	75,000
	125,000
At 3.0% (official rate of interest) =	3,750
Less: excess rent	(700)
Benefit	3,050

Use of the accommodation for business purposes

2.29   The accommodation might include either:

- a separate area specifically built for business use (eg a shop with a flat where clearly the shop is not living accommodation); or

- a separate area which, although part of the main house, is set aside exclusively for business use.

In either of these cases relief from the tax charge can apply where that element of the property is considered to meet the condition of being used wholly, exclusively and necessarily for the performance of their duties of employment (*ITEPA 2003, s 364* and see **2.18**).

Houses outside the UK

2.30   Houses outside the UK will not have a UK rateable value and so the general meaning of 'annual value' will apply in such cases (*ITEPA 2003, s 110* and see **2.27**) with the benefit then being calculated in the normal way as set out above.

However, an overseas property might escape this charge altogether. In many cases a 'personal' purchase of an overseas 'holiday home' will be made through a company, often to meet the requirements of local law. It could be argued that if the home was used by the owner/director of the company then a benefit charge might arise, but legislation confirms that no charge will apply where:

● the company is wholly owned by the directors/other individuals (ie shares cannot be owned in a trust unless it is a bare trust – that is one which is transparent for UK tax law), and

● the company has an interest in the overseas property which gives it exclusive rights to enjoy the property (which can include a 'time share' arrangement), does not have any other significant assets and does not undertake any activity unrelated to the property,

There are anti-avoidance rules which attack any artificial manipulation of this relief (*ITEPA 2003, ss 100A–100B*).

Other accommodation-related matters

2.31   As well as the provision of the accommodation, the employee might have other costs met by the employer such as council tax or heat and light. It is important to identify any such items as these will be taxed as pecuniary liabilities of the employee (see **2.16**).

Certain assets specifically relating to the accommodation may also be provided (for example furniture, electrical items etc) and these will produce a separate chargeable benefit under (ITEPA 2003, s *205*) although this charge did not apply to lower-paid employees for 2015/16 and earlier and continues to not apply to lower-paid ministers of religion for 2016/17 onwards.

This charge may still arise even though the benefit of the accommodation itself is exempt (see **2.21**) but in those cases, the benefit chargeable is limited to 10% of the net earnings of the employment less any contributions made by the employee (*ITEPA 2003, s 315*).

> **Focus**
>
> Issues on accommodation often arise due to lack of understanding of when a charge arises and how the tax bill is calculated. Anyone in an organisation responsible for offering or organising accommodation should be aware that tax issues need to be considered 'up front'.

It should be noted that the provision of living accommodation to an employee on or after 6 April 2016 under a fair bargain will still be taxable (*ITEPA 2003, s 97(1A)* and see **2.16**).

Cars, vans and related benefits

2.32   The provision of cars and vans for employees is subject to 'standalone' rules within *Chapter 6* of the benefits code. The provisions are wide reaching and have impacted on many decisions as to whether vehicles are provided by employers, which vehicles are provided and how vehicles are provided.

The basic charging provision is broadly that where a car or van is made available for private use by an employee (or a member of his family) by reason of employment but without the employee taking ownership of the car then, unless the car falls to be taxed in some other way (ie as general earnings), the provision of the car will produce a taxable benefit (*ITEPA 2003, s 114(1)*)).

Made available by reason of employment does not include circumstances where the employer:

- is an individual and the vehicle is made available in the normal course of the employer's domestic, family or personal relations (*ITEPA 2003, s 117(2)*); or

- carries on a vehicle hire business and the vehicle is of the same kind that would normally be available to hire by members of the public and it is made available to an employee on normal commercial terms in their capacity as a member of the public (*ITEPA 2003, s 117(3)*).

However, following on from the case of *HMRC v Apollo Fuels Limited [2016] EWCA Civ 157* changes were made to the legislation to ensure that the provision of a car or van to an employee on or after 6 April 2016 under a fair bargain will still be taxable (*ITEPA 2003, s 114(1A)*).

The case centred around the question as to whether a charge should arise under *Chapter 6* of the benefits code in respect of a car which was leased to an employee from his employer on arm's length commercial terms, including the requirement for the employee to pay lease charges at full market value. HMRC accepted that the employee did not derive any financial benefit from the lease but nonetheless considered a charge under *Chapter 6* still arose.

The basic principle behind the car leasing schemes (and that of many other similar ones) was that so long as a sufficient number of employees were members, the economies of scale allowed for each of them to lease a car at a reasonable cost. Assuming that they used their car for business purposes, and a sufficient number of business miles were travelled, then the leasing costs would be covered somewhat by the payments they received under the AMAPs scheme (see **2.33**). The outcome was that they were not subject to a benefit on the car, but did in fact pay market value under the terms of the lease.

The Court of Appeal found in favour of the taxpayer, in that no charge arose on the provision of the cars as the employees received no benefit in the ordinary sense of the word. That said, the change in legislation introduced on the back of this brings to an end many car leasing schemes of this nature, or at least in their previous form. This whole saga may appear to the layman as nothing more than HMRC taking the ball home with them after losing the game fair and square.

2.33   Business mileage

Where a private car is used for business purposes, an employer may reimburse the employee for the costs of business journeys. HMRC publish a rate of 'approved mileage allowance payments' (AMAPs) which an employer can pay employees each year without having to report them to HMRC or pay any tax on them (*ITEPA 2003, ss 229–236*).

The current rates are:

Tax – rates per business mile

Type of vehicle	First 10,000 miles	Above 10,000
Cars and vans	45p	25p
Motorcycles	24p	24p
Cycles	20p	20p

Business mileage is calculated by combining miles done in all vehicles of the same type so, if an employee changes his car or van, he does not start a new 'first 10,000 miles'.

If the allowances paid to an employee exceed the approved amount for the tax year, then the employer must report the excess amount on Form P11D for income tax purposes. There are slightly different rates for national insurance purposes (in that there is no reduced rate for cars and vans for over 10,000 miles) but where these are exceeded, Class 1 national insurance will need to be applied at the time of the payment (and not Class 1A via the Form P11D).

If the allowances paid are less than the approved amount for the tax year, the employee will be able to get tax relief (called mileage allowance relief, or MAR) on the unused balance of the approved amount. See 43.9 for the NIC treatment of mileage payments .

Full details of these arrangements can be found in the HMRC manuals at EIM31200.

Where an employee is provided with a company car but not provided with fuel (see **2.49**) then different tax free mileage rates apply (see www.gov.uk/ government/publications/advisory-fuel-rates). This is due to the fact that the AMAP rates cover not only the fuel required for the business journey but also the cost of wear and tear on the employees' vehicle.

What is a car?

2.34   The legislation defines a car as a 'mechanically propelled road vehicle' unless it is:

- a goods vehicle; or

- a vehicle which is not commonly used as (and not suitable for use as) a private vehicle; or

- a motor bike or an invalid carriage as defined in the *Road Traffic Act 1988, s 185(1)*.

(*ITEPA 2003, s 115(1)*)

A goods vehicle is one which is primarily designed to carry goods or materials. This will cover what would normally be described as commercial vehicles (eg lorries, vans, etc).

Whilst in many cases this is a straightforward matter, complications can arise where the vehicle is a 'multi–purpose vehicle' (for example a four-wheel drive off-road vehicle that might – at least in some people's minds – be used for fun at the weekends) or double cab pick-ups which are able to seat four people in a similar manner to a 'normal' road car. Where there is doubt, it is important to look carefully at the specifications of the vehicle to arrive at the proper classification.

It is also important to stress that the test is based on how the vehicle is constructed, not on how it is used. An estate car remains a car even though someone might use it all the time to transport goods.

What does 'made available for private use' mean?

2.35   The phrase takes its normal dictionary definition, but care must be taken to distinguish between cases where the car is not available and cases where the employee is not in a position to use it because of his own circumstances (*ITEPA 2003, s 143*).

So if a car is at the body shop for repair after a crash, or the employee has no access (and cannot demand access to) the keys for the car, then it is not available, but if the car was sat on the employee's drive not being used because of illness, holiday, etc, then the car would still be available for use.

> **Focus**
>
> A trap often fallen into is to assume that if a car is not used then no tax charge will arise. It is the availability of the car, not whether the car is actually used, that will determine if a tax charge arises.

Which family members are included here?

2.36   The car will still give rise to a benefit on the employee (assuming it passes the other tests) if it is provided to a member of their family or household (which includes domestic staff and guests).

Care needs to be taken to identify any cases where the car is provided to a family member because of their *own* employment. Where that is the case, the tax charge will fall on them personally.

Ownership of the car

2.37   The car benefit rules apply where the employee does not own the car himself. Part ownership agreements (under which the employer passes on some capital interest in the car) or leasing agreements (where the employer 'rents' the car to the employee – see **2.32**) do not take the car out of the benefit rules. Payments of this nature may have an impact on the quantum of the benefit (see **2.44** and **2.48**).

Other costs related to the car

2.38   The benefit arising on the provision of the car includes the associated day to day running costs (eg insurance, road fund license and maintenance) but not fuel (see **2.49**). Separate charges may arise from the provision of a chauffeur and the payment by the employer of fines or charges (eg parking fines) which are the responsibility of the driver.

Cases where the car benefit charge will not apply

2.39   In some narrow situations a car benefit will not be charged and these include:

● Where the car is not allowed to be used privately, and is not used privately (ie other than for business travel). As one may suspect this relief is only granted in exceptional cases and HMRC will need explicit proof that the prohibition is legally enforceable and cast iron evidence that no private use has occurred (*ITEPA 2003, ss 118, 171(1)*).

● Where the car is a 'pool car' (*ITEPA 2003, s 167*). Some businesses have cars or vans available for use by numerous employees for business purposes. For example, a joinery firm may have a car housed at its business premises which is used by employees to run to the local builder's merchant to pick up small items purchased for specific jobs. A similar exemption is available for pool vans (*ITEPA 2003, s 168*).

Where this is the case, the car or van will not fall to be taxed under the benefit rules, as long as certain conditions apply. These are:

o the vehicle was made available to, and actually used by, more than one employee;

o it was made available to the drivers by reason of their employment;

o it was not ordinarily used by one employee to the exclusion of the others;

o any private use of the vehicle was merely incidental to the business use. This can be a difficult test to meet but the approach adopted by HMRC is to look at any case where the private element is 'plainly subordinate' to the business use. They use the example of an employee making an early morning start on a business journey where they take a pooled car home the previous evening. They say:

'Considered in isolation, the office to home journey is private use, but in these circumstances it is plainly subordinate to the business journey the next day. It is undertaken to facilitate the business trip. It is thus merely incidental to the business use' (EIM23455);

o the vehicle was not normally kept overnight at or near the home of an employee.

The tests are 'all or nothing' tests; fail one and the vehicle cannot qualify as a pool vehicle.

Focus

HMRC will look carefully at any claim that a car is a pool car, so full and accurate records must support this treatment.

- Where the car is provided to a disabled employee, defined as an employee who has:

  'a physical or mental impairment with a substantial and long-term adverse effect on their ability to carry out normal day to day activities' (*ITEPA 2003, s 246(4)*).

  In such cases, the normal car benefit charge will not apply only if the following conditions are met:

  o the car has been adapted for the employee's special needs or, in the case of an employee who because of disability can only drive a car that has automatic transmission, it is such a car;

  o the car is prohibited from being used apart from:

    – business travel (*ITEPA 2003, s 171(1)*);

    – travelling to and from work (ie 'ordinary commuting'), including where the journey is for practical purposes substantially ordinary commuting, or

    – travel to undertake a business training course,

  o and, in the tax year under consideration, the car is only used in this way;

  o the car is an emergency vehicle – such as a police car – and there are suitable restrictions on private use (*ITEPA 2003, s 248A*).

  o the car is provided to a lower-paid minister of religion (see **2.14**).

Cars used by employees in the motor trade

2.40 In cases where the employee is employed in the motor trade HMRC have issued guidance to deal with certain practical problems which arise when considering car benefits. Details of their approach to test and experimental cars, demonstrator vehicles and cases where there are frequent changes of car can be found at EIM23800.

Calculating the benefit

2.41 If a car benefit arises the amount of the benefit is calculated by multiplying the price of the car and accessories by the appropriate percentage (*ITEPA 2003, s 121*). Example calculations follow and more details are provided on the terminology used at **2.42** *et seq*.

Example 2.15 – Car benefit calculation (1)

John is provided with a car for the whole tax year by his employer which he is able to use for private as well as business journeys, as long as he makes a payment of £20 per month. He makes a capital contribution of £1,600 to the car. The car has a list price (including standard accessories, VAT, number plates and delivery) of £18,250. It is a petrol engine car with a published CO_2 emissions figure of 128gm/kg.

As a manufacturer's option, metallic paint is provided for the car at a cost of £350.

	Calculation	£
1	Take the list price of the car	18,250
2	Add any extra accessories in the car manufacturer's price list	
	Metallic paint	350
	Price of the car including accessories	18,600
3	Deduct any capital contribution	(1,600)
	Price after capital contribution deduction	17,000
4	Apply appropriate percentage	
	Based on CO_2 emissions (rounded down to nearest 5gm/kg)	
	125 gm/km = 22% for 2016/17	22%
	Annual car benefit before deductions £17,000 x 22% = 3,740	
5	Deductions	
	Monthly payment for private use 12 × £20 =	(240)
	Taxable benefit for year	3,500

Example 2.16 – Car benefit calculation (2)

Jane has a similar car to John (with the same 'spec' on delivery and same contributions deal). Immediately after she has the car delivered she has an additional sound system fitted at cost to her employer of £600. This sum is added at step 2 to the above computation, increasing the price of her car including accessories to £19,200. The percentage calculations are applied to that figure.

Example 2.17 – Car benefit calculation (3)

In the second year John has the car, he has an accident and the car is off the road for 45 days being repaired. He does not have a replacement car, using public transport and lifts from friends and family in this period.

The tax benefit calculation for that year is as follows:

	£
Car benefit as above (before deduction for monthly contributions)	3,740
Less deduction for unavailability at 45/365 × £3,740 =	(461)
Revised benefit before personal contributions	3,279
Deduction for personal contributions	(240)
Taxable benefit for the year	3,039

The price of the car

2.42   This is not the actual price paid for a car but rather its original UK 'list price' as published by the manufacturer. Occasionally a car will have no list price (for example it might be a foreign import not normally sold in the UK). In such cases a 'notional price' is used, which is effectively the price which would reasonably have been expected to be the list price (*ITEPA 2003, s 124*).

In some cases the list price will be very low compared to the car's current value. For example, a vintage car may have been originally sold for a few hundred pounds but now may be worth many thousands. To deal with this there are special rules that apply to 'classic cars'. These are cars which are more than 15 years old (at the end of the tax year in question) with a market value of more than £15,000 (*ITEPA 2003, s 147*).

Where this sum exceeds the figure calculated under the normal procedure (including any reduction for any capital contribution by the employee – see **2.44**) then that market value is used in the computation.

There are also special rules where the car in question is manufactured as a road fuel gas car (*ITEPA 2003, s 146*).

Accessories

2.43   The list price covers 'standard' specification cars. Often a car is offered with 'extras' for additional payment and the costs of these are added on to the list price in calculating the car benefit (*ITEPA 2003, ss 125–131*).

Capital contributions

2.44   Where the employee pays towards the acquisition of the car (or, for example, pays personally for additional accessories), the amount he pays is deducted from the full list and additional accessories price when calculating the benefit (*ITEPA 2003, s 132*).

If there is an agreement to pay something back to an employee who has made a capital contribution when the car is sold, the detail of any such agreement should be considered. If the agreement says that the employee would simply get his proportion of any sale proceeds back, then his full original capital contribution will go to reduce the car benefit. If, however, the employee has a right to a fixed sum on any sale, then this amount is not taken as a capital contribution but as a loan, not reducing the car benefit.

Capital contributions can indicate that an employee is paying to access a car to his personal preference, or a 'better' car. This should not be confused with cases where the employee makes a general contribution for the use of the car. These have a different impact on the benefit calculation (see **2.48**).

The 'appropriate percentage'

2.45   The total of the list price plus accessories less capital contribution is multiplied by a percentage, based on the car's CO_2 emissions. This is known as the appropriate percentage (*ITEPA 2003, ss 133–142*).

For diesel cars a 3% supplement is added to the appropriate percentage, subject to an overall cap of 37% (*ITEPA 2003, s 141*). This adjustment was due to be repealed with effect from 6 April 2016 (*FA 2014, s 24*) however this has now been delayed (*FA 2016, s 10*) and it is not expected to be brought in until 6 April 2020.

Reductions for the car not being available for use

2.46   As mentioned above, a car benefit will only apply if the car is made available for private use. Where the car is not available then a reduction can apply to the calculated benefit charge. So if the car is only made available or is withdrawn part way through a tax year, the car benefit charge will be adjusted proportionately (*ITEPA 2003, s 143*).

Where a car is temporarily unavailable in a tax year (for example, if it is in the body shop undergoing extensive repairs) there will only be a reduction in the benefit charge if that period is at least 30 consecutive days (*ITEPA 2003, s 143(2)*).

In many cases, where a vehicle is off the road, a replacement car will be provided. Where this is the case and the original car is off the road for more than 30 days then benefit calculations will be needed for both cars in the tax year. But where the original car is off the road for less than 30 days (perhaps the more common situation) then the original car will be considered as fully available even though a replacement car is being used. In theory this means the employee has two cars potentially chargeable but the rules prevent any 'double' charge to tax as long as the replacement car is not 'materially better' than the original car (*ITEPA 2003, s 145*).

Shared cars

2.47   Rarely a car might be made available to more than one employee, but not under arrangements which make the car a pool car (see **2.39** above).

In those cases the car benefit will be divided between the employees on a 'just and reasonable' basis (*ITEPA 2003, s 148*).

Payment for private use

2.48   Where, as part of the agreement for the provision of the car, the employee is required to pay for the private use of the car (and actually makes such a payment in that tax year), then the sum paid is deducted for the car benefit as calculated above. Care needs to be taken that the agreement is to pay for private use and not for some other reason, even if the payment relates to the car. For example, a requirement that the employee makes a contribution to the costs of insurance (perhaps to cover the additional costs of allowing family members to drive the car) will not pass this test. Only payments for the *actual* use of the car will qualify (*ITEPA 2003, s 144*).

Car fuel

2.49   In addition to the benefit charge on the provision of a car, a separate charge will apply where fuel is provided for that car, unless either all fuel used for private motoring is required to be (and is in fact) reimbursed by the employee or fuel is only made available for business travel (*ITEPA 2003, ss 149–153*).

The charge is calculated by:

- taking a fixed sum set annually by legislation (for 2016/17 this is £22,200);

- multiplying this by the appropriate percentage as set out in **2.45** above (*ITEPA 2003, s 150*).

This basic charge can be reduced proportionately where:

- the car is unavailable for part of a tax year (see **2.46**);

- the provision of fuel (whether completely or for private use) is stopped in the tax year;

- the car is shared (*ITEPA 2003, s 152*).

Focus

The car fuel charge is an 'all or nothing' charge. Rolling the wheels of the car once on a private journey will bring the full tax charge into play. Small errors can therefore have large tax downsides.

HMRC publishes rates (see www.gov.uk/government/publications/advisory-fuel-rates) which should be used when employees reimburse their employer for private mileage.

Vans

2.50 The legislation for vans is written in similar terms to the car legislation (that is a benefit will arise where the van is made available for private use by an employee, or a member of his family, by reason of employment but without the employee taking ownership), and similar reductions to any such benefit apply in the following case:

- periods when the van is unavailable (*ITEPA 2003, s 156* and see **2.46**);

- shared vans (*ITEPA 2003, s 157* and see **2.47**); and

- payment for private use (*ITEPA 2003, s 158* and see **2.48**).

But there are key differences, such as:

- the van charge will not apply where the private use is insignificant (see **2.52**);

• the van charge is calculated on a different basis (see **2.53**).

What is a van?

2.51   A van is defined as a 'mechanically propelled road vehicle' which is:

• a goods vehicle (being a vehicle 'of a construction primarily suited for the conveyance of goods or burden of any description'); with

• a design weight of no more than 3,500kg (ie not a heavy goods vehicle); and

• not a motor cycle.

People are not 'goods or burden' so a minibus will not be a van (*ITEPA 2003, s 115*).

Restrictions on private use

2.52   A van benefit will only apply if there is actual private use of the vehicle and this is not insignificant (*ITEPA 2003, s 114(3A)*). Insignificant for this purpose is not defined within the legislation and will therefore take its ordinary meaning. In particular, HMRC guidance on this matter is that the measure of whether private use is insignificant should be considered in respect of qualitative, quantitative and absolute terms over the tax year (see HMRC employment income manual EIM22745).

In addition to this broad test, there is a further test at *s 155(1B)* excluding any benefit where the 'restrictive private use' condition is met. This condition comprises the *commuter use* test and the *business travel* test both of which must be met throughout the tax year (or part thereof where the van is made available).

The *commuter use* test is met where a van is made available to an employee under terms which prohibit private use (other than that which is insignificant) other than normal 'commuting' and, in practice, no such additional private use is made of the van. This is a major difference between the van benefit rules and the car benefit rules (*ITEPA 2003, s 155(5)*).

The *business travel* test is met where the van is provided and used mainly for business travel (*ITEPA 2003, s 155(7)*).

So a van benefit charge will not arise where a van is provided primarily for business trips (eg to undertake a delivery round) as long as the only private use allowed and in fact undertaken is getting to and from home and the normal place of work (eg the warehouse where packets for delivery are picked up) with the occasional insignificant private uses (eg one or two trips a year to the local recycling centre to dispose of personal goods).

Measuring the van benefit

2.53   Where the van charge applies it is based on a flat rate (£3,150 for 2016/17) unless the van cannot under any circumstances emit CO_2 by being driven (eg a wholly electrically propelled van). In such cases, only a proportion of the flat rate is brought into account – 20% for 2016/17 increasing to 90% by 2021/22 (*ITEPA 2003, ss 155(1B)–(1C)*).

Any charge will be subject to any available deductions (see **2.50**).

Van fuel

2.54   Where fuel is provided for a van then a separate van fuel benefit may apply. This is based on a flat rate published in legislation. The rate for 2016/17 is £594 (*ITEPA 2003, s 161*).

The benefit is reduced to nil in cases where all fuel used for private motoring is required to be (and is in fact) reimbursed by the employee or fuel is only made available for business travel.

A van fuel benefit will not arise where the van itself is exempt from charge because the restrictive private use condition is met (see **2.52**) or where the van cannot under any circumstances emit CO_2 by being driven.

The van fuel benefit will be adjusted proportionately where the van is unavailable for part of a tax year, the provision of fuel is stopped in the tax year or the van is shared.

Beneficial loans

2.55   Where an employee or a relative of an employee is provided with a 'taxable cheap loan' by their employer or certain other persons then a taxable benefit will arise (*ITEPA 2003, s 175*) subject to certain exceptions (see **2.56**).

A *taxable cheap loan* is one on which either no interest is paid, or the interest paid is less than that which would be due at the official rate of interest (*ITEPA 2003, s 175(2)*).

It should be noted that the provision of beneficial loans to an employee on or after 6 April 2016 under a fair bargain will still be taxable (*ITEPA 2003, s 173(1A)* and see **2.16**).

Exceptions

2.56   The beneficial loan rules will not apply where:

- The loan is one where any interest paid would have qualified for tax relief (for example, if the loan was to borrow money to buy an interest in a closely controlled company). These are known as qualifying loans (*ITEPA 2003, s 178*).

- The total amount of the loan (or loans) is no more than £10,000 at any point within the tax year (previously £5,000 before 6 April 2014) although partial relief may still be available where there is more than one loan in place and although the overall total of those loans exceeds that amount, the total of non-qualifying loans does not (*ITEPA 2003, s 180*).

- The loan is made to a relative of the employee and it can be shown that the employee himself derived no benefit from the loan, but note that any benefit could be non-financial, such as a feeling of relief that the financial problems of a relative have been resolved by the making of the loan (*ITEPA 2003, s 174(5)(b), (6)*).

- The loan is to an employee to cover business expenses, it does not exceed £1,000, is repaid within six months of the date it was made and the employee regularly accounts for these expenses (*ITEPA 2003, s 179*).

- The loan is made by an employer whose business is advancing money and the employee is getting the same deal as members of the public (*ITEPA 2003, s 176*).

- Loans to lower-paid ministers of religion (see **2.14**).

The chargeable amount

2.57   Where a beneficial loan is made, the tax charge is based on the difference between the interest that would have been paid had interest been charged at the official rate of interest and the amount actually paid. This figure is normally worked out using an averaging method but a 'day-by-day' calculation can be used as an alternative (*ITEPA 2003, ss 182–183*).

Loans written off

2.58   If a loan is 'written off' by an employer and the only reason the loan has been written off is because the borrower is an employee then the amount written off is taxable under the normal rules of *ITEPA 2003, s 62* (see **2.4** above).

If the write off is due at least in part to some other reason (perhaps, for example, the write off of a loan to someone who has left the business) then *s 62* may not apply. In this case *ITEPA 2003, s 188* will bring the write off into charge to tax as long as the loan was originally made because of the employment of the borrower.

But care needs to be taken where the borrower was a participator (usually meaning a shareholder) and the lending company is a closely controlled company (which almost all owner-managed businesses are). In these cases any loan will attract a corporate tax charge on the company under *CTA 2010, s 455*. If such a loan is written off a separate charge to income tax will arise on the employee under *ITTOIA 2005, s 415* as if this was akin to a dividend. If a charge under *s 415* arises then *s 188* will not apply (by virtue of *ITEPA 2003, s 189*).

No charge will apply if:

- a loan to a relative of an employee is written off and it can be shown that the employee himself derived no benefit from the write off; or

- the loan is written off on the death of an employee.

Reporting benefits

2.59 Benefits can be accounted for and reported in several different ways:

- year-end reporting on Form P11D;

- in year payrolling of benefits; and

- by way of a PAYE settlement agreement (PSA).

Before 6 April 2016, there was also the potential to apply to HRMC for a dispensation in order to prevent the need to report benefits which were eligible for a claim for income tax relief by the employee (see **2.17**).

Forms P11D

2.60 The employer must make a return of benefits provided in the tax year on Form P11D by 6 July following the end of the tax year.

A Form P11D is completed for each employee provided with benefits, unless the benefits are exempt or are reported by one of the other routes noted at **2.59**. It is important to ensure that the benefits are reported in the correct section of the form, as only certain benefits attract Class 1A NIC.

The Forms P11D for each employee are submitted to HMRC along with a summary Form P11Db which sets out the Class 1A NIC liability of the company and also includes a declaration which must be made by the company. These forms can be submitted in paper form or electronically.

Full details of the reporting requirements are outside the scope of this book but can be found on the HMRC website at www.gov.uk/employer-reporting-expenses-benefits/overview.

The exemption from certain benefits for individuals who were in lower-paid employment was removed from 6 April 2016 (see **2.14**) and as a consequence reporting under the Form P9D is no longer required. Any benefits which are no longer exempt will instead be reported on the Form P11D.

Payrolling of benefits

2.61 Since 6 April 2016 it has been possible for certain benefits to be dealt with through the payroll system, rather than to report them at the end of the year on Forms P11D. This should ensure that the correct amount of income tax is paid on those benefits in the tax year in which they are received.

Under this system, the cash equivalent of the benefits are included on the payroll system as part of the employee's gross pay, allowing for the income tax due on the benefits to be collected over the tax year. The payrolling of the benefit does not deal with the national insurance liability though and this must be reported (and paid) after the end of the tax via the Form P11D(b).

Payrolling of benefits is optional and employers wishing to use this method must register with HRMC before the start of the tax year. Once done, HMRC will remove the value of any benefits being payrolled from the employee's tax code, so as to ensure that the employee is not taxed twice on the same benefit.

Further details can be found at www.gov.uk/guidance/paying-your-employees-expenses-and-benefits-through-your-payroll.

PAYE settlement agreement

2.62 A PSA is a method for the employer to account directly to HMRC for the tax cost of some benefits which would be difficult or impossible to accurately report as part of the year end procedure. Such items are limited to:

- minor items, such as a small present for an employee to mark a wedding;

- irregular items, such as expenses of a spouse occasionally accompanying an employee abroad;

- items where it is impracticable to operate PAYE on or to determine a value for P11D purposes, such as the cost of catering at an internal lunchtime meeting which is attended by numerous employees.

PSAs are annual agreements, and employers will need to renew the agreement with HMRC each tax year – this must be done before 6 July following the end of the relevant tax year.

Under a PSA it is the employer who settles the income tax liability of the employees and for this purpose, the benefit is 'grossed-up' – ie the income tax liability is based not only upon the value of the benefit provided to the employee, but also on the value of the employee's income tax liability settled by the employer.

Class 1B NIC is charged on the total value of the benefit and the income tax thereon (see **43.37**).

The employer must provide HMRC with a calculation of the income tax and national insurance due under the PSA by 6 July following the end of the relevant tax year. HMRC will then issue a payslip confirming that amount and the payment must then be made by 22 October following the tax year if paid electronically (or 19 October if paid by cheque).

Further details can be found at www.gov.uk/paye-settlement-agreements/overview.

PAYMENTS ON LEAVING EMPLOYMENT

2.63   When an employee leaves employment, additional payments may be made. This might be the case, for example, if a redundancy occurs, someone leaves by mutual agreement with the employer, or has to finish work because of ill health. If a payment is made on termination of employment, a careful analysis of any payment is needed to establish if special tax rules apply.

Payments taxed as normal remuneration

2.64   The first thing to consider is if the payment falls to be taxed under the normal rules of *ITEPA 2003, s 62* (see **2.3** *et seq* above). Any payment made to a departing employee who is paid under the contractual arrangements which exist between the employee and the employer will fall to be taxed under *s 62*. So, for example:

- payments of salary whilst someone works a notice period,

- a 'bonus' payment to ensure continued work up to the actual date of departure, and

- an additional reward for 'good work over the years'

will all fall to be taxed under the normal rules of *s 62*.

One issue which causes much debate relates to payments which are made where someone is given notice but is required to stop work immediately, even though the employment contract requires a period of notice to be given. These pay in lieu of notice (or PILON) payments are covered in more detail below but the key is to establish whether the payment is made because of a contractual arrangement (for example, the application of a clause within the employment contract). If so, then *s 62* will apply. If not then other, more advantageous, rules may apply (see below).

What are 'contractual payments'?

2.65   The issue of what formally constitutes a contract is a legal concept beyond the scope of this publication but for tax purposes the following explanation may help. All employees and employers enter into an agreement which governs the work which the employee agrees to do and the rewards which the employer agrees to provide. This agreement can be verbal but usually the terms are contained within a written employment contract. In addition, there may be other documents which set down the terms of the contract. These might include staff handbooks, letters of appointment, welfare pamphlets and collective agreements with a trade union.

In addition, there may be payments which are made because of the normal 'custom or practice' of an employer. For example, an employer might make a £500 'gift' to anyone leaving the firm after working for 15 years or more. This is not written down but it becomes the norm.

All these payments will be taxed under the provisions of *s 62*.

What if the 'normal remuneration' tax rules do not apply?

2.66   If the nature of the payment means that *s 62* does not apply then the next step is to consider if any other charging section applies.

On termination it is often the case that the employer will make a payment to ensure the departing employee is bound not to compete against the former employer, or is otherwise restricted, at least for a period after departure. Payments for restrictive covenants are specifically brought into tax by legislation as income *(ITEPA 2003, ss 225, 226)*.

In addition, a payment is sometimes made on a termination near retirement age. This can fall to be characterised as a payment of an 'unapproved' retirement benefit which again is brought into tax by specific legislation *(ITEPA 2003, s 394)*.

Only if the payment does not fall to be taxed under any of the above rules will the payment be dealt with under legislation which can give some relief from tax on termination payments.

The 's 401' rules

2.67 Special rules apply to deal with payments made on termination of an employment that are not otherwise chargeable to tax *(ITEPA 2003, s 401)*.

The rules will cover:

● payment of compensation on termination of an employment, whether through resignation, redundancy, death, illness, etc;

● payments of 'damages' because of a breach of the terms of an employment contract;

● redundancy payments, both statutory and any 'top up' payment;

● 'golden handshakes';

● payments in lieu of notice where there is no contractual entitlement to receive, or reserved right to make, such a payment.

It is vital to establish the true nature of the payment before applying the *s 401* rules, as descriptions of payments can often be misleading. It is the true nature of the payment which will determine the tax treatment of the payment, not what it is called.

For the *s 401* treatment to apply the payments must stem from the termination of employment. It is not enough just for the payments to be made at the same time as the termination.

The £30,000 exemption

2.68 If the *s 401* rules apply then in most cases the first £30,000 of any payment will be exempt from tax. It is not surprising, therefore, that the background to any such payment will be carefully considered by HMRC before accepting that the *s 401* rules can be used *(ITEPA 2003, s 403(1))*.

It is wrong to say that any payment on termination will benefit from this exemption, and great care should be taken to ensure that the nature of the payment actually leads to application of the *s 401* rules.

Focus

The £30,000 tax-free amount is not automatic as each case must be carefully considered to establish the reason why a payment has been made. NIC rules are different and no £30,000 limit exists for appropriate payments.

It was announced at the Budget 2016 that following a review of termination payments by the Office of Tax Simplification and a subsequent public consultation in 2015, legislation will be brought into the Finance Bill 2017 to 'tighten up the rules' in this area to 'prevent manipulation' and to align the rules applying to income tax and NIC (so that NIC will arise on these payments in circumstances where income tax is due). These changes are expected to take effect from April 2018.

100% exemption on termination through death, injury or disability

2.69   Where the termination is due to the death, injury or disability of the employee different rules can apply making the payment totally free from tax (*ITEPA 2003, s 406(a), (b)*).

The death of an employee is clearly straightforward to demonstrate but termination because of injury and disability can prove contentious.

'Injury' covers both the physical and the psychological. So for this rule someone who falls off a ladder will be in the same position as someone who has a nervous breakdown. If those unfortunate events lead to the individual leaving employment, a payment made on that termination may be paid free of tax.

HMRC will examine the facts of any such situation very carefully and will need to be convinced that the circumstances behind any such payment merit the 'tax free' treatment. They will rest their review on the findings in the tax case of *Hasted v Horner* ChD 1995, 67 TC 439. In this case two tests were established that must be passed for the treatment to apply. These are set out in the HMRC manual as follows:

- there must be an identified medical condition that disables or prevents the employee from carrying out the duties of the employment. Medical evidence confirming the precise nature of the disability must therefore be seen in all cases and it must be clear that the nature of the disability prevented the employee carrying out the specific duties of the employment; and

- the payment must be made on account of that disability and on account of nothing else. This means that the facts demonstrate that was the sole motive of the payer. In the typical case the payer will confirm that is so but the description given by the parties is not determinative if the facts indicate other motives exist. If, for example, the employer is unaware of the disability when the employee leaves, then the payment cannot be made on account of disability. Similarly, if any part of the payment is a reward for specific services, or due on termination regardless of the cause, it cannot be on account of disability.

In the recent case of *Moorthy v HMRC [2016] UKUT 0013 TCC* it was confirmed that the scope of this exemption does not extend to injury to feelings.

NIC

2.70   Any payment which qualifies for the *s 401* treatment will be fully exempt from National Insurance as such payments are not earnings. There is currently no £30,000 limit on this NIC exemption although it has been announced that this be changed from April 2018 (see **2.68**).

Non-cash benefits on termination

2.71   Quite often on the termination of an employment the individual will continue to enjoy, at least for a period, non-cash benefits. An example of this would be the continued use of a company car (*ITEPA 2003, s 415*).

The *s 401* rules cover both cash payments and non-cash benefits provided on termination. The £30,000 exemption applies first to the cash element with any remaining part of the exemption then applying to the cash equivalent of the benefit.

Non-cash benefits are taxed under *s 401* (subject to the application of the exemptions) when they are used or enjoyed. So, for example, a car which remains available for an ex-employee might give rise to a charge to tax for some time after the employee has left employment (*ITEPA 2003, s 403(3)*).

Payments to pension schemes

2.72   On termination, part of the leaving 'package' might involve a contribution to a pension fund. If the pension fund is a registered pension scheme or an employer-financed retirement benefit scheme then such a contribution will be outside the *s 401* rules and free of tax. It does not count towards the £30,000 exemption. Care must be taken not to breach any pension fund rules or the limits imposed on annual or lifetime contributions for tax purposes in such cases and advice should be sought from a pension specialist (*ITEPA 2003, s 408*).

Payment of legal costs

2.73   On termination the departing employee may need to take legal advice to protect his position, for example where the terms under which the employee is to leave the company are set down in a written compromise agreement. If the employer pays or contributes to these legal costs then such payments are accepted as being outside the terms of *s 401*, and are tax free, provided that the payment goes directly to the lawyer (unless the payment is made under a formal court order, in which case it will be exempt even if it goes directly to the departing employee) (*ITEPA 2003, s 413A*).

Outplacement counselling

2.74   When an employee leaves employment through, say, redundancy, it is not uncommon for the employer to pay for advice and assistance to help the employee deal with trauma of being without a job and to provide ideas and guidance on how to get back into economic activity.

Subject to certain limitations (for example the employee must have been in employment with the employer for two years and the service must be available to all similar employees) these costs do not form part of a taxable termination package and as such they do not count towards the £30,000 exemption (*ITEPA 2003, s 310*).

Foreign service

2.75   If the employee has worked overseas, any termination payment may be either fully or partly exempt from tax (*ITEPA 2003, s 413*).

If the employee's earnings are taxed as if he was not resident in the UK and:

- 75% of his period of service is foreign service, or

- if he has been working abroad for ten years or more, the last ten years of his total service has been foreign service, or

- if he has been working abroad for 20 years or more, 50% of his service (including ten of the last 20 years) is foreign service,

then any termination payment will be fully exempt.

If the employee does not qualify for full exemption under these rules, a proportion of his termination payment may still be exempt if some of his employment ranks as foreign service (*ITEPA 2003, s 414*).

Redundancy

2.76   Redundancy payments will always fall within the rules of *s 401*, benefiting from the £30,000 exemption. This will be the case even where the employer has published 'procedures' for making redundancy payments which might, at first glance, appear to constitute a contractual right which would bring payments into the *s 61* rules.

But great care must be taken to properly identify payments to ensure they fall within the definition of redundancy. A full technical explanation of this is beyond the scope of this publication but the key point is that a redundancy occurs when the position the employee occupies disappears. Where an individual moves aside to allow a continuing position to be occupied by another individual there is no redundancy.

It is also important to identify, even where there is a genuine redundancy, the nature of all the payments made on departure. If other payments are made at the same time (for example a payment to continue to work up until the redundancy date or a contractual payment in lieu of notice) then these payments are not redundancy payments and the tax treatment must be considered on their own terms.

PAYE and the payment of tax

2.77   If a termination package results in some of the payment being taxable and some not then the PAYE rules oblige the employer to deduct the correct amount of tax at source. Taxable payments made before the departure of the employee will be processed through the payroll in the normal way.

Taxable payments made after departure (either because they are contractual or are in excess of any exempt amount) are also taxed through payroll using code OT.

The employee should also comply with the requirements of the self-assessment tax return procedures in connection with any such termination payments.

THE 'DISGUISED REMUNERATION' REGIME

2.78   Since April 2011 there have been rules to attack arrangements under which employees are rewarded through third parties (such as trusts or other vehicles) which avoid or defer the payment of income tax. This legislation also covers unregistered pension schemes.

In outline, if third party arrangements are put in place to give a reward to an employee these rules act to ensure that an income tax charge arises, unless the specific arrangements are excluded from these rules. The rules are designed to catch tax avoidance arrangements, not certain recognised 'mainstream' reward plans (*ITEPA 2003, Pt 7A*).

These rules will only apply where a third party is involved. Direct payments from an employer to an employee will not be caught by these rules (but will, of course, be covered by the mainstream legislation above).

But note that the rules do catch situations where the employer is acting as a trustee or where payments are made by an employer under unregistered pension arrangements.

Common schemes which will be impacted by these rules will include the use of employee trusts or Employer-Financed Retirement Benefits Schemes (EFRBS) which provide, for example, loans which allow individuals to enjoy the benefit of money which has not been through the tax 'mill'. This may well impact on a number of high profile schemes which have been marketed and reported on in the press over the last year.

But the legislation should not catch some more mainstream arrangements. Registered pension schemes and approved employee share schemes will be protected as will ordinary commercial transactions.

In addition, benefits under 'all employee' plans that are genuinely available to substantially all employees will be outside these rules, as long as they cannot be accessed by only a few chosen individuals.

It should be noted that these rules are in addition to the General Anti-Abuse Rule (see **54.5**).

APPENDIX: COMPANY CAR BENEFIT CHARGES – 2014/15 TO 2016/17

(ITEPA 2003, s 139; Finance Act 2010, ss 58, 59; Finance Act 2011, s 51)

Table of appropriate percentages – 6 April 2014 to 5 April 2019

2.79

CO$_2$ emissions (g/km)	2018/19	2017/18	2016/17	2015/16	2014/15
0	13	9	7	5	0
1 – 50	13	9	7	5	5
51 – 75	16	13	11	9	5
76 – 94	19	17	15	13	11
95 – 99	20	18	16	14	12
100 – 104	21	19	17	15	13
105 – 109	22	20	18	16	14
110 – 114	23	21	19	17	15
115 – 119	24	22	20	18	16
120 – 124	25	23	21	19	17
125 – 129	26	24	22	20	18
130 – 134	27	25	23	21	19
135 – 139	28	26	24	22	20
140 – 144	29	27	25	23	21
145 – 149	30	28	26	24	22
150 – 154	31	29	27	25	23
155 – 159	32	30	28	26	24
160 – 164	33	31	29	27	25
165 – 169	34	32	30	28	26
170 – 174	35	33	31	29	27
175 – 179	36	34	32	30	28
180 – 184	37	35	33	31	29

185 – 189	37	36	34	32	30
190 – 194	37	37	35	33	31
195 – 199	37	37	36	34	32
200 – 204	37	37	37	35	33
205 – 209	37	37	37	36	34
210 and more	37	37	37	37	35

Notes

1   *Round down* – Before applying the appropriate percentage listed above, the emissions figure should be rounded down to the nearest multiple of five, except that rounding does not apply to cars with emissions below 95/km.

2   *Diesel cars* – These are subject to the 3% supplement up to a maximum of 37% for 2015/16 and onwards, and 35% for 2014/15 and earlier (see **2.45**).

3

Self-employment

SIGNPOSTS

- **Scope** – All individuals who are carrying on a trade, profession or vocation, whether alone or in partnership, are treated as self-employed and have to register with HMRC under self-assessment (see **3.1–3.3**).

- **What is 'trading'?** – The question as to whether a trade is being carried on or not depends on the facts in each case (see **3.4–3.6**).

- **How profits are calculated** – The income tax charge is based on the profits per the accounts as adjusted for tax purposes. For this purpose, accounts are required to be prepared in accordance with UK generally accepted accounting principles which is based on the accruals basis, although some small businesses do have the option to use the cash basis (see **3.7–3.17**).

- **How profits are taxed** – The tax year in which profits fall to be taxed is governed by the rules concerning basis periods and specific provisions apply to the opening and closing years of trade (see **3.18–3.24**).

- **Partnerships** – A partnership is generally not considered to be a separate legal entity for tax purposes and there are special provisions for determining how taxable profits of the partnership are allocated to the individual partners. Specific rules apply to salaried members of limited liability partnerships and partnerships consisting of mixed members (see **3.25–3.33**).

- **Loss relief** – Where a business makes a taxable loss, reliefs are available to deduct the loss from other income and gains or to carry it forward to be deducted from future profits of the same trade. Restrictions apply to limit relief for such losses arising from tax avoidance arrangements and in the case of non-active traders. Losses arising from a partnership may also be restricted to the level of a partners' capital contribution (see **3.34–3.47**).

- **Construction Industry Scheme (CIS)** – The CIS makes it compulsory for both actual and deemed contractors to register under the scheme with HMRC before making any payments to subcontractors (unless they are employees) under a contract for construction operations (see **3.48–3.56**).

- **Appendix: Time limits for claims and elections** – See table at the end of the chapter (see **3.57**).

INTRODUCTION

3.1   An individual who starts his own business is treated as self-employed for tax purposes provided the business is not operated from within a limited company and the services provided do not rank as an employment (see **Chapter 2** above).

The taxpayer will need to register the business with HMRC (see **1.6**).

If the individual goes into business with other individuals and a partnership is formed, the individual will still be treated as self-employed but it is the partnership which will be responsible for registering the business with HMRC and filing tax returns (see **3.26**).

Tax will be payable on the profits from the trade, profession or vocation which are charged to income tax in accordance with the provisions laid down in the *Income Tax (Trading and Other Income) Act 2005 (ITTOIA 2005)*.

The scope of the tax charge covers all trade profits (which includes profits from a profession or vocation):

- arising to a UK resident wherever the trade is carried on;

- arising to a non-UK resident either:
    - from a trade carried out wholly in the UK; or
    - from the activities located in the UK if the trade is carried on partly in the UK and partly abroad.

    (*ITTOIA 2005, ss 5, 6*)

Note that if a person ceases to be UK resident he is treated for income tax purposes as having ceased the trade at the time he becomes non-UK resident and, if he continues to trade in the UK, as having started up a new trade immediately afterwards (*ITTOIA 2005, ss 17, 852(6)–(7) and 854(5)*).

The person who is liable to the tax charge is the person who receives or who is entitled to receive the profits (*ITTOIA 2005, s 8*).

Business records need to be kept of all transactions so that an accurate return of income can be made (see **1.36**). Tax is charged on the full amount of the profits for the tax year which are based on the profits in the basis period. The general rule is that the basis period for the tax year is the period of 12 months ending with the accounting date in that tax year. The specific rules regarding basis periods are laid down in the legislation (*see* **3.18**).

A person who is self-employed will be liable to pay National Insurance contributions (NICs). Class 2 contributions are payable at a fixed rate per week. The liability for Class 4 contributions is based on the taxable profits assessable in the tax year and is calculated as part of the income tax computation. See **Chapter 44** for NIC and the self-employed.

STARTING A BUSINESS

Responsibilities as a self-employed taxpayer

3.2   Anyone who is self-employed is personally responsible for paying the tax and NIC liabilities arising from their business. It is therefore necessary to inform HMRC of chargeability to tax by registering for self-assessment. On registration a unique tax reference number (UTR) is issued to the individual.

A person becomes self-employed whether he is operating as a sole trader or working in partnership. However, the process for registering with HMRC varies as follows:

1   Sole traders registering for self-assessment and NICs can do so online where they have previously not been registered for self-assessment (www.gov.uk/new-business-register-for-tax) or by completing Form CWF1 (www.gov.uk/government/publications/self-assessment-and-national-insurance-contributions-register-if-youre-a-self-employed-sole-trader-cwf1) where they are already part of the 'self-assessment system' and have a UTR.

2   Partnerships:

   - A partnership is treated as a separate entity for tax purposes. Therefore the partnership itself needs to be registered for self-assessment. The partnership must nominate a representative partner who will be responsible for submitting the partnership tax return.

   - A new partnership needs to be registered for self-assessment using Form SA400 (www.gov.uk/government/publications/self-assessment-register-a-partnership-for-self-assessment-sa400) although Limited Liability Partnerships are registered from their Companies House registration.

- It is the individual partners though who are responsible for paying the tax and NIC liabilities allocated to them, not the partnership, so each partner must also register separately.

- A new partner needs to register for self-assessment and Class 2 NICs using Form SA401 (www.gov.uk/government/publications/self-assessment-register-a-partner-for-self-assessment-and-class-2-nics-sa401) unless they are not an individual in which case Form SA402 is used (www.gov.uk/government/publications/self-assessment-register-a-partner-for-self-assessment-if-theyre-not-an-individual-sa402).

It is recommended that HMRC is notified as soon as the business has started. The strict deadlines are as follows:

- The time limit to register for Class 2 NICs is within three months of the commencement of the business. A person will be liable to a penalty, based on a percentage of the contributions lost, if notification has not been made by 31 January following the end of the tax year.

- The time limit to notify HMRC for income tax purposes is by 5 October following the end of the tax year in which the chargeability to tax arose. Penalties can be charged for late notification (*FA 2008, Sch 41*) of up to 100% of the tax due though in practice if the tax has been paid within 12 months of the due date for payment and an unprompted disclosure made, the penalty can be mitigated in full.

For further details on penalties, see **53.1**.

The business may also need to register as an employer if it is intending to take on employees so that it can enrol for PAYE (see **2.9**).

Registration for VAT must also be considered. There is an obligation to register for VAT if the turnover of taxable goods and services of the business is expected to exceed £83,000 (the annual registration limit from 1 April 2016) in the first 30 days alone or was over £83,000 for the last 12 months. It may be to the business's advantage to register voluntarily (see **Chapter 38**).

Registration for PAYE and VAT may be done online at the same time as the individual registers with HMRC for self-assessment (www.gov.uk/new-business-register-for-tax).

It is the duty of both sole traders and individual partners to submit an income tax return where requested to HMRC, to report their self-employed income (see **Chapter 1**). The business profits of sole traders are reported on the self-employment supplementary pages in either the short or full version of the tax return. The form of tax return required will depend on the complexity of the tax affairs and the annual turnover of the business.

The partnership supplementary pages need to be completed by a partner to disclose his share of the taxable profits of the partnership and any other taxable partnership income (as taken from the partnership return) and again these are available in both the short and full versions. The partnership tax return, which needs to be submitted by the representative nominated partner, is dealt with at **3.26**.

> **Focus**
>
> Business records must be kept of all business transactions including supporting documentation so that complete and accurate returns can be made. It is a legal requirement to keep adequate records for a specified time (see **1.36–1.38** and **Chapter 55**).

Deciding whether to operate as a sole trader, partnership or limited company

3.3   When starting a business, a question which needs to be addressed is: Which is the most suitable vehicle for the business? Should the business be unincorporated or be carried out through a limited company? If the business is to be run jointly, should a formal partnership be formed and, if so, would a limited liability partnership be advantageous or not? Or is it best to start as a sole trader and then incorporate once the business has been established?

The answers to these questions will depend not only on the tax issues but also on a variety of other commercial factors, including any additional administrative burdens and any particular regulatory requirements of the trade, profession or vocation.

What is a trade?

3.4   In many cases it will be quite clear that the activities of a business constitute a trade. However, there are also many occasions when the situation is not so clear cut. For example, the occasional buying and selling of personal possessions through the internet may not be regarded as trading, whereas the setting up of a website (or the use of an online platform such as eBay) to market items that are being purchased and then advertised for resale at a marked up price may well be considered a trading activity.

The question of whether a person is trading is important in establishing whether a charge to income tax exists. Moreover, if a transaction is deemed to be a trading activity rather than simply the sale of a chargeable asset, the income tax rules will apply, rather than the capital gains tax rules. This will lead to the application of different rules on the deductibility of expenses and availability of losses, different reliefs potentially being available and different rates of tax applying – all of which will impact on net tax payable.

There is anti-avoidance legislation for certain transactions in land that may need to be considered when land is being bought and sold. This is a complex area and care needs to be taken to make sure that the provisions do not apply.

How to identify activities as trading

3.5   The legislation defines trade so as to include 'any venture in the nature of trade' (*ITA 2007, s 989*).

Although the word 'venture' could catch a one-off transaction, the definition is not that helpful in clarifying exactly how to identify trading activities, as opposed to, say, a capital disposal or simply organising one's own investments by the buying and selling of shares. It has been left to case law, drawing conclusions from individual circumstances, to provide the main indicators of when trading activity takes place.

These indicators are often referred to as the 'badges of trade' and were reviewed in the case of *Marson v Morton* ChD 1986, 59 TC 381. This gives us a number of guidelines to consider when deciding if a business is trading or not: it is necessary to look at the specific facts of each particular situation as well as considering the case in its totality. It is recommended to seek specialist advice, when the situation is not clear.

The relevant extracts from this case are set out at **19.1** but in summary the 'badges of trade' (and some comments thereon) include:

1   *Profit-seeking motive* – Was there an intention to make a profit? Was this the reason why actions have been taken, or taken in a particular way? Was the project demonstrably 'commercially viable'? Or did an advantage accrue simply by chance? Was a profit made despite the stated original motivation of the taxpayer?

2   *Type of asset* – Were the goods acquired of a kind that would be subject to further processes, eg raw materials subjected to a manufacturing

process? Or were they of the type to be acquired for personal pleasure, like, perhaps, a boat? What were the reasons for the purchase of the asset? Was it:

- for the taxpayer's own use or consumption, or
- as an investment, or
- possibly to yield income and resale at profit (*CIR v Fraser* CS 1942 24 TC 498).

3   *Repetition of transactions* – Were sales regularly made and of the same kind of items and at a level that suggests an on-going trading activity? Is this a hobby that has developed into a trade?

4   *Asset modification* – Were the assets altered or improved before being sold on? Were purchases bought in bulk and the items then sold on in smaller lots?

5   *Circumstances of asset sale* – Were the sales conducted in a commercial manner, eg a shop or website set-up, the business advertised or a sales person taken on?

6   *Lapse of time between purchase and sale* – Were the items purchased and sold on fairly quickly, suggesting that they were acquired for a 'quick profit' rather than as an investment?

7   *Finance* – Was money borrowed to fund the purchase, possibly on disadvantageous terms which would require the borrower to repay the loan quickly?

8   *How was the asset acquired* – Was it inherited or received as a gift or was it purchased?

It is also worth noting that profits from illegal trading activities are still chargeable to income tax.

Miscellaneous income

3.6   *ITTOIA 2005* also contains provision (in *Pt 5*) for the taxation of miscellaneous income. These rules apply to receipts that are taxable but are not trading income; for example, monies received by a writer for occasional articles written. This can be compared to the tax treatment of monies received by a journalist who regularly writes articles, which are taxable as part of his professional or vocational work.

HOW ARE TAXABLE PROFITS MEASURED?

The legislation

3.7 *ITTOIA 2005, Pt 2 (Trading Income)* sets out the rules which need to be applied in order to arrive at the taxable profits for a trade, profession or vocation. These rules also apply to the calculation of profits of a property business but subject to the limitations listed (*ITTOIA 2005, s 272(1), (2)*).

The taxation of property income, which includes the profits from a property business, is dealt with in **Chapter 8**.

Outline of steps to be taken

3.8 The starting point for calculating taxable profits is the profits per the accounts. The legislation lays down basic rules for the basis on which the accounts must be prepared, which include the requirement that accounts have to be prepared in accordance with UK generally accepted accounting practice (*ITTOIA 2005, s 25*).

Adjustments to the profits then have to be made in accordance with the provisions that restrict certain deductions and allow other specified items. The most important of these restrictions is that expenditure has to be wholly and exclusively for the purposes of the business (see **3.15(2)**). Where no specific provisions or principles exist that affect a particular item of income or expenditure, there is no need to make an adjustment as it is the accounting practice that prevails and thereby determines the tax treatment of the item.

No deductions can be made for capital expenditure but certain expenditure may qualify for capital allowances (see **Chapter 4**). Capital allowances claimed are treated as a trading expense (or where there are only balancing charges, these are treated as a trading receipt) in arriving at taxable profits for the accounting period (*CAA 2001, s 2*). Relief for capital expenditure may also be available if on disposal of the asset, any gain is chargeable to capital gains tax, in which case the cost of the asset can be deducted from the sale proceeds (see **Chapter 12**).

HMRC guidance

3.9 For clarification of how the profits are calculated, the HMRC Business Income Manual (BIM) is a useful resource (www.hmrc.gov.uk/manuals/bimmanual/index.htm). It provides detailed guidance on HMRC's interpretation of the rules and common practice when measuring taxable profits.

HMRC has also produced 'toolkits' to cover specific areas where mistakes are commonly made. The current toolkits that relate to business profits are:

- *Business Profits* (www.gov.uk/government/publications/hmrc-business-profits-toolkit)

- *Capital v Revenue Expenditure* (www.gov.uk/government/publications/hmrc-capital-vs-revenue-expenditure-toolkit)

- *Private and Personal Expenditure* (www.gov.uk/government/publications/hmrc-private-and-personal-expenditure-toolkit).

These are available to download and include hyperlinks to more detailed guidance if needed. Care must always be taken though in using the advice offered as the application of the toolkits depends on the law at the relevant time and on the precise facts. They are generally updated annually.

Specific trades

3.10   Certain trades are dealt with on a different basis from the general rules (*ITTOIA 2005, ss 9–16*). They include such trades as farming and market gardening, visiting performers and divers and diving supervisors.

There are also other trades where specific practices are applied when calculating taxable profits.

Detailed guidance on how to measure the profits of particular trades can be found at BIM50000.

ACCOUNTS PREPARATION

General

3.11   The accounts are prepared from the books and records of the business. It is a legal requirement for the taxpayer to maintain adequate records in order to be able to submit a complete and accurate return of the taxable income of the business to HMRC (see **1.36–1.38**).

The accounts have to be prepared in accordance with UK generally accepted accounting practice (UK GAAP). **Chapter 59** gives some background information on some of the key areas of UK GAAP that are relevant for tax purposes.

In a nutshell, the profits of a business per the accounts are derived from:

- turnover (business income);

- *less* business expenditure (excluding capital expenditure).

If the business is registered for VAT, the receipts and expenses are normally included net of VAT.

Accruals basis

3.12   One of the fundamental requirements of UK GAAP is that the accounts are prepared on an accruals basis (see **59.4**). This means that transactions are reflected in the accounts in the period in which the right to the income arose and the legal liability for expenses was incurred. It is irrelevant when the cash was received or when the expenditure was paid for.

If the business is accounting for VAT on a cash basis, it is important to make sure that adjustments are made for transactions occurring around the year end so that the income and expenditure not yet received or paid for is included in the accounts.

In the case of *Smith v HMRC* [2011] STC 1724, it was held that accounts that were not prepared under UK GAAP relevant at the time constituted 'negligent conduct': note that the behaviour of the taxpayer affects the level of penalties charged for errors made in the returns, although the term careless is now used in the legislation instead of negligent (see **53.8**).

However, unincorporated small businesses can elect to prepare their accounts on the cash basis, rather than the accruals basis (see **3.13**).

Example 3.1 – Accounts adjustments

Andy set up a new business selling vintage clothes on 1 December 2015. He prepared his first set of accounts himself which are made up to 30 June 2016 and showed a profit of £12,000. He has treated payments made from the business bank account as deductions against profit and included all monies received by 30 June 2015 in turnover (he has not elected for the cash basis). The draft accounts are presented to his accountant and Andy is surprised to see that the profit figure, as revised by the accountant, now stands at £15,000.

The adjustments that have been made are:

		£
Profits per draft accounts		12,000
Adjustments		
1	Increase in turnover for additional sales made pre year end	1,125
2	Cost of sales reduced by closing stock	1,500

3	Business rates reduced by the prepayment proportion	1,800
4	Accountancy charges included for services provided	(1,000)
5	Expenses reduced by excluding cost of new laptop	475
	Profits per final accounts	15,900

Notes – Reasons for adjustments

1   Andy had sold vintage clothes to a friend, Beth, who had started up her own online business. At 30 June 2016, Beth still owed Andy £1,125. The date that determines when the sales should be included in turnover is the date the contract is made. The date the cash is received is not relevant.

2   Andy had deducted from his profits all payments made for clothes bought. However, in his shop on 30 June 2016 were clothes costing £1,500. This closing stock has to be excluded from total cost of sales as these costs cannot be matched against sales made in the accounting period. Relief will be available for these costs in the period in which they are sold.

3   The business rates of £2,400 for the year were paid in full in April 2016. However, only the proportion relating to the period up to 30 June 2016 can be claimed as a deduction: thus the payment covering the nine-month period from July 2016 to March 2017 has to be disallowed and will be deducted in the June 2017 accounts.

4   Accountancy charges of £1,000 for services provided to the business relating to the period ended 30 June 2016 can be claimed as a deduction even though the invoice was not raised until after the year end.

5   The cost of the laptop cannot be claimed as an expense against revenue as it is a capital item and will still have value at the year end, although tax relief can be claimed through capital allowances (see **Chapter 4**).

Cash basis and simplified expenses for small businesses

3.13   Since 6 April 2013 certain small businesses have been able to elect to use a simpler cash basis to work out their taxable income. In contrast to the accruals basis (see **3.12**), the cash basis computes the profits by bringing in all business receipts and deducting all allowable business payments within the period of account for a given tax year in which they were received or paid. No adjustments are made for debtors, creditors or stock, apart from in the year in which the business enters or leaves the cash basis when transitional rules apply to ensure that income is only taxed once and relief for expenditure is only claimed once (*ITTOIA 2005, Pt 2, Ch 3A*).

A flat rate simplified expense scheme for certain business expenses was introduced at the same time as the cash basis although this is available to all unincorporated businesses, whether or not they adopt the cash basis (*ITTOIA 2005, Ch 5A*). This scheme allows a taxpayer to deduct flat rate expenses rather than the actual expense incurred and applies only to the following categories:

- Vehicles – a flat rate for mileage can be claimed instead of the actual cost of buying and running a vehicle (eg insurance, repairs and fuel). The current rate is 45p per mile for the first 10,000 miles and 25p per mile thereafter. The rate applies equally to cars and goods vehicles but cannot be used where a claim has previously been made for capital allowances in respect of the vehicle.

- Working from home – rather than claiming a proportion of utility expenses for costs incurred in connection with the use of a home for business purposes, a flat rate can be claimed based upon the number of hours per month the home is used for business purposes. This allowance does not cover telephone and internet costs, which can be claimed in the usual way.

- Living at business premises – where the taxpayer lives at the business premises (for example, in the running of a guesthouse) an adjustment is required to reflect the split of expenses incurred between business and private use. A flat rate adjustment can be used instead of apportioning the actual expenses – this is calculated as a monthly adjustment based upon the number of people living at the premises.

Although the legislation was introduced following a recommendation by the Office of Tax Simplification, it is strongly recommended that taxpayers become familiar with all the complexities of the cash basis before electing to use it. This is necessary not only to make sure that the taxable profits under the new system have been correctly computed under the transitional rules but also that it is in the taxpayer's best interests to make the switch. Guidance can be found at BIM70000.

A main summary of the cash basis rules and points to watch out for are:

- *The election* – The election to opt for the cash basis is made on the individual's tax return for sole traders and on the partnership return for businesses operated by a partnership.

- *Who qualifies* – Self-employed individuals and partnerships can choose the cash basis, provided that the turnover of the business does not exceed the annual VAT threshold (£83,000 for 2016/17) or twice the threshold if the person is a recipient of universal credit. The threshold applies to the turnover of all businesses held by one person in that tax year. There is legislation that deals with what to do when the thresholds are exceeded and when it is possible to opt out of the scheme. There are also specific exclusions from using the cash basis (*ITTOIA 2005, s 31A–C*).

- *Effect on loss relief* – No sideways loss relief can be claimed if when calculating taxable income a negative result arises (see **3.42**). Such losses can only be carried forward and set against future profits of the same business whilst the cash basis is used.

- *Transitional rules* – These cover the situation when a business moves into or out of the cash basis or ceases to trade. The intention is to make sure income, expenses and stock are treated in a logical way so that no items are taxed or claimed twice. Where adjustments result in an addition to income, it is spread evenly over the next six years, with the option of an election being made to bring it forward (*ITTOIA 2005, ss 226–240*).

- *Interest on cash borrowings* – *ITTOIA 2005, s 51A* introduces the general rule which prohibits a deduction for interest paid on a loan in calculating the profits on a cash basis. However, *ITTOIA 2005, s 57B* does allow a deduction of up to £500 for such disallowable interest.

- *Capital expenditure (excluding cars)* – With the exclusion of expenditure on cars, expenditure on any item that would have otherwise qualified as plant and machinery for capital allowance purposes is able to be deducted under the cash basis and any proceeds received on the subsequent sale of the assets included in income (*ITTOIA 2005, ss 33–33A*). However, care needs to be taken when switching to the cash basis as there are specific provisions to deal with assets on which capital allowances have previously been claimed (*ITTOIA 2005, Pt 2, Ch 17A*). There are also specific rules dealing with assets bought on hire purchase and the adjustments that may need to be made when switching to or from cash basis.

- *Cars* – The provisions enabling a deduction for capital expenditure (*ITTOIA 2005, s 33A*) do not apply to the purchase of cars. The taxpayer still has the option of claiming capital allowances and motor expenses paid (less any adjustment for private use) in the usual way or he can choose to adopt the flat rate simplified expenses scheme.

- *Goods for own use* – there is no requirement to bring into account as a receipt the value of any goods taken for personal use. Instead, a just and reasonable adjustment should be made, for example, the cost of such goods might be disallowed as an expense.

It should be stressed that expenses can only be claimed as a deduction if they are qualifying business expenses, that are:

- incurred wholly and exclusively for the purposes of the business (see **3.15(2)**); and

- incurred in respect of expenditure which is not capital in nature (see **3.15(1)**) – with the exception for the cost of certain expenditure which would otherwise qualify as expenditure on plant and machinery as detailed above.

Turnover (business income)

3.14 It is important to ensure that income from all sources is included and that adequate records are kept as evidence that the income reported is a true reflection of business activities.

Particular care needs to be taken to ensure that systems are in place to record all cash transactions. A risk area would be expenditure or drawings taken by the proprietor from cash sales: if the cash sales are not correctly recorded then the profits would be understated. The HMRC toolkit on 'Business Profits' highlights the risk areas when income has not been fully accounted for and advises on how to mitigate the risks.

Another consequence of inadequate records is where deposits of non-business receipts (such as loans or gifts) are paid into the bank account and for which no supporting documentation has been kept. In the event of an enquiry being opened, HMRC would take the view that such deposits constituted business income unless it could be proved otherwise.

The turnover should not include any items for capital receipts such as the sale of a car or compensation proceeds received for the loss of an asset. Instead, these items should be included in the accounts as a profit or loss on disposal. A tax adjustment would then be made to remove the debit or credit from the profits and the proceeds of sale would either be dealt with through the capital allowances computations, if capital allowances had been claimed on the asset disposed of (see **Chapter 4**) or in computing any chargeable gain if the disposal falls within the capital gains tax legislation (see **Chapter 12**).

Expenditure – rules restricting deductions

3.15 In calculating the profits of the trade (including professions and vocations) certain deductions made in the accounts are restricted for tax purposes and the amounts that do not qualify as a tax deduction will need to be added back in the tax computation to arrive at taxable profits (*ITTOIA 2005, ss 33–55B*).

Care will need to be taken to ensure that the correct tax treatment is followed and the first step in achieving this is to identify expenses that may be restricted. This is a complex area and there may be the need to seek further advice. It is often necessary to look at case law and compare the facts of different cases with the facts of the particular expense in question to decide what is and is not allowable.

Detailed guidance can be found at:

- BIM30000 Measuring the profits (general rules) – accountancy and tax, stock, VAT, capital or revenue, wholly and exclusively;

- BIM40000 Measuring the profits (specific rules and practices) – receipts and deductions.

The first two rules covered by the legislation restricting deductions are of a more general nature (*ss 33* and *34*) whereas the subsequent rules deal with specific items (*ss 35–55B*):

1   *Capital expenditure (s 33)*

- Expenditure of a capital nature is not allowed as a deduction (*s 33*); the term 'capital' is not defined in legislation and as such has been left to the courts to decide. In board terms though, it can be considered in terms of any item of expenditure on the acquisition of an asset or advantage for the enduring benefit of the business.

- Clearly expenditure on the purchase of a fixed asset would be considered to be capital in nature, but so would the cost of any significant improvement to that asset along with any costs associated with acquiring the asset. But capital expenditure extends far beyond the acquisition of fixed assets – it can include, for example, costs incurred in establishing or altering the capital structure of the business (including forming, varying or dissolving a partnership or converting a partnership to an LLP) and in certain cases a payment made to exit an onerous contract. The answer to whether a payment is capital in nature will turn on the specific facts of the case.

- The HMRC 'capital v revenue expenditure' toolkit lists the main areas where common errors are made. It is necessary to review specific expense headings in order to identify any items of a capital nature; these would include legal and professional costs, repairs and renewals and finance costs.

2   '*Wholly and exclusively' (s 34)*

- Expenditure has to be 'wholly and exclusively for the purposes of the business' in order to qualify as a deduction. If there was a dual purpose in incurring the expenditure and the proportion incurred

109

for the purposes of the trade can be identified, then this proportion can remain as a deduction but an add-back will be required to cover the non-business element. HMRC have highlighted this as an area where errors commonly occur in their toolkit 'private and personal expenditure'.

- The potential problem areas include:

  ○ Travel and subsistence:

    This is an area of potential confusion as there is often a lack of understanding as to what constitutes business and personal expenditure. For example, travel from home to the normal work place is ordinary commuting and such expenditure is of a personal nature and does not qualify for a business deduction.

    Where a journey is undertaken for both business and pleasure (a dual purpose), the restriction of the deduction will depend very much on the facts: for example, was the personal element only incidental to the business trip or was it the other way round?

    In situations where the travelling expenses do qualify, related subsistence expenses will also qualify (*ITTOIA 2005, s 57A*). Detailed records should be kept of business journeys as evidence of the basis of the claim for business expenditure.

  ○ Personal bills paid and withdrawals of monies for the proprietor's or partner's own use, either from the business bank account, by the business credit card or out of cash must be identified and cannot be claimed as a deduction from profits. These amounts should be debited instead to the partner's current or capital account.

    Even if monies withdrawn have been described as 'wages' or where a fixed share of a partner's profits is referred to as a 'salary' they are not allowable deductions – they are simply a withdrawal of profits. However, this is not the case for certain salaried members of LLPs (see **3.30**).

    Expenditure may have been incurred for both business and personal purposes, such as using the home as an office or paying the interest on a car loan which is used for both private and business use. Only the business proportion can be claimed.

  ○ Wages paid to family members that are not commensurate with their duties will need to be adjusted for, for example if

110

the owner's husband acts as a secretary and gets paid twice the market rate then the excess should be added back.

○   Services that have been provided by the business to the owner or partner cannot be claimed as a deduction, for example the servicing of the owner's car by their garage business. Note that it is the costs of the services provided (namely wages and materials and any associated expenses) that need to be added back and not the market value of the service that would have been charged to a third party.

3   *Rules regarding specific expenses*

These rules dealing with specific items can be found in *ITTOIA 2005, ss 35–55B* and are summarised as follows:

- *Bad and doubtful debts (s 35)* – Only specific debts that are identified as bad or estimated to be bad are allowable. General provisions (ie a percentage of debtors over a certain age) or provisions for slow payers (ie the customer who always pays late) are not allowed.

- *Unpaid remuneration (ss 36–37)* – Where the accounts include an expense for employee wages that have not been paid nine months after the end of the period of account, the deduction needs to be added back for tax purposes.

- *Employee benefit contributions (ss 38–44)* – These rules set out the conditions when deductions are allowed for arrangements that provide benefits to employees through a trust scheme or other arrangement.

- *Business entertainment and gifts (ss 45–47)* – The general rule is that no deduction is allowed for expenses incurred in providing entertainment or gifts, with the following exceptions:

  (i)   It is the trader's business to provide entertainment and it is provided in the ordinary course of his business;

  (ii) The entertainment is provided for employees (which would generally be assessed on the employee as a taxable benefit – see **2.14**) unless the entertainment is provided for others and the provision of entertainment to the employees is incidental to the provision of others; or

  (iii) Generally gifts that do not cost the trader more than £50 and carry a conspicuous advert for the trader, and are not food, drink, tobacco or a token or voucher exchangeable for gifts. Gifts cannot be provided to employees unless they are also provided to others and their provision to the employees is incidental. The restriction of £50 applies to the costs of all gifts given to the same person in the same basis period.

- *Car or motor cycle hire (ss 48–50B)* – Hire charges are restricted where the vehicle's CO_2 emissions exceed 130g/km. The restriction is calculated as 15% of the hire charges.

- *Social security contributions (s 53)* – No deductions are allowed for the payment of either Class 2 or Class 4 NIC.

- Penalties, interest and VAT surcharges are not allowable deductions (*s 54*), nor are crime related payments (*s 55*).

Expenditure – rules allowing deductions

3.16 These rules lay down the deductions that are allowed for specific expenses (*ITTOIA 2005, Pt 2, Ch 5*). They include provision for:

- Pre-trading expenses (*s 57*) incurred for the purposes of the trade in the seven years before the trade began can be claimed as a deduction, by being treated as expenses on the start date. Clearly, they must be deductions that would have qualified had they been incurred after the trade commenced.

- Incidental costs of finance where the loan interest qualifies (*s 58*).

- Replacement and alteration of trade tools where the original cost did not qualify as a deduction on the grounds that it was of a capital nature (*s 68*).

- Employees seconded to charities and educational establishments (*ss 70–71*).

- Counselling and retraining expenses (*ss 73–75*) and redundancy payments, etc (*ss 76–80*).

- Scientific research – for trades only, not professions or vocations (*ss 87–88*).

- Expenses connected with patents (*s 89*) and designs or trademarks (*s 90*).

- Expenses connected with foreign trades (*ss 92–94*).

- Certain payments to salaried members of an LLP (*s 94AA*) where they are deemed to be employed rather than self-employed (see **3.30**)

Focus

Find out about how the business is conducted and the type of expenses that are paid before completing the computation of taxable trading profits.

A complete and accurate return is made when only allowable deductions are claimed and all income has been correctly included.

Computation of trading income – example showing tax adjustments made

3.17

Example 3.2 – Calculating taxable profits

John Smith is a UK trader who commenced trade on 1 June 2015. His profit and loss account for the year to 31 May 2016 was as follows:

	£	£
Sales		150,000
Deduct purchases	75,000	
Less: stock at 31.5.16	(15,000)	60,000
Gross profit		90,000
Deduct:		
Salaries	28,000	
Depreciation	2,700	
Motor expenses	4,500	
Travel and subsistence	1,800	
Rent and rates	7,500	
Office expenses	2,800	
Heat and light	1,600	
Advertising and promotion	1,100	
Entertainment	475	
Bank interest and charges	150	
Legal and accountancy fees	1,300	
Repairs and renewals	600	
Bad debts	3,522	
Sundries	205	56,252
Net profit		33,748
Loss on sale of office equipment		(200)

Rent received	700
Bank interest received (net)	80
Profit	34,328

Additional information

(a)   *Sales* – Goods with a sales value of £300 were given to a friend who runs a garage in exchange for free servicing of a sports car owned by Mrs Eileen Smith, John's wife.

(b)   *Stock* – Goods that cost £250 were thought to have gone missing at the year-end but were found a few weeks later.

(c)   *Salaries* – Included in salaries is a bonus of £1,000 that was promised to the sales manager but which has never been paid.

(d)   *Motor expenses* – This includes the insurance, servicing, tax and repair costs of £2,500 on John Smith's private car. From business mileage records kept (which exclude home to work), the business use proportion is 40%.

(e)   *Travel and subsistence* – This includes the cost of £700 on a trip for John and Eileen Smith to Paris to celebrate their wedding anniversary, during which they also intended to visit a potential supplier who unfortunately was unavailable.

(f)   *Office expenses* – Mobile telephone costs of which £300 relate to non-business use.

(g)   *Advertising and promotion* – This includes the cost of £180 for entertaining potential customers.

(h)   *Entertainment* – This includes £100 spent in taking all the staff out for a Christmas meal.

(i)   *Repairs and renewals* – This includes £500 in respect of the replacement of various old tools. No deduction had been claimed when the tools were first purchased and the tools are similar in design to the original tools.

(j)   *Bad debts* – A provision of £250 has been made of 10% against all debts that are more than six months old. The balance of the charge relates to specific write-offs of debts that are known to be bad.

(k)   *Sundries* – Parking fines totalling £60 are included.

(l)   *Capital allowances* – the total claimed for the year to 31 May 2016 was £1,200.

Trading income computation – Year to 31 May 2015

	£	£
Profit per the accounts		34,328
Add:		
Sales that have been omitted	300	
Stock that was excluded in error	250	
Unpaid bonus	1,000	
Private proportion of motor expenses	1,500	
Paris trip expenses incurred primarily for private purposes	700	
Mobile telephone costs – personal element	300	
Entertainment included in advertising and promotion	180	
Entertainment costs excluding staff entertainment	375	
Bad debts provision	250	
Parking fines	60	
Loss on disposal	200	
Depreciation	2,700	
		7,815
		42,143
Deduct:		
Rent received	700	
Bank interest received	80	
		(780)
		41,363
Capital allowances		(1,200)
Trading income profit		40,163

HOW ARE PROFITS TAXED?

Basis of assessment

3.18   The rules governing the basis of assessment are set out in *ITTOIA 2005, Pt 2, Ch 15*. The income tax charged in a tax year is based on the profits of the business earned in the basis period. The general rule is that the basis period for a tax year is the period of 12 months ending on the accounting date, which is the date to which the accounts are drawn up (*ITTOIA 2005, s 198*). The accounting date chosen can be any date in the tax year and this is the date that is then adopted for subsequent years. It is possible to change the accounting date but there are restrictions (see **3.23**).

Focus

Normally a business will be taxed on the profits based on the accounts ending in the tax year; for example where the accounts are prepared to 30 June, the profits for the year ended 30 June 2016 will be charged to tax in the tax year 2016/17.

Opening years of a new business

3.19   When a business starts to trade, or (when an individual joins a partnership, see **3.27**) there are special rules to tax the opening years of trading. The profits that are taxed are those that fall into the following basis periods:

- Year 1: from the date the trade started to the following 5 April (*ITTOIA 2005, s 199*).

- Year 2: dependent on the accounting date (*ITTOIA 2005, s 200*):

  1   If the accounting date falls less than 12 months from the date the trade started, then the basis period is 12 months from the start date.

  2   If the accounting date falls more than 12 months from the date the trade started, then the basis period is 12 months ending on the accounting date in the tax year.

  3   If there is no accounting date in the tax year, then the basis period is the same as the tax year, that is the 12 months from 6 April to 5 April.

- Year 3: normally 12 months to the accounting date ending in the tax year (the general rule).

If the trade ceases at any time during these years, the rules governing the basis period on cessation of the business apply.

Example 3.3 – Taxable profits of a new business

Stephen starts to trade on 1 December 2015 and prepares accounts to 30 June; the first period of account is for seven months to 30 June 2016. His trading profits (as adjusted for tax purposes and after capital allowances) for the first three accounting periods are:

	£
Seven months to 30 June 2016	14,000
Year ended 30 June 2017	36,000
Year ended 30 June 2018	29,000

His taxable profits for the first four years are as follows:

	Basis period		£	£
2015/16	1.12.15 to 5.4.16	£14,000 × 4/7		8,000
2016/17	1.12.15 to 30.11.16:			
	1.12.15 to 30.6.16		14,000	
	1.7.16 to 30.11.16	£36,000 × 5/12	15,000	29,000
2017/18	1.7.16 to 30.6.17			36,000
2018/19	1.7.17 to 30.6.18			29,000

Overlap relief (see **3.21** below) accrues where profits are 'taxed twice' under the commencement rules, as follows:

1.12.15 to 5.4.16, 4 months taxed in 2015/16 and in 2016/17	8,000
1.7.16 to 30.11.16, 5 months taxed in 2016/17 and in 2017/18	15,000
Total overlap relief accrued	23,000

Closing years for a business that ceases to trade

3.20   When a trade permanently ceases (or when an individual leaves a partnership, see **3.27**) the basis period commences immediately after the end of the basis period for the previous tax year and ends on the date of cessation. This is not the case where a person starts a business and ceases to trade in the same tax year – in such cases the basis period is the period of trading (*ITTOIA 2005, s 202*).

When a business ceases to trade, a claim to deduct 'overlap relief' is allowed (see **3.21**).

Example 3.4 – Cessation of trading

Mary ran a restaurant and made up accounts to 31 January each year. The business ceased on 31 July 2016. The taxable profits for the period ended 31 January 2016 were £75,000 and for the six months period up to the date of cessation were £30,000. She had overlap relief accrued of £18,000.

2016/17	Basis period for the year of cessation	£
	1.2.16 to 31.7.16	
	Profits of	30,000
	Less overlap relief	(18,000)
	Profits assessable	**12,000**

Note – The basis period for 2015/16 remains unchanged being the 12 months ended 31 January 2016.

Overlap relief

3.21   The way that profits are taxed in the early years of a business means that the same profits may be taxed twice. This is because the same period of account may fall into two basis periods. The period of account which overlaps is known as the overlap period. The overlap profit is the profit that arises in the overlap period (*s 204*).

It is worth noting that if a business has always made up accounts to 5 April then there will have been no overlap period and thus no overlap relief on cessation.

A record of the overlap profits should be kept as it can be many years from the start of the business to the date it ceases and the opening year's returns may have been discarded. There is a box on the self-employment pages of the tax return in which to enter the overlap relief being carried forward although it is not obligatory.

The overlap relief can be deducted from the profits in the final tax year of trading (*s 205*). If there is a change in the accounting date before then, some of the overlap relief may already have been utilised if the basis period was longer than 12 months.

It should be noted that the limit on income tax reliefs that can be claimed in any one tax year (see **9.6**) does not apply to the extent that trade loss relief is attributable to deductions of overlap relief.

See **Example 3.3** for how the overlap profit is calculated and **Example 3.4** as to how overlap relief is claimed.

> **Focus**
>
> Keep a permanent record of the overlap profits – it will be needed when the business ceases or the accounting date is changed.

Overlap losses

3.22   If a loss arises in the overlap period, then the amount in Year 2 is excluded from the computation so that relief is not given twice (*s 206*). The amount would be nil for overlap purposes and a claim for loss relief could be made (see **3.42–3.49**).

Change of accounting date

3.23   Certain conditions must be met for a change of accounting date to apply otherwise it will not be recognised by HMRC who will continue to tax the profits for the 12-month periods ending on the original accounting date (*s 216(4)*).

The main points are that:

- HMRC must be notified in time (normally by 31 January following the tax year of change);

- the first accounts to the new accounting date must not exceed 18 months; and

- there must have been no change of date in the five preceding tax years (unless HMRC are satisfied that the change is for commercial reasons).

There are specific rules governing the basis periods to be applied and these can be found in *ITTOIA 2005, s 214–219*. There is also provision for the deduction for overlap profit on the change of accounting date (*ITTOIA 2005, s 220*). Guidance on the computation of profits and examples can be found at BIM81035–81090.

The rules in this area are complicated and the following example illustrates one situation.

Example 3.5 – Change of accounting date

A business has been trading for many years preparing accounts to 5 April each year until 5 April 2016. In 2016/17 accounts are prepared for a (short) period of three months from 6 April 2016 to 30 June 2016.

The basis periods are:

2015–2016	12 months to 5 April 2016
2016–2017	12 months to 30 June 2016
2017–2018	12 months to 30 June 2017

The change of accounting date occurs in 2016/17. As the new accounting date is less than 12 months after the basis period for the previous year, the basis period for 2016/17 is the 12 months ending with the new accounting date (30 June 2016).

The nine-month period from 1 July 2015 to 5 April 2016 is an overlap period. The profits for this overlap period will qualify for overlap relief in a later year.

Post-cessation receipts

3.24   Income tax is charged on post-cessation receipts arising from a trade. They are defined as any sums received after a person has permanently ceased to trade (including a partner who has ceased his notional trade) which arise from the carrying on of the trade before cessation (*ITTOIA 2005, ss 241–253*). An election can be made to have the receipt treated as received in the tax year the trade ceased, as this may be beneficial to the taxpayer, but is restricted to amounts received in the six years after cessation (*ITTOIA, s 257*).

The legislation allows a deduction of a loss, expense or debit against post-cessation receipts, provided that the deduction would have been allowed against trading profits had the trade not ceased and it has not already been claimed as a deduction when the trade was carried on (*ITTOIA 2005, ss 254, 255*).

PARTNERSHIPS

3.25   A partnership is the relationship which subsists between persons carrying on a business in common with a view to profit and these can take several forms:

●   *English partnership* – these are referred to as 'general partnerships' and are the most commonly used form of partnership. Partners are themselves jointly liable for the debts incurred by the partnership while they are a partner. These partnerships are governed by the *Partnership Act 1890* and are not a separate legal entity from the partners.

- *Scottish partnership* – these are also governed by the *Partnership Act 1890* and although they are a separate legal entity from the partners, it is the partners who are both jointly and severally liable for the debts incurred by the partnership while they are a partner.

- *Limited partnership* – these partnerships have both general and limited partners and are not a separate legal entity from the partners. The general partners are liable for all debts of the firm while the liability of limited partners is capped at the amount to which they have contributed capital to the partnership. Limited partners cannot bind or take part in the management of the partnership otherwise their limited liability will be lost. These are governed by the *Limited Partnership Act 1907*.

- *Limited liability partnership (LLP)* – these were introduced by the *Limited Liability Partnership Act 2000* and are in effect a hybrid between a company and a partnership. They offer the *veil of incorporation* of a company (ie a separate legal entity and limited liability) yet the flexibility of a partnership. Partners in an LLP are generally referred to as 'members'

Persons carrying on businesses, whether trades or not, in partnership are referred to collectively as a 'firm' (*ITTOIA 2005, s 847(1)*) and a firm is not to be regarded for income tax purpose as an entity separate and distinct from the partners unless otherwise indicated (*ITTOIA 2005, s 848*).

As such it is the partners (and not the partnership) which is liable to tax on any income and gains of the partnership. These are adjusted for tax in the normal way (see **3.7** *et seq*) and shared between the partners in accordance with the terms of the partnership agreement (whether written or verbal).

This is the case even for an LLP (which is in fact a separate legal entity) so long as the LLP is carrying on a trade, profession or business with a view to a profit (*ITTOIA 2005, s 863*). An LLP will continue to be treated in this way through periods of temporary cessation of the business and during a winding up so long as it is not connected to tax avoidance. Where this condition is not met an LLP will be subject to corporation tax.

Companies in partnership are subject to corporation tax on their share of profit (see **17.1**) although special rules can apply to mixed partnerships (see **3.22**).

The tax treatment of English partnerships and Scottish partnerships is identical – further references in this chapter to general partnerships applies equally to both Scottish partnerships.

Partnership tax return

3.26   Although a partnership is not itself subject to tax, it is required to register with HMRC (see **3.2**) and submit an annual tax return.

The partnership return must include the names of all the partners of the firm during the tax year. The trading profits (or losses) for the accounting period ended in the tax year (as adjusted for tax purposes) along with any other partnership income and gains arising in the tax year, must be included in the return and allocated between each of the partners.

Any expenses borne personally by an individual partner and not included within the partnership accounts but which were incurred by the partner in connection with the business and meet the requirements as allowable deductions (see **3.15**) need to be taken into account in calculating the profit share of that partner. The same treatment applies for capital allowances claimed on assets purchased personally by an individual partner and which have been used for business purposes.

The requirements for when the partnership return needs to be submitted is the same as for personal tax returns (see **10.1** and **50.2**). Penalties for failure to notify, for late submission and for incorrect returns are the same too (see **Chapter 53**).

Calculation of each partner's share of taxable profits

3.27   The taxable profits of an accounting period are allocated to each of the partners in line with the profit sharing arrangements that apply to that period of account. Profit sharing arrangements made include:

- a fixed share of profits for one or more of the partners, such as where:

  o a partner is paid a fixed share and is not entitled to any further share in the profits – these are sometimes referred to as a 'salaried partner' although this term can be misleading and in particular, specific rules can apply to treat a 'salaried members of an LLP' as an employee (see **3.30**); or

  o a partner is paid a prior fixed share (such as a seniority allowance for a general practitioner) and is also entitled to share in any remaining profits;

- interest payable at an agreed rate on capital introduced.

All prior claims to profits are deducted from total profits with the remaining balance then being allocated between the partners in their profit sharing ratios. This allocation cannot increase or create a loss for a partner: if this happens, this 'notional' loss must be re-allocated among the other partners.

In determining the assessable profits for each partner and the basis period to which they are applied, each partner's share of the firm's trading profits or losses are treated as profits or losses of a trade carried on by a partner alone – this is referred to as the 'notional trade', as opposed to the 'actual trade' that the partnership is carrying on (*ITTOIA 2005, s 852(1)*).

A partner starts to carry on a notional trade either when the partnership itself starts to actually trade or, if later, when he joins the partnership. Likewise, a partner permanently ceases to carry on a notional trade when he leaves the partnership or when the actual trade ceases, if earlier. A partner will continue to carry on the notional trade, even alone if all the other partners have left, and will continue to do so until the actual trade permanently ceases (*ITTOIA 2005, s 852(5)*).

Example 3.6 – Allocation of partnership income

Clare, Helen and Sarah trade in partnership. They share profits in the ratio of 2:2:1. They are allocated sums of £25,000, £25,000 and £40,000 respectively as a prior share of profit. The partners are also entitled to interest of £500 per year on the capital they have introduced. The partnership makes a taxable profit in the year to 31 March 2016 of £250,000. The profits are allocated for tax purposes as follows:

	Total	Clare	Helen	Sarah
	£	£	£	£
Prior share of profit	90,000	25,000	25,000	40,000
Interest on capital	1,500	500	500	500
Balance of profits (2:2:1 ratio)	158,500	63,400	63,400	31,700
Chargeable on partners for 2015/16	250,000	88,900	88,900	72,200

Example 3.7 – Allocation of notional loss

If, in **Example 3.6** above, the taxable profits of the partnership were only £25,000 the allocation would be as follows:

	Total	Clare	Helen	Sarah
	£	£	£	£
Salary	90,000	25,000	25,000	40,000
Interest on capital	1,500	500	500	500

Balance of profits (2:2:1 ratio)	(66,500)	(26,600)	(26,600)	(13,300)
	25,000	(1,100)	(1,100)	27,200
Reallocation of notional loss		1,100	1,100	(2,200)
Chargeable on partners for 2015/16	25,000	nil	nil	25,000

As Clare and Helen have the same profit sharing ratio, the loss is equally allocated from them to Sarah.

Non-trading income which has been taxed at source

3.28   Taxed income is charged to tax on the individual partners for the tax year in which it arises and not by reference to the basis period. Thus any taxed income that has been included in the income of the partnership accounts is excluded when arriving at the profits of the accounting period.

The actual amounts of the taxed income that arise in the tax year are then separately recorded in the partnership tax return, together with any tax deducted at source.

Non-trading income received untaxed

3.29   The partner is treated as if his share of untaxed income of the partnership was the profit or loss of a 'notional business' carried on by him alone. The notional business includes all untaxed income, such as property income or untaxed interest and any relievable losses from non-trade sources (*ITTOIA 2005, s 854*).

The income is included in the same accounting period as the trading income and the same basis periods are used to determine the income assessable on an individual partner; in other words, this income will be subject to the same opening and closing years as his trading income (*ITTOIA 2005, s 855*).

The partnership tax return will need to have details entered for all untaxed income received in the accounting period.

Focus

Non-trading income needs to be excluded from the taxable trading profits and dealt with separately on the partnership tax return.

Salaried members of LLPs

3.30   Where in effect a member of an LLP is providing services to the LLP on terms similar to that of employment (the 'salaried members test'), they will be treated for tax purposes as if they are employed under a contract of service and so will be taxed as if they were an employee of the LLP (*ITTOIA 2005, s 863A*) in the same way as any other employee (see **Chapter 2**).

From the LLP's perspective, payments to salaried members will be subject to PAYE and will be an allowable deduction from the partnership profits (subject to the normal restrictions – see **3.15**).

These rules apply only to members of an LLP and the rules for all other partnerships remain unaltered.

> **Focus**
>
> The *Limited Liability Partnership Act 2000, s 4(4)* created the assumption of self-employed status for all members of an LLP. This somewhat bizarre status has been exploited and abused and there was growing evidence of whole workforces being transferred to LLPs to avoid employment status, especially amongst low-paid and migrant workforces. The legislation seeks to block and counteract these perceived abuses.

3.31   The salaried members test

The salaried members test is met where at any time each of Conditions A–C are satisfied, as follows:

- *Condition A* – this is a test as to whether the profits received by the member are in fact a 'disguised salary' and is met if at least 80% of the amount payable to the member is:

  - fixed;

  - if variable, is variable without reference to the overall profit and loss of the LLP; or

  - is not in practice affected by the overall amount of the profit and loss of the LLP.

  HMRC guidance makes clear that bonus payments linked to individual performance or profit centres will not be treated as variable (as they are not linked to the overall profit or loss of the LLP) whereas points earned for individual performance or profit centre performance that are then linked to the overall profit and loss of the LLP will be acceptable.

This is a forward looking test which should be considered on the basis of the arrangements in force at the time that the salaried members test is being considered (*ITTOIA 2005, s 863B*).

- *Condition B* – this is a test of whether the member has significant influence over the affairs of the LLP and will be met where the mutual rights and duties of the members do not provide this (*ITTOIA 2005, s 863C*).

  This calls for a review to be made of the role played by the member in the business of the LLP, both by way of the partnership agreement but also what actually happens in practice. HMRC guidance makes clear that the key issue is whether the member contributes to high level decision making and suggests that a salaried member is unlikely to have any real say in the business. The guidance acknowledges that even a full equity member might have little say in a large LLP whose affairs are managed by an executive committee, and that in these circumstances the equity member would have little influence over the affairs of the LLP – that said, a full equity member in those circumstances would be expected to fail Condition A and Condition C and therefore fall outside of these provisions.

- *Condition C* – this test considers the level of investment made by the member and is met if, at the relevant time, the member's capital contribution to the LLP is less than 25% of any disguised salary (*ITTOIA 2005, s 863D*).

  HMRC guidance makes clear that a distinction has to be drawn between a contribution to the capital of the LLP (which is regulated by the LLP agreement and is treated as a permanent endowment to the firm) and the member's day-to-day current account, the balance of which is disregarded for these purposes.

  The key question is whether the funds provided by the member form part of a long-term funding of the firm, no matter what terminology might be applied in the LLP agreement. HMRC are alive to the possibility of circular transactions and this is dealt with in the detailed guidance on this provision.

  The condition C test is applied:

  - at the beginning of each tax year, or if later when the individual becomes a member;

  - when there is a change in the contribution; or

  - on any change in circumstances which might affect whether the test is met.

Example 3.8 – Salaried members of an LLP

The BIG LLP was founded by three individuals, B, I and G, who make all the major decisions in the business and they have invested all but a nominal amount of the capital. B, I and G are entitled to the residual profits.

B, I and G bring in some junior members who are paid a fixed monthly sum plus an annual discretionary bonus which is typically 20% to 30% of their annual fixed compensation.

The junior members are all salaried members, satisfying Conditions A, B and C. Whilst the bonus is sometimes more than 20% of the reward package, this is set without reference to the profits of the firm but is instead based wholly on their own fixed share. In addition, the individuals have no real influence and no capital contribution.

The legislation contains anti-avoidance rules (*ITTOIA 2005, s 863G*) to prevent use of artificial structures or arrangements designed to circumvent this legislation. In particular, the rules deal with:

● an individual personally performing services for the LLP at a time when he is not a member;

● providing services to the LLP via a company; and

● arrangements designed to ensure that the mixed membership partnership legislation (see **3.32**) does not apply.

HMRC have issued detailed guidance and examples on the application of these provisions which can prove useful when considering if and how the salaried member test applies to real world cases (www.gov.uk/government/publications/salaried-member-rules-legislation-day-technical-note-and-guidance).

Mixed partnerships

3.32   The rules relating to mixed partnerships apply equally to all types of partnership. A mixed partnership is broadly one containing both individual and non-individual partners, typically companies but the legislation is widely drafted to include other non-individual entities, for example trusts and other LLPs.

Partnerships are seen as offering greater flexibility than other business structures such as limited companies but generally have tax disadvantages in that partners are subject to income tax and NIC on all profits attributed to them (whether withdrawn or not) at rates which are significantly higher than corporate tax rates.

This led to planning designed to combine the flexibility of partnerships with the tax advantages of companies and in its simplest form, this worked by allocating profits to a corporate partner – these would be subject to corporation tax and could either continue to be used by the partnership or be paid to the company to be 'moneyboxed' and withdrawn at a later time.

These provisions apply to block such planning by reallocating profits from *non-individual partners* to individual *partners* where certain conditions are met.

Excess profit allocations

3.33 The legislation applies where the partnership makes a profit for tax purposes and a profit share is allocated to non-individual partners and either Condition X or Y applies (*ITTOIA 2005, s 850C(1)*).

- *Condition X* – The profit allocated to the non-individual partner (B) represents deferred profits of an individual partner (A).

  For this purpose, deferred profits are any profits of the individual member that are held back for whatever reason and are initially allocated to a non-individual member with the result that the tax paid in that period is lower than it would have been had those profits been allocated to the individual member – in short, these are profits which are intended to be paid to the individual at a later time.

- *Condition Y* – non-individual partner's (B) profit share exceeds the appropriate notional profit and the individual partner (A) meets the 'power to enjoy' conditions in relation to any element of the profit share allocated B.

  There is very little distinction between the situation where the non-individual partner does nothing but receives an allocation of profits and the situation where the non-individual partner does something, brings something or has something which merits an allocation. When calculating the appropriate notional profit for Condition Y, the legislation allows for a limited return on capital (*ITTOIA 2005, s 850C(11)*) and consideration for services (*ITTOIA 205, s 850C(15)*) to be taken into account rather than the amount that the non-individual partner could expect to receive if he was a third party.

  As for the individual's power to enjoy those profits, the test is satisfied only if any one of three conditions is met (*ITTOIA 2005, s 850C(18)*):

  ○ the individual partner and the non-individual partner are connected – for this purpose the general and widely defined test of connected in *ITA 2007, s 993* applies, with the exception that persons are not simply connected through being partners;

○ the individual partner is party to arrangements, the main purpose of which is to secure that an amount of profits allocated to the non-individual partner are subject to corporation tax rather than income tax; or

○ any of the enjoyment conditions are satisfied – these consider whether the individual or a person connected with them is in a position to enjoy the benefits of the profits allocated to the non-individual partner and are widely drawn and catch profit shares, benefits and artificial growth in capital values provided directly or indirectly and at any time (*ITTOIA 2015, s 850C(20)*).

The legislation imposes a reasonableness test and A's profit share is increased on a just and reasonable basis by so much of the amount of B's profits as it is reasonable to suppose is attributable to A's deferred profits or A's power to enjoy. The reallocation of business profit includes investment income, not just trading or professional income.

Example 3.9 – Using a corporate member to defer tax

The XYZ LLP has three individual members: Mrs X, Mrs Y and Mrs Z. The LLP is very profitable. In order to reduce the amount of profits which are taxed at higher income tax rates, a company, XYZ Ltd, becomes a corporate member of the XYZ LLP. XYZ Ltd is fully owned by Mrs X, Mrs Y and Mrs Z.

XYZ Ltd does not provide any services and only a nominal amount of capital.

Mrs X, Mrs Y and Mrs Z allocate sufficient profits to themselves to utilise their personal allowances and allocate the balance of the profit to XYZ Ltd. The profit share allocated is invested or retained in the partnership by the company member as additional partnership capital or advances.

Mrs X, Mrs Y and Mrs Z meet the enjoyment conditions in relation to the sums allocated XYZ Ltd. They will be taxed on an additional share of profits, split on a just and reasonable basis, equal to the profit share allocated to XYZ Ltd, less a sum representing an appropriate notional return on the nominal amount of capital introduced by XYZ Ltd.

This arrangement may also meet Condition X since it has a main purpose of securing corporation tax treatment on the profit.

Provisions ensure that an individual is not taxed on the same profits twice, both under the mixed partnership legislation and when amounts are received from the non-individual partner – for example, on a distribution made by a corporate partner (*ITTOIA 2015, s 850E*). These rules effectively provide that where the non-individual partner makes payments to the individual partner out of profits taxable on the individual partner, those amounts are not taken into account in calculating the tax liability of the individual partner. Practical difficulties may arise over a period of time in identifying such payments in the records of the non-individual partner and substantiating the nature of any specific payment and it would seem sensible to carefully record (and possibly minute) the nature of any payments. The legislation also contains anti-avoidance provisions and applies equally to individuals who are not partners but carry out work for a partnership and their role is *de facto* that of a partner (*ITTOIA 2015 s 850D*).

HMRC have issued detailed guidance on these provisions which can help understand how they apply in practice (www.gov.uk/government/publications/mixed-membership-partnership-aifms-and-asset-disposal-rules-legislation-day-technical-note-and-guidance).

Focus

The legislation is widely drafted and is designed to counter most or all planning techniques associated with the use of partnerships/LLPs and corporate vehicles, however configured, and the legislation should be carefully considered before embarking on (or unwinding) any such planning.

To give a simple example, it would be thought that unwinding a structure with individual partners and a corporate partner by way of the individuals ceasing to be partners would avoid these rules from that point forward. However, even though the result would be a partnership with only one corporate partner, the anti-avoidance provisions of *s 850D* could apply to tax the individuals under the mixed partnership rules.

RELIEF FOR LOSSES

Outline

3.34 If losses are made by a business, the legislation provides for those trading losses to be offset against trading profits and also, provided the qualifying conditions are met, against other income (*ITA 2007, Pt 4*).

Losses are usually calculated in the same way as business profits and using the same basis periods and the loss relief available is:

- against general income ('sideways relief') (*ITA 2007, ss 64–70*)

- against capital gains in certain circumstances (*ITA 2007, s 71*);

- early trade losses relief ('sideways relief') (*ITA 2007, ss 72–74*);

- carry forward trade loss relief (*ITA 2007, ss 83–88*);

- terminal trade loss relief (*ITA 2007, ss 89–94*).

Relief for trading losses against general income

3.35   As long as the business is conducted on a commercial basis with a view to the realisation of trading profits (*s 66*), the losses can be relieved as follows (*s 64*):

- against the total income in the tax year the loss arises; and/or

- against the total income arising in the preceding tax year.

The taxpayer can decide which year the losses are set against first although they cannot limit the claim so as to, for example, preserve their personal allowance.

Relief is not normally available for losses made by farming or market gardening businesses which also made losses in the previous five years, as calculated before capital allowances (*ss 67–69*).

The available loss is restricted by the limit on income tax relief (see **9.6**) and the restrictions to losses from self-employment (**3.40**).

The time limit for claiming the loss relief is the first anniversary of 31 January following the tax year in which the loss was made.

Losses set against gains

3.36   The relief under *s 64* is extended to allow losses to be offset against capital gains arising in the year in which the loss arose and the preceding year (*s 71*). Claims are subject to the restrictions to losses from self-employment (**3.40**).

The loss must first be set-off against other income (*s 64*) and must then be reduced by any other reliefs already claimed in respect of the loss (eg *s 72* relief for early year losses).

The loss can be set-off against the net capital gains arising in the year so that capital losses brought forward do not have to be used first.

Example 3.10 – Trading losses and capital gains

John has been trading profitably for many years and makes up his accounts to 30 September. He has recently made losses of £5,000 and £45,000 respectively in the two years ended 30 September 2015 and 2016.

He decided to sell his holiday home in July 2016 and made a capital gain of £48,000. He has capital losses brought forward of £12,000 from the sale of shares in May 2015. Other income includes rental income of £10,000 and £8,000 respectively in the two years ended 5 April 2016 and 2017.

He claims relief for the trading losses as follows:

2015/16	£
Loss arising in the year	5,000
Carried forward against future profits	5,000

Note – The rental income of £10,000 will be covered by his personal allowances so no advantage would be gained by claiming loss relief in this year against other income.

2016/17	£
Loss arising in the year	45,000
Offset against rental income	(8,000)
Loss available to be claimed under *s 71*	37,000
Capital gain	48,000
Less: s 71 claim	(37,000)
Gain remaining	11,000
Less: annual exemption	(11,000)
Taxable gain	nil

Note – The capital losses brought forward have not been claimed as it is more beneficial to utilise the annual exemption and retain the availability of the losses for carry forward.

Relief for losses arising in the early years of trading

3.37   The loss relief for new businesses can be particularly advantageous, when funds could be tight, as tax paid by an individual in the three years before the business was started may be available for repayment (with interest), depending on the level of losses arising in the first four years of the new business. The claim can be made by a sole trader or partner.

The legislation (*ITA 2007, s 72*) provides that:

1   An individual may make a claim for early trade loss relief if the individual makes a loss in a trade:

   (a)   in the tax year in which a trade is first carried on by the individual; or

   (b)   in any of the next three tax years.

2   The claim is for the loss to be deducted in calculating the individual's net income for the three tax years before the one in which the loss is made.

All of the loss arising in a particular tax year is included in the claim and must be deducted from total income in the previous three years, starting with the earliest year first, unless there is insufficient income, in which case the unused losses can be included in any other loss relief claim. It is not possible to confine the claim to, say, one year only.

In order for the trading loss to qualify for this relief, the trade must be commercial. The relevant legislation (*s 74(2)*) provides that a trade is commercial if it is carried on throughout the basis period for the tax year:

(a)   on a commercial basis; and

(b)   in such a way that profits could reasonably be expected to be made in the basis period or within a reasonable time thereafter.

As it may be difficult to prove to HMRC that this section has been complied with (eg if losses occurred in all of the first four years) it is advisable to retain business plans to demonstrate when profits are, or were, envisaged.

The available loss is restricted by the limit on income tax relief (see **9.6**) and the restrictions to losses from self-employment (**3.40**).

The time limit for claiming the loss relief is the first anniversary of 31 January following the tax year in which the loss was made.

Example 3.11 – A difficult start for a new business

Peter started a trade as a plasterer on 1 November 2015 and prepared accounts to 31 October 2016. Prior to setting up the new business, he was employed by Big Builders Ltd, at a salary of £20,000 and had no other income.

Peter's new business made losses in the first three years with his trading losses (as adjusted for tax purposes and after taking account of capital allowances) being calculated as:

	£	£
Year ended 31 October 2016 – Loss	36,000	
Year ended 31 October 2017 – Loss	12,000	
Year ended 31 October 2018 – Loss	24,000	
The losses for tax purposes are:		
2015/16 (1.11.15 to 5.4.16)	36,000 × 5/12	15,000
2016/17 (y/e 31.10.16)		36,000
Less: losses already allocated to 2015/16		(15,000)
		21,000
2017/18 (y/e 31.10.17)		12,000
2018/19 (y/e 31.10.18)		24,000

Loss relief for earlier years is available as follows:

	2015/16	2016/17	2017/18	2018/19
	£	£	£	£
Losses available	15,000	21,000	12,000	24,000
Set against total income:				
2012/13	15,000	5,000		
2013/14		16,000	4,000	
2014/15			8,000	12,000
Unrelieved losses	nil	nil	nil	12,000

Note – Revised total income for all three years has been reduced to nil and there are unrelieved losses available for set-off against any other income in either the current year (2018/19), the preceding year (2017/18) or available to carry forward against profits of the same trade.

Focus

When losses are claimed against other income, the individual circumstances of the taxpayer will determine which type of relief will give the greatest reduction in the tax liability or the maximum repayment of tax and interest supplement. You have up to a year after filing the tax return showing the loss to make the decision (and longer if you filed the return before 31 January).

Losses carried forward against future trade profits

3.38   Any unrelieved trading losses can be carried forward and set off against subsequent profits of the same trade that is carried on by the same owner. In calculating the individual's total income, the losses are deducted from the trading profits arising in the first subsequent tax year with any losses still unrelieved being carried forward to the following tax year (*ITA 2007, s 83*).

If a business is transferred to a limited company, there is also relief available to utilise any unrelieved losses of the business existing at the time of incorporation.

The sole trader or partner may carry forward these losses and offset them against their first available income derived from the company: the losses are set off against earnings first, then investment income.

In order to qualify, the individual must have been allotted shares in the company (and has kept at least 80% of them) and the company continues the same trade (*ITA 2007, s 86*; BIM85060). The claim must be made within four years of the end of the tax year in which the transfer occurs.

Relief for losses on the permanent cessation of a trade

3.39   On the permanent discontinuance of a trade, any losses arising in the 12 months up to the date of cessation can be relieved under the terminal loss provisions (*ITA 2007, s 89*).

A partner is treated as having ceased his notional trade when he steps down from the partnership (*ITTOIA 2005, s 852(4)*): his share of the partnership losses arising in the last 12 months is included in the terminal loss relief claim.

The loss includes any unrelieved trading charges and overlap relief (see **3.21**). In addition, a partner can also increase his loss by any interest paid that would normally qualify for tax relief under *ITA 2007, s 383* but was not relieved due to insufficient net income.

The calculation of the terminal loss will be based on any unrelieved trading losses arising in either of the following two periods (with any profits being ignored):

- the period from 6 April to the date of cessation; or

- the period from one year prior to the date of cessation to 5 April.

The terminal loss can be set-off against any trading profits in the year of cessation and carried back to the three previous years. The loss is deducted from profits of the final tax year and then carried back against the later years first.

The claim must be made within four years of the end of the tax year in which it occurs.

In addition, post-cessation trade relief may be claimed for any 'qualifying payment' made or 'qualifying event' occurring in relation to a debt owed to that person within seven years of the cessation of the trade (*ITA 2007, ss 96–99*). The qualifying payments are in the nature of dealing with claims against the business such as remedying defective work, payments for damages and professional fees incurred. It should be noted that post-cessation trade relief is restricted by the limit on income tax relief (see **9.6**).

Restrictions to losses from self-employment

3.40   A raft of provisions have been introduced over recent years in an attempt to prevent the use of contrived schemes to generate trade losses which can then be utilised against an individual's other income (by way of sideways relief under *s 64*– see **3.35** and **3.37**) and gains (see **3.36**). These provisions were introduced in several stages – each change closed down a specific 'loophole' only for another to be found shortly after which then needed to be closed down. As a result, the legislation in this area is particularly complex and it has the potential to apply to individuals who have sustained genuine commercial losses.

General restriction

3.41   A general restriction applies to any person carrying on a business (as a sole trader or in partnership) where the losses arise as a consequence or in connection with a tax avoidance arrangement. In such cases no relief is available for that loss by way of sideways relief or against gains (*ITA 2007, s 74ZA*).

Unlike some more of the specific restrictions detailed below, this general restriction applies not only to losses of a trade but also to losses from a profession or vocation.

Non-active individuals

3.42   There are restrictions where trading losses are incurred by an individual (other than a partner) carrying on a trade in a non-active capacity (*ITA 2007, s 74A*).

An individual is in a non-active capacity where they do not spend on average at least ten hours a week personally engaged in activities of the trade on a commercial basis and with a view to realising a profit. Where these provisions apply, the amount of loss relief available to offset against other income or gains is restricted to a monetary limit of £25,000 in any one tax year.

It should be noted that this restriction applies to losses from carrying on a trade only, and not for losses incurred from carrying on a profession or vocation.

Non-active partners

3.43   There are restrictions for non-active partners of a general partnership or an LLP (similar to those applying to non-active individuals) where trading losses are incurred by an individual in respect of a trade carried on by the firm (*ITA 2007, s 103C*).

An individual is a non-active partner where they do not spend on average at least ten hours a week personally engaged in carrying on the firm's trading activities on a commercial basis and with a view to realising a profit. Where these provisions apply, the amount of loss relief available to offset against other income or gains in any one tax year is restricted to the lower of:

- the loss available for the period – after restriction under *s 107* (see **3.45**) or *s 110* (see **3.44**); and

- £25,000.

This restriction applies in total to all losses incurred in the year in the capacity of a non-active partner. So for example, where an individual is a non-active partner in two different partnerships, it is the combined loss from both of those partnerships that is compared to the £25,000 limit.

As with the restriction for non-active individuals, this applies to losses from carrying on a trade only, and not for losses incurred from carrying on a profession or vocation.

Losses in early years of trading

3.44   A general restriction applies to limit the loss available to any individual who is a partner in a firm (whether a general partnership or an LLP) to their capital contribution in the case of losses in the early years of trade under *s 72* (*ITA 2007, s 110*).

What constitutes a capital contribution for this purpose is complex, but in broad terms is the total of:

- the amount of capital which the member has contributed to the LLP as capital which has not been withdrawn;

- the amount of the individual's share of profits from the trade which have not been withdrawn from the partnership nor added to capital; and

- any additional amount which the member may have to contribute on a winding to the LLP.

However, in calculating the capital contribution, any amount contributed for the main purpose of obtaining relief against other income or gains (*ITA 2007, s 113A*) or any contributions where the economic benefit is borne by someone else (*ITA 2007, s 114* and *SI 2005/2017*) are excluded.

The restriction under these provisions is calculated on a cumulative basis, by comparing the total relief for any loss from the partnership used by the member against other income and gains up to and including the relevant period against the member's capital contribution at the end of the relevant period.

It should be noted that this restriction applies to losses from carrying on a trade only, and not for losses incurred from carrying on a profession or vocation.

Members of LLPs

3.45   Similar provisions to those applying to losses of earlier years apply to members of LLPs generally – the key difference to these provisions is that when calculating the capital contribution, no account is taken of any share of profits from the trade which have not been withdrawn from the partnership nor added to capital (*ITA 2007, s 107*).

These provisions apply only where the provisions of *s 110* do not apply.

Other provisions

3.46   There are further provisions which can apply to restrict losses for limited partners (*ITA 2007, s 102(1)(a)*), certain corporate partners (*CTA 2010, ss 55–61*), individuals involved in film partnerships (*ITA 2007, s 115*) and mixed partnerships (*ITA 2007, s 116A*) although the scope of this book does not allow for these to be considered here.

> **Focus**
>
> Loss relief against other income and gains for trading losses ('sideways relief') can be restricted in many ways. The facts need to be established before a claim is submitted to make sure the legislation is complied with.

General HMRC guidance

3.47 HMRCs income tax losses toolkit (www.gov.uk/government/publications/hmrc-income-tax-losses-toolkit) covers the most common errors made in loss relief claims and further guidance can be found within Helpsheet HS227 Losses (www.gov.uk/government/publications/losses-hs227-self-assessment-helpsheet). The key areas where particular care needs to be taken are:

- To ensure that all trading losses have been correctly calculated, having been adjusted by any requisite tax adjustments.

- That an accurate record is kept of all losses incurred, the amounts upon which relief has been claimed and the amount of any unused relief. This will act as a safeguard not only to ensure that no losses are left unclaimed but also that relief has not been claimed twice.

- That each partner claiming loss relief claims only the share appropriate to his own individual circumstances. Particular care needs to be taken when a partner joins or leaves the partnership (see BIM82230).

- When losses are set against total income (or chargeable gains), it is an 'all or nothing' claim: this may result in personal allowances (or the annual capital gains tax exemption) not being utilised.

> **Focus**
>
> All necessary documentation must be kept to support claims for losses – certificates of income tax deducted (P60, bank interest on other income), the business plan to demonstrate that the business is commercially viable and an accurate record of losses made and claimed to date.

CONSTRUCTION INDUSTRY SCHEME

Introduction

3.48 The Construction Industry Scheme (CIS) provides for certain payments made to subcontractors under construction contracts, which are not contracts of employment, to be made after amounts have been deducted for tax.

The legislation governing the CIS is contained in the *Finance Act 2004, Pt 3, Ch 3*, in regulations and other supplementary provisions.

Guidance that is offered on the gov.uk website includes:

- Construction Industry Scheme Reform Manual – showing how payments are taxed since April 2007 (www.gov.uk/hmrc-internal-manuals/construction-industry-scheme-reform);

- Detailed information on how the system operates can be found by following the CIS link on the home page (www.gov.uk/what-is-the-construction-industry-scheme);

- Booklet CIS340 – a comprehensive guide for contractors and sub-contractors (www.gov.uk/government/publications/construction-industry-scheme-cis-340).

In addition, HMRC's CIS Helpline can be contacted on 0300 200 3210 from 8am to 8pm Monday to Friday and 8am to 4pm on Saturday.

The scheme was introduced as most workers in the construction industry did not have employment contracts and therefore no tax was being deducted from the payments made to them (unlike employees whose pay is subject to PAYE).

The general rules that determine a person's employment status still apply to construction workers. Thus, the first step before any payments are made is to ascertain whether the person being taken on is treated for tax purposes as employed or self-employed. This will depend on the specific terms and conditions of each engagement; a person may be an employee under one contract and self-employed under another. The scheme does offer guidance on how to make this decision.

For further information on employment and self-employment indicators, see **2.2**.

Who does the scheme apply to?

3.49 The scheme applies to payments by a contractor to a subcontractor under a contract for construction operations. A contract is a legally binding agreement or arrangement, which may be written or verbal. The scheme does not apply to payments made under an employment contract.

It applies to all businesses in the construction industry, whether they operate as sole traders, in partnership or through limited companies. It also includes any business whose main activity is not construction but whose average annual expenditure on construction operations over a three-year period exceeds £1 million. Such businesses are known as 'deemed contractors' (under *FA 2004, s 59*). CIS does not apply to private householders.

Non-resident contractors and non-resident subcontractors have to register under the scheme for construction work carried out in the UK.

What are construction operations?

3.50   *FA 2004, s 74* gives the 'meaning of construction operations' as covering 'construction, alteration, repair, extension, demolition or dismantling' of buildings or structures (*s 74(2)(a)*) and the same wording is applied for construction operations on any works forming part of the land, such as walls, road works and drainage systems (*s 74(2)(b)*).

Section 74(2)(c) goes on to cover installations, such as heating or lighting systems, in a building or structure but limits the construction operations in this case simply to the installation and not its repair or extension. Thus payments for the installation of air-conditioning, for example, would be within the scheme but contracts for its repair and maintenance would not.

The legislation contains a list of what constitutes construction operations, and a list of what does not (*FA 2004, s 74*, which may be extended by regulations).

Detailed guidance for specific types of work can be found in the HMRC manual (CISR14330).

Contractors

3.51   A contractor is a business or other concern that pays subcontractors for construction work. A contractor intending to carry out construction work must register his business with HMRC under the scheme.

The contractor must first establish whether the subcontractor is in fact an employee or not to see whether payments made to him are within the CIS.

A person could be both a contractor and subcontractor at the same time. If he contracts with a contractor to do work, he is a subcontractor. If he then subcontracts some of that work to others, he is a contractor. This situation could apply to a gang leader who has arranged a contract and is paid for it directly and then pays the members of the gang himself for doing the work.

A contractor is referred to as a 'main contractor' if the business itself is in construction and as a 'deemed contractor' if the business falls within the scheme as it spends more than £1 million a year on construction expenditure.

Verification process and payment

3.52   Before any payments under the construction contract are made, the contractor must contact HMRC as part of the verification process. Details need to be provided of the subcontractor (name, type of business, UTR, NI number) in order to obtain a verification reference number and to find out what rate of tax (if any) is to be applied.

The only time this is not necessary is if the subcontractor has already been included on the contractor's CIS return in the current or two previous tax years. HMRC will advise which of the following rates to use:

- Gross payments can be made to subcontractors who have registered for gross payments.

- Tax is deducted at the basic rate from payments made to persons registered for payment under deduction.

- Tax is deducted at the higher rate for persons who have not registered. The higher rate for 2016/17 is 30%.

The contractor should carry on applying the deduction rates that have been advised unless informed otherwise by HMRC.

The payment on which the tax is calculated includes any payments for travelling and subsistence. It excludes the cost of materials supplied by the subcontractor, VAT (if the subcontractor is VAT registered) and any amount equal to the Construction Industry Training Board (CITB) levy.

All payments fall within the scheme, whether they are paid directly to the subcontractor or not, and whatever form the payment takes: cash, cheque, credit card, advance, 'sub' or loan. If a single contract covers several tasks, of which not all fall within the meaning of construction operations, the whole contract is still treated by HMRC as to be paid within the scheme.

An appropriate statement must be provided to the subcontractor within 14 days of the end of every tax month (by the 19th), as specified by the regulations and includes the verification number given for the subcontractor and details of the payments made and tax deducted. No statement is required if the subcontractor is paid gross but it is good practice to provide one.

Monthly returns

3.53   All contractors have to submit monthly returns, CIS300, to HMRC. No annual returns are required. The tax month end is the fifth day of the month. The procedures and regulations are as follows:

- Monthly returns must be filed electronically: either using HMRC's free CIS online service, commercial CIS software or for large employers by using the electronic data interchange (EDI). To do this, the contractor needs to register for the CIS online service.

- The returns must contain details of subcontractors (including the verification number) with payments made plus tax deducted and declarations that employment status has been considered and that all subcontractors have been verified, as need be.

- Returns no not have to be filed for months where no payments have been made, but HMRC must be informed that no return is due.

- The deadline for filing the returns is 14 days after the tax month end, (which is by the 19th of the month),

- Payment to HMRC of the tax deducted must be made within 14 days of the month end (ie the 19th of the following month) or within 17 days if paid electronically (ie the 22nd of the following month). Quarterly payments can be agreed if the amounts are under certain limits.

- Penalties are imposed for late submission of returns – a fixed penalty of £100 is charged is a return is 1 day late, a further fixed penalty of £100 is charged if the return is remains outstanding after 2 months and this is then increased to the greater of £300 or a tax-geared penalty if outstanding six months later, which is charged again six months later if the return is still outstanding.

- If an incorrect return is made, HMRC should be informed by phone (0300 200 3210). The action that needs to be taken to correct the return will depend upon the type of error made, as explained in the HMRC guidance notes (CIS 340). A penalty may be charged if the mistake was caused through negligence or intent.

Contractors operating as limited companies, who also have employees and so operate PAYE, should offset each month any CIS deducted from their own income against their PAYE liabilities as well as against the CIS deductions they have made from payments to their own subcontractors in arriving at the amount due to be paid to HMRC. Any excess CIS deductions are carried forward each month until the end of the tax year when a claim for repayment can be made.

Only companies can use this arrangement to reclaim CIS deductions taken from payments and not individual contractors or partnerships.

Since the introduction of the Real Time Information system for PAYE (see **2.10**), such company employers will need to complete a monthly Employment Payment Summary (EPS) to show the adjustment to the amount of PAYE due to be paid to HMRC for CIS deductions taken off income received.

Records

3.54   Records need to be kept for at least three years after the end of the tax year to which they relate. The records must be available for inspection by HMRC and a penalty of up to £3,000 may be charged for non-compliance.

Sub-contractors

3.55   Sub-contractors must apply to HMRC for registration under the scheme. If they do not register, tax will be deducted at the higher rate. Registration will be either for gross payment or for payment under deduction depending on whether the conditions for gross payment status are met or not (see **3.56**).

As a self-employed person, the sub-contractor must complete his own self-assessment tax return to report on the profits from his business. All tax deducted under the scheme can be offset firstly against his income tax liability and then his Class 4 NIC liability with any overpayment of tax to be refunded.

It is extremely important that records are kept, including the monthly statements provided by the contractor. This is particularly important if tax has been deducted at the higher rate as the verification number will be needed to match up the tax suffered with the contractor's returns.

Focus

Sub-contractors are treated as self-employed when paid under construction contracts which are not considered to give them employment status. They need to register for self-assessment (see **3.2**) and file annual tax returns as well as registering within the CIS. All records of payments received from contractors and tax deducted must be kept plus documentation for any other receipts or expenditure to enable them to make a complete and accurate return of their income.

Requirements for registering for payments to be received gross

3.56   The business needs to meet certain conditions before the subcontractor qualifies for payments to be received gross (*FA 2004, s 64, Sch 11; SI 2004/2045, reg 28(1)*).

- *Business test* – The business needs to carry out construction work, or provide labour for construction work, in the UK and operate through a bank account.

- *Turnover test* – It must be likely that the turnover (based on relevant payments net of VAT and after deducting the cost of materials supplied) will exceed the minimum turnover threshold which is:

    ○   for individuals operating as sole traders, £30,000;

    ○   for partnerships, the lower of £30,000 per partner or at least £100,000 for the whole partnership;

    ○   for companies, the lower of £30,000 per 'relevant person' (being a director or beneficial owner of shares in a close company) or £100,000 for the whole company (unless the company is a close company).

- *Compliance test* – The business has complied with all its tax obligations. This covers the compliance obligations not just of the business itself but also the self-assessment returns of the sole trader, partners, partnership and company directors of a close company.

Certain lapses are allowed. See the HMRC guidelines for more detail.

The business will be subject to an annual compliance review by HMRC, known as an 'On-going Tax Treatment Qualifying Test'. The purpose of the review is to check that the business still qualifies for gross payment status. The test is automatic and computer generated and considers the tax compliance history of the contractor.

HMRC have the right to cancel a registration for gross payment if the person:

- would now be refused were an application to be made;

- has made an incorrect return; or

- has failed to comply with any provisions (whether as a subcontractor or contractor) including making payments of tax on time.

The cancellation takes effect from 90 days after HMRC have made the determination to withdraw gross payment status.

If the reason for the cancellation is due to fraudulent behaviour, either at the time of the application or in an incorrect return or the subcontractor has knowingly failed to comply with the provisions, the cancellation is immediate.

APPENDIX: TIME LIMITS FOR CLAIMS AND ELECTIONS

(TMA 1970, s 43(1))

3.57

1   Claims must be made on the tax return or by an amendment to the return. Except where another period is expressly prescribed, a claim for relief in respect of income tax must be within four years after the end of the tax year.

2   Specific exceptions in respect of business profits and losses include the following:

Provision	**Time limit**
Averaging of profits of farmers or creative artists (*ITTIOA 2005, s 222(5)*)	First anniversary of 31 January after end of second tax year to which the claim relates
Stock transferred to a connected party on cessation of trade to be valued at higher of cost or sale price (*ITTOIA 2005, s 178(4)*)	First anniversary of 31 January following the tax year of cessation
Herd basis (*ITTOIA 2005, s 124(2); CTA 2009, s 122(2)*)	First anniversary of 31 January following the tax year in which the first relevant period of account ends
Change of accounting date (*ITTOIA 2005, s 217(2)*)	Filing date for the relevant tax return
Post-cessation relief (*ITTOIA 2005, s 257(4); ITA 2007, s 96(4)*)	First anniversary of 31 January following the tax year
Furnished holiday lettings: averaging of letting periods (*ITTOIA 2005, s 326(6)*)	First anniversary of 31 January following the tax year
Furnished holiday lettings: grace period election (*ITTOIA 2005, s 326A(5)*)	First anniversary of 31 January following the tax year

Provision	Time limit
Current and preceding year set-off of trading losses (*ITA 2007, s 64(5)*)	First anniversary of 31 January following the loss-making year
Three year carry back of trading losses in opening years of trade (*ITA 2007, s 72(3)*)	First anniversary of 31 January following the tax year in which the loss is made
Relief for trade, etc losses against capital gains of the year in which the loss was made or the previous year (*TCGA 1992, s 261B(8)*)	First anniversary of 31 January following the tax year in which the loss was made

4

Capital allowances

SIGNPOSTS

- **Scope** – Tax relief is available for some capital expenditure through capital allowances, which apply to various categories of qualifying costs. Capital allowances are generally available for expenditure incurred under hire purchase arrangements (see **4.1–4.3**).

- **Plant and machinery** – The most common capital allowance claims are on plant and machinery. However, identifying plant can be difficult and its meaning has largely developed through case law (see **4.4–4.5**).

- **Plant and machinery allowances** – Expenditure is 'pooled' and writing down allowances are claimed on the balance of the pool at the end of the period. The annual investment allowance provides for 100% relief in the year of expenditure, although this is limited and not available on all assets. Certain expenditure qualifies for 100% 'first year allowances' (see **4.6–4.9**).

- **Plant in buildings and integral features** – plant and machinery allowances cannot be claimed on buildings, but there may be items of plant which form part of the building upon which allowances can be claimed. Care needs to be taken when acquiring a second hand building to ensure the maximum allowances available are preserved (see **4.10–4.13**).

- **Motor cars** – special rules also apply to expenditure on cars (see **4.14–4.15**).

- **Disposals** – The disposal of plant and machinery can result in further allowances or a clawback of allowances previously claimed (see **4.16–4.17**).

- **Other allowances and reliefs** – Capital allowances are available under special provisions which apply to various types of qualifying expenditure, these include business premises renovation allowance and research and development expenditure (see **4.18–4.20**).

- **Other capital expenditure reliefs** – Relief is available for certain other capital expenditure, including of remediation of contaminated land (see **4.21**).

- **Other issues** – Specific rules cover situations such as partnerships. There is also some interaction between the capital allowances rules and capital gains tax (see **4.22–4.24**).

- **Appendix: Plant and machinery allowance rates** – Tables of writing down allowances and annual investment allowance are included at the end of this chapter (see **4.25–4.26**).

INTRODUCTION

4.1   As a general rule, capital expenditure is not an allowable deduction in computing profits for tax purposes, whereas revenue expenditure is. The question of whether expenditure is on capital or revenue account is not always straightforward.

For capital expenditure, capital allowances are available where a person who carries on a *qualifying activity* incurs *qualifying capital expenditure*. Not all capital expenditure 'qualifies' for this purpose.

Allowances are available on capital expenditure under the following categories:

- plant and machinery;
- business premises renovation;
- mineral extraction;
- research and development;
- know-how;
- patents; and
- dredging.

The main allowances encountered in practice are those on plant and machinery. Some of the other allowances are dealt with briefly at the end of this chapter. Persons with a specific interest in claiming any of the allowances set out above should refer to more specialist works, such as *Capital Allowances: Transactions and Planning 2016/17* published by Bloomsbury Professional.

There are certain concepts which are common to all the systems of allowances, and these will be considered first.

Capital expenditure

4.2   Capital allowances are due when a person carrying on a *qualifying activity* incurs *qualifying expenditure* and, as a result, an asset belongs to him. For this purpose, a *qualifying activity* includes trades, professions, vocations, employment and property rental activity. *Qualifying expenditure* is capital (rather than revenue) expenditure; that is, expenditure which has not been written off to profit and loss account (validly).

> **Example 4.1 – Capital v repairs**
>
> Jim runs the Morrison Hotel. He gets planning consent to extend the dining room by the construction of a 'conservatory style' extension. During the course of the work, the carpets and doors in the existing dining room are damaged by the builders, and Jim replaces them. The expenditure on the conservatory creates a new asset, or a larger asset, and is therefore capital, but the replacement of the carpets and doors (provided there is no significant element of upgrade) is classed as a repair.

Where the only element of improvement results from using modern materials for the replacement work (for example, wiring to modern standards, or replacing wooden windows with UPVC), HMRC will usually accept that this is repair work. However, new installations (such as broadband connections) may well be regarded as capital.

Where the work involves substantial alterations to a building, any small elements that might otherwise be regarded as repairs are treated as part of the overall improvements.

Finance leases and hire purchase

4.3   The question of whether an asset is acquired under a finance lease, or under hire purchase, is not always straightforward to determine. However, it is key to determining who is entitled to capital allowances – in broad terms, it is the 'owner' of the asset who is able to claim the capital allowances.

An asset under finance lease is generally treated as belonging to the lessor for capital allowance purposes, however this is not the case where the lease is a 'long funding lease'. A long funding lease is effectively looked upon as a transaction where the lessee acquires an assets and the lessor finances the purchase – in these cases it is the lessee who benefits from the capital allowances (see **59.10**).

An asset acquired under hire purchase is generally treated as belonging to the purchaser, who is then able to claim capital allowances. However, where an asset is acquired under hire purchase, the asset must be brought into use before capital allowances are available. Contracts that allow for the 'purchaser' to acquire title to the asset will generally be treated as giving rise to a hire purchase contract, provided that the end purchase price is not unrealistically large.

Focus

Contracts need to be reviewed carefully to determine whether the acquisition is by finance lease, long funding lease or hire purchase. In cases where it is not clear, clarity may be able to be sought from the finance provider – they will have considered the nature of the transaction in order to determine which party is eligible to claim capital allowances as this will impact upon their tax position and therefore influence how they structured the cost of the agreement.

Example 4.2 – Hire purchase asset

Jethro, a farmer, decides to buy a new combine harvester under hire purchase terms. He prepares accounts to 31 March each year. He enters into a contract in February and the combine harvester is delivered on 1 March. His employees begin training in the use of the combine harvester in May, with a view to harvesting crops in late August/September. The combine harvester has not been brought into use by 31 March, so no allowances are available in the year the contract is signed.

It should be noted that HMRC have been known to take an extremely restricted view as to when the asset is brought into use within the meaning of *CAA 2001, s 67*. HMRC may seek to argue that the asset is not brought into use until it is used to make profits for the trade. In the author's view, this is open to challenge.

For example, if Jethro (above) prepared accounts to 30 June, HMRC might seek to deny allowances in the year of acquisition on the basis that the combine harvester is not brought into use to make profits until harvest time.

PLANT AND MACHINERY

4.4   The first question to ask is what plant and machinery actually is. One of the judicial pronouncements on this vexed question was as follows:

'The philosopher statesman, Balfour, is reported to have said it was unnecessary to define a Great Power because, like an elephant, you recognised it when you met it. Unhappily plant in taxing and other statutes is no elephant (although I suppose an elephant might be plant).' Stephenson LJ in *Cole Bros Limited v Phillips* Hl 1992, 55 TC 188 at p 220.

The question of what constitutes plant has been developed through case law, rather than statutes. Plant is part of the *apparatus with which* a business is carried on, rather than the *setting in which* a business is carried on. It also performs some form of *function* in the trade. This definition has led to many tax cases over the years, mostly surrounding the question of what constitutes plant installed in a building (and whether a 'building' is in fact plant in its entirety). This is discussed at **4.10** below. Other plant and machinery includes the machinery used in production in, for example, a factory, furniture and fittings, computer equipment and other items used in the trade.

There is some guidance in statute as to what is and is not plant (see *CAA 2001, ss 21–23*).

Plant and machinery – case law

4.5   The following are examples of some of the items held to be, and not to be, plant.

Plant

- Hulk (old ship) used for coal storage: *John Hall Junior & Co v Rickman* [1906] 1 KB 311

- Moveable office partitions: *Jarrold v John Good & Sons Ltd* CA 1962, 40 TC 681

- Dry dock: *CIR v Barclay Curle & Co Ltd* HL 1969, 45 TC 221

- Swimming pools: *Cooke v Beach Station Caravans Ltd* Ch D 1974, 49 TC 514

- Artificial football pitches: *CIR v Anchor International Ltd* CS 2004, 77 TC 38 – *but not* all weather racing tracks: *Lingfield Park 1991 Ltd v Shove* CA 2004, 76 TC 363, or putting greens at a golf course: *Family Golf Centres Ltd v Thorne* [1998] SSCD 106 (Sp C 150)

- Lighting and décor in certain premises: *CIR v Scottish & Newcastle Breweries Ltd* HL 1982, 55 TC 252

- Control room to house security equipment: *B & E Security Systems Ltd v HMRC* FTT [2010] UKFTT 146 (TC).

Not plant

- General lighting: *J Lyons & Co Ltd v Attorney-General* ChD 1944, 170 LT 348; [1944] 1 All ER 477 (this is a war damage compensation claim case)

- Shop fronts, tiles, raised floors (unless specifically installed to house plant): *Wimpy International Ltd v Warland; Associated Restaurants Ltd v Warland* CA 1988, 61 TC 51

- General lighting and associated wiring (but note that these are now treated as integral features: see **4.7** below): *Cole Bros Ltd v Phillips* HL 1982, 55 TC 188

- Ship used as floating restaurant: *Benson v Yard Arm Club Ltd* CA 1979, 53 TC 67

- Building housing car wash machinery (the machinery itself was held to be plant): *Attwood v Anduff Car Wash Ltd* CA 1997, 69 TC 575.

Whilst it is not always easy to follow the distinction between the various cases, the key test is that those items held to be plant will perform some function in the trade, rather than simply being the place in which the trade is carried on.

Practitioners may find HMRC's capital allowances toolkit helpful – this reflects HMRC's understanding of the relevant legislation and case law, and in particular what constitutes plant and machinery (www.gov.uk/government/publications/hmrc-capital-allowances-for-plant-and-machinery-toolkit).

> **Focus**
>
> Use the toolkit to guide decision making, but apply decided cases in preference to toolkit answers.

PLANT AND MACHINERY ALLOWANCES

4.6   Plant and machinery allowances can be claimed in different ways and the rate of allowances available will depend upon the nature of the assets acquired. Allowances claimed will be treated as a deduction from the profits of the qualifying activity (see **4.2**).

Writing down allowances

4.7   The main form of allowances are known as writing down allowances (WDA). Qualifying expenditure is added to a 'pool' and WDA are calculated by reference to the balance of expenditure on each pool at the end of the period – the main types of pool and applicable rates are:

- *main pool* – this is the default pool where expenditure will be allocated unless it is required to be allocated elsewhere. The rate of WDA applicable to the main pool is 18%.

- *special rate pool* – expenditure on integral features (see **4.11**), certain cars (see **4.14**) and long life assets are allocated to this pool and attract a reduced rate of WDA at 8%.

Where the period of account is shorter than 12 months, the WDA will be reduced proportionality. Where the period exceeds 12 months, the capital allowance computation will be prepared on the basis of two separate periods – the initial 12 months and then the remainder of the period.

Where the balance of expenditure on any pool is less than or equal to the 'small pool limit' of £1,000, the business can claim a writing down allowance of full amount of that balance, rather than 18% or 8%.

Annual investment allowances

4.8   A business can claim an annual investment allowance (AIA), for each year in which it carries on business. This allows a business to claim 100% allowances for capital expenditure within the AIA limit in the year of purchase. The business can allocate AIA as it wants, and may choose to prioritise expenditure on integral features which would otherwise be allocated to the special rate pool and attract a lower rate of WDAs.

The AIA limit has fluctuated significantly in recent years – with effect from 1 January 2016 the AIA limit is reduced from £500,000 to a new 'permanent' level of £200,000. Details of the limit applicable before this time can be found at **4.26**.

The balance of any expenditure not covered by the AIA is added to the appropriate pool and will be subject to WDAs.

There are restrictions on the nature of expenditure upon which the AIA can be claimed, and in particular, it cannot be claimed on expenditure incurred in respect of a car (see **4.14**).

There are complicated rules to ensure that multiple claims for AIA cannot be made by one person or group of businesses and these can affect:

- a person controlling 'related' unincorporated businesses;
- a company which carries on more than one qualifying activity;
- 'related' singleton companies; or
- a group of companies.

For this purpose, 'related' means that one or both of the following tests are met:

- the shared premises condition; and
- the similar activities condition.

Complex transitional rules apply where a business's accounting period spans the date upon which there is a change in the AIA limit. In these case, the accounting period is essentially treated as comprising more than one period for AIA purposes. The AIA limit has to be calculated by prorating the limits on a monthly basis. Each period's expenditure must then be reviewed by reference to a secondary test. HMRC have published a guidance on these provisions which can be found here www.gov.uk/guidance/annual-investment-allowance-limit-changes-during-accounting-periods.

Example 4.3 – Period spanning the AIA limit change 31 December 2015

Genesis Limited has a 31 March 2016 year end.

The AIA limit is split over two periods.

Period 1	1 April 2015 – 31 December 2015	9 months at £500,000 pa	£375,000
Period 2	1 January 2016 – 31 March 2016	3 months at £200,000 pa	£50,000
	AIA limit		£425,000

The maximum AIA for this period is £425,000. However, there is a secondary limit which restricts the level of any claim for AIA in the period from 1 January 2016 to 31 March 2016 to the pro rata limit for that period (ie £50,000). There is no maximum claim limit for AIA for the period from 1 April 2015 to 31 December 2015 other than the overall maximum for the period of £425,000.

Example 4.4 – Calculating allowances

Vince is a farmer who likes to plough his own furrows. He spends £525,000 in January 2015 within his accounting period to 31 December 2015 on three combine harvesters. He purchases no other plant or equipment in the year. Vince gets allowances of:

AIA limit (1 January 2015 – 31 December 2015) – £500,000

The £525,000 exceeds the limit for the year so AIA is restricted to £500,000.

The balance of £25,000 is subject to 18% writing down allowance, giving him total writing down allowances of £4,500. In the following year, the

155

remaining expenditure of £20,500 is subject to writing down allowances at 18%.

In Year 1 Vince will be able to deduct £504,500 (£500,000 + £4,500) from his profits before capital allowances.

In Year 2 Vince will be able to deduct £3,690 (18% of £20,500) from his profits before capital allowances.

Focus

Plan the timing of expenditure to maximise use of annual investment allowances where possible. If substantial capital expenditure is planned, consider changing the year end to maximise the availability of AIA.

First year allowances

4.9   Certain expenditure qualifies for 100% first year allowances, mainly capital expenditure intended to improve the environment (without counting towards the AIA limit). The qualifying plant includes:

- energy saving equipment (as included on the 'energy technology product list');

- water saving equipment (as included on the 'water efficient technologies product list');

- low emission cars (currently cars with less than 95g/km);

- zero emission goods vehicles;

- gas, biogas and hydrogen refuelling equipment;

- environmentally beneficial plant and machinery (again certified as above);

There are various restrictions to these allowances and in particular, the plant should not be used for leasing or within a dwelling house. Further details (including links to the relevant lists) can be found on the HMRC website (www.gov.uk/capital-allowances/first-year-allowances).

Focus

Where you incur capital expenditure on environmentally friendly plant, check the list to see if it qualifies.

PLANT IN BUILDINGS AND INTEGRAL FEATURES

4.10   Many buildings include a substantial element of plant and machinery. Therefore, where a business has incurred capital expenditure on the construction or purchase of a building to be used for the purpose of a qualifying activity, there is an opportunity (often overlooked) to claim substantial tax relief.

Deciding what expenditure can actually qualify as plant and machinery is not always clear and the first point to consider is the definition of terms within the legislation (*CAA 2001, ss 21–23*).

Section 21 provides that expenditure on provision of plant and machinery does not include expenditure on the provision of a building. It goes on to define certain items (known as *List A*) which are treated as buildings. These include walls, floors, ceilings, doors, gates, shutters, windows and stairs. *Section 22* provides similar provisions with regard to structures and sets out a *List B* which includes tunnels, bridges, viaducts, aqueducts, embankments, cuttings, hard standing, railways, tramways, car parks, etc. These lists are not exhaustive.

Section 23 then provides a list of items which are unaffected by those two sections (in other words, those items which can be treated as plant and machinery) and sets out a *List C. List C* runs to 33 items and includes a number of items which one would normally expect to be included as plant, such as manufacturing or processing equipment, storage equipment including cold rooms, cookers, washing machines, dishwashers, refrigerators and similar equipment, sound insulation for a particular trade, computers, telecommunications and surveillance systems. There are some perhaps less expected items, such as caravans for holiday lettings, moveable partitions, decorative assets provided for the enjoyment of the public in hotels, restaurants and similar trades, cold stores, silos for temporary storage, or storage tanks. These largely follow decided cases in this area. The overall thrust of the legislation is to prevent the ambit of 'plant' in buildings from becoming any wider.

> **Focus**
>
> The abolition of industrial buildings allowances and agricultural buildings allowances (which provided allowances on the cost of certain buildings) makes it vital to identify and maximise any claim for plant and machinery allowances for items within such buildings.

Integral features

4.11   The concept of 'integral features' was introduced from April 2008 and provides that expenditure on the provision or replacement of integral features is deemed to be plant (*CAA 2001, s 33A*). The items that qualify as integral features are defined at *s 33A(5)* and are:

- electrical systems including lighting systems;

- cold water systems;

- space or water heating systems;

- systems of ventilation, air cooling or air purification (air conditioning) and any floor or ceiling comprised in such a system;

- lift, escalator or moving walkway;

- external solar shading.

It will be noted that a number of the items listed above have previously been held not to be plant in decided cases (cold water plumbing, lighting and electrical wiring being the most important). The changes therefore resulted in a significant extension of the scope of plant in buildings.

Where expenditure is incurred on an integral feature which amounts to more than 50% of the cost of replacing that integral feature, the expenditure is treated as capital expenditure on the provision of that feature.

Integral features are allocated to the special rate pool and therefore attract the lower rate of WDAs, however a business can choose to allocate its AIA against expenditure on integral features.

Example 4.5 – Making the correct claims

Ed constructs a commercial building in the 12 months ended 31 December 2015, and plant totalling £1,000,000 is identified in the building, as follows:

	£	
Electrical wiring and lighting	100,000	(IF)
Plumbing and water systems	100,000	(IF)
Lifts	150,000	(IF)
Air conditioning and central heating	150,000	(IF)
Telephone exchange	150,000	(P)
Fire and burglar alarm system	150,000	(P)
Fitted furniture	200,000	(P)

Of this, £500,000 is 'normal' plant (P) and £500,000 is integral features (IF). Ed wants to maximise his allowances. He therefore attributes the entire £500,000 annual investment allowance against integral features, claiming

---

£90,000 of writing down allowances (£500,000 at 18%) on the general plant which is added to the main pool. His total allowances are:

	£
Annual investment allowance	500,000
Main pool - WDA	90,000
	590,000

Allowances on the purchase of a building

4.12   Historically, it was possible for the purchaser of a second hand building to make a claim for capital allowances in respect of any plant within the building at the time of acquisition – certain conditions had to be met but it was often difficult for HMRC to challenge such claims as they were unable to obtain the relevant information from the vendor.

Since April 2012, in order for such claims to be made the vendor and purchaser must either agree a value for plant and machinery under *CAA 2001, s 198* (a written election made within two years of sale), or have the value determined by a Tribunal. Once accepted by HMRC, the *s 198* election is irrevocable, and fixes the disposal proceeds of the seller for plant on which he claimed allowances, and the purchase price for the purchaser of that plant.

Since April 2014 the rules have been tightened further – a purchaser can only claim allowances on items where the vendor (if eligible to do so) has actually claimed allowances. This may well push more property owners into claiming allowances due on fixtures.

Focus

The new rules mean it is vital that tax advisors consider claims for allowances as part of the process of acquiring new commercial property. Much more care will be needed in completing Section 19 of the Commercial Property Standard Enquiries form (previously often poorly completed by solicitors).

In particular, where a vendor has not previously made a claim for capital allowances on plant within the building, and they are entitled to, it may be possible to agree a claim is made immediately before the sale, so that a *s 198* election can be made and the purchaser can then benefit from the allowances.

Leased buildings

4.13   Where a taxpayer incurs capital expenditure on plant for a leased building (perhaps because they hold a long lease) the plant is deemed to belong to them, and therefore capital allowances are available.

There are complex rules to allocate allowances, where it is possible that more than one person has spent the money, but generally they go to the lowest interest in the building, in other words the person who holds an interest on which any other interests potentially entitled to allowances are reversionary.

MOTOR CARS

4.14   Special rules apply for capital allowances which can be claimed on motor cars. In particular:

- expenditure on cars cannot qualify for the AIA (see **4.8**)

- cars with an emission level exceeding 130g/km are added to the special rate pool and benefit from reduced WDAs (see **4.7**)

- cars with an emission level not exceeding 95g/km: 100% (see **4.8**)

The grams per kilometre are shown on the V5 car registration certificate.

What is a car for capital allowances purposes?

4.15   A car is a mechanically propelled road vehicle unless it is:

- built in such a way that it is mainly suitable for transporting goods; or

- not commonly used or suitable for use as a private vehicle.

See *CAA 2001, s 268A.*

As a result of this definition, vans and lorries are not cars, but motor homes are. Motor cycles are not treated as cars for capital allowance purposes.

> **Focus**
> Employers purchasing car fleets will often want to focus on cars with lower emission levels, to give higher rates of allowance. For very low emission cars, 100% FYAs may be due.

DISPOSALS

4.16   Where plant and machinery is disposed of, the seller must bring the proceeds into account – this is done by deducting them from the pool to which the original expenditure on that asset was allocated.

If this results in a negative figure in the pool, this is treated as a balancing charge (addition to taxable profits). Where plant is sold together with other assets, a just and reasonable apportionment of the proceeds is to be made.

On the cessation of the qualifying activity, once all disposal proceeds of all assets have been allocated to the relevant pool, a balancing adjustment will arise – where the balance of the pool is a negative figure, a balancing charge will arise; where the balance on the pool is a positive figure, a balancing allowance will arise (a deduction from taxable profits).

Where fixed plant (including integral features) is sold as part of a building, the relevant amount taken to the pool in respect of the assets will be the consideration allocated to that plant by way of the joint election under *CAA 2001, s 198* or the value determined by the Tribunal (see **4.12**).

The legislation also sets out the disposal value that should be used in specific cases, which may include the use of market value (*CCA 2001, s 61*).

Transfers between connected parties

4.17   The capital allowances code contains extensive provisions to prevent the exploitation of allowances when assets and businesses are transferred between connected parties.

For transfers of trades between companies under (75%) common ownership, the provisions of *CTA 2010, ss 948* provide that the capital allowance pools are effectively transferred to the transferee company ensuring that no balancing allowances or charges arise.

OTHER ALLOWANCES

4.18   This section provides a brief introduction to some other types of allowances currently available. It is intended to alert the reader to the existence of such allowances, and explain when they may be available, rather than to provide a comprehensive guide to what is a complex subject of limited application. Further guidance can be found in HMRC's Capital Allowances Manual.

Focus

Be aware of the potential for claiming these allowances in appropriate cases.

Business premises renovation allowances

4.19 Business premises renovation allowances (BPRA) (*CAA 2001, ss 360A–360Z4*) are available where 'qualifying expenditure' is incurred on a 'qualifying building'. Where available, 100% initial allowance is allowed for qualifying expenditure in the year in which it is incurred. This allowance can be deferred, with a 25% writing down allowance claimed on any expenditure for which the initial allowance was not claimed. Balancing adjustments are made if the property is sold within seven years of coming back into use.

Qualifying expenditure is expenditure on converting or renovating a qualifying building that will be used (or available for letting) for the purpose of a trade, profession or vocation, or as an office. But it does not include acquisition costs, extension costs, development of adjoining buildings, or acquisition of plant and machinery other than fixtures.

A qualifying building (or part of a building) is one in a 'disadvantaged area', which has been unused for at least a year at the date the renovation or conversion work starts. Prior to that it should have been used for business purposes, and not as a dwelling.

The relief was originally introduced for a limited period of time and although this period was extended, it is due to expire 1 April 2017 for corporation tax purposes and 6 April 2017 for income tax purposes.

Further details can be found on HMRC website, including a link to a 'postcode checker' to determine whether a building is within a disadvantaged area (www. gov.uk/guidance/business-premises-renovation-allowance-bpra).

Research and development expenditure

4.20 Capital allowances are available where a trader incurs capital expenditure on research and development undertaken directly by him, or on his behalf, related to the trade (see *CAA 2001, ss 437–451*). When the trade has not yet started, allowances are available if the person actually begins to carry on the trade connected with the research and development.

The allowance is equal to the whole of the expenditure and is given for the chargeable period within which the expenditure is incurred or when the trade commences, whichever is the later. If the asset is sold or the trader ceases to own it, a balancing charge will generally occur.

Qualifying expenditure is capital expenditure incurred by a person on carrying out, or providing facilities for carrying out, research and development. The research and development may be directly undertaken by him or on his behalf for the benefit of a trade he is carrying on, or one he has subsequently started to carry on. The expenditure can include buildings.

Research and development take the definition as per general accepted accountancy practice.

OTHER CAPITAL EXPENDITURE RELIEFS

Remediation of contaminated or derelict land

4.21   Where a company carries on a trade or a UK property business, and incurs expenditure on land for the purpose of remedying contamination or dereliction of the land, it can claim additional relief. There is 100% allowance for capital expenditure, or a 150% deduction for qualifying land remediation expenditure, with the option to convert part of any loss attributable to land remediation relief into a payable tax credit.

The intention was to abolish this relief with effect from 1 April 2012 but after consultation this relief has been retained.

OTHER ISSUES

Partnerships

4.22   Where capital expenditure is incurred by a partnership, this qualifies for capital allowances as it would have qualified if owned by an individual. In considering whether the asset is owned by the partnership, one considers the following factors:

- Is the asset held in the partnership name or in trust for the continuing partners?

- Where the capital expenditure was incurred as a result of a written contract, who is party to the contract?

- Was the expenditure invoiced to the partnership?

- Was payment made from the partnership bank account or otherwise with partnership monies?

- Does the asset appear in the partnership accounts?

The treatment of allowances

4.23   Individual partners are assessed to tax separately on their respective share of the partnership profits, on the basis of a 'notional trade' (see **3.27**). Capital allowances are treated as trading expenses of the period of account for the partnership business, and therefore form part of the profits of the notional trade. Where a partner acquires an asset personally for use in the partnership's trade, any capital allowances available on that asset are calculated separately from the partnership assets, but included as part of the profit of the notional trade of that partner (see **3.26**).

Interaction with capital gains tax

4.24   Where a trader has claimed capital allowances on plant installed in the building, in order that a purchaser of that building to claim any capital allowances on that plant, a joint election under *CAA 2001, s 198* must be made (see **4.12**)

Where capital allowances have been given and not reclaimed in respect of a building, whereas this does not affect the computation of a capital gain, any loss on the sale of the building is restricted by reference to the capital allowances claimed.

This is best illustrated by way of an example.

Example 4.7 – Effect of a *s 198* election (1)

Robert constructs a commercial building costing £1 million, and claims capital allowances on expenditure of £300,000. Some years later he sells the building to Jimmy for £1.5 million, and agrees with Jimmy that a joint *CAA 2001, s 198* election will be made to treat the sale proceeds of the plant as £100,000.

Robert retains the total net capital allowances of £200,000 (£300,000 less £100,000) and his capital gain is £0.5 million. Jimmy can claim capital allowances on £100,000.

Example 4.8 – Effect of a *s 198* election (2)

Robert buys another building for £1 million and, again, claims capital allowances on expenditure of £300,000. Some years later he sells the building to John for £900,000, and agrees with John that the *CAA 2001, s 198* election should be made to transfer the plant at a value of £100,000.

> Robert again retains his capital allowances of £200,000, but the capital loss of £100,000 on the building is restricted to nil because of capital allowances already claimed. John can claim capital allowances on the expenditure of £100,000.

APPENDIX: PLANT AND MACHINERY ALLOWANCE RATES

Writing down allowances (WDAs)

(CAA 2001, s 56)

4.25

	Main rate	Special rate
	%	%
From April 2012	18	8
April 2008 to April 2012	20	10
Before April 2008	25	–

Notes

1   *Changes* – The changes in WDA rates from 1 April 2012 (corporation tax) or 6 April 2012 (for income tax) were made by *FA 2011, s 10*.

2   *Straddling periods* – For chargeable periods which straddle the above relevant dates, the rate of WDA is a hybrid of the rates before and after the changes.

3   *Further information* – guidance for taxpayers is found at www.gov.uk/capital-allowances/overview. Technical guidance is found in the HMRC Capital Allowances manual at CA23220.

Annual investment allowance (AIA)

(CAA 2001, s 51A)

4.26

Expenditure incurred in period	Maximum AIA
	£
From 1 January 2016	200,000
From April 2014 to 31 December 2015	500,000

From 1 January 2013 to 31 March/5 April 2014	250,000
From April 2012 to 31 December 2012	25,000
April 2010 to April 2012	100,000
April 2008 to April 2010	50,000

Notes

1   *Chargeable periods* – The AIA is given for a chargeable period. As a general rule, the annual limit is proportionately increased or decreased for chargeable periods longer or shorter than 12 months.

2   *Maximum AIA entitlement* – For chargeable periods which straddle the relevant dates in the table, the maximum AIA entitlement is subject to adjustment (see **4.8**). Further guidance can be found at www.gov.uk/guidance/ annual-investment-allowance-limit-changes-during-accounting-periods.

3   *Non-qualifying* – The AIA cannot be claimed by a trust or by a partnership where one or more members is a company, and there are anti-avoidance provisions restricting entitlement to the AIA in certain circumstances (*CAA 2001, ss 38A, 51B–51N*).

4   *Exclusions* – The AIA is not due (for example) in respect of the purchase of cars, and it cannot be claimed for the period when the trade ceases (*CAA 2001, s 38B*).

5

Share incentives

- **Unapproved share options** – A tax charge can arise in respect of share options which are not approved by HMRC. This does not normally apply on the grant of the option, but may do so when the option is exercised (see **5.27–5.30**).

- **Tax-advantaged share option schemes** – A number of share incentive plans offer tax advantages if certain conditions are satisfied. The enterprise management incentives (EMI) plan is designed for small and medium sized companies (see **5.32–5.33**). Company share ownership plans (CSOPs) offer advantages for shares with a market value on grant not exceeding £30,000 (see **5.34–5.36**). Save As You Earn (SAYE) schemes broadly allow employees to save in order to pay for shares when exercising share options (see **5.37–5.38**). A share incentives plan (SIP) is an 'all employee' plan, which can provide for 'free' shares to be given to employees, 'partnership' shares to be bought on favourable terms, and also allow employees to receive 'matching' and 'dividend' shares (see **5.39–5.44**). Employee Shareholder Plans are the newest arrangement providing for limited income tax and capital gains tax relief in exchange for the employee giving up certain employment rights (see **5.45**).

- **Readily convertible assets** – Whether any charge arising in relation to a share incentive is subject to national insurance and whether PAYE should be operated in order to collect any income tax will depend upon whether the shares are readily convertible assets (see **5.46**).

- **Reporting requirements** – There are numerous reporting requirements which must be complied with when offering share incentives (see **5.47**).

EMPLOYEE SHARE INCENTIVES IN GENERAL

5.1   Businesses may wish to reward, retain and incentivise their employees in a number of ways. Rewards in the form of cash or benefits will be taxed under the rules outlined in **Chapter 2** above. Where companies use share-based incentives, although a charge to tax as earnings can arise under the normal charging provisions (*ITEPA 2003, s 62*) additional rules under *ITEPA 2003, Pt 7* can also apply to impose a tax charge on acquisition or at a later time on the occurrence of certain events.

Transfer of shares or options?

5.2   Share incentives may be delivered either by transferring shares outright to an employee or by giving the employee an option to buy the shares under defined arrangements. Options granted to employees give rise to legally binding obligations and rights for the employer and employee and should not be confused with more general 'promises' to provide an equity share in the company at some stage in the future.

Understanding the actual agreements between the employer and employee will be vital in establishing which tax rules apply.

Fully taxed or tax-advantaged incentives

5.3   If share based incentives are being used by employers it is important to consider if the arrangements being used qualify for any tax-advantaged treatment. Examples of arrangements which may qualify for this more beneficial treatment are covered below.

Any arrangements falling outside the tax-advantaged plans will fall to be taxed as 'employment-related securities' or 'employment-related securities options'.

Employment-related securities and employment-related securities options

5.4   The legislation in this area covers 'securities' that are defined to include:

- shares;
- contracts of insurance;
- loan stock (both company and government);
- warrants;
- certificates conferring rights to securities held by others;
- units in a collective investment scheme;
- futures; and
- contracts for difference.

(*ITEPA 2003, s 420*)

For the purposes of this chapter, the words 'shares' can be read to cover all securities.

Options are dealt with separately (see below) but in both cases the legislation within *ITEPA 2003, Pt 7* will only apply if the shares or options are 'employment-related'. This is defined in legislation which, in basic terms, confirms that this covers any case where any person acquires a share or is granted an option by reason of an employment of that person or any other person.

It should be noted that the person who obtains the shares or is granted an option does not have to be the employee through whose employment the interest in the shares or option arose, and in such cases the tax charge would be on the employee not on the recipient of the shares or option.

Who does the legislation apply to?

5.5   The legislation applies to all directors, employees and office holders.

The legislation also confirms that, subject to some narrow exemptions (see below), shares and/or options, given or granted by any past, present or future employer to an employee will be deemed to stem from that employment. This prevents, say, the directors/founders of a business claiming that they escape the legislation because they got their shares not as employees but because they set the business up. But any such shares may well be of limited value and/or the founders might have paid full value for the shares. In such cases the shares will be employment-related securities but the tax charge on them will clearly be nil (*ITEPA 2003, s 421B*).

Situations where these rules don't apply

5.6   Some situations give rise to a full or limited exemption from the employment-related securities rules. These include:

- *Family or personal relationships* – The 'deeming provision' in **5.5** above is removed where the right or opportunity to benefit from a share is provided to an individual in the 'normal course of the domestic, family or personal relationships' of that person (*ITEPA 2003, ss 421B(3), 471(3)*).

  HMRC confirm their approach to this at ERSM20220. In most cases, a 'gift' of shares to a family member who works in the family business will be covered by this exception but the case can be harder to prove where the individual concerned is an unrelated close friend. In this context HMRC say:

    'Personal relationships can also include friendships and it is not unknown for a proprietor to pass on his business to a long-time employee with whom he has developed close personal ties. The principal question to be asked is would an employer trying to reward or incentivise the employee have passed over such shares to him/her, or is the reason more personal than an employer/employee relationship.'

A rule of thumb might be that this exception would apply in cases where the person giving the share can say about the recipient of the share 'he's like a brother to me' and mean it.

- *Death of the employee* – Shares fall outside the definition of employment-related securities on death, meaning that there is no charge under this section on or after the employee's death. But note that the death of an associate of the employee does not prevent a charge and if the chargeable event occurs before the date of death then the charge will still apply (*ITEPA 2003, ss 421B(6), 477(2)*).

- *Seven years after employment ceases* – Securities cease to be employment-related securities seven years after the employee leaves employment. But note that any option granted before cessation of employment remains an employment-related securities option without any application of this seven-year rule (*ITEPA 2003, s 421B(7)*).

- *Employee-controlled companies* – If the shares in a company are held for the benefit of the company's employees and the employees control the company through that shareholding then (subject to all such shares being subject to the same rights and restrictions) there is an exemption from a charge under the rules which apply to restricted securities, convertible securities, securities acquired for less than market value or charges related to post-acquisition benefits from those securities (see below). But importantly the exemption will not apply if the shares have been part of some tax avoidance arrangement (*ITEPA 2003, s 421H*).

- *Public offers* – Shares which employees benefit from which are part of a public offer will not be caught by the rules governing restricted securities, convertible securities and securities acquired for less than market value (*ITEPA 2003, s 421F*).

- *Approved share schemes* – These have their own rules (see below).

The residence exemption that was previously included within these provisions (*ITEPA 2003, s 421E*) was repealed with effect from 6 April 2015 and replaced by new provisions which broadly bring the taxation of employment related securities for non-UK residents in line with other employment income (*ITEPA 2003, ss 41F–41L*).

Focus

Almost always, when a director or employee of a company is given a share reward, the employment-related securities legislation will apply, but check carefully where family members are involved.

TAX ON THE ACQUISITION OF EMPLOYMENT-RELATED SECURITIES

5.7   On acquisition of an employment-related security an income tax charge will arise based on the difference between what is paid for the shares and what the shares are worth. They are taxed under the 'money's worth' rules (see **2.6**). But see **5.8** below for how this rule may be modified in some cases.

Money's worth and market value

5.8   These two concepts normally give the same answer but are used in different parts of the legislation. Charges on the acquisition of shares are made under *ITEPA 2003, s 62*, which uses the concept of 'something capable of being converted into money or something of direct monetary value'.

Other charges on shares (see below) directly link back to a definition of market value in the capital gains tax legislation which is based on what might reasonably be expected to be obtained from a sale in the open market (*TCGA 1992, s 272*).

In the vast majority of cases these two values will be the same but if in any case the market value under the capital gains tax rule is greater than the money's worth value under the *s 62* rule, then any excess value would be brought into charge to income tax by *ITEPA 2003, Ch 3C*, under the rules governing securities acquired for less than market value. The *s 62* charge on the money's worth basis will always take precedence over the *Ch 3C* rules.

Modified rules for particular circumstances

5.9   The characteristics of the shares acquired can lead to the application of different rules. This includes

- *Shares that might be forfeited* – A charge to income tax will generally not arise where the share acquired is subject to a potential forfeiture of the share if that restriction will cease within five years of the date of acquisition (*ITEPA 2003, s 425(2)*).

  Such shares will be subject to an income tax charge when any restrictions are lifted, varied or the shares are sold (see **5.10** below). An election can be made to ignore this rule and bring into tax the full value of the share (ignoring the impact of the forfeiture restriction) when the shares are acquired. See **5.12** below.

- *Shares which are convertible* – Where any additional value in the share due to its conversion is ignored in calculating the income tax charge on acquisition (*ITEPA 2003, s 437(1)*).

'RESTRICTED SECURITIES'

5.10   Specific rules apply to 'restricted securities'. The legislation defines 'restricted securities' very widely and so the rules will apply where there is any restriction on a share (included in any agreement, contract, agreement, etc) which means that the market value of the share is altered. There are three major sorts of restriction which are dealt with in the legislation:

- *Risk of forfeiture* – This is where a share runs the risk of being taken away from the employee and this reduces the value of the share. For example, an employee might have a share in a company that he would have to sell back to the company if he was to leave employment.

- *Restriction on freedom to retain or sell the shares or to exercise certain share rights* – This covers situations where the employee cannot freely keep or sell a share, keep the proceeds of any sale, benefit from dividends or vote.

- *Potential disadvantages in respect of the securities* – This covers any other restrictions to the disadvantage of the employee. For example, there may be a requirement that the employee can receive dividends and vote, but must always pay the dividends back to the company and vote as instructed.

It is important to establish whether the shares concerned are subject to restriction or whether the characteristics of the share are simply 'generic' to that class of shares in the company. If the characteristics of the share are enshrined in the Articles of the company as applying to all shares of that class, and an employee gets one of those shares, then there is no 'restriction' (see ERSM30310).

> **Example 5.1 – What is a 'restriction'?**
>
> If Joe Smith is given shares in his employer's company and there is a side letter saying he must not sell those shares for three years that is clearly a restriction to which this legislation applies. But if Joe gets a non-voting B share in the company, with the share rights set out in the articles, there is no restriction on such a share – all shareholders of this class of share would have shares with this characteristic.

A common issue arises where employees have to sell their shares back to the company on leaving employment. In such cases this characteristic would only apply to employees, and not necessarily all shareholders, and so this would be a restriction to consider under this legislation.

The charge to income tax

5.11   If restricted securities are being considered then an income tax charge will arise if there is a 'chargeable event' (*ITEPA 2003, s 426*).

There are three such events (*ITEPA 2003, s 427*):

● The release of all restrictions from the shares, whilst they are still owned by the employee or a connected party such as a spouse.

● The variation of any of the restrictions, whilst they are still owned by the employee or a connected party such as a spouse – this also covers the release of some restrictions and not others.

● The disposal of the shares to an unconnected person, before all the restrictions have been lifted.

In all these cases an income tax charge will arise (*ITEPA 2003, s 428*) based on a rather daunting formula which is explained in full in the HMRC manuals at ERSM30400.

This is a complex area but to understand the detailed examples in the HMRC manual it might be helpful to understand what the legislation is trying to do.

When a restricted share has been acquired by the employee a charge would have arisen on the money's worth basis as set out at **5.8** above. This would have looked at any difference between what was paid for the share and the actual market value (or 'AMV') of the share at the time of acquisition. The AMV taken into account will reflect any characteristics of the share at that time, for example the sort of restrictions talked about in **5.10** above.

If you were to ignore the impact of such restrictions on the market value of that same share, then it is reasonable to expect that the market value would be greater – this is referred to as the unrestricted market value (or 'UMV').

The difference between these two values (the UMV and the AMV) is not ordinarily subject to tax on the acquisition of the share, although see **5.12** where an election is made. Potentially, therefore, the employee has a share which could give extra value if those restrictions are released, varied or the share is sold to someone to whom the restrictions have no impact. It is this potential additional value which these rules look to tax when a chargeable event occurs.

The legislation uses a complex rule to calculate the additional value. A simple example of this is as follows

---

Example 5.2 – Calculating the charge (1)

Rashid acquires shares in his employer's company for £500. These shares are restricted securities, in that if Rashid leaves employment within three years he must offer to sell the shares back to the company for £500.

Due to this restriction, the AMV of the shares acquired is considered to be £1,200.

The UMV of the shares at that time is £2,000.

Rashid sells his shares in the company for £10,000 after holding them for five years.

The events give the following tax treatment:

Year 1 – Shares bought

Shares have been bought for £500 that are worth (ie have an AMV of) £1,200. But there is no income tax charge on this 'discount' because the shares are subject to a forfeiture clause that will expire within five years – see **5.9** above.

Year 3 – Selling restriction lifted

This is a chargeable event (see **5.11** above). At this stage the UMV has risen to £4,000 and as there are no other restrictions remaining, the AMV of the shares is also £4,000.

Applying the formula set out in *ITEPA 2003, s 428* the charge arising at this time is calculated as:

UMV × (IUP – PCP – OP) – CE = charge

4,000 × (0.75 – 0 – 0) – 0 = £3,000

See ERSM30400 for explanation of this calculation.

Year 5 – Shares sold

The shares are sold for £10,000. This sum is subject to the capital gains rules. The tax charge will be based on the consideration for sale (£10,000)

---

less the cost of the shares and the sums chargeable to income tax during the ownership of the shares, as follows:

	£	£
Consideration		10,000
Less: cost	500	
Year 3 income tax charge	3,000	
Total costs (excluding dealing costs)		(3,500)
Chargeable to capital gains tax		6,500

(Subject to offset of annual exemption, losses, etc.)

So what this legislation achieves is to bring into charge to income tax the proportion of the value of the shares that is not paid for on acquisition. The example illustrates this if we consider the following:

Rashid bought shares with an unrestricted market value of £2,000 but only paid £500 for them. In effect he received a discount of 75%. By applying the legislation an income tax charge arises as shown of:

	Unrestricted market value	Taxable sum	%
Year 1	2,000	nil	0
Year 3	4,000	3,000	75
Total % charged			75

So the full percentage discount enjoyed by Rashid has been brought into charge across the period of ownership as the restrictions have been lifted. His actual tax cost varies, of course, with the changing value of the shares.

Elections to ignore restrictions

5.12   Elections can be made to ignore the above rules and replace them with a tax charge based on the full value of the shares on acquisition and/or chargeable event. The rules are as follows:

●   Election on the acquisition of a forfeitable security where the restrictions will cease within five years (see **5.9** above).

The employer and employee may jointly elect that a charge arises on the actual market value on acquisition of the forfeitable security so that the rules outlined in **5.10** above do not apply. This joint election must be 'in a form approved by the Board of Inland Revenue' and HMRC publish forms which are suitable for this purpose. An election must be made within 14 days of the acquisition of the shares and cannot be revoked once made. Any election does not need to be sent to HMRC but must be kept by the employer and employee (*ITEPA 2003, s 425(3)*).

- Election on the acquisition of any restricted security (including a forfeitable security) under which all or any chosen restrictions can be ignored in calculating the value of the share. This gives the taxpayer the opportunity to identify and exclude from the charge set out in **5.11** above, any specific restrictions which are anticipated to be lifted (which would give rise to an increase in the tax bill assuming the shares rose in value) (*ITEPA 2003, s 431(1) or (2)*).

  The same rules on the nature and timing of the election apply as shown in the above paragraph dealing with *ITEPA 2003, s 425(3)*.

- Election can be made on any 'chargeable event' after acquisition to ignore the impact of any remaining restrictions, effectively bringing them into charge at that time instead (*ITEPA 2003, s 430*).

Once again the same rules on the nature and timing of the election apply as shown in the above paragraph dealing with *ITEPA 2003, s 425(3)*.

Example 5.3 – Calculating the charge (2)

If in **Example 5.2** Rashid had elected to ignore the restrictions on his shares when he acquired them he would have been charged as follows:

Year 1 Acquisition – Income tax charged on the difference between the UMV of the shares (£2,000) and the amount he pays for those shares (£500).

So he is charged to income tax on £1,500 in Year 1.

When the restrictions on the shares are lifted in Years 3, no further income tax charge arises.

On disposal of the shares Rashid would be chargeable to capital gains tax as follows:

	£	£
Consideration		10,000
Less: cost	500	

Year 1 income tax charge	1,500	
Total costs (excluding dealing costs)		(2,000)
Chargeable to capital gains tax		8,000

(Subject to offset of annual exemption, losses, etc).

Without making the election, Rashid would be subject to tax on £9,500. Of this, £3,000 would be chargeable to income tax with the remaining £6,500 being chargeable to capital gains tax (see **Example 5.2**).

On making the election, Rashid would still be subject to tax on a total of £9,500 although only £1,500 would be chargeable to income tax with the remaining £8,000 being chargeable to capital gains tax.

Given the differential in income tax and capital gains tax rates (and the potential for Rashid to qualify for entrepreneurs' relief on the disposal), the election in this case would be beneficial as the total tax bill would be reduced. Rashid would however have to find the funds to pay the tax bill 'up front' in Year 1.

But the answer won't always be that simple.

Example 5.4 – Whether to make an election

Jasmine is offered a similar deal to Rashid by her employer, with similar restrictions and values as in the above example. She buys the shares for £500 but, in her case, the restrictions are not released and when the business is sold the shares are actually only worth £100.

If no election is made there will be no charge to income tax on acquisition, no charge to income tax during her holding the shares and a capital loss on disposal of the shares of £400 (£500 cost less £100 sale proceeds).

If an election was made, however, Jasmine will pay income tax up front on acquisition on £1,500, but will get no 'relief' for this tax other than through an increased capital loss on the sale (which will then be £1,900 – being £500 cost plus £1,500 charged to income tax less £100 sale proceeds). Clearly in that case making an election is a bad decision!

CONVERTIBLE SECURITIES

5.13   Another set of tax rules apply where shares are converted from one sort of share to another sort of share. When this happens any benefit will be charged to tax as employment income.

A security will be convertible if it:

- carries on acquisition an entitlement for the shareholder to convert it (either with or without conditions that need to be met) into a security of a different description; or

- is granted such an entitlement after acquisition; or

- some other agreement allows the securities to be converted by someone else other than the shareholder (*ITEPA 2003, s 436*).

These rules will apply even if the conversion happens 'automatically' after a period of time.

Focus

These are very complicated rules and specialist advice should be taken in all cases involving this sort of share. The explanations which follow give a flavour of the problems that arise.

Charge to income tax

5.14 On acquisition of a convertible security, any value which is due to the potential conversion is ignored in calculating the initial income tax charge.

Example 5.5 – Tax charge on acquisition of loan stock

Harry's employer gives him loan stock of £500 nominal value (on which he will get interest of 3% per year) which after three years will convert to 50 shares in the company. At the time of the investment 50 shares in the company are worth £4,000.

The loan stock is worth £3,000, but without the right to convert to shares it would only be worth £2,500.

The income tax charge on acquisition is based on £2,500, ignoring the value in the loan stock because of the right to convert. The underlying value of the shares is also ignored (*ITEPA 2003, s 437(1)*).

This rule may be modified where the arrangements form part of an avoidance arrangement, where the full value of the security will be brought into charge if the value is greater than the 'reduced value' as calculated above.

Chargeable events

5.15   There will also be a tax charge on any of the following events after the acquisition of a convertible security:

- the actual conversion of the securities into securities of a different description;
- the disposal of the convertible securities otherwise than to an associated person;
- the release of the entitlement to convert the securities in return for consideration;
- the receipt by an associated person of a benefit in respect of the entitlement to convert the securities (*ITEPA 2003, s 439(3)*).

The phrase 'associated person' can be confusing as the same phrase means something different in other parts of the tax legislation. Here, this generally means the employee plus his immediate family or household (*ITEPA 2003, s 421C*). So it catches arrangements where someone married or living with an employee gets the shares. As the HMRC manuals somewhat quaintly put it, 'The broad coverage of "household" is intended to include modern personal relationships beyond the traditional family within marriage' (ERSM20250).

Calculating the tax charge

5.16   In similar fashion to the rules on restricted securities, the legislation sets down a formula based approach to establish the taxable sum on a chargeable event. The rules on this can be found at ERSM40080 (*ITEPA 2003, s 441*).

Example 5.6 – Tax charge on conversion

Using **Example 5.5** you will recall that Harry holds loan stock. He converts this to shares after holding the loan stock for three years. At that stage the shares he gets in the company are worth £4,750. The loan stock is worth £3,000 but after ignoring the impact of the conversion rights the loan stock would only be worth £2,500. Harry pays an additional £100 to the employer at the date of conversion.

The amount of the gain is calculated by using the formula set out at *ITEPA 2003, s 441(2) and* explained at ERSM40080 as:

CMVCS – (CMVERS + CC) = charge

£4,750 – (£2,500 + £100) = £2,150

The effect of this rule is that tax is charged on the additional value Harry receives on the conversion of the securities.

Example 5.7 – Sale before conversion

In the above example, if Harry sold his loan stock for £3,000 before conversion (at the time when ignoring the impact of the conversion rights the loan stock would only be worth £2,500) the gain would be calculated by using the formula set out at *ITEPA 2003, s 441(3) and* explained at ERSM40080 as:

DC – CMVERS = charge

£3,000 – £2,500 = £500

The effect of this rule is that tax is charged on the value Harry gets from the sale of the conversion rights.

Example 5.8 – Release of conversion right

If prior to conversion Harry agrees to accept a sum of £400 from his employer to give up the right to convert the loan stock to shares, that £400 would be the gain. If instead of cash Harry was given an asset, the gain will be the market value of that asset (*ITEPA 2003, s 441(4)*).

Exceptions

5.17   The exceptions set out in respect of the restricted security provisions at **5.6** above apply equally to the convertible security provisions.

Convertible securities which are also restricted

5.18   Where a security is both convertible and restricted, HMRC take the view that unless these securities form part of some avoidance arrangement they are content for the more flexible restricted securities rules to apply (see ERSM40030).

SECURITIES WITH ARTIFICIALLY DEPRESSED VALUE

5.19   This rule attacks avoidance of tax in cases where the value of the shares is artificially depressed by more than 10% as a result of things done otherwise than for genuine commercial purposes, generally within a seven year period ending at the time of the chargeable event.

The legislation can bite on the occurrence of the following chargeable events:

- on the acquisition of securities;
- on a restricted securities chargeable event;
- on a convertible securities chargeable event;
- on the disposal of securities for more than market value;
- on any securities benefits not otherwise subject to tax.

The tax charge

5.20 A charge will arise on the occurrence of one of the chargeable events listed above to replace the depressed value with the true market value (see ERSM50100 *et seq*).

However, where the securities are restricted securities a chargeable event under *ITEPA 2003, s 427* is deemed to occur on the following occasions:

- just before the cancellation of the security or a disposal that does not qualify as a chargeable event, and
- on 5 April each year.

The period considered for assessing whether things have been done to artificially depress the value of securities is extended in the case of forfeitable securities, to commence seven years before the date of acquisition of those securities and end on the date of the chargeable event. (*ITEPA 2003, ss 446E(3)–(4)*).

SECURITIES WITH ARTIFICIALLY ENHANCED VALUE

5.21 This rule attacks avoidance of tax in cases where the value of the shares is artificially enhanced by more than 10% as a result of things done otherwise than for genuine commercial purposes (*ITEPA 2003, Pt 7, Ch 3B*).

The tax charge

5.22 Where the rule applies, the tax charge will be based on the increase in the value of the shares by way of the artificial enhancement (see ERSM60100).

The measure of whether there has been an artificial enhancement to the value of the shares is assessed for each tax year, and therefore an annual tax charge can arise.

Legislation is in place to prevent charges under this section producing a 'double tax charge' in cases where the securities, for example, subsequently fall into the charge under the restricted securities legislation dealt with at **5.10**.

SECURITIES ACQUIRED FOR LESS THAN MARKET VALUE

5.23   In normal circumstances, when an employee acquires a share for less than its market value the general employment tax rules (*ITEPA 2003, s 62*) apply to give an income tax charge on the 'money's worth' principle (see **2.6**).

In some cases this charge may not apply, for example if:

● the residence rules impact to prevent a general tax charge; or

● the shares are part paid; or

● there is some mismatch between the money's worth value and the full market value of the share.

In any case where this happens legislation comes into play which catches any discount that escapes the general employment tax rules (*ITEPA 2003, s 446Q*).

The tax charge

5.24   This legislation applies where an employee pays less than the actual market value for shares or acquires them under terms giving an obligation to make further payments for the shares. The tax charge is based on the difference between:

● what is paid by the employee; and

● the actual market value of the shares (assuming any future obligations to pay had already been met).

This sum is then charged as if it was a notional loan to the employee, on which there is an annual charge under the beneficial loans legislation (see **2.55**) and a final charge on sale of the shares or write off of the outstanding sums due.

These rules will not apply in the cases excluded from charge as outlined in **5.6**.

SECURITIES DISPOSED OF FOR MORE THAN MARKET VALUE

5.25   Where an employee's shares are disposed of for more than their market value, the extra sum paid is charged to income tax. This can arise where:

● the employer buys back the shares at an enhanced value;

● the employer makes a payment on a sale to a third party;

- employees are able to sell their shares at a higher price than other shareholders (perhaps during a sale of their employing company); or

- the employee swaps shares for more valuable securities.

(*ITEPA 2003, Part 7, Ch 3D*)

The impact of these rules can be seen in the case of *Grays Timber Products Ltd v HMRC* (sometimes cited as *Company A v HMRC*) [2010] STC 782. In that case the company's managing director had been allotted shares in its holding company under an arrangement that on a sale of the holding company he would receive substantially more per share than the other shareholders. The director argued that the market value of his shares would be impacted by this 'side agreement' and so when he sold his shares and received his sale proceeds, the whole of those proceeds would fall to be taxed under the capital gains tax regime.

Unfortunately for the taxpayer the Supreme Court decided that the market value of the shares can only be determined by those features which are intrinsically linked to the share itself, in other words the feature would have to attach to the share whoever holds it. In the *Grays Timber* case the feature which gave the director an enhanced payment on his share disposal would not remain attached to the share in the hands of its new owner. So the additional sum per share he received over and above the other shareholders was held not to be a payment falling under the capital gains tax regime but rather a payment chargeable to income tax under *ITEPA 2003, Ch 3D*.

This illustrates the need to carefully establish what rights attach to all similar shares in a company (perhaps through the articles and memorandum of association) and those rights which are personal to the shareholder.

POST-ACQUISITION BENEFITS FROM SECURITIES

5.26 There is further legislation that will bring into charge any benefits arising from employee shares that are not otherwise caught by the general legislation. Any benefits caught by these rules are taxed as income of the employee in the year they are received (*ITEPA 2003, Pt 7, Ch 4*).

'UNAPPROVED' SHARE OPTIONS

5.27 As with all the matters discussed in this chapter, the rules on 'unapproved' share options (options not falling within the tax advantaged schemes mentioned below) also cover options over other securities. The majority of cases are likely to involve share options and so the rules are discussed here in the context of such options.

A share option does not involve the transfer of a share to an employee. It is also not simply a vague 'promise' to allow an employee to acquire a share at some stage in the future. A share option is a legally binding agreement giving the employee the right to acquire shares in the company under agreed terms of price, date, etc. Normally this legal right will be set out in a formal option agreement.

There are three basic steps to consider relating to the tax treatment of unapproved share options. These are:

- the grant of an option;

- the exercise of the option;

- the sale of the shares acquired.

Care should be taken to ensure that each of these steps is considered separately as they are governed by distinct tax rules.

Grant of unapproved options

5.28   The general rule is that no charge to tax will arise on the grant of an option (*ITEPA 2003, s 475*). The only exceptions to this rule will be for certain rare grants of options at a discount under a CSOP scheme (see below, and *ITEPA 2003, s 475(2)*) or where the option is granted to a non-UK resident employee (where a charge may arise under the normal employment income provisions of *ITEPA 2003, s 62*). A detailed review of such cases is outside the scope of this publication.

Exercise of unapproved options

5.29   The legislation does not actually use the word 'exercise' as the rules also cover cases where shares come to an individual without them having to take any 'action' to obtain the shares (for example, where shares are automatically delivered to an executive under a long-term incentive plan). The rules also cover situations where the option is released for a payment or a benefit, but the most common situation will be where an employee takes up an option right by exercising the option.

In these cases the chargeable amount arising on the exercise of an option is in effect based on the market value of the shares passing to the employee on exercise less any costs such as the option price paid. The legislation at *ITEPA 2003, s 478* follows the draftsman's recurring obsession of defining everything by way of a formula, using the calculation explained at ERSM48400.

Example 5.10 – Exercising the share option

In May 2014, Betty Jackson's employer granted her an option to buy 3,000 shares at a price of £2 per share, the option to be exercisable if she remained an employee of the company for two years. She paid £10 as consideration for the grant of the option.

Betty exercised the option in June 2016 when shares were worth £4 per share.

Betty's tax charge will be based on:

		£
Value of shares at exercise: 3,000 × £4	=	12,000
Less cost of shares: 3,000 × £2	=	(6,000)
Less sum paid for the grant of the option		(10)
Share option gain charged to income tax in 2016/17	=	5,990

Depending upon the nature of the shares acquired pursuant to the option, they may themselves be subject to the earlier provisions of this chapter (for example, if they were restricted securities).

Sale of shares

5.30   On the sale of shares acquired through the exercise of options, the normal capital gains tax rules apply. Confusion can often arise if the exercise of an option is followed immediately by the sale of the shares, but these are two distinct and separate transactions which have their own tax consequences.

TAX ADVANTAGED OPTION SCHEMES

5.31   There are a number of share incentive plans which give tax advantages. These include:

- Enterprise Management Incentive (EMI) schemes;

- Company Share Ownership Plans (CSOP);

- Save As You Earn schemes (SAYE);

- Share Incentive Plans (SIP);

- Employee Shareholder Plans.

Enterprise Management Incentive (EMI) schemes

5.32   These are tax advantaged share option schemes designed for small and medium sized companies. The essence of the scheme is that no tax charge will arise on the grant of an option nor (normally) on the exercise of the option, but rather a capital gains tax charge will arise on the eventual sale of the shares.

To qualify for this treatment the option must be granted for genuine commercial reasons, such as to encourage the recruitment, retention and reward of key individuals within a company (*ITEPA 2003, Sch 5, para 4*).

There are numerous specific requirements that must be met before the EMI tax advantages will apply. These include:

1   General requirements

- An employee may not be granted qualifying options over shares with a total value of more than £250,000 (for options granted prior to 16 June 2012 the limit was £120,000 and for options granted before 6 April 2008 the limit was £100,000). The value of any unexercised CSOP options held by the employee must be included in this figure. For this purpose the value of the shares is the market value of the shares assuming there were no restrictions. The value of shares can be agreed with HMRC in advance of any option grants (*ITEPA 2003, Sch 5, para 5*).

- The total value of shares under EMI options granted by a company cannot exceed £3 million at any time (*ITEPA 2003, Sch 5, para 7*).

2   Relating to the company

- EMI options can only be issued by independent companies, meaning a company that is not a 51% subsidiary. In addition, the company issuing the EMI options must only have qualifying subsidiaries, meaning that no other person can control or have arrangements in place to control, more than 50% of any subsidiary (*ITEPA 2003, Sch 5, para 9*).

- The company's gross assets must not exceed £30 million at the date of any EMI option grant. For companies within a group this test is applied to the group as a whole (*ITEPA 2003, Sch 5, para 12*).

- A qualifying company must have fewer than 250 full-time equivalent employees at the date on which a qualifying EMI option is granted (*ITEPA 2003, Sch 5, para 12A*).

- A qualifying company must have a permanent establishment in the UK (as defined by *CTA 2010, Pt 24, Ch 2*). This rule replaced the requirement for the company to be carrying on a trade wholly or mainly in the UK, which applied to EMI options granted prior to 16 December 2010 (*ITEPA 2003, Sch 5, para 14A*).

- The trade carried on by the company must not be an 'excluded activity' such as:

  o dealing in land, commodities or futures, or shares, securities or other financial instruments;

  o dealing in goods, otherwise than in the course of an ordinary trade of wholesale or retail distribution;

  o banking, insurance, money-lending, debt-factoring, hire purchase financing or other financial activities;

  o leasing (including letting ships on charter, or other assets on hire);

  o receiving royalties or other licence fees;

  o providing legal or accountancy services;

  o property development;

  o farming or market gardening;

  o holding, managing or occupying woodlands, any other forestry activities or timber production;

  o shipbuilding, coal and steel production;

  o operating or managing hotels or comparable establishments or managing property used as a hotel or comparable establishment;

  o operating or managing nursing homes or residential care homes, or managing property used as a nursing home or residential care home;

  o providing services or facilities for another excluded business which is controlled by the provider of the services or facilities.

(*ITEPA 2003, Sch 5, paras 16–23*)

3 Relating to the employee

- Employees can only be granted EMI options if they work:

  o at least 25 hours each week, or

  o if less, 75% of their working time

for the company granting the option (or for its qualifying subsidiary). These tests are based on average working time so an employee on flexible hours can still qualify. When looking at the 75% test, the measurement is made against all paid work (including any self-employed work). Time off ill, etc still counts as working hours for these tests (*ITEPA 2003, Sch 5, para 26*).

188

- The employee must not have, before the grant of an EMI option, a material interest in the company, being defined as controlling more than 30% of the shares of the company or having rights over 30% or more of the assets of the company on a winding up. Options over shares (other than existing EMI options) are counted in this test, as are shares or assets controlled by associates such as a spouse or parent.

A common error is to assume that an EMI option cannot be granted over more than 30% of the shares in a company to an employee. This can be done, as the test of material ownership is made immediately before the grant of the options, not after (*ITEPA 2003, Sch 5, para 28*).

4   Other requirements

- The shares under option must be ordinary shares which are fully paid up and not redeemable (*ITEPA 2003, Sch 5, para 35*).

- The options must be exercised within ten years of the date of grant for the tax advantages to apply (*ITEPA 2003, Sch 5, para 36*).

- The option must be written and must include:
  ○   the date of the grant of the option;

  ○   that it is granted under the provisions of *ITEPA 2003, Sch 5*;

  ○   the number of shares that may be acquired;

  ○   the price the employee will pay;

  ○   when and how the option may be exercised;

  ○   any restrictions on the shares;

  ○   any performance conditions related to the option; and

  ○   whether there is a risk of forfeiture.

  Often this is achieved by the company establishing a general 'plan' under which individual options are granted, linking the option to the company's memorandum and articles of association (*ITEPA 2003, Sch 5, para 37*).

- Options must not be transferable (*ITEPA 2003, Sch 5, para 38*).

- No adjustments can be made to an option after grant that would increase the market value of the shares under option or result in any of the other qualifying conditions failing to be met. Minor adjustments to the option can be made after grant but not if they change the agreement fundamentally, for example by changing the number of shares under option, the price payable or the terms under which the option can be exercised (*ITEPA 2003, s 536*).

- Options can be 'rolled over' into new options in cases where there is a company reorganisation. This must be done within six months of the date of the reorganisation (*ITEPA 2003, Sch 5, Part 6*).

- HMRC must be notified of any grant of an EMI option within 92 days of the grant (*ITEPA 2003, Sch 5, para 44*). This notification must be given electronically and the option holder must make a declaration that they meet the statutory requirements relating to commitment of working time. This must be retained by the company (and produced if requested by HMRC) with a copy given to the optionholder within seven days of signature.

Taxation of EMI options

5.33   No income tax charge will arise on the exercise of an EMI option as long as the rules are complied with and the price paid for the acquisition of the shares is at least the market value of those shares at the date of the option grant.

If the option is granted at a discount, then an income tax charge will arise on exercise.

Example 5.11 – Exercise of EMI option granted at a discount

Alan is granted an option to acquire 1,000 shares in his employer's company at a price of £5 per share. At the date of grant the shares are worth £8 per share.

He exercises the option when the value of the shares has risen to £10 per share.

Alan has an income tax charge at the date of exercise on the discount as follows:

			£
Market value at date of grant	£8 × 1,000	=	8,000
Less price paid on exercise	£5 × 1,000	=	(5,000)
Total discount subject to income tax		=	3,000

Note – If Alan sold these shares for £10 each, his base cost for capital gains tax purposes would be based on £8 per share.

These rules are modified where there is a fall in the market value of the shares between the date of grant and the date of exercise, so that the lower value is brought into account. So if in the above example the share price had been £7 at the date of exercise, Alan would have had an income tax charge based on a discount of £2,000 (£7 – £5 × 1,000).

Finance Act 2013 allows entrepreneurs' relief on any capital gains made:

- on the sale of shares sold on or after 6 April 2013, and

- which were acquired by the exercise of an EMI option on or after 6 April 2012,

without the need to have the 5% shareholding level normally required.

In addition, the 12-month holding period for these shares to qualify for entrepreneurs' relief will run from the date of the grant of option. The other rules relating to entrepreneurs' relief must, of course, be met. For further guidance on entrepreneurs' relief see **Chapter 14** below.

An income tax charge will also arise if the options are exercised more than 90 days after a 'disqualifying event'. These events will include:

- the loss of independence of a company that has granted an option;

- the company ceasing to meet the trading activity test;

- the employee ceasing to work for the company, or otherwise ceasing to meet the working time requirement;

- a variation in the terms of the option that increases the market value of the shares or makes the option cease to meet the requirements of *ITEPA 2003, Sch 5*;

- changes to the share capital of the company impact on the value of the shares under option or make the option cease to meet the requirements of *ITEPA 2003, Sch 5*.

> **Focus**
>
> EMI schemes represent a continuing opportunity to bring the wider workforce into company share ownership, and can be a very useful tool in aligning employees' motivations with that of principal shareholders.

Company Share Ownership Plans (CSOP)

5.34   These plans are tax advantaged share option schemes and, no tax charge will arise on the grant of the option, nor (normally) on the exercise of the option, but rather a capital gains tax charge will arise on the eventual sale of the shares.

The total market value of shares over which options have been granted under that particular or any other CSOP scheme must not exceed £30,000 as measured at the date of grant of the particular options (*ITEPA 2003, Sch 4, para 6*).

The option price payable under the CSOP plan must be set at the time of grant and must not be less than the market value at the date of grant (*ITEPA 2003, Sch 4, para 22*).

A CSOP option cannot generally be exercised with the tax advantages in the first three years after grant and must be exercised no later than the tenth anniversary of the grant (*ITEPA 2003, s 524*).

Need for approval

5.35   Historically there was a formal approval procedure that had to be followed before CSOP options could be granted. However, from 6 April 2014, CSOP plans in common with other tax advantaged plans, have been moved to a 'self-certification' basis, with no need for upfront 'approval' of a scheme. Indeed, the word 'approved' is dropped from the legislation and replaced with the phrase 'Schedule 4', being the Schedule in *ITEPA 2003* that gives the requirements for the tax relief to apply.

The notification of a new CSOP scheme must be given by 6 July after the end of the tax year in which they began, so for plans started in 2016/17, HMRC must be notified by 6 July 2017. Notifications are required to be made electronically and require the company to make a declaration that the *Sch 4* rules have been complied with.

The key features of a CSOP scheme that must be met are:

- For schemes in existence before 6 April 2014, the purpose of the scheme had to be to provide benefits in the form of share options to employees and directors and no features could be included in the plan that are neither essential nor reasonably incidental to that purpose.

  This 'purpose test' is amended from 6 April 2014 to require that a CSOP's purpose must be to provide benefits in the form of share options, and must not provide benefits outside the statutory rules, which means, for example, they must not provide a cash alternative to employees in respect of these options.

  For CSOPs in operation before 6 April 2014 but continuing after that date, the change will only apply if, and from the time of the first occasion on which, any provision of the scheme is altered (*ITEPA 2003, Sch 4, para 5*).

- Only full-time directors and qualifying employees of the company (or group company) can be granted options. Full-time directors are normally those working 25 hours per week or more (*ITEPA 2003, Sch 4, para 8*).

- No one may be granted a CSOP option if they (either on their own or with associates such as spouses, parents children, etc) have (or have had in the previous 12 months) a material interest in a close company (that is one controlled by owner directors or where the ownership is in the hands of five or fewer people) where the CSOP scheme allows for shares in that close company (or another company under its control) to be acquired.

  Material interest was defined as having an interest in (either through ownership or having an option over) 30% of the ordinary share capital of the company (*ITEPA 2003, Sch 4, para 9*).

- The CSOP option must be over ordinary share capital of the company (*ITEPA 2003, Sch 4, para 16*) and the shares must be fully paid-up and not redeemable (*ITEPA 2003, Sch 4, para 18*). There are also limits on the restrictions which the shares are subject to, to ensure that there is little scope for manipulation of the shares (*ITEPA 2003, Sch 4, para 19*).

- The options must be non-transferable (*ITEPA 2003, Sch 4, para 23*).

The need for care

5.36　There are numerous other rules that must be met if a CSOP is to successfully obtain the available tax advantages and with the introduction of self-certification employers will no longer have the safety net of HMRC 'approval' to their schemes. Specialist advice should be sought on these plans, particularly as HMRC are highly likely to start reviewing schemes with a view to penalising employers who get things wrong in this complex area.

> **Focus**
>
> The more restrictive nature of CSOP plans mean they have less attraction than, say, EMI schemes, but in cases where the profile of the company does not work for EMI schemes (eg because of a workforce of more than 250) then these plans may be helpful. Companies with existing CSOPs will need to be alert to the need to make amendments to the rules of the CSOP to reflect the changes in legislation from 6 April 2014.

Save As You Earn schemes (SAYE)

5.37　Unlike EMI and CSOP schemes (see **5.32** and **5.34**) SAYE plans must be offered to all employees for the tax advantages to be obtained. Under these plans, employees are offered a share option with the ability to set the price at a discount to the full market value. At a similar time the employees set up a savings plan which receives contributions from them over a set period of three or five years. At the end of the savings period a bonus may be paid into the plan, and the accumulated funds are then used to pay the option price on exercise of the option. Alternatively the funds can be taken in cash (*ITEPA 2003, Sch 3*).

The general requirements that need to be met for a SAYE scheme to qualify include the following:

- The options must be over ordinary shares of the company which has set up the scheme, or the company which controls it. There are similar 'purpose' test rules as for CSOP schemes (see **5.35** above) (*ITEPA 2003, Sch 3, paras 18–22*).

- The price payable on the exercise of a SAYE option is fixed at the time of grant and must not be less than 80% of the market value at the grant date (*ITEPA 2003, Sch 3, para 28*).

- A SAYE savings contract must be entered into when the options are granted under which the employee agrees to save a fixed amount per month for a fixed number of months. This sum is deducted from net pay (*ITEPA 2003, Sch 3, paras 23–25*).

- The monthly amount saved must fall between set limits. These limits are currently £5 and £500. The amount saved each month cannot be altered. The savings must be for either 36 or 60 months (three or five years).

- Theoretically a tax-free bonus is paid at the end of the savings period, although from 27 December 2014 the rates of bonus have been nil for all plans.

- Up to a total of six monthly contributions may be postponed with the savings contract being extended by one month for each contribution postponed.

- An individual may exercise an option before the savings plan has matured in some circumstances (such as a company reorganisation), but this may result in the options being treated as unapproved options.

- Scheme rules must confirm what happens on cessation of employment through death, illness, injury, redundancy or retirement or for any other reason.

- These plans will fall under the self-certification rules for tax advantaged plans from 6 April 2014. The latest reporting rules are covered at **5.46**.

Tax charges on SAYE schemes

5.38   If an SAYE option is exercised after the third anniversary of the grant then there will be no income tax charge on the exercise of the option.

If an option is exercised before the third anniversary because of the employee leaving employment through injury, disability, redundancy or retirement then there will still be no income tax charge. If an option is exercised before the third anniversary for some other reason, then the option will be treated as an unapproved option (see **5.29**).

If the shares acquired through the exercise of an option are sold, the capital gains tax rules will apply. But it is possible to transfer shares coming out of a SAYE scheme into an Individual Savings Account (ISA) within 90 days of exercising the SAYE option.

Example 5.12 – Buying and selling SAYE scheme shares

John joins his employer's SAYE scheme and saves over a three-year period. At the start of the scheme the share price is £1 per share.

At the end of the three-year period John has a savings pot of £4,000. The share price has risen to £1.75 per share.

John's position is as follows:

SAYE Share option exercised over 4,000 shares at £1 per share

John then holds 4,000 shares worth £7,000.

He may sell these immediately and realise a gain of £3,000 (which will be subject to capital gains tax – although he may have his annual exempt amount or losses to offset against this).

He may, alternatively, decide to hold onto these shares either directly or through his share ISA (with the transfer to be done within 90 days of the exercise).

Focus

These plans remain popular despite several alternative plans having been launched since SAYE plans came into being in the 1980s. Companies with existing SAYE plans will need to be alert to the need to make amendments to the rules to reflect the changes in legislation from 6 April 2014.

Share Incentive Plans (SIP)

5.39   A SIP is a tax advantaged share acquisition plan. It is an 'all employee' plan designed to be used for the whole of a workforce (*ITEPA 2003, Sch 2*).

Shares can be provided to an employee under this plan either as:

- free shares – given to employees; or
- partnership shares – bought on favourable terms by the employee.

Plans can offer a mixture of both methods of share acquisition (*ITEPA 2003, Sch 2, para 2*).

In addition, an employee may receive matching shares and dividend shares. These are explained below.

Whilst the plan must be open to all employees who are employed by the company (or the group) establishing the scheme and the offer must be 'on the same terms' to all employees, the number of shares offered can be varied to reflect, for example, remuneration, length of service or work performance against set criteria (*ITEPA 2003, Sch 2, para 8*).

There are similar 'purpose' test rules as for CSOP schemes (see **5.35** above).

Until 2013 any employee with a 'material interest' in the company could not participate in a SIP (*ITEPA 2003, Sch 2, para 19*) however, this rule has now been abolished.

Any shares used in the plan must be fully paid up and not redeemable (*ITEPA 2003, Sch 2, para 28*).

Free shares

5.40   Each qualifying employee can receive up to £3,600 worth of free shares in each tax year. The value of the shares is taken at the date the award is made. Performance criteria can be linked to these awards, but they must comply with the detailed legislation. Employees must be told what these performance criteria are for the scheme to qualify.

After the award of free shares these must be held for a minimum period of three years in a plan trust. The company can extend this to any period up to five years from the date of award of the shares. All shares in the same award must have the same holding period and the period cannot be increased after the award (*ITEPA 2003, Sch 2, para 36(2)*).

The holding period will end early if the employee leaves the company, but the plan rules can provide for the shares to be forfeited in such a case (*ITEPA 2003, Sch 2, para 36(5)*).

Partnership shares

5.41   This involves the employee entering into a partnership agreement which provides for a deduction from pre-tax salary, using those funds to buy shares. The agreement must show the amount to be deducted and the frequency of deduction (eg weekly, monthly).

The maximum deduction is the lower of £1,800 or 10% of salary.

Monies deducted must be used to buy shares within 30 days of the deduction, unless the scheme sets out an 'accumulation period' (of up to 12 months) during which the deducted funds are saved in a SIP trust. In such cases the shares must be bought within 30 days of the end of the accumulation period. If interest is earned on any such accumulated funds it belongs to the individual employee and will be subject to income tax.

Funds which are withdrawn in cash by an employee from this pot will be subject to tax and NIC collected through a PAYE deduction (which in practical terms is normally administered by the employer on behalf of the trustees) (*ITEPA 2003, s 503*).

Matching shares

5.42   If an employee acquires partnership shares (see **5.41** above) the employer may 'match' those shares with additional free shares. This can be done up to a ratio of two matching shares for each partnership share (*ITEPA 2003, Sch 2, para 60(2)*).

The matching shares must be of the same class and carry the same rights as the partnership shares they match, must be awarded on the same day as the partnership shares they match and must be awarded to all those who take part in the award on exactly the same basis (*ITEPA 2003, Sch 2, para 59(1)*).

Matching shares must then meet the same requirements of minimum holding period, etc as other free shares (see **5.40**).

Dividend shares

5.43   Dividends paid on shares held in the SIP trust may be reinvested in further shares. These are called dividend shares (*ITEPA 2003, Sch 2, para 62(3)(b)*). From 6 April 2013 there is no cap on the amount of this reinvestment (*ITEPA 2003, Sch 2, para 64*).

Any dividends not reinvested must be paid to the employee as soon as practicable (*ITEPA 2003, Sch 2, para 69*).

Dividend shares must be held for three years for the tax advantages to apply (*ITEPA 2003, Sch 2, para 67*).

Taxation of SIP shares

5.44 When shares come out of a plan into the hands of the employee there will generally be no income tax if the shares are taken when an employee leaves the company because of the following (*ITEPA 2003, s 498*):

- injury, disability, redundancy;
- a transfer under the TUPE rules;
- change in control of the company;
- retirement on or after the age specified in the plan;
- death.

In other cases the tax rules vary depending on what sort of shares are in point and how long they have been in the SIP trust. Essentially:

- For free and matching shares:
  - shares held less than three years will be subject to income tax based on the market value of the shares at the date they come out of the plan;
  - shares held for three years but less than five years will be subject to income tax based on the lesser of the market value of the shares at the date of award and the date they come out of the plan;
  - shares held for five years or more will have no income tax charge.

  PAYE will be applicable to any such taxable sums.

- For partnership shares:
  - shares held less than three years will be subject to income tax based on the market value of the shares at the date they come out of the plan;
  - shares held for three years but less than five years will be subject to income tax based on the lesser of the partnership money used to buy the shares, and the market value of the shares at the date they come out of the plan;
  - shares held for five years or more will have no income tax charge.

  PAYE will be applicable to any such taxable sums.

- For dividend shares:
  - dividends reinvested into additional shares are not liable to income tax in the hands of the employee;
  - dividend shares held for less than three years will give rise to an income tax charge based on the cash dividend used to acquire

those shares. The participant will also be entitled to the appropriate tax credits.

○ shares held for three years or more will have no income tax charge.

(*ITEPA 2003, s 500 et seq*)

Shares kept in the plan until sale will be free of any capital gains tax charge (*TCGA 1992, Sch 7D, para 2*).

> **Focus**
>
> Unlike SAYE plans, SIP plans can result in employees losing 'real' money if they invest in partnership shares. It is vital that the 'downsides' as well as the 'upsides' of all such plans are fully explained to any potential participant. Companies with existing SIP plans will need to be alert to the need to make amendments to the rules to reflect the changes in legislation from 6 April 2014.

Employee shareholder plans

5.45 Employee shareholder status provides certain tax advantages in respect of shares acquired by employees in exchange for the giving up of certain employment rights.

The key conditions required in order for this status to be available are that:

- The shares issued must be those of the employer or parent company.

- The employee or an individual connected with them must not have a material interest in that company, broadly defined as a 25% interest in the voting rights (*ITEPA 2003, s 226D and TCGA 1992, s 236D*).

- The shares awarded to the employee must have a market value of at least £2,000 although there is no upper limit to the value of shares which can be awarded (*ITEPA 2003, s 226A*).

- The employee must pay no consideration for the award of shares.

- The employee must be provided with independent legal advice funded by the employer in respect of the employment rights they are required to give up in exchange for the shares.

Where the relevant conditions are met, the employee can benefit from the following tax reliefs:

- Income tax will not be chargeable on the first £2,000 of share value received by an employee shareholder – any value above that amount will be subject to income tax in the usual way (*ITEPA 2003, ss 226A(1)–(3)*);

- Capital gains tax will not be chargeable on the first £50,000 of shares received by an employee shareholder – this is measured by reference to the market value of the shares at the time of acquisition, ignoring any restrictions attached to the shares which may reduce that. For arrangements entered into after 16 March 2016, a lifetime limit of £100,000 is introduced in respect of the capital gains tax exemption (*TCGA 1992, s 1A*);

- The cost of the independent legal advice funded by the employer will not be a taxable benefit (*ITEPA 2003, s 326B*).

There is no requirement for the employee to continue in employment or to hold the shares for a minimum period in order for them to benefit from the tax relief available.

(*Employment Rights Act 1996, s 205A*; *ITEPA 2003, ss 226A–226D*; *TCGA 1992, ss 236B–236G*)

For full details of the income tax position, see www.gov.uk/government/publications/guidance-on-the-income-tax-treatment-of-employee-shareholder-shares.

For full details of the capital gains tax rules, see www.gov.uk/government/publications/guidance-on-the-capital-gains-tax-treatment-of-employee-shareholder-shares.

READILY CONVERTIBLE ASSETS

5.46   The reference in this chapter to any charge to tax arising in respect of share incentives has generally only been to income tax, however consideration needs to be given to how such a charge is applied and whether any liability to national insurance arises.

For this purpose, it needs to be determined whether the liability to tax arises in respect of securities which are readily convertible assets (or RCAs):

- Where the securities are RCAs, then the liability arising will be in respect of income tax (deductible via PAYE) and national insurance.

- Where the securities are not RCAs, then the liability arising will only be in respect of income tax and this will be reportable and payable through the normal self-assessment tax system.

Securities will be RCAs where they are listed on a recognised stock exchange or where there are arrangements in place (or an understanding that there will be such arrangements in the future) to allow for the securities to be traded, ie they can quite easily be converted into cash.

Securities which do not meet this definition will be deemed to be RCAs where the company is not able to benefit from a corporation tax deduction in respect of the amount subject to tax upon the employee (see **19.10**). Two common examples of where corporation tax relief is not available, and securities are deemed to be RCAs are where:

- The company is under the control of another unlisted company – this could be the case where securities in a subsidiary company are awarded to employees of that company as a way to link their incentive to the company for which they work.

- The shares are not actually acquired by the employee – this is seen on a purchase of own shares by a company, so where for example the consideration for the purchase is considered to be more than market value the employment related security charge arising (see **5.28**) would be subject to PAYE and NIC.

Where the securities are RCAs and the tax liability arising is not deducted, or is unable to be deducted in full, from the employee through the PAYE system a benefit in kind charge can arise. To avoid this change, the employee must repay the full amount which has not been deducted to the company within 90 days of the charge arising. A benefit in kind will be charged on any amount outstanding at that point – any subsequent repayment after the 90 day period is not able to remove or reduce this charge (*ITEPA 2003, s 222*).

REPORTING REQUIREMENTS

5.47   There are a number of reporting requirements in respect of the share incentives, which must now be reported to HMRC electronically. Before a company can make an electronic return, they must first have access to online services with HMRC and have activated the employment related securities service.

Annual returns are required to be filed by 6 July following the relevant tax year and although these are made electronically, they are frequently still referred to using the old paper form references:

- Shares obtained by reason of employment (otherwise than those provided through tax advantaged schemes) and any subsequent chargeable events (formerly Form 42)

- Tax advantaged schemes under EMI (formerly Form EMI40), CSOP (formerly Form 35), SAYE (formerly Form 34) and SIP (formerly Form 39)

In addition to the annual returns, certain other events must be notified within a certain time frame including:

- Registration, self-certification and notification of changes to the key features of CSOP, SAYE or SIP schemes.

- Grant of EMI options - care should be taken to ensure EMI schemes are registered promptly after setting up the scheme as any new option grants will need to be notified within 92 days of grant date.

In addition, an employee who has taxable income from unapproved or tax advantaged schemes which has not be subject to PAYE should include this on their self-assessment return on the supplementary pages (SA101). HMRC Help sheet HS305 includes detailed guidance on the items to be returned.

If the shares or options are in an unquoted company, then it may be necessary for the employer to agree the value with Shares and Assets Valuation, a specialist department of HMRC.

Where a SIP or an EMI scheme is being operated there are a number of occasions when a valuation is needed and this will involve completing Forms VAL230 for a SIP and VAL231 for an EMI scheme.

6

Pensions, state benefits and tax credits

SIGNPOSTS

- **Pension changes** – since 2014 radical changes to pensions gave people greater freedom over how to access their defined contribution pension savings through a 'flexi-access drawdown account' but withdrawals may have different tax treatments (see **6.2**).

- **Scope** – Most pension schemes are now registered pension schemes which may be set up by an employer for employees or for individuals who may be self-employed or employed (see **6.3–6.5**).

- **Upper limits** – There are annual and lifetime allowances for contributions to registered pension schemes. Tax charges generally arise if these limits are exceeded (see **6.6–6.13**).

- **Tax charges** – Registered pension schemes are normally exempt from tax on income and gains, but tax liabilities can be incurred in some circumstances. Pension income is also taxable (see **6.14**).

- **State benefits, etc** – Certain state benefits (eg jobseeker's allowance) are taxable income, whereas other state benefits (eg attendance allowance) are not. For state benefits, see **6.15**.

- **High income child benefit charge** – There is a charge on an individual whose income exceeds £50,000 and either he or his partner has received child benefit in that tax year (see **6.16**).

- **Tax credits** – The working tax credit and child tax credit are non-taxable state benefits, which can be complex to calculate in practice. Both credits are administered by HMRC (see **6.17**).

- **Appendix: Registered pension scheme tax charges** – A table showing potential tax charges in connection with registered pension schemes is included at the end of this chapter (see **6.18**).

INTRODUCTION

6.1   A complete analysis of the complex world of pensions is beyond the scope of this book but what follows is an outline of the changes introduced by the *Taxation of Pensions Act 2014* and the *Finance Acts 2014* and *2015* (which amended the legislation on pensions found in *Pt 4* of the *Finance Act 2004*) and the main tax issues arising on pensions.

The process of reform may still continue as there are various consultation documents in progress, such as the 'capping of early exit charges for members of occupational pension schemes'. The introduction of Lifetime ISAs introduces a new route for pension savings, encouraging individuals to save out of taxed income attracting a 25% government bonus that when paid out is tax-free (see **7.23**)

REGISTERED PENSION SCHEMES

Pensions – withdrawals

6.2   Since 2015/16 and the changes introduced with the *Taxation of Pensions Act 2014*, members of defined contribution schemes are no longer required to purchase annuities but instead are allowed to access their savings more flexibly from a new 'flexi-access drawdown account'. Subject to the scheme rules, individuals are now able to access their pension pot savings from the age of 55 as and when they wish: amounts withdrawn as pension are taxed at their marginal rates and amounts withdrawn as lump sums continue to be tax free up to 25% of the fund (or up to the lifetime allowance limit if lower). Members may also be able to take a series of 'uncrystallised funds pension lump sums' rather than withdraw the full lump sum entitlement in one go if their pension scheme provides this option.

Before the changes introduced in 2014 on flexible withdrawals from defined contribution schemes, amounts withdrawn that breached the permitted draw down pension rules were treated as unauthorised payments and taxed at 55%.

Members of a defined benefits scheme (as opposed to a defined contributions scheme) continue to draw their pensions unaffected by the recent changes. Payments made to them on retirement are based on defined benefits (usually final salary) and not on the amounts held in the pension pot at the date of retirement. They are still entitled to a tax -free lump sum (assuming their lifetime allowance has not been exceeded) and pension payments continue to be taxed at the marginal rate of income tax as they are added to their total taxable income each year.

The government website gives further information on the administration of pensions, as well as the tax relief on paying into a pension scheme and tax on pensions (at www.gov.uk/topic/business-tax/pension-scheme-administration).

Pensions – contributions

Background

6.3   The pensions regime was significantly reformed with effect from 6 April 2006 ('A' Day). The motive behind this was to simplify the position which had become very complicated with different rules for occupational pension schemes, retirement annuities and personal pensions. In addition, the intention was to give individuals the opportunity to save for their retirement in a flexible way.

Unfortunately, the reality is that the position is *still* very complicated as provisions have been brought in since 'A' Day primarily to restrict the use of pension schemes in tax planning by wealthy individuals.

Post 'A' Day pension provision is centred on registered pension schemes which have replaced approved occupational and personal pension schemes.

The main legislation on pension schemes is in *Finance Act 2004, Pt 4*. There is also a manual dealing with registered pension schemes on the HMRC website (at www.hmrc.gov.uk/manuals/ptmanual/index.htm).

A registered pension scheme is simply a tax-favoured pension scheme which benefits from tax reliefs on its investment income and gains, so that no tax is due on most rent, interest and dividends, and members (and contributing employers, if relevant) can obtain tax relief on contributions.

There are very few restrictions on who can be a member of a registered pension scheme but in order to benefit from tax relief on contributions, an individual must have earnings from employment or self–employment which are subject to UK tax.

Occupational or public service pension schemes

6.4   Under these schemes, which are basically registered pension schemes set up by an employer for his employees, the employer usually takes the pension contributions from pay before deducting tax (but not National Insurance contributions). The employee therefore only pays tax on the net sum, in effect providing tax relief at source for these contributions.

If the employer does not deduct the contributions from gross pay, then refer to the section on personal pensions below.

GPs and dentists who contribute to a public service pension scheme should claim tax relief through their self-assessment tax return.

Personal pensions

6.5   Personal pensions are registered pension schemes for individuals who are self-employed or whose employer has not made any pension provisions for employees.

Under these schemes, pension contributions are paid out of net pay (ie income which has suffered income tax). The pension provider will claim tax back from the government at the basic rate of 20%. In practice, this means that for every £80 paid into your personal pension, the total amount added to the pension pot is £100. If an individual pays tax at higher or additional rates, the balance of any relief will in most cases be claimed back through the tax return. This will also apply to any scheme (such as a retirement annuity plan set up before 1988) where there is no relief at all claimed at source by the provider.

A non-taxpayer can still pay into a personal pension scheme and benefit from basic rate tax relief (20%) on the first £2,880 of contributions. In practice, this means that the £2,880 contribution will generate additions to the pension pot of £720 and so increase it to £3,600. No tax relief will be given for contributions above this amount. A proviso should be added that the availability of the tax relief depends on the type of pension scheme being operated: a contract-based scheme typically uses 'relief at source', enabling the tax boost, but a significant number of schemes are 'trust-based' using a 'net pay' method and so the non-taxpayer will not get the tax advantage.

Similar rules apply if someone funds another person's pension pot. For example, an individual may put money into the pension fund of a spouse, child or grandchild and the pension holder (not the payer of the contribution) will get tax relief. This could be used to fund a non-taxpaying person so that a contribution to a fund in their name of £2,880 a year becomes £3,600 with tax relief. These payments will only be acceptable in schemes which allow such contributions from third parties.

Limits on tax relief for contributions

6.6   There is no limit on the number of registered pension schemes an individual can invest in and get tax relief on, although:

- contributions must not exceed 100% of earnings each year; and

- the contributions must be made before the age of 75; and

- the cap on the maximum amount saved each year must not be breached. If it is, a charge to income tax arises, known as the annual allowance charge (see **6.10**).

The annual allowance

6.7 This annual allowance is set each year and has reduced significantly in the recent past, as follows:

Tax year	Annual allowance
2016/17 onwards	£40,000 (but tapered reduction to £10,000 for high income individuals, see **6.9**)
2015/16	£40,000 (but may be £80,000 in some cases, see below)
2014/15	£40,000
2013/14	£50,000
2012/13	£50,000
2011/12	£50,000
2010/11	£255,000
2009/10	£245,000

With the alignment of pension input periods introduced by the *Finance (No 2) Act 2015* (see **6.10**), there were transitional rules to cover the tax year 2015/16 to make sure no-one was penalised by the change (insertion of *s 228C* into *FA 2004*). The rules split the tax year into pre- and post-alignment periods, before and after 8 July 2015, whereby the annual allowance was doubled to £80,000 in the pre-alignment period and any unused allowance in this earlier period could be carried forward to the post-alignment period up to a maximum of £40,000. There may therefore have been scope for some individuals to benefit from this higher allowance by making additional pension contributions before 5 April 2016.

Unused annual allowance available for carry forward

6.8 If an individual has pension savings of more than £40,000 for a tax year, he may still not be liable for an annual allowance charge for that year. With effect from 2011/12, as long he has been a member of a registered pension scheme for the period of claim, even if no contributions have been made, he can carry forward any annual allowance that he has not used in the previous three tax years to the current tax year on a first in, first out basis (*FA 2004, s 228A*).

Example 6.1 – Unused annual allowance carried forward

Zoe is self-employed and has paid contributions of £40,000, £20,000 and £30,000 to her pension arrangement in the last three years. This year, 2016/17, her business has record profits of £105,000 and she decides to top up her pension scheme. She has no other income so her annual allowance is £40,000 as she is not a high income individual.

She has unused annual allowances of £40,000 and can make a contribution of up to £80,000 without penalty.

Reduction of annual allowance for high-income individuals

6.9   The *Finance (No 2) Act 2015* introduced a tapered reduction to the existing annual allowance of £40,000 for high-income individuals with effect from 6 April 2016. These are defined as individuals with adjusted income of over £150,000 and threshold income of over £150,000 less the normal annual allowance, currently £40,000.

Adjusted income is net income (as defined by Steps 1 and 2 of *ITA 2003, s 23* – see **1.16**) plus the value of any pension savings less the sum of any lump sum death benefits received by the taxpayer in the tax year. Pension savings include both employers' contributions and those made by the taxpayer and for defined benefit schemes they incorporate any increase in the value of the pension (see **6.12**).

The annual allowance is reduced by £2 for every £1 of adjusted net income that exceeds £150,000. This tapering applies until income reaches £210,000 when the allowance remains at £10,000.

It is the threshold income that provides the income floor so individuals with income below the threshold income will not be affected. This means that in 2016/17 a taxpayer whose income is £110,000 or less (regardless of the value of their pension contributions) will be entitled to the full £40,000 allowance, but there are provisos; for example, if an individual enters into salary sacrifice or flexible remuneration arrangements on or after 9 July 2015 in order to reduce their threshold income, the amount given up will be added back to their income. In addition, there are anti-avoidance provisions to prevent income from being reduced in one tax year (to below the threshold so that the individual becomes entitled to a higher annual allowance) and then increased by an equivalent amount in a different tax year.

Individuals subject to the tapered annual allowance will still be able to carry forward any unused allowances from the three previous tax years.

Example 6.2 – Tapering of annual allowance for high income individual

In 2016/17, George has a salary of £135,000. His employer contributes 12.5% (£16,875) into his defined contribution pension scheme and George adds a further 5% (£6,750). George has no other income or tax reliefs.

208

George's net income exceeds the threshold income of £110,000 (£150,000 – £40,000) as his salary less his own pension contribution of £6,750 totals £128,250.

His adjusted net income is based on his salary of £135,000 (before relief for pension contributions he has paid) plus the value of his employer's contribution of £16,875, which gives £151,875. As this exceeds the limit of £150,000, his annual allowance is reduced by £1 for every £2 over the limit, so by £937 ((£151,875 – £150,000) × ½). His reduced annual allowance will be £39,063 (£40,000 – £937). His total pension savings are £23,625 (£16,875 + £6,750) so he will not be subject to the annual allowance charge.

The annual allowance charge

6.10   If pension savings exceed the annual allowance, an annual allowance tax charge will arise. The excess will be added to annual taxable income. Tax will be charged at the marginal rate appropriate to the total amount of taxable income and must be included in a self-assessment tax return (on page 4 of the supplementary pages).

Pension savings are described in the legislation as 'the total pension input amount'. The limits imposed by the annual allowance apply to all registered pension schemes and include both contributions made by individuals and their employers.

It is not always a straightforward matter to calculate the excess of pension savings over the annual allowance as:

- the amount of pension savings depends on the type of scheme, such as defined contributions or defined benefits (see **Examples 6.4–6.6** below);

- the amount of annual allowance available depends on the date the 'Pension Input Period' (PIP) ends (see **Example 6.3** below) though with the alignment of all PIPs with the tax year as from 2016/17, this now only affects how the unused allowance carried forward had been calculated. (*Finance (No 2) Act 2015*)

To establish the position, the level of contributions (pension savings) in a 'pension input period' (PIP) must be worked out for each scheme of which the taxpayer is a member. A PIP normally runs for 12 months but it can be for a greater or lesser period. The scheme administrators will be able to confirm the PIP for each scheme. The *Finance (No 2) Act 2015* in aligning the pension input periods with the tax year, as from 6 April 2016, introduced transitional rules for 2015/16 (see **6.6** and **Example 6.3**).

Example 6.3 – Pension input period

Mr B makes a pension contribution of £50,000 on 1 October 2013 and again on 1 October 2014. The PIP date for his scheme is 30 June each year.

The contribution paid in October 2013 was relieved in 2013/14, the tax year it was paid. The payment was made during a PIP ended on 30 June 2014 which is in the tax year 2014/15 when the annual allowance was £40,000 and so exceeds by £10,000 the annual allowance. An annual allowance charge of £10,000 will arise.

The contribution paid in October 2014 was relieved in 2014/15. The contribution is into a PIP ended on 30 June 2015 and so falls into the tax year 2015/16 which is covered by the transitional rules. As it was paid in the 'pre alignment' period up to 8 July 2015, the enhanced annual allowance is £80,000 and so no annual tax charge arises. In fact, Mr B has unused allowance of £30,000 available to carry forward to the 'post alignment' period should he wish to make additional contributions before 5 April 2016. Alternatively, the unused allowance can be carried forward for future years.

Calculating pension savings (the 'pension input amount') for defined contribution schemes

6.11 The measurement of the savings each year will depend on the type of scheme involved.

For personal pensions, the figure is simply the amount of contributions in the period, grossed up to cover the basic rate tax.

Example 6.4 – Working out gross contributions

Natalie pays £400 a month into a personal pension. Her savings are grossed up to £500 a month by applying credit for basic rate tax at 20% (ie £400 × 100/80 = £500), meaning her total savings in the year will be 12 × £500 = £6,000.

For occupational pension schemes, the value of contributions made by the employer must be included to establish the total savings in the year. For a money purchase or defined contribution scheme, the savings will be the total of employer and employee contributions.

Example 6.5 – Employee and employer contributions

Jack is paid a salary of £80,000 a year and contributes 4% to his defined contribution pension scheme. His employer adds a further 5%. Jack's total pension savings in the year are:

	£80,000 × 4%	=	£3,200
plus	£80,000 × 5%	=	£4,000
Total savings in the year		=	£7,200

Calculating pension savings for defined benefit schemes

6.12   For defined benefits schemes, sometimes known as final salary schemes, the savings figure for the year is based on the increase in the value of the pension over the PIP, not just the amount of the contributions in the year (*FA 2004, ss 234–236*). This can involve a complex calculation and the figures will normally be provided by the pension administrator but HMRC provide an online calculator which can assist in getting to the figures for planning purposes. This can be found at www.gov.uk/tax-on-your-private-pension/annual-allowance and then click on the annual allowance calculator link.

Example 6.6 – Calculating the pension saving

Jermaine is a member of a scheme that gives him a pension of 1/60th pensionable pay for each year of being a scheme member with the option of commuting pensions for a lump sum.

At the start of the PIP, Jermaine's pensionable pay is £50,000. He has 15 years' service at the start of his pension input period.

Find the amount of pension entitlement at the start of the input period.

This is calculated as 15/60 × £50,000 = £12,500.

Multiply result by 16.

£12,500 × 16 = £200,000

Increase amount for CPI (Consumer Price Index – assumed to be 3%).

A 3% increase brings the opening value to £206,000.

At the end of the PIP, Jermaine's pensionable pay has increased by 10% to £55,000 and his pensionable service is now 16 years.

Find annual rate of pension.

This is calculated as $16/60 \times £55,000 = £14,667$.

Multiply result by 16.

$£14,667 \times 16 = £234,672$

Jermaine's pension saving for this arrangement is the difference between his opening value and closing value. This is £28,672 (£234,672 − £206,000).

Focus

A member of a defined benefit scheme can find that a salary increase during a year may have the unexpected result of creating an annual allowance charge.

The lifetime allowance

6.13 When a pension matures, up to 25% of the available funds can be taken as a tax-free lump sum, provided the pension scheme rules allow it, and the total fund is within the 'lifetime allowance' for the year in which benefits are taken. The lifetime allowance amounts for recent years are as follows:

Tax year	Lifetime allowance
2018/19 onwards	£1 million plus CPI inflation
2016/17 & 2017/18	£1 million
2014/15 & 2015/16	£1.25 million
2013/14	£1.5 million
2012/13	£1.5 million
2011/12	£1.8 million
2010/11	£1.8 million
2009/10	£1.75 million

The lifetime allowance is the maximum amount of pension and/or lump sum that can be paid out from a registered pension scheme which can benefit from tax relief. This figure is tested at any stage when benefits begin to be drawn or at age 75 if this is earlier (known as a 'benefit crystallisation event').

If a pension scheme provides benefits above the lifetime allowance, a tax charge will arise. This will be based on the excess of the pension benefits over the lifetime allowance (*FA 2004, ss 214–215*).

The charge is at the rate of 55% of the amount chargeable that constitutes a 'lump sum' and at 25% on the 'retained amount'. These rates can be varied by Treasury Order. The chargeable amount is not to be treated as income for any purpose of the *Tax Acts*.

Finance Act 2016 provides that an individual is entitled to claim for further protections as a result of the reduction in the lifetime allowance from £1.25m to £1m from 6 April 2016, as long as certain conditions are met. The decision whether to fix the allowance is a complex one as it limits the ability to accrue further pension benefits. Specialist advice should be sought from the pension administrator as well as a tax adviser.

Example 6.7 – Lifetime allowance exceeded

Theo starts to draw his pension in 2016/17. His total pension benefit in the year is £1.9 million which is in excess of the lifetime allowance of £1 million. He will pay tax on the £900,000 excess.

If the excess is retained to be paid out as future pension income, the rate of the charge is 25%, but if the excess is taken as a lump sum the rate is 55%.

Tax charges on a registered pension scheme

6.14   As explained above, a registered pension scheme is normally exempt from tax on its income and gains and therefore the administrator should not be troubled by tax. There are, however, a number of circumstances when tax liabilities can arise.

As mentioned above, there can be an annual allowance charge if pension savings exceed the annual allowance, taking account of unused allowance in the previous three years.

Also as mentioned above, there can be a tax charge if the benefits in a scheme exceed the lifetime allowance.

In view of the privileged tax status given to a registered pension scheme, there are detailed and complicated rules governing the payments and transactions which are permitted. Tax charges can arise if the registered pension scheme breaches one of these rules, for example by making an 'unauthorised payment' which could be a loan to a company connected to a member but not a 'sponsoring employer'. There is also a charge if a registered pension scheme is de-registered by HMRC as a result of breaches of rules; the charge effectively claws back the tax exemption which has been enjoyed by the scheme.

A summary of the tax charges is set out at the end of this chapter.

Focus

The tax reliefs given to registered pension schemes are very valuable and HMRC will pursue schemes which break the rules. The tax charges and surcharges which can arise can be huge as they are intended to claw back the tax benefits accruing over the life of the scheme.

STATE BENEFITS

6.15   It is beyond the scope of this work to provide a comprehensive review of all state benefits, but in the context of taxation the following lists might help identify if a benefit is taxable or not. Care should be taken as the benefit system is undergoing review and the benefits available may change from time to time, and significant changes are taking place between now and 2022.

Taxable state benefits include:

- bereavement allowance
- certain payments of incapacity benefit (from the 29th week of payment)
- contributions based employment and support allowance
- certain payments of income support
- pensions payable under the industrial death benefit scheme
- carer's allowance
- jobseeker's allowance
- state pension
- graduated retirement benefit
- statutory sick pay
- statutory maternity pay
- statutory paternity pay
- statutory adoption pay
- widowed parent's allowance

- widow's pension paid to widows whose entitlement arose before 9 April 2001.

Non-taxable state benefits include:

- attendance allowance
- job grant (replacing back to work bonus)
- bereavement payment
- child benefit (but see **6.16** below)
- child tax credit
- cold weather payments
- council tax reduction (sometimes called council tax support)
- constant attendance allowance
- disability living allowance and personal independence payments
- discretionary housing payments
- emergency assistance payments
- exceptionally severe disablement allowance
- free TV licence for over-75s
- guardian's allowance
- housing benefit, administered by local authorities
- incapacity benefit for first 28 weeks of entitlement, taxable thereafter
- income-related employment and support allowance
- income support, certain payments
- industrial injuries disablement benefit (reduced earnings allowance)
- maternity allowance
- pensioner's Christmas bonus
- reduced earnings allowance
- retirement allowance
- social fund payments to people on a low income to help with maternity expenses and funeral costs,
- state pension credit
- universal credit (see note below).

- war widow's pension
- winter fuel payment
- working tax credit
- young person's bridging allowance

(*ITEPA 2003, Pts 9, 10:* see Tables A for taxable benefits (*s 660*) and Table B for wholly exempt (*s 677*))

Universal Credit is being introduced in stages across the country, with completion expected by 2022. It is a new single monthly payment for people who are looking for work or on a low income, which will eventually replace:

- income-based jobseeker's allowance;
- income-related employment and support allowance;
- income support;
- child tax credits;
- working tax credits;
- housing benefit.

High income child benefit charge

6.16   Although child benefit is not subject to income tax, an income tax charge is levied on an individual whose adjusted net income exceeds £50,000 in a tax year and who is, or whose partner is, in receipt of child benefit. This is known as the high income child benefit charge (*ITEPA 2003, Ch 8, ss 681B–681H*). The mechanics of the charge are to gradually claw back the child benefit paid out from those individuals, to whom the legislation applies, who have adjusted net incomes of between £50,000 and £60,000. This means that for anyone whose adjusted net income exceeds £60,000, the charge equals the child benefit paid.

The charge was introduced on 7 January 2013 and applies to tax years 2012/13 onwards. For those for whom the tax charge applies, there is an option to opt out of receiving the child benefit. If the child benefit continues to be received, even for a week, by an individual, or his spouse or partner, and the income of one of them exceeds £50,000 in that tax year, then the spouse or partner with the higher income will be liable to the high income child benefit charge. The Revenue needs to be informed of the liability and this can be done by completing the relevant boxes on page 5 of the income tax return. If the individual does not submit tax returns, it will be necessary to register for self-assessment in order to be able to do so and this must be done by 5 October following the end of the tax year in which the charge arises (see **1.6**). The charge will be collected via PAYE where possible or, if not, via the normal self-assessment system.

The legislation defines 'partner' as someone you are either married to or in a civil partnership with (and not separated under a court order or separated where the separation is likely to be permanent) or someone with whom you are living as if they were your husband or wife or as if they were your civil partner. If the charge falls on the person who is not in receipt of the child benefit, it applies only to those weeks when the partnership was in existence. There are also rules governing the situation where the child is not living with the parent who is claiming the child benefit.

'Adjusted net income' is broadly taxable income before deducting any personal allowances or reliefs but adjusted by deducting the gross equivalent of any pension contributions paid net of basic rate tax or any gift aid donations.

The amount of the charge is 1% of the amount of 'child benefit entitlement' for every £100 of the chargeable person's adjusted net income over £50,000 (see **Example 6.8** below). In other words, a sliding scale gradually claws back the child benefit that has been received so that if the person's income is £60,000 or over, all of the child benefit will have been effectively repaid. See **11.14** for possible planning opportunities.

It is possible to opt in and opt out of receiving the child benefit: an election can be made to stop the payments and then be revoked at a later date. Only the person who is entitled to the child benefit can make the election. The election can be revoked retrospectively so that it is treated as never having been in force during that tax year and the claimant has two years from the end of the tax year to do so (*Social Security Administration Act 1992, s 13A; Social Security Administration (Northern Ireland) Act 1992, s 11A*). It is always recommended to claim child benefit and then make the election not to receive it, even when a child is born to a family where the income of one of the partners is well above £50,000 per annum. This is because entitlement to child benefit has other non-tax effects: for example, the person who is entitled to child benefit will receive Class 3 NIC credits as a carer for looking after children under 12, which could count towards their entitlement to state pension. In addition, the child will automatically receive a National Insurance number on reaching age 16.

See www.gov.uk/child-benefit-tax-charge for further information, including links to online forms for making and revoking an election.

Focus

Make sure you register your entitlement to child benefit, even if you make an election not to receive it. In this way you will protect your entitlement to the basic state pension if you have a child under 12 and do not pay sufficient National Insurance contributions already.

Example 6.8 – Calculation of the charge

In 2016/17, Jane, who was a single parent, was in receipt of child benefit throughout the year for her two children. She has a part-time job earning £15,000 a year. On 23 September 2016, her partner, John, moved in. John received a salary of £60,000 and paid £1,000 a year in gift aid donations. They lived together until 1 January 2017 when they split up and John moved out.

John's adjusted net income is £58,750 (being £60,000 less the donation grossed up of £1,250) which exceeds the £50,000 limit and so he is liable to the charge. He is only liable to the charge in the 13 whole weeks they lived together, with the week starting on the Monday, 26 September.

The child benefits received for the two children were £34.40 per week, giving a total received in the period when Jane and John were living together of £447.20. The charge is 1% of £447.20 for every £100 of John's income above £50,000. John's income exceeds the limit by £8,750 and therefore the charge is £391.30 ((£447.20 × 1%) × (£8,750/100)).

TAX CREDITS

6.17   Tax credits are 'top-up' payments made via the tax system to individuals who are responsible for at least one child or young person (child tax credit) or are in work but are on a low income (working tax credit) and usually live in the UK. Neither form of tax credit is taxable. These payments are being replaced by universal credit (UC) which is being introduced in stages between now and March 2022. It is expected that tax credits will be closed to new claims by early 2017 and that most existing claims will be transferred to UC by May 2020.

It is important to keep abreast of the changes to universal credit as the new rules will be different in terms of qualification rules and income measurement, particularly in relation to self-employment. When tax credits are replaced by universal credit, responsibility for their administration will pass back to the DWP although HMRC will stay play an important role in providing their Real Time Information on a regular basis to the DWP so that UC claims can be amended by DWP in 'real time'.

As set out above, there are currently two types of tax credits:

- *working tax credit* (WTC) – primarily for people who work for more than 30 hours per week (aged 25–59 who do not have children) or more than 16 hours per week, (for single parents or those aged over 60 or disabled or whose partner is disabled) or usually more than 24 hours per week (for couples between them with a child, with one partner working more than 16 hours per week); and

- *child tax credit* (CTC) – paid to someone aged 16 and over who is responsible for a child under 16 or under 20 if in approved education or training

The calculation of tax credits is complicated. The government website has an online calculator which allows you to check if you are entitled to tax credits and how much you might receive (www.gov.uk/tax-credits-calculator).

The child tax credit is made up of two elements:

- the family element which is paid to any family responsible for at least one child (maximum £545 pa); and

- the child element which is paid for each child or young person in the family (maximum usually £2,780 pa although this can be more for a disabled child).

The calculation of working tax credits is complex but basically your income is compared to a threshold (currently £6,420 for WTC and £16,105 for CTC) and if it is less, you will get full working tax credits; if more, your entitlement will be reduced. The reduction is 41% of any income falling above the designated threshold which is then applied to the maximum rate for all elements. Despite the government's original intention to increase the taper rate and halve the thresholds, these remained the same.

The working tax credit is also made up of a number of elements, some of which are:

- the basic element (maximum £1,960 pa);

- the couples element (maximum £2,010 pa);

- the lone parent element (maximum £2,010 pa).

Child tax credits and working tax credits are claimed for the first time by contacting the HMRC Tax Credits Helpline on 0345 300 3900, who will send you a form.

Tax credits are awarded for a complete tax year (or from the date of claim if claimed within a tax year) and are paid directly into a bank or building society account weekly or monthly. If your circumstances change within the period of award, you must tell HMRC immediately as it might affect your entitlement.

Tax credits need to be renewed each year and the deadline is 31 July. Claimant will be sent a renewals pack by HMRC, either stating 'check now' or 'reply now'. The renewals process enables HMRC to finalise the tax credits paid for the tax year just ended as well as renewing the claim for the current tax year. Claims can be renewed by post, by phone or online by registering with the Government Gateway. Failure to renew will result in the payments being stopped.

> **Focus**
>
> When you receive a renewal pack from HMRC regarding your tax credits, it is important to check all the details are correct and tell the tax credit office by 31 July of any errors or the payments may stop and you could be fined. You must also make sure you renew the claim if required to do so by the same deadline. ,

APPENDIX: TAX CHARGES ON PAYMENTS FROM REGISTERED PENSION SCHEMES

(FA 2004, Pt 4, Ch 5)

6.18

Charge	Rates
Lifetime allowance charge *(FA 2004, s 215)*	• 55% – if the amount over the lifetime allowance is paid as a lump sum • 25% – if the amount over the lifetime allowance is not taken as a lump sum
Annual allowance charge *(FA 2004, s 227)*	Marginal rate of income tax, that is 20%; 40%; 45%
Unauthorised payments charge *(FA 2004, s 208)*	40%
Unauthorised payments surcharge *(FA 2004, s 209)*	15%
Short service refund lump sum charge *(FA 2004, s 205; SI 2010/536)*	• 20% on first £20,000; • 50% on amount over £20,000

Serious ill-health lump sum charge (see Note 2) (*FA 2004, s 205A*)	To 2014/15: 55% From 2015/16: 45%
Special lump sum death benefits charge (see Note 3) (*FA 2004, s 206*)	To 2014/15: 55% From 2015/16: 45% From 2016/17: Recipient's marginal rate of income tax or 45%
Authorised surplus payments charge (*FA 2004, s 207*)	35%
Scheme sanction charge (*FA 2004, s 240*)	15%–40%
De-registration charge (*FA 2004, s 242*)	40%

Notes

1   *Serious ill-health lump sum charge* – The charge (in *FA 2004, s 205A*) was introduced with effect for 2011/12 and subsequent tax years, in respect of lump sums paid on or after 6 April 2011 (*FA 2011, Sch 16, para 102*) for payments to pension scheme members who have reached the age of 75 years.

2   *Special lump sum death benefits charge* – FA 2004, s 206 is amended by *Finance (No 2) Act 2015*, for payments made after 6 April 2016, by restricting the 45% charge on payments to 'non qualifying persons' only, as long as the payment is made within 2 years of the pension scheme administrator's being aware of (or would be expected to have known of) the member's death. The effect of this is that for most payments, the 45% charge is removed and the payments will be taxed as pension income at the beneficiary's marginal rate of income tax. Where payments are made to a personal representative, who is a non-qualifying person, the charge must be paid but if the payment is then passed on to a beneficiary who is an individual, it is treated as income in the hands of the beneficiary and the tax charge under this section can be deducted from the income tax charged on their total income. Note that, as from 5 April 2015, in most instances, when a member dies under the age of 75, the lump sum death benefits are exempt from tax. The charges referred to apply when the member dies after reaching their 75th birthday.

7

Savings and investments

SIGNPOSTS

- **Interest received** – Individuals are liable to tax on interest in the
  tax year it is paid or credited. The person receiving or entitled to the
  interest is generally liable to tax, although special rules can apply in
  the case of joint accounts of spouses or civil partners (see **7.1–7.3**).

- **Savings income changes** – The *Finance Act 2016* introduced a
  new personal savings allowance giving a nil rate of tax to basic rate
  taxpayers on their first £1,000 of savings income (£500 for higher
  rate taxpayers). In addition, most interest payments from banks and
  building societies no longer suffer tax at source but are paid gross.
  These measures are effective from 6 April 2016 (see **7.4**).

- **Tax rates** – There are specific rules to establish the order in which
  an individual's income is taxed, which determines what rate of tax
  applies to the savings income (see **7.5**).

- **Dividends** – These (and certain other company distributions) are
  broadly taxed on individuals at special rates. The *Finance Act 2016*
  introduced radical changes to the taxation of dividends effective
  from 6 April 2016 whereby dividends no longer carry a basic rate tax
  credit, the tax rates have been changed and individuals are entitled to
  a dividend allowance of £5,000 taxed at a rate of 0% (see **7.7–7.11**),

- **Other savings and investments** – Special rules apply income tax to
  a variety of financial instruments and circumstances (see **7.12–7.18**).

- **Life assurance** – Income tax charges can arise on gains from certain
  life assurance products, such as 'non-qualifying' life policies (see
  7.19).

- **Tax favoured investments** – Some investments benefit from special
  exemptions which make them tax-efficient, such as Individual Savings
  Accounts (ISAs) and Enterprise Investment Scheme (EIS) shares (see
  7.20–7.29).

- **New Help to Buy and Lifetime ISAs** – These new ISAs give savers
  a government bonus to help buy their first home and to boost their

pension savings. See **7.22–7.23** on how they work and from which dates they operate.

- **Appendix: ISA allowances** – A table of ISA investment limits is included at the end of this chapter (see **7.29**).

INTEREST

7.1   The following guidelines deal with tax on interest for individuals. For companies see **Chapter 20**.

When is interest taxed?

7.2   Interest is taxable in the tax year that it is paid, or credited to an account which can be drawn on. Care should be taken not to include any interest earned but unpaid or un-credited. The test is really when the interest can be accessed by the individual who is entitled to it (*ITTOIA 2005, s 370*).

Example 7.1 – Interest on accumulated savings

Dennis has a bank savings account, on which interest is credited every 31 December. He can withdraw money from the account but has actually just left the funds to accumulate in the account for a number of years.

The fact he has not drawn any money out does not prevent the interest earned being taxed in the tax year it is credited, so that interest credited on 31 December 2016 will fall to be taxed in the tax year 2016/17.

Interest can in practice often be treated as arising when it becomes due and payable. However, if a taxpayer does not actually receive interest (or have it credited to an account) until a later date, it does not form part of his taxable income until it is received.

Example 7.2 – Taxable on receipt

Margaret makes a loan of £10,000 to a friend to help her start a florist's business. They agree that the florist will pay interest at a rate of 3% each year, on 30 September, and will repay the £10,000 after five years.

The business struggles in the first couple of years and Margaret doesn't actually receive any payment from the florist in the first two years. Finally,

---

the florist gets a deal to supply a local wedding organiser and this improves her cash flow. Margaret receives payment of three lots of interest on 30 September 2016. The whole of this sum is taxable in 2016/17.

Who is taxable?

7.3 The person receiving, or who is entitled to receive, the interest will be liable to tax on that interest.

Anyone receiving interest income in a representative capacity, such as an agent or bare trustee, has no entitlement to that interest and as such should not be taxed on it (*ITTOIA 2005, s 371*).

Where a joint account is held by spouses or civil partners, the interest entitlement will be split 50:50, unless an election is made to split the interest in a proportion that reflects the true beneficial entitlement between the parties.

The election is made by making a joint declaration on Form 17 (which can be downloaded from the HMRC website (www.gov.uk)) and submitting it to HMRC. It is necessary to submit evidence of beneficial ownership with the form.

A couple can make a different choice for each investment that they own jointly. In some cases they can choose to be taxed on their actual entitlement; in others they can accept the standard 50:50 basis.

Where married couples or civil partners elect not to be taxed 50:50, the normal rules of beneficial ownership apply.

Once a declaration is made it remains in force until the couple's interests in the property or income change, or they stop living together as a married couple or as civil partners (this also includes the death of a spouse or partner). Fresh declarations can be made to reflect the new actual position.

The declaration takes effect from the date the Form 17 was signed provided that it is received by HMRC within 60 days of that date.

It should be noted that the 50:50 splitting rule does not apply to partnership income, income from furnished holiday lets and distributions from shares in a close company.

HMRC's view is that a declaration cannot be made where the property is owned as beneficial joint tenants, as the couple do not own the property in shares at all, but are entitled jointly to the whole of both the property and the income

(TSEM9850). This would include joint bank accounts, although these are no longer specifically mentioned on Form 17.

In any other case where the joint holders are not married or in a civil partnership, the holders will be taxed on their actual beneficial interest in the account (*ITA 2007, s 836*).

If interest is paid on a sum invested in a child's name by a parent or step-parent, then if interest above £100 per annum is earned it will be deemed to be the income of the parent.

Note that this rule does not apply to gifts from grandparents or other relatives or friends. (There may be inheritance tax consequences of gifts – see **Part 4**).

> **Focus**
>
> Care needs to be taken to identify when interest is received, whose interest it is and to ensure the source of the interest is disclosed to HMRC. Penalties may apply if this is not done.

Personal Savings Allowance

7.4   The *Finance Act 2016* introduces a savings allowance that is taxed at the savings nil rate (*ITA 2007, ss 12A and 12B as inserted by FA 2016, s 4(1)*). The individual's entitlement to the savings allowance depends on whether they are basic, higher or additional rate taxpayers.

- For basic rate taxpayers the allowance is £1,000.

- for higher rate taxpayers the allowance is £500

- For additional rate taxpayers the allowance is nil.

The savings nil rate of tax is applied to the savings income that is covered by the allowance. The excess is then taxed at the marginal rate.

> **Example 7.3 – Applying the Personal Savings Allowance**
>
> In 2016/17, Peter has a salary of £42,700. He receives an interest distribution from an authorised unit trust of £900. His tax liability for the year is:
>
> | | £ | £ |
> |---|---|---|
> | Salary | | 42,700 |
> | Interest | | 900 |

Total income			43,600
Less Personal Allowance			(11,000)
Taxable income			32,600
Income tax due on salary	31,700	20%	6,340
Income tax due on savings:	500	0%	-
	400	40%	160
Total taxable income	32,600		6,500
Total tax charge			

The balance of Peter's basic rate band of £300 (£32,000 less £31,700) is used up by his savings income that falls into his personal savings allowance which is taxed at 0%. Peter is only entitled to a PSA of £500 as part of his income is higher rate income.

Savings income includes not only interest from banks and building societies and other providers, such as credit unions and National Savings and Investment but also includes:

- interest distributions (but not dividend distributions) from authorised unit trusts, open-ended investment companies and investment trusts

- income from government or company bonds

- most types of purchased life annuity payments

It does not include interest from Individual Savings Accounts (ISAs) which are already tax-free.

Rate of tax

7.5   In addition to the Personal Savings Allowance (PSA) which gives a 'savings nil rate' of tax, there is also a 'starting rate for savings' band of £5,000 which is taxed at 0% (this 0% rate is effective from 6 April 2015 when it reduced from 10%). However, there are conditions limiting when it applies: **see 1.18.** ((*FA 2014, s 3*).

The ordering rules for the different sources of income received by an individual are found at *ITA 2007, s 16* and broadly speaking are as follows:

- the lowest slice is the individual's non-saving income; earnings, benefits, pensions, business profits and property income, which is effectively taxed first;

226

- followed by savings income; such as bank and building society interest; and

- dividends are treated as the highest part of the individual's total income.

A key point to note is that 'saving income' is taken as being taxed after other income such as employment income or trading profit, so that the personal allowance of an individual may be 'used up' by other income. In other words, the 0% starting rate is only relevant for the recipients of interest whose non-saving income does not exceed their personal allowance plus the £5,000 starting rate limit Based on the tax bands and rates for the tax year 2016/17 this applies as follows:

- taxable savings income that is within the £5,000 starting rate band is taxed at 0% (but only if the rate band has not been used up by other income as noted above);

- taxable savings income for individuals who have no higher rate income is taxed at the savings nil rate of 0% up to the PSA of £1,000

- taxable savings income (included with any other income) that falls within the basic rate band, that is within £32,000 less the £5,000 starting rate band less the PSA of £1,000 is taxed at 20%;

- taxable savings income for individuals who have no additional rate income is taxed at the savings nil rate of 0% up to the PSA of £500

- taxable savings income (included with any other income) that falls within the higher rate band, that is £150,000 less the PSA of £500 less the basic rate band of £32,000 is taxed at 40%;

- taxable savings income (included with any other income) above the £150,000 income tax band is taxed at 45%.

For an example of how this works in practice, see **1.19** and **Example 1.3.**

Care should be taken to identify any interest or other payments which fall outside the tax net, such as interest on SAYE schemes (see **5.40**), interest on ISA plans, NS&I Index linked savings certificates and premium bond winnings. But note that returns from alternative finance arrangements such as Mudaraba, Sukuk or Wakala will fall to be treated as interest for these purposes.

Tax deducted from interest payments

7.6 Prior to 6 April 2016, interest may have been paid under deduction of tax at basic rate, 20% in recent years. Banks and building societies were required by law to deduct this tax at source unless the taxpayer had formally registered to receive the interest gross. This requirement has been removed by

Schedule 6 of the *Finance Act 2016* (*ITA 2007 s 851* omitted). Where tax has been deducted from interest and a reclaim is due, this can be done by using Form R40. Claims must be made within four years of the end of the tax year to which the claim relates. See **1.29–1.31** for claiming a tax refund.

Care must be taken by anyone in receipt of interest income to make sure HMRC has been correctly notified where there may be a charge to tax, particularly those taxpayers who may not be registered for self-assessment (see **1.6**). Prior to 5 April 2016, when basic rate tax was usually deducted at source, this was only necessary where additional tax was due because the taxpayer was a higher rate taxpayer. As interest is now paid gross, a tax liability could arise for even a basic rate taxpayer if their savings income exceeded their personal savings allowance. Interest must be declared on a tax return (if one is issued) together with details of any tax deducted at source.

Another potential pitfall to watch out for is that individual taxpayers who make charitable donations may find that they no longer pay sufficient tax to cover the tax attributable to their gift aid donations and would be liable for the shortfall. This is more likely to arise with banks and building societies paying interest gross and the introduction of the personal savings allowance. HMRC has issued new Gift Aid declaration wordings to highlight the issue.

Focus

Now that most savings income is paid gross, individuals who do not usually file tax returns need to take extra care to find out if they need to notify HMRC of any tax liability.

Banks, and other institutions, now offer a range of reward payments, as well as interest payments, and some of these are taxable – individuals will need to clarify the tax treatment with their banks.

DIVIDENDS

7.7 Dividends are distributions of profit from a company to its shareholders. The relevant tax legislation (*ITTOIA 2005, Pt 4*) charges tax on:

- dividends and other distributions from a UK company;
- dividends from non-UK resident companies;
- 'stock dividends';
- amounts released from loans from a close company to its participators.

In this chapter we will talk mainly about the tax treatment of cash dividends from a UK company to a UK individual.

The tax position on dividends received from foreign companies is dealt with later in **58.3**. Broadly they are taxed in a similar way to UK dividends. In most cases dividends will be paid to a shareholder but the legislation is written so that it will cover any person to whom any distribution is made, or treated as made and any person receiving or entitled to the distribution (*ITTOIA 2005, s 385*).

In some cases, in privately owned companies, dividend waivers will be made. These are often used to allow one shareholder, or group of shareholders, to be paid a dividend whilst another shareholder or shareholders decide they do not wish to have a distribution of the profit. To be effective the waiver must be in place before the shareholder becomes entitled to a dividend.

Key points include:

● a formal deed of waiver should be created which must be signed, dated, witnessed and lodged with the company. It can cover a shareholder's entitlement to either a single or a number of dividends, perhaps for a defined time;

● to ensure that a waiver is in place before the shareholder becomes entitled to it, an interim dividend must be waived before it is paid but a final dividend must be waived before it is approved at an AGM.

HMRC will be less likely to attack these arrangements if there is a demonstrable, and stated, commercial rationale for the waiver and the waiver is a 'one off' rather than an annual event!

Calculating the tax liability on dividends

7.8   From 6 April 2016, the taxation of dividends changed in three ways:

● Dividends no longer carry a 'tax credit'

● Individuals have a dividend allowance of £5,000 on which dividend income is taxed at 0%

● The dividend tax rates have changed and have effectively increased by 7.5%

Example 7.7 compares the change in tax liabilities between 2015/16 under the old regime and 2016/17 in which the new rules operate.

Abolition of tax credit

7.9   Before 6 April 2016, each dividend payment carried a non-repayable 'tax credit' which covered a basic rate taxpayer's tax liability. The tax credit was 1/9th of the value of the dividend, and the combined dividend and tax credit was known as dividend income (*ITA 2007, s 19*).

From 6 April 2016, no 'tax credits' are attached to dividends. The dividend received is simply the taxable income on which the dividend rates are applied. So a basic rate taxpayer can no longer assume that no tax liability arises on dividends received: broadly speaking, if they are in receipt of dividend income exceeding the dividend allowance of £5,000 the excess will be taxed at 7.5%. There will be exceptions when taxpayers can benefit from the starting rate for savings -see Example **1.3** in **1.19**

Example 7.5 - Taxation of dividends in 2016/17 compared with 2015/16 for a basic rate taxpayer

Jenny owns 100 shares in Robert Enterprises Limited. A dividend was declared in June 2015 of £9 per share and again in June 2016 of £9 per share. (For the purposes of this example, it is assumed her dividend allowance is already covered by other income and that she is a basic rate taxpayer).

	2015/16 £	2016/17 £
Net dividend	900	900
Tax credit (1/9)	100	none
Gross dividend	1,000	900
Tax at	10%	7.5%
Tax charge	100	67.50
Less tax credit	(100)	none
Tax payable	nil	67.50

New Dividend Allowance

7.10   The new dividend allowance for individuals applies for the tax year 2016/17 onwards (*ITA 2007, s 13A as inserted by FA 2016*). It is *not* simply a tax -free allowance on the first £5,000 slice of dividend income as this would mean that the first £5,000 of dividend income could be ignored in the personal tax computation. Rather it is a nil rate band that is applied to the first £5,000 of dividend income. Dividends within your allowance will still count towards your basic or higher rate bands, and may therefore affect the rate of tax that you pay on dividends you receive in excess of the £5,000 allowance. This is best illustrated by an example.

Example 7.6 – application of dividend allowance

Mary received dividends of £7,500 in 2016/17. She also received a salary of £147,000.

	£		£
Salary			147,000
Dividends			7,500
Taxable income			154,500
Income tax charge:			
On non-dividend income	32,000	20%	6,400
	115,000	40%	46,000
On dividend income	5,000	0%	-
	2,500	38.1%	952.50
Total tax			53,352.50

Although Mary still has £3,000 of her higher rate band (£118,000–£115,000) remaining, this is used up by the first £3,000 of her dividend allowance which is taxed at the dividend nil rate.

Dividend tax rates

7.11   The rate of tax applying to a dividend payment will depend on the marginal rate of the taxpayer receiving the dividend, remembering that dividend income is charged to tax as the last slice of income – see the example below. From 2016/17, dividend income is taxed at:

● On the first £5,000 at the dividend nil rate of 0% and the excess at

● for basic rate taxpayers at the dividend ordinary rate of 7.5% (previously 10%)

● for higher rate taxpayers at the dividend upper rate of 32.5% (previously 32.5%) and

● for additional rate taxpayers at the dividend additional rate of 38.1% (previously 37.5%).

Taking into account the tax credit that was available, the effective rates of taxation on dividends prior to 6 April 2016 were 0%, 25%, and 30.55% for basic, higher and additional rate taxpayers respectively.

Example 7.7 – Comparison of tax rates on dividend income between 2015/16 and 2016/17 for a higher rate taxpayer

Lawrence was self-employed with taxable profits of £50,000 in each of the years ended 31 March 2016 and 2017. He also had dividend income of £25,000 in each year. As a higher rate taxpayer the tax due on his dividends was:

	2015/16	2016/17
	£	£
Dividends	25,000	25,000
(90% of the dividend income)		
Tax credit	2,778	
(10% of the dividend income)		
Dividend income	27,778	25,000
(dividend paid plus tax credit for 2015/16)		
Dividend nil rate		0%
Dividend higher rate	32.5%	32.5%
Tax charge on dividend income	32.5%*27,778=	0%*5,000+32.5% *20,000 =
	9,028	6,500
Less tax credit	(2,778)	
Extra tax due	6,250	6,500

Focus

The tax treatment of dividends has changed significantly since 6 April 2016. The rate of tax on dividends needs careful calculation, and will vary dependent on the level of dividends received and the overall income of the taxpayer.

OTHER SAVINGS INCOME

7.12   Whilst this publication looks at the main rules on interest and dividend income, there are a number of other forms of savings income which have separate rules. This section identifies some of these types of income and gives an outline of the tax rules applying. Further advice may be needed if you come across these sorts of income in practice.

Deeply discounted securities

7.13　The HMRC manuals (at SAIM3010) describe these as:

'government securities and commercial bonds and loan stock, where the amount paid on redemption is higher than the price at which they were issued. The difference is the discount and represents the whole or part of the reward to the holder of the security for the use of the money borrowed by the security issuer. Where certain conditions apply, the tax rules ensure that gains on such securities are taxed as income, rather than as capital gains.'

The tax rules are in *ITTOIA 2005, ss 427–460*. Income tax is chargeable on profits arising on disposals in the tax year. Disposal is defined to include redemption, transfer by sale, exchange or gift, and conversion into shares. Profit on disposal is simply the excess of the amount received over the amount paid. No account is normally taken of any incidental costs of acquisition or disposal (*ITTOIA 2005, ss 437, 439*).

There is normally no relief for losses arising on such transactions (*ITTOIA 2005, ss 453–456*).

In some cases market value will replace the actual prices of the securities. This will apply where there are transfers as follows (*ITTOIA 2005, s 440*):

● other than at arm's length;

● between connected persons;

● for consideration not wholly in money or money's worth;

● on death;

● by a personal representative to a legatee.

It should be noted that these rules will not apply where the security is issued merely to satisfy a 'qualifying earn-out right', for example where deferred consideration is paid by way of a loan note (*ITTOIA 2005, s 442*).

Accrued income scheme

7.14　The accrued income scheme gives a freestanding income tax charge on accrued interest on the transfer of a security. The legislation applies to marketable securities, such as government or corporate bonds, but does not apply to shares in a company. Companies owning securities are not caught by these rules but are taxed under the loan relationships legislation (see **Chapter 20**).

Depending on whether the sale of the securities is with or without the accrued interest (sometimes called 'cum-dividend' or 'ex-dividend') the sum is treated as a payment to or by either the transferor or the transferee. Payments in the tax year are aggregated. Any excess of payments received over payments made is charged to income tax as accrued income profits for the tax year. If a loss is made it is relievable by being set against the actual interest received.

Any amount taxable as income is removed from both the sale and purchase considerations of the securities for capital gains tax purposes.

Individuals whose total holdings do not exceed £5,000 are excluded from these rules as are certain other individuals such as financial traders, non-residents, charities, etc (*ITTOIA 2005, Pt 4*).

Collective investment schemes

7.15   A collective investment scheme is one where investors 'pool' their assets and invest in a managed portfolio. These funds may either be 'authorised' or 'unauthorised'.

'Authorised' funds are chargeable to corporation tax, with individuals paying income tax on the distributions from the fund.

In 'unauthorised' funds, income arising to the trust is regarded as income of the trustees (rather than the unit holders) and assessed to tax according to the sources of income concerned. Income tax is chargeable at the basic rate and not at the dividend ordinary rate or savings rate. The trustees are treated as making a 'deemed payment' to the unit holder and as deducting basic rate income tax from that payment so that unit holders are treated as receiving payments, from which income tax has been deducted. These rules do not apply to:

- enterprise zone property unit trust schemes;
- charitable unit trusts;
- limited partnerships;
- approved profit sharing schemes.

There are special rules for the taxation of offshore funds (*TIOPA 2010, Pt 8*).

Stock dividends

7.16 This is where a company offers its shareholders the alternative of receiving additional shares in the company rather than a cash dividend. They may also be known as 'scrip dividends' or 'bonus issues'.

The rules do not apply to normal bonus issues which involve the capitalisation of reserves and allotment to shareholders of bonus shares pro-rata to existing holdings.

Up to 5 April 2016 tax was charged on the cash equivalent of the stock dividends issued grossed up at the dividend ordinary rate (*ITTOIA 2005, s 409–414*). From 6 April 2016 the notional 10% dividend tax credit is abolished therefore there is no need to gross up the dividend before charging tax.

UK Real Estate Investment Trusts

7.17 A UK Real Estate Investment Trust (REIT) is a company or group that carries on a property rental business and meets a number of tests. If the conditions are met, a special tax regime may apply where the business consists of at least 75% property rental. In those cases rental income is exempt from corporation tax and no capital gains arise on the disposal of the rental properties.

One of the principal conditions is that the REIT must distribute 90% of its rental profits from its tax-exempt property rental business and pay these distributions under deduction of basic rate income tax. This means that tax falls not on the REIT company but on the shareholder in that company.

But note that if other, non-rental profits are distributed, these will be treated as normal dividends and the shares in the REIT company will remain subject to capital gains tax (*CTA 2010, Pt 12*).

Interest included in damages for personal injury

7.18 Any damages, award or settlement in respect of personal injuries or death may include an element of interest. 'Personal injuries' will include any disease or impairment of a person's physical or mental condition.

Any such damages included in an award of a UK court, or in an out-of-court settlement are exempted from tax. Awards by a foreign court will also be exempt from tax as long as the interest is exempt from tax in the country in which the award is made (*ITTOIA 2005, s 751*).

> **Focus**
>
> Complicated rules apply in all these areas and care will be needed to get the correct answer if you are faced with such situations.

Life assurance

7.19 Up to 14 March 1984, there were income tax reliefs for premiums paid under life assurance policies. Policies taken out after that date did not qualify for relief and from 6 April 2015 all policies cease to qualify for relief.

There are, however, income tax charges on gains from certain life assurance policies. HMRC Helpsheet 320, which can be downloaded from the gov.uk website, is available to assist in deciding what needs to be returned.

A detailed review is beyond the scope of this book but the following is an overview.

Policies taken out post-1984 which were for a period of ten years or more or for the whole of life and on which premiums were payable regularly are usually 'qualifying policies' on which no tax charge arises. If in doubt the insurer should be able to confirm the position. For policies taken out or varied after 12 March 2012 the premiums payable must be less than £3,600 per year. The most common example of a 'non-qualifying' policy is a single premium life insurance policy which is one where a substantial amount is paid to the insurer at the beginning of the policy. Additional premiums may also be payable. This type of policy pays out a lump sum on its maturity or if the assured (or another life assured) should die. The assured may also withdraw sums or a loan may be made by the insurer. This type of policy is very likely to result in a taxable gain.

A gain will arise if during the year withdrawals are made or cash is received on surrender, maturity or death or an assignment or other change of ownership of a UK life policy.

In each insurance year the assured can withdraw up to 5% of the premium paid into a single premium policy without a gain accruing in that year, however, the 5% withdrawals come into the calculation of any chargeable event when the policy ends.

UK insurers are obliged by law to issue a chargeable event certificate if there has been a taxable event in a year. However, if it is necessary to calculate the gain or check the insurance company's calculations, the position is in outline as follows.

The gain is calculated as the difference between the proceeds received on surrender or maturity plus any previous withdrawals less the premiums paid and any previous chargeable gains.

For basic rate taxpayers, no further tax is due. Higher rate taxpayers will have tax to pay but 'top-slicing relief' reduces the tax payable in that the gain is divided by the number of years that the policy has been in force to determine the tax rate for the whole gain.

Example 7.8 – Income tax on a chargeable event

Mr Thomas purchases a single premium bond in 20010/11 for £10,000.

He takes annual withdrawals of £500 for six years under the 5% rule.

He cashes in the bond in 2016/17 and receives £13,000.

The gain is £ ((13,000 + 3,000) – 10,000) = £6,000.

If the taxpayer has £200 of his basic rate band left after all other income and allowances are taken into account, the tax payable on the chargeable event will be calculated as:

		£		£
Gain per year on 6-year policy				1,000
Tax at basic rate	200 @ 20%			40
Tax at higher rate	800 @ 40%			320
Total				360
Less basic rate tax	1,000 @ 20%			200
Tax due on £1,000				160
Tax due on £6,000				960

TAX-EFFICIENT INVESTMENTS

Individual savings accounts (ISAs)

7.20   There are a few investments which benefit from special rules which can make them very tax-efficient. This may not mean that they are good investments for a particular tax payer but that is outside the scope of this work.

One of the best known tax-efficient investments is the Individual Savings Account (ISA).An ISA is basically a savings arrangement in cash and/or stocks and shares which benefits from an exemption from income tax and capital gains tax. There are limits to the amounts that can be subscribed in each tax year and the limit for 2016/17 is £15,240, increasing to £20,000 in 2017/18.

Under the old ISA rules, which applied before 1 July 2014, the investor was restricted in the amounts that could be invested in cash ISAs but now the investment can be made in any combination of cash and/or stocks and shares up to the relevant limit. ISAs are only available to individuals who are over 18 (or over 16 for cash ISAs). So an individual aged between 16 and 18 can invest up to £15,240 in 2016/17 in a cash ISA but not in a stocks and shares ISA. This is in addition to any amounts invested into a Junior ISA.

Since ISAs were introduced only for over 18s and partly to compensate for the end of the Child Trust Fund (CTF), Junior ISAs were introduced from 1 November 2011. All UK resident children (under 18) who do not have a CTF account are eligible to open a Junior ISA. Again, investments can be held in cash or stocks and shares and all income and gains are tax-free. There is a limit of £4,080 on annual contributions for 2016/17. Income arising from a sum paid by a parent into his child's Junior ISA is not taxed as the parent's income.

There are no statutory restrictions on withdrawing funds from an ISA for adults, although banks and building societies often have rules on specific accounts. And from 6 April 2016, savers can withdraw and replace funds from their cash ISAs without it counting towards their annual subscription limit for that year. In contrast, funds placed in a Junior ISA are locked in until the child reaches the age of 18 at which point the account will automatically become an adult ISA.

From 3 December 2014, on the death of an individual who holds an ISA account, his or her spouse or civil partner can inherit the ISA, retaining the tax advantages. From 6 April 2016, the surviving spouse will also be able to invest in that ISA up to the limits the deceased spouse would have been entitled to, as well as investing in their own ISA.

Innovative Finance ISA

7.21   This is a new type of ISA for peer to peer lending. They were introduced to give investors more choice and flexibility and to encourage competition in the banking sector by diversifying the available sources of finance. The rates of interest will be higher than cash ISAs to reflect the fact that the investment does carry risk.

These ISAs should have been available from 6 April 2016 but, at the time of writing, only a handful of companies had won approval to offer them.

Help to Buy ISA

7.22 A new product was launched from 1 December 2015. First time buyers who save with the new Help to Buy ISA will have their savings topped up by an additional 25% from the government (up to a maximum of £3,000) when they come to purchase their new home. The application for the extra 25% of their savings from the government will be made by their solicitor or conveyancer. There needs to be a minimum saved of £1,600 before the saver will qualify for the 25% bonus and the bonus must be claimed within 12 months of closing the account.

The initial deposit into the savings account can be anything up to £1,200 and thereafter up to £200 per calendar month may be deposited up to a maximum of £12,000.

The scheme is only available for the purchase of a home in the UK where it is intended to live and for those who do not already own a home, either in the UK or elsewhere. It not available to acquire property intended for letting. The property price must not exceed £250,000 (or £450,000 within London). The property must be purchased with a mortgage.

If the property is being purchased with someone else, each first time buyer can apply for their own Help to Buy: ISA.

The Help to Buy: ISA will be open for new savers until 30 November 2019, and open to new contributions until 2029.

Savers will be able to pay into a Help to Buy: ISA as well as a Lifetime ISA but will only be able to use the government bonus from one of their accounts to buy their first home. See **7.23** below for the new Lifetime ISAs and how funds can be transferred from the Help to Buy: ISA in 2017/18 only.

Lifetime ISA

7.23 Lifetime ISAs were introduced in the 2016 Budget to be available from April 2017. These are intended to help individuals purchase their first home and to provide pension savings in their retirement. Deposits of up to £4,000 per annum will benefit from a 25% government bonus.

They are available for people aged 18 and under the age of 40. Savers can make Lifetime ISA contributions and receive a bonus up to the age of 50. Full or partial withdrawals can be made from age 60. The withdrawal (including the bonus) can be used for any purpose, and will be paid free of tax. Funds can remain invested and any interest and investment growth will be tax-free.

7.23   *Savings and investments*

Any contributions to Lifetime ISAs are limited by the overall £20,000 annual ISA subscription limit. Transfers can be made from existing cash and stock ISAs to help fund the Lifetime ISA and, as with other transfers, are not affected by the annual ISA limit.

For 2017/18 **only**, it will be possible to transfer Help to Buy: ISA savings into a Lifetime ISA. For Help to Buy: ISA savings made before April 2017 that are transferred across, the £4,000 annual contribution limit does not apply and these funds will all be entitled to the 25% bonus. For the transfer of Help to Buy: ISA savings made after April 2017, the annual contribution limit of £4,000 is applied and these transfers are taken into account together with the direct contributions paid into the Lifetime ISA in ensuring the £4,000 limit is not exceeded. See example **7.9**.

Example 7.9 Bonus on transfer of Help to Buy: ISA savings in 2017/18 to Lifetime ISA

Megan opened a Help to Buy: ISA in February 2016 with an initial deposit of £1,200. She saved £200 per month until September 2017. In June 2017 she opened a Lifetime ISA with an initial deposit of £500 and saved a further £2,000 in January 2018. In October 2017, she closed her Help to Buy: ISA and transferred all the funds to her Lifetime ISA. As her contributions after April 17 totalled £3,700 she could only make a further saving of £300 before 5 April 2018 without exceeding her annual Lifetime ISA allowance of £4,000.

At the end of the tax year in April 2018, the government bonus paid into her Lifetime ISA was £1,950 based on the following:

Pre April 2017 savings transferred from her Help to Buy: ISA.	£3,800 at 25%	£950
Savings in 2017/18 limited to £4,000		
Post April 2017 savings transferred from Help to Buy: ISA	£1,200	
Lifetime ISA contributions	£2,800	
	£4,000 at 25%	£1,000
Total bonus received		£1,950

Further information can be found at: www.helptobuy.gov.uk/help-to-buy-isa/how-does-it-work.

Focus

If you are saving to buy your first home, consider opening a Help to Buy or Lifetime ISA to benefit from the 25% government bonus. If you already have a Help to Buy:ISA, consider opening a Lifetime ISA in April 17 and transferring your savings before 5 April 2018 to benefit from the relaxation of the annual limit for transfers in 2017/18 only.

Enterprise Investment Scheme

7.24   Another tax-favoured investment is shares in a company which qualifies under the Enterprise Investment Scheme (EIS). Information on the income tax reliefs for EIS investments is available on the gov.uk website.

The EIS offers tax incentives if you invest in shares in smaller, unlisted companies.

Subject to satisfying all the relevant conditions, including retaining the shares for three years, an individual investing in an EIS company can reduce his income tax liability in the tax year in which the shares are issued by 30% of the amount invested.

The maximum subscription by an individual in a tax year is £1 million. Relief is claimed on a Form EIS3 which is supplied by the company and must be claimed within five years of 31 January after the end of the tax year.

It is possible to elect to claim the relief in the previous tax year; this is also dealt with on the EIS3.

The main conditions are outlined below:

- Throughout the relevant three-year qualifying period, an EIS company must be an unquoted company with only fully-paid issued shares, be a trading company, carrying on a qualifying trade, have a permanent establishment in the UK and not be a 51% subsidiary of another company, or otherwise be under the control of another company.

- The investor cannot be 'connected' with the EIS company, ie he cannot own more than 30% of the shares, directly or indirectly. Investors cannot normally be paid directors or employees of the EIS company at the time of the issue of shares. Otherwise, qualifying investors can in certain circumstances be paid for their work, provided the total remuneration package is 'normal and reasonable'.

- The money raised by the EIS share issue must be wholly used for the qualifying business activity and schemes that involve guarantees or exit arrangements will not attract tax relief

- From 18 November 2015 there are a number of changes. There are restrictions on existing shareholders claiming relief and the money raised cannot be used to acquire a business. In addition in some cases the relief is restricted by the age of the company in that the investment must be made within 7 years of making their first commercial sale or 10 years if the company is a knowledge-intensive company. A new cap has also been introduced on the total amount of investments a company may raise under EIS, VCT or other risk finance investment, of £12 million or £20 million for knowledge-intensive companies.

The *Finance (No. 2) Act 2015* included legislation placing a time limit on the availability of relief: only shares issued before 6 April 2025 will be eligible for relief (*ITA 2007, s 157(1)(aa)*). However, the Treasury retain the power to amend the end date (*s 157(1A)*).

Seed Enterprise Investment Scheme

7.25   The Seed Enterprise Investment Scheme (SEIS) was introduced in the *Finance Act 2012* as an extension to the EIS and applies to shares issued after 6 April 2012. It was originally intended to end on 5 April 2017 but has now been extended without time limit.

The main rules are contained in *ITA 2007, Pt 5A* and *TCGA 1992, ss 150E–150G, Sch 5BB*.

The rationale behind the SEIS was to encourage investment in very small start-up companies which by their nature are high risk investments.

The main conditions for the investors are:

- individual investors can subscribe up to £100,000 in a year and get income tax relief of 50% of the amount invested (irrespective of their marginal tax rate);

- the relief can be claimed in the year of investment or can be carried back to the previous year;

- the individual cannot control the company and must have a stake of less than 30% and can be a director but not just an employee;

- SEIS shares are exempt from CGT after a three-year qualifying period;

- there is an exemption for gains in 2014/15 and subsequent years that are invested in SEIS shares (this relief was restricted to half the qualifying reinvested amount for gains in 2013/14).

The main conditions for the company are:

- it must be a UK unquoted company carrying on a 'new business' which means a trade which is less than two years old (whether or not it was previously carried on by another entity);

- it must have 25 or fewer employees and assets of up to £200,000;

- the maximum investment under the SEIS is £150,000 cumulatively in any three-year period;

- the company must carry on a qualifying business.

The conditions for relief are complicated as is the interaction with EIS, and HMRC have published guidance at (www.gov.uk/guidance/seed-enterprise-investment-scheme-background). Information can also be found in the HMRC's Venture Capital Schemes Manual.

Venture Capital Trusts

7.26   Another tax-favoured investment is the Venture Capital Trust Scheme (VCT) which started on 6 April 1995 and was designed to encourage individuals to invest *indirectly* in a range of small higher-risk trading companies, whose shares and securities are not listed, by investing through VCTs. By investing in a VCT, you are able to spread the investment risk over a number of companies.

VCTs are run by fund managers who are usually members of larger investment groups. VCTs must be approved by HMRC and have to meet a number of conditions.

Individual investors in a VCT may be entitled to various income tax and capital gains tax reliefs and VCTs are exempt from corporation tax on any gains arising on the disposal of their investments.

The main income tax reliefs are:

- exemption from income tax on dividends from ordinary shares in VCTs;

- income tax relief at the rate of 30% of the amount subscribed for shares issued in the tax year.

The shares must be new ordinary shares and must not carry any preferential rights or rights of redemption at any time in the period of five years beginning with their date of issue. The tax relief for the amount subscribed is available in the tax year in which the shares were issued, provided that you hold them for at least five years.

Legislation was introduced in the *Finance Act 2014* to restrict an individual's entitlement to VCT income tax relief where investments are conditionally linked in any way to a VCT buy-back, or have been made within six months of a disposal of shares in the same VCT.

Social investment tax relief (SITR)

7.27   The *Finance Act 2014* introduced social investment tax relief for individual investors who invest in cash in new shares or in new qualifying debt investments in qualifying social enterprises (an unquoted community interest company, community benefit society or a charity with less than 500 equivalent full-time employees) on or after 6 April 2014 and before 6 April 2019 (*ITA 2007*, new *Pt 5B* and *TCGA 1992, ss 255A–255E* as inserted by *FA 2014*)).

Income tax relief is available at 30% up to a maximum investment of £1 million per annum. From 2015/16, any unused relief can be carried back to the previous year. On disposal of the investment, any chargeable gains are exempt from capital gains tax and any capital losses allowable. Capital gains tax deferral relief is available on any gains arising on disposals of assets in the period 6 April 2014 to 5 April 2019 which are reinvested into qualifying social investments.

Premium bonds

7.28   The maximum holding is £50,000 and the prizes are not taxable.

APPENDIX: INDIVIDUAL SAVING ACCOUNTS

(ITTOIA 2005, Pt 6, Ch 3; SI 1998/1870, reg 4)

7.29

	2016/17 Age 18 and over	2015/16 Age 18 and over	20/14/15 Age 18 and over	2013/14 Age 18 and over
Overall limit	£15,240	£15,240	£15,000	11,520
Cash limit	n/a	n/a	n/a	£5,760
Junior ISA	£4,080	£4,080	£4,000	£3,720

Notes

1   *Period from 6 April 2014 to 30 June 2014* – The overall limit applying to this period before the introduction of the new ISAs was £11,880, with the maximum cash deposit of £5,940.

2   *Young people* – Whether or not a person aged 16 to 18 already holds a Junior ISA (see Note 3 below), they may invest in an adult cash ISA up to the cash limit, but not in a stocks and shares ISA.

3   *Junior ISA* (JISA) – These became available from 1 November 2011 to UK resident children (under 18s) who do not have a Child Trust Fund (CTF) account. The investment limit can be divided between cash and stocks and shares. When the holder reaches the age of 18, a JISA becomes an adult ISA (*ITTOIA 2005, s 695A*).

4   From April 2017, the new overall ISA limit will be £20,000 which covers contributions to a Lifetime ISA, cash ISA, stocks and shares ISA and Innovative Finance ISA.

8

Land and property

SIGNPOSTS

- **Scope** – Rents and various other receipts from land or property in the UK are brought into charge as income, less deductions for allowable property business expenses. Separate tax return supplementary pages for individuals deal with income from land and property abroad (see **8.1–8.2**).

- **Expenses** – Deductions are generally allowed for expenses incurred 'wholly and exclusively' for the purposes of the lettings business. Capital allowances can also be claimed for certain capital costs where the property is commercial. 'Wear and tear allowance' is available to landlords of furnished residential accommodation to cover the depreciation of plant and machinery such as furniture, fridges, etc (see **8.3–8.12**).

- **Losses** – Property business losses are generally carried forward and set off against future property income of the same business, subject to certain exceptions (see **8.13**).

- **Furnished holiday lettings** – These lettings are treated as a trade for some tax purposes, with potentially beneficial tax consequences. However, a number of conditions must be satisfied for this tax treatment to apply (see **8.14**).

- **Non-resident landlords** – Rent from UK property paid to non-resident landlords is subject to deduction of UK basic rate income tax at source, unless permission is given by HMRC for gross payment (see **8.15**).

- **Rent-a-room relief** – This relief generally applies to individuals who provide furnished residential accommodation in their own home (see **8.16**).

- **Foreign property income** – This is calculated and taxed in broadly the same way as income from land and property in the UK, although UK and overseas lettings businesses are taxed separately, and the losses of one are not deductible from profits of the other (see **8.17**).

- **Lease premiums** – Part of the premium granted on a short lease is treated as income of the landlord, and as deductible rent for the tenant (see **8.18**).

- **Record keeping** – Landlords are required to keep records of income and allowable expenditure (see **8.19**).

- **Annual Tax on Enveloped Dwellings** – From 2013, an annual tax is levied on certain high value dwellings owned by companies and there is an associated CGT charge (see **8.20**).

- **Appendix: Furnished holiday lettings** – A table of 'qualifying holiday accommodation' periods is included at the end of this chapter (see **8.21**).

INTRODUCTION

8.1   For corporation tax purposes, companies are taxed on rental profits under generally accepted accounting principles, as explained in more detail in **21.2**. This chapter deals with income tax issues for individuals, partnerships and trusts.

The main statutory provisions taxing property income are in *ITTOIA 2005, Pt 3* (*ss 260–364*). The HMRC website has a separate manual on property income. There is also a toolkit for property rental income on the HMRC website at www.gov.uk/government/publications/hmrc-property-rental-toolkit.

UK property income is returned on the SA105 supplementary tax return pages, and there are notes to SA105 to assist with this. There are also Helpsheets – HS223 (Rent-a-room) and HS253 (Furnished holiday lettings).

Foreign property income is returned on the SA106 supplementary pages and there are notes to SA106 to assist with this.

All self-assessment forms are available from the HMRC website (www.gov. uk/self-assessment-tax-returns).

In principle, the taxation of property income is simple. All rents and similar receipts from the exploitation of land or property in the UK are brought in as income, and then the business expenses incurred in earning the income, other than capital expenses, are deducted. Subject to specific rules the profits are calculated under generally accepted accounting principles (GAAP).

It is also possible to claim capital allowances on certain capital expenditure when the property is commercial (rather than residential) (see **Chapter 4**).

Where the property is outside the UK, the rents are treated as overseas property income and it is taxed as foreign income. However, the computational rules are similar (see **8.17**).

Where a non-resident investor owns UK property, the rents are subject to income tax (whether or not the investor is a company). The special rules are discussed below (see **8.15**).

There are four types of property income:

- UK property income;

- overseas property income;

- UK furnished holiday lettings income;

- overseas furnished holiday lettings income.

For a UK resident, all four types of income are subject to UK tax, and assessed on the basis of income arising in the tax year (ended 5 April), except where rental income arises in a partnership (or LLP) which is also carrying on a trade, where the accounts basis is used. The income and expenses of each type of property are combined to form a single property business of that type.

> **Focus**
>
> Where an individual carries on property businesses both on his own account and as a member of a partnership (including an LLP), the individual and partnership businesses are treated as two separate property businesses, so there may be a further separate property business to report. This impacts on the set off of profits and losses.

PROPERTY INCOME

8.2 Rental income from furnished, commercial and domestic premises, or from any bare land, is taxable as property income. When a property is let furnished, any separate income obtained for use of the furniture are receipts of the business. Similarly, service charges are treated as rental income.

There are a number of less common receipts:

- property exploitation activities, including rent charges, ground rents and similar;

- premium and other lump sums received on the grant of short leases: this means leases of 50 years or less – the rules on this are extremely complex;

- reverse premiums;

- income from granting sporting rights (this might include fishing or shooting permits);

- income from allowing waste to be buried or stored on land;

- income from letting other people use land – for example, a film crew pays to film on land;

- grants received from local authorities or similar contributions towards revenue expenses;

- rental income received through enterprise zone trust schemes;

- income from caravans or houseboats where these are stationary;

- service charges;

- refunds or rebates of business expenses which have been allowed;

- deposits taken from tenants (to the extent not repaid); and

- insurance recoveries.

EXPENSES

8.3

Focus

Expenses are deductible if they are incurred wholly and exclusively for the purposes of the letting business. Where expenditure has two purposes, for example business and private, and part of this is obviously for the purpose of the business, usually an appropriate proportion of the expenses will be deductible.

Some expenses are considered in more detail below but the following items are potentially allowable expenses:

- business rates;

- council tax;

- water rates;

- ground rents;

- property and contents insurance;

- services provided, such as gardening, cleaning, communal hot water;

- fees paid to an agent for rent collection, advertising and admin;

- professional fees for renewing a short lease or evicting an unsatisfactory tenant;

- exterior and interior painting;

- damp treatment;

- stone cleaning;

- roof repairs;

- repairs to any machinery supplied with the property.

Repairs

8.4   In conducting a property business, there are particular issues with the deduction of property repairs. For this purpose, a repair (as opposed to an improvement) means the restoration of the property by replacing component parts of it. For example, if tiles are blown off the roof by a storm, the cost of replacing those tiles is a repair.

Examples of tax deductible repairs would include:

- painting and decorating (both internal and external);

- stone cleaning;

- damp and rot treatment.

- mending broken windows, doors, furniture, etc;

- repointing; and

- replacing roof slates.

The purchase of the property cannot be regarded as a repair (this is always capital). Where a property is bought in a run-down condition and has to be 'repaired' in order to get it into a lettable state, the cost of those 'repairs' may be regarded for tax purposes as part of the acquisition cost of the building, and therefore not deductible. However, if the properties had been let out before undertaking the repairs, or the run-down state did not affect the purchase price, it is more likely that the repairs will be accepted as deductible. This is very much a question of fact.

Where the property in question is commercial rather than residential, it may be possible for the purchaser to claim capital allowances on plant and machinery installed in the building. This is dealt with in more detail in **Chapter 4**.

Focus

The cost of improvements to a building is regarded as capital, but it is not always easy to tell whether expenditure on a property relates to repairs or improvements. HMRC have given some guidance (PIM2020; see www. hmrc.gov.uk/manuals/pimmanual/PIM2020.htm) which states that, where the effect of expenditure is simply to replace existing elements of the building with more up-to-date elements (for example, rewiring to current standards, replacing wooden windows with UPVC windows) this will generally be regarded as repairs. However, where there is an element of alteration (for example, a conservatory is constructed, which includes wiring and windows) this will be regarded as an improvement.

Rent payable and council tax

8.5   Where the landlord himself pays rent (for example, where the landlord sublets part of his business premises), an appropriate proportion of the rent paid will be allowable. Similarly, where the landlord remains responsible for business rates, an appropriate proportion will be allowable. However, for residential dwellings, it is normally the responsibility of the inhabitants to pay council tax, because council tax depends on the number of persons within the dwelling. This is not normally regarded as tax deductible, unless the landlord is paying council tax in respect of an empty property, a house in multiple occupation, or any other property where it is customary for the landlord to pay the council tax. See also PIM2030 (www.hmrc.gov.uk/manuals/pimmanual/PIM2030.htm).

Insurance premiums

8.6   Insurance premiums covering the following risks are allowable if paid for the purposes of the rental business:

● a risk of damage to the property;

● a risk of damage to contents; and

● loss of rent.

Advertising expenses

8.7   The cost of advertising to find a lessee for the property is normally tax deductible against the rent.

Bad debts

8.8   Bad debts are normally tax deductible to the extent that they are clearly irrecoverable, or can reasonably be said to be doubtful.

Common parts

8.9   If the landlord owns a block of flats, there are generally separate parts of the building which are not let to individual tenants, but are used by them in common (for example, corridors, lifts, etc). The landlord can deduct expenditure on the upkeep of these common parts from his rental business income.

Finance costs

8.10   Where an investor borrows money to buy land or property for letting, or to repair, improve or alter that property, such interest is deductible from letting income. Where the interest is partly used to fund the purchase or repair of let property, and partly for other purposes, an apportionment is required.

From 6 April 2017, interest relief is gradually being withdrawn, in favour of a basic rate tax credit for interest expense. For higher rate taxpayers, the effective tax rate on rental profits will therefore exceed the headline rate. The provisions are phased in over four years. In some cases, where the investor is highly geared, this could take the effective tax rate to over 100%, and the investor will need to consider the appropriate course of action.

> **Example 8.1 – Allowable interest costs**
>
> Frank buys a cottage for £200,000 which he occupies, and spends a further £100,000 on constructing an annex, which he lets to his mother at full market rent. All the costs are funded by borrowing.
>
> Frank can claim relief on one-third of his interest costs.

Where a property investor incurs fees or charges to take out loans to buy a property, these are normally deductible, provided they relate wholly and exclusively to property let out on a commercial basis (*ITTOIA 2005, s 272*).

Capital allowances

8.11   Following the abolition of industrial buildings allowances and agricultural buildings allowances, only that part of a property which qualifies as plant and machinery will be subject to any allowances. It should be noted that, for dwelling houses, capital allowances are not available to set off against rental income.

Replacement of domestic items relief

8.12 Instead of capital allowances, where a landlord let out residential property on a furnished basis, he was entitled up to 2015/16 to a wear and tear allowance of 10% of the 'net rent' on the furnished letting, to provide some relief for depreciation of the furniture, plant and machinery in the property.

The net rent is the rent less charges and services that would often be paid by the tenant but are paid by the landlord, for example council tax, water rates, etc.

Focus

The 10% deduction was given to cover the sort of plant and machinery that a tenant would provide in unfurnished lettings such as furniture (beds and chairs), TVs, fridges, carpets, curtains, cooker, washing machine. It doesn't matter if the landlord does not provide all of these things but the accommodation must be genuinely furnished.

The wear and tear allowance was simple to claim and meant that the taxpayer got a deduction every year even if they did not have to replace furniture every year. If you did claim the wear and tear allowance, you could not claim for the cost of replacing some assets; that is the only relief that you could have for furniture and plant.

The Government has announced the end of the 10% wear and tear allowance from April 2016. The new system gives tax relief for the replacement of furnishings and other domestic items. The main practical difference is that landlords will need to keep records of the money they spend replacing domestic items in order to claim relief. The relief does not extend to fixtures, although replacement fixtures may qualify as repairs in many instances.

LOSSES

8.13 Losses from property investment business can be carried forward and set off against future property income from the same business (after combining businesses of the same type, as discussed in **8.1** above). Where an individual carries on property businesses of different types or both as an individual and as a partner, he cannot set off losses from one against the other directly.

Where the loss arises from excess capital allowances or the business has a relevant agricultural connection, such a loss may be set off against general income.

Example 8.2 – Profits and losses – no offset

Johnny owns property which he lets out, and is a partner in a trading partnership with his brother Edgar. The partnership trades from part of Winter House, and the rest of Winter House is let out. This is treated as rental income, rather than letting of surplus trading premises (which would be part of trading income). No capital allowances are due.

If Johnny's own let property makes a loss, this cannot be set off against income from letting Winter House (PIM1030; see www.hmrc.gov.uk/manuals/pimmanual/PIM1030.htm). If that loss arose from capital allowances or was increased by them, the loss might be set against Johnny's total income.

FURNISHED HOLIDAY LETTINGS

8.14   For the purposes of tax allowances, in particular capital allowances, it should be noted that furnished holiday lettings are treated as a trade for some tax purposes. As a result, capital allowances will be available on plant and machinery installed in the property and any gain on disposal is potentially subject to entrepreneurs' relief.

In order to qualify as a holiday let, the property must be available for letting to the general public as holiday accommodation for a period of at least 210 days (140 for periods of account commencing before 5 April 2012) and actually let for at least 105 days in that period (70 days for periods of account commencing before 5 April 2012).

From 2011/12, the furnished holiday letting rules are also extended to properties situated in the European Economic Area.

Where a person has a number of units which are let for holiday purposes, each of them must separately satisfy the availability condition but if some are individually let for less than the limit (70 or 105 days as appropriate), the landlord can test the letting condition against the average occupancy of the units (*ITTOIA 2005, s 326*). This is an averaging election for under-used holiday accommodation which must be claimed before one year from 31 January following the year of assessment.

A table of 'qualifying holiday accommodation' periods is included at the end of this chapter.

NON-RESIDENT LANDLORDS

8.15   Where a landlord resident outside the UK lets UK-situ property, the rental income is subject to UK taxation (and standard double taxation treaties give the UK priority taxing rights). Either the tenant will pay rent direct to the landlord, or he will pay it to a letting agent, who passes the rent on to the landlord.

Where rent is paid to such a landlord, the payer (tenant or agent) must deduct UK basic rate income tax, unless he has received permission to pay the rent gross (Form CAR PTI), and account for the tax quarterly to HMRC.

In order to get Form CAR PTI, the landlord must apply to HMRC under the non-resident landlord scheme and demonstrate that:

● his UK tax affairs are up to date; or

● he never has had any UK tax obligations; or

● he does not expect to be liable to UK income tax; and

● he will undertake to comply with self-assessment rules. (Where a letting agent is involved, they often deal with the self-assessment return as part of their work.)

If the landlord receives the income under deduction of tax, and the tax deducted exceeds his actual liability, he may file a return in order to claim a refund of the excess.

For disposals after 5 April 2015, a non-resident disposing of UK residential property (but not property such as nursing homes or student accommodation) is liable to UK CGT. Principal Private Residence (PPR) relief is available in the normal way (see **Chapter 14**), but a house can only be a person's PPR if he or members of his family spend sufficient time there in a tax year (which may give rise to conflicts with the new residence rules).

RENT-A-ROOM RELIEF

8.16   Rent-a-room relief applies where a taxpayer provides furnished residential accommodation in their only or main home. For example, the taxpayer takes in a lodger. There are two types of relief. The first is full exemption, which is available if the gross letting receipts are £7,500 (£4,250 up to April 2016) or less (this is approximately £144 per week). Clearly, however, the taxpayer cannot claim any of the letting expenses if the income is exempt. If the receipts exceed £7,500, there is an alternative basis of taxation, which taxes the excess of the gross receipts over £7,500, as taxable rental income, but again without deducting any expenses.

Example 8.3 – How the relief works

David lets a room to Tina in his main home for £200 per week. The apportioned costs of letting this room are agreed at £50 per week. Tina occupies the room for the full 52 weeks in the year.

The normal taxable income would be £7,800 (52 weeks of £150 profit) but David can claim to reduce the taxable income to £300 (£7,800 minus £7,500) under rent-a-room relief.

FOREIGN PROPERTY INCOME

8.17   As mentioned above, income from overseas property lettings is calculated and taxed broadly in the same way as income from lettings in the UK.

The income must be returned on the supplementary foreign pages of the self-assessment tax return.

As with income from a UK rental business, the net profit (or loss) for all overseas property lettings are calculated by adding up all the rental income and deducting all the allowable expenses. The expenses which are allowable are governed by the same rules as expenses of a UK property business which are discussed above.

By aggregating the results of all overseas property lettings, losses from one overseas property are automatically offset against the profits from the others.

Focus

If you make a loss overall, you can offset it against future years' overseas rental profits.

UK and overseas letting businesses are taxed separately and losses from one cannot be offset against the profits from the other.

If foreign tax is charged on overseas rental income you can usually claim credit for it against the UK tax due or you can treat the foreign tax as an expense and deduct it from overseas rental income.

LEASE PREMIUMS

8.18   Where a short lease (ie a lease for a period of less than 50 years) is granted and a premium is paid, some of that premium is treated as income in the hands of the landlord and deductible rent in the hands of the tenant. The income element of the premium received is taxed on the landlord in the year of receipt.

It should be noted that these rules on premiums only relate to the grant of leases, not premiums for the assignment of leases, which are dealt with under the CGT rules.

The premium is reduced by 2% for each complete year of the lease after the first, and the resulting amount is taxable as income of the rental business so:

- where the lease is for less than two years, the full premium is taxable as income;

- 98% of the premium is taxable as income if the lease is for two but less than three years;

- 96% is taxable if the lease is for three but less than four years, etc.

The formula used is:

$r = p - ((p \times y)/50)$

r = rent;

p = premium;

y = number of complete years in the lease apart from the first.

Normally the number of complete years in the lease is treated as the term for which it was granted, but there are rules which treat a lease as being for a different period in some cases. If, for example, prior to 1 or 6 April 2013, there is a break clause in the lease, after which there will be a large increase in rent which makes it unlikely that the lease will continue beyond the break clause date, the lease will be treated as if it ended on the date of the break clause. This provision has been removed for 2013/4 onwards.

Conversely, where the lease is likely to be extended on very favourable terms, the lease will be treated as continuing beyond its end date.

Where the landlord is an intermediate landlord, and pays a premium to his landlord to secure a grant of the lease, and this is a short lease, an appropriate proportion of that payment can be deducted from the rental or premium income. If the end tenant also pays a premium, the intermediate landlord can deduct the premium paid from the premium received. Otherwise relief is spread over the rental period. HMRC's Property Income Manual (at PIM2300 *et seq*) sets out the full rules in great detail.

257

RECORD KEEPING

8.19   As a landlord, it is necessary to keep records of the rent you charge and receive, any services charged separately and the dates each property is rented out. Records should also be kept of all allowable expenses including invoices for revenue and capital costs, if you are claiming capital allowances or Replacement of Domestic Items Relief. There may also be rent books, receipts and bank statements. If the rent-a-room scheme is used, you do not need to keep a record of expenses as they cannot be claimed.

When completing a self-assessment form for UK property income for 2015/16, expenses can be grouped as a single item if the income is less the £82,000; otherwise expenses have to be shown separately. Even if income is less than £82,000, it is necessary to retain records for six years in case HMRC needs to see them.

Property income of less than £2,500 can be taxed by adjusting the landlord's PAYE code.

ANNUAL TAX ON ENVELOPED DWELLINGS (ATED)

8.20   ATED is a new tax imposed from 1 April 2013 on companies which own 'expensive' dwellings (valued at £2 million or more, or £1 million from 6 April 2015), which are let to persons connected with the owner of the company. The valuation date is the later of the date of acquisition or 1 April 2012. The value must be self-assessed, and there are penalties if the value is incorrect. HMRC require a specific value (not 'in the region of …'). Properties will need to be revalued every five years.

The returns must be done by 30 April in each year, and payment made on that date.

Tax bands depend on the property values, as follows:

Property value	Annual tax 2014/15	Annual tax 2015/16	Annual tax 2016/17
£500,000 to £1,000,000	0	0	3.500
£1,000,001 to £2,000,000	0	£7,000	7,000
£2,000,001 to £5,000,000	£15,400	£23,350	23,350
£5,000,001 to £10,000,000	£35,900	£54,450	54,450
£10,000,001 to £20,000,000	£71,850	£109,050	109,050
£20,000,001 and over	£143,750	£218,200	218,200

Where the property only falls within the ATED rules for part of the year, the tax charge is apportioned. A prior ruling can be sought on the valuation of the property if required. Where a property is subject to an ATED charge, any disposal of that property is subject to CGT at 28% on the ATED element of the gain. Only ATED losses of the same or previous years can be set off against such gains.

APPENDIX: FURNISHED HOLIDAY LETTINGS

(*ITTOIA 2005, ss 323–326A; CTA 2009, ss 265–268A*)

'Qualifying holiday accommodation' periods

(*ITTOIA 2005, s 325; CTA 2009, s 267*)

8.21

Condition	During the relevant period
Available for commercial letting	210 days (140 days for 2011/12 and earlier years)
Actually let commercially	105 days (70 days in 2011/12 and earlier years) A period of longer-term occupation is not a letting as holiday accommodation (see below)
Pattern of occupation	No more than 155 days of longer-term occupation

Notes

1   '*Qualifying holiday accommodation*' – Accommodation which is let during the tax year (or accounting period, for companies) is 'qualifying holiday accommodation' for that year or accounting period if the 'available for letting', ' actual letting' and 'pattern of occupation' conditions are all satisfied.

2   *Period of longer-term occupation* – This is a continuous period of more than 31 days during which the accommodation is in the same occupation, other than under circumstances that are not normal.

3   '*Relevant period*' – The 'relevant period' is determined as follows (*ITTOA 2005, s 324; CTA 2009, s 266*):

 • Accommodation not let by the individual or company as furnished accommodation in the previous tax year (or in the 12 months immediately before the accounting period, for companies) – 12 months beginning with the first day in the tax year or accounting period on which it is so let.

- Accommodation let by the individual or company as furnished accommodation in the previous tax year (or in the 12 months immediately before the accounting period, for companies) but not in the following tax year (or not in the 12 months immediately after the accounting period, for companies) – 12 months ending with the last day in the tax year or accounting period on which it was so let.

- Any other case – The tax year (or 12 months ending with the last day of the accounting period, for companies).

4   *Averaging election* – An individual or company who lets several properties as furnished holiday accommodation can elect for the number of days actually let to be averages over one or more of the properties, such that all the properties reach the minimum threshold of 105 days actually let for the relevant tax year (or accounting period, for companies) (see *ITTOIA 2005, s 326; CTA 2009, s 268*).

5   *'Period of grace' election* – This can be used from 2011/12 where a property has qualified as FHL either on the actual days let or because of the use of an averaging elections in the previous tax year (or accounting period, for companies). The owner can elect to treat the property as continuing to qualify for up to two later years or accounting periods, even though it does not satisfy the 'letting condition' of 105 days in those years or accounting periods. The election must be made in the first tax year or accounting period in which the letting condition is not met (see *ITTOIA 2005, s 326A; CTA 2009, s 268A*).

6   *Further information* – See HMRC's Property Income Manual at PIM4113, and also Helpsheet HS253 'Furnished Holiday Lettings' in respect of individuals etc (www.gov.uk/government/publications/furnished-holiday-lettings-hs253-self-assessment-helpsheet).

9

Allowances, reliefs and deductions

SIGNPOSTS

- **Tax calculation** – An individual's income tax liability is calculated in stages, as set out in the tax legislation (see **9.1**).

- **Personal allowances** – Nearly every individual who lives in the UK is entitled to an income tax personal allowance and it is possible in limited circumstances to transfer part of the allowance to a spouse or civil partner. There are a number of other allowances available to reduce an individual's income tax liability (see **9.2–9.5**).

- **Limit on income tax reliefs** – The amount by which an individual can reduce their taxable income by claiming certain reliefs is restricted in certain cases (see **9.6**).

- **Loan interest** – Tax relief is available for interest paid on certain loans, such as loans to buy an interest in a close company, or to invest in a partnership (see **9.7–9.13**).

- **Donations to charity** – The gift aid scheme allows charities to claim back basic rate tax paid by the donor, and higher and additional rate taxpayers to claim additional tax relief, in respect of qualifying donations (see **9.14**).

- **Deductions which reduce tax** – Certain forms of relief give a reduction in tax liability by a specified percentage (see **9.15**).

- **Appendix: Personal allowances and reliefs** – A table of amounts for 2016/17 and earlier years is included at the end of this chapter (see **9.16**).

INTRODUCTION

9.1   The calculation of an individual's income tax liability proceeds in stages, and can be broadly summarised as follows (*ITA 2007, s 23*):

- *Step 1* – Aggregate all their income that is chargeable to tax to arrive at 'total income'.

- *Step 2* – Take off deductions such as losses and allowable interest to arrive at 'net income'.

- *Step 3* – Deduct allowances such as personal allowances to arrive at 'taxable income'.

- *Step 4* – Calculate the income tax liability on each component of income.

- *Step 5* – Aggregate the income tax liabilities calculated at *step 4*.

- *Step 6* – Deduct from this items which give a reduction in income tax (such as EIS relief).

This chapter highlights the main allowances, deductions and reliefs which can be claimed in calculating an individual's income tax liability although further information can be found at www.gov.uk/topic/personal-tax/income-tax and also in *Income Tax 2016/17* (part of the *Core Tax Annuals* series, published by Bloomsbury Professional).

PERSONAL ALLOWANCES

9.2 There are several allowances available to individuals in order to reduce their income which is subject to income tax. However, certain allowances (including the personal allowance, blind person's allowance and married couples allowance) are not available to non-UK domiciled individuals who adopt the 'remittance' basis of tax under *ITA 2007, ss 809B* and *809G* (see **Chapter 57**).

Personal allowance

9.3 Most people living in the UK are entitled to an income tax personal allowance (*ITA 2007, ss 35 and 56*). This is the amount of income which can be received each year without having to pay tax on it.

The standard personal allowance for 2016/17 is £11,000 although this will be withdrawn at a rate of £1 for every £2 that the individual's income exceeds £100,000. The effect of this abatement for 2016/17 is that where an individual's income exceeds £122,000 their personal allowance will be withdrawn in full.

> **Example 9.1 – Restricted personal allowance for high income**
>
> Paul is the managing director of a family-run bakery company. He is aged 55. His income is:
>
> Salary   £110,000

Car and medical insurance benefits as per P11D   £9,000

Total income   £119,000

The income limit for the personal allowance is £100,000.

Paul's excess income over the allowance is £119,000 – £100,000 = £19,000. His personal allowance of £11,000 for 2016/17 is reduced by £9,500, being £1 for every £2 of this excess. So his personal allowance is reduced to £1,500.

Example 9.2 – No personal allowance

32-year-old Mildred runs a successful PR company and earns £124,000 a year in 2016/17.

Her excess earnings over the £100,000 limit (£124,000 – £100,000 = £24,000) mean that the whole of her personal allowance is eliminated, as the calculated reduction in the allowances (£12,000, being £1 for every £2 of this excess) exceeds the total available allowance of £11,000 for the year.

The basic personal allowance will rise to £11,500 for 2017/18 (*FA 2016, s 3*).

Individuals born before 5 April 1938 or between 5 April 1938 and 5 April 1948 were previously eligible for an age-related allowance, abated where an individual's income exceeded the age-related allowance income limit. This is no longer available from 6 April 2016 as the standard personal allowance exceeds the level at which the age-related allowances were set (see **9.17**).

Marriage allowance

9.4   Since April 2015, a spouse or civil partner is able to transfer 10% of their standard personal allowance to their spouse or civil partner.

The allowance can only be transferred from a spouse or civil partner whose income falls below the personal allowance to their spouse or civil partner who is liable to income tax at the basic rate of tax, thus the benefit of the allowance for 2016/17 is £220 (ie £11,000 x 10% = £1,100 @ 20%).

Further details can be found at www.gov.uk/marriage-allowance.

Other personal allowances

9.5   There are several other personal allowances available to individuals:

- *Blind person's allowance* – This allowance is available to individuals who are registered blind or severely sight impaired and is added to the standard personal allowance. The allowance can be transferred in part or full to a spouse or civil partner and the rate of the allowance for 2016/17 is £2,290. Further details can be found at www.gov.uk/ blind-persons-allowance.

- *Married couples allowance* – Although the married couples allowance was abolished with the introduction of independent taxation, couples where at least one of the spouses or civil partners was born before 6 April 1935 can continue to claim the relief. The maximum allowance for 2016/17 of £8,355 is relieved at a rate of 10%. It is reduced by £1 for every £2 of income over the age-related allowance limit of £27,700 to a minimum figure of £3,220.

- *Dividend allowance* – Introduced with effect from 6 April 2016 dividends falling within the dividend allowance will not be subject to income tax. This allowance is structured as a nil rate band rather than an exemption, so any income falling within this allowance will continue to erode the tax band within which it falls. The dividend allowance is set at £5,000 for 2016/17 (see **7.10**).

- *Savings allowance* – Introduced with effect from 6 April 2016 interest falling within the personal savings allowance will not be subject to income tax. This allowance is structured as a nil rate band rather than an exemption, so any income falling within this allowance will continue to erode the tax band within which it falls. The savings allowance is set at £1,000 for basic rate taxpayers and £500 for higher rate taxpayers for 2016/17 (see **7.4**).

- *Rent-a-room relief* – This relief provides a limited exemption from income tax on the rental income received for providing residential accommodation in your only or main home. The level of rent-a-room relief is set at £7,500 for 2016/17 (see **8.16**).

LIMIT ON INCOME TAX RELIEFS

9.6   The total amount of income tax relief an individual can claim at *step 2* (see **9.1**) in any one tax year is limited to the greater of £50,000 or 25% of the individual's adjusted net income (*ITA 2007, s 24A*). The reliefs that are included in the restriction are:

- *Trade losses* – Set against general income (*ITA 2007, s 64*), relief for early years (*ITA 2007, s 72*) and post-cessation trade relief (*ITA 2007, s 96*).

- *Property losses* – Set against general income (*ITA 2007, s 120)* and post-cessation property relief (*ITA 2007, s 125).*

- *Employee losses* – Claimed against general income (*ITA 2007, s 128)* and former employees' deductions for liabilities (*ITEPA 2003, s 555).*

- *Share losses* – On non-EIS/SEIS shares (*ITA 2007, Pt 4, Ch 6)* and on deeply discounted securities (*ITTOIA 2005, ss 446–448 and 453–456).*

- *Qualifying loan interest* – For interest paid on certain loans (*ITA 2007, Pt 8, Ch 1* and see **9.7**).

The legislation sets out the method of computing the limit and also explains how to calculate 'adjusted net income' as adjustments may need to be made depending on the taxpayer's pension arrangements and any charitable donations.

Example 9.3 – How the limit is computed

Lucy's total income for 2016/17 is £160,000. She claims relief for trading losses of £40,000 made in 2016/17 against her total income for that year and also for qualifying loan interest of £20,000. Lucy's relief limit is £50,000 as this is the greater of £50,000 and 25% of her income (ie £40,000).

As Lucy's claim for relief exceeds her relief limit, she can choose how best to apply the reliefs. The qualifying loan interest can only be claimed in the year it is paid and therefore she claims all of this relief of £20,000. The remaining relief available is £30,000 for the trading losses, leaving excess losses of £10,000 that can either be carried back and set against general income in 2015/16 (provided this does not mean her limit was exceeded in that previous year) or can be carried forward against future profits of the same trade.

TAX RELIEF FOR INTEREST PAID

9.7

Focus

Tax relief is available for the interest cost of certain loans. Relief is given as a deduction in the tax year in which the interest is paid.

For clarity, these rules do not apply to loans which are taken out by a business on which the interest will normally be claimed as an allowable deduction in computing the profits of the business.

The loans on which relief may be claimed are detailed below. Such relief is subject to certain restrictions, and in particular where the loan is made to a person as part of arrangements designed to reduce their income tax or capital gains tax liability (*ITA 2007, s 384A*).

Loans to buy plant or machinery

9.8   A partner in a partnership can claim relief for the interest paid on a loan to buy plant or machinery used in the partnership's business and an employee can claim relief for the interest paid on a loan to buy plant or machinery for use in carrying out the duties of the employment (*ITA 2007, ss 388–391*).

Loan to buy interest in a close company

9.9   Relief is available for interest paid on a loan applied:

- in acquiring any part of the ordinary share capital of a close company;

- in lending money to a company, which is used wholly and exclusively for the purposes of its business or that of any associated close company;

- in paying off another loan if interest on that loan would have been eligible for relief if it had continued.

There are a number of other conditions which need to be met as well as restrictions that can prevent the relief (*ITA 2007, ss 392–395*) and in particular the relief is not available where the company is a close investment holding company (see **18.2**).

Loan to buy interest in employee-controlled company

9.10   Relief is available for interest paid on a loan obtained by an individual for acquiring shares in an unquoted trading company or the holding company of a trading group which is an employee-controlled company (defined as one where more than 50% of the issued ordinary share capital of the company and more than 50% of the voting power in the company are beneficially owned by individuals who are full-time employees of the company).

The individual must be a full-time employee of the company and the shares must be acquired either before or no later than 12 months after it became employee-controlled. A number of other conditions must also be met (*ITA 2007, ss 396–397*).

Loan to invest in a partnership

9.11   Relief is available to an individual for interest on a loan to acquire an interest in a partnership or to provide a partnership with capital or a loan. This relief is prevented where the individual is either a limited partner in a limited partnership or a member of an investment LLP and in certain cases where the individual withdraws capital from the partnership (*ITA 2007, ss 398–400*).

Loan to invest in a co-operative

9.12   Relief is available for interest paid on a loan used for acquiring shares in a co-operative body or in lending money to that body which is used wholly and exclusively for its business (*ITA 2007, ss 401–402*).

Loan to pay inheritance tax

9.13   Relief is available for interest paid on a loan taken out by the personal representatives of a deceased person to pay inheritance tax (*ITA 2007, ss 403–405*).

DONATIONS TO CHARITY

9.14   Donations to a charity (or a community amateur sports club) can be made under the gift aid scheme, under which the charity can claim back the basic rate tax paid by the donor and higher rate taxpayers can claim additional tax relief.

Gift aid can be claimed on gifts of money, which include cash, cheque (when cleared), direct debit, credit or debit card, etc. Only donations from individuals qualify and the sum can be in sterling or any other currency.

But the following will *not* qualify for gift aid:

- gifts from a company;
- the write-off of a loan;
- sums paid on behalf of another person;
- conditional gifts requiring repayment or purchases of items from a donor;
- payments for goods or services;
- sums which a person is obliged to pay; and
- gifts by way of voucher.

Focus

In addition, there must be no significant benefit provided to the donor (or anyone connected to the donor such as a spouse or relative).

The measurement of whether a benefit is 'significant' or not is set out in the following chart:

Amount of donation	Maximum value of benefits
£0–£100	25% of the donation
£101–£1,000	£25
£1,001+	5% of the donation
	(up to a maximum of £2,500)

The charity can claim back sums as set out in the following example.

Example 9.5 – Tax relief for gift aid donation

Freddie makes a gift aid payment of £500 to Alcohol Research UK. The charity will claim back the basic rate tax deemed to have been deducted from the payment, as follows:

Net payment £500 (being equivalent to £625 less 20% basic rate tax of £125).

The charity can claim back £125.

Freddie pays tax at the higher rate of 40% and can therefore claim the difference between the tax deemed to have been deducted at source and his actual tax rate, as follows:

Total gross payment = £625

Basic rate tax deemed deducted at source £625 × 20% = £125

Higher rate tax to be claimed back £625 × (40% – 20%) = £125

DEDUCTIONS WHICH REDUCE TAX

9.15   The four main deductions which reduce tax are:

- *Enterprise Investment Scheme (EIS)* – If an individual subscribes for shares which qualify under the EIS, then in the tax year in which the shares are issued, his tax liability is reduced by 30% of the amount subscribed (see **7.24**).

- *Seed Enterprise Investment Scheme (SEIS)* – Subscriptions for shares which qualify under the SEIS will give tax relief at 50% of the amount subscribed (see **7.25**).

- *Venture Capital Trust (VCT)* – Subscriptions to a VCT reduce a taxpayer's liability by 30% of the amount subscribed (see **7.26**).

- *Social investment tax relief (SITR)* – Qualifying social investments reduce a taxpayer's liability by 30% of the amount invested (see **7.27**).

These income tax reliefs operate by reducing the individual's tax liability for the year, with the maximum relief available being to restrict the tax liability to nil.

APPENDIX: PERSONAL ALLOWANCES AND RELIEFS

(ITA 2007, Pt 3)

9.16

	2016/17 £	2015/16 £	2014/15 £	2013/14 £
Personal allowance				
Personal allowance	11,000	10,600	10,000	9,440
Income limit for personal allowance	100,000	100,000	100,000	100,000
Age-related allowances				
Personal allowance				
Born between 6 April 1938 - 5 April 1948	N/A	10,600	10,500	10,500
Born before 6 April 1938	N/A	10,660	10,660	10,660
Married couple's allowance				
Minimum allowance	3,220	3,220	3,140	3,040
Maximum allowance	8,355	8,355	8,165	7,915
Income limit for age-related allowances	27,700	27,700	27,000	26,100
Marriage allowance	1,100	1,060	N/A	N/A
Blind person's allowance	2,290	2,290	2,230	2,160
Savings allowance				
Basic rate taxpayer	1,000	N/A	N/A	N/A

Higher rate taxpayer	500	N/A	N/A	N/A
Dividend allowance	5,000	N/A	N/A	N/A
Rent-a-room relief	7,500	4,250	4,250	4,250

Notes

1   *Reduction in personal allowances* – Personal allowances are reduced if 'adjusted net income' (as defined in *ITA 2007, s 58*) exceeds £100,000, by £1 for every £2 above the £100,000 threshold, irrespective of the taxpayer's age (*ITA 2007, s 35*).

2   *Personal allowances* – The *Finance (No 2) Act 2015* sets the personal allowance for 2016/17 at £11,000 and the *Finance Act 2006 sets the personal allowance* for 2017/18 at £11,500.

3   *Abatement of age-related allowances* – The age-related personal allowance and the married couple's allowance are subject to abatement to the extent that income exceeds the income limit, by £1 for every £2 of income above the limit. Age-related personal allowances for individuals can be reduced below the basic personal allowance if income exceeds £100,000.

4   *Phasing out of age-related allowances* – The age-related personal allowances have not been increased since 2013/14 and were withdrawn from 6 April 2016 given that the standard personal allowance exceeded their limit at that time.

5   *Married couple's allowance* – The rate of tax relief for the married couple's allowance is 10% (*ITA 2007, s 45*). The marriage must have taken place before 5 December 2005 and at least one party to the marriage must have been born before 6 April 1935. The maximum allowance is available so long as the individual's income does not exceed the income limit for age-related allowances.

6   *Marriage allowance* – the marriage allowance provides for a limited transfer of the personal allowanced from one spouse or civil partner to the other. The taxable income of the transferor must fall below the personal allowance and the taxable income of the transferee must fall within the basic rate band.

7   *Personal savings allowance* – interest falling within the personal savings allowances will not be subject to income tax. The allowance is structured as a nil rate band of tax rather than an exemption.

8   *Dividend allowance* – dividends falling with the dividend allowance will not be subject to income tax. The allowance is structured as a nil rate band of tax rather than an exemption.

10

Tax in retirement – an overview

SIGNPOSTS

- **Scope** – Tax in retirement generally follows the taxation rules that apply to all individuals. Certain sources of income are common among retired individuals (see **10.1**).

- **State pension** – The state retirement pension is in fact taxable, although it is paid without deduction of tax (see **10.2**).

- **Occupational pensions** – These are also in general fully taxable and tax is collected under the PAYE system. Most individuals living in the UK are entitled to a basic personal allowance; retired individuals may be entitled to a higher age-related allowance (see **10.3–10.4**).

- **Investment income** – Retired individuals are taxed on interest, dividends and other investment income in the same way as other individuals (see **10.5–10.6**).

- **Other taxes** – The capital gains tax rules apply to retired individuals in the same way as other taxpayers. Inheritance tax often becomes an increasingly important consideration for individuals as they advance towards retirement and beyond (see **10.7–10.8**).

INCOME TAX

10.1   When someone reaches state pension age they no longer pay national insurance contributions, but the income tax rules will still apply. This chapter looks at some specific tax issues as they relate to retired individuals.

The first step will be to identify what sources of income are taxable and what are non-taxable. There are no special rules for people who have reached the state pension age and as with all other taxpayers it is important to carefully identify the tax treatment of any money received. Common taxable sources include:

- earnings from working as an employee (part time or full time) or as a self-employed person;

- pensions, including state pension, and annuities from private pensions;

- interest paid by banks and building societies, etc;

- dividends from shares;

- income from letting out property;

- some state benefits, such as bereavement allowance;

- income from trusts.

Some common non-taxable benefits include:

- pension credit;

- some state benefits, such as disability living allowance;

- winter fuel payment;

- war pensions;

- lottery or premium bond wins;

- industrial injuries benefits;

- interest paid on individual savings accounts (ISAs);

- some National Savings and Investments products.

STATE RETIREMENT PENSION

10.2   State retirement pension is taxable, but regular monthly payments of pension are paid without tax being deducted at source. Any tax on such payments may be collected through an increased tax deduction on other income sources as explained below.

Individuals reaching state pension age before 6 April 2016 who wished to defer taking a state pension could choose to take the extra state pension due to them as a one-off lump sum. The 'no tax deducted' treatment may vary if a lump sum is paid. The lump sum will be taxed at the highest marginal income tax rate of the individual who claims it in the year it is paid, and the Department of Work and Pensions will ask for information on the marginal income tax rate before paying the lump sum, deducting tax as appropriate before payment.

It is important to note that when working out the marginal income tax rate for this purpose, any capital gains in the year are ignored, so an individual could make a substantial capital gain in the year they receive a pension lump sum but may still only pay lower levels of income tax on that lump sum.

Example 10.1 – Calculating the marginal income tax rate

Alan is entitled to a state pension lump sum in tax year 2015/16 of £10,000.

In 2015/16 he has income of:

Earnings from his business	£29,600
State pension	£6,440

His tax free personal allowance for 2015/16 is £10,600, meaning that his total income less allowances is £29,600 + £6,440 – £10,600 = £25,440

In the same year Alan sells a flat he used as a second home and makes a gain chargeable to capital gains tax on the sale of £30,000.

In working out the tax due on the pension lump sum the capital gain is ignored, meaning that the tax due and deducted from the £10,000 will be 20%. Alan therefore gets a net figure of £8,000 from the DWP.

Your lump sum will not affect the rate at which you are already paying income tax – it will be taxed at the same rate.

Focus

As the monthly state pension is paid tax free, any tax due on this pension will be collected through some other method. Often this is done by increasing the tax deducted from payments of occupational pensions, using the PAYE coding system. This can cause some confusion as at first glance the total tax deducted from an occupational pension can appear high.

Example 10.2 – Taxing the state pension

Judith is 71 and receives a company pension of £12,000 a year and a state pension for 2016/17 of £6,204. She is entitled to a tax-free allowance of £11,000 for that year.

Her state pension is paid without deduction of tax but her company pension is taxed to take account of her state pension as follows:

	£	£
Company pension		12,000
Allowances due	11,000	
Less: used against state pension	(6,204)	

Allowances therefore available to set against company pension	(4,796)
Total taxable company pension	7,204

OCCUPATIONAL PENSIONS AND RETIREMENT ANNUITIES

10.3 Occupational pensions can either be from a former employer's pension scheme, or from a personal pension plan. Pension plans that were set up before July 1988 deliver payments in the form of a 'retirement annuity'.

All occupational pensions and retirement annuities are taxed 'at source'. HMRC inform the pension payer via a coding notice of the level of tax allowances to be applied to the pension sending a similar notice to the pensioner taxpayer.

Focus

As with all such notices, care needs to be taken to check that the correct tax is actually being deducted, as HMRC do not have an unblemished record on these matters!

If a dispute arises about the tax due and you think that HMRC should have already collected the correct tax because they already had all the necessary information and they have failed to use this information, then in some limited circumstances HMRC may agree not to collect it. This is currently under Extra Statutory Concession A19. Where both a state pension and an occupational pension are being received, the occupational pension will be used to recover the tax due on both pensions.

Example 10.2 above illustrates how the occupational pension is taxed.

Special rules apply to foreign pensions, which are defined as pensions paid by or on behalf of a person who is outside the United Kingdom to a person who is resident in the United Kingdom. Unless the pension concerned is dealt with on the remittance basis, the taxable amount of a foreign pension is 90% of the actual amount arising in the tax year (*ITEPA 2003, s 573*).

AGE ALLOWANCE

10.4 A key item in the example above is the personal allowance available to the individual. Nearly everyone who lives in the UK gets a personal allowance that allows them to receive some income free of tax. In the 2016/17 tax year, the standard personal allowance for income tax is £11,000. For people born before 6 April 1938 there was a higher tax-free allowance (known as the age allowance) which could be reduced depending on the person's annual income, as shown below. This is no longer relevant to 2016/17 and the personal allowance is £11,000 whether you are born before or after April 1938.

For 2015/16 there were two levels of personal allowance, both of which had income limits:

Basic personal allowance	£10,600	income limit	£100,000
Born before 6 April 1938	£10,660	income limit	£27,700

The income limits operate as follows:

For those born before 6 April 1938:

● compare the 'adjusted net income' to the income limit (£27,700 for 2015/16);

● if it exceeds £27,700 but is not more than £100,000, the age-related personal allowance is reduced by £1 for every £2 over the limit until the basic allowance of £10,600 is reached.

Regardless of when a person was born, for every £2 earned over £100,000 the personal allowance continues to fall by £1 with no cut-off point. For the tax year 2016/17, this can reduce the personal allowance to zero if income is £122,000 or more.

INTEREST PAID ON SAVINGS

10.5 The first consideration is whether the account which is paying the interest is taxable or tax-free. Almost all accounts will produce taxable income but individual savings accounts (ISAs) and some National Savings products are tax-free.

Before 6 April 2016, taxable interest on savings was normally subject to a deduction at source of 20% tax, with any higher rate tax due to be accounted for separately. Non-taxpayers (for example those people whose income is below the personal allowance), could apply for interest to be paid without deduction by completing Form R85.

From April 2016, this has changed and interest will normally be paid gross (see **7.6**).

DIVIDENDS

10.6 Dividend income paid on shares or unit trusts was paid with an associated tax credit up to 5 April 2016 so that only higher and additional rate taxpayers had any further tax to consider.

This position changed in April 2016. See **Chapter 7** regarding these rules.

CAPITAL GAINS TAX

10.7 The normal capital gains tax (CGT) rules apply to all individuals (see **Part 2**).

CGT will apply to assets that are acquired as a gift or are inherited. In these cases, the 'base cost' of the asset for the CGT calculation on the asset sale is based on the market value of the asset when ownership passed to the recipient. Where the asset is inherited, the market value is measured at the date of death, not the actual date of transfer.

Example 10.4 – Capital gains tax on property sale

Raj inherited a city centre flat which had been owned by his father. The flat was bought ten years earlier for £190,000 and is worth £300,000 at the time of his father's death.

Raj sold the flat a year later for £325,000.

He will have a capital gain of £25,000 (which may be mitigated depending on Raj's own position in the tax year of sale, using, for example, his annual CGT exemption).

Of course, any house which is lived in by the owner as his main residence is not subject to CGT on sale – see **Part 2**.

INHERITANCE TAX

10.8 A full explanation of the inheritance tax (IHT) rules is given at **Part 4**.

In outline, the first £325,000 of an estate is exempt from IHT (this is called the 'nil-rate band' – because tax is charged at 0%!).

The value of the estate above this figure is charged at 40%.

On death any unused part of an individual's nil-rate band can be passed on to their surviving spouse/civil partner.

Assets that pass on death between spouses or civil partners are generally exempt from IHT.

11

Income tax planning

SIGNPOSTS

- **Scope** – Some tax planning arrangements are more complicated than others, and some may require tax specialist help (see **11.2**).

- **Incorporating a business** – Sole traders or individual partners may benefit from certain tax advantages by operating their business through a company, depending on the particular circumstances (see **11.2–11.3**).

- **Property Investment Businesses** – Consider using a company rather than owning the property personally (see **11.4**).

- **Tax-efficient investments** – Some savings and investment opportunities offer certain tax advantages, subject to various conditions and limits. These include pensions, ISAs, EIS and VCTs, as well as qualifying life assurance policies (see **11.6–11.11**).

- **Loan interest relief** – Tax relief is available for interest paid in respect of certain categories of borrowing (see **11.12**).

- **High income child benefit charge** – The clawback of child benefit makes dividing income efficiently in a family more important and improves the cost effectiveness of some expenses (see **11.14**).

- **Anti-avoidance** – Tax planning may be affected by anti-avoidance provisions including GAAR (see **11.19**), or by general anti-avoidance principles established through case law (see **11.16**).

- **Other issues** – Commercial considerations must be taken into account when tax planning (**11.20**). In addition, some business sectors may be affected by specific rules dealing with personal service companies (**11.18**). Tax planning involving losses is potentially restricted in certain situations, and individuals may be affected by the 'cap' which applies to some reliefs, including certain business losses (**11.13**). There is also legislation requiring tax avoidance schemes to be disclosed to HMRC in defined instances (see **11.19**).

INTRODUCTION

11.1   This chapter covers the more straightforward methods by which a taxpayer might mitigate his income tax liability.

It should be noted that many tax mitigation schemes are highly complex, and require specialist support to ensure they are implemented correctly. Many of these arrangements do not deliver an absolute saving, simply deferring the tax and in such cases assessing the true benefit can be difficult. In most cases, such schemes will be heavily scrutinised by HMRC. Such schemes are outside the scope of this book.

INCORPORATION

11.2   When setting up a new business, the decision needs to be made as to whether the business should be operated through a company or as a sole trader or in partnership. There are many commercial considerations which can influence the business structure which should be adopted. For example, in some cases the business's customers will require that it is operated through a limited company.

Focus

For many businesses, there can be a significant advantage in operating through a company under which the proprietor takes a limited amount of remuneration and supplements his income from dividends paid to the company, as shown in the following example. However, the position must be examined taking into account the taxpayer's particular circumstances.

Example 11.1 – Sole trader vs company

Joe is planning to open a general store and his business model indicates that he will make profits of £50,000 in each year. He has no other income.

As a sole trader his tax for 2016/17 will be as follows:

Income tax	£	£
Profits	50,000	
Personal allowances	(11,000)	
Taxable income	39,000	
Tax at basic rate	32,000	6,400.00
Tax at higher rate	7,000	2,800.00
Total tax		9,200.00

National Insurance

Class 2 (abolition planned)	145.60
Class 4 on £8,060 to £43,000	3,144.60
Excess	140.00
Total NI	3,430.20.
Total tax and NI	12,630.20
	(25.3% of profits)

If Joe formed a company and took a salary of £11,500, and withdrew the rest of the profit as a dividend, the position would be:

	£	£
Company position		
Profits (before salary)		50,000
Less: salary	11,500	
and employer's NI [(a)]	468[(1)]	(11,968)
Profit before tax		38,032
Corporation tax [(b)]		(7,606)
Profits available for distribution		30,426
Joe's position		
Income tax		
Salary	11,500	
Dividend	30,426	41.926
Personal allowance		(11,000)
Taxable income		30,926
Tax at basic rate	500	100.00
Tax at dividend ordinary rate	30,426	2,281.95
Less dividend allowance	5,000	(375.00)
Income tax [(c)]		2,006.95
National Insurance [(d)]		412.80[(2)]
Total tax and NI (a+b+c+d)		10,493.75
		(21.0% of profits)
Saving by incorporation		**2,136.45**

Notes

1 £11,500 – £8,112 (secondary threshold) at 13.8%.
2 £11,500 – £8,060 (primary threshold at) 12.0%.

Transfer of assets (including goodwill)

11.3   Prior to 3 December 2014, transferring a business from a partnership or sole trader to a company could secure a significant advantage by transferring the goodwill into the company at market value. This transfer would have been subject to capital gains tax but because of entrepreneurs' relief (see **14.7**) the rate of tax would have only been 10%. Some commentators indicate that this could still be advantageous even if the rate of CGT payable is 20%. The government has also prevented the transferee company claiming a deduction for amortisation of goodwill. The position is therefore more complicated.

However, entrepreneurs' relief would still be available for transferring other capital assets into the company. This might, for example, include the business premises, although the SDLT position would need to be considered. In this way, the new business owners would have a loan account which they could draw on, having paid the 10% tax on the transfer of the property. The profits net of corporation tax can be distributed to the proprietors without any further tax charge.

There has always been concern with regard to these arrangements that there is a potential risk of a double charge to tax because if the company makes a further capital gain on disposing of the property, it will be liable to corporation tax on that gain, and the proprietors would be liable to further tax on extracting that profit. This would need to be examined in detail.

With incorporation it is always important to examine all of the aspects of the business and ensure that the business has actually been transferred. Transferring land and buildings into the company will require the appropriate legal transfer documentation. Similarly, any business licences need to be transferred in to ensure that the ownership of the business is in the right place.

Property rental businesses

11.4   From 6 April 17, relief for interest paid by businesses letting residential property, carried on by individuals, partnerships and trusts will be restricted. The relief is being reduced over 4 years to the basic rate of income tax. It could therefore be attractive for the business owner to transfer the business to a company where the profits will be subject to corporation tax after interest has been deducted. Any distribution to the shareholders would be taxed at their marginal rate for dividend income.

Any capital repayments on borrowing in the company would be repaid out of profits charged at CT rates rather than personal rates.

This might be achieved by a transfer of the business to the company in exchange for an issue for shares, but a number of factors need to be considered, including:

- whether the business qualifies as a business within the meaning of *TCGA 1992, s 162*;

- how any loans should be transferred to the company;

- whether the value of the business is sufficient to absorb any inherent gains in the properties, so there is no tax charge on transfers on the incorporation.

It is also necessary to address the question of potential double charges to tax referred to at **11.3** above. One advantage of this type of incorporation is that the base cost of the properties to the new company is their market value at the time of incorporation, so this would potentially save tax on properties sold after the incorporation. The base cost of the shares to the business owners would be reduced, so that the latent gains would crystallise when those shares are disposed of, either by gift or sale.

Although the new rules for interest relief do not apply to commercial property letting, there may still be advantages in incorporation, such as being able to repay borrowing out of income which has not suffered the higher rates of income tax.

Focus

If the business to be incorporated is operated by a partnership, then the curious rules which apply to SDLT and partnerships might mean that there may not be any SDLT charge on the incorporation. If these rules do not apply, it is likely that SDLT will be due on the market value of the properties being transferred, which could be significant; but potentially the cost could still be outweighed by the long-term benefit, particularly where there are significant borrowings.

Other tax issues

11.5   If there are losses available to carry forward in the original business these are not transferred to the company. If the consideration for the transfer of the trade consists wholly or mainly of shares the losses can be carried forward by the trader or partner and set against income derived from the company, provided he retains the shares (*ITA 2007, s 86*; BIM 75500).

There are other points to be taken into consideration, before deciding to use a company:

- retained profits are taxed at the corporate rate;

- pension provision (see **11.8**);

- potential double charges to CGT on assets owned by a company; that is the company is liable to tax on any gains and the shareholders are also liable when those gains are paid out to them;

- compliance with company law;

- need to operate PAYE;

- unwinding the structure if it proves inefficient (but see the new relief for disincorporation at **26.11**);

- the anti-avoidance regime (**11.16**).

TAX-EFFICIENT INVESTING

11.6   The first consideration in ensuring that investments are tax efficient is to maximise the family's tax allowances. For an individual, there will be no choices to make in this area, but for a family where only one of the partners has significant amounts of income, making investments in the name of the other partner can save a significant amount of tax. If, for example, the high earning partner has surplus cash to invest, any income will be taxed at his marginal rate. However, if the investments are made in the name of the lower earning partner, the income might be absorbed by personal allowances or lower rate bands.

If the income arises from dividends, possibly from a private company, there may be no additional tax in the hands of the junior partner in the family, whereas there could be a significant tax liability if the difference were paid to the higher earner. Any planning in this area would take into account the changes to dividend taxation which came in from April 2016.

Focus

Similarly, if grandparents wish to provide funds to support the family, it might be advisable to invest such funds for the benefit of the grandchildren rather than the intermediate generation, because the grandchildren will have their own personal allowances and bands of income tax. This might be achieved by way of a formal trust or the provision of funds for the grandchildren held by the parents as bare trustees.

However, it is important that the arrangements are properly documented. See the discussion below (**11.16**) about the settlements legislation which might limit the effectiveness of such arrangements where gifts are provided to benefit minor children by their parents or gifts of income to spouses.

Joint investments

11.7   Where investments are made jointly, the general rule is that the income from those investments is shared equally between husband and wife or civil partners. However, if the husband and wife do not share the income equally and do not wish for it to be taxed equally between them, then HMRC can be notified of the different proportions. It is necessary for each spouse's personal share of the income to match his personal share of the capital. The notification to HMRC will be on Form 17 and will state the proportions by which they hold the asset and that the income should be taxed on the basis of their appropriate shares.

Example 11.2 – Husband and wife: jointly owned property

Mr and Mrs Smith own a property jointly on which they receive £15,000 a year in rent. Mrs Smith is a higher rate taxpayer but Mr Smith has a limited amount of savings income and does not use all of his personal allowances. Without any planning, Mrs Smith will be taxable at 40% on half the rent at a cost of £3,000 per annum, while Mr Smith would be able to use the balance of his personal allowance and only be liable to tax at 20% on the excess.

If Mrs Smith transfers the whole of her property interest to Mr Smith, then he will be taxed on all of the rent. Alternatively if they agree to share the property as to both capital and income in a different ratio, say one third to Mrs Smith and two thirds to Mr Smith, they can make a declaration on Form 17 of the basis on which they hold the property, so that Mr Smith will be taxed on two-thirds. It is important that they share both capital and income in the same proportions. This topic is discussed in further detail in HMRC's Trusts and Estates Manual, at TSEM9800 onwards.

If the property constitutes furnished holiday lettings (taxable as a trade), then the income is taxed according to how a husband and wife decide to share income. It is not necessary for the shares of income and capital to be in the same ratio or to submit Form 17.

HMRC require evidence of how the property is held, such as a declaration of trust (TSEM9851). HMRC's view is that a declaration cannot be made where the property is owned as beneficial joint tenants, as the couple do not own the property in shares at all, but are entitled jointly to the whole of both the property and the income (TSEM9850). HMRC now appear to accept that joint bank accounts can be held in unequal shares, although providing evidence of this could be difficult.

Pensions

11.8 As contributions to pension funds attract income tax relief and the income and gains arising from pension fund investments are tax free, they have clear tax saving advantages over other investments. However, when the pension income is withdrawn the pension is taxable, subject to a right to commute, broadly, 25% of the fund to a tax-free sum on retirement; the precise position will depend on the pension scheme rules.

Tax relief on pension contributions are limited to the greater of £3,600 or the scheme member's relevant UK earnings for the tax year. The latter figure is broadly:

- employment income;
- income from trades, professions or vocations;
- income from furnished lettings businesses; and
- certain other amounts arising from intellectual property.

The minimum figure of £3,600 only applies where income tax relief is given by deduction at source, so provides for a net contribution of £2,880 for each tax year.

It is possible to contribute more than the amount allowable for income tax relief, but no tax relief would be available on the excess. There are no provisions to allow premiums paid in one year to be treated as contributions for an earlier or later year where there may be more income.

The relevant earnings limit does not apply to contributions made by the scheme member's employer. Therefore the employer could contribute amounts greater than earnings although the annual allowance limits must be considered. This would be of particular interest to taxpayers who are employees or directors of their own companies.

It should be noted that employee contributions are not eligible for relief for National Insurance purposes. It may therefore be worth considering entering into a salary sacrifice arrangement with the employer under which the employee agrees to a reduced basic remuneration in return for the employer contributing more to the employee's pension scheme. Not only will this save the employee National Insurance on his salary, but also it will reduce secondary contributions due by the employer. The employer saving might well be shared with the employee. The implications of Auto Enrolment need to be considered.

At the time of writing, there is concern that significant tax may be lost to the Treasury by schemes seeking to exploit the new freedom to take benefits largely at the member's discretion. The member over retirement age might agree to sacrifice the major part of his salary in return for a contribution by his employer. He would then take benefits from the scheme (tax free in part at least) to supplement his take-home pay. This would save income tax and National Insurance. The relaxation took effect from 5 April 2015.

With all salary sacrifice arrangements, the other consequences of agreeing to reduce salary must be considered; such as potential entitlement to benefits (for example maternity pay) or the ability to apply for a mortgage. It is important that under these arrangements the employee generally agrees to take a reduced salary so that the contract of employment is varied in order to provide for a different remuneration package. If the contract is not properly varied, then the salary sacrifice would be ineffective and National Insurance would be due.

In addition to the earnings limit, there are two further limits on pension contributions. The Annual Allowance is (considered at **6.7**) and the Life Time Allowance (considered at **6.13**). The rules are complex and must be fully appreciated.

Focus

For contributions after 5 April 2011, it is possible to bring forward unused annual allowance from the three previous years of assessment, provided that the taxpayer was a member of a registered pension scheme in those tax years.

Example 11.3 – Using the annual allowance

Fred's pension inputs for the year ended 5 April 2016 are £60,000, but he was a member of the pension scheme in the previous year when he only contributed £20,000. He was not a member of any other schemes therefore he can bring forward £20,000 to 2015/16 and will not breach the annual allowance.

If he had not been a member of a scheme in previous years or has used up his annual allowances for those years, he would have been liable to an annual allowance charge on the excess at his marginal rate of tax – £8,000 if he was a higher rate taxpayer for the year in question.

From 5 April 2016, the annual allowance will be progressively reduced where the taxpayer's income exceeds £150,000 so that it will only be £10,000 where the income exceeds £210,000 (see **6.8**). At the same time, pension input periods are be aligned to 5 April. Where the taxpayer's income varies, it may be possible to mitigate the effect, if he can control the timing of his income.

In most cases there should be no difficulty claiming a deduction for the whole contribution paid by a private company to a pension fund for its employees. However, the contribution must be incurred wholly and exclusively for earning profits. HMRC may challenge excessive contributions which don't represent a fair reward for services provided, such as to benefit a shareholder, or member of his family, where the scheme member has little influence on the results of the business. There are also rules which mean that relief for very large irregular contributions must be spread over a number of years.

Individual savings accounts

11.9   An individual is entitled to make investments in an Individual Savings Account (ISA). The income and gains from such investments are free of both income tax and capital gains tax.

The accounts are no longer split in two forms (stocks and shares accounts and cash accounts) and the fund can be transferred between stock and shares and cash as the investor chooses.

In any tax year, an individual may subscribe up to the overall limit, currently £15,240 (there is a plan to increase this to £20,000 from 6 April 2017).

While there is no tax relief for putting the investment into the ISA, there is no tax charge when the income or capital is later withdrawn, so they potentially offer similar advantages to pensions, although the amounts which can be invested are lower.

Since 6 April 2016, if money is withdrawn from an ISA, it can be returned to the fund, provided that the net contribution is within the annual limit. When one spouse or civil partner dies after 3 December 2014, it is possible to pass the benefits of an ISA to the surviving spouse or civil partner.

> **Focus**
>
> It is also possible to set up a junior ISA for any child under 18 who does not have a child trust fund. Even if the income is provided by a parent, it is not taxed on them. The annual limit for 2016/17 is £4,080.

> Again any income and gains of the fund are tax free, but in this case the fund is locked until the child reaches 18, so this is a long-term savings plan rather than something that parents can use to save for school fees for when the child starts secondary school.

EIS/SEIS/VCTs

11.10   The government offers various incentives for investing in expanding companies in the form of shares. The first, an Enterprise Investment Scheme (EIS), offers a 30% income tax relief for investments in the shares of a single company.

For example, if Joan invests £100,000 in June 2016, she can deduct £30,000 from her 2016/17 tax liability, but if this eliminates her total tax charge, any excess EIS relief will not create a tax repayment. From 5 April 2012 the limit on EIS investments by an individual for any one year is £1 million. It is possible to treat part of the investment in one tax year as if it had been incurred in the previous tax year.

There are detailed rules regulating what shares can qualify and the type of businesses involved and to ensure that the investor is not connected with the company and does not receive any value from the company in the relevant period. Normally to retain the relief, the investor must retain the shares for a minimum period of three years.

Provided the conditions continue to be satisfied throughout the relevant periods, any capital gains tax on the disposal of the shares is exempt from tax.

These investments are inherently risky, hence the significant tax advantages offered. There are various schemes operated to make EIS more widely available – for example, investment in companies set up to produce films or television programmes. Many of these schemes are structured to make the investment risk lower, but it is important to consider what the real rate of return on the investment is likely to be, because the returns often quoted take into account the income tax relief assumed to be obtained and the investor may not recover the full amount of the original sum invested.

In addition to income tax relief and exemption from income and gains, it is also possible to use the EIS scheme to defer capital gains arising on other assets until the EIS investment is realised.

Focus

A smaller scale scheme – the Seed Enterprise Investment Scheme (SEIS) – was launched with effect from 6 April 2012. This is aimed at investments in smaller companies and the amount of investment is limited to £100,000 for a single year or £150,000 over two or more years into a single company. However, the income tax relief is at 50% irrespective of the taxpayer's marginal rate.

There is also a capital gains tax advantage for investments made in SEIS companies as existing capital gains can be rolled into the shares and effectively become exempt. Prior to 5 April 2013, 100% of the gain could be 'rolled over' and from 6 April 2013, 50% of the gain can be rolled over.

Venture Capital Trusts (VCTs) enable shareholders to get similar relief to that found for EIS, but over a spread of companies by investing through a trust. Income tax relief is given on eligible investments at 30%. There is a limit of £200,000 which can be invested in a single year in the scheme. Any income and gains on qualifying shares are exempt, provided the conditions continue to be satisfied throughout the relevant period.

There are similar schemes for investments in social enterprises (*ITA 2007, Pt 5B*) and community investment finance institutions (*ITA 2007, Pt 7*).

Other savings products

11.11   National Savings and Investments offer a range of tax free products such as National Savings Investment bonds and premium bonds. It is necessary to determine whether these give a better return than other tax-free savings, although the limits may be higher, so a combination of products is probably advisable. Clearly premium bonds effectively represent a gamble and it is necessary to hold a significant amount of bonds in order to win prizes on a consistent basis.

Qualifying life assurance policies, where regular savings are made for at least ten years, give a tax-free return to the investor, although there will be taxes and costs within the fund.

There are also other life assurance products (non-qualifying policies) which are not exempt, and the taxpayer is taxed on any gain made on the policy. With this type of policy it is normally possible to make 5% withdrawals each year of the policy without paying a tax charge, although any excess will be subject to a chargeable event gain. If the policy is UK-based, the gain will normally be assumed to be net of basic rate tax, so that only higher or additional rates will be payable. The notional tax credit is not repayable. These policies are effective if they are used to defer the gains until a year in which the policy owner is liable to tax at only the basic rate.

The calculation of gains on chargeable events is complex and withdrawals at the wrong time can generate significant tax charges without any economic return. It is therefore advisable to check before taking any withdrawals from such a policy as to what the chargeable event might be and whether top slicing relief would be available to mitigate the tax liability. Often these policies are sold as blocks of smaller policies rather than one large policy. It may be more advisable to cash in a single policy rather than take a withdrawal from every policy in the block.

It is also possible to attain small tax-free gains from investments through Friendly Societies which offer a number of life assurance products, some of which will be free of tax. However, the tax-free products will be limited to fairly small amounts by way of premium. These policies usually last for ten years.

OTHER ISSUES

Borrowings

11.12   Tax relief for borrowing is now rather restricted and in particular is no longer available for funds borrowed to finance the purchase of a taxpayer's home.

However, borrowing to finance a trade is allowable. Therefore, if a taxpayer borrows to finance such a business, tax relief will be available against the profits, or possibly by set off against general income. Although relief is available for borrowing for a property rental business, rules are being phased in which will restrict that relief on loans to finance buy-to-let properties, particularly for higher-rate taxpayers.

It is usually possible to borrow to enable the business to distribute its profits to the proprietor, but if the effect is to overdraw the proprietor's capital account, interest relief may be restricted.

Focus

If the proprietor introduces a capital asset into the business, for example appropriating his house to a property letting business, the capital introduced will be the value of the asset at the time. If the business later borrows to enable that capital to be repaid, HMRC will allow a deduction for the interest (see BIM45700 *et seq*).

There are special rules for loans to invest in close companies and partnerships. These give a standalone interest relief. The application of these rules is more complex, and in particular there are rules which reduce relief if capital is returned to the borrower. Therefore special attention is required if relief is to be obtained and not lost. It should be noted that these rules require that the borrowing is not on overdraft.

It is also important to distinguish between the purpose of the loan, which determines whether relief is due, and any security given, which does not. Although relief should be available on the eligible portion of a mixed loan, it will be more straightforward to determine the amount of interest relief available if there are separate loans, in particular when allocating repayments.

Losses

11.13 Over recent years many arrangements have exploited the generous set off rules for losses. As a result significant restrictions have been placed on the use of tax losses, particularly where the taxpayer's involvement in the business giving rise to the losses is limited, or by way of partnership. Where losses may be available, a full review of the rules is required to see whether there is any restriction. Since 6 April 2013, there is a general cap on some forms of tax relief (such as losses) to £50,000 or 25% of total income (see **9.7**).

Focus

In some cases claims for loss relief may not be fully effective: where the whole of a loss must be used, it might be relieved only at basic rate or against income covered by allowances or other reliefs. Therefore, wherever possible the timing of losses should be reviewed, for example by disclaiming capital allowances, as well as timing the claims to fall into the most effective year. Also avoid creating other deductions such as pension contributions in loss-making periods.

High income child benefit charge

11.14 Where a family is claiming child benefit and one of the members of the family has adjusted net income of over £50,000, the 'partner' with the higher income is subject to the high income child tax benefit charge. As this depends on the number of children, the additional tax rate can be significant – for example 17.88% if there are two children. This gives a marginal rate of 57.88%.

If the income is shared more evenly between the 'partners', this charge might be reduced or eliminated. If a couple's joint income is £80,000, all their child benefit will be lost if their income is split £60,000:£20,000, but they will not lose any if the split is £50,000:£30,000. Therefore getting the couple's income into the right hands is even more important.

Certain costs, in particular pension contributions and gift aid, reduce adjusted net income and therefore attract tax relief at more than 40% in the band of income from £50,000 to £60,000 for families with children.

Timing of income and expenses

11.15   The timing of income and expenses can also produce savings where this can be controlled. For example a shareholder in a family company can ensure that he does not lose his personal allowance by deferring a dividend or bonus which would otherwise take his income over £100,000. Retired taxpayers may be able to use flexible pension drawdown to control the timing of their income.

For 2016/17, a taxpayer will suffer a marginal rate of tax at 60% on non-dividend income, if the taxable income falls between £100,000 and £122,200. Consider making pension contributions (see **Chapter 6**) or gift aid donations. The marginal rate on dividend income is more difficult to assess because of interaction with the other tax bands, but could be as high as 52.5%.

Similar considerations apply to the use of the use of the savings allowance.

TAX AVOIDANCE

11.16   With all tax planning, it is as well to check what tax avoidance legislation might apply.

In respect of spreading the income around the family to minimise the tax rates, it is important to consider the settlements legislation found in *ITTOIA 2005, s 624* onwards. In particular, these rules treat income arising to another person as that of the settlor under the arrangements if that settlor has retained an interest under the settlement. For example, if a taxpayer creates a discretionary trust, he will be taxed on the income of the trust if he may benefit, even if the possibility is remote (such as the property coming back to him as all other possible beneficiaries have died). These rules extend the definition of settlement beyond formal trusts to all forms of arrangement where one person has provided funds to generate income which is payable to the other person or persons.

For this purpose, a settlement involves arrangements where the settlor provides bounty (*IRC v Plummer* HL 1979, 54 TC1).Therefore it does not extend to purely commercial arrangements.

There is an exemption from this legislation where the gift consists of an outright gift to the taxpayer's spouse or civil partner, provided that the gift is not effectively a right to income.

> **Focus**
>
> The settlements legislation also applies to situations where the settlor's minor children benefit from the arrangement. There is an exemption where the total income arising from such arrangements to each child in any one tax year does not exceed £100. 'Children' includes step-children but excludes married children.

HMRC apply these rules widely and were successful in applying the legislation in the joint cases, See *Young v Pearce* and *Young v Scrutton* [1996] STC 743 where preference shares were issued to the taxpayer's wives on which substantial dividends were declared. In contrast, there was held to be no settlement in the case of *Jones v Garnett* [2007] STC 1536 where it was held that the legislation did not apply to arrangements under which Mr Jones and his wife were both shareholders of their company, Arctic Systems.

In the first two cases, the husbands arranged for the wives to own preference shares which were held to be essentially a right to income, as the shares had minimal entitlement to capital. In the second, Mrs Jones had ordinary shares in Arctic Systems, entitling her to the same rights as her husband. HMRC also sought to argue that, as Mr Jones was the breadwinner for the company, there was a settlement in that the arrangement gave Mrs Jones a disproportionate share of the income. The House of Lords accepted this but also accepted Mr Jones' argument that the transfer of a share to her was an outright gift which was not solely a right to income.

Similarly, it is also worth considering whether any of the arrangements put in place might be caught as artificial where some step has been inserted to achieve a particular objective which can be disregarded by the courts along the line of cases that started with *Furniss v Dawson* HL 1984, 55 TC 324.

Incorporation

11.17 On the question of incorporation, in addition to ensuring that the business is effectively transferred to the company and goodwill is properly valued, there are two particular anti-avoidance rules to consider. These are:

- sale of occupation income (*ITA 2007, s 773*); and

- transfers of income streams (*ITA 2007, s 809AZA*).

Both of these sections seek to prevent income being converted to capital. It should be noted that the first section does not apply to trades, so they would have no bearing on the incorporation of a trading company but would potentially apply to the incorporation of a professional practice. There is a let out (*s 784*) for sales of going concerns unless those are structured so the price paid represents a capitalisation of future earnings.

The transfer of income streams legislation is designed to ensure that, where the transferor disposes of the right to receive income without disposing of the asset which produces that income, he is taxed on the capital sum as income rather than capital and therefore does not avoid the income tax liability. This is a sweep-up clause to close the gaps in areas of legislation where such a rule does not already apply. Clearly it should not apply to a straightforward incorporation, but might catch a situation under which an agreement was made by a sole trader to sell the right to the income from the business to a company for a capital sum, while retaining the business structure.

IR35

11.18   Where an individual provides personal services to a client through an intermediary, if the arrangements are such that he would have been an employee of the client had he been engaged directly, the IR35 legislation (*ITEPA 2003, Pt 2, Ch 8*) deems there to be notional payments of remuneration by the intermediary to the worker on which PAYE and National Insurance will arise. If the worker is engaged directly by the client, then it would be the client's responsibility to operate PAYE and National Insurance. However, if the client creates an intermediary structure such as a company, that intermediary will be required to operate those taxes, which could effectively transfer the obligation from the client to the worker.

In such circumstances, it may not be sensible to incorporate the business. However, in a number of industries such as information technology, clients will often only deal with corporate suppliers so that the risks fall on the suppliers.

In May 2012, new guidance notes were published by HMRC which set out the basic risk factors suggesting when the IR35 rules might apply, but this guidance was removed in May 2015. Their current guidance can be found at www.gov. uk/guidance/ir35-find-out-if-it-applies. The issues are often finely balanced and professional advice should be taken if the position is not clear.

From 5 April 2013 the rules will apply equally to office holders.

DOTAS/GAAR

11.19   There are rules governing the disclosure of tax avoidance schemes (DOTAS) under which there are obligations for promoters of schemes which meet certain hallmarks to disclose those schemes to HMRC. Where such a disclosure is made, HMRC will normally allocate a reference number which the promoter must pass on to clients who have used the arrangement.

A taxpayer who has obtained a tax advantage from a scheme must quote the reference number of the scheme on his self-assessment return.

Where tax planning is undertaken after *Finance Act 2013* received Royal Assent (17 July 2013), the general anti-abuse rule (GAAR) must be considered. HMRC can use this to strike down arrangements which it considers abusive, even if they meet the terms of the law. This should not apply to arrangements which have been accepted prior to the rule being introduced (see **54.3**).

In addition, HMRC now have power to collect tax lost as a result the use of a scheme even if the position has not been finally agreed between the taxpayer and HMRC, where the scheme has similar features to an arrangement which the courts have ruled ineffective.

COMMERCIAL CONSIDERATIONS

11.20 It is always worth remembering that the most important objectives should be to maximise the commercial return on any investment and minimise the risks to capital. This may arise in a number of ways:

- a lower rate of real return might be the cost of choosing a tax efficient investment;

- there may be a greater risk of loss of the capital from tax efficient investments;

- there may be family risks with transferring income to other family members such as divorce or simple profligacy if you lose control of the asset;

- it may be necessary to tie up the capital for longer periods to benefit from the tax reliefs, and there might be commercial cancellation fees or significant tax costs to unwind the structures early;

- the tax-efficient products may be more difficult to understand and to therefore determine whether they are appropriate for your circumstances.

Part 2
Capital Gains Tax

12

Capital gains tax (CGT) – outline

SIGNPOSTS

- **Scope** – CGT broadly applies to individuals who are resident in the UK. However, from 6 April 2015 CGT is charged on gains made by non-residents from UK residential property (see **8.15**). CGT is also charged on trustees, but not companies (the latter pay corporation tax on chargeable gains). The main rates of CGT for individuals from 6 April 2016 are 10% and 20% (previously 18% and 28%) (see **12.1–12.2**).

- **Disposals** – CGT is charged on the total gains on all disposals in a tax year, but not disposals of exempt assets (see **12.3–12.4**).

- **Gains and losses** – Capital losses are calculated in the same way as capital gains. Some disposals are treated as being made for market value, while others are treated as taking place on a 'no gain, no loss' basis. Allowable expenditure is deducted in calculating the gain or loss. Special rules apply to the disposal of assets held on 31 March 1982. Unused capital losses can generally be carried forward against future gains (see **12.5–12.7**).

- **CGT reliefs and the annual exemption** – Various forms of CGT relief defer or eliminate capital gains, if the relevant relief conditions are satisfied. Also each individual has an annual tax free allowance for CGT (see **12.8–12.9**).

- **Compliance** – Persons who are chargeable to CGT and do not already complete a tax return must notify HMRC by 5 October following the end of the tax year. However, gains do not need to be notified to HMRC if certain conditions are satisfied. Tax returns must be filed, and CGT payments made, within statutory time limits (see **12.10**).

- **Appendix: Rates and annual exemptions** – A table of CGT rates and exemptions for 2016/17 and earlier tax years is included at the end of this chapter (see **12.11**).

INTRODUCTION

12.1   The main legislation governing CGT is in the *Taxation of Chargeable Gains Act 1992* (*TCGA 1992*), and unless otherwise stated, all references to tax legislation in **Chapters 12–16** are to *TCGA 1992*.

CGT is charged on chargeable gains made by individuals and trustees. Companies are taxed on chargeable gains but their gains are subject to corporation tax not CGT (*TCGA 1992, s 8*) (see **17.2**).

Individuals who are resident in the UK are liable to CGT on disposals of all assets whether the assets are in the UK or elsewhere (*TCGA 1992, s 2(1)*).

Non-residents trading in the UK are liable to CGT on gains on business assets in the UK (*TCGA 1992, s 10*). In addition, from 6 April 2015 non-residents are liable to CGT on gains made from UK residential property (see **8.15**)

Residence and domicile are dealt with later in the book (see **Chapters 56** and **57**).

CGT for trustees including the residence of trustees is dealt with in **Part 5**.

CGT rates

12.2   From 6 April 2008 to 22 June 2010, CGT was charged at a flat rate of 18%.

From 23 June 2010 the following CGT rates applied:

- 18% for individuals if the gain is within their unused basic rate income tax band;
- 28% for individuals for gains outside their basic rate income tax band;
- 28% for trustees and personal representatives;
- 10% for gains qualifying for entrepreneurs' relief (see **14.7**).

From 6 April 2016 the new rates of CGT are:

- 10% for individuals if the gain is within their unused basic rate income tax band;
- 20% for individuals for gains outside their basic rate income tax band;
- 20% for trustees and personal representatives;
- 10% for gains qualifying for entrepreneurs' relief and investors' relief (see **14.7**).

The previous rates of capital gains tax (18% and 28%) will continue to apply to gains on residential property that does not qualify for private residence relief (see **14.1**).

(*TCGA 1992, s 4*)

DISPOSALS – OUTLINE

Types of disposal

12.3   CGT is charged on the total gains on all disposals in a year of assessment subject to deductions for losses and the annual exemption (see **12.9**). Gains on all disposals are chargeable gains unless a particular exemption or relief is relevant (see **Chapter 14**).

A disposal occurs when you cease to own an asset. This could result from:

* a sale whether for full value consideration or not;

* a gift or transfer;

* an exchange;

Certain payments received in respect of the loss of or damage to an asset, for example insurance proceeds, may also be treated as a disposal (*TCGA 1992, s 22*).

Exempt assets

12.4   Certain assets are exempt from CGT so that no chargeable gain or allowable capital loss arises on disposals of exempt assets..

Examples of assets which are exempt for CGT are:

* funds in sterling (*TCGA 1992, s 21(1)(b)*);

* foreign currency bank account withdrawals or transfers, with effect from 6 April 2012 (*TCGA 1992, s 252*). Previously, an exemption applied to foreign currency for an individual's personal expenditure outside the UK;

* private motor cars but not personalised number plates (*TCGA 1992, s 263*);

* chattels (tangible moveable assets) disposed of for less than £6,000 (see **15.4**);

* lottery prizes, betting winnings, premium bond prizes (*TCGA 1992, s 51*);

- life assurance policy proceeds paid to the original policy owner (*TCGA 1992, s 210*).

There is no disposal when you inherit an asset on the death of an individual until you dispose of the asset. It may be necessary to obtain information from the executors of the deceased's estate to find out how to calculate the gain or loss on a later sale (*TCGA 1992, s 62*).

> **Focus**
>
> CGT does not only arise on sales at market value but also on sales for less than market value and gifts. CGT can also be due when a capital sum is received in respect of an asset.

CALCULATING GAINS AND LOSSES

Actual and 'deemed' proceeds

12.5   The gain or loss on each individual asset is computed separately. All gains and losses in a tax year are then aggregated. Whether any tax is due on the aggregate gain depends on whether any relief is available against the gain. Gains may also be reduced or eliminated by the annual exemption or by losses.

The gain or loss on a disposal is calculated by taking the actual proceeds realised (or in some cases the deemed proceeds) and deducting from it the allowable expenditure:

- In the straightforward case of a sale at full market value, the actual sales proceeds are used in the calculation. However, in the case of a gift of an asset, the sales proceeds are deemed to be the market value at the date of gift (*TCGA 1992, s 17*).

- Some disposals are treated as taking place at no gain or loss (see **13.3**).

- Disposals made for less than full market value consideration are also treated as being made for full open market value, again unless they are deemed to take place at no gain or loss (*TCGA 1992, s 17*).

- Transactions between connected persons are also deemed to take place at market value (*TCGA 1992, s 18*).

An individual is connected with his spouse or civil partner and with any relative of himself or of his spouse or civil partner, and with the spouse or civil partner of any such relative (*TCGA 1992, s 286*).

'Relative' for this purpose means brother, sister, ancestor or lineal descendant.

If an individual is a partner in a partnership, he is connected with his business partners and each other's spouses, civil partners and relatives except in connection with acquisitions and disposals of partnership assets made pursuant to bona fide commercial arrangements.

If an individual is a trustee, he is connected with the settlor of the trust, any person connected with the settlor, and any company connected with the settlement.

Allowable expenditure

12.6 The allowable expenditure which is deducted from the sales proceeds falls under four categories (*TCGA 1992, s 38*):

- The base cost or original acquisition cost of the asset.

- Improvement expenditure incurred for the purpose of enhancing the value of the asset and reflected in the state of the asset at the time of disposal.

- Expenditure incurred in establishing title to the asset.

- Incidental costs of acquisition or disposal.

In some cases, the base cost of an asset may not be the historical cost. For example, if the asset has been acquired as a gift or on a transfer between connected parties at less than market value then the market value used as sale proceeds for the transferor is the base cost to the transferee.

Special provisions also apply to the disposal of assets acquired before 31 March 1982 where the acquisition cost for tax purposes is re-based to the asset's market value on 31 March 1982 (*TCGA 1992, s 35*).

Example 12.1 – Sale of shares

In June 2000, you buy some shares for £2,500 and sell them for £12,500 in May 2016.

	£
Sales proceeds	12,500
Base cost	(2,500)
Gain	10,000

303

Example 12.2 – Sale of property

In March 2000, you buy a holiday home for £200,000. Stamp duty and legal costs incurred on the acquisition were £2,000.

In 2005, you spend £10,000 on an extension to the property.

In June 2016, you sell the property for £350,000 and incur fees from estate agents and solicitors of £3,000.

	£	£
Sales proceeds		350,000
Incidental costs of disposal		(3,000)
Net proceeds		347,000
Base cost	200,000	
Incidental costs of acquisition	2,000	
Improvements	10,000	(212,000)
Gain		135,000

Focus

The gain or loss is calculated by deducting allowable expenditure from proceeds. In some cases the proceeds are deemed proceeds rather than actual proceeds. Special rules apply to transactions between 'connected' persons.

Losses

12.7   Broadly, capital losses are calculated in the same way as capital gains so you make a loss if you sell an asset for less than your acquisition cost, including costs of acquisition, disposal and improvement (*TCGA 1992, s 16*).

If an asset is exempt from capital gains tax then a loss on its disposal cannot be an allowable capital loss. This would apply for example to a loss on disposal of a motor car.

Capital losses incurred in a tax year are firstly set off against gains of the same tax year. Any losses not utilised can then be carried forward for set off against gains of subsequent years (*TCGA 1992, s 2(2)*).

A loss on a disposal to a connected person is deductible only from chargeable gains arising on other disposals to the same person (*TCGA 1992, s 18(3)*).

Individuals are usually entitled to an annual exemption for capital gains tax which means that there is no liability to capital gains tax if your aggregate gains for the tax year are below the annual exemption for that year (see **12.9**). Capital losses in a tax year are set against gains in the same tax year even if the result is that some or all of the annual exemption is wasted.

Capital losses brought forward from earlier years are deducted only to the extent that they are needed to reduce the net gains to the annual exemption for the tax year. Any unused losses can be carried forward to future tax years (*TCGA 1992, s 3(5A)*).

Example 12.3 – Capital gains and losses

In 2016/17, Mr A makes two capital disposals resulting in a loss on shares in X plc of £2,000 and a gain on a holiday home of £22,000.

He has capital losses carried forward from earlier years of £10,500.

	£	£
2016/17		
Capital loss		(2,000)
Capital gain		22,000
Net gain		20,000
Capital losses brought forward	(10,500)	
Utilised to reduce gain to annual exemption	8,900	(8,900)
		11,100
Less: Annual exemption		(11,100)
Gain		0
Losses carried forward to 2017/18	(1,600)	

There are no general provisions allowing capital losses to be carried back against the gains of earlier periods (*TCGA 1992, s 2(3)*).

However, there is a special provision for capital losses realised by an individual in the tax year of his death under which losses in excess of gains in the year of death may be carried back against capital gains in the three preceding tax years (*TCGA 1992, s 62(2)*).

RELIEFS – OUTLINE

12.8   There are a number of reliefs against capital gains tax which can reduce, eliminate or defer capital gains tax.

An important relief for individuals is private residence relief which means that if you sell your own home you don't usually pay capital gains tax on any gain you make (see **14.1**). However, private residence relief and the other reliefs available all have detailed conditions which need to be studied to make sure that they are available in any particular case.

Annual exemption

12.9   Individuals have an annual tax-free allowance for CGT purposes: the annual exemption (*TCGA 1992, s 3*).

The annual exemption for the tax year 2016/17 is:

£11,100 for each individual;

£5,550 for most trustees.

If your aggregate gain for the tax year is above the annual exemption, you will be subject to CGT on the excess. Aggregate gains below the annual exemption will not be taxable.

COMPLIANCE (REPORTING AND PAYMENT OF CGT)

12.10

Focus

If CGT is due or a capital loss has accrued which you wish to carry forward and you have not received a notice to complete a tax return, you are required to notify HMRC that you are chargeable before 5 October after the end of the tax year (*TMA 1970, s 7(1)*).

If you normally complete a tax return, you will need to complete some additional pages to return capital gains and losses.

You do not need to report gains on assets that are exempt from CGT, such as private motor cars or your private residence (in most cases).

You do not need to report gains if all of the following conditions are met:

- There is no CGT to pay.

- The total gains (before you deduct any losses) are equal to or lower than the annual exemption, ie £11,100 for 2016/17.

- The total disposal proceeds are no more than four times the annual exemption, ie £44,400 for 2016/17.

The return must be submitted by the filing date which is 31 January following the end of the tax year for electronically submitted returns. For paper returns, the deadline is 31 October following the end of the tax year.

Non-residents disposing of UK residential property after 5 April 2015 must report the disposal to HMRC within 30 days of the disposal.

CGT is payable by 31 January following the end of the tax year.

The Autumn Statement 2015 announced that from April 2019 a payment on account of tax due on a disposal of residential property must be made within 30 days of the date of disposal.

Interest is charged on overdue tax from the due date to the date of payment at a rate set by HMRC. CGT which is paid more than 28 days late is also subject to a surcharge of 5% with an additional 5% surcharge if the tax is paid more than six months late.

APPENDIX: RATES AND ANNUAL EXEMPTIONS

(TCGA 1992, ss 3, 4, Sch 1)

12.11

Tax year	Annual exempt amount		Tax rate paid by		
	Individuals, personal representatives (PRs) and trusts for disabled	General trusts	Individuals within:		Trustees and PRs
			Basic rate band	Higher tax bands	
	£	£	%	%	%
2016/17	11,100	5,550	10	20	20
2015/16	11,100	5,550	18	28	28
2014/15	11,000	5,500	18	28	28
2013/14	10,900	5,450	18	28	28
2012/13	10,600	5,300	18	28	28
2011/12	10,600	5,300	18	28	28
2010/11 (23 June 2010 to 5 April 2011)	10,100	5,050	18	28	28
2010/11 (6 April to 22 June 2010)	10,100	5,050	18	18	18
2009/10	10,100	5,050	18	18	18

Notes

1   *Remittance basis users* – From 2008/09, an individual who claims to use the remittance basis for a tax year is not entitled to the annual capital gains exemption for that year *(ITA 2007, s 809G)*. However, the annual exempt amount remains available where the remittance basis applies without a claim – eg where the individual's unremitted foreign income and gains are less than £2,000 for the year *(ITA 2007, s 809D)*.

2   *Personal representatives* – The annual exemption is available to personal representatives in the tax year of death and the following two years *(TCGA 1992, s 3(7))*.

3   *Trustees* – The annual exemption for trustees is divided by the number of qualifying settlements created by one settlor, subject to a lower limit of 10% of the annual exemption for individuals for that tax year (*TCGA 1992, Sch 1, para 2*).

4   *2010/11* – In this year the CGT rates changed with effect from 23 June 2010, but the annual exempt amounts were not changed and applied for the whole tax year.

5   *Entrepreneurs' relief rate* – A 10% rate of capital gains tax applies from 23 June 2010, in respect of gains qualifying for entrepreneurs' relief (*TCGA 1992, s 169N(3)*).

6   *Investors' relief rate* – A 10% rate of capital gains tax applies from 6 April 2016, in respect of gains qualifying for investors' relief (*TCGA 1992, s 169VC(2)*).

7   *Residential property gains* – From 6 April 2016 gains arising on the disposal of residential property are taxed at 18% where they fall within the basic rate band and 28% where they fall within the higher or additional rate band.

8   *Earlier years* – For 2007/08 and earlier tax years, capital gains were taxed as the top slice of income at income tax rates.

13

Disposals

SIGNPOSTS

- **Scope** – There are rules for CGT to determine the time of disposal under a contract. Disposals for CGT purposes may be actual or 'deemed' and certain disposals are treated as taking place at no gain or loss (see **13.1–13.3**).

- **Part and 'small' disposals** – In calculating the gain or loss on a part disposal, a proportion of allowable expenditure can be taken into account. Special treatment is available in respect of 'small' disposal proceeds in certain circumstances (see **13.4–13.5**).

- **Compensation** – If compensation or damages are derived from the right to take court action, the disposal of that right can result in a capital gain. However, by concession the receipt is treated as derived from the underlying asset, if there is one (see **13.6**).

TIME OF DISPOSAL

13.1   Where an asset is sold under the terms of a contract, for capital gains tax purposes the disposal takes place when contracts are exchanged and not when the contract is completed (*TCGA 1992, s 28*).

However, if the contract is never completed, there is no disposal (CG14261).

If the contract is conditional, the disposal takes place when the condition is satisfied.

In the case of a disposal where there is no corresponding acquisition, the time of the disposal is the time when the proceeds are received (*TCGA 1992, s 22*).

ACTUAL AND DEEMED DISPOSALS

13.2   An actual disposal occurs when you cease to own an asset.

Capital gains tax rules treat certain transactions as 'deemed disposals'.

There is a deemed disposal when a capital sum is derived from an asset, even though there is no change in ownership of the asset (*TCGA 1992, s 22*).

An example of this is a rights issue on quoted shares. The shareholder may decide not to take up the rights and instead sell the rights for cash. The cash received is treated as a part disposal of the shareholding even though there is no actual disposal of the shares.

Another instance where there is a deemed disposal is a negligible value claim (*TCGA 1992, s 24(2)*) (see **14.22** for more details).

> **Focus**
>
> There is no deemed disposal for CGT on death. There may be inheritance tax due but for CGT purposes the personal representatives acquire the deceased's assets at market value at the time of death. Assets transferred to a legatee by the personal representatives are treated as transferred at the same market value which becomes the legatee's base cost for CGT. Disposals of assets to third parties by the personal representatives are liable to CGT in the normal way.

NO GAIN, NO LOSS DISPOSALS

13.3 Certain disposals are treated as taking place at no gain or loss. This means that the allowable expenditure for the person selling the asset is treated as their sales proceeds. It is also treated as allowable expenditure for the person acquiring the asset.

> **Focus**
>
> The most common example of this is transfers between husband and wife or between civil partners (*TCGA 1992, s 58(1)*).

> **Example 13.1 – Inter-spouse/civil partner transfer**
>
> Mrs A owns a buy-to-let property which she acquired in 2005 for £80,000. She decides to transfer it to her husband, Mr A, in 2010 when it is worth £100,000 and he sells it to Mr C in 2016 for £110,000.
>
> There is no gain or loss on the transfer to Mr A, who is deemed to acquire the asset for £80,000.

On the sale to Mr C, Mr A's basic allowable expenditure is £80,000 together with any incidental costs of acquisition or disposal such as legal and estate agents' fees.

PART DISPOSALS

13.4　For capital gains purposes, a disposal includes a part disposal, which could be the disposal of a physical part of the asset or realising part of the value of an asset (*TCGA 1992, s 21(2)*).

In order to compute the gain on a part disposal, it is necessary to determine the allowable expenditure that can be deducted in the calculation (*TCGA 1992, s 42*).

Unless costs can be identified specifically to the part sold or the part retained, the costs attributed to the disposal are the following fraction of the total allowable costs:

$$\frac{A}{A+B}$$

Where

A is the proceeds for the part disposal; and

B is the value of the part retained.

Example 13.2 – Part disposal of land

Mr C bought land in 2000 for £100,000. In 2016, he sells about half of the land for £80,000. The value of the land retained is £120,000.

	£	£
Sales proceeds 2016		80,000
Cost of land 2000	100,000	
Attribute costs using A/(A+B) formula		
A	80,000	
B	120,000	
A/(A+B)	0.4	
Attributable costs (0.4 × £100,000)		(40,000)
Gain		40,000
Cost of land retained (£100,000 less £40,000)		60,000

SMALL DISPOSAL PROCEEDS

13.5   The receipt of a capital sum derived from an asset is a disposal for capital gains tax even though the person paying the capital sum does not acquire an asset.

There is provision for a taxpayer receiving a capital sum in respect of shares to elect that there is no disposal for capital gains tax purposes if the capital sum is either less than 5% of the value of the asset or £3,000. If the election is made, the capital sum is deducted from the allowable costs for future disposals (*TCGA 1992, s 122*).

Example 13.3 – Treatment of small capital sum

Mrs A has 2,000 £1 shares in Bank plc, which cost £20,000 in 2005. In 2016, Bank plc reduces its share capital to 50p shares and Mrs A receives a capital sum of £1,000.

Since the capital sum is less than £3,000, Mrs A can elect that there is no disposal and the allowable cost of the shares in Bank plc for future disposals is reduced by £1,000 to £19,000.

Note – This would only usually be advantageous to Mrs A if she has other gains to use her annual exemption against.

There is a similar relief for capital sums derived from assets other than shares under which a claim can be made that there is no disposal for CGT if the capital sum is:

●   wholly applied in restoring the asset; or

●   small as compared with the value of the asset.

Small for this purpose means 5% or less or up to £3,000 if greater. A similar relief applies to small part disposals of land but with different limits.

If this treatment is adopted, the capital sum is deducted from the cost of the asset to be used in any later sale (*TCGA 1992, s 23*).

COMPENSATION

13.6   If a person receives compensation or damages as a result, for example, of a court case, he is treated as having disposed of the right to take action. This could result in a capital gain (*Zim Properties Ltd v Proctor* ChD 1984, 58 TC 371).

Following the *Zim Properties* case, the tax position on compensation and damages was clarified (ESC D33).

If the compensation arises because an asset has been totally or partially lost, destroyed or damaged, any compensation received can be treated as deriving from the asset rather than the right to take action. Provided the asset would be subject to capital gains tax, the receipt of compensation is treated as a disposal or part disposal of the asset. The provisions for small disposal proceeds (see **13.5** above) may also be relevant.

Focus

Sometimes compensation is received and there is no asset that it can be related back to, for example a claim against a professional person for negligent advice or actions in respect of private or domestic matters. In these cases, the compensation is usually exempt from CGT under ESC D33. From 27 January 2014, only the first £500,000 of such compensation is automatically exempt. A claim can be made for relief above that amount but HMRC will not normally give relief.

14

Reliefs

SIGNPOSTS

- **Private residence relief** – A gain on the disposal of one's only or main residence is usually exempt from CGT. A CGT liability may arise in certain situations, eg following periods of absence, although some absences are permitted within limits. If more than one property is used as a residence, an election is available to specify the main residence. Non-residents may be liable to UK CGT on the sale of a residential property unless it qualifies for Private Residence Relief (see **14.4**). 'Lettings relief' may be available if all or part of the property is rented out at some stage of ownership, up to a maximum of £40,000 (see **14.1–14.6**).

- **Entrepreneurs' relief** – This relief can reduce the CGT rate to 10% on gains from qualifying business disposals of up to £10 million, if certain conditions are satisfied. A claim is required (see **14.7– 14.12**). Budget 2016 introduced a new investors' relief, similar to entrepreneurs' relief but for external investors (see **14.13**).

- **'Holdover' relief** – Two forms of holdover relief are available, one for gifts of business assets, and the other for certain disposals including gifts on which inheritance tax is chargeable (see **14.14–14.15**).

- **Rollover relief** – Traders may claim rollover relief if proceeds from the disposal of qualifying business assets are reinvested in replacement ones, subject to certain conditions (see **14.16–14.19**).

- **Incorporation relief** – A specific relief applies to defer gains arising broadly where sole traders or partners incorporate their business by transferring it to a company in return for shares. The relief is automatic if the relevant conditions are satisfied, although an election is available to opt out of it (see **14.20**).

- **Other reliefs** – Some forms of investment offer certain CGT advantages, such as the Enterprise Investment Scheme and Venture Capital Trusts (see **14.21–14.24**).

- **Appendix: Entrepreneurs' relief** – A table of relief limits for the current and earlier years is included at the end of this chapter (see **14.25**).

PRIVATE RESIDENCE RELIEF

What is a dwelling-house?

14.1   A gain on the disposal of a property which is, or has at any time in the individual's period of ownership been, his only or main residence is exempt from capital gains tax (*TCGA 1992, s 222*).

There is no definition of what can be a 'dwelling-house' in the terms of the legislation so it can be a house, a flat or even a caravan or houseboat.

A 'dwelling-house' could be made up of more than one property. A detached garage or children's playroom would usually be part of the dwelling-house and it is possible that cottages occupied by domestic staff may also be part of a dwelling-house.

What are gardens or grounds?

14.2   The exemption is also extended to garden or grounds for 'occupation and enjoyment with that residence' (*TCGA 1992, s 222(1)(b)*).

The garden or grounds should normally be less than 0.5 hectares unless a larger area is required for enjoyment of the dwelling-house (*TCGA 1992, s 222(3)*).

'Garden or grounds' is not defined in statute. HMRC regard a garden based on a dictionary definition as:

'a piece of ground, usually partly grassed and adjoining a private house, used for growing flowers, fruit or vegetables, and as a place of recreation' (CG64360).

Grounds are suggested to be:

'Enclosed land surrounding or attached to a dwelling house or other building serving chiefly for ornament or recreation.'

Based on the above, agricultural land used for a trade is not part of the garden or grounds but paddocks and orchards and overgrown land may be part of the garden or grounds.

What is a residence?

14.3   There is no definition in the legislation of 'residence'.

In simple terms, 'A residence is a place where somebody lives' as stated by Nourse J in *Frost v Feltham* Ch D 1980, 55 TC 10. A residence may be in the UK or abroad.

It appears that residence is a matter of quality rather than quantity and HMRC will not suggest any minimum period of occupancy which will mean that a property qualifies as a residence (CG64435).

In a recent case involving a number of residences and relationship breakdowns, a property occupied for only eight weeks qualified for private residence relief (*Richard James Dutton-Forshaw v HMRC* [2015] UKFTT 478).

In some limited circumstances from 6 April 2015 the taxpayer may have to meet a 'day count test' in order to qualify for the relief (see **14.4** below).

> **Focus**
>
> The exemption applies in full if the property has been the individual's main residence throughout the period of ownership although relief was always given for the final 18 months of ownership. Before 6 April 2014, the final period exemption was 36 months. Periods of ownership before 31 March 1982 are ignored (*TCGA 1992, s 223(1)*).

If the property has not always been the main residence, then the relief is available for a fraction of the gain. The fraction is calculated as the period of main residence (including the last 18/36 months of ownership even if not the main residence then) divided by the total period of ownership (*TCGA 1992, s 223(2)*).

Permitted periods of absence

14.4   Certain periods of absence are 'permitted' and can be ignored in the calculations (*TCGA 1992, s 223(3)*):

- periods of absence for any reason which in total do not exceed three years;

- any period throughout which the taxpayer was employed outside the United Kingdom; and

- periods of up to four years in total when the taxpayer could not reside in the property because of the requirements of his employment.

In all cases it is important that the property is the main residence before and after the absence, although this is relaxed in certain cases where the individual is unable to return to the property by reason of their employment.

Example 14.1 – Absence whilst working abroad

Amy purchased a house in August 2000 from which date it was used as her only residence until February 2001 when she moved to Dubai to work for her employer. She returned to the UK in August 2006 when she again occupied the house as her only residence.

In February 2007 she decided to put the house up for sale and moved back to live with her parents in their house. Unfortunately her house was not sold until August 2016 when a gain of £90,000 was realised.

	Years	£
Gain		90,000
Total period of ownership		
August 2000 – August 2016	16.0	
Total period of residence		
August 2000 – February 2001	0.5	
August 2006 – February 2007	0.5	
Permitted absence		
February 2001 – August 2006 (overseas employment)	5.5	
February 2015 – August 2016 (last 18 months)	1.5	
	8.0	
Relief – 8.0/16		(45,000)
Chargeable gain		45,000

From 6 April 2015, non-UK residents are subject to UK capital gains tax on gains on disposals of UK residential property. If the property is the seller's main home then Private Residence Relief may be available against the gain.

As a part of the introduction of these provisions, there are new rules *which apply to UK residents as well as non-residents* which can restrict the availability of the relief where the property is located in a different territory to the one in which the taxpayer is resident. A residence owned by a UK or non-UK resident will only be capable of qualifying for PPR if it is located in a territory in which the individual, their spouse or civil partner is resident or, where it is located in a different territory, the individual meets the 'day count test' in relation to the residence.

The day count test will be met if the individual or their spouse/civil partner spend at least 90 days in the property in the tax year (although no one day can be counted twice by virtue of the individual and their spouse/civil partner both being there at the same time).

Where the individual or their spouse/civil partner has an interest in more than one dwelling in the territory in which the property is located, days spent in those other dwellings can be aggregated with days spent in the property in question to determine whether the 90-day threshold is met. But you can only nominate *one* property for Private Residence Relief.

Where the individual owns the property for only part of a tax year, the 90-day threshold in the day count test will be reduced pro rata.

If the 90-day rule is not met, the individual will be counted as away from the property for that tax year.

> **Focus**
>
> A non-resident individual who wishes to make sure they satisfy the day count test so that a property qualifies for PPR will have to be careful that they do not prejudice their residence status under the Statutory Residence Test; for example days spent in the UK is crucial in the sufficient ties test (see **56.4**).

More than one property

14.5   For the purpose of private residence relief, an individual and his spouse (or civil partner) can only have one main residence at any time (*TCGA 1992, s 222 (5)*).

> **Focus**
>
> If a taxpayer owns several properties which are used as residences, then he may elect to specify which property is the main residence.
>
> The election must be made within two years of acquiring a second residence.
>
> If no election is made, a main residence will be determined based on the facts.

Let properties

14.6   Normally private residence relief will not apply to an investment property, such as a 'buy-to-let' property.

14.7 *Reliefs*

There is a provision which disapplies private residence relief if a house was bought for the purpose of realising a gain (*TCGA 1992, s 224(3)*).

There is a specific 'lettings relief' which applies if a taxpayer has let the whole or part of his residence as residential accommodation for part of the period of ownership. Up to £40,000 of the gain which would otherwise be taxable can be exempt (*TCGA 1992, s 223(4)*).

Example 14.2 – Lettings relief in action

Charlotte sells her house making a gain of £60,000. 60% of the house has been used as her main residence and 40% has been let.

	£	£
Gain on sale of property		60,000
Private residence relief 60% of £60,000		(36,000)
Gain on let part		24,000
Letting relief		
Lowest of:		
Statutory limit	40,000	
Private residence relief	36,000	
Gain on let part	24,000	(24,000)
Gain		0

Focus

Private residence relief was the subject of much press coverage in relation to the MPs' expenses scandal. With the reduction of the final period relief and the changes relating to properties abroad, the relief is now being restricted, possibly in response to this publicity.

ENTREPRENEURS' RELIEF

Entrepreneurs' relief limits

14.7   Entrepreneurs' relief was introduced for disposals after 6 April 2008 (*TCGA 1992, s 169H*) to replace taper relief but, it was modelled more on retirement relief in that each individual has a lifetime cap on relief. Also certain assets which qualified for taper relief do not qualify for entrepreneurs' relief.

When entrepreneurs' relief was first introduced, the lifetime cap was only £1 million but it has been gradually increased to £10 million for disposals after 5 April 2011 which makes it a very valuable relief (*TCGA 1992, s 169N*).

For previous relief limits please see the table at the end of this chapter.

Qualifying disposals for entrepreneurs' relief

14.8   Entrepreneurs' relief is available against gains on 'qualifying disposals' which fall into one of the following categories (*TCGA 1992, s 169I*):

A sole trader, who has owned a business for at least 12 months, sells:

- the whole or part of his business; or

- assets used in his business and sold within three years of cessation of the business.

A partner in a business who:

- sells the whole or part of his interest in the assets of the partnership which he has owned for at least 12 months; or

- sells assets used in a sole trader business to the partnership which is taking over his business and the disposal takes place with three years of the date of cessation of the business and the individual has owned the business for the 12 months before cessation.

A shareholder who sells shares or securities in his personal trading company and:

- the shareholder owned at least 5% of the ordinary share capital and controlled at least 5% of the voting rights;

- the shareholder is an officer or employee of the company (or another company in the same group); and

- these conditions are satisfied throughout the 12 months before the disposal.

A recent case (*Castledine v HMRC* [2016] UKFTT 0145) considered the test of ownership of 5% of the ordinary share capital. The company had A ordinary shares, B ordinary shares, preference shares and deferred shares in issue and the taxpayer held 5% of the share capital if the deferred shares were excluded, but only 4.99% of the share capital if the deferred shares were taken into account. He was denied entrepreneurs' relief because for this purpose ordinary share capital means all the company's issued share capital (however described), other than capital the holders of which have a right to a dividend at a fixed rate but have no other right to share in the company's profits. The deferred shares had to be brought into the calculation despite the fact that they had no voting rights, no rights to dividends and were probably worthless.

For this purpose, a company is a trading company if its activities do not include to a substantial extent activities other than trading activities. 'Substantial' in this context means more than 20%. This 20% test should be applied over turnover, asset base, expenses and time spent by management and employees over a period but it is also necessary to look at the business in the round. It is possible for the company to apply to HMRC under the non-Statutory Clearance procedure in cases where they have been unable to confirm to a shareholder that the company is trading for entrepreneur relief.

Focus

There are potential problems where a trading company has large cash balances. Assuming that these have built up from trading operations and they are not actively managed, then HMRC do not usually take the view that there is a non-trading activity. However if the balances are very large, it is necessary to look carefully at the 20% test above to see if the status is prejudiced.

Finance Act 2015 included a number of changes to entrepreneurs' relief which were intended to block perceived abuses, in particular individuals exploiting the joint venture provisions in order to qualify for the relief where in reality, they were not beneficially entitled to a 5% interest in the trading company. Unfortunately, this impacted on some genuine commercial arrangements and changes in *Finance Act 2016* reverse these changes with effect from 18 March 2015 by introducing new definitions of trading company and trading group for entrepreneurs' relief purposes.

Practically this means that for an individual who owns 20% of the shares in a company (A) which has a 40% interest in a trading company (B):

- A is treated as carrying on a part of the business of B for the purpose of determining the trading status of A; and

- The individual has an effective interest of 8% (20% of 40%) in B, more than 5% and therefore may qualify for the relief.

A shareholder claiming entrepreneurs' relief against gains on shares in his personal company does not have to work full time in order to qualify as an officer or employee and can be a non-executive director or the company secretary.

To help employee shareholders who would not otherwise qualify for entrepreneurs' relief (as they do not pass the 5% test) entrepreneurs' relief has been extended to apply to the disposal by an employee or officer of a company of shares in that company (or a company in the same trading group) when the shares meet the requirements of the Enterprise Management Incentive (EMI) scheme. (*FA 2013, Sch 24*).

Associated disposals

14.9   Relief is also available for gains on 'associated disposals' which are disposals of assets owned by the individual but used in the business of a partnership or personal company and the following conditions are satisfied (*TCGA 1992, s 169K*):

- the individual had made a qualifying disposal of his interest in the partnership or shares in the personal company; and

- the disposal was part of withdrawal from participation in the business of the partnership or company; and

- the assets were used in the business of the partnership or company for 12 months before the disposal.

Previously there was no guidance on a minimum size for the withdrawal from the business and there was a potential for ER to be obtained when there was no substantial withdrawal. From 18 March 2015, gains on personal assets used in a business carried on by a company or a partnership, will not be 'associated disposals' unless they are disposed of in connection with a disposal of at least a 5% shareholding in the company, or a 5% share in the partnership assets. *Finance Act 2016* makes it clear that the disposal of shares or a share of partnership assets may be to persons connected with the claimant, such as family members. Also, the requirement that the material disposal be of a certain minimum size may not apply if the claimant is disposing of all his or her interest in the partnership.

Entrepreneurs' relief can also apply to disposals by trustees of shares in a trading company or assets used in a business subject to various conditions (see **34.12**).

How entrepreneurs' relief works

14.10

Example 14.3 – Sole trader

In August 2016 you dispose of your manufacturing business which you had owned for the last ten years. You make gains on the business assets as follows:

Factory premises – £1,200,000

Goodwill – £1,250,000

The gains on the factory premises and the goodwill are aggregated and will together qualify for entrepreneurs' relief which will be due in respect of the total gain of £2,450,000.

Example 14.4 – Retiring partner

You have been a partner with three other persons in a trading business for several years. Each partner had a 25% interest in the partnership's assets.

On 31 December 2016 you retire and dispose of your 25% interest in the assets of the business, which continues, to the other partners. You make gains of £1,250,000 on the disposals of your 25% share of the business goodwill and premises.

All of your gains will qualify for entrepreneurs' relief because you have disposed of the whole of your interest in the assets of the partnership.

Example 14.5 – Disposal of shares

In September 2016 you dispose of the shares you had owned for the last ten years in a trading company of which you were a director. You owned 25% of the shares of the company that entitled you to 25% of the voting rights.

You made a gain of £800,000 which will qualify for entrepreneurs' relief.

Example 14.6 – Associated disposal

Following on from the previous example, you also personally owned the premises from which the company has traded for ten years. Throughout that period the company paid you a full market rent for the use of these premises.

When you sold your shares you disposed of the premises to the remaining shareholders making a gain on the 'associated disposal' of £300,000 which prima facie qualifies for entrepreneurs' relief.

However, because a full market rent was paid to you for the business use of the property, a proportion of the gain relating to the premises will not attract relief. Only the period for which rent was paid after 5 April 2008 is taken into account in restricting the amount of the £300,000 gain which qualifies for relief. This would be 8½ of the ten years the property was in use for the business. A 'just and reasonable' figure in these circumstances would be:

Total gain on the sale of the premises £300,000

Gain accruing for 8½ years of use from April 2008 to September 2016

£300,000 × 8.5/10 = £255,000

Gain on premises eligible for entrepreneurs' relief £300,000 less £255,000, ie £45,000.

Claiming and calculating the relief

14.11

Focus

Entrepreneurs' relief must be claimed by the taxpayer so he can decide whether to save his lifetime allowance for a later gain if other reliefs are available (*TCGA 1992, s 169M*).

Entrepreneurs' relief is usually claimed on the self-assessment tax return. If this is not done for some reason, it can be claimed by completing the form in Helpsheet HS275.

The relief is given for gains up to 22 June 2010 by reducing the capital gain by 4/9ths on which tax is charged at 18%. After that date, gains on which entrepreneurs' relief is available are taxed at 10%.

When entrepreneurs' relief is not available

14.12   Entrepreneurs' relief is not available against gains on buy-to-let residential properties although it is available against gains on properties used in a furnished holiday lettings business that qualifies to be treated as a trade.

If relief is claimed under the associated disposals provisions, relief will be restricted or eliminated if rent was charged on the asset being sold (see **Example 14.6** above).

A sale of assets without the sale of the business or the cessation of trade does not qualify for entrepreneurs' relief. This potentially affects, for example, a farmer selling off a parcel of land and continuing to farm on his remaining land.

An individual may make a disposal of shares in a personal company and be able to defer the gain by receiving shares or qualifying corporate bonds (QCBs) in another company. If he does this he may not be able to satisfy the conditions for entrepreneurs' relief when later on he realises the new shares or QCBs. There are provisions which allow the individual to take entrepreneurs' relief on the original disposal rather than defer the gain (*TCGA1992, s 169Q*).

With effect from 3 December 2014, a new *section 169LA* was inserted in *TCGA 1992*, so that where goodwill is transferred to a close company and the transferor has shares in the company, entrepreneurs' relief will not be available. *Finance Act 2016* contains amendments to these rules which are backdated to 3 December 2014 and allow entrepreneurs' relief to be claimed in this situation provided that the claimant holds less than 5% of the acquiring company's shares.

In the past this was often used as a tax-efficient route for incorporation as the individual only paid tax at 10% on the gain and could draw down the director's loan account created on incorporation without any further personal tax liabilities. If other chargeable assets are transferred into a company on incorporation, entrepreneur relief would still be available on those assets even if the individual owns more than 5% of the acquiring company's shares.

Focus

Entrepreneurs' relief can reduce the CGT rate from 20% to 10% if the relevant conditions are met. However, sales of assets without the sale of a business do not qualify. Commercial properties let on the open market also fail to qualify. In addition, entrepreneurs' relief can no longer be claimed on goodwill transferred to a company on incorporation.

Employees with small shareholdings in their employer may not qualify due to the 5% test unless the shares have been acquired under an EMI scheme.

INVESTORS' RELIEF

Extension of entrepreneurs' relief to external investors

14.13   In a surprise move, the *Finance Act 2016* introduces a new relief for external investors in unlisted trading companies so that qualifying individuals can benefit from a 10% rate of CGT subject to a lifetime cap of £10 million. The new relief, which is called investors' relief, is intended to encourage long-term investment in unlisted trading companies.

The relief is for individuals (including individuals who jointly subscribe for shares) who are not "relevant employees" of the company during the qualifying period. A person who is an unremunerated director may qualify if they have not previously been connected with the company or involved in carrying on any part of the activities of the company in any way. Furthermore, an individual who subsequently becomes an employee may fall outside of the definition of a relevant employee and therefore benefit form this relief – the conditions which must be met include that the employment must not commence within 180 days of the start of the qualifying period and there must have been no reasonable prospect (ie it was more likely than not) of them becoming a employee within that period.

There are detailed rules governing the relief but the main conditions are:

- The shares must be newly issued fully paid up ordinary shares subscribed for with new consideration by the individual making the disposal; and

- The investment must be in an unlisted trading company, or an unlisted holding company of a trading group; and

- The shares must be subscribed for by the individual for genuine commercial reasons and not for the avoidance of tax; and

- The shares must have been issued by the company on or after 17 March 2016 and have been held continually for a period of at least three years commencing on or after 6 April 2016 and ending on the date of the disposal.

The relief is also available to trustees of a settlement but the amount of relief is attributed to a qualifying beneficiary's own individual lifetime limit.

This relief can be contrasted with entrepreneurs' relief which is only available to officers and employees (**14.8**). The £10 million lifetime limit for entrepreneurs' relief and investors' relief are independent of each other.

Focus

Although the 10% rate of tax appears attractive to individuals who would normally pay tax on capital gains at the higher rate of 20%, there are other investment routes, such as the Enterprise Investment Scheme which offer income tax relief for the investment *and* exemption from CGT on disposal (**14.23**).

HOLDOVER RELIEFS

Gift relief

14.14   A gift of an asset or a sale at less than market value is treated as a disposal with deemed proceeds of market value (see **12.5**). This raises obvious problems as the person making the gift may not have the funds to pay the capital gains tax. In view of this there have in the past been various forms of 'gift relief' of which only two now remain.

The first one is a holdover relief for gifts of business assets (*TCGA 1992, s 165*).

If this relief applies, the person making the gift (the transferor) and the recipient (the transferee) may elect to holdover the gain so that the transferee's allowable expenditure on the asset is reduced by the gain. Effectively the transferee takes over the gain.

The relief applies to disposals by an individual and the trustees of a settlement other than as a bargain at arm's length to a UK resident transferee of qualifying assets which are basically:

- assets used in a trade carried on by the transferor or his personal company;

- shares in an unlisted trading company (shares dealt in on AIM, Plus-traded and Plus-quoted markets are not regarded as listed but shares dealt in on Plus-listed are) or in the transferor's personal company.

Holdover relief is not available if the transferee is not resident in the UK and the relief can be clawed back if the transferee ceases to be resident within six years of the gift unless he has gone abroad to work for a period of up to three years.

In the case of a gift of shares, the relief does not apply if the transferee is a company.

A 'personal company' for this purpose is one where the transferor held at least 5% of the voting rights.

Further information on this relief can be found in HMRC Helpsheet HS295 (available from www.gov.uk/government/publications/relief-for-gifts-and-similar-transactions-hs295-self-assessment-helpsheet) which includes the form which must be completed to make a claim.

Example 14.7 – Gift of business assets

Mr A ran a repair business as a sole trader. He decides to give the business premises to his son, Mr B, when they are worth £50,000. The premises cost £20,000 so the gain based on market value is £30,000.

Mr A and Mr B decide to claim holdover relief so that Mr A does not have to pay tax on the gain.

Mr B will have an allowable cost of £20,000 for capital gains tax for any future disposal of the premises.

Relief on gifts on which IHT is due

14.15   The second type of holdover relief is a relief for gifts between individuals or trustees of a settlement on which inheritance tax is chargeable (*TCGA 1992, s 260*).

Gifts between individuals are usually 'potentially exempt transfers' and are not chargeable to inheritance tax in the terms of this relief. Therefore this relief mainly applies to transfers to and from trusts.

Focus

It should be noted that the relief still applies even if no inheritance tax is payable on the gift because the transfer is within the inheritance tax nil rate band.

ROLLOVER RELIEF

Qualifying assets

14.16   Rollover relief applies to the replacement of business assets and enables traders to defer chargeable gains on the disposal of qualifying assets when they reinvest the sales proceeds in other qualifying assets for use in the business (*TCGA 1992, s 152*).

Focus

The replacement assets must normally be acquired within one year before and three years after the disposal of the old assets. The relief must be claimed.

Qualifying assets for the purpose of this relief include the following (*TCGA 1992, s 155*):

- land and buildings;
- fixed plant or machinery which is not part of a building;
- ships, aircraft and hovercraft and satellites, space stations and spacecraft (including launch vehicles);
- goodwill;
- milk, potato, ewe and suckler cow premium and fish quotas.

Although the relief is in terms of 'reinvesting' the proceeds, the actual funds do not have to be traced from the sale to the purchase.

Use of the assets

14.17   The old and new assets must all have been used in the trade. If the asset is used only partly in the trade or only used in the trade for part of the period of ownership then apportionment is necessary to determine the amounts which can be rolled over (*TCGA 1992, s 152(6), (7)*).

It is not necessary for the replacement asset to be used in the *same* trade as the asset which has been sold. For example, a taxpayer could sell a building which he used in a car repair business and buy a new building to be used as a restaurant (*TCGA 1992, s 152(8)*).

Neither do the assets have to be of the same type. For example, a taxpayer could sell a building used as a warehouse and reinvest in fixed plant to be used in his factory.

If the sale of the old asset or the purchase of the replacement asset are delayed so that the time periods allowed for the relief are not satisfied, the taxpayer can apply to have the periods extended (*TCGA 1992, s 152(3)*).

Who can claim rollover relief?

14.18   The relief applies to individuals carrying on a trade either as a sole trader or as a partner and to trading companies.

It is also extended to an individual who is replacing an asset he owns personally that is used in the trade of his personal company but the old asset and the replacement asset must be used by the same personal company. A rollover relief claim is not precluded by payment of rent for the use of the asset. A personal company for this purpose is one in which the taxpayer can exercise at least 5% of the voting rights (*TCGA 1992, s 157*).

Example 14.8 – Rollover relief on business premises

Mr A sells his business premises for £50,000 realising a gain of £30,000. He immediately buys new premises for £90,000 and makes a claim for rollover relief.

The whole of the £30,000 gain is postponed.

The cost of the new premises for capital gains tax purposes is £60,000 (£90,000 less the rolled over gain of £30,000).

Example 14.9 – Partial claim

Mr A sells his business premises for £100,000 making a gain of £50,000. He buys new premises for £80,000 and makes a claim for rollover relief as the purchase was within three years of the sale.

£20,000 of the sale proceeds for the old property has not been reinvested. Therefore £20,000 of the gain on the old premises is chargeable.

The remainder of the gain, £30,000 (£50,000 less £20,000) can be rolled over into the new premises which will have a cost for capital gains tax of £50,000 (£80,000 less £30,000).

Note – Mr A should review his position in the three years following the disposal to see if there is any later expenditure which could be used to roll over the gain of £20,000.

The new asset is depreciating

14.19 There are special rules which apply if the new (replacement) asset is a 'depreciating asset': basically an asset with a life of less than 60 years. This will apply to fixed plant and machinery or a lease on a property for less than 60 years (*TCGA 1992, s 154*).

In this case the gain is still postponed but only until the earliest of:

- ten years from when you bought or acquired the new asset; or

- the date you stop using the new asset in your trade; or

- the date you sell or dispose of the new asset.

Example 14.10 – Postponement of gain

Mr A sells his business premises for £125,000 making a gain of £20,000. He acquires new business premises on a 30-year lease on 1 August 2016 for £135,000 and claims to rollover the gain of £20,000 into the new premises.

The leased premises are used in his business until they are sold on 1 July 2022.

The gain can only be postponed until the earliest of:

• 31 July 2026 (ten years from the date the leased premises were acquired);

• 1 July 2022 (the date he stopped using the leased premises); or

• 1 July 2022 (the date of sale).

So the gain is postponed until 1 July 2022 and must be included in the tax return for 2022/23.

Note – If Mr A acquires a non-depreciating asset to be used in his business before 1 July 2022, he can make a further rollover relief claim to set the gain against this asset.

INCORPORATION RELIEF

14.20 If you incorporate a business by transferring a business currently carried on by a sole trader or partnership to a company, there will normally be disposals for capital gains tax purposes of the business assets. It is possible to defer the gains arising using incorporation relief (*TCGA 1992, s 162*).

In order for the relief to apply, the business, including all of the assets of the business (other than cash), must be transferred as a going concern in return for shares in the company it is transferred to. Sometimes the owners of a business may prefer to keep some business assets in their own name such as business premises but this will mean that this relief cannot apply.

If the conditions are met, the cost of the shares acquired is reduced by the postponed gain.

The relief is given automatically and there is no need to make a claim.

If the consideration is not only shares but, for example, includes a loan account, then the relief will be restricted and some of the gain will remain taxable.

HMRC do not treat the assumption of business liabilities by the transferee company as consideration for the transfer, however, this is not extended to include personal liabilities such as the tax liabilities of the unincorporated business (ESC D32).

Example 14.11 – Incorporation of sole trader's business

Mr A transferred all of his business to a company which also took over the liabilities. The consideration for the transfer was 1,000 shares valued at £130,000.

The assets and liabilities of the business were:

	Value	Gain
	£	**£**
Premises	100,000	23,000
Stock	35,000	
Debtors	17,000	
	152,000	23,000
Trade creditors	(22,000)	
	130,000	23,000

All the gain can be deferred as the consideration is wholly in shares

Cost of shares for capital gains tax	130,000
Less postponed gain	(23,000)
Revised cost for capital gains tax	107,000

In some circumstances, a taxpayer may not want the relief to apply, for example if the tax on the gain on incorporation could be reduced by entrepreneurs' relief. If this is the case, he can submit an election (*TCGA 1992, s 162A*).

Focus

The main corporation tax rate of 20% in financial year 2015 and 2016 makes incorporation attractive when personal income tax rates can be up to 45%.

Incorporation relief often means that a business can be incorporated without crystallising CGT liabilities. There is some relief for disincorporation (*FA 2013, s 58*) (see **26.10**).

OTHER RELIEFS

Loans to traders

14.21 A simple debt arising from a straightforward loan from one person to another is not normally within the scope of capital gains tax. This means that you cannot be assessed on a gain but neither can you obtain relief for a loss (*TCGA 1992, s 251*).

There is a special relief which allows you to claim a capital loss on a loan to a trader if the loan cannot be repaid. The loan must have been used wholly for trade purposes and have become irrecoverable. You cannot claim if the borrower was your spouse or civil partner either when the loan was made or subsequently (*TCGA 1992, s 253*).

The relief is extended to cover the situation where, instead of making a loan to the trader yourself, you act as guarantor for a loan. If the loan becomes irrecoverable and you have to pay up under your guarantee, you may claim an allowable loss. The conditions for relief are similar to those which apply to losses on loans to traders but a claim has to be made within four years of the end of the tax year in which a guarantee payment is made (*TCGA 1992, s 253(4)*).

Example 14.12 – Loan for business which fails

Ella lends £25,000 to her sister, Lara, to start a hair and beauty salon. After trading successfully for a couple of years, the business fails. £5,000 of the loan is repaid but £20,000 is irrecoverable.

Ella can claim an allowable loss of £20,000.

Focus

There is no time limit in which to make the claim for a loss on a loan. The loss will arise either at the time you make the claim or, if you specify when you make your claim, at an earlier time that falls in either of the two previous tax years, provided all the necessary conditions for relief are satisfied at the date you make the claim and at the earlier time.

Negligible value claims

14.22 If you own an asset which has become of little value, you would not usually be able to claim a capital loss since there has been no disposal of the asset. In order to help with this situation, it is possible to make a negligible value claim. You are then treated as though you had sold the asset and immediately re-acquired it at its value at the time the claim is made.

You must still own the asset when you make the claim and the asset must have become of negligible value while you owned it. An asset is of negligible value if it is worth next to nothing (*TCGA 1992*, s *24(1A)*).

If you make a negligible value claim during the tax year 2016/17, any loss resulting from the deemed disposal will arise in that year, unless you specify an earlier time falling in the two previous tax years at which the deemed disposal should be treated as occurring.

HMRC publish a list of shares which have been quoted on the London Stock Exchange and have been accepted as being of negligible value for this purpose (www.gov.uk/negligible-value-agreements-to-30-june-2014).

For other assets it may be necessary to complete HMRC Form CG34 which will allow HMRC to check the value you have used in the claim.

There is an HMRC Helpsheet (HS286) dealing with negligible value claims.

Example 14.13 – A successful claim

In July 2016, Mr A is notified that his shares in Aeron plc are worthless. He bought the shares in 2005 for £15,000. Mr A knows that he has made capital gains in 2016/17 so makes a negligible value claim which is accepted.

He has a capital loss of £15,000 to set against his gains.

Enterprise Investment Scheme

14.23   The Enterprise Investment Scheme (EIS) offers tax incentives if you invest in shares in smaller, unlisted companies. Income tax relief is available if you invest in shares through the EIS subject to satisfying various conditions over a qualifying period (see **7.17**).

The EIS also provides some CGT reliefs:

● Deferral relief, when you reinvest a gain on any asset in shares under the Enterprise Investment Scheme (*TCGA 1992, Sch 5B*). If you make a gain by disposing of something that is liable to CGT and invest your gain in EIS shares, you can delay paying CGT on the amount of the gain equal to the amount you invested. To receive this relief there is a period in which you must invest in EIS shares – between one year before and three years after disposing of your original assets. Income tax relief does not have to be claimed in respect of the EIS shares and, for deferral relief, you can be connected with the EIS company ie you can control more than 30% of the company.

- For disposals after 3 December 2014, new rules in *Finance Act 2015* allow gains which satisfy the normal conditions for Entrepreneurs' Relief at the time of the disposal but which are instead deferred into investments which qualify under the EIS (or Social Investment Tax Relief), to benefit from Entrepreneurs' Relief when the gain is realised for example on the disposal of the EIS shares or the SITR investment.

- Exemption from CGT when you sell or dispose of EIS shares (*TCGA 1992, s 150A(2)*). If you qualified for income tax relief on shares under the EIS and claimed the relief, any gain when you sell those shares will not be subject to CGT if both of the following apply:

  o the income tax relief has not since been recovered;

  o you have held your shares for at least three years.

The importance of claiming the income tax relief was emphasised in the case of *Ames* [2015] TC 04523.

Focus

The EIS company has to satisfy HMRC that it meets the requirements for EIS relief. At the end of this process, the company can issue Form EIS3 to the investors. In general, claims for EIS relief are made on the self-assessment tax return but if claiming the deferral relief, it is necessary to complete the claim on the Form EIS3 and submit it to HMRC.

Venture Capital Trust

14.24   A Venture Capital Trust (VCT) is a company which invests in small unlisted companies. An individual investor can claim income tax relief on a subscription for shares issued by an approved VCT. The relief is withdrawn if the investor disposes of the shares within five years or the VCT loses its approval within that period. Dividends from a VCT are, subject to annual subscription limits, exempt from income tax.

A gain or loss accruing to an individual on a disposal of ordinary shares in a company which was a VCT throughout his period of ownership is not a chargeable gain or an allowable loss. The shares must have been within the permitted maximum investment when they were acquired. The permitted maximum subscription is £200,000 (*TCGA 1992, s 151A; ITTOIA 2005, s 709(4)*).

APPENDIX: ENTREPRENEURS' RELIEF

(*TCGA 1992, ss 169H–169S*)

14.25

Date of qualifying business disposal	Lifetime limit
From 6 April 2011	£10 million
23 June 2010–5 April 2011	£5 million
6 April 2010–22 June 2010	£2 million
6 April 2008–5 April 2010	£1 million

Conditions

1 The relief broadly applies to qualifying disposals by an individual or certain trustees on or after 6 April 2008 of:

- all or part of a trade carried on alone or in partnership;

- assets of such a trade following cessation; or

- shares or securities in the individual's 'personal company', where the company is a trading company (or the holding company of a trading group) and the individual is an officer or employee of the company (or of a trading group member) (see *TCGA 1992, ss 169H, 169I*); and

- the relevant conditions are met throughout a period of at least one year ending with the date of disposal or cessation of trade (see *TCGA 1992, s 169I*).

2 A personal company is one in which the taxpayer holds at least 5% of the ordinary share capital and controls at least 5% of the voting rights of the company.

3 Trustees can claim relief on the disposal of settlement business assets if a qualifying beneficiary has an interest in possession in the whole or a relevant part of the settled property, where all the conditions for the relief are satisfied by the beneficiary (see *TCGA 1992, s 169J*).

4 Transitional rules apply to allow relief to be claimed in some circumstances where a gain made before 6 April 2008 is deferred

using QCBs, EIS or VCT and becomes chargeable on or after that date (*FA 2008, Sch 3, paras 7, 8*).

5   From 6 April 2013, gains made on shares acquired through exercising EMI options on or after 6 April 2012 can qualify for entrepreneurs' relief, even if the taxpayer holds less than 5% of the ordinary share capital of the company.

Calculation of relief

- For disposals arising on and after 23 June 2010, the net gains qualifying for entrepreneurs' relief are charged at the rate of 10%.

- For disposals made from 6 April 2008 to 22 June 2010, the qualifying net gains are reduced by 4/9ths before being charged to tax at the flat rate of 18%.

15

Particular assets and situations

SIGNPOSTS

- **Shares and securities** – The identification of which shares have been sold can involve a process known as 'pooling' (see **15.1**).

- **Land and buildings** – Specific rules apply to the calculation of gains in respect of certain leases (see **15.2**).

- **Options** – Options are assets for CGT purposes, and there are particular rules for dealing with them (see **15.3**).

- **Chattels and wasting assets** – A gain on the disposal of a 'chattel' is exempt if the proceeds are less than £6,000. If the proceeds exceed that amount, the chargeable gain is limited. As a general rule, no chargeable gain arises on the disposal of a 'wasting asset' (ie an asset with a predictable life of no more than 50 years) if it is a chattel (see **15.4**).

- **Debts** – A simple loan from one person to another is normally outside the scope of CGT in the hands of the original creditor (although loss relief can be claimed for irrecoverable loans to traders, if certain conditions are satisfied). There is an exception for a 'debt on a security'. Many securities are 'qualifying corporate bonds', and are exempt from CGT (see **15.5**).

SHARES AND SECURITIES – 'POOLING'

15.1   An individual may have acquired shares in a particular company on a number of occasions at different prices. If some of the shares are sold, it is necessary to be able to identify which shares have been sold and how much expenditure can be deducted from the proceeds in calculating the gain or loss.

The rules for identifying shares have been changed a number of times since CGT was introduced. The current rules which apply to disposals by individuals after 6 April 2008 re-introduce the concept of 'pooling' under which shares in the same company and class held by the same person in the same capacity are now generally treated as a single pool of shares.

Focus

When looking at a disposal of shares they are to be identified with acquisitions by the same person of shares of the same class in the same company in the following order:

1   acquisitions on the same day as the disposal;

2   acquisitions within 30 days after the day of disposal (to prevent 'bed and breakfasting');

3   all other shares in the pool.

Example 15.1 – Disposal of 'pooled' shares

Mrs A sold 1,000 ordinary shares in AAC plc on 1 August 2016 for £50,000.

Before the sale her shareholding in AAC plc was made up as follows:

			Cost
			£
11 July 2000 bought	1,000	shares	40,000
5 September 2006 bought	2,000	shares	95,000
Total	3,000		135,000

The 1,000 shares sold are assumed to be out of the 'pool' of shares and are taken as being 1/3 (1,000/3,000) of the holding.

The gain is calculated as:

2016/17	£
Proceeds	50,000
Cost £135,000 × 1/3	(45,000)
Gain	5,000

LAND AND LEASES OF LAND

15.2   Land and buildings or an interest in land are assets for CGT purposes. Despite this, in some circumstances, a profit on disposal of land may be taxed as income if the transaction is viewed as a trading transaction rather than the disposal of an investment.

If an interest in freehold land is sold, subject to the possibility mentioned above of the profits being taxed as income, the CGT position is reasonably straightforward.

Sometimes rather than selling the freehold interest the owner may grant a lease of property for a period. Normally rent will be paid on a lease and there may be a 'lease premium' which is a capital sum paid for the grant of a lease. A person who has a lease of a property may grant a sub-lease out of his lease or may assign the lease to another person. For tax purposes, leases are categorised as 'long' (50 years or more) or 'short' (less than 50 years).

Focus

There are special rules for dealing with the tax implications of these types of transactions. This book only looks at the situation of a grant of a long lease or a short lease out of a freehold. Other situations are covered in *Capital Gains Tax 2016/17* (published by Bloomsbury Professional).

The grant of a long lease out of a freehold interest or another long lease is treated as a normal capital disposal, however, the calculation recognises that the freeholder will get the property back at the end of the lease and so is taxed as a part disposal (see **13.4** above) where A is the premium received and B is the residual value retained by the landlord plus the value of the right to receive the rent. (*TCGA 1992, Sch 8(2)*).

Example 15.2 – Grant of a long lease

Mr B bought a freehold property in April 2000 for £200,000. In 2016, he decided to grant a 60-year lease of the property to Mr C for a premium of £120,000 and annual rent of £10,000 pa.

It was agreed that the value of the freehold reversion was £60,000 and the value of the right to receive the rent was £60,000.

Mr B's gain on the grant of the lease is calculated as:

	£
Proceeds	120,000
Allowable cost:	
fraction A/(A+B) is 120,000/(120,000+60,000+60,000)	
ie ½ of the original cost of £200,000	(100,000)
Gain	20,000

The calculation of the gain on a grant of a short lease out of a freehold or a long lease is modified as part of the premium for the grant is taxed as income (see **Chapter 8**) and is therefore excluded from the calculation. This is easiest to show in an example.

Example 15.3 – Grant of a short lease

Mr C bought a freehold property for £45,000 some years ago.

In 2016, he granted a 46-year lease for a premium of £35,000 and a market rent.

The value of the freehold reversion was £50,000 (including the right to receive the rent).

	£
The amount taxed as income is:	
The premium	35,000
Less: the premium × (no. of years of the lease – 1)/50 ie £35,000 × (46–1)/50	(31,500)
	3,500
The calculation of the gain is:	
Premium received	35,000
Less: taxed as income	(3,500)
	31,500
Allowable cost	
(A – amount taxed as income)/(A+B) × cost	
ie (35,000–3,500)/(35,000+50,000) × 45,000	(16,677)
Gain	14,823

OPTIONS

15.3   An option is an asset for CGT (*TCGA 1992, s 21(1)(a)*).

Therefore the grant of an option is the disposal of an asset, namely the option.

A grant of an option is not treated as a part disposal of the asset that the option relates to.

The exercise of an option is not treated as a disposal of the option but the granting of the option and the transfer of the asset subject to the option are treated as a single transaction (*TCGA 1992, s 144(1)*).

Example 15.4 – Grant and exercise of option

Mrs C granted an option to Mr D in May 2015 for £7,000 under which he could acquire property E for £70,000 within two years of the grant of the option. In August 2016, Mr D exercised the option. Mrs C had purchased property E in 2000 for £50,000.

Grant of option 2015/16	£
Proceeds	7,000
Cost	0
Chargeable gain (subject to annual exemption)	7,000
Exercise of option 2016/17	
Proceeds for property	70,000
Proceeds for option	7,000
	77,000
Cost	(50,000)
Chargeable gain	27,000

As a consequence of the option being exercised, the grant of the option ceases to be a chargeable event, the gain in 2015/16 is reduced to nil and any tax paid no the grant of the option is refunded or set off (CG12317).

CHATTELS AND WASTING ASSETS

15.4   A chattel is a tangible moveable asset such as a painting or jewellery. A gain on the sale of a chattel is exempt from CGT if the disposal proceeds are less that £6,000. If the proceeds are more than £6,000, the chargeable gain is limited to five-thirds of the excess (*TCGA 1992, s 262*).

Example 15.5 – Chattel exemption

In August 2016, you sold an antique, which originally cost £2,000, for £7,500.

The amount received is £1,500 more than the £6,000 exemption limit.

You multiply £1,500 by five-thirds getting a figure of £2,500.

The actual gain on sale of the asset was £7,500 less £2,000, £5,500.

You only pay CGT on the lower amount of £2,500 and not on the actual gain.

Focus

In order to prevent taxpayers avoiding CGT by splitting up sets of assets and selling them in batches to keep the proceeds below £6,000, articles can be deemed to be a single asset if they are sold to the same person or connected persons.

A wasting asset is an asset with a predictable life of less than 50 years. In general, there is no chargeable gain on the disposal of a chattel which has a predicable life of less than 50 years unless capital allowances could have been claimed on them. Assets that are wasting assets but are not chattels and therefore not covered by the exemption include for example leases of land and other assets for less than 50 years.

Plant and machinery is always accepted as a wasting asset. There was a recent Court of Appeal decision on this (*Executors of Lord Howard of Henderskelfe (dec'd) v HMRC* [2013] UKUT 129) in which it was held that a painting informally loaned to Castle Howard was plant and therefore a wasting asset exempt from capital gains tax.

In view of this decision, legislation was included in *Finance Act 2015* so that from April 2015, this exemption is disapplied if the asset has only become plant through use in the trade, profession or vocation of a person other than the person making the disposal.

On the disposal of a wasting asset which does not qualify for the exemption, the allowable expenditure on acquisition of the asset is restricted. It is assumed that the cost of the asset less any scrap or residual value is written off evenly over the predictable life. This is achieved by applying the following multiples (*TCGA 1992, s 46*):

● the period of ownership of the asset; and

● the predictable life.

For leases of land, the rule in *s 46* is overruled by the table in *TCGA 1992, Sch 8*.

Example 15.6 – Sale of wasting asset

In August 2015, Mrs C bought a wasting asset for £20,000. When the asset was bought, it had a predictable life of ten years, and an estimated scrap value of £5,000. In August 2016, Mrs C sold the asset for £19,000.

	£	£
Sales proceeds		19,000
Cost	20,000	
Cost written off during ownership		
Original cost £20,000 less scrap value £5,000 = £15,000		
Period of ownership 1 year		
Predictable life 10 years		
So restrict £15,000 by 1/10th	1,500	
		(18,500)
Gain		500

DEBTS

15.5　A simple debt arising from a straightforward loan from one person to another is not normally within the scope of capital gains *tax* (*TCGA 1992, s 251*). This means that an individual who is the original creditor cannot be assessed on a gain on a simple debt and cannot get relief for a loss. However, you may be able to claim a loss if a loan to a trader goes bad (see **14.21**).

Securities are loans to companies which are formalised. They may be called 'debts on security' or loan stock. Securities are chargeable assets for the original lender in general. However, many securities are 'qualifying corporate bonds' and are therefore exempt from CGT.

16

Planning and other issues

SIGNPOSTS

- **Partnerships** – Individual partners are broadly subject to CGT on disposals of partnership assets on the basis that they each own an interest in those assets (see **16.1**).

- **Companies** – Capital gains made by companies are calculated using largely the same rules as for individuals (although indexation allowance is also available for companies), but they are liable to corporation tax rather than CGT. There is a special relief for disposals of substantial shareholdings by companies (see **23.7**). There are specific rules for groups of companies (see **23.4**), and also in respect of company reconstructions and reorganisations (see **16.2–16.3**).

- **Planning and anti-avoidance** – Basic CGT planning includes making full use of available reliefs and exemptions, such as the annual CGT exemption. More complicated CGT planning may be restricted by various pieces of anti-avoidance legislation (see **16.4–16.5**).

PARTNERSHIPS

16.1   Partnerships, limited liability partnerships and Scottish partnerships are treated as transparent for CGT. Each partner has to return any CGT disposals on the basis that they own an interest in the partnership assets (HMRC Statement of Practice D12).

The main occasions when partners have CGT disposals are:

- When the partnership has disposed of an asset during the year, for example if it sold its business premises. Each partner is treated as owning a fractional share of the partnership assets, the fraction determined usually from the partnership agreement.

- When there has been a change in the partnership during the year, for example the admission of a new partner resulting in a reduced partnership share to the old partners. If the firm's assets have not been re-valued and there is no direct payment of consideration outside the partnership, there will be no gain or loss for the old partners.

* When a partner leaves a partnership. If the partner leaving receives consideration from the other partners or a third party then there will be a disposal on which there may be a gain. If the disposal is to the other partners and no consideration is received, there will not normally be any gain or loss.

Example 16.1 – Sale of partnership property

Mr A and Mrs B are equal partners in a business partnership. The partnership bought a warehouse in January 2005 for £120,000. The warehouse is sold in September 2016 for £140,000.

Mr A and Mr B both need to return a gain of £10,000 based on sales proceeds of £70,000 and costs of £60,000.

Example 16.2 – Sale of goodwill

Mr C, Mr D and Mr E are in partnership based on equal shares of one third each. The only chargeable asset of the partnership is goodwill which is not shown in the balance sheet.

The partners decide to sell the business to a third party as a going concern and receive £300,000 for the goodwill. Mr C and Mr D have no allowable expenditure on goodwill as they were the original partners who set the business up. Mr E became a partner later and paid £25,000 to Mr C and £25,000 to Mr D for goodwill.

When Mr E became a partner, Mr C and Mr D will each have been taxed on a gain of £25,000 arising from the sale of goodwill to Mr E.

On the sale to the third party, the partners will have capital gains as follows:

	Mr C	**Mr D**	**Mr E**
	£	**£**	**£**
Proceeds (1/3 of £300,000 each)	100,000	100,000	100,000
Allowable expenditure	0	0	(50,000)
Gain	100,000	100,000	50,000

347

COMPANIES – OUTLINE

16.2   Gains on disposals of chargeable assets by a company are calculated largely based on the same rules as are used for gains realised by individuals.

However, companies can claim a deduction from their capital gains for indexation allowance which is intended to compensate for the effect of inflation. Indexation allowance was introduced from March 1982 and was originally available to all taxpayers, but from April 1998 it is no longer available for individual taxpayers (*TCGA 1992, ss 53–54*).

If a company has a gain before indexation then it can be reduced by indexation allowance but indexation cannot be used to create or increase a loss.

Focus

Indexation allowance is calculated by applying the increase in the retail prices index between acquiring the asset and selling it to the allowable expenditure on the asset. HMRC publish the retail prices index and indexation factors (see www.gov.uk/government/collections/corporation-tax-on-chargeable-gains-indexation-allowance-rates).

Example 16.3 – Sale of company property

ABC Ltd bought a property in November 2007 for £200,000 and sold it in February 2016 for £300,000.

The indexation factor from November 2007 to February 2016 is 0.24.

	£
Proceeds	300,000
Cost	(200,000)
Unindexed gain	100,000
Indexation 0.24 × £200,000	(48,000)
Gain	52,000

Capital gains made by a company are aggregated with other profits made in its accounting period and are subject to corporation tax at the rate applying for that period.

Transfers of chargeable assets between companies which are members of a group can generally be made so that no gain or loss arises. A group is basically a company and its 75% subsidiaries (*TCGA 1992, s 171*).

There is also a special relief for disposals of substantial shareholdings by companies. If a trading company X Ltd has owned at least 10% of the share capital of another trading company Y Ltd for 12 months or more, a disposal by X Ltd of the shares in Y Ltd is exempt so that there is no chargeable gain but also there can be no allowable loss (*TCGA 1992, Sch 7AC*) (see **23.7**).

COMPANY RECONSTRUCTIONS AND REORGANISATIONS

16.3   A company may wish to reorganise its share capital so that all the shareholders receive new shares in exactly the same proportion as the old shares. There is no CGT charge on this transaction (*TCGA 1992, ss 126–127*).

An extension to this relief can apply in the case of a reconstruction where one company is 'taken over' by another company (*TCGA 1992, s 135*).

If Company B issues shares in exchange for shares in Company A and:

- after the exchange Company B owns more than 25% of the ordinary share capital of Company A; or

- the issue of shares is the result of a general offer to the members of Company A; or

- after the exchange Company B holds the greater part of the voting power of Company A

then the shareholders in Company A are treated as if the new shares received are the same asset as the old shares with the same base cost.

Example 16.4 – Disposal of shares on takeover

Mrs C buys 1,000 shares in Newcall plc for £2,000 in January 2007. Newcall plc is taken over by Telcall plc on 1 December 2015 and Mrs C receives 2,000 shares in Telcall plc in exchange for her Newcall plc shares.

Mrs C is not treated as making a disposal of the Newcall plc shares on 1 December 2015. Instead her Telcall plc shares are treated as acquired in January 2007 at the same cost (£2,000) as her shares in Newcall plc.

Similar provisions apply where a company enters into a scheme of reconstruction under which another company issues shares to its shareholders.
Again the new shares received are treated as replacing the old shares and
inheriting their cost (*TCGA 1992, s 136*).

PLANNING POINTS

16.4 CGT planning should be primarily aimed at maximising the use of
reliefs and exemptions available.

Focus

Taxpayers in general and in particular higher rate taxpayers should try to
use their annual exemption each year. This might involve bringing forward
disposals of assets so that they fall into an earlier tax year or restricting a
claim for deferral relief. They may need to liaise with their stockbrokers on
making suitable sales from an investment portfolio.

Asset transfers between spouses living together (or civil partners) can also
be used to reduce the tax bill. For example, if an individual is contemplating
selling the shares in a family trading company, he could gift a small number
of shares to his wife and to each of his adult children. No tax should arise on
the gifts as the transfer to his wife is a no gain no loss transaction (see **13.3**)
and holdover elections can be made for the gifts to his children (see **14.14**).
When the sale goes ahead, the proceeds paid to his wife and children may be
tax-free due to availability of the annual exemptions and, if taxable, may be
taxed at a lower rate than if no transfers had taken place. Such transfers may
be challenged if they take place when the sale negotiations are at an advanced
stage. It is also possible to use gifts between spouses to make maximum use of
Entrepreneur Relief.

If an individual anticipates having a substantial gain in a year, they should
review their assets (with their stockbroker, if appropriate) to see if any assets
are standing at a loss which could be crystallised by making a negligible value
claim. The loss can then be set against the gain.

ANTI-AVOIDANCE – OUTLINE

16.5 There are a number of routes which HMRC can use to challenge
attempts by a taxpayer to avoid or reduce a liability to capital gains tax.

First there is the line of cases which resulted in the '*Ramsay* principle'. In
essence where a preordained series of transactions is entered into to avoid tax,

it is necessary to look at the end result and not at the particular transactions in isolation. This may mean that the arrangements are ineffective.

There are also requirements to disclose details to HMRC of certain schemes which are intended to result in a tax advantage. In order to determine if an arrangement falls within this legislation it is necessary to see if it has any of a number of 'hallmarks'. In most cases it is the promoter of the scheme who has the duty to disclose. This is known as DOTAS (disclosure of tax avoidance schemes).

In addition, a general anti-abuse rule (GAAR) was introduced in *Finance Act 2013*. GAAR is targeted at artificial and abusive arrangements that are complex and/or novel and are outside that contemplated when formulating the relevant tax legislation. So there must be a tax arrangement entered into in order to obtain a tax advantage and the arrangement must be 'abusive', ie it cannot reasonably be regarded as a reasonable course of action, having regard to all the circumstances. If the GAAR applies, the tax advantage can be counteracted on a 'just and reasonable' basis; for example, if a scheme created losses, the losses would not be allowed. Further details of DOTAS and GAAR are set out in **Chapter 54**.

There are many specific pieces of anti-avoidance legislation impacting on CGT. The most general one is the targeted anti-avoidance rule under which a capital loss is not allowed if it results from arrangements for which the main purpose was securing a tax advantage (*TCGA 1992, s 16A*).

Other anti-avoidance provisions relate to specific reliefs and exemptions and are intended to prevent transactions being structured so as to fall into a particular relief or exemption.

For example, principal private residence relief is denied if the property was acquired wholly or partly for the purpose of realising a gain on its disposal (*TCGA 1992, s 224(3)*).

Another example is splitting up disposals of assets over several transactions so that each individual disposal would fall into the chattels exemption (see **15.4** above). This could also apply, for example, to splitting a sale of a set of furniture over several lots where the total proceeds are less than the value of the whole set if it was sold complete. If this provision is in point, it is necessary to look at all of the transactions together and recalculate the proceeds. (*TCGA 1992, ss 19, 20*).

In addition to the above, note should be taken of the targeted anti-avoidance rules preventing individuals benefiting from capital treatment on winding up in certain cases, and the provisions relating to transactions in securities. See 26.9 for further details.

Part 3
Corporation Tax

17

Corporation tax

SIGNPOSTS

- **Scope** – Corporation tax is levied on companies which are UK resident or trading in the UK (see **17.1–17.4**).

- **Losses** – These can be utilised in a variety of ways, depending on the nature of the business from which they are derived (see **17.5**).

- **Accounting periods** – These are the periods for which corporation tax is charged. They are generally 12-month periods during which a company is carrying on a business (see **17.6**).

- **Corporation tax rates** – Up to 31 March 2015, the rates depended on the level of profits and the number of 'associated companies' (see **17.7–17.8**).

- **Compliance issues** – A company must make a return of its income and gains within 12 months of the end of its accounting period (see **17.9**).

- **Appendix: Rates of corporation tax** – A table of corporation tax rates is included at the end of this chapter, including announcements in respect of future years (see **17.10**).

INTRODUCTION

Scope of corporation tax

17.1   Corporation tax is a tax on the income and chargeable gains, together known as profits, of companies that are resident in the UK (*CTA 2009, s 2*).

A company for this purpose means any body corporate or unincorporated association but does not include a partnership, local authority or local authority association (*CTA 2010, s 1121*). This means that clubs and societies that are unincorporated associations are liable to corporation tax.

17.1 *Corporation tax*

A partnership is the relationship which subsists between persons carrying on a business in common with a view to profit (*Partnership Act 1890*). Although an English partnership is not a separate legal entity a Scottish partnership is (*Partnership Act 1890, s 4(2)*) and in both cases it is the partners who are taxed on their shares of profit and not the partnership itself. The partners' status determines whether they are liable to income tax or corporation tax, as such, an individual partner will be subject to income tax on their share of profits while a corporate partner will be subject to corporation tax on theirs.

Limited partnerships and limited liability partnerships (LLPs) are not within the definition of partnership in the *1890 Act* as they are formed in pursuance of an Act of Parliament and so excluded by *s 1(2)(b)* of that Act, and therefore are prima facie within the charge to corporation tax. However, limited partnerships (and in most circumstances LLPs) are treated as transparent and it is the partners who are liable.

Persons carrying on businesses, whether trades or not, in partnership are referred to collectively as a firm (*CTA 2009, s 1257*) and a firm is not to be regarded for corporation tax purposes as an entity separate and distinct from the partners unless otherwise indicated (*CTA 2009, s 1258*).

The treatment of LLPs follows this by treating all the activities as if they were carried on in partnership by its members and not by the LLP if it carries on a trade or business with a view to profit (*CTA 2009, s 1273*). This treatment continues during a temporary cessation of the business and during a winding up if it is not connected to tax avoidance (*CTA 2009, s 1273(3), (4)*). So LLPs that are not carrying on a trade or business with a view to profit are within the charge to corporation tax.

Non-resident companies are only chargeable to corporation tax on the profits of a trade carried on through a permanent establishment in the UK. Corporation tax is assessed and charged on the full amount of profits arising in an accounting period. Non-resident companies which have a UK source of income such as rent are chargeable to income tax at the basic rate and are not liable to corporation tax. For a discussion of company residence, see **24.1**.

The UK means Great Britain and Northern Ireland (*Interpretation Act 1978, Sch 1*) and extends to the mean low water mark. It is deemed to include the territorial sea for the purposes of the *Corporation Tax Acts (CTA 2010, s 1170)*. The territorial sea of the UK generally extends to 12 nautical miles from the low water mark around the coast (*Territorial Sea Act 1987, ss 1* and *4(2)*). The Isle of Man and the Channel Islands are not part of the UK and where they are within 24 nautical miles of the UK the territorial sea extends to the median line. The Isles of Scilly, Isle of Wight, islands off the Welsh coast and the Northern and Western Islands of Scotland are all part of the UK.

Oil exploration and exploitation activities on the UK sector of the continental shelf are treated as if they were activities carried on through a permanent establishment in the UK (*CTA 2009, s 1313*).

The corporation tax legislation has now been completely separated from income tax legislation and is contained mainly in the *Corporation Tax Acts* of *2009* and *2010* (*CTA 2009 and CTA 2010*). International matters are contained in the *Taxation (International and Other Provisions) Act 2010* (*TIOPA 2010*).

The charge to corporation tax

17.2   The charge to corporation tax applies to the aggregate amount of profits and gains for an accounting period, as reduced by available losses (see **17.5**). Particular rules apply to how profits and gains from different sources are calculated:

- the profits of a trade (*CTA 2009, s 35*);

- the profits of a property business (*CTA 2009, s 209*);

- the profits from its loan relationships (*CTA 2009, s 295*); and

- miscellaneous income (*CTA 2009, s 932*) (which covers income not otherwise within the charge to corporation tax *CTA 2009, s 979*).

- the total amount of the chargeable gains for an accounting period as computed in accordance with the principles applying for capital gains tax (*TCGA 1992, s 8*).

17.3   A company's profits are calculated by reference to the company's accounts but as adjusted for a number of items. For example:

- Depreciation of fixed assets is not allowable but instead there is a system of capital allowances that give relief for the cost of the assets.

- Gains on the disposal of fixed assets are calculated using normal capital gains tax rules but can be reduced for inflation by the use of an indexation allowance.

Further details regarding the adjustments required to be made to accounting profits can be seen at **19.2**.

Example 17.1 – Pro forma tax computation

Westing Limited

Corporation Tax Computation

		Trading £	Property £	Other £	Gains £	Total £
Profit per accounts		21,000	(5,500)	5,000	25,000	45,500
Add back:						
	Depreciation	2,000				2,000
	Legal fees re new lease		15,000			15,000
	Interest payable	8,000	2,000			10,000
Less:						
	Capital allowances	(3,000)	(1,500)			(4,500)
	Indexation allowance				(5,000)	(5,000)
Total profits		28,000	10,000	5,000	20,000	63,000

17.4 Profits from mutual trading are not, however, taxable. For there to be a mutual trade, the contributors to the mutual surplus, as a class, must be identical to the participators in the surplus and the common fund must be owned by them. On a winding up the surplus must go back to the contributors in proportion to their contribution. However, in practice HMRC only require the current contributors and those who ceased within five years to be considered (BIM24115). It is not membership of a body that is important so a non-member who is a contributor and who is entitled to share in the surplus will not jeopardise mutual trading status (*Ayrshire Employers Mutual Insurance Association Ltd v CIR* HL 1946, 27 TC 331).

LOSSES – OUTLINE

17.5 Losses can be set off against profits in a variety of ways depending on the nature of the losses and the activities carried on by the company. Loss utilisation is dealt with below under the appropriate heading. See also HMRC's toolkit on company losses (www.hmrc.gov.uk/agents/toolkits/ct-losses.pdf).

The following is a summary:

Type of loss	Current year	Carry forward	Carry back	Group relief
Trading losses *(see 19.12)*	Against total profits	Against profits from the same trade	Against total profits - 1 year (extended to 3 years in respect of terminal losses)	In same year
Non-trading loan relationship losses (see 20.8)	Against total profits	Against non-trading profits	Against total profits - 1 year	In same year
UK Property business losses (see **21.4**)	Against total profits	Against total profits	No	In same year
Overseas property business losses (see **21.4**)	No	Against overseas property income only	No	No
Surplus expenses of management (see 22.4)	Against total profits	Against total profits	No	In same year

Example 17.2 – Pro forma tax computation: utilisation of losses

Westing Limited

Corporation Tax Computation

	Trading £	Property £	Other £	Gains £	Total £
Income and gains	28,000	10,000	5,000	20,000	63,000
Management expenses					
b/fwd	(15,000)				

current	(12,000)					
	(27,000)	(27,000)				(27,000)
Non trading loan relationship deficit						
b/fwd	(50,000)	(1,000)	(10,000)	(5,000)	(20,000)	(36,000)
current	(30,000)					
Taxable total profits		Nil	Nil	Nil	Nil	Nil

Notes

1 The management expenses have to be set off first against total profits before the non-trading loan relationship losses (*CTA 2009, s 1219; CTA 2010, s 4(2)*).

2 There are surplus non-trading loan relationship losses of £14,000 brought forward which can be carried forward to the next period for set off against non-trading profits. The current year non-trading loan relationship losses of £30,000 can be group relieved (*CTA 2010, s 99*) if there is a group company with sufficient profits or carried forward to the next period.

Changes were announced at the Budget 2016 with regards to the utilisation of corporate losses arising on or after 1 April 2017. A more flexible system is proposed, relaxing the current restriction on the use of losses which are carried forward, so that they may be set against profits from other streams and from other companies within a group.

Restrictions were also announced in respect of large companies, which from 1 April 2017 will limit the set off of brought forward losses in a year where it makes substantial profits.

These changes are still to be consulted on and full details about how they will work are not expected until the release of the Finance Bill 2017.

ACCOUNTING PERIODS

17.6 An accounting period of a company begins when the company comes within the charge to corporation tax or immediately after the end of the previous accounting period if the company is still within the charge to corporation tax. A UK resident company is treated as coming within the charge to corporation tax when it starts to carry on business if it would not otherwise be within the charge to corporation tax. An investment company that only receives dividends from other UK companies is treated as starting to carry on business when it first acquires shares in a non-dormant company (CTM01420). If a chargeable gain or an allowable loss accrues to a company at a time when the company does not otherwise have an accounting period, then an accounting period starts at that time (*CTA 2009, s 9*).

An accounting period ends on the first occurrence of a number of circumstances. These include the ending of 12 months from the beginning of the accounting period, an accounting date of the company, the end of any period for which the company does not make up accounts, the company starting or ceasing to trade, the company coming or ceasing to be within the charge to corporation tax in respect of a trade or if it carries on more than one trade in respect of all trades, the company beginning or ceasing to be UK resident, the company ceasing to be within the charge to corporation tax, the company entering into administration, and the company ceasing to be in administration (*CTA 2009, s 10*).

Specific rules apply to determine the date upon which an accounting period begins and ends in respect of companies being wound up (*CTA 2009, s 12*).

In cases where accounts are made up to varying dates where they are normally no more than four days from a mean date, HMRC will accept each period of account as if it were made up to the mean date (CTM01560).

Profits are apportioned between the financial years in which the accounting period falls on a time basis (*CTA 2010, s 1172*). However, for long accounting periods it is permissible to use other methods of apportionment, such as the actual results in a period, where it is necessary to do so (*CTA 2009, s 52* and the case of *Marshall Hus & Partners Ltd v Bolton* (1980) 55TC539. See also CTM01405).

Example 17.3 – Accounting periods

Brae Limited was incorporated on 15 November 2014 and started to trade on 5 December 2014. It makes up its accounts to 31 March each year.

Its first accounting period is the period from 5 December 2014 to 31 March 2015.

Its next accounting period will be the 12 months to 31 March 2016.

CORPORATION TAX RATES

17.7   The corporation tax rate is set for each financial year. The financial year 2014 means the 12-month period ending on 31 March 2015. The rates are as follows:

Financial year	Full rate	Small profits rate	Marginal rate
2014	21%	20%	21.25%
2015	20%		
2016	20%		
2017 to 2019	19%		
2020	17%		

A more comprehensive table of corporation tax rates is included at the end of this chapter.

Prior to 2015 the full rate of corporation tax applied where a company had profits of £1.5 million or more and the small companies' rate applied where the profits were £300,000 or less. For profits between these limits the marginal rate applied. Close investment holding companies (see **18.2**) could not benefit from the small profits rate.

Associated companies

17.8   Prior to the financial year 2015, provisions were in place to prevent a larger business being split over a number of companies so that each company was taxed at the small profits rate.

These provisions applied to ensure that where companies were under common control, known as associated companies, the limits were divided by the number of companies that were associated with each other.

With the equalisation of corporation tax rates from that time, this has largely become of academic interest only. However, the provisions are still relevant for accounting periods that straddle 1 April 2015 as the periods before and after 1 April are treated as two separate accounting periods for the purpose of applying these rules. Detailed commentary on these provisions can be found in the Tax Guide 2015/16 and earlier editions.

The concept of associated companies is still relevant for deciding whether a company is 'large' for determining whether quarterly payments of corporation tax are required (see **50.5**) and for determining the rates are which corporation tax is charged on ring fence profits from oil activities, although from 1 April 2015, both of these apply where there are 'related 51% group company' rather than 'associated companies'.

COMPLIANCE ISSUES

Corporation tax returns

17.9   The company must make a return of its income and gains to HMRC on Form CT600, which should be supported by computations of the company's tax position and statutory accounts for the period. These must be filed electronically within 12 months of the end of the accounting period. For long periods of account, the filing date is 12 months from the end of the period of account (*FA 1998, Sch 18, para 14*). A period of account is the period for which the statutory accounts are drawn up.

A company can change its accounting reference date, that is the date to which it draws up its accounts, by giving notice to the Registrar of Companies of its new accounting reference date and whether the period is to be shortened or extended. Where a period has been extended it may not be extended again within five years of an earlier extension, subject to limited exceptions. An accounting reference period cannot be extended so as to exceed 18 months (*CA 2006, s 392*).

Focus

From 1 April 2011, accounts and tax computations that are also filed with the return must be tagged with the iXBRL language to enable them to be automatically read by a computer (*FA 1998, Sch 18*) (*Income and Corporation Taxes (Electronic Communications) Regulations 2003, SI 2003/282* and *Revenue Directions*).

HMRC operate a policy of not requiring clubs and unincorporated associations which do not expect their annual corporation tax liability to exceed £100 and run exclusively for the benefit of its own members to file a corporation tax return (*COM23110*). However, excluded from this policy are privately owned clubs run by their members as a commercial enterprise for personal profit, housing associations, trade associations, thrift funds, holiday clubs, mutual insurance arrangements and subsidiaries of charities.

APPENDIX: RATES OF CORPORATION TAX

(CTA 2010, Pt 2, Ch 2, 3; Pt 3)

17.10

	Financial year commencing 1 April				
	2020	**2017 to 2019**	**2015 & 2016**	**2014**	**2013**
Small profits rate	N/A	N/A	N/A	20%	20%
Small profits rate can be claimed by qualifying companies with profits not exceeding	N/A	N/A	N/A	£300,000	£300,000
Marginal relief lower limit	N/A	N/A	N/A	£300,000	£300,000
Marginal relief upper limit	N/A	N/A	N/A	£1,500,000	£1,500,000
Standard fraction	N/A	N/A	N/A	1/400	3/400
Main rate of corporation tax	17%	19%	20%	21%	23%
	2012	**2011**	**2010**	**2009**	**2008**
Small profits rate	20%	20%	21%	21%	21%
Small profits rate can be claimed by qualifying companies with profits not exceeding	£300,000	£300,000	£300,000	£300,000	£300,000
Marginal relief lower limit	£300,000	£300,000	£300,000	£300,000	£300,000
Marginal relief upper limit	£1,500,000	£1,500,000	£1,500,000	£1,500,000	£1,500,000
Standard fraction	2/200	3/200	7/400	7/400	7/400
Main rate of corporation tax	24%	26%	28%	28%	28%

Notes

1   *Formerly known as* – Prior to 1 April 2010, the 'small profits rate' was known as the 'small companies' rate', 'marginal relief' as 'marginal small companies' relief', and 'standard fraction' as 'marginal small companies' relief fraction'.

2   *Main rates* – The small profits rate has been abolished from 2015 which removes the need for marginal relief (*FA 2013, s 6*).

3   *Patent box* – For accounting periods beginning on and after 1 April 2013, any company can elect for a reduced rate of corporation tax to be applied to all profits attributable to qualifying intellectual property. The reduced rate of 10% is being phased in, with the full benefit only being available from 1 April 2017 (see **25.9**).

4   *Profit thresholds* – The lower and upper limits for the small profits rate and marginal relief purposes are reduced proportionately for accounting periods of less than 12 months. The limits are also divided by the number of associated companies carrying on a trade or business for all or part of the accounting period (*CTA 2010, s 25*). The small profits rate does not apply to 'close investment holding companies' (*CTA 2010, s 18(b)*).

5   *Unit trusts and OEICs* – These companies are subject to corporation tax set at the basic income tax rate charged for the tax year beginning on 6 April in that financial year (*CTA 2010, ss 614, 618*). For financial years 2008 to 2016 the applicable tax rate is 20%.

6   *Oil and gas* – For companies with ring-fenced profits from oil-related activities, the small profits rate for financial years 2007 to 2016 is 19% and the ring fence fraction is 11/400 (*FA 2011, s 6*). The main rate of tax for ring fence profits for financial years 2008 to 2016 is 30%.

7   *Above the line R&D* – For qualifying expenditure incurred on and after 1 April 2013, large companies can claim an above the line research and development credit at the rate of 10% (*FA 2013, Sch 14*) and 11% for expenditure incurred on and after 1 April 2015 (*FA 2015, s 27*).

18

Close companies

SIGNPOSTS

- **Scope** – A close company is broadly a company controlled by a small number of individuals (see **18.1**).

- **Close investment holding company** – Such a company does not exist wholly or mainly to trade or let property to unconnected parties (see **18.2**).

- **Benefits to participators** – These may be taxed as dividends, where the participator is not taxed on them as employment income (see **18.3**).

- **Loans to participators** – These generally require the company to pay an amount to HMRC, which is repayable to the company to the extent that the loan is repaid, released or written off (see **18.4**).

WHAT IS A CLOSE COMPANY?

18.1   A close company is a UK-resident company that is controlled by five or fewer participators, or any number of participators if those participators are all directors. A participator is essentially a shareholder or someone who has lent the company money. Any rights and powers that a person's relatives or business partners have are attributed to them for this purpose. Relatives include spouses, civil partners, parents or remoter forebear, children or remoter issue and brothers and sisters, but not spouses of relatives (*CTA 2010, s 439*). Relatives and business partners are called 'associates'.

Control of a company includes possession of the greater part of the share capital, the greater part of the voting power, entitlement to the greater part of the income if it were to be distributed, or the greater part of the assets on a winding up. If two or more persons together satisfy these conditions they are treated as having control (*CTA 2010, s 450*). This is extended to include future entitlement as well as present entitlement (*CTA 2010, s 451*).

Example 18.1 – A close company

Belmont Limited is owned as to 30% by John Hillswick, 20% by Peter Quarff and 50% by Alan Sumburgh.

Belmont Limited is a close company, and would still be close if John's holding were in fact owned by ten individuals who owned 3% each, as Peter and Alan between them control 70%.

Non-resident companies, companies controlled by the Crown, certain companies controlled by non-close companies, and quoted companies in which shares carrying at least 35% of the voting rights are held by the public are not to be treated as close companies (*CTA 2010, ss 442–445*).

CLOSE INVESTMENT HOLDING COMPANIES

18.2   A 'close investment holding company' is a close company that does not exist wholly or mainly for the purposes of carrying on a trade or for the letting of land and buildings to unconnected third parties (*CTA 2010, s 34*).

The consequences of a company being a close investment holding company are:

● The company cannot benefit from the small profits' rate of corporation tax (see **17.6**), although with the equalisation of corporation tax, this in no longer relevant from 1 April 2015.

● Tax relief available to an individual to buy an interest in or loan money to a close company is not available where that close company is a close investment holding company (see **9.9**).

BENEFITS TO PARTICIPATORS

18.3   Benefits in kind provided to participators of a close company who are not taxed on them as employees are treated as dividends and taxed on them accordingly (*CTA 2010, s 1064*).

However, if the participator is a company which owns at least 51% of the company providing the benefit, or both are 51% subsidiaries of another company, then the benefit is not treated as a dividend as long as all the companies are UK resident (*CTA 2010, s 1066*).

> **Example 18.2 – Car provided to a participator**
>
> Adrian Nesting owns 25% of Sandwick Limited which provides him with a car. He is not a director or employee of that company and not charged to tax on the benefit of the car as employment income.
>
> The cash equivalent of the benefit, as calculated under the rules for employment income, will be taxed on him as a dividend.

LOANS TO PARTICIPATORS

18.4   A close company that makes a loan to any of the following can be subject to tax on the value of that loan under the 'loans to participator' provisions (*CTA 2010, s 455*):

- A participator of the company, or an associate of such a participator.

- A trustee of a settlement where at least one of the trustees or beneficiaries is a participator in the company, or an associate of such a participator.

- A partnership, whether limited or otherwise, where at least one partner is an individual who is a participator in the company, or an associate of such a participator.

Loans by companies to employee shares schemes and employee benefit trusts can be caught if the trust or the trustees hold shares or they make payments to shareholders to buy their shares (see CTM61525).

The purpose of these provisions is to prevent participators benefiting from company funds loaned to them, rather than declaring a divided upon which they would be subject to income tax.

For loans made before 6 April 2016 the rate of tax charged was 25%, which corresponded with the effective rate of income tax arising on a dividend paid to a higher rate taxpayer.

Following the changes to the taxation of dividends with effect from 6 April 2016 (see **7.8**), the rate of tax has increased to 32.5% in respect of any loans made on or after that date.

The tax charge is based upon the value of the loan outstanding at the year end, although relief is given where that balance is reduced within nine months of the year end.

The tax will be repaid nine months after the end of the accounting period in which repayment or write off of the loan is made (*CTA 2010, s 458*). Where only part of the loan is repaid or written off, only a proportion of the tax corresponding to that part is repaid.

> **Example 18.3 – Loan to a participator**
>
> Mr Bell is the sole shareholder of Clapper Ltd. On 1 May 2016, Clapper Ltd loans £100,000 to Mr Bell. The company's year end is 30 June 2016, and at that time, the balance of the loan outstanding amounts to £80,000. By the 31 March 2017, Mr Bell has repaid further amounts and the outstanding loan is £30,000.
>
> In this case, it is the amount outstanding on 31 March 2017 (nine months after the year end) that is relevant. As the loan was provided after 6 April 2016, the rate applicable under *CTA 2010 s 455* is 32.5% and the charge amounts to £9,750. This falls due for payment on 1 April 2017.
>
> Assuming the remaining balance of the loan is repaid before 30 June 2017, the tax paid will be able to be reclaimed by the company on 1 April 2018.

If a loan to a participator is written off, no corporation tax relief is available for the write-off (*CTA 2009, s 321A*).

> **Focus**
>
> Loans to participators also arise from directors' overdrawn loan accounts. HMRC have produced a directors' loan account toolkit which may be helpful in identifying amounts that should be included in such loan accounts (www.hmrc.gov/agents/toolkits/dla.pdf).

Whether a bonus which cannot be drawn because of a restriction but which is taxable (under *Rule 3(a)* of *ITEPA 2003, s 18(1)* (see **19.7**)) can be taken into account in determining whether an account is overdrawn will depend on the facts (see CTM61565 for a discussion on aggregating accounts).

Dividends are brought into account in the case of interim dividends when they are actually paid but for final dividends when they are payable.

The legislation is extended to cover attempts to sidestep it. Where a close company makes a loan which does not otherwise give rise to a tax charge and a person other than the close company makes a payment or transfers property to, or releases or satisfies a liability of, a participator in the company or an associate of that participator then the loan is treated as made to that person (*CTA 2010, s 459*).

It also catches the case where the participator is a participator in a company that controls the close company (*CTA 2010, s 459(4)*). It might be possible to avoid this section if it can be shown that the arrangements were made by a person in the ordinary course of a business carried on by that person (*CTA 2010, s 459(3)*).

Example 18.4 – Loans to participators: extension of rule

Edward would like to recover the £1 million that he has lent to his company Cunningburgh Limited which it uses as working capital in its trade. Edward also owns Mainland Limited which has surplus cash. Mainland therefore lends Cunningburgh £1 million which it uses to repay £1 million to Edward. So Mainland now funds Cunningburgh and Edward has been repaid in full.

Unfortunately this is caught by *s 459* and Mainland will have to pay £325,000 to HMRC (assuming that the loan was provided after 6 April 2016).

Section 459 can also cause difficulties for management buy outs where, for example, a Newco acquires shares in Target, Target lends funds to Newco and Newco uses the cash to pay the shareholders in Target for their shares. The conditions for *s 459* are satisfied and a tax liability arises. This could be avoided if the shareholders are removed from the share register first or Target pays a dividend (rather than lending funds) to Newco.

A further extension of *s 455* treats a loan by a company controlled by a close company as if it were made by the close company (*CTA 2010, s 460*). This would catch an arrangement where the subsidiary was a non-resident company (which as we have seen is not to be treated as a close company by *s 442*).

Benefits conferred on participators or their associates as a result of tax avoidance arrangements are also caught (*CTA 2010, s 464A*), as are attempts to repay loans and then take them out again which will result in restrictions on repayment of the tax (*CTA 2010, ss 464C, 464D*). The repayment restrictions apply to repayments of at least £5,000 and new loans made within 30 days but where the loan repayment is at least £15,000 there is no time limit if there is an intention, or arrangements have been made, to make a fresh loan.

A benefit-in-kind charge may also arise on an individual where they are in receipt of a loan from a close company (see **2.55**).

19

Trading companies

SIGNPOSTS

- **What is 'trading'?** – The 'badges of trade' point to whether an activity amounts to trading (see **19.1**).

- **Trading profits** – These are calculated in accordance with generally accepted accounting practice and are adjusted for items that are not allowable or taxable (see **19.2–19.11**).

- **Trading losses** – These can be utilised by set-off against other profits in the same year, carried back one year for set-off against any profits of that year and carried forward for offset against future profits from the same trade (see **19.12**).

TRADING – OUTLINE

19.1 To establish whether there is a trade being carried on, it is necessary to look at the so-called badges of trade. These were spelt out by the Vice Chancellor in the High Court in the case of *Marson v Morton* Ch D 1986, 59 TC 381 (at p 391) as follows:

'The matters which are apparently treated as a badge of trading are as follows:

(1) That the transaction in question was a one-off transaction. Although a one-off transaction is in law capable of being an adventure in the nature of trade, obviously the lack of repetition is a pointer which indicates there might not here be trade but something else.

(2) Is the transaction in question in some way related to the trade which the taxpayer otherwise carries on? For example, a one-off purchase of silver cutlery by a general dealer is much more likely to be a trade transaction than such a purchase by a retired colonel.

(3) The nature of the subject matter may be a valuable pointer. Was the transaction in a commodity of a kind which is normally the subject matter of trade and which can only be turned to advantage

by realisation, such as referred to in the passage that the Chairman quoted from *Reinhold* (34 TC 389). For example, a large bulk of whisky or toilet paper is essentially a subject matter of trade, not of enjoyment.

(4)   In some cases attention has been paid to the way in which the transaction was carried through: was it carried through in a way typical of the trade in a commodity of that nature?

(5)   What was the source of finance of the transaction? If the money was borrowed that is some pointer towards an intention to buy the item with a view to its resale in the short term; a fair pointer towards trade.

(6)   Was the item which was purchased resold as it stood or was work done on it or relating to it for the purposes of resale? For example, the purchase of second-hand machinery which was repaired or improved before resale. If there was such work done, that is again a pointer towards the transaction being in the nature of trade.

(7)   Was the item purchased resold in one lot as it was bought, or was it broken down into saleable lots? If it was broken down it is again some indication that it was a trading transaction, the purchase being with a view to resale at profit by doing something in relation to the object bought.

(8)   What were the purchasers' intentions as to resale at the time of purchase? If there was an intention to hold the object indefinitely, albeit with an intention to make a capital profit at the end of the day, that is a pointer towards a pure investment as opposed to a trading deal. On the other hand, if before the contract of purchase is made a contract for resale is already in place, that is a very strong pointer towards a trading deal rather than an investment. Similarly, an intention to resell in the short term rather than the long term is some indication against concluding that the transaction was by way of investment rather than by way of a deal.

However, as far as I can see, this is in no sense decisive by itself.

(9)   Did the item purchased provide enjoyment for the purchaser (for example, a picture), or pride of possession, or produce income pending resale? If it did, then that may indicate an intention to buy either for personal satisfaction or to invest for income yield, rather than do a deal purely for the purpose of making a profit on the turn. I will consider in a moment the question whether, if there is no income produced or pride of possession pending resale, that is a strong pointer in favour of it being a trade rather than an investment.

I emphasise again that the matters I have mentioned are not a comprehensive list and no single item is in any way decisive. I believe that in order to reach a proper factual assessment in each case it is necessary to stand back, having looked at those matters, and look at the whole picture and ask the question – and for this purpose it is no bad thing to go back to the words of the statute – was this an adventure in the nature of trade? In some cases perhaps more homely language might be appropriate by asking the question, was the taxpayer investing the money or was he doing a deal?'

See also HMRC's Business Income Manual (at BIM20205) and **3.5**.

Focus

Was this an adventure in the nature of trade? In some cases perhaps more homely language might be appropriate by asking the question, was the taxpayer investing the money or was he doing a deal?

A trade starts when the company opens its doors for business even though it may not immediately receive any income.

A trade is not very helpfully defined as including 'any venture in the nature of trade' (*CTA 2010, s 1119*). It is a narrower concept than activity or business – not every activity that a company carries on is a business and not every business carried on is a trade. A business that does not amount to trading would include holding properties as investments to receive the rent rather than making a profit from buying and selling them.

Example 19.1 – Whether a company is carrying on a business

A company's claim to small profits rate was affected by whether its associated company was carrying on a trade or business. The associated company had received bank interest on its deposit account but had not carried out any other activity during that accounting period.

The Court of Appeal agreed with the Special Commissioner decision that it 'was in a state of suspended animation and carried on no trade or business during the relevant period.

Despite receiving interest, this did not mean that the company was carrying on an investment business (*Jowett v O'Neill & Brennan Construction Ltd* 70 TC 566; [1998] STC 482). For the meaning of associated companies see **17.7**.

TRADING PROFITS

19.2 Corporation tax is charged on profits of companies and profits means income and chargeable gains. The profits of the trade must be calculated in accordance with UK generally accepted accounting practice (GAAP).

However, no deduction is allowed for items of a capital nature and for other items for which there are rules specifically restricting deductions (*CTA 2009, s 2*) as explained below.

Capital expenditure

19.3 Capital expenditure is expenditure that brings into existence an asset for the 'enduring benefit' of the trade and, subject to anything to the contrary in the Corporation Taxes Acts is not deductible (*CTA 2009, s 53*; see the case of *Atherton v British Insulated and Helsby Cables Ltd* HL 1925, 10 TC 155).

The above case concerned an initial payment into a staff pension fund which was held not to be deductible as it was a capital payment to set up the pension fund.

Depreciation of capital assets is not an allowable deduction for computing trade profits (see **59.13**). Instead, there is a system of capital allowances on plant and machinery (see **4**).

'Wholly and exclusively'

19.4

> **Focus**
>
> To be deductible, expenditure has to be incurred wholly and exclusively for the purpose of earning profits in the trade and no deduction is allowed for losses not connected with or arising out of the trade (*CTA 2009, s 54*).

An identifiable part or identifiable proportion of the expenditure incurred wholly and exclusively for the purposes of the trade may be deducted, however expenses which have been incurred for a dual purpose are not allowable. Losses from other activities may in fact be deducted when calculating the taxable profits but not when calculating the profits from the trade.

Expensive car hire

19.5   Expenditure on car hire is restricted by 15% for cars with emissions of 130g/km (160 g/km up to 6 April 2013) or more. Electric cars are not restricted in this way.

Entertainment

19.6   Deductions are not allowed for business entertainment except where the entertainment is provided for employees (*CTA 2009, ss 1298* and *1299*).

Business gifts are generally not allowable (*CTA 2009, s 1298*) however this is subject to certain exceptions, for example small gifts incorporating a conspicuous advertisement for the company, unless the gift is food, drink, tobacco or a voucher exchangeable for goods (*CTA 2009, s 1300*).

Unpaid remuneration

19.7   Remuneration that is not paid within nine months of the year end is not deductible until the period in which it is paid (*CTA 2009, s 1288*).

Remuneration is 'paid' when it is credited to an account on which the employee is free to draw unless the employee is a director in which case the rule applies even if he is not free to draw on the account (*ITEPA 2003, Rule 3(a) of s 18(1), s 686(1); CTA 2009, s 1289(4)*; see also EIM42310).

Pension contributions

19.8   The amounts paid into a registered pension scheme are allowable for tax purposes in the period in which they are paid. The payments must be wholly and exclusively incurred for the purposes of earning profits in the trade.

Spreading may be required where contributions are paid for two successive chargeable periods and the payment in the second period exceeds the payment in the first period by more than 210%.

In such cases, spreading is only required where the payments in the second period exceed 110% of the payments in the first period (the 'relevant excess') by £500,000.

Where this relevant excess is between £500,000 and £1 million, 50% of the relevant excess is relieved in the following period. Between £1 million and £2 million, one third of the relevant excess is relieved in the following year and one third the year after. For relevant excesses of £2 million or more, 25% is relieved in each of the next three years (*FA 2004, s 197* and PTM043400).

Example 19.2 – Spreading of tax relief for pension contributions

In the year to 31 December 2015, a contribution is paid to a registered pension scheme of £1 million, which is allowed for that year, and £2.9 million is paid in the following year.

The contribution of £2.9 million in the second year is greater than 210% of the contributions in the first year (£1 million × 210% = £2.1 million) therefore spreading needs to be considered.

The relevant excess is £1.8 million (£2.9 million less 110% of £1 million) so needs to be spread over three years.

The company can benefit from a deduction of £1.7 million in the year ended 31 December 2016, being 110% of the contribution in the first year (£1.1 million) plus one third of the amount needed to be spread (£0.6 million).

A further deduction of £0.6 million is allowed in both the year ended 31 December 2017 and the year ended 31 December 2018.

Payments to Employee Benefit Trusts (EBTs)

19.9   Payments into an EBT are not allowable deductions in the paying company until the benefits are taxed on the employees if they are not provided within nine months of the year end (*CTA 2009, ss 1290–1296* and BIM44570).

Deductions for employee share acquisitions

19.10   A company that grants share options or awards shares to its employees can claim a corporation tax deduction equal to the amount on which the employee is chargeable to income tax, or would be chargeable if the shares were not received under an approved share scheme. Corporation tax relief is given in the period in which the employee acquires the shares (*CTA 2009, Part 12*).

TAX COMPUTATION FOR A TRADING COMPANY

19.11   The following is a typical tax computation to arrive at the adjusted trading profit with references to the paragraph where the treatment is discussed:

Example 19.3 – Corporation tax computation

	£	£
Profit per accounts		10,000
Add back		
Depreciation (**59.14**)	2,000	
Unpaid remuneration (**19.7**)	4,000	
Capital expenditure written off (**19.3**)	1,500	
General dilapidations provision (**59.6**)	5,000	
Future loss provision (**59.7**)	20,000	
Entertaining customers (**19.6**)	1,000	
Pension closing less opening accrual (**19.8**)	1,200	
FRS 102, s 28 adjustment re: increase in pension		
scheme deficit charged to P/L (**59.15**)	15,000	
Expensive car lease disallowance (**19.5**)	2,500	
Loss on sale of car (**59.14**)	3,000	
		55,200
Less		
Capital allowances (**19.3**)	2,100	
R&D additional 125% of £40,000 spent (**25.8**)	50,000	
		(52,100)
Taxable profit		13,100
Less		
Trading loss brought forward		(5,000)
		8,100
Group relief (**23.2**)		(2,000)
Profits chargeable to corporation tax		6,100
Corporation tax at 20%		1,220
Tax payable under *CTA 2010, s 455* on £10,000		
loan to a participator (**18.4**)		3,250
Tax chargeable		4,470

LOSSES

19.12   Trading losses can generally be set against any profits arising in the same year (including non-trading profits and capital gains), be carried forward against future profits from the same trade or carried back for one year to set against any profits for that year (including non-trading profits and capital gains).

In the final year of trading, any terminal loss may be carried back three years against any profits.

Losses can also be surrendered to other group companies (see **23.2**) or consortium members (see **23.3**) for periods corresponding to the period in which the loss crystallised.

> **Focus**
>
> Where there is a change of ownership of a company, losses incurred before the change of ownership can be lost if there is either a major change in the nature or conduct of the trade within any period of three years or the scale of activities has become small or negligible and the change happens before any significant revival of the trade (*CTA 2010, s 673*).

A change of ownership does not generally include interposing another company between a subsidiary company and its parent company, or between a parent company and its shareholders (*CTA 2010, ss 723, 724* and *724A*).

There are further rules to stop arrangements involving hiving down trades to new subsidiaries which then are sold to a third party and which might then be further hived down to a new subsidiary of the purchasing company (*CTA 2010, s 676*).

From 18 March 2015, contrived arrangements aimed at relieving or refreshing carried forward trading losses, non-trading loan relationship deficits and management expenses are prevented where the tax value of the arrangements is greater than their commercial value (*CTA 2010, ss 730E – 730H as inserted by FA 2015, Sch 3*).

Example 19.4 – Carry forward and back of trading losses

Norwick Limited	Y/e 31.12.2013	Y/e 31.12.2014	Y/e 31.12.2015
	£	£	£
Trading profit	100,000		50,000
Trading loss		(120,000)	
Loss carry back	(100,000)	100,000	
Loss carry forward		(20,000)	(20,000)
Adjusted profit	0	0	30,000

Changes were announced at the Budget 2016 with regards to the utilisation of corporate losses arising on or after 1 April 2017 (see **17.5**).

20

Loan relationships

SIGNPOSTS

- **Scope** – A 'loan relationship' broadly exists between a creditor and debtor in respect of a money debt, where the debt arises from the lending of money. Income and expenses related to them are taxed/relieved under the loan relationship rules (see **20.1**).

- **Debits and credits to be brought into account** – Changes were introduced from 1 January 2016 which effect the general rule as to when debits and credits are to be brought into account (see **20.2**). There are specific provisions which amend this general rule in certain circumstances, such as loan relationships between connected companies, relief for impairment losses, credits arising on the release of debts and the timing of relief for interest not paid within 12 months of the end of the relevant accounting period (see **20.3–20.6**). Changes in the way loans are accounted for under FRS 102 will potentially impact upon the tax treatment of interest free or non-market loans (see **20.7**).

- **Losses** – Non-trading loan relationship deficits may be utilised in a number of different ways. Debits and credits arising in relation to trading loan relationships are treated as part of the trading results and related losses are therefore treated as part of any trading loss arising (see **20.8**).

SCOPE OF LOAN RELATIONSHIP RULES

20.1 A loan relationship is that which exists between a creditor and debtor in respect of a money debt and the debt arises from the lending of money (*CTA 2009, s 302*).

A money debt is a debt which (*CTA 2009, s 303*):

(a) falls to be settled:

    (i) by the payment of money,

(ii)   by the transfer of a right to settlement under a debt which is itself a money debt, or

(iii)   by the issue or transfer of any share in any company;

(b)   has at any time fallen to be so settled; or

(c)   may at the option of the debtor or the creditor fall to be so settled.

Further rules treat certain relationships as loan relationships (*CTA 2009, part 6*).

Focus

Some of the rules governing loan relationships are extended to cover 'relevant non-lending relationships' which include interest bearing trade debts, judgement debts (where they carry statutory or other interest) and deferred consideration on capital disposal (where it carries interest or an exchange difference can arise). The amounts to be taken into account are the interest, exchange difference and impairment loss but not the debt itself.

There are also special rules to deal with Islamic finance, referred to as alternative financing arrangements (*CTA 2009, ss 501–520*).

The loan relationship rules apply to the exclusion of any other legislation in respect of the matters covered by those rules except for a number of specified matters such as the transfer pricing rules (*CTA 2009, s 464*).

The F(No2)A 15 introduced a number of changes to the loan relationship provisions in order to modernise them and also as a consequence of the changes to the accounting framework with the introduction of FRS 102. The majority of these changes take effect in relation to accounting period commencing on or after 1 January 2016, although there are a number of transitional provisions to deal with loan relationships in existence before that time.

Reference within the legislation to companies which are party to a loan relationship are to debtor companies (or companies with a debtor relationship) and creditor companies (or companies with creditor relationship) and unfortunately this can lead to much confusion. For this purpose, a debtor company is the company in debt, i.e. the company holding the loan relationship as a liability (or creditor) on their balance sheet. The definition of a creditor company is the reverse.

DEBITS AND CREDITS TO BE BROUGHT INTO ACCOUNT

20.2   Loan relationship debits and credits include interest paid and received on loans, the write down (or 'impairment') of loans if they have become bad or doubtful and any expenses incurred in bringing the loan relationship into existence.

For accounting periods commencing before 1 January 2016 the general principle was that all loan relationship debits and credits recognised in the company's accounts in accordance with UK GAAP were to be brought into account for tax purposes. This would include amounts recognised in the profit and loss account (or income statement) as well as amounts recognised directly to reserves (for example the statement of total recognised gains and losses) or direct to equity.

For accounting periods commencing on or after 1 January 2016 the general principle is that only amounts recognised in a company's accounts as an item of profit or loss are to be brought into account. Amounts which are initially taken to reserves and are subsequently recycled to profit and loss will be taxed when recycled.

Given the change in approach there is the potential for amounts to be brought into account twice – first when they are taken to reserves in an accounting period commencing before 1 January 2016 and then when recycled to profit and loss in an accounting period commencing on or after that date. Transitional provisions prevent this by bringing into account an amount equal and opposite to that which could be accounted for twice. This adjustment is brought into account over a five year period, commencing with the first period to which these new provisions apply (*F(No2)A 15, Sch 7, Paras 115–119*).

Connected companies

20.3   Special rules apply to loan relationships between connected companies to prevent issues arising from asymmetries between the accounting policies of such companies. In particular, these rules apply to impairment losses and late paid interest between connected companies.

Focus

For this purpose, companies are connected for an accounting period if one controls the other or both are controlled by the same person at any point in that accounting period (*CTA 2009, s 466*).

'Control' means the power of a person to secure that the affairs of the company are conducted in accordance with the person's wishes by means of shareholding, voting power, or powers in the articles or any other document regulating the company or any other company (*CTA 2009, s 472*).

Impairment losses – debits to be brought into account

20.4   The general rule is that all debits arising from the impairment of a debt are to be brought into account.

This rule is modified for loan relationships between connected companies. In these cases, no debit is to be brought into account (*CTA 2009, s 354*) unless the creditor company is under statutory insolvency measures (*CTA 2009, s 357*) or the impairment loss arises on the release of the debt in consideration for an issue of shares, and the connection between the companies only arises by virtue of that share issue (*CTA 2009, s 356*).

Release of debts – credits to be brought into account

20.5   The general rule is that all credits arising on the release of a debt are to be brought into account, however this is modified in several circumstances as set out below.

Where the loan relationship is between connected companies, to reflect that fact that any debit recognised by the creditor company is not brought into account, any credit recognised on the release of a debt by the debtor company is generally not taxable. However, particular rules apply to deem a release of the debt and bring the credit into charge where either, two companies party to a loan relationship become connected at a time when the debt is impaired or, a company acquires the debt at undervalue and is connected with the debtor. These prevent the exploitation of the connected company rules in cases where the impairment arises before connection.

With regards to loan relationships between companies which are not connected, a credit arising on the release of a debt is also not taxable where:

- The release is part of formal insolvency procedures (*CTA 2009, ss 322(3) and (5)*), or

- The release is in consideration of the issue of ordinary share capital of the debtor company (*CTA 2009, s 322(4)*), even where the value of the shares issued is substantially lower than the value of the loan released.

With regard to the second point here, HMRC state at CFM33202:

'There is no requirement for the shares issued by the debtor company to be held for any particular length of time. Indeed, regulatory capital requirements may lead a bank to sell on the shares received as part of a debt/equity swap.

Commonly any on-sale of the shares will be to an unconnected third party. On the other hand there may, for example, be arrangements (contractual or other) in place for the lender to divest itself immediately of the shares to a company connected with the borrower for nominal consideration. If so, the consideration the lender receives may be the cash it gets, not the shares; the release of the debt may be entirely gratuitous and a realistic view of the transaction may be that the shares are issued merely to obtain a tax advantage for the debtor company.'

But if the companies become connected as a result of the share issue, there is a deemed release of an amount of the debt equal to the impairment and the credit in the borrower may be taxable *(CTA 2009, s 362)*. This can be avoided where the debt is released within 60 days of the companies becoming connected, the connection arises from an arm's length transaction and at the point immediately before the companies became connected it was reasonable to assume that without the connection and associated arrangements, there would be a material risk of the debtor company being unable to pay its debts at some point within the next 12 months *(CTA 2009, s 362A)*.

Two further exemptions were introduced by F(No2) A 2015 in respect of debts between unconnected companies where they are released or substantially modified on or after 1 January 2015. These exclude the credit being brought into account where it is reasonable to assume that without that release or substantial modification of the debt, there is a material risk that the company will be unable to repay its debts at some point in the next 12 months *(CTA 2009, s 322(5B) and s 323A)*.

A modification is considered as 'substantial' if it is treated as such for accounting purposes. This could apply where there is a refinancing of the debt and GAAP requires the refinanced debt to be accounted for at fair value, resulting in a credit being taken to profit and loss.

The measure of whether a company is unable to repay its debts is by reference to either the fact that it is unable to repay them as they fall due, or the value of the company's assets is less than the amount of its liabilities *(CTA 2009, s 323(A1) and s 362A(5))*.

Unpaid interest

20.6   Interest payable on debts that is unpaid more than 12 months after the end of the accounting period is allowed only when paid if it is not brought into account by the creditor under the loan relationship rules and the parties are connected in one of the following circumstances *(CTA 2009, Pt 5, Ch 8)*:

(a)   the loan is from a participator;

(b)   the loan is made by the trustees of an occupational pension scheme.

Without this rule, interest would be allowed as a deduction when it accrued but the lender would either only be taxed on it when received (because they are outside the loan relationship rules) or would not be taxed upon it at all (because they are outside the scope of UK tax entirely).

Before 1 January 2016, additional restrictions applied in certain cases where the creditor was resident in a tax haven.

Interest-free and non-market loans

20.7 The introduction of FRS 102 will see a change in the way that many loan relationships are accounted for, as compared to the way in which they were accounted for under 'old UK GAAP' where FRS 26 was not applied.

The key difference is that initial recognition of loans will be at the present value of future expected cash flows or fair value, rather than face value. These values will be the same in many cases, but generally not where the debt is entered into on non-market terms (e.g. interest free loans).

In such cases, the accounting treatment will generally require the loan to be recognised on the balance sheet at its discounted value / fair value with the difference between this and its face value (the 'discount') being taken to equity. Over the term of the loan notional interest will be accounted for through profit and loss – the result of this is that at the end of the term, the value of the debt on the balance sheet will have accreted to face value and the total of the notional interest taken to profit and loss will be equal to the discount originally taken to equity.

From a tax perspective, consideration needs to be given to the tax treatment of the discount when it is taken to equity and the notional interest when it is taken to profit and loss. This is very much dependent upon the position of the parties to the loan relationship, and given the variables it is not possible to cover the detail here. HMRC published detailed guidance on this matter in October 2015 (www.gov.uk/government/publications/corporation-tax-treatment-of-interest-free-loans-and-other-non-market-loans) which will be included within their Corporate Finance Manual in due course.

LOSSES

20.8 Trading loan relationship debits are treated as expenses of the trade to which they relate (*CTA 2009, s 297*) and so form part of any trading loss (see **19.12**).

Non-trading loan relationship losses can be set against any profits in the same accounting period, carried back one year against profits in that period, or carried forward against non-trading profits in future periods.

See also the restrictions on the carry forward of losses where there are contrived arrangements to utilise them, set out at **19.12** above.

Example 20.1 – Utilisation of non-trade relationship losses

Uyeasound Limited is a company which carries on a trade and also lets commercial property. It has trading profits in the year to 31 December 2016 of £5,000 and has a profit in its property business of £10,000.

It has an interest charge in that year of £20,000 on a loan to buy the property which is therefore not a trading expense but is a non-trading loan relationship loss.

It can set £5,000 of this loss against its trading profit in that year and set £10,000 against its property income. It can carry forward the balance of £5,000 and set it off against its property profits or any other non-trading profits in the future.

Shell companies that do not carry on a trade, property or investment business but that have non-trading loan relationship losses cannot carry them forward to a period after a change of ownership (*CTA 2010, ss 705A–705G*).

21

Property businesses

SIGNPOSTS

- **Property businesses** – A property business generates income from land, although whether the letting of property amounts to a business depends on the facts (see **21.1**).

- **Scope** – Property income is calculated in the same way as trading income, with some extra rules to deal with matters like lease premiums (see **21.2–21.3**).

- **Losses** – The losses from a UK property business can be utilised by set-off against other profits in the same year or carried forward against other profits. Losses from an overseas property business can only be used against profits from that overseas property business (see **21.4**).

PROPERTY BUSINESSES – OUTLINE

21.1   The profits of a UK resident company's property business are liable to corporation tax. 'Property business' means a UK property business or an overseas property business (*CTA 2009, s 204 (1)*).

A UK property business consists of a business that generates income from land in the UK, such as rent, and every transaction which the company enters into for that purpose otherwise than in the course of such a business (*CTA 2009, s 205*).

An overseas property business is similarly defined but in respect of land outside the UK (*CTA 2009, s 206*).

Whether the commercial letting of property to a third party constitutes a business or not depends on the facts. The relevant cases are *American Leaf Blending Co v Director-General of Inland Revenue (Malaysia)* [1978] 3 All ER 1185 and *HMRC v Salaried Persons Postal Loans Ltd* [2006] EWHC 763 (Ch).

In the case of *Salaried Persons Postal Loans Ltd*, it was held that a company whose sole activity was the continuation of the letting to one tenant of former trading premises after it ceased to trade was not carrying on a business. This was based on a finding of fact by the Special Commissioners, which the Revenue was not able to overturn on appeal.

The case of *American Leaf Blending* is similar, but they let their premises to a succession of lessees and carried on other activities. They were held to be carrying on a business.

This issue can be of particular importance in deciding whether a limited liability partnership (LLP) is treated as opaque and taxed as a company or whether it is treated as transparent with the partners being taxed on their share of its profits (see **17.1**).

PROPERTY BUSINESS PROFITS

21.2   Profits from a property business are broadly calculated on the same basis as trading profits (*CTA 2009, s 210*). All the lettings from UK property are treated as a single UK property letting business and similarly for overseas properties the lettings are treated as a single overseas property business.

Premiums received on short leases are subject to tax partly as capital and partly as income calculated by reference to the length of the lease (*CTA 2009, ss 215–247*). For a one-year lease the whole of the premium is taxable as income, and for a 51-year lease none of the premium is taxable as income. The amount treated as income is the premium less one fiftieth of the premium for every year other than the first of the lease. So for an 11-year lease the income element of the premium is four-fifths. The capital element, in this case one-fifth, is treated as a part disposal for capital gains tax (see also **8.18**).

The payer may be able to claim a deduction for the income part over the duration of the lease as a trading expense or against property income (*CTA 2009, ss 62–67, 231–234*).

Where under the terms of the lease the tenant is obliged to carry out work on the premises, the amount by which the landlord's estate or interest is increased as a result is charged to tax as a premium (*CTA 2009, s 218*).

Deductions

21.3   Capital allowances are available in respect of assets in the let property (except where the let property is a dwelling house) and on other assets used in a property business such as office equipment.

Prior to April 2016 an election could be made in respect of furnished residential lettings for a wear and tear allowance equal to 10% of the rental income (after deducting certain expenses normally borne by the tenant) to make up for the fact that capital allowances are not available on assets used in a dwelling house,

From April 2016, all landlords of residential dwelling houses (whether the property is furnished or not) will be able to deduct the costs they actually incur on replacing furnishings, appliances and kitchenware in the property. The relief given will be for the cost of a like-for-like, or nearest modern equivalent, replacement asset, plus any costs incurred in disposing of the old asset and acquiring the new asset, less any proceeds received for the asset being replaced (*CTA 2009, s 250A as introduced by FA 2016, s 73*).

Repair expenditure is an allowable expense as long as it is not capital. This rules out expenditure on buying property and also on improvements. Acquiring an asset in a dilapidated state which needs expenditure to be incurred to put it into a position where it can be let will be capital. Expenditure to put right normal wear and tear even though this is incurred soon after the property is acquired is allowable as revenue expenditure (PIM2020).

Legal and agents' fees incurred in buying property and legal fees incurred in drawing up the first lease are capital, unless the lease is for a year or less. Legal fees for short lease renewals (i.e. less than 50 years) are, however, generally revenue expenditure as long as the renewed lease is broadly similar to the old one. Ongoing accountancy fees including those for agreeing the tax liability of the company and valuations for insurance purposes are allowable as revenue items (PIM2205).

LOSSES

21.4   Losses from a UK property business are available to set against the total profits of the accounting period and any excess can be carried forward and treated as a UK property business loss for the following period, which is able to be set against total profits for that period (*CTA 2010, s 62*).

If, however, the company ceases to carry on a UK property business, but continues to be a company with investment business, any unused losses can be carried forward as expenses of management and these are dealt with at **22.3** below.

Losses from an overseas property business, however, may only be carried forward and set off against the profits of that overseas property business (*CTA 2010, s 66*).

Focus

Loss relief is only available whether to a UK or overseas property business if it is carried on a commercial basis. This means that it must be carried on with a view to making a profit or so as to afford a reasonable expectation of making a profit (*CTA 2010, ss 62–67*).

22

Companies with investment business

SIGNPOSTS

- **Scope** –The profits of companies with investment business are calculated and charged to tax according to the rules governing that income, as are losses. There is a potential restriction for losses in certain circumstances involving a change of ownership (see **22.1–22.2**).

- **Management expenses** – Such expenses are incurred in the making and managing of investments, subject to certain exclusions such as expenses deductible in computing trading or property business profits (see **22.3**).

- **Surplus management expenses** – These can be utilised against current year income and the surplus carried forward and treated as if it were surplus for the following year (see **22.4**).

TAXATION OF PROFITS

22.1 A company with investment business is one whose business consists wholly or partly of making investments (*CTA 2009, s 1218B*). The investments could typically include shares in subsidiaries, shares in other companies, property investments, and portfolio investments. The income could therefore include such matters as dividends from shares which may in fact not be taxable, trading income (see **19**), rent which will be taxed under the property business heading (see **21**), miscellaneous income, and interest which will generally be dealt with under the heading of loan relationships (see **20**).

In calculating the total profits of a company with investment business, a deduction is allowed for its expenses of management.

LOSSES

22.2

> **Focus**
>
> Losses can take the form of excess management expenses, trade losses, property losses, or loan relationship debits and these are dealt with under the appropriate headings.

Losses are restricted where there is a change in the ownership of a company with investment business (*CTA 2010, ss 679–684*) and either:

- A significant increase in the capital of the company.

- A major change in the nature or conduct of the trade carried on by the company in the period of three years before and three years after the change.

- A change of ownership occurs after the scale of activities has become small or negligible and before any significant revival of the business.

For there to be a significant increase in the capital of a company, the increase must be at least £1 million and equate to at least 125% of the capital before the increase. Capital includes share capital, share premium, debts and accrued interest on the debts (CTA 2010, ss 688–691).

MANAGEMENT EXPENSES

22.3   Expenses of management cover expenses incurred in the making and managing of investments but exclude items of a capital nature (*CTA 2009, s 1219(3)(a)*). Also excluded are expenses that are deductible in computing the profits of a business such as a trade or a property business (*CTA 2009, s 1219(3)(b)*) and business entertaining (*CTA 2009, ss 1298, 1299, 1300*).

Although at first sight it might appear that such expenses must necessarily be capital and so be disallowed, this is not necessarily the case, and helpfully HMRC have issued clarification in their Company Taxation Manual at CTM08250:

> 'The fact that the investments of a company with investment business are likely to be held on capital account does not create a presumption that the expenses of managing those investments are themselves capital. Ordinary recurring expenditure which otherwise satisfies the tests in Section [1219] is very unlikely to be of a capital nature.

For example, we would generally expect regular, on–going costs of employment of staff in a department managing a company's investments to be non-capital.

It is also worth noting that if expenses are debited in a statement of 'capital' profits and losses in financial accounts, or in a statement that combines revenue and 'capital' items, that does not in itself exclude them from deduction as expenses of management. Section [1255] covers this point.

For details of where the capital/revenue divide might fall in the context of acquisitions and disposals, see CTM08260.'

The annotated text of CTM08260 is as follows:

'Expenditure related to acquisition of investments

Expenditure on appraising and investigating investments will in general be revenue in nature. However, the process of appraisal will eventually reach the stage where the company will decide which, if any, companies it is seeking to acquire.

Expenditure up to the point at which a decision is made to acquire a particular investment will generally be non-capital. For example, expenses incurred on obtaining preliminary reports and profit forecasts for a number of investment options, such as any prudent investor might obtain, are not capital expenditure because at this point the company is merely appraising its investment opportunities.

Once the decision to acquire is made then the expenditure is capital in nature and therefore disallowed by [*CTA 2009, s 1219(3)*].

The point at which a decision to acquire is made will depend on the particular facts in each case. In the context of a take–over the making of any offer to the target company, including an indicative or conditional offer, would suggest that a decision to acquire that investment has been made and any expenditure incurred thereafter would be capital in nature.

A success fee is likely to be capital in nature. It is also unlikely to be an expense of management on first principles. [This is dealt with in more detail at CTM08190 which is not reproduced here.]

Expenditure connected with the disposal of an investment

Similar considerations apply where it is a disposal rather than an acquisition that is being considered. Once it has been decided to dispose of an investment in some way, any costs incurred after that point will be costs of the disposal and therefore capital. We would generally consider the decision to dispose of an asset to be the point at which a decision was taken to market it.

Abortive expenditure

An abortive acquisition or disposal is no different, in terms of the nature of expenditure, from a successful acquisition/disposal. If the expenses would be capital if the asset were acquired, they would not change their nature because the attempt to acquire it was unsuccessful.

Project development costs

Expenditure up to the point at which a decision has been made to go ahead with the investment will generally be non-capital.

It will normally be the case that once the phase of the project has been reached at which it is not a question of whether it will go ahead, but how, then the expenses will be capital from that point.'

There are a number of specific items that are allowed as management expenses even though they may be capital in nature for example the cost of setting up certain employee share schemes (*CTA 2009, s 1221*).

Expenses of management of investments held for an unallowable purpose are not allowable. Unallowable purpose means a purpose that is not a business or other commercial purpose or for the purpose of activities that are not within the charge to corporation tax. Investments held in connection with arrangements for securing a tax advantage are also held for an unallowable purpose (*CTA 2009, s 1220*).

Surplus management expenses

22.4   Management expenses and qualifying charitable donations (so far as they are made for the purposes of the company's investment business) which are unable to be deducted in full in the period are treated as surplus management expenses. These are added to any surplus management expenses brought forward from earlier accounting periods and are treated as expenses of management for the following accounting period (*CTA 2009, s 1223*).

This means that they can be set against both income and gains of the same or future accounting period.

Example 22.1 – Utilisation of management expenses

Belmont Limited has a trading profit of £120,000, UK property income of £30,000 and dividends of £20,000 from its share portfolio of UK companies. It has expenses of management of £5,000.

Its taxable profit is the aggregate of its trading profit and UK property income (being £150,000) less management expenses giving a taxable profit of £145,000 on which it will pay corporation tax. The UK dividend income is exempt (*CTA 2009, s 931B*).

23

Groups of companies

SIGNPOSTS

- **Scope** – A company and its 75% subsidiaries form a group (see **23.1**).

- **Losses** – These can be surrendered by a group company and used by another group member (see **23.2**). Losses can also be used by a consortium member (see **23.3**).

- **Capital assets** – Transfers of capital assets between group members can take place without a corporation tax charge on any gains that might otherwise arise. Capital losses can be surrendered as well, although the definition of group is modified for these purposes (see **23.4**). However, anti–avoidance provisions in the form of a degrouping charge prevent use of the 'envelope trick' (see **23.5**).

- **Intangible assets** – Transfers of intangible assets between group members can also take place without a corporation tax charge. The relief is very similar, although not identical, to that applying to the transfer of capital assets (see **23.6**).

- **Substantial shareholdings exemption** – Gains on disposals of substantial shareholdings are exempt, where certain conditions are satisfied (see **23.7**).

WHAT IS A 'GROUP'?

23.1   There are different definitions of group for different purposes but here we are concerned with a group for group relief which enables losses to be surrendered between group members.

Two companies are members of the same group if one is the 75% subsidiary of the other or both are 75% subsidiaries of a third company (*CTA 2010, s 152*). Companies do not have to be UK resident to be members of a group. A company is the 75% subsidiary of another company if at least 75% of its ordinary share capital is beneficially owned directly or indirectly by the other company (*CTA 2010, s 1154(3)*). In addition, it must be beneficially entitled to at least 75% of the distributable profits and beneficially entitled to 75% of assets available to the shareholders on a winding up (*CTA 2010, s 151*).

The existence of arrangements under which a third party could acquire the whole or part of one of the group members needs to be taken into account in deciding whether it remains a member of the group for group relief purposes (*CTA 2010, ss 171 et seq*).

Arrangements for the transfer of a group member out of the group are to be ignored where the arrangements are in normal commercial usage and not designed to avoid tax (*CTA 2010, ss 155A and 155B*). This would cover such matters as using shares as security under a mortgage and commercial terms of a joint venture agreement.

GROUP RELIEF

23.2

> **Focus**
>
> A company can surrender trading losses, excess capital allowances, non-trading loan relationship deficits, charitable donations, UK property business losses, management expenses and non-trading losses on intangible fixed assets to another group member to set against its total profits in the same accounting period (*CTA 2010, s 99*).
>
> However, the amount of losses from qualifying charitable donations, UK property businesses, excess management expenses and non-trading intangible fixed assets that can be surrendered as group relief are restricted to the excess over the company's gross profit for the period. The gross profit is the profit before any deduction for losses (*CTA 2010, s 105*).

Losses cannot be carried forward to a future accounting period and surrendered in that period. However, proposals were announced at the Budget 2016 to relax this restriction in respect of losses arising on or after 1 April 2017 (see **17.5**).

There are complicated rules to restrict the ability of a non-resident company to surrender its losses against profits of a UK-resident company.

A claimant company's profit has to be reduced by any trading losses brought forward in calculating the maximum group relief to which it is entitled (*CTA 2010, s 45*).

Where the accounting periods of the claimant and the surrendering company do not coincide, it is the losses of the overlapping period that need to be calculated and these can be surrendered up to the amount of the claimant company's profits for that overlapping period. Apportionments are done on a time basis (*CTA 2010, ss 139, 140*).

A claim for group relief must be made in a company tax return or an amendment to a return (*FA 1998, Sch 18, paras 10, 66–77A*).

Example 23.1 – Group relief

	Muness Ltd	Valhalla Ltd
	£	£
Trading profit/(loss)	50,000	(10,000)
Less: trading loss b/fwd	(20,000)	
	30,000	
Group relief	(10,000)	10,000
Profits chargeable to		
Corporation tax	20,000	nil

CONSORTIUM RELIEF

23.3 Group relief is also available between members of a consortium.

A company is owned by a consortium if it is not a 75% subsidiary of another and at least 75% of its ordinary share capital is owned by companies each of which owns at least 5% (*CTA 2010, s 153*).

Example 23.2 – A consortium

Hermaness Limited has issued share capital of 100 ordinary shares. Baltasound Limited owns 50 shares, Eshaness Limited 30 shares, Saxa Limited 16 shares and Mousa Limited four shares.

Baltasound, Eshaness and Saxa own between them 96 shares and each own at least 5% so they form a consortium.

Mousa, however, owns less than 5% so is not a member of the consortium.

If Hermaness owned 90% or more of another trading company, that would also be treated as owned by the consortium.

CHARGEABLE GAINS

Transfer of assets

23.4   Capital assets can also be transferred between members of a group without a liability to corporation tax on any chargeable gains that might otherwise crystallise.

For this purpose, the definition of a group is slightly modified and introduces the concept of a principal company (*TCGA 1992, s 170*). A group consists of a principal company and its 75% subsidiaries together with each subsidiary's 75% subsidiaries, etc. The principal company cannot be the 75% subsidiary of any other company and any companies that it owns indirectly must be effective 51% subsidiaries of it.

Furthermore, the provisions around the existence of arrangements for group relief purposes (see **23.1**) do not apply for the definition of a group for corporation tax on capital gains (*TCGA 1992, s 170(8)*).

Example 23.3 – Capital gains group

Burrafirth Limited owns 75% of Valsgarth Limited which in turn owns 75% of Clibberswick Limited and which in turn owns 75% of Eshaness Limited. Burrafirth Limited is owned by individuals.

Burrafirth Limited, Valsgarth Limited and Clibberswick Limited form a group but not Eshaness Limited, as it is not a 51% subsidiary of Burrafirth Limited. Burrafirth Limited holds an effective interest of 42.19% in Eshaness Limited ($75\% \times 75\% \times 75\% = 42.19\%$).

Neither can Eshaness be a member of Valsgarth's group because Valsgarth cannot be a principal company as it is a 75% subsidiary of Burrafirth. Nor can it be a member of Clibberswick's group because this is a 75% subsidiary of Valsgarth.

The whole or part of a capital gain or loss in one company can be transferred to another company in the group by means of a joint election no later than two years after the end of the accounting period of the company in which the gain or loss was made (*TCGA 1992, s 171A*). This enables a brought forward loss in the company to which the gain is transferred to be utilised against that gain. However, there must be a disposal of assets to a person; it is not sufficient that, for example, loan notes have been repaid giving rise to a gain (*DMWSHNZ*

Ltd (in members' voluntary liquidation) v Revenue & Customs Commissioners [2015] EWCA Civ 1036).

The ability to transfer losses can be useful, for example where one company in a large group is used to warehouse capital losses so that they can be tracked.

DEGROUPING CHARGES

23.5   Without some anti-avoidance rules it would be very easy to use what was known as the 'envelope trick' to sell an asset to a third party without paying any corporation tax on any gain. This worked by setting up a subsidiary, transferring the asset to the subsidiary and then selling the subsidiary to the third party.

These arrangements are caught by deeming the subsidiary company which has acquired the asset to have disposed of the asset and immediately reacquired it (*TCGA 1992, s 179(3)*). This gives rise to a gain in the subsidiary which is liable to tax.

However, where the degrouping charge arises by reason of a disposal of shares in the subsidiary holding the asset, the charge to tax will fall on the vendor company, by way of an adjustment to the disposal proceeds. This can enable another relief, the substantial shareholding exemption (see **23.7**), to apply where relevant. The charge to tax can also be avoided where use can be made of the reconstruction provisions.

> **Focus**
>
> Can matters be planned to exempt a degrouping charge by means of the 'substantial shareholding exemption'? This exemption is outlined below.

INTANGIBLE ASSETS

23.6   The transfer of intangible assets between group members is tax neutral. For the purposes of the intangible fixed asset regime, group is defined in a similar way as it is for capital gains tax and uses the concept of a principal company (see **23.4** and *CTA 2009, ss 764–773*).

There is a degrouping charge that falls on a transferee company that leaves the group within six years of it acquiring an intangible asset from another group member (*CTA 2009, s 780*). The charge is calculated by reference to the market value of the asset at the time of its transfer and crystallises immediately before the company leaves the group.

The degrouping charge can be avoided where use can be made of the reconstruction provisions (*CTA 2009, s 817*). However, as the degrouping charge arises on the transferee company, the substantial shareholding exemption (see **23.7**) cannot protect against it.

OTHER RELIEF

The substantial shareholding exemption

23.7 The disposal by a company of shares in a subsidiary in which it owns at least 10% of the ordinary share capital is exempt from tax if the shares have been held for at least one year. This is known as the substantial shareholding exemption (SSE), and is of course subject to a number of conditions (*TCGA 1992, Sch 7AC*).

The company making the disposal must be a trading company or the holding company of a trading group and must remain so immediately after the disposal. The company being disposed of must also be a trading company or the holding company of a trading group. The shareholding must entitle the shareholder to at least 10% of the profits available for distribution and on a winding up to at least 10% of the assets available for distribution to the equity holders.

For SSE purposes, the general definition of a chargeable gains group (see **23.4**) is amended to substitute 51% for 75%. When considering whether a group is a trading group, companies which do not form part of the chargeable gains group may therefore need to be considered. Caution is also necessary here as a group will not be the same group if a new holding company is interposed between the parent company and its members.

The disadvantage of this relief is that losses on the disposal of interests in companies are not allowable. Consequently, there are rules to prevent the conditions for the relief being breached by, for example, the company ceasing to trade before being sold. The relief is therefore extended to cover situations where the relief would have been available if the disposal had been made at any time in the period of two years prior to the actual disposal.

The relief will also apply where the company making the disposal is not a trading company or the holding company of a trading group immediately after the disposal and is wound up as soon as is reasonably practical in the circumstances.

The relief is also extended to holdings of shares in a joint venture company, that is, a company in which five or fewer persons hold at least 75% of its ordinary share capital. A person includes a company (an individual is a natural person and a company is a legal person).

Example 23.4 – Substantial shareholding exemption

Herma Limited is a trading company that owns the whole of the share capital of Saxa Limited which is also a trading company and which it has owned for ten months. Herma has been approached by a third party to sell Saxa at a price that would give rise to a considerable profit.

If it sells it now the profit will be taxable but if it delays the exchange of contracts for a couple of months the gain will be exempt.

Focus

A delay in selling a subsidiary until the conditions for relief are satisfied could secure the substantial shareholding exemption.

Note that the date of disposal is the date of the contract where the contract is unconditional and not the later date of completion. A conditional contract is one that is subject to a condition precedent, that is a condition precedent to the formation of the contract, and the disposal takes place if and when the condition is satisfied.

An example of such a condition would be if the sale of Saxa in the above example was subject to Saxa obtaining planning permission for the development of one of its sites. A condition subsequent, such as the satisfying of various terms of the agreement, does not make the contract conditional for tax purposes. Such a condition subsequent could include the delivery of Saxa's books and records to the purchaser on completion.

If Herma in the above example did not carry on its own trade but was merely the holding company of Saxa then to secure the substantial shareholding exemption it would need to be wound up as soon as was practicable following the sale of its subsidiary.

The one year holding period of shares for the SSE to apply is in certain cases treated as satisfied in the case of a company setting up a subsidiary and hiving down assets used for its trade to the subsidiary for use in its trade. As long as the parent company used the asset in its trade during the last 12 months before it transferred it, then it is treated as having held the shares during that 12-month period. This is extended to cover an asset held by another company as long as the three companies were members of the same group when the asset was transferred and the transferring member was a member of the same group when it used the asset in its trade (*TCGA 1992, Sch 7AC, para 15A*). Note that

401

the transferring member must have been a member of a group when it used the asset so a stand-alone company would not satisfy the condition but if it had a dormant subsidiary during that period it would seem that would avoid the bear trap.

This is a useful extension of the SSE as it may enable a degrouping charge to be avoided and for the disposal of a trade to a third party without crystallising any charge to corporation tax.

The Government announced at the 2016 Budget that they will undertake a review of the SSE provisions as they consider them to be in need of modernisation. A consultation was released in May 2016 to seek views on whether the provisions were still delivering the original policy objective and whether there could be changes to the provisions in order to simplify them and ensure international competitiveness. At the time of writing, a response was yet to be issued from HMRC on the comments received from the process.

24

Foreign matters

SIGNPOSTS

- **Company residence** – A company is resident in the UK if it is incorporated here or its central management and control is exercised here. A non-resident company must have sufficient presence in the form of a permanent establishment in the UK to be taxed here (see **24.1–24.2**).

- **Controlled foreign companies** – There are rules aimed at the prevention of tax avoidance by sheltering profits in a foreign subsidiary (see **24.3**).

- **Transfer pricing** – These rules are designed to prevent tax avoidance by manipulating prices. All UK companies are within the scope of these provisions, but small and medium-sized companies are only subject to them in certain circumstances (see **24.4**).

- **Double taxation relief** – Relief is given for foreign tax suffered on a company's profits. The UK has a network of double tax treaties with other territories, but where there is no treaty, unilateral tax relief is generally available (see **24.5**).

- **Diverted profit tax** – These provisions are aimed at arrangements which seek to avoid UK corporation tax by avoiding a taxable presence in the UK or undertaking operations with a lack of economic subsistence. They impose a 25% tax charge on profits from such activities (see **24.6**).

- **Profits from trading in and developing UK land** – The *Finance Act 2016* overhauled the anti-avoidance provisions relating to profits derived from land and extended them to ensure that offshore property developers are taxed on their profits from UK land in the same way as UK property developers (see **24.7**).

COMPANY RESIDENCE

24.1 A company is resident in the UK if it is incorporated in the UK (*CTA 2009, s 1114*) or its central management and control is exercised from the UK *(De Beers Consolidated Mines Ltd v Howe* HL 1906, 5 TC 198 and *Bullock v The Unit Construction Co Ltd* HL 1959, 38 TC 712). The central management and control test is based on case law and does not appear in any tax legislation. Central management and control is the highest level of control of the business of a company and may be different from the place where the day-to-day operations of the company are carried out. Where the directors exercise central management and control and the place where they meet to exercise this control is in the UK, the company will be UK resident. The obvious ruse of appointing non-UK resident directors will be ineffective, leaving aside the place of incorporation test, in making a company non-resident if they are acting under orders from UK resident individuals.

In the case of a UK resident company with a subsidiary incorporated abroad, HMRC take the view that as long as the UK resident parent only exercises the control it has as a majority shareholder in general meetings of its subsidiary, such as appointing and dismissing its directors, then the subsidiary will not be treated as managed and controlled by its parent.

However if it 'usurps the functions of the board of the subsidiary or where that board merely rubber stamps the parent company's decisions without giving them any independent consideration of its own' then the subsidiary will be treated as UK resident.

There is a helpful Statement of Practice SP 1/90 issued by HMRC that sets out their views on company residence from which the above quote is drawn.

Example 24.1 – Company residence

Baltasound Limited is incorporated in Jersey but all its operations are carried out in the UK and its directors are all UK resident.

However they hold their annual formal board meeting in Sark ('the Sark lark'). Unless there are some exceptional factors at play here, the company will be regarded as UK resident.

Obtaining a deduction for the costs of travel and accommodation might also be problematical as they would have to be shown to be incurred wholly and exclusively for the purpose of earning profits of the company.

Even if the company could be shown to be managed and controlled abroad, its profits from its UK trading operations would be subject to UK corporation tax (see **17.1** above and **24.2** below).

Focus

Rather than challenge whether the company is genuinely non-resident, HMRC may invoke the anti-avoidance provisions now contained in *ITA 2007, Pt 13, Ch 2* (Transfer of Assets Abroad).

Where these provisions apply, the company's profits can be taxed on the individual shareholders at their marginal rate of tax which may be as much as 45%.

BRANCHES AND PERMANENT ESTABLISHMENTS

24.2 As mentioned at the beginning of this chapter, a non-resident company can only be liable to corporation tax if it carries on a trade in the United Kingdom through a permanent establishment.

A permanent establishment is defined in *CTA 2010, s 1141*. It is either a fixed place of business in which the business of the company is wholly or partly carried on, or if it has an agent that habitually exercises authority in the UK to do business on behalf of the company.

In particular, a fixed place of business includes:

- a place of management,
- a branch,
- an office,
- a factory,
- a workshop,
- an installation or structure for the exploration of natural resources,
- a mine, an oil or gas well, a quarry or any other place of extraction of natural resources, and
- a building site or construction or installation project.

Independent brokers and investment managers are not regarded as permanent establishments subject to certain conditions being satisfied.

Activities of a preparatory or auxiliary nature, such as the storage, display or delivery of goods, or for collecting information for the company are not regarded as sufficient for a company to have a permanent establishment.

Example 24.2 – No permanent establishment

Haroldswick SARL is a French construction company which has secured a contract to build some houses in the UK. The work takes ten months.

Under the terms of the UK/France tax treaty, the company does not have a permanent establishment in the UK because the building site does not last for more than 12 months and so is not liable to UK tax.

Similarly if the company was UK resident and the contract was to build houses in France, it would not be liable to French tax on the profits.

Focus

An election can be made to exempt profits from a foreign permanent establishment of a UK company from UK corporation tax (*CTA 2009, s 18A*). The election takes effect from the start of the next accounting period and is then irrevocable.

Small companies' profits from countries which do not have a full tax treaty (that is one not containing a non-discrimination clause) are excluded from this exemption as are capital gains of close companies.

Anti-avoidance rules prevent it from being used to avoid a balancing charge on the sale of fixed assets that have qualified for capital allowances and to avoid tax on profits that have been artificially diverted from the UK.

CONTROLLED FOREIGN COMPANIES

24.3   The controlled foreign company rules are designed to stop a company from sheltering from UK tax, overseas profits in a foreign subsidiary located in a tax haven.

A controlled foreign company (CFC) is a non-resident company controlled by persons resident in the UK (*TIOPA 2010, 371AA(3)*). Control can be either by means of shareholding or rights contained in the articles (legal control) or having the ability to receive more than 50% of: the proceeds of sale of the share capital, the income if distributed, or the assets on a winding up (economic control). A company that is controlled by two persons, one of whom is resident and the other non-resident, is also a CFC if they each have at least a 40% interest but the non-resident does not have more than a 55% interest (*TIOPA 2010, Pt 9A, Ch 18*).

A CFC charge can only apply to certain specified profits that pass through a CFC charge gateway (*TIOPA 2010, s 371BB*). There are five heads of profits that are specified and detailed rules to determine which, if any, head applies. They include general profits, trading and non-trading finance profits, captive insurance profits and profits from certain types of financial institution.

Five exemptions may apply to remove a CFC charge as follows:

- the exempt period;
- the excluded territories;
- the low profits;
- the low profit margin; or
- the tax exemption

The exempt period applies in cases where foreign subsidiaries are acquired and allows a period of grace, generally 12 months, for any reorganisation to take place that may be necessary to prevent a CFC charge arising. However if there is a CFC charge in the next period the exempt period exemption is lost (*TIOPA 2010, Pt 9A, Ch 10*).

The excluded territories exemption applies to CFCs resident in Australia, Canada, France, Germany, Japan, or the USA. It also applies to a wider list of countries subject to various additional tests (*Controlled Foreign Companies (Excluded Territories) Regulations 2012, SI 2012/3024* which came into force on 1 January 2013) (*TIOPA 2010, Pt 9A, Ch 11*).

The low profits exemption applies where the pre-tax *accounts* profits are not more than £500,000 and the amount of those profits representing non-trading income is not more than £50,000. The pre-tax accounts profits are adjusted for any transfer pricing adjustments required and reduced by any dividends that would be exempt from UK tax, property income profits, and capital profits and losses. Alternatively, the adjusted *taxable* total profits can be taken rather than the accounts profits if they are below the limits. There are, in addition, rules to stop fragmentation schemes and group mismatch schemes and the use of CFCs to provide the services of UK individuals in the UK (*TIOPA 2010, Pt 9A, Ch 12*).

The low profit margin exemption applies if the pre-tax accounts profit is not more than 10% of relevant operating expenditure. The pre-tax accounts profits are adjusted as for the low profits exemption but also by adding back interest expense (*TIOPA 2010, Pt 9A, Ch 13*).

The tax exemption applies where the local tax is at least 75% of what the UK tax would be if the CFC were UK resident. The local tax is confined to tax charged by reference to profits, so excludes turnover taxes and excludes tax on capital gains. There are a number of anti-avoidance measures so for example the exemption does not apply to designer rate taxes under the laws of Guernsey, Jersey, the Isle of Man and Gibraltar whereby the CFC can choose its own rate of tax (*TIOPA 2010, Pt 9A, Ch 14*).

A CFC charge can only be made on a UK resident company which, together with connected or associated persons whether resident or not, has at least 25% of the CFC's profits apportioned to it (*TIOPA 2010, Pt 9A, Ch 2*).The full rate of corporation tax is applied to the amount apportioned less any creditable foreign tax that is available.

Guidance on the rules is contained in HMRC's International Manual (INTM191000).

TRANSFER PRICING

24.4   The purpose of the transfer pricing legislation is to ensure that profits are not diverted outside the UK tax net by means of transactions between connected persons that are not at arm's length (*TIOPA 2010, Pts 4, 5*). Where the provisions apply, arm's length prices are substituted for the actual prices at which transactions have taken place for the purpose of computing the company's tax liability.

However, in order not to discriminate against companies in the EU, all large UK companies are within the scope of these provisions even though the transactions might be with other UK resident companies. Small and medium-sized companies are only obliged to use arm's length prices on transactions with companies which are resident in countries that do not have double tax agreements with the UK which contain non-discrimination articles. These will generally be transactions with companies in tax havens. Small and medium-sized companies can opt into the rules if they wish and HMRC can make a direction to a medium-sized company following an enquiry that it must use arm's length prices in computing its tax liability. HMRC can also make a direction to a small and medium-sized company which is party to a transaction that is relevant to a patent box claim.

A small company is one with less than 50 employees and with either up to €10 million turnover or balance sheet total. A medium-sized company is one with less than 250 employees and with up to €50 million turnover or up to €43 million balance sheet total. Consequently a company with 50 or more employees cannot be a small company and one with 250 or more employees is large (*TIOPA 2010, s 172*, Annex to Commission Recommendation 2003/361 EC of 6 May 2003; (see also HMRC's International Manual INTM412080).

International tax arrangements of large international groups have been under significant media and parliamentary scrutiny. Following the release of the final reports by the Organisation for Economic Co-operation and Development (OECD) in relation to the Base Erosion and Profit Shifting (BEPS) project, the *Finance Act 2016* amends the UK transfer pricing provisions to align these to the revised OECD transfer pricing guidance. The main changes to the OECD guidance is to align outcomes with value created, and in particular it addresses issues relating to intangible assets and contracts where the risks and profits are not supported by the activities. This should help to rebalance some of the arrangements being scrutinised, for example where intellectual property and other intangible assets are held offshore.

DOUBLE TAXATION RELIEF

24.5   Relief is available for foreign tax suffered on profits which are subject to tax in the UK (*TIOPA 2010, Pts 2, 3*). Where there is a double tax treaty between the UK and the foreign country, the treaty sets out how relief is to be given. Where there is no tax treaty, unilateral tax relief is generally available.

Foreign tax is usually allowed as a deduction against the UK tax on the same profits but any excess cannot be recovered. Where there is no UK tax on the profits, foreign tax can usually be allowed as a deduction in computing the UK taxable profits. Foreign taxes that are based on turnover rather than profit are not eligible for double tax relief.

Some tax treaties allow credit to be given for tax that would have been payable were it not for some special exemption. This is known as tax sparing relief.

Tax treaties very often provide for a lower withholding tax on dividends, interest and royalties payable between the parties to the treaty. For example, the new treaty between the UK and China reduced the rate of withholding tax on dividends from China to the UK to 5% from profits arising after 1 January 2014. This rate will apply where the shareholder owns directly at least 25% of the Chinese company.

Foreign dividends received by the UK companies are now generally exempt from UK tax (see **25.1**).

Example 24.3 – Foreign dividends

Urafirth Limited has a subsidiary in China from which it received a dividend prior to the new treaty provisions coming into force. The dividend is Yuan 10,000,000 from which 10% withholding tax is deducted and which, when

---

converted into sterling, equals a net £900,000. No further tax is payable in the UK and neither can the £100,000 withholding tax be recovered.

However, under the new treaty provisions the new rate of 5% withholding tax would give a £50,000 saving.

DIVERTED PROFITS TAX (DPT)

24.6   Diverted profits arising on or after 1 April 2015 are liable to a new tax at the rate of 25%. It is not corporation tax, it is not self-assessed and is outside of the UK's tax treaty network.

The DPT targets:

- arrangements which avoid a UK permanent establishment (PE) by a person carrying on activity in the UK in connection with supplies of goods and services by a non-UK resident company to customers in the UK; and

- arrangements which lack economic substance and are primarily to counteract arrangements that exploit tax differences between different countries.

The DPT is set at a higher rate than that which a company would be subject to corporation tax so as to encourage companies with arrangements which would fall within the scope of the tax to restructure their operations.

There are limited exemptions from the regime, including for small and medium-sized companies and companies with limited UK-related sales or expenses (where they would otherwise be within the provisions aimed at avoiding a PE).

PROFITS FROM TRADING IN AND DEVELOPING UK LAND

24.7   An offshore property developer will be subject to UK tax on the profits arising from the development of UK land. In most cases, offshore property developers would be considered to be carrying on that trade through a permanent establishment in the UK. If this was not the case then they may still have a residual UK income tax charge in respect of UK source trading profits, or alternatively, a charge to diverted profit tax (see **24.6**) may arise.

New provisions were introduced with effect from 5 July 2016 in relation to offshore property developers to ensure that they are taxed in the same way as UK property developers. These are aimed at structures put in place in order to avoid a charge to UK tax on such transactions under the provisions highlighted above.

The new provisions extend the territorial scope of corporation tax to include any non-UK resident company that carries on a trade of dealing in or developing UK land. The profits of such a trade will be chargeable to UK corporation tax irrespective of where they arise (*FA 2016, s 76*).

Anti-avoidance rules will apply for the intervening period between the announcement of these new provisions at the Budget on 16 March 2016 and their introduction date. These are aimed to prevent companies avoiding the new charge by either using arrangements to 'rebase' the value of the land before the introduction of the charge or otherwise entering any other arrangements the main or one of the main purposes of which is to avoid such a charge.

The government have also confirmed that they will consider the introduction of a withholding tax on such profits to ensure full compliance with the new rules as necessary.

In addition to these new provisions, the *Finance Act 2016* overhauled and extended the transactions in land anti-avoidance provisions, which can charge gains arising on the disposal of land to income tax rather than capital gains tax (*FA 2016, s 77*).

The detailed scope of these provisions cannot be covered within this book, but it is worth noting that one key change is to replace the 'sole or main objective' test with a 'main purpose' test. The change in the level of this threshold raised significant concern, particularly with buy to let landlords – would the long-term intention of selling a buy to let property to realise a gain be considered as meeting the main purpose test?

Assurance was gained from HMRC by the National Landlords Association that this is not the intention of the legislation and that buy to let landlords should generally not be caught by these provisions. They will, as they would have been under the previous legislation, be subject to income tax on profits arising from the development of a property before it is sold or any profit relating to a 'slice of the action' on a subsequent development (see www.landlords.org.uk/news-campaigns/news/nla-reassures-members-over-new-land-tax-changes-no-additional-impact-on-landlord).

Equivalent provisions were introduced at the same time for income tax purposes (*FA 2016, ss 78–79*).

25

Particular matters

SIGNPOSTS

- **Distributions** – Dividends received by a company are generally exempt from tax unless caught by anti-avoidance rules. Dividends are the most common type of distribution but there are others, such as on a company purchase of own shares (except in the case of an unquoted company where certain conditions are satisfied) and distributions in the course of a liquidation in normal circumstances (see **25.1–25.5**).

- **Construction industry scheme** – Payments by contractors to subcontractors in the construction industry are subject to a special tax regime, which broadly requires the payments to be made under deduction of tax, unless the subcontractor is registered to receive them gross (see **25.6**).

- **Intangible fixed assets** – The tax treatment of intangible fixed assets depends upon when the asset was acquired. Certain assets fall within the capital gains regime while others are broadly taxed in accordance with the accounting entries (see **25.7**).

- **Research and development** – Relief for research and development, which advances science and technology through the resolution of scientific or technological uncertainty, is available with an uplift of up to 130% (see **25.8**).

- **Patent box** – Profits from patents will be subject to a lower rate of tax (ie effectively 10%) where certain conditions are satisfied (see **25.9**).

- **Worldwide debt cap** – Interest relief can be restricted for large groups of companies under the worldwide debt cap rules. These provisions are due to be replaced from 1 April 2017 (see **25.10**).

DISTRIBUTIONS

Dividends

25.1   A dividend is a particular type of distribution and is usually paid in cash out of distributable reserves to the shareholders. There are a number of other matters that are included in the definition of distribution (*CTA 2010, s 1000*). A company's distributable reserves are essentially its business profits after tax which it has not yet distributed. A distribution is not an allowable deduction for corporation tax.

> **Focus**
>
> For tax purposes, an individual is liable to income tax on dividends but they are generally tax free to a corporate shareholder because of a number of specific exemptions (*CTA 2009, s 931A(1)*).

The exemptions depend on whether the company receiving the dividend is small or not under the EC definition (*CTA 2009, s 931S(1)* and Annex to Commission Recommendation 2003/361 EC of 6 May 2003). A company is small if it has less than 50 employees and either turnover or balance sheet total of less than €10 million. A dividend received by a small company is exempt if it is from a UK company or from a company resident in a territory with which the UK has a double tax treaty that contains a non-discrimination clause. A dividend received by a company that is not small is exempt if it is from a company which it controls or from a portfolio investment in which it owns less than 10%. There are a number of other conditions to stop the exemption from being used for tax avoidance.

Return of capital

25.2 A return of share capital, including a share premium account, is an income distribution for the purposes of corporation tax if credited to the profit and loss account before being paid out (*CTA 2010, s 1027A*). However, if paid out directly *without* being credited to the profit and loss account first, it is a capital distribution.

> **Example 25.1 – Distributions**
>
> Mavine Limited is owned by an investment company, Mousa Limited, which acquired it when Mavine was a quoted company with a view to turning it around and selling it on when conditions were more favourable.
>
> Mavine has a large share capital of £200 million and a deficit on its distributable reserves of £150 million. It is now profitable again and Mousa wants to sell it. As a first step it tidies up its balance sheet by reducing the share capital to £25 million and, more by luck than judgement and without

consulting the company's in-house tax department, crediting distributable reserves with £175 million. Distributable reserves are now £25 million.

Mavine declares a dividend of £25 million which it pays to Mousa. This is not taxable in Mousa's hands. If Mavine had only credited its reserves with £150 million and paid the balance of £25 million to Mousa, Mousa would have a capital gain of £25 million less an appropriate proportion of the cost of acquiring Mavine's shares. The gain would not be covered by the substantial shareholding exemption dealt with at **23.7** because Mousa is not a trading company.

However, if Mavine had been owned by individuals this accounting treatment might be more appropriate.

Purchase of own shares

25.3   A purchase by a company of its own shares is a distribution but for an unquoted private trading company, or the holding company of a trading group, this does not apply if certain conditions are satisfied (*CTA 2010, ss 1033–1048*). The individual vendor shareholder must be:

●   UK resident;

●   have held the shares for five years;

●   must reduce his holding, and those of his associates by 25% bearing in mind that in doing the calculations there is a reduced amount of share capital in issue after the buyback (*CTA 2010, s 1037*) (associates are defined in *CTA 2010, s 1059*); and

●   must not be connected with the company after the buyback (*CTA 2010, ss 1042, 1062*).

Focus

Most importantly it has to be demonstrated that the buyback is for the purpose of benefitting a trade carried on by the company or any of its 75% subsidiaries. HMRC's Statement of Practice SP2/82 comes to the rescue here and gives some examples that would generally be accepted as benefitting the trade. For example, a controlling shareholder who wishes to retire as a director and who might otherwise sell his shares to someone who might not be acceptable to the other shareholders. He can also retain a 5% shareholding for sentimental reasons.

A trading company is for this purpose a company whose business consists wholly or mainly of carrying on a trade or trades. A trading group means a company which has one or more 75% subsidiaries and whose businesses (taken together with those subsidiaries) consist wholly or mainly of carrying on a trade or trades. Trade for this purpose does not include dealing in shares, securities, land or futures (*CTA 2010, s 1048*).

A company must pay for the shares when it acquires them (*Companies Act 2006, s 691(2)*) although since 30 April 2013 this has been relaxed in connection with employee share schemes (*Companies Act 2006 (Amendment of Part 18) Regulations 2013, SI 2013/999*). Payment can also be in kind as well as cash although HMRC may need convincing of this (*Roof-Bond Ltd v Douglas* [2000] 1 BCLC 401). If the company does not have the funds to buyback all of the shares, the shareholder can make it a loan beforehand so it can use the cash to buy the shares. However, the loan plus any shares retained must be less than 30% of the loan capital and share capital of the company following the buyback in order that the individual does not fail the connection test (*CTA 2010, ss 1042, 1062*). In the case of a company with a small number of valuable shares this might not be possible without a prior bonus issue of shares (*Tax Bulletin 21*). Alternatively, the contract for the sale of the shares can provide for completion to be staggered over a period of time for different tranches of shares. If the contract is unconditional the shares are treated as disposed of when the contract is made but for company law purposes no debt arises until the completion date and so does not constitute loan capital (*CTA 2010, s 1063*).

There is a statutory advance clearance procedure which is explained in SP2/82 and which lists the information required to be given in the clearance application (*CTA 2010, s 1044*). The purchase of own shares must be notified to HMRC within 60 days of the payment (*CTA 2010, s 1046*).

Exempt distributions

25.4   The transfer by a company of the shares in one or more of its 75% subsidiaries can be an exempt distribution if a number of conditions for demergers are satisfied (*CTA 2010, ss 1073–1099*).

The companies must be trading and not investment companies and none of the companies can be acquired by third parties. There are further provisions dealing with the transfer of trades to other companies which issue shares to the original shareholders. An exempt distribution is not liable to income tax in the hands of the shareholders.

Liquidation distributions

25.5   Liquidation distributions are also not treated as distributions and are dealt with below at **26.7**.

CONSTRUCTION INDUSTRY SCHEME

25.6   Certain payments made by companies carrying out construction operations to its subcontractors have to be made under deduction of tax. (*FA 2004, ss 57–77*). Subcontractors can register to be paid gross otherwise a deduction of 20% for registered subcontractors, or 30% for unregistered subcontractors, has to be made. Payments for materials or payments that are employment income in the hands of the recipient are not subject to the deduction. For more information, see **3.50** above and see also HMRC's guide for contractors and subcontractors (CIS340).

INTANGIBLE FIXED ASSETS

25.7   Intangible fixed assets include goodwill, patents and trademarks and their tax treatment for corporation tax purposes is dependent upon when the assets were created or acquired:

- Pre-April 2002 assets – assets created or acquired before 1 April 2002 are treated as capital assets. Any profit or loss arising on their disposal is brought into account under the provisions of *TCGA 1992* and a capital gain or loss will arise. There is provision to rollover such gains into intangible fixed assets acquired on or after 1 April 2002.

- Post-April 2002 assets – assets acquired on or after 1 April 2002 fall within the provisions of *Part 8, CTA 2009* and generally fall to be taxed in accordance with the amounts charged or credited in the accounts, although this is now subject to certain restrictions.

Anti-avoidance provisions apply to prevent pre-April 2002 assets held by a related party being 'converted' to a post-April 2002 asset in order to benefit from the relief available under *Part 8* (*CTA 2009, s 882*).

The tax relief available under *Part 8* was restricted with regards to acquisitions of relevant assets (which include goodwill, customer information and unregistered trademarks) from an individual or partnership where they were connected with the acquiring company and the acquisition was made on or after 3 December 2014.

Further restrictions were made with regards to the acquisition of relevant assets by a company on or after 8 July 2015. These prevent any relief for amortisation of these assets under *Part 8* although allow for relief for any loss crystallised on their realisation as a non-trading debit (*CTA 2009 816A*).

For post-April 2002 assets unaffected by these two restrictions, relief is available for the amortisation of these assets charged in the accounts or an irrevocable election can be made to write them off at 4% per annum on a straight line basis. The sale of such assets will give rise to a profit or loss calculated by reference to their tax written down value and the proceeds. There are provisions for rollover relief into intangible assets acquired.

The recent changes to the relief under *Part* 8 coupled with the loss of the 10% capital gains tax rate on the disposal of goodwill by an individual to a connected company have taken away some of the advantages of incorporating a business (see **14.13** and Example 25.2 in the Tax Guide 2014).

RESEARCH AND DEVELOPMENT

25.8   Research and development (R&D) occurs when a project seeks an advance in science or technology. Guidance on the meaning of R&D issued by the government (CIRD 81900) states that the activities that are R&D are those that directly contribute to the advance, through the resolution of scientific or technological uncertainty. Relief is given for R&D expenditure that is revenue expenditure for tax purposes. Capital expenditure may qualify for R&D allowances (see **4.20**).

Focus

An additional deduction can be claimed for revenue expenditure on R&D for small- and medium-sized enterprises (SMEs). This is 130% for expenditure incurred from 1 April 2015, previously 125% for expenditure incurred on or after 1 April 2012. So the total deduction is now 230% of the expenditure. To the extent that this gives rise to a loss, which cannot be utilised in the previous or current accounting period, the company can claim a tax refund of 14.5% of the loss for expenditure incurred on or after 1 April 2014 or 11% for expenditure incurred on or after 1 April 2012.

Relief is not available under the SME scheme to the extent that the expenditure:

- Attributable to the R&D project exceeds the cap of €7.5 million (*CTA 2009, s 1113*).

- Is subsidised by a third party (*CTA 2009, s 1052(5)*).

- Relates to R&D which the SME has been contracted to carry out by another person (*CTA 2009, s 1052(6)*).

Due to its generosity, relief under the SME scheme is notified state aid (i.e. state aid which is notified to and approved by the European Commission). As such, any project which is in receipt of any other form of notified state aid is excluded from relief under the SME scheme on any expenditure (i.e. not just to the extent to which it is subsidised).

To the extent that any expenditure is prevented from qualifying for relief under the SME scheme for these reasons, relief may generally be claimed under the scheme for large companies as detailed below (*CTA 2009, s 1068 and CTA 2009 ss 104C–104I*). For R&D work subcontracted to the SME relief is not available under the large company scheme if the work is contracted to it by another SME.

For periods ending before 1 April 2016, large companies were able to claim an additional deduction of 30% but if this gave rise to a loss there was no option to claim a payable tax credit as there was for an SME. However, for expenditure incurred after 31 March 2013, a claim can instead be made under the Research and Development Expenditure Credit (RDEC) scheme for a credit which is added to the taxable profit and is also deducted from the resulting tax liability. So for a company with no corporation tax liability the credit will be received in full. The credit was originally 10% but this was increased for expenditure incurred on or after 1 April 2015 to 11%. Both large company schemes were available in the period from 1 April 2013 to 31 March 2016, but only the RDEC is available from 1 April 2016.

A useful comparison of the different schemes is given in CIRD80250.

For the purposes of R&D, a medium-sized company is one with less than 500 employees and with up to €100 million turnover or up to €86 million balance sheet total. A small company is one with less than 50 employees and with either up to €10 million turnover or balance sheet total (*CTA 2009, ss 1119, 1120*).

The specialist R&D units of HMRC are available to provide support and assistance in making claims and the locations of these units are listed at CIRD80350.

Example 25.2 – R&D relief

Jarlshof Limited manufactures solar panels but its profits are being hit by imports of cheap panels from China. It is investigating an alternative technology for generation of electricity using the thermoelectric effect which will do away with the need for special panels and should theoretically enable the efficiency to be greatly improved at a much reduced cost.

It is a medium-sized company and in its year to 31 March 2016 it expects to spend £100,000 on researching this technology. Its profit for the year is expected to be £50,000 before accounting for this expenditure.

Whether the expenditure is capitalised or written off immediately (*FA 2004, s 53*) the company can claim a deduction for this in the year plus a further £130,000. This gives rise to a tax loss of £180,000 and so the company can use the loss against its future profits or carry it back for one year.

Alternatively, if it cannot carry it back, it can claim a tax refund of £26,100, being 14.5% of this loss. Without the relief it would have paid tax on £50,000 and would have obtained tax relief on the £100,000 expenditure for the periods in which it was written off in its accounts.

PATENT BOX

25.9   From 1 April 2013, an election can be made for part of the profits from qualifying patents held by companies to be taxed at 10%. The relief is being phased in over five years so the full benefit of the 10% rate will only be available from April 2017.

This relief will apply to patent royalties and profits from the sale of products which have exploited the patents whether generated from existing intellectual property (IP) or new IP. The 10% rate will not apply to any part of the profits that relate to the routine return (i.e. the return which could be expected to be made, but for the benefit of the IP) or the marketing return (i.e. the element of the profit generated from marketing activities). A simple adjustment for the marketing return is available for smaller claims and this will avoid brand valuation.

However, in order to comply with the Organisation for Economic Co-operation and Development (OECD) framework under Action 5 of the Base Erosion and Profit Shifting (BEPS) project, a revised patent box regime is introduced from 1 July 2016 (*CTA 2010, Pt 8A, Chapter 2A*).

The revised regime is based on a 'nexus' approach, but is otherwise very similar to the original regime. In broad terms, the nexus approach requires the IP to have been developed by the company making the patent box claim, thereby preventing the transfer of IP into UK group companies in order to benefit from the relief. In the majority of cases this approach will result in a reduced claim being available as compared to the original regime.

Any company which has made a claim under the original regime in respect of IP generated before 1 July 2016 can continue to claim under that regime until 1 July 2021. Any IP generated on or after 1 July 2016 will only be able to benefit from relief under the revised regime.

WORLDWIDE DEBT CAP

25.10   As dividends from overseas subsidiaries are generally tax free, an upstream loan to the parent by a foreign subsidiary at a commercial rate of interest could be used to avoid tax. The interest paid could give rise to a tax deduction in the UK and the corresponding interest received by the subsidiary could be paid back to the parent as a tax free dividend. The worldwide debt cap rules were enacted to stop large groups from doing this (*TIOPA 2010, Pt 7*). Small and medium-sized groups are unaffected by these debt cap rules.

Where they apply, interest relief is restricted if the interest expense is more than 75% of the worldwide group's gross debt. However, there is a corresponding reduction in the interest income of group members although there can be circumstances where the reduction is less than the add back. The rules are complicated, the tax yield is minimal, and they are expected to be repealed in 2017.

For this purpose a group is 'large' if:

- it has 250 or more employees; or

- its turnover is more than €50 million and its balance sheet total is more than €43 million.

This is from the European Commission definition (*TIOPA 2010, s 344*).

It was announced at the Budget 2016 that a restriction on the deductibility of corporate interest in line with the OECD framework under Action 4 of the BEPS project will be introduced with effect from 1 April 2017. It is proposed that a fixed ratio rule will apply, limiting the corporation tax deduction for net interest expenses to 30% of a group's UK earnings before interest, tax, depreciation and amortisation (EBITDA). A de minimis threshold is proposed so that these new provisions will only apply where the net UK interest expense of the group exceeds £2 million. On introduction of these provisions, the worldwide debt cap will be repealed.

26

Corporation tax planning

SIGNPOSTS

- **Year-end tax planning** – There are a number of issues and tax planning opportunities to consider at or before the company's year-end (see **26.1**).

- **Reconstructions** – Company reconstructions can benefit from certain forms of statutory tax relief, for the individual shareholder and company, depending on the particular circumstances. There are statutory clearance procedures available in some cases (see **26.2–26.6**).

- **Distributions on a winding up** – The liquidation of a company has potential tax implications for the shareholders and the company itself. Special treatment applies to distributions in the course of a company's dissolution, if certain conditions are satisfied. A new targeted anti-avoidance rule introduced from 6 April 2016 can lead to distributions which would otherwise be treated as capital being charged to income tax (see **26.7–26.9**).

- **Disincorporation relief** – Relief is available to companies on the disposal of their businesses to shareholders (see **26.10**).

YEAR-END PLANNING

26.1   The following are some of the matters that should be considered:

- Paying dividends rather than bonuses. For a private company owned by the directors, a comparison between paying a dividend or bonus will usually favour a dividend even though for 2016/17, with the higher dividend tax rates, it may be more marginal. To be deductible, bonuses have to be paid within nine months of the year-end.

- Accelerating capital expenditure might be beneficial to obtain tax relief in an earlier period, although availability of AIA relief must also be considered (see **Chapter 4**).

- Interest on a loan from a participator or the trustees of an occupational pension scheme is only allowed if paid within nine months of the year end (see **20.6**).

- Will the company be large and have to pay quarterly corporation tax instalments (see **50.5**).

- If there are loans to directors outstanding consider how these can be repaid within nine months after the year-end to avoid a 32.5% tax liability on the company (see **18.4**).

- Make sure that pension contributions have been paid in the accounting period otherwise relief will not be due for that period (see **19.8**).

- Consider any time limits for claims and elections that may be needed.

RECONSTRUCTIONS

26.2   Where a company is carrying on two or more businesses, the shareholders may wish to have the businesses in separate companies because perhaps they want to sell one of the businesses or the shareholders wish to split the businesses between themselves.

Focus

There are a number of ways that this can be achieved tax free using special relieving provisions. However there are a number of tax charges that can apply and there is no overall provision that covers these. Each case has to be looked at and a suitable plan worked out to ensure that no liability arises.

Transfer of trade for shares

26.3   A company can transfer a trade with its related assets to another company in exchange for the transferee issuing shares to the shareholders of the transferor. The assets are treated as transferred at such a value as will not give rise to a capital gain subject to complying with the provisions of *TCGA 1992, s 139*.

However if the shareholders are individuals this can give rise to a deemed dividend taxable on them at their highest income tax rate.

Avoiding a dividend

26.4   A deemed dividend can be avoided if the statutory demerger rules can be used (see **25.4**) however these do not apply if the purpose of the demerger is to sell one of the resulting companies to third parties or the activities of the company to be demerged are not all trading activities.

In such cases it may be necessary to consider an alternative route by way of a liquidation (otherwise known as section 110 reconstruction) or a reduction in share capital – these are commonly referred to as non-statutory demergers or reconstructions. Both of these alternatives rely upon the distribution being a capital distribution (rather than an income distribution) so that the benefit of the capital gain reorganisation provisions (*TCGA 1992, ss 126 et seq*) apply.

Although a reconstruction by way of liquidation or capital reduction can in most cases be achieved in a tax efficient way they rely upon a number of separate stand-alone relieving provisions to ensure that there are no adverse tax consequences on either the company or the shareholders.

In addition to income tax, corporation tax and capital gains tax, it is also important to ensure that the exemptions and relieving provisions for stamp duty and stamp duty land tax are considered (see **Chapter 47** and **48**).

Preparing for a reconstruction

26.5   Prior to a non-statutory reconstruction it may be necessary to put a new company (Newco) between the shareholders and the company being reconstructed (Target). This can be achieved tax free by way of a share exchange. Newco acquires the shares held by the shareholders in Target and issues its own new shares to them (*TCGA 1992, s 135*).

It is also common to partition the shares in a company before undertaking a reconstruction; for example one group of shareholders may be given A shares which are only interested in business A and the other shareholders B shares that are only interested in business B.

The different elements of the business may also be transferred into separate companies to facilitate the reconstruction. A company can transfer a trade or part of a trade to another company both of which are at least 75% owned by the same persons without the trade being treated as ceasing. This enables losses and capital allowances relating to that trade to carry over into the successor company (*CTA 2010, ss 940A–957*). Losses can be restricted if liabilities are left behind in the transferor company. The ownership test looks at the period starting two years before the transfer and one year after rather than ownership on the date of the transfer. See also **19.12** for further restrictions on losses where there is a change of ownership.

Capital assets can also be transferred, although care does need to be taken to avoid any de-grouping charges (see **23.5** and **23.6**) or claw-back of relief for stamp duty land tax (see **47.8** *et seq*).

Statutory clearances

26.6 It is advisable to use the statutory clearance mechanism where it is available for all the steps in a reconstruction to demonstrate to HMRC that they are being carried out for bona fide commercial reasons. This will provide comfort that the anti-avoidance provisions will not be invoked that might otherwise prevent the relieving provisions from applying.

Focus

The HMRC guidance on clearances and approvals (www.hmrc.gov.uk/cap/) helpfully pulls together information relating to clearances and addresses for submission.

Example 26.1 – A company reconstruction

Unst Limited is owned equally by two brothers, Andrew and Brian. The company owns and operates two caravan parks at Sandwick and Toft. The brothers have decided to split the company up as they can no longer agree on how it should be run. Andrew wants to continue to run Sandwick and Brian wants to continue to run Toft.

The first step is to partition the shares in Unst into A shares, held by Andrew, and B shares held by Brian. The A shares entitle Andrew to the Sandwick business and the B shares entitle Brian to the Toft business. Brian forms a new company Toft Limited which acquires the Toft business for which it issues shares to Brian. Brian's B shares in Unst are now worthless, as they are not interested in the remaining business in Unst, and can be cancelled.

As both businesses are trades, rather than investments, the statutory demerger rules should apply and so clearances from HMRC should be forthcoming with the effect that the transactions can be done tax free at both the company and shareholder level.

DISTRIBUTIONS ON A WINDING UP

Liquidations

26.7 When a company goes into liquidation it ceases to trade, and its accounting period ends and a new one commences. It also loses the beneficial ownership of its assets but this is ignored for determining the composition of any capital gains tax group of which it was a member (*TCGA 1992, s 170(11)*).

Distributions made by the liquidator to the shareholders are not treated as income distributions but as capital distributions subject to capital gains tax (*CTA 2010, s 1030*) although there are certain anti-avoidance provisions which can override this general treatment (see **26.9**).

Dissolutions

26.8   Legislation was introduced (*CTA 2010, s 1030A*) to replace a concession (Extra-Statutory Concession C16) which enables a company to pay out its remaining assets to its shareholders after it has ceased to trade as a capital distribution, without the expense of a formal liquidation. If the distribution is not more than £25,000 it will be treated as within *s 1030* and so taxed as capital in the hands of the shareholder.

Although company law treats such a return of share capital as an unauthorised distribution so that the Crown can recover it as *bona vacantia*, the Treasury Solicitor's Department confirmed in November 2011 that it will not attempt to recover any unauthorised distributions of share capital of any amount prior to dissolution.

For a 'belt and braces' approach, the share capital can be reduced to a negligible level by means of a capital reduction authorised under the *Companies Act 2006* before striking off. The procedure for doing so is relatively straightforward.

Example 26.2 – Capital treatment on ceasing a business

Wadbister Limited has been trading for many years as a bookshop but has seen its business decline with the advent of e-books. The owner decides to call it a day and cease when its lease expires. The company sold off its remaining stock and fixed assets, paid all its bills and collected what it was owed and now only has cash in the bank. It has share capital of £100 and reserves of £19,900 matched by cash of £20,000.

After it has been inactive for three months, the company applies to the Company Registrar to be struck off and pays out all of the cash to the owner.

The striking-off and dissolution of the company takes place within two years of the cash being paid out and so none of it is a distribution and it falls to be treated as a capital gain. The owner is entitled to entrepreneurs' relief so only pays 10% capital gains tax.

Targeted anti-avoidance rule

26.9   New anti-avoidance provisions were introduced in relation to distributions made on or after 6 April 2016 to prevent individuals benefiting from capital treatment on a winding up in certain cases.

Specifically, these provisions are aimed at circumstances where within two years of the winding up the individual receiving the distribution carries on (whether as a sole trader, in partnership or via a company), or is involved with, a similar trade or activity to that which was previously carried on by the company. For this purpose, the individual's involvement in a similar trade or activity will only be relevant where that trade or activity is carried on by a person connected to them, or a company controlled by such a person.

These provisions will only apply where immediately before the winding up the individual held at least a 5% interest in the company and at sometime within the two years before the winding up the company was a close company.

A final condition ensures that the distribution will only be subject to income tax where it is reasonable to assume that a main purpose of the winding up was the avoidance or reduction of an income tax charge.

These provisions are drafted very widely and there is the potential for may unsuspecting transactions to be caught.

There is no statutory clearance mechanism within these provisions and HMRC has confirmed that they will not generally provide clearance under the non-statutory clearance system where the question is concerning the 'main purpose' test, which is the most subjective element which taxpayers are likely to need assurance on.

Detailed guidance is yet to be published by HMRC, although they have provided three examples that are reproduced in part below.

Example 26.3 – distribution in a winding up

Example 1

Mr A has been the sole shareholder of a company which carries on the trade of landscape gardening for ten years. Mr A decides to wind up the business and retire. Because he no longer needs a company he liquidates the company and receives a distribution in a winding up. To subsidise his pension, Mr A continues to do a small amount of gardening in his local village.

When viewed as a whole, these arrangements do not appear to have tax as a main purpose. It is natural for Mr A to have wound up his company because it is no longer needed once the trade has ceased. Although Mr A continues to do some gardening, there is no reason why he would need a company for this, and it does not seem that he set the company up, wound it up and then continued a trade all with a view to receive the profits as capital rather than income. In these circumstances, Mr A's distribution in the winding up will continue to be treated as capital.

Example 2

Mrs B is an IT contractor. Whenever she receives a new contract, she sets up a limited company to carry out that contract. When the work is completed and the client has paid, Mrs B winds up the company and receives the profits as capital.

It looks like there is a main purpose of obtaining a tax advantage. All of the contracts could have been operated through the same company, and apart from the tax savings it would seem that would have been the most sensible option for Mrs B. Where the distribution from the winding up is made on or after 6 April 2016, in these circumstances the distribution will be treated as a dividend and subject to income tax.

Example 3

Mrs C is an accountant who has operated through a limited company for three years. She decides that the risk involved with running her own business is not worth her effort, and so decides to accept a job at her brother's accountancy firm as an employee. Her brother's firm has been operating for eight years. Mrs C winds up her company and begins life as an employee.

Looking at the arrangements as a whole it is not reasonable to assume that they have tax advantage as a main purpose. Mrs C's company was incorporated and wound up for commercial, not tax, reasons; although she works for a connected party it is clear that the other business was not set up to facilitate a tax advantage because it has been operating for some time. In these circumstances, the distribution from the winding up will continue to be treated as capital, absent any other considerations.

Although these examples give some indication of what HMRC sees as the scope of the provisions, they are very limited and, as ever, are only guidance. The examples are very much at the extremes of the scale, and there are many other possible situations which you could perceive that would fall within the gray area between these. The clear message is to proceed with caution in such cases until further guidance is produced or a more detailed understanding is gained as to how HMRC will approach the provisions in practice.

This targeted anti-avoidance rule is in addition to the much wider reaching transactions in securities provisions which aim to counteract an income tax advantage in cases where one of the main purposes of the transaction was to obtain that advantage.

However, unlike the transactions in securities provisions which must be invoked by HMRC, any charge arising under this targeted anti-avoidance rule is required to be self-assessed by the individual.

DISINCORPORATION RELIEF

26.10   In order to help small businesses that no longer want to operate as limited companies, it is possible to transfer a business out of a company tax efficiently for a limited period. From 1 April 2013 until 31 March 2018, a company can transfer its business as a going concern to some or all of the shareholders who are individuals without triggering any liability to corporation tax if a claim is made. All the assets of the business except cash have to be transferred. The value of goodwill and any interest in land held as a fixed asset cannot exceed £100,000 (*FA 2013, s 59*).

However the market value of what the shareholders receive less any money paid by them will be treated as an income distribution and taxed on them accordingly as dividends and there is no special relief to prevent this tax charge. The implications of this will have to be weighed up and it may be necessary for the shareholders to pay market value for what they are receiving. If the company is then left with cash of up to £25,000, the procedure in *CTA 2010, s 1030A* may be able to be used to pay this part to the shareholders as capital. After setting off their base cost of their shares any gain will be liable to capital gains tax and benefit from entrepreneur's relief if the conditions are satisfied. This is dealt with at **26.8**.

If the company is put into liquidation before the business is transferred out to avoid the tax charge on the income distribution then there is the question of whether the transfer is the transfer of a going concern as a liquidator's duty is to realise the assets for the benefit of the creditors rather than to carry on a trade. The relief only applies where there is a transfer of a going concern.

To qualify for the corporation tax relief, the individual shareholders must have held the shares for a minimum of 12 months and they must not be acting as members of a limited liability partnership. If the transfer is done by way of contract, the date on which the transfer takes place is the date when the contract becomes unconditional. If the transfer is effected by more than one contract then it is the date of the contract that transfers the goodwill that is relevant.

Example 26.3 – Using disincorporation relief

Professor John Gillmore has wound down his scientific advisory business that he carries on through a limited company and wishes to continue on a smaller scale without using his company to reduce the administration that having a company entails. The goodwill, which has an original cost of nil, is valued at £10,000 and the remainder of the assets have minimal value. The company ceases to trade and transfers the business to him. A claim for disincorporation relief is made so that the gain on the disposal of the goodwill, computed by reference to its market value, is not taxable.

The value of the goodwill is deemed to be a dividend and John will be subject to income tax on this in the year of disincorporation.

Part 4
Inheritance Tax

27

Inheritance tax (IHT) – outline

SIGNPOSTS

- **Scope** – IHT is the UK's wealth transfer tax and is charged on transfers of value made by an individual (see **27.1**).

- **Domicile** – Identifying the domicile of an individual is key to determining their exposure to IHT. There are different types of domicile, and the concept of 'deemed domicile' for IHT purposes (**27.2–27.3**).

- **IHT rates and the nil-rate band** – IHT is charged at different rates depending on whether the transfer is made in lifetime or on death. A threshold (often called the 'nil-rate band') is intended to protect small estates from liability (see **27.4–27.5**).

- **Transfer of value** – This is a wider concept than an obvious transfer such as a lifetime gift, and can include transactions which reduce the value of your estate. In particular, you are treated as making a transfer of value on your death (see **27.6–27.7**).

- **Reliefs and exemptions** – There are a number of exemptions and reliefs available which can reduce or eliminate IHT (see **27.8**).

- **Compliance** – The administrative provisions governing returns and payments are complex, although there are some limited exceptions to the IHT reporting requirements in some cases. The payment of IHT by a donor results in a further fall in the value of his estate, so it is necessary to 'gross-up' the gift by the tax (see **27.9–27.10**).

- **Double tax relief, etc** – Since other jurisdictions have similar wealth transfer taxes, it is possible that IHT and another transfer tax could be charged on the same property. However, the IHT legislation provides for a measure of relief. In some circumstances, the same property could be subject to IHT twice, but there are double charge relief provisions to deal with this (see **27.11–27.12**).

- **IHT may be due on transfers into trusts and also during the lifetime of trusts** (see **Chapter 35**).

- **Appendix: IHT thresholds and rates** – A table of IHT thresholds and rates is included at the end of this chapter (see **27.14**).

All references in this chapter are to IHTA 1984, unless otherwise stated.

LIABILITY TO IHT

27.1   IHT is charged on transfers of value made by an individual that are not exempt transfers. For a chargeable transfer to occur, the following conditions must apply (*IHTA 1984, s 2(1)*):

- must be a transfer of value (**27.6**);

- must be a transfer made by an individual;

- must not be an exempt transfer (**28.1**); and

- must not be a potentially exempt transfer (**29.2**).

In addition, charges may arise in respect of settled property (see **Chapter 35**) and transfers by close companies, but these charges are made by reference to an individual.

DOMICILE AND DEEMED DOMICILE

27.2   IHT is levied on:

- all chargeable transfers of assets (UK and foreign) made by persons domiciled in the UK;

- all chargeable transfers of UK assets made by persons not domiciled in the UK.

Types of domicile

27.3   Domicile is a complex topic and it is first necessary to establish the actual domicile of the taxpayer and then consider whether he is deemed to be domiciled in the UK. A person's domicile is the place where he ultimately intends to reside or to which he tends to return.

There are three types of legal domicile:

- *domicile of origin* – acquired at birth, normally from the father;

- *domicile of choice* – acquired when the individual abandons his existing domicile and resides in another state, intending to remain there indefinitely;

- *domicile of dependence* – acquired at a time when the individual is incapable of choosing his own domicile, now usually because of his age, so his domicile is dependent on that of another person.

Where a person makes a chargeable transfer but he was not domiciled in the UK under normal rules, they may still be deemed to be domiciled in the UK (*s 267*):

- Any person who was domiciled in the UK will continue to be treated as being domiciled in the UK for a further three years after he ceases to be domiciled in the UK under normal rules.

- Any person who has been resident in the UK for 17 of the previous 20 fiscal years, ending with the year of the chargeable transfer, is deemed to be domiciled in the UK for IHT purposes.

In addition, under legislation included in the *Finance Act 2013, s 177*, it is possible for individuals who are domiciled other than in the UK and who are married or in a civil partnership with a UK domiciled person, to elect to be treated as UK-domiciled for IHT purposes (see **28.6**).

The government intends to include provisions in Finance Act 2017 changing to the rules on domicile from April 2017. The period before being treated as UK domiciled will be reduced to 15 years and individuals born in the UK with UK domicile will be deemed UK domiciled in any year that they are resident here. In relation to the deemed 15 year rule:

- (a)   counts years when the taxpayer is under 18 years of age.

- (b)   The deemed status is not passed from parent to child.

In relation to Settled property

- (a)   For long term residents who created settlements while they were non-UK domiciled there will be no change to the current treatment of trust assets for IHT. In these circumstance, the UK trust assets are chargeable and the foreign assets (excluded property) are not.

- (b)   Any foreign assets settled into trust by returning UK domiciles while they are domiciled elsewhere, would no longer be excluded property in relation to events on or after 6 April 2017 whilst the settlor meets the residence condition

> **Focus**
>
> Domicile is a very important issue now as there are many UK residents who do not have a UK domicile of origin. Despite this, their overseas assets may still be chargeable to UK IHT if they have adopted a UK domicile of choice or are UK deemed domiciled by virtue of residence in the UK.

IHT RATES AND THRESHOLD

27.4   IHT is charged at two different rates, depending on whether the transfer is made during the person's lifetime or in the death estate:

Lifetime transfers	20%
Death estate	40%

In 2012, the government introduced an incentive to encourage charitable legacies on death which can reduce the normal rate of 40% to 36%. This is covered in more detail at **28.30** below.

Transfers made within seven years of death may suffer an additional IHT charge on death but for transfers between three and seven years after making a gift, taper relief reduces the amount of IHT that would become due (see **28.13**).

Quick succession relief can also reduce the tax liability where IHT is charged twice within a five-year period (see **28.14**).

Threshold (nil rate band)

27.5   The amount of IHT depends on the taxpayer's cumulative total transfers within a seven-year period (*s 7*). The cumulative transfers up to the threshold or nil rate band (NRB) are taxed at 0%, and the excess is charged at the lifetime rate or death rate as appropriate.

The threshold for recent years is shown in **27.14** below.

For deaths after 8 October 2007, the estate may benefit from the NRB of the deceased's former spouse or civil partner (see **30.8**).

> **Focus**
>
> The NRB is intended to keep small estates out of the scope of IHT. However, due to the increases in value of property over the past 25 years,

many individuals whose main asset is their home may be exposed to IHT, even though they do not consider themselves to be wealthy.

From April 2017, a further relief will be introduced where the estate includes the taxpayer's home, provided it is given to children and remoter issue. This will be phased in over a period of 4 years so that for deaths in 2017/2018 the maximum additional amount will be set at £100,000, rising to £125,000 for 2018/2019, £150,000 for 2019/2020 and to £175,000 for 2020/2021. This may also be transferred to a surviving spouse or civil partner. As part of this measure the nil rate band is to remain frozen at £325,000 until 2020/2021 (see **30.9**).

TRANSFERS OF VALUE

27.6   A 'transfer of value' is any disposition made by a person as a result of which the value of his estate immediately after that disposition is less than it would be but for that disposition; and the amount by which it is less is the value transferred by the transfer (*s 3(1)*). The value transferred may be different from the value received by the donee.

Example 27.1 – Transfer of value greater than benefit received

Joan is the controlling shareholder of a private company with 51% of the shares; she gives her son 2%.

The value of the transfer will be the difference in value between a 51% holding and a 49% one, rather than the usually much lower value of a 2% shareholding.

A 'disposition' covers any act by which a person transfers (or disposes of) property (or cash), including both the creation and the release of any debt or right which results in a reduction the value of his estate.

In addition to its normal meaning, 'disposition' is specifically extended to cover the following:

- transfers made by associated operations (*s 268*) (see **29.8**);

- failure to exercise a right (*s 3(3)*);

- alteration of rights attaching to a close company's share/loan capital (*s 98*).

> **Example 27.2 – Failure to act can be a transfer of value**
>
> John has the right to take up a bonus issue of shares in a company of which he is a shareholder.
>
> Failure to exercise that right would be a transfer of value.

Transfers by individuals during their lifetimes are in many cases assumed to be exempt unless the individual dies within seven years. These are referred to as potentially exempt transfers (PETS) (*s 3A*). See **29.2** for more detail. This does not apply in all cases and transfers other than to individuals (eg to companies) and into most trusts are immediately chargeable (chargeable lifetime transfers or CLT's) (see **Chapter 29**).

There are special provisions (in *IHTA 1984, Pt IV*) dealing with transfers of value by close companies. The effect of these provisions is to apportion the transfer of value to the participators of the close company.

Death is a special occasion of charge, outlined below.

> **Focus**
>
> It is important for wealthy clients or their professional advisers to keep records of gifts that they make even if the gifts would be PETs as the person administering their estate on their eventual death will need this information.

IHT ON DEATH – OUTLINE

27.7   The death of any person is treated for IHT purposes as though, immediately before death, that person had made a transfer of value equal to the value of his chargeable estate (*ss 4, 5*). In addition to any assets the deceased was able to dispose of personally, this would include any property where the deceased had an interest as joint tenant, which passes to the surviving joint tenants.

Certain settlements in which the deceased had an interest in possession are treated as part of the deceased's estate but the trustees are liable for the IHT due on trust property.

RELIEFS AND EXEMPTIONS – OUTLINE

27.8   There are a number of reliefs and exemptions available for transfers which may normally fall to be transfers of value for IHT purposes such as:

- Nil-Rate Band (**NRB**) (**27.5**);

- Residence Nil-Rate Band (**RNRB**) (**30.9**);

- double taxation relief (**27.11**);

- exempt transfers such as the annual allowance, small gifts, transfers between spouses (**28.1–28.11**);

- quick succession relief (see **28.14**);

- business property relief (see **28.15–28.20**);

- agricultural property relief (see **28.21–28.27**);

- woodlands relief (see **28.28**);

- national heritage property (see **28.29**);

- reduced rate for charitable gifts (see **28.30**);

- post-death reliefs (see **30.5**).

In addition, property which is classified as 'excluded property' is outside the scope of IHT.

Excluded property includes property situated outside the UK owned by an individual who is not UK domiciled, and certain other property (This is covered in more detail at **28.12**).

IHT COMPLIANCE

IHT returns

27.9   Every person making a chargeable transfer must deliver an account (for each chargeable occasion) to HMRC specifying all appropriate property and its value. The time limits for submitting these accounts are the later of the following (*s 216*):

- 12 months from the end of the month in which the chargeable transaction occurs; and

- three months from the date on which the person first becomes liable for the tax due.

For transfers on death, the personal representative must deliver the appropriate account and specify all property which formed part of the deceased's estate immediately before his death, along with the value of that property. They must also give full details of any chargeable transfers made by the deceased within the seven years prior to death (*s 216(3)*). Tax has to be paid by the end of six months after the person died. After this the estate has to pay interest. IHT can be paid in instalments over 10 years on things that may take time to sell, e.g property and some types of shares.

For chargeable events occurring after 5 April 2014, the trustees of relevant property settlements must deliver the IHT account six months after the end of the month in which the chargeable event occurs (*s 216(6)*) and pay the tax by the end of the same period (*s 226*).

However, no trust return is required in relation to any settlement, if a full and proper account of the property has already been delivered in relation to it.

There are limited exceptions to these reporting requirements where the event would not give rise to a tax charge, although not all cases where no tax is due are exempt from reporting. It should be noted that if probate is required, even if an estate is excepted from the need to file a return, a Return of Estate Information (Form IHT205 in England and Wales) will be required by the probate registry. Details of exceptions can be found in the 'Inheritance Tax (Delivery of Accounts) (Excepted Estates) Regulations'. For trusts the exemptions can be found in the 'Inheritance Tax (Delivery of Accounts) (Excepted Settlements) Regulations', In general there is more scope for claiming exemption for a trust than for an individual.

IHT payments

27.10   The IHT legislation establishes the person (or persons) who may be liable for any IHT arising from a chargeable transfer. In general, all persons who have benefited from the relevant assets may become liable. Those persons who have the most immediate interest, eg the transferor or personal representatives, take primary liability (*ss 199–203*).

The tax on an estate of a deceased person could be underpaid if a PET made by the deceased during the seven years prior to his death remains undiscovered until after the estate has been fully administered. In such cases, HMRC will not usually pursue underpaid tax where the personal representative:

- has made the fullest possible enquiries;
- has done everything in his power to make full disclosure; and
- has fully distributed the assets of the estate and obtained a certificate of discharge before any lifetime transfers came to light.

For chargeable lifetime transfers (CLTs) where the transferor (generally) pays the IHT due, if he is the person who suffers the tax, grossing up is necessary.

Example 27.3 – Effect on transfer of value of the donor paying the tax

Fred wins the lottery and creates a settlement for his grandchildren in 2010 by transferring £500,000 to the trustees. He has never made significant gifts in the past. He intends to pay any IHT arising.

His transfer of value and the tax due are as follows:

	£
Cash payment to settlement	500,000
Annual exemption (including amount brought forward)	6,000
	494,000
Nil rate band available	325,000
Net amount chargeable at lifetime rate (20%)	169,000
Tax 20%/(100%–20%) = 25%	42,250
Reconciliation	
Fall in value of Fred's estate	
Cash	500,000
Tax	42,250
	542,250
Annual exemption	6,000
Nil rate band	325,000
Taxable at 20%	211,250
Tax	42,250

Focus

IHT is charged on the fall in value of the transferor's estate, so if he pays any tax due that will increase that fall, so the tax will need to be grossed up.

For transfers on death, the trustees account for the tax due on any part of the deceased's estate which is represented by settled property. The cost, however, will ultimately be met by the remainderman since it reduces the capital available for distribution.

For the free estate (assets that an individual is free to dispose of) on death:

- IHT on both realty (land and buildings) and personalty (other property such as personal, moveable objects) is to be paid out of the residue;

- property situated outside the UK bears its own tax.

Should a will dictate that a specific legacy is to be 'free of tax' (or similar wording), the tax relating to that gift will be payable out of the residue of the estate. In this case, property situated outside the UK may not bear its own tax.

DOUBLE TAX RELIEF

27.11   There may be occasions where assets are held which would be subject to IHT in the UK, and also the equivalent to IHT (or is chargeable on or by reference to death or lifetime gifts) in another country. In some cases, there will be double taxation agreements to cover this, however, where no double taxation agreement exists, relief will be given on a unilateral basis (*ss 158–159*).

The relief will take the form of a credit for part or all of the foreign tax and is set against the UK IHT payable on the transfer. As with other taxes, this credit can never exceed the amount of the UK IHT chargeable on the assets in question (*s 159*).

The amount of the credit given is dependent on the situation of the property:

- Where the property is situated in the foreign country charging the tax but not situated in the UK, the credit given will be equal to the tax charged in the foreign country.

- Where the property:

  o is situated in neither the UK nor the foreign country, or

  o is situated in both the UK and the foreign country (different countries may determine the location of the property according to different rules),

  the credit is computed by reference to the formula $(A \times C)/(A+B)$

  Where:

  A = amount of IHT

  B = overseas tax

  C = whichever of A and B is the smaller.

There are further rules dealing with cases where tax is imposed by two or more overseas territories.

DOUBLE CHARGES RELIEF

27.12   There may be situations where a potential double charge could arise, in particular:

●   where the property transferred by a failed PET has been gifted back to the transferor and is part of his estate for IHT;

●   where property was transferred, but subject to a reservation, so that it is included as a transfer in the deceased's cumulative total and as part of his estate;

●   where property has been transferred and the transferee has made a loan to the transferor, which cannot be deducted by virtue of *FA 1986, s 103*.

The *Inheritance Tax (Double Charges Relief) Regulations 1987*, *SI 1987/1130* provide relief for these double charges. The regulations also set out examples of how the relief is intended to operate.

FURTHER INFORMATION

27.13   Further information on IHT can be found:

●   on HMRC's website (www.gov.uk/topic/personal-tax/inheritance-tax);

●   in HMRC's inheritance tax manual (www.hmrc.gov.uk/manuals/ ihtmanual);

●   there is also an 'IHT toolkit' (www.gov.uk/government/publications/ hmrc-inheritance-tax-toolkit-2014-to-2015).

APPENDIX: INHERITANCE TAX (IHT) THRESHOLDS AND RATES (LIFETIME TRANSFERS AND TRANSFERS ON DEATH OR WITHIN SEVEN YEARS BEFORE DEATH)

27.14

Period	Upper limit £	Rate of tax	Grossing up rate for each £ over the upper limit
6 April 2009–5 April 2021	325,000	20% on gross lifetime transfers over the cumulative upper limit	1/4 for net lifetime transfers
2008/09	312,000		
2007/08	300,000		
2006/07	285,000		
2005/06	275,000		
2004/05	263,000		
2003/04	255,000		
2002/03	250,000		
2001/02	242,000		
2000/01	234,000		
1999/2000	231,000	40% on transfers on death over the cumulative upper limit	2/3 for net transfers on death (not bearing own tax)
1989/99	223,000		
1997/98	215,000		
1996/97	200,000		
1995/96	154,000		
10 March 1992 to 5 April 1995	150,000		
6 April 1991 to 9 March 1992	140,000		
1990/91	128,000		
1989/90	118,000		
15 March 1988 to 5 April 1989	110,000		
17 March 1987 to 14 March 1988	90,000		
18 March 1986 to 16 March 1987	71,000		

Notes

1   *What is covered* – The above rates and thresholds apply to lifetime transfers and transfers on death or within seven years before death.

2   *Nil rate band* – The IHT threshold (or 'nil rate band') is set at £325,000 for the tax years 2010/11 to 2020/21 inclusive.

4   *Charity discount* – A lower IHT rate of 36% can apply to a deceased person's estate, where 10% or more of the net estate has been left to charities and/or registered community amateur sports clubs, with effect for deaths on or after 6 April 2012 (*IHTA 1984, Sch 1A*).

5   *Debts* – For deaths occurring on or after 17 July 2013, a debt by the deceased will only be taken into account if it is actually discharged out of the estate on or after death (*IHTA 1984, s 175A*).

28

Reliefs and exemptions, etc

SIGNPOSTS

- **Exemptions** – IHT exemptions can be split between those exempting transfers of value during the taxpayer's lifetime (eg the annual exemption and normal gifts out of income) and those exempting transfers of value at all times (eg the spouse or civil partner exemption and gifts to charities) (see **28.1–28.11**).

- **Excluded property** – Certain property is excluded from an IHT charge (see **28.12**).

- **Reliefs** – IHT reliefs can broadly be distinguished between those reducing the value charged (eg business property relief) and those reducing the tax due (eg taper relief) (see **28.13–28.31**).

- **Business property relief** – This important and valuable relief reduces the value transferred by a transfer of value by a specified percentage. The current rates of BPR are 100% and 50%, with the actual rate depending on the type of business property. The relief may be claimed if certain conditions are satisfied, but it can be inadvertently restricted or denied in some cases (see **28.15–28.20**).

- **Agricultural property relief** – This relief operates on a similar basis to business property relief. It applies a percentage discount (100% or 50%) against the agricultural value of agricultural property transferred in certain circumstances (see **28.21–28.27**).

- **Other reliefs** – Other forms of IHT relief include 'related property relief' and 'fall in value' relief (see **28.31**).

- **Appendix: Business and agricultural property relief** – A table summarising the rates of business and agricultural property relief is included at the end of this chapter (see **28.32**).

All references in this chapter are to IHTA 1984, unless otherwise stated. 'PET' means potentially exempt transfer and 'CLT' means chargeable lifetime transfer.

EXEMPT TRANSFERS

28.1   There are a number of exemptions which are deductible from transfers of value in arriving at the amounts chargeable to IHT, commonly known as exempt transfers.

These are generally considered under two headings:

- those which apply through the operation of limits and which are available for lifetime transfers only, such as:
    - annual exemption (*s 19*),
    - small gifts exemption (*s 20*),
    - normal expenditure out of income (*s 21*), and
    - gifts in consideration of marriage (*s 22*);
- exemptions which apply because of the status of the recipient and are available for both lifetime and death transfers, including:
    - transfers between spouses and civil partners (*s 18*),
    - gifts to charities (*s 23*),
    - gifts to political parties (*s 24*),
    - gifts to housing associations (*s 24A*), and
    - gifts for national purposes (*s 25*).

Annual exemption

28.2   Transfers of value made by a transferor in a single tax year are exempt to the extent that the total of the values transferred by them does not exceed £3,000. Where the transfers of value exceed this amount, the first £3,000 will be taken to be exempt.

If the total transfers are less than £3,000, the unused part of that exemption may be carried forward to the following year. In that following year, that year's exemption is to be used *before* any unused amount brought forward. There is no further carry forward if the amount brought forward cannot be used in the second year.

Example 28.1 – Carry forward of annual exemption

Arthur made the following gifts:

2012/13	£1,800
2013/14	£4,000
2014/15	£4,500

For 2012/13, the gift is covered by his annual exemption, leaving £1,200 to carry forward.

For 2013/14, the gift is covered by the 2013/14 exemption plus £1,000 of the amount brought forward. There is no balance to carry forward.

For 2014/15, the gift is reduced by £3,000 leaving £1,500 which may give rise to a charge. The excess relief from 2012/13 of £200 is lost.

The exemption is applied on a chronological basis where there are multiple transfers of value in the year. For multiple transfers on the same day, any exemption will be apportioned in the ratio of the values transferred (after applying any other exemptions).

To ensure that the annual exemptions are not allocated against PETs (which may never become chargeable and therefore wasting the exemption), where possible the transferor should make any chargeable lifetime transfers before any PETs planned for the same year (*s 19*).

Focus

When planning gifts, ensure that the annual exemption is used each year and chargeable transfers (even within the nil rate band) are made earlier in the year than PETs.

Small gifts exemption

28.3   Transfers of value made by a transferor as outright gifts to any one person are exempt if the values transferred by them do not exceed £250 in any one year.

This exemption is not available at all for use against larger gifts where the total value transferred to any one person exceeds £250 (*s 20*).

Example 28.2 – Birthday and Christmas gifts

Bertha makes the following gifts in 2013/14:

Christmas presents to Joshua, Jacob and Jeremiah of £100 each.

She also gives them birthday presents of £100, £150 and £200 respectively.

The gifts to Joshua and Jacob are covered by the small gifts exemption, but no part of the gifts to Jeremiah is as they exceed £250 in total.

Normal expenditure out of income

28.4   A transfer of value is an exempt transfer where the taxpayer can show that the transfer meets all three of the following conditions (*s 21*):

- that it formed part of the transferor's normal expenditure;

- that (taking one year with another) it was made out of his income; and

- that, after the transfer, the transferor was left with sufficient income to maintain his usual standard of living.

This exemption does not apply to certain payments of premiums on a life policy where these are linked to an annuity and certain annuities do not count as income for this purpose (*s 21(2), (3)*).

It is important to be able to show that the expenditure is 'normal' for the taxpayer. This will usually be tested only after death, so will require documentary evidence or a clear pattern of gifts.

However, the gifts don't need to follow a rigid pattern as to timing or amount. In *Bennett v CIR* [1995] STC 54 the taxpayer instructed the trustees of a settlement to pay any income in excess of her needs to her children. In the first year the trustees paid £9,300 to each child and in the following year they paid £60,000 to each child. There were no further payments as the donor died suddenly. The High Court held that the payments were part of a settled pattern intended to last for a sufficient period to be considered normal, despite there being only two payments.

It is important that the transfer is out of income and not out of capital realised to make the gift. Similarly transfers of capital assets will not count unless these were purchased from income for the specific purpose of making the gift and they meet the other conditions.

HMRC also require the claimant to demonstrate that the taxpayer had sufficient income to meet his normal expenditure after the gifts.

Gifts such as those in **Example 28.2** are likely to be within this exemption. If a taxpayer does not require the income from an investment, he might instruct the payer to direct the income thereafter to those he wishes to benefit.

Focus

This is potentially a very valuable relief, but considerable thought should be given during the transferor's life to establishing that a normal pattern exists, the gifts are out of income and there is evidence to present to HMRC when the time comes.

Gifts in consideration of marriage

28.5   Transfers of value made by a single transferor in consideration of marriage (or civil partnership) are exempt where they do not exceed the following limits (*s 22*):

- £5,000 in the case of a gift by a parent to one of the parties to the marriage;

- £2,500 in the case where the transferor is a more remote ancestor;

- £2,500 in the case of a party to the marriage;

- £1,000 in any other case.

Where the annual exemption is also available, the marriage exemption should be deducted before the annual exemption.

This relief has potential for a significant total sum to be given. If all the parents and grandparents contribute the maximum, each party to the marriage could receive £20,000, before any other exemptions.

The relief covers gifts into trust as well as outright gifts. While settling a relatively small sum is not likely to be economic, the relief can be deducted from the value of a larger gift.

Transfers between spouses and civil partners

28.6   Where property is transferred between spouses or civil partners, it will generally be treated as an exempt transfer to the extent that the property in question becomes comprised in the estate of the transferor's spouse (*s 18*). This exemption also applies where no property is actually transferred but the estate of the transferee has increased.

There is a restriction to the inter-spouse transfer exemption where the transferor is domiciled in the UK but the transferee is not UK domiciled. This applies on a cumulative basis to all transfers of value made by the transferor to the other spouse or civil partner since 1974. (Before 1 January 1974, a woman acquired her husband's UK domicile upon marriage, so this restriction was not applicable.) If both spouses or partners are non-UK domiciled, or if the spouse making the transfer is non-UK domiciled but the recipient spouse is domiciled in the UK, there is no restriction to the spouse exemption.

Prior to 5 April 2013, the exemption was restricted to £55,000, where the transferee was non-UK domiciled. The *Finance Act 2013* amends the IHT treatment of transfers between UK-domiciled individuals and their non-UK domiciled spouse or civil partners for transfers after 6 April 2013 in two ways:

● the cap will be increased to the amount of the nil-rate band; and

● under a new election, individuals not domiciled in the UK and who are married or in a civil partnership with a UK-domiciled person, will be able to elect to be treated as UK-domiciled for IHT purposes.

Focus

As this is an exemption, it applies to transfers of value, which might otherwise be PETs. Therefore the allowance will be used up more quickly than is at first apparent. It will always be necessary to look back to the date of the marriage where the relief is restricted in this way, not just the last seven years.

Making the election brings the non-domiciled spouse's world-wide estate into charge to IHT so requires careful consideration.

Gifts to charities

28.7   A transfer of value to a charity, either as an outright gift or a gift into a settlement, is exempt. This applies to both lifetime and death transfers (*s 23*) and covers the whole of the value transferred by the transferor rather than the value in the hands of the charity (SP E13).

Charities which qualify for the exemption are those which qualify as charities for corporation tax or income tax purposes. In general, foreign charities do not qualify as they are excluded from registration under the *Charities Act 1960*. However, the relief now extends to charities located in the UK or an EU member state or specified country, which includes Iceland and Norway (*FA 2010, Sch 6*; *SI 2010/1904*).

Property will be treated as having been given to a charity if it becomes the property of the charity, or if it is held in trust for only charitable purposes.

Gifts to political parties

28.8   Transfers to qualifying political parties are exempt from IHT (*s 24*). A qualifying political party is one which, at the last general election before the transfer:

- had two members of the party elected to the House of Commons; or

- had one member of the party elected to the House of Commons and a total of 150,000 votes were given to candidates who were members of the party.

HMRC's Statement of Practice SP E13 also applies to transfers to political parties (see **28.7**).

Gifts for national purposes

28.9   A transfer of value is exempt where the property transferred passes to any of a number of prescribed national institutions (*s 25*). These include:

- the National Gallery;

- the British Museum;

- the National Museums of Scotland;

- the National Museum of Wales;

- the Ulster Museum.

Also included are a wide range of universities, art galleries, museums and libraries throughout England, Scotland, Wales and Northern Ireland (*Sch 3*).

Gifts to housing associations

28.10   A transfer of value in respect of land (within the UK) given to a registered housing association is exempt (*s 24A*).

Dispositions for family maintenance

28.11   Maintenance payments for spouses, children and other dependants are not treated as transfers of value in the following circumstances (*s 11*):

- the payment is by one party to a marriage for the benefit of the other. This includes dispositions made on the occasion of separation (or any subsequent variation of such a disposition); or

- the payment is for the maintenance, education or training of a child of either party to the marriage. This will apply up to the end of the fiscal year in which the child reaches the age of 18 or, if later, ceases to undergo full-time education/training; or

- the payment represents a reasonable provision for the care and maintenance of a dependent relative.

EXCLUDED PROPERTY

28.12   When establishing the value of lifetime transfers and the estate on death, no account is to be taken of excluded property.

Excluded property comprises the following:

- property situated outside the UK which is owned by a non-UK domiciled person (*s 6(1)*);

- certain property situated outside the UK which is held in a settlement created by a person who was not domiciled in the UK at the time it was made (*s 48(3)*);

- holdings in authorised unit trusts and shares in open-ended investment companies which are owned by a non-UK domiciled person (*s 48(3A)*);

- reversionary interests (*s 47*);

- certain government securities (*s 6(2)*);

- certain savings held by persons domiciled in the Channel Islands or the Isle of Man (*s 6(3)*);

- money which could have been paid to a deceased's personal representatives under certain pension arrangements but instead an annuity is paid to his dependants (*s 152*);

- certain overseas pensions, gratuities and lump sum payments on death (*s 153*);

- property of a person in the armed forces who dies on active service (*s 154*) or emergency service personnel who die as a result of dealing with or responding to emergency circumstances (*s 153A*));

- a 'relevant decoration or award' – usually made to a member of the armed forces or emergency services (*s 6(1B)*);

- emoluments and tangible movable property of members of overseas forces posted to the UK (*s 6(4)*).

In the July 2015 Budget, it was announced that rules will be included in FA 2017 to ensure that all UK residential property is within the charge to IHT, even where it is held through offshore structures (such as an overseas company) where it is excluded property under current law. This will apply from April 2017.

TAPER RELIEF

28.13   IHT is chargeable on gifts made in the seven years before death at a rate of 40%, which will include any tax (or further tax) arising on PETs or CLTs. However, should the transferor die more than three years after making a gift, taper relief can be applied to the amount of IHT (not the value transferred) that would become due.

Time between the date of gift and the date of death	Taper relief percentage	Proportion of tax due
3 to 4 years	20%	80%
4 to 5 years	40%	60%
5 to 6 years	60%	40%
6 to 7 years	80%	20%

If on death it becomes necessary to recalculate the tax due on transfers made by the deceased in the previous seven years, and taper relief means that the IHT due as a result of his death will be less than the tax that has already been paid, there will be no further tax to pay, but no repayment will be due.

Example 28.3 – Reduction in tax on failed PET

In May 2006, Clarence gave his son £400,000, and he died in November 2011, leaving the balance of his estate (£400,000) to his daughter. The IHT due will be as follows:

	£
Gift to son	400,000
Less: annual exemptions	(6,000)
Chargeable	394,000
Taxable at 40% (after NRB of £325,000)	69,000
Tax at 40% before taper relief	27,600
Taper relief – 60% (5–6 years)	16,560
Tax payable by Clarence's son	11,040
Tax on the estate at 40%	160,000

Focus

Taper relief reduces the tax due not the transfer of value, so does not affect the amount of the NRB available for later transfers.

Example 28.4 – No refund of tax paid on original gifts when recomputed tax is lower

In June 2009, Danielle settled £350,000 on discretionary trusts for her grandchildren. She died in May 2015. She paid the IHT on setting up the trust herself.

The original tax due creating the trust was as follows:

	£
Amount settled	350,000
Less: annual exemptions	(6,000)
Chargeable	344,000
NRB	(325,000)
Amount chargeable at 25% (grossed up)	19,000
Tax paid	4,750

Recomputed tax following Danielle's death:

	£
Gross value transferred (£344,000+£4,750)	348,750
NRB	(325,000)
Amount chargeable at 40%	23,750
Tax due	9,500
Less: taper relief – 60% (5–6 years)	(5,700)
	3,800
Less: tax paid	(4,750)
Further tax due	nil

The difference of £950 is not reclaimable.

There is no NRB to set against Danielle's estate.

QUICK SUCCESSION RELIEF

28.14　Quick succession relief (QSR), also known as 'successive charges relief' is designed to give a degree of relief where successive charges to IHT arise within a five-year period.

QSR is available where an estate taxable on death reflects the benefit of property received within the previous five years under a transfer on which tax was (or has become) payable (*s 141*).

For settlements, QSR may also arise on lifetime transfers as well as on death. However, the transferor must have had an interest in possession in the settled property, by reference to which the later transfer is determined, the value of the first transfer must have been determined by reference to that property and the first transfer must have included making the settlement or occurred after it was made.

The IHT payable on the second transfer is reduced by a credit for the tax on the first transfer according to the formula:

$$\text{Credit} = AP \times T \times \frac{G - T}{G}$$

Where:

T is the tax charged on the earlier transfer;

G is the gross value of the earlier transfer; and

AP is the appropriate percentage as shown below:

Years between the two transfers	Percentage reduction
1 year or less	100
1 to 2 years	80
2 to 3 years	60
3 to 4 years	40
4 to 5 years	20
Over 5 years	0

Example 28.5 – Relief for tax suffered on failed PET

In May 2009, Eric is given a painting worth £35,000 by his uncle who has already used all of his allowances and his NRB.

In March 2011 his uncle died, leaving Eric to pay £14,000 tax on the failed PET.

In December 2012, Eric died leaving his estate (including the painting) to his nephews and nieces. His estate after exemptions and reliefs was valued at £400,000.

The estate will be able to deduct £6,720 calculated as follows:

$$80\% \times 14,000 \times \frac{35,000 - 14,000}{35,000}$$

BUSINESS PROPERTY RELIEF

28.15   Business property relief (BPR) operates by giving a reduction of a specified percentage against the value of any 'relevant business property' which is the subject of a transfer (*Pt V, Ch 1*).

- The relief is available for any type of transfer, covering both lifetime transfers and transfers on death.

- There is no upper limit to this relief.

- The relief can apply to all business property and is not restricted to transfers of UK property.

- The relief is mandatory – it does not have to be formally claimed.

Where a lifetime transfer of business property is made, the percentage reduction takes place prior to any required grossing up and before giving effect to any of the lifetime exemptions that may be available. The relief is set against the value transferred.

There are two basic conditions which must be observed in order for the relief to be available:

- the property transferred must be relevant business property (*s 104(1)*) (see **28.16**); and

- the property must (usually) have been owned throughout the two years prior to the transfer (*s 106*).

Relevant business property

28.16   The property on which the relief is available can be divided into six main categories as set out below:

- **100% Relief**

    o   a business or an interest in a business (does not apply to the assets used within a business (but see *HMRC v Nelson Dance Family Settlement Trustees* [2009] EWHC 71 (Ch)) (*s 105(1)(a)*);

    o   unquoted securities which (either by themselves or in conjunction with other holdings owned by the transferor and related property) gave the transferor control of that company immediately before the transfer (*s 105(1)(b)*);

    o   unquoted shares (*s 105(1)(bba)*).

457

- **50% Relief**
  - quoted shares and securities which (either by themselves or in conjunction with other holdings owned by the transferor and related property) gave the transferor control of that company immediately before the transfer (*s 105(1)(cc)*);
  - land, buildings, plant or machinery owned by the transferor which, immediately before the transfer, was used wholly or mainly for the purpose of a business carried on either:
    - by a company controlled by the transferor, or
    - by a partnership in which the transferor is partner (*s 105(1)(d)*);
  - land, buildings, plant or machinery owned by a settlement which, immediately before the transfer, was used wholly or mainly for the purposes of a business carried on by the person who was then beneficially entitled to an interest in possession in that settlement (*s 105(1)(e)*).

'Business' includes professions and vocations, but excludes activities not carried on for gain (*s 103(3)*).

In the case of a partnership, it is only the transferor partner's share of the business which attracts the relief. It does not matter that the partner in question may be only a sleeping or limited partner. It should be noted that a partner's interest is a 'chose in action', rather than an interest in the underlying assets.

Focus

It is important to note that the capital account of a retired partner does not qualify for BPR (*Beckman v CIR* Sp C [2000] SSCD 59 (Sp C 226)).

This is often an issue where a partnership cannot afford to repay the whole of a retiring partner's capital account so it is agreed that it is repaid over a period as cashflow allows.

BPR is not to be given if the business consists wholly or mainly of one or more of the following:

- dealing in shares or securities;
- dealing in land or buildings;
- making or holding investments.

However, *sub-s (4)* brings back into the relieving provisions businesses which are wholly market makers or discount houses carried on in the UK. It also ensures that holding companies of companies eligible under *sub-s (3)* also qualify.

These rules exclude companies which carry on mainly investment activities from relief, but if the company is wholly or mainly trading the shares may qualify in full. Some care is required in the case of groups of companies because the value attributable to shares in an investment company within the group are excluded when valuing the shares in the holding company (*s 111*).

Example 28.6 – Effect of investment activity on BPR

Pericles & Co Limited (which is unquoted) runs a substantial furniture retail trade, but it has let out a shop, which it no longer has use for, to a pub group which has converted it to use in its business. It is accepted that this property letting activity represents less than half of Pericles's activities. BPR will be available for the whole value of Pericles's shares.

However, if Pericles transferred the letting business to a separate wholly owned subsidiary, then BPR would be restricted. This restriction is carried out by valuing the shares in the first instance including the property letting business to determine the transfer of value and then excluding that business to determine the amount eligible for BPR. The element not eligible for relief may be more or less than the proportion of the business represented by that activity, depending on its influence in valuing the shares.

If the letting business grows, then BPR would be lost when the letting activity represents more than half of the overall business.

There are similar restrictions for assets not used in the business, such as surplus cash or assets held for the personal use of the shareholders (*s 112*).

In assessing whether a business is wholly or mainly carrying on excluded activities, it is necessary to assess the position in the round. There are a number of cases on this subject in particular:

- *Martin and Horsfall (Executors of Violet Moore deceased) v IRC* (Sp C [1995] SSCD 5 (Sp C 2)) and *Burkinyoung (Executor of BL Burkinyoung deceased) v IRC* (Sp C [1995] SSCD 29 (Sp C 3)) – whether property letting was a business or mainly investment.

- *McCall and Keenan (PRS of McClean Deceased) v RCC* [2009] STC 900 – whether letting land on grazing licences was a business or mainly investment.

- *IRC v George* [2003] EWCA Civ 1763 – whether a business of running a caravan site was mainly an investment activity.

- *IRC v Farmer* [1999] STC (SCD) 321 – whether a farming business with substantial letting activity was mainly an investment activity.

- *Brander v Revenue and Customs Commissioners* [2010] UKUT 300 (TCC) – whether a landed estate (not held by a company) was a single business.

- *HMRC v Nelson Dance Family Settlement Trustees v RCC* [2009] EWHC 71 (Ch) – held that the transfer of an asset out of a business was eligible for BPR, even though the asset transfer did not constitute a business or part of a business in itself.

- *Revenue and Customs Commissioners v Lockyer and another (personal representatives of Pawson, deceased)* [2013] UKUT 50 (TCC) – held that a furnished holiday letting business did not qualify for BPR despite significant services provided for guests.

Although *s 267A* treats the members of a limited liability partnership as entitled to a share of its underlying assets, HMRC's view is that in determining whether the business is an investment business you should look at the business as a whole. Therefore, BPR may not be due if the partnership or LLP only makes passive investments in unquoted trading companies, even though the shares would attract relief if held by the partners personally.

There is an HMRC clearance service for IHT issues. Details can be found at: www.gov.uk/non-statutory-clearance-service-guidance.

Minimum period of ownership

28.17   The transferor must have owned the business property throughout the two years immediately prior to the transfer. This rule applies to all of the categories of business property. However, there are special rules for replacement property (see **28.18**) and successions (see **28.19**).

It is only necessary to hold the property actually being transferred (or its replacement) throughout the two-year period. It is not necessary for the transferor to have had control of a company throughout the last two years in order to qualify for the 50% relief for controlling shareholdings in quoted companies. The only necessity is for him to have owned the shares actually being transferred for that period (IHTM25172).

Example 28.7 – Loss of control

Freda controls 60% of the votes attached to the shares of a quoted company.

She would be entitled to 50% relief on a transfer of, say, a 15% holding (provided that the 15% being transferred has been owned for two years or is replacement property) even if she had only recently acquired control because of an acquisition of further shares or a change in the votes attached to her shares or those of the other shareholders.

There is no requirement that the business is the same throughout the two-year period, although there must be a business during that time (IHTM25303). What is less clear is whether the business needs to qualify throughout that period, but it is likely that HMRC will challenge cases where it did not.

Example 28.8 – Change of business

Gerald owns shares in an unquoted company which originally ran a warehousing business, but when the market dried up, he started using the premises for indoor go-kart racing.

The change of trade does not affect the period of ownership.

Replacement property

28.18 Property which has not yet been owned for two years can still qualify for relief if:

- it replaced other property which would itself have qualified for the relief as relevant business property; and

- taken together, both sets of property have been owned by the transferor for at least two of the five years immediately prior to the transfer.

However, it should be noted that the amount of relief that can be obtained in these circumstances will be limited to the amount that there would have been if the original property had not been replaced (*s 107*).

Example 28.9 – Limitation of relief for replacement property

Harold owned a company which ran a saw mill for many years. In 2010, he sold the shares for £1 million.

In 2011, he used the proceeds together with savings to buy shares in trading companies listed on AIM for £2 million.

He died shortly afterwards.

The AIM shares would have qualified if he had lived for two years after buying them. He can claim BPR using the replacement property rules, but the relief will be limited to £1 million.

Successions and successive transfers

28.19   Where the transferor acquired the business property following the death of another individual, his period of ownership is deemed to run from the date of that death. Where the individual was his spouse (or civil partner), ownership is considered to have commenced when the spouse acquired the property provided that the inter-spouse transfer takes place on death (*s 108*).

Business property held for less than two years at the date of a transfer (and which did not replace other business property) may still meet the two-year ownership test under legislation intended to deal with premature deaths. The relief is still available for property which would qualify for BPR (apart from the ownership period), provided that:

- the transferor (or his spouse) acquired the property as a result of a previous transfer in respect of which business property relief was due; and

- either the acquisition or the present transfer arose on a death (*s 109*).

Other points

28.20   Where BPR is claimed on a lifetime transfer (whether a CLT or PET), the relief may not be available where the transferor dies within seven years (see **29.5**).

Also BPR will not be available where the property in question is subject to a binding contract for sale (*s 113*). This can cause problems if there are agreements in place to deal with the continuation of the business where a shareholder or partner dies.

Focus

It may be possible to preserve BPR and protect the ownership of the business by using put and call options rather than a binding agreement for sale.

AGRICULTURAL PROPERTY RELIEF

28.21 Agricultural property relief (APR) operates on a similar basis to BPR by giving a deduction against the 'agricultural value' (as opposed to market value) of 'agricultural property' which is the subject of a transfer. It is applied before other exemptions and before any grossing up (*Pt V, Ch 2*).

Example 28.10 – Importance of being able to claim BPR, rather than APR

Ingrid owns 30 acres of farmland which she has let to Julian on a ten-year lease. He grows crops on it. She has planning permission to erect some houses on the land. Taking into account planning permission, the land is worth £1.8 million but the agricultural value is only £180,000.

She is only entitled to APR on £180,000. If she farmed the land herself, she could claim BPR on the full value.

As with BPR:

- it is available for any type of transfer, and covers both lifetime transfers and transfers on death;

- there is no upper limit to the relief;

- the relief is mandatory – it does not have to be formally claimed.

Definition of agricultural property

28.22 'Agricultural property' is defined as:

- agricultural land or pasture; and

- includes woodland and any building used in connection with the intensive rearing of livestock or fish, occupied with agricultural land; and

- also includes cottages, farm buildings and farmhouses of a character appropriate to the agricultural land.

463

HMRC broadly follow the definition of agriculture in the *Agricultural Tenancies Act 1995* which defines 'agriculture' as including horticulture, fruit growing, seed growing, dairy farming and livestock breeding and keeping, the use of land as grazing land, meadow land, osier land, market gardens and nursery grounds, and the use of land for woodlands where that use is ancillary to the farming of land for other agricultural purposes.

The breeding and rearing of horses on a stud farm is treated as agricultural for this purpose (*s 115(4)*).

Relief is limited to property in the UK, Channel Islands, Isle of Man or the EEA.

The 'agricultural value' of any agricultural property is determined to be the value of the property if it were subject to a perpetual covenant preventing it from being used for anything other than agriculture (*s 115(2)–(5)*).

To qualify for APR, the land must be occupied for agricultural purposes; in most cases this should be fairly apparent. However, it is worth noting that pasture used for leisure purposes, such as grazing for horses kept for riding, does not qualify.

The most difficult area for APR is obtaining relief for farmhouses. It would be rare for a farmhouse to qualify for BPR, so APR is a valuable relief, although in many cases the agricultural value of the property may be much less than full market value.

The first point is to demonstrate that the house in question is the place from which the farm is managed. With larger farms there may be a separate office from which the farm is run, particularly if a farm manager is employed by the business.

The second issue is whether the house is of a character appropriate to the farm. There is a long list of cases dealing with this issue, including:

- *Arnander (Executors of McKenna Deceased v HMRC* [2006] SpC 0565;

- *Lloyds TSB (Personal representative of Antrobus) v IRC* [2002] STC (SCD) 468;

- *Lloyds TSB Private Banking (Executor of Miss R Antrobus deceased) v Twiddy* Lands Tribunal [2006] RVR 138;

- *Rosser v IRC* [2002] STC (SCD) 311.

HMRC regularly challenge claims for APR on farmhouses, in particular where the value of the house is a large part of the overall value of the farm. They compare the nature of the house with the nature of other farmhouses in the locality, and the relative size of the land farmed. They will also seek to deny relief where the income does not appear to support the running of the farmhouse. They also challenge whether the house is occupied for agriculture in cases of lifestyle or elderly farmers.

Conditions for relief

28.23   In order to qualify for relief, there is a minimum requirement in terms of the period of the transferor's occupation or ownership. The relief is only available if the agricultural property was either:

- occupied by the transferor for agricultural purposes throughout the period of two years ending with the date of the transfer; or

- owned by the transferor throughout the period of seven years ending with that date and has been occupied throughout that period (whether by the transferor or by another) for agricultural purposes (*s 117*).

Rate of relief

28.24   Given that the property satisfies the above test, the percentage reduction in the value transferred is:

- 100% where the donor is owner/farmer;

- 100% where the donor leases the land to another farmer and either:

  ○   vacant possession is available within 24 months, or

  ○   the lease began after 1 September 1995;

- any other cases – 50% (*s 116(2)*).

Strictly speaking, the period in which vacant possession must be obtained is 12 months, but it is extended to 24 months by ESC F17.

Replacement agricultural property

28.25   Where occupied agricultural property was a replacement for other agricultural property, the two-year occupation requirement is treated as satisfied if the current agricultural property and any agricultural property which it replaced were occupied by the transferor for agricultural purposes for periods which together amount to at least two years falling within the five years ending with the date of transfer (*s 118(1)*).

Where the owned agricultural property was a replacement for other agricultural property, the seven year ownership requirement is treated as satisfied if the current agricultural property and any agricultural property which it replaced were both owned by the transferor and occupied (by him or another) for agricultural purposes for periods which together amount to at least seven years falling within the ten years ending with the date of transfer (*s 118(2)*).

However, it should be noted, that the amount of relief that can be obtained in these circumstances will be limited to the amount that there would have been if the original property had not been replaced (*s 118(3)*).

Successions

28.26   Where a transferor has inherited agricultural property on the death of another, he is deemed to have owned it from the date of death. If he subsequently occupies the property, he is deemed to have occupied it since the date of the death (*s 120*).

If the land was inherited from the transferor's spouse, he is deemed to have owned it and occupied it for periods during which his spouse owned it and occupied it.

The succession rules also allow agricultural property to qualify for APR if:

- the property was acquired by way of a transfer qualifying for APR; and

- either the earlier transfer or the current transfer was a transfer on death; and

- the property was occupied for agricultural purposes at the time of the later transfer either by the current transferor or by the personal representatives of the earlier transferor.

Other points

28.27   Where APR is claimed on a lifetime transfer (whether a CLT or PET), the relief may not be available where the transferor dies within seven years (see **Chapter 29**).

Also APR will not be available where the property in question is subject to a binding contract for sale (*s 124*). This can cause problems on death where there are agreements in place to enable the continuation of the business where a shareholder or partner dies.

APR is available on controlling interests in farming companies but only up to the amount attributable to the agricultural value of property (*s 122*).

HMRC's view is that the ownership and occupation of the agricultural property must be the same for APR to be available, which is a particular issue where farmhouses are concerned. Doubt is cast on this view by a recent case – *Revenue and Customs Commissioners v Joseph Nicholas Hanson (Trustee of William Hanson 1957 Settlement)* [2013] UKUT 224 (TCC).

WOODLANDS RELIEF

28.28 If any part of a person's estate immediately before his death is attributable to the value of land in the UK on which trees or underwood are growing:

- the value of the trees and underwood (but not the value of the land itself) can be excluded when determining the value of that person's property transferred on his death; but

- IHT is chargeable on any later disposal of the trees or underwood, unless any other reliefs are available (*s 125(1), (2)*).

If the woodland qualifies for APR, woodland relief is not available, but APR (or BPR if available) would usually be more beneficial.

HERITAGE PROPERTY

28.29 In order to preserve and protect national heritage for the benefit of the public, the government introduced the conditional exemption tax incentive scheme.

Under the scheme, no IHT (or CGT) is paid when an asset which qualifies for exemption passes to a new owner on death or is gifted. In order to get the exemption, the new owner must agree to:

- look after the item;
- allow the public access to it;
- keep it in the UK – if it is moveable.

If the owner doesn't keep to the agreement, the exemption is withdrawn and they will have to pay tax on the asset. They will also have to pay tax if they sell the asset.

The main types of assets that qualify as national heritage property are:

- outstanding historical buildings, estates and parklands and works of art, furnishings, sculptures, etc linked to such historical buildings;

- land that is needed to protect the character and amenities of these buildings;

- land, including buildings, of outstanding scenic, historic or scientific interest;

- paintings, portraits, drawings, watercolours, furniture, sculptures, books, manuscripts, ceramics, etc of artistic, historic or scientific interest in their own right;

- scientific collections or other items not yielding income, of important national, historic, artistic or scientific interest.

An offer can be made to settle some or all of the IHT and interest owed by transferring national heritage property to the Crown, but such offers are rarely accepted. The rules for this are complex, and each item will be dealt with on a case-by-case basis. In the rare cases where an offer is accepted, all of the IHT due must be paid in advance through any of the usual means. After the payment has been made, the asset can be transferred to the Crown, after which HMRC will repay the IHT paid.

REDUCED RATE FOR CHARITABLE GIFTS

28.30 To encourage giving to charity, there is relief available for deaths occurring on or after 6 April 2012. Broadly, the relief means that provided that 10% of the base line amount chargeable to IHT on a death is donated to charity, the rate of tax on that component of the chargeable estate is taxed at 36% rather than 40% (*Sch 1A*).

This relief is not sufficient to mean that the other beneficiaries from the estate would be better off by making such a donation, but where the deceased already has made a significant gift to charity in his will, it might be possible to reduce the IHT by increasing that legacy, with the result that the other beneficiaries receive more than they would have done.

Example 28.11 – Increasing existing legacy to reduce IHT

Bradley leaves £50,000 in his will to his local cycling club, a registered community sports club. When he dies, his estate is worth £850,000. He is unmarried and has made no previous transfers of value.

The IHT on his estate will be as follows:

	£
Value of estate	850,000
Legacy to cycle club	(50,000)
Taxable estate	800,000
NRB	(325,000)
Taxable	475,000
Add back charitable legacy	50,000
Baseline amount	525,000

As the legacy is less than 10% of the baseline, the net estate is taxed at 40%, so the IHT due is £190,000.

If the legacy was increased to £53,000, then the calculation would become:

	£
Value of estate	850,000
Legacy to cycle club	(53,000)
Taxable estate	797,000
NRB	(325,000)
Taxable	472,000
Add back charitable legacy	53,000
Baseline amount	525,000

The legacy is now more than 10% of the baseline, so the net estate is taxed at 36% and the IHT due is £169,920. The cycle club gets £3,000 more but the IHT is reduced by £20,080, which means the other beneficiaries receive £17,080 more.

HMRC accept that the beneficiaries of an estate may wish to enter into an instrument of variation under *s 142* to achieve this result, and their guidance confirms that this is perfectly acceptable (IHTM45011). The guidance also confirms that the benefit that the parties receive as a result of the reduced IHT is not normally consideration for the purposes of *s 142(3)* (IHTM45039).

HMRC also recognise that taxpayers may wish to include a clause in their will so that any legacy to charity is of such an amount to secure that the provisions apply. They have provided draft wording in their guidance at IHTM45008 and, their officers are currently instructed that they should not challenge the use of that wording, but any variation is likely to come under scrutiny.

For the purposes of the relief, the amounts chargeable to IHT are broken down into four components (*Sch 1A, para 3*):

- *settled property* – that is, any property which is held in a settlement but is included in the deceased's estate for the purposes of calculating IHT, such as interests in possession which were created before 22 March 2006;

- *survivorship property* – that is, property which passes to another joint owner because he survives the deceased;

- *property subject to a gift with reservation*; and

- *the general component* – everything else chargeable to IHT on the death.

The reduced rate applies to each component separately and the gift to charity must exceed 10% of the baseline amount calculated for that component.

Generally, instruments of variation will only be tax efficient in respect of the general component, so it would not be possible to bring the other components within the relief post-death. Any settlement would require provisions that at least 10% of the settled property passed to a charity on the death of the life tenant for that component to benefit. Property subject to a gift with reservation could never benefit independently as the charge is on a notional interest in property which already belongs to another person.

It is unlikely that property passing by survivorship would attract the relief, unless the property was held jointly with a charity. If an instrument of variation is carried out to break the survivorship terms of property post-death, the property nevertheless remains in the survivorship component, even if as a result of the instrument the property in question then forms part of the residue of the deceased's estate.

Where the deceased's estate has several items within one of the components, such as multiple interests in possession or property passing by survivorship, the property is aggregated within that component. If part of that property passed to charity as a result of the death, then the other items making up that component may then benefit from the reduced rate depending on the circumstances. Therefore if an instrument of variation was made to sever joint property and direct it to charity, this might enable the other elements of the survivorship component to benefit.

Recognising the difficulties that may arise from the above, it is possible to aggregate components. For example, if there was a gift to charity out of the general component such that the general component benefited from the reduced rate, it might be possible merge the gift with reservation and general components and apply the reduced rate to both – as long as the gift to charity was significant enough to be 10% of the combined baseline. The election must be made within two years of death for this to apply (*Sch 1A, paras 7, 8, 9*).

To calculate the baseline amount, the following steps are taken (*Sch 1A, para 5*):

Step 1 – Calculate the chargeable transfer in respect of the component. This is computed after all exemptions and reliefs, such as spouse exemption or business property relief, and in particular any gift to charity.

Step 2 – Deduct from this figure the appropriate proportion of the available nil rate band. The available nil rate band is the nil rate band including any transferred nil rate band, after deducting any lifetime chargeable transfers which must be brought into account. Where there is more than one component in the estate, the available nil rate band is apportioned between the components in proportion to the chargeable transfers for each component.

Step 3 – The charitable legacy is then added back to the previous figure to arrive at the baseline amount. If the charitable legacy exceeds 10% of the baseline amount, then the reduced rate applies to that component.

Example 28.12 – General component and GWR component

Nicola (who never married) died leaving an estate worth £545,000. She left £35,000 to charity. Ten years before she died, she gave her house to her children, but they have let her continue to live there. On her death it was valued at £340,000.

471

For IHT her estate would be taxed as follows:

	Free estate	Gift with reservation	Total
	£	£	£
Value of estate	545,000	340,000	885,000
Legacy to charity	(35,000)		(35,000)
Taxable estate	510,000	340,000	850,000
NRB	(195,000)	(130,000)	(325,000)
Taxable	315,000	210,000	525,000
Add back charitable legacy	35,000	–	35,000
Baseline amount	350,000	210,000	560,000

For the general component (the free estate in this case), the charitable legacy is 10% of the baseline, so that component is taxed at 36% and the GWR is taxed at 40%, meaning that the total tax will be £197,400 (£113,400 + £84,000).

Example 28.13 – Merged components

Olivia died leaving an estate worth £600,000. Her husband died some years previously and left legacies which used 70% of his NRB. Olivia left £56,000 to charity. Ten years before she died she gave her house to her children, but they have let her continue to live there. On her death it was valued at £340,000.

	Free estate	Gift with reservation	Total
	£	£	£
Value of estate	600,000	340,000	940,000
Legacy to charity	(56,000)		(56,000)
Taxable estate	544,000	340,000	884,000
NRB (£325,000 * 130%)	(260,000)	(162,500)	(422,500)
Taxable	284,000	177,500	461,500
Add back charitable legacy	56,000	–	56,000
Baseline amount	340,000	177,500	517,500

As the charitable legacy is more than 10% of the baseline amount for the general component, that component will be taxed at 36%. There is no charitable gift for the gift with reservation, so that gift would be taxed at 40%. However, by electing to merge the components in time, Olivia's personal representatives and her children can secure that the reduced rate also applies to the GWR component as the charitable legacy of £56,000 is greater than 10% of the two components combined (£517,500). This saves tax of £7,100 (4% × £177,500).

In some instances the potential benefit of the reduced rate might exceed the costs of determining the true values of the property in the estate, which will be necessary to confirm that the charitable legacy exceeded the baseline amount. It is therefore possible to disclaim this relief, provided an election is made within two years of death. If an election is not made, then presumably HMRC can insist on the valuations being carried out – a departure from their normal practice.

There can be further complications with this relief, particularly in cases where:

- the legacy is to be determined at such an amount as to ensure that the reduced rate applies; and

- it is necessary to consider the interaction of other reliefs with specific legacies, such as APR and BPR; or

- certain legacies are specified to be free of tax so that they need to be grossed up to determine where the tax falls.

HMRC have created a calculator to assist with this process, which can be found at www.hmrc.gov.uk/tools/iht-reduced-rate/calculator.htm.

OTHER RELIEFS

28.31 *Related property relief* – If related property is sold to an unconnected person within three years after the death for less than the related property valuation, a claim may be made to recalculate the tax on death without reference to the related property (*s 176*) (see **30.7**).

Fall in value relief – If following a PET or chargeable transfer, the value of the property transferred is less at the time of the transferor's death, relief may be available so that when calculating the IHT on the transfer the lower value can be used (*s 131*).

There are other reliefs only applicable post-death for sales of shares and sales of land and these are covered at **30.5**.

APPENDIX: AGRICULTURAL AND BUSINESS PROPERTY RELIEF

(IHTA 1984, Pt V, Chs 1, 2)

28.32

Agricultural property (Notes 1, 2)		Business property	
Nature of property	**Disposals from 6 April 1996**	**Nature of property**	**Disposals from 6 April 1996**
	%		%
Vacant possession or right to obtain it within 12 months	100	Business or interest in a business	100
Tenanted land with vacant possession value (Note 3)	100	Quoted company: controlling shareholding	50
Agricultural land let on or after 1 September 1995	100	Unquoted company: controlling shareholding	100
Any other circumstances	50	Unquoted company: shareholding more than 25%	100
		Unquoted company: shareholding 25% or less	100
		Unquoted securities: control holding	100
		Settled property used in life tenant's business (Note 4)	100/50
		Land, buildings, machinery or plant used by transferor's company or partnership	50

Notes

1   *EEA states* – IHT due or paid from 23 April 2003 in respect of agricultural property located in a qualifying EEA state at the time of the chargeable event is eligible for relief (*FA 2009, s 122*).

2   *Grazing land* – If land is let to graze animals or take grass from land for a season, and vacant possession reverts to the landowner within a year, any agricultural property relief due will be at the 100% rate (IHTM24142).

3   *Old tenancies* – Land let on a tenancy commencing before 10 March 1981 may qualify for relief at 100% in certain circumstances, ie broadly if the transferor owned the land before 10 March 1981, the land would have qualified for relief (under *FA 1975, Sch 8*) had it been transferred before that date, and the transferor did not have vacant possession (or entitlement to it) from then until the date of death/transfer (*IHTA 1984, s 116(2), (3)*).

4   *Settled property* – The higher rate applies if the settled property is transferred with the business on death (see IHTM25243).

5   *Deductions for debts* – Where a debt is incurred on or after 6 April 2013 to acquire an asset on which relief is due under APR, BPR or woodlands relief, the debt must be first deducted from the value of that asset before any excess debt is deducted from the value of the total estate (*IHTA 1984, s 162B*).

29

Lifetime transfers

SIGNPOSTS

- **Scope** – Certain transfers of value are exempt for IHT purposes, but some exemptions are only available for lifetime transfers (see **29.1**).

- **PETs and CLTs** – Potentially exempt transfers (PETs) are IHT-free provided that the donor survives for seven years after the gift. Chargeable lifetime transfers (CLTs) such as transfers into most trusts and transfers by close companies are always chargeable to IHT, even if at a nil rate of tax. Further IHT may be due if the donor dies within seven years of the CLT (see **29.2–29.3**).

- **Valuation** – The value of a transfer is the amount by which the donor's estate is reduced which may be different from the value of the asset acquired by the donee (see **29.4**).

- **Business and agricultural property relief** – For gifts on which business and agricultural property relief has applied, certain conditions must be satisfied for BPR and APR to be preserved, should the donor not survive for seven years (see **29.5**).

- **Gifts with reservation** – In some situations, anti-avoidance rules can apply to treat assets given away as remaining part of the donor's estate for IHT purposes, subject to certain exceptions (see **29.6**).

- **Pre-owned assets** – The pre-owned assets tax regime was introduced because of the growth in IHT schemes often involving the family home, and imposes an income tax charge on the value of the benefit retained, subject to certain exemptions and exclusions (see **29.7**).

- **Associated operations** – An anti-avoidance rule broadly provides that for transactions made by way of two or more linked operations, the combined effect on the transferor's estate is taken into account and treated as made at the time of the last transfer (see **29.8**).

All references in this chapter are to IHTA 1984, unless otherwise stated.

LIFETIME EXEMPTIONS

29.1   As indicated at **28.1**, lifetime exemptions generally fall into two categories:

- those which apply through the operations of limits and which are available for lifetime transfers only:

  o   annual exemption,

  o   small gifts exemption,

  o   normal expenditure out of income,

  o   gifts in consideration of marriages;

- exemptions which apply because of the status of the recipient and are available for both lifetime and death transfers:

  o   transfers between spouses,

  o   gifts to charities,

  o   gifts to political parties,

  o   gifts for national purposes.

POTENTIALLY EXEMPT TRANSFERS

29.2   Before 22 March 2006, a potentially exempt transfer (PET) was defined as a transfer of value, which is not otherwise covered by an exemption, made by an individual to:

- another individual; or

- an accumulation and maintenance trust; or

- an interest in possession trust; or

- a disabled trust.

On or after 22 March 2006, a PET is a transfer of value, which is not otherwise covered by an exemption, made by an individual to:

- another individual; or

- a disabled trust; or

- a bereaved minor's trust on the termination of an immediate post-death interest *(s 3A(1), (2))*.

Generally, the above provisions also apply to transfers on the lifetime termination of an interest in possession held by an individual where the property is treated as part of his estate for IHT (see **35.19** and **35.20**).

The legislation specifies that a transfer of value to an individual is a PET to the extent that the value transferred is attributable to property which becomes part of the estate of that individual or the value by which that individual's estate is increased. This suggests that a transfer of a minority holding from a majority stake may not qualify in full, because of the differing valuations, but HMRC do not take this point.

A PET becomes an exempt transfer if the transferor survives a further seven years from the date the transfer is made, otherwise the PET will become a chargeable transfer (*s 3A(4)*).

A PET is assumed to be exempt until the transferor dies. Therefore no tax will be payable at the time when the transfer is made or any other time in the seven-year period (*s 3A(5)*).

Although tax is not payable until the transferor dies, the value of the transfer is fixed at the time the PET is made. It is not recalculated using values at the time of the donor's death, unless the value of the property gifted has decreased during the period and a claim is to be made for relief for that decrease. When computing the tax on death, the rates in force at the date of death are used.

Example 29.1 – Simple failed PET

Julius gave his son Keiran all of his shares in a quoted company valued at £500,000 in January 2010. He died in December that year. At that date the shares were worth £750,000.

No tax would have been payable at the time of the gift, but on Julius's death the transfer would become chargeable. Keiran is liable for tax of £67,600 (40% × (£500,000 – £6,000 – £325,000)). This assumes that Julius had no prior transfers to take into account.

Although the transfer proves to be taxable, the early transfer saves tax because the growth in value escapes IHT (although it may mean more CGT is paid in due course as Keiran's base cost for CGT will be £500,000 not £750,000). The gift also uses the annual exemption.

Focus

While PETs are not chargeable during the donor's life, they will have to be considered if he dies within seven years so a record must be maintained for consideration when later transfers are planned and in order to determine the charge on death.

The donee should consider whether he may be liable for tax on the gift if the donor dies.

CHARGEABLE LIFETIME TRANSFERS

29.3 Those transfers which may be exempt from IHT have been set out above. Any other lifetime transfers will be chargeable lifetime transfers (CLTs). The main transfers which can never be PETs and so will always be treated as CLTs are:

● transfers into most trusts on or after 22 March 2006; and

● close company transfers which are treated as having been made by the company's shareholders.

CLTs are charged at the lifetime rate, to the extent that they exceed the NRB. As with PETs, if the transferor dies within seven years, the tax position is revisited and further tax may be due. The position is similar to that for PETs, although with CLTs tax may have arisen on the earlier transfer.

Example 29.2 – Chargeable transfer within seven years of death

In June 2006, Leonora settled £330,000 on discretionary trusts for her grandchildren. She died in May 2009. She paid the IHT on setting up the trust herself.

The original tax due creating the trust was as follows:

	£
Amount settled;	330,000
Less: annual exemptions	(6,000)
Chargeable	324,000
NRB	(285,000)
Amount chargeable at 25% (grossing up applies)	39,000
Tax paid	9,750

	£
Recomputed tax following Danielle's death	
Gross value transferred (£324,000 + £9,750)	333,750
NRB	(325,000)
Amount chargeable at 40%	8,750
Tax due	3,500
Less: tax paid	(9,750)
Further tax due	nil

No further tax is due, but neither is there a repayment.

If the settlement had been made more than three years before Leonora died, taper relief would have been available if any further tax was due.

Focus

If property settled is eligible for APR or BPR, there may be no IHT on the original transfer because the value transferred is nil or falls within the nil rate band. The trustees need to be aware that in determining the rate of tax for exit charges within the first ten years APR or BPR will be not be available (see **35.15**).

VALUATION ISSUES

29.4   The value of transfers is not the value of the gift in the hands of the donee but the fall in value of the donor's estate, which may be significantly different.

Example 29.3 – Loss of control of unquoted trading company

William owns 51% of the ordinary shares of Windsor Limited. When his brother Harry joins the board, William gives him 2% of the shares so that Harry meets the qualifying requirement under the articles.

It is agreed that a 2% holding is worth £75,000. However, a 51% holding is valued at £6.6 million and a 49% holding at £5.1 million.

The fall in the value of William's estate is £1.5 million, which is the value of the transfer for IHT.

The related property rules discussed at **30.4** also need to be considered. If in the above example William only held 45% before the transfer, but his wife held 6%, a gift of 2% by either of them would have the same result.

The difference between the fall in value of the donor's estate and the value of the asset acquired by the donee is most likely to be an issue for gifts of shares in unquoted companies, as in the example above. This is because the value per share of shares in unquoted companies is often different for different percentage shareholdings. For example a controlling holding is considered to be more valuable than a minority shareholding, This point is irrelevant for quoted shares, which have a standard value irrespective of the number of shares.

The valuation of unquoted shares is a difficult area and is something which HMRC regard as high risk so they will often enquire into the value offered by the taxpayer. Another area where valuations are important is land, and HMRC will expect a properly qualified surveyor to have considered land valuations which are included in an IHT return.

For IHT purposes, the value of a life assurance policy is generally its open market value. However, where the transfer is not on the death of the transferor, the value of such a policy is the greater of:

- the aggregate premiums paid to date; or

- its open market value.

This is the case whether the transferor is the life assured or not. Any surrender value applicable to the policy is not relevant. The value of the premiums paid is taken net of life assurance relief, if any (*s 167*).

GIFTS BENEFITING FROM BUSINESS OR AGRICULTURAL PROPERTY RELIEF

29.5   The value of transfers may be affected by BPR and APR. However, as most lifetime gifts are PETs, the reliefs may only be relevant on the death of the donor. BPR and APR are covered in depth at **28.15–28.27**.

When planning lifetime transfers which will benefit from these reliefs it is important to consider the additional conditions which must be satisfied if relief is to be available should the transferor die within seven years.

For BPR, the basic rule is that the transferee must retain property until he dies, until the transferor dies or for seven years (whichever is sooner), and throughout that period the property must be relevant business property. The second condition does not need to be met where the property consists of certain types of share (*s 113A*).

> **Example 29.4 – Failed PET ceasing to qualify for BPR**
>
> In January 2012, Malcolm gives his son Norbert 15,000 shares in Torside Brewing Ltd, an unquoted trading company. HMRC's Shares and Assets Valuation Division determine that the fall in Malcolm's estate is £400,000, as he previously had a controlling stake.
>
> In November 2012, Norbert receives an offer of £1 million from Mega Brewing plc and sells the shares. Malcolm dies shortly afterwards.
>
> Had Norbert retained the shares there would be no IHT to pay. However, as the shares have been sold, he will be liable for IHT of £27,600. The loss of BPR will also affect the IHT arising on the rest of the estate as the NRB will have been used.

There are replacement property rules for this purpose in *s 113B*. These are stricter than those for the ownership period test (**see 28.18**) as the whole of the net proceeds of sale must be re-invested in property eligible for BPR within three years of the disposal. They also require that the acquisition is on arm's length terms.

However, they permit some scope for post-death action. Provided that the replacement property is acquired within the three-year period, the replacement can be acquired after the transferor's death.

In the above example, Norbert has until November 2015 to acquire suitable replacement property, and avoid the tax charge.

For APR purposes, the basic rule is that the transferee must own property until he dies, until the transferor dies or for seven years (whichever is sooner), and where:

- the property is not shares or securities of a company, it must be agricultural property immediately before the later death and have been occupied for the purposes of agriculture throughout that period; or

- the property is shares or securities of a company, throughout that period the agricultural property for which APR was available on the original transfer must have been owned by the company and have been occupied for the purposes of agriculture (*s 124A*).

Again there are rules for replacement property similar to those for BPR.

Focus

If the beneficiary of any gift of property eligible for APR or BPR is thinking of disposing of it, he will need to consider the potential additional cost created if the donor were to die.

GIFTS WITH RESERVATION

29.6 It might be tempting for a donor to give away 'ownership' of property to another individual but still retain an interest in that property. A typical example of this would be a parent who gifts his house to a child, but then remains in residence. To counter such actions, the special gifts with reservations provisions were introduced (*FA 1986, s 102*).

Property given away on or after 18 March 1986 is subject to a reservation if:

- actual possession/enjoyment of the property is not immediately assumed by the transferee; or

- the property is not enjoyed to the entire exclusion, or virtually to the entire exclusion of the transferor; or

- the property is not enjoyed to the entire exclusion, or virtually to the entire exclusion of any collateral benefit to the transferor whether arising by contract or otherwise (*FA 1986, s 102(1)*).

The use of the phrase 'or virtually to the entire exclusion' is intended to severely limit any benefit the donor might receive if he wishes to exclude the property from his estate for IHT. However, HMRC ignores limited visits to the property which is the subject of the gift (*Revenue Interpretation 55*).

If an individual makes a gift of an asset but reserves a benefit for himself, he will be treated for IHT purposes at the time of his death as though he were still beneficially entitled to that asset. If the reservation expires before his death, the transfer will be deemed to have been made at the time the reservation expired (*FA 1986, s 102*) and is a PET (*FA 1986, s 102(4)*).

The gifts with reservations provisions were extended in relation to gifts of interests in land from 9 March 1999, to deal with certain IHT arrangements broadly involving individuals making gifts of land whilst continuing to enjoy a benefit from it (*FA 1986, ss 102A–102C*).

There are a number of exemptions available, in particular:

- certain gifts covered by other IHT exemptions (see *FA 1986, s 102(5), such as* covers transfers between spouses amongst others);

- gifts of a share of property which they occupy with the transferee (*FA 1986, s 102B*);

- where the use of the asset is for full consideration (*FA 1986, Sch 20, para 6(a)*);

- where the donor moves back into property given away, because he needs to live there to be cared for as a result of sickness or age, and the circumstances could not have been foreseen at the date of the gift (*FA 1986, Sch 20, para 6(b)*).

A gift, to which the reservation of benefit rules are deemed to apply, is still a transfer of value at the time of the gift. The usual rules will determine whether this is a chargeable transfer. However, there are provisions (*IHT (Double Charges Relief) Regulations 1987, SI 1987/1130; IHT (Double Charges Relief) Regulations 2005, SI 2005/3441*) to ensure that any element of double charge will be eliminated, as the asset will be included in the transferor's death estate.

In this case, the total IHT payable following the death must be calculated in two ways:

- by ignoring the lifetime transfer and taxing the property as part of the deceased's estate at death; or

- by charging the lifetime transfer and leaving the property out of the estate.

The IHT payable is then the higher of these two amounts. Should they result in identical tax liabilities, the first calculation is used and the property is included in the estate at death to establish where the IHT liability falls.

Where the gift was a CLT, credit can be taken for the lifetime tax paid, but only to the extent that it does not exceed the tax on death in respect of that property and no excess tax can be reclaimed.

Example 29.5 – Gifts with reservation remaining in estate at death

Oliver (who is divorced) gives his house to his son Peter in March 2010, but carries on living there until he dies in February 2013. In March 2010 the property was worth £400,000. At the date of his death it is worth £475,000. His remaining estate is worth £500,000.

	£	£
Calculation ignoring lifetime transfer		
Gift of house to Peter (ignored)		
Value of house on death		475,000
Estate		500,000
		975,000
Tax	325,000	nil
	650,000	260,000
Calculation ignoring the house		£
Gift of house to Peter		400,000
Less annual exemptions		(6,000)
		394,000
Tax on failed PET		
Tax	325,000	nil
	69,000	27,600
Estate (excluding house)		500,000
Tax on estate		200,000
Total tax		227,600

HMRC will choose the first option, so the tax will be £260,000 in total.

Where both the original gift was made and the reservation is lifted less than seven years before the date of death, there would be two charges arising:

- the original gift would be taxed using the full scale at the date of death; and

- the PET which arose as a result of the reservation being lifted would have become chargeable.

In this case, the total tax payable in consequence of the death must be computed on two bases:

- by ignoring the original gift and charging the PET as a result of the reservation having ceased; and

- by charging the original gift and ignoring the subsequent PET.

485

The IHT payable is then the higher of these two amounts. Should they result in the identical tax liabilities, the first calculation is used and the property is included in the estate at death to establish where the IHT liability falls.

Where a reservation is released and a PET subsequently becomes chargeable, HMRC consider that the annual exemption is not available.

Example 29.6 – Reservation lifted in the seven years before death

If Oliver gave up the use of the house in January 2011 when the house was worth £350,000, then the position would be as follows:

	£	£
Calculation ignoring original gift		
Gift of house to Peter (ignored)		
Value of house on release of reserved benefit		350,000
Tax	325,000	nil
	25,000	10,000
Estate		500,000
Tax at 40%		200,000
Total tax		210,000
Calculation ignoring the deemed PET when benefit released		
Gift of house to Peter		400,000
Less: annual exemptions		(6,000)
		394,000
Tax on failed PET		
Tax	325,000	nil
	69,000	27,600
Estate		500,000
Tax on estate		200,000
Total tax		227,600

HMRC will choose the second option, so the tax will be £227,600 in total.

HMRC have produced a list of examples covering reservation of benefit and associated issues (*Tax Bulletin*, November 1993).

Although HMRC have sought to limit cases where gifts with reservation are effective, some arrangements still work for IHT purposes. Such arrangements are outside the scope of this work. However, in those cases, it is necessary to consider the charge on pre-owned assets (see **29.7**).

> **Focus**
>
> While the property gifted is treated as part of the transferor's estate for IHT purposes, it is not in fact part of his estate. Therefore there is no uplift in the market value of the assets for CGT purposes.
>
> Thus, in the above example, Peter's base cost will be £400,000, not £475,000. He will therefore be liable to CGT on a gain of £75,000 if he sells the property for 'probate' value in order to pay the IHT.

There are rules to ensure that the legislation is still effective where the property is replaced. However, there is no equivalent to the 'contribution condition' in the pre-owned asset rules, so straightforward gifts of cash are not caught under the GWR rules.

PRE-OWNED ASSETS

29.7   As a counter to contentious IHT planning arrangements, many of which involved the family home, the pre-owned assets tax (POAT) charge was introduced, with effect from 6 April 2005. The charge was aimed at devices such as 'lease carve-out' (as in *Lady Ingram's Executors v CIR* [1999] STC 37), 'double trust' schemes and 'reversionary lease' schemes.

The POAT charge applies to persons who continue to derive a benefit from an asset that they either previously owned or they have provided the funds for another person to purchase that asset (unless full consideration is given for the benefit). Individuals caught by the POAT rules face an income tax charge on the deemed value of the benefit, unless they elect to include the value of the relevant property in their estate for IHT purposes or unravel the arrangement.

The rules are found in *FA 2004, Sch 15*.

The charge falls under three heads:

- land – *Sch 15, para 3*;

- chattels – *Sch 15, para 6*;

- intangibles – *Sch 15, para 8*.

For land, the charge applies where the taxpayer occupies land previously given away (the disposal condition) or purchased with funds he has supplied (the contribution condition). The basic amount chargeable is the rental value of the property for the period during which the taxpayer occupies the property. This will be reduced by any rent paid under a legal obligation and in cases where the value of the property is higher than the taxpayer's gift.

For chattels, the charge applies where the taxpayer is in possession of or has use of a chattel (for example, a painting) previously given away (the disposal condition) or purchased with funds he supplied (the contribution condition). The basic amount chargeable is 'notional' interest on the value of the chattel for the period during which the taxpayer has use of the chattel. This would be reduced by any rent paid under a legal obligation and in cases where the value of the property is higher than the taxpayer's gift. The interest rate is set by regulations and currently equates to the 'official' rate of 3% (3.25% before 6 April 2015).

As well as taxing direct gifts, the provisions also apply where the original property is replaced, or where property acquired with a cash gift is replaced. However, they don't apply in cases where a cash gift is used to improve an existing asset.

Example 29.7 – Direct gift

Bart gave his daughter Lisa a house in Dorset in 1987 (as he had moved to Carlisle), which she lived in as her home for many years.

However, in 2006 she left the property and began letting it out.

In 2010, Bart wished to visit his old haunts and agreed to pay his daughter £500 per month to use it during the summer.

It is agreed that the annual rental value is £18,000, so Bart would be liable for a charge of £1,000 per month. However, this will be exempt provided that he spends less than five months in the house in any tax year and he is not liable to other POAT charges under the de minimis rule – see below.

Example 29.8 – Cash gift

Charles gives his daughter Patricia £250,000 to buy a house. Some years later she sells that house and buys a larger one.

In 2011 Charles moves into one of Patricia's spare rooms as he prefers the neighbourhood.

> It is accepted that he has full use of the house, and the rental value is agreed at £8,000.
>
> Charles will be liable to tax on this sum.

For intangibles, the charge applies to intangible property held in a settlement where the taxpayer has an interest in the settlement and in consequence is liable to income tax on income arising in that settlement under *ITTIOA 2005, s 624*. However, in deciding whether the settlor has an interest in the settlement, references to his spouse or civil partner in *ITTOIA 2005, s 625* are ignored.

The property subject to tax is anything the taxpayer settled or added later, or derived from such property. It only applies to intangible property, such as shares or other rights, including cash. As the settlor may be taxed on income and gains arising from such property, there is an element of double taxation. This is reflected in the charge. The basic amount chargeable is 'notional' interest on the value of the intangibles for the period less any tax payable by the taxpayer under various provisions (*FA 2004, Sch 15, para 9*). The relief for that tax is at the taxpayer's marginal rate – not the full amount of the tax. The interest rate is set by regulations and currently equates to the 'official' rate of 3% (3.25% before 6 April 2015).

Example 29.9 – POAT charge on intangibles

Audrey is chargeable to tax on the income of a trust as settlor, but it is agreed she is not within the GWR rules. In 2011/12 the only asset was cash of £300,000 which represents property she settled. The income for the year was £15,000 on which Audrey pays tax of £6,000.

She is also liable for tax under POAT on £6,000 (£300,000 at 4%, being £12,000, less £6,000 tax on the trust income) – giving rise to a further charge of £2,400 if she is a higher rate taxpayer.

There are certain exclusions from the POAT provisions, including genuine arm's length sales and where an asset still counts as part of the donor's estate under GWR. A disposal of a part share of a property at arm's length is also an excluded transaction. This covers genuine equity release arrangements with arm's length providers.

Where the total amount chargeable under these provisions is not more than £5,000, the whole is exempt (*FA 2004, Sch 15, para 11*).

29.8 *Lifetime transfers*

Where there is a period of seven years (or more) between a cash gift and the donor first occupying a property bought with that cash, the donor's occupation of the property will not trigger a POAT charge.

> **Focus**
>
> Assessing whether it is more tax efficient to suffer any tax due under these rules or elect to have the relevant asset included in the estate of the donor will depend on several factors, including how long the property will be enjoyed by him, whether the charge can be mitigated by restricting his use each year and whether any other planning might reduce the potential IHT.

ASSOCIATED OPERATIONS

29.8   Transfers are said to be 'associated' if they affect the same property or form a chain of linked operations. This covers operations taking place at different times, or a number of steps taking place at the same time. It should be noted that it is not necessary for the operations to be made by the same person (*s 268(3)*).

Where the associated operations provisions are in point, the transfer of value is treated as having been made at the point in time that the final step was carried out.

> **Example 29.10 – Transfer of shares in unquoted company**
>
> Quentin gives away three blocks of shares in his unquoted property company, in which he originally held 60% as follows:
>
> | | |
> |---|---|
> | January 2012 | 19% |
> | February 2013 | 5% |
> | June 2014 | 26% |
>
> The transfers will typically have different values per share transferred because of the loss of control. HMRC may seek to treat the transactions as a single transfer of value in June 2014.

30

IHT on death

SIGNPOSTS

- **Scope** – On death, IHT is charged on the value of the deceased person's estate, although any IHT is generally limited to UK assets in the case of non-UK domiciled persons. The charge applies to all property that the deceased was free to dispose of, plus various other assets which are considered to be part of his estate (see **30.1–30.2**). Certain deductions are allowed, but some restrictions are imposed as an anti-avoidance measure (see **30.3**).

- **Related property** – In valuing the deceased's estate, a special rule requires that 'related property' owned by the deceased's spouse or civil partner and certain other persons is taken into account (see **30.4**).

- **Reliefs and exemptions** – Various forms of IHT relief and certain exemptions may be claimed on death, depending on the circumstances (see **30.5**).

- **Who pays the IHT and how much?** – The amount of IHT may depend on who inherits and who pays the tax, so gifts may require 'grossing up' for IHT, and reliefs may need to be apportioned (see **30.6**).

- **Post-death reliefs** – Losses on the sale of certain assets following death may result in IHT relief being available, if certain conditions are satisfied (see **30.7**).

- **Transferable nil rate band** – This allows all or part of an unused nil rate band to be transferred to a surviving spouse or civil partner. Some care may be required in order to maximise the IHT benefit where there are multiple partners (see **30.8**).

- **Residence Nil Rate Band** – This new relief will be phased in from 5 April 2017 and provides an additional relief of £100,000 in 2017–2018 rising in stages to £175,000 in 2020-2021 where the transferor passes value arising from his main residence to descendants (see **30.9**).

- **Appendix: Distribution of intestate estates** – A table setting out the rules for England and Wales is at the end of the chapter (see **30.10**).

All references in this chapter are to IHTA 1984, unless otherwise stated. 'PET' means potentially exempt transfer and 'CLT' means chargeable lifetime transfer.

THE ESTATE ON DEATH

30.1   On the death of any individual, he is deemed to have made a transfer of value equal to the value of his estate, immediately before his death (*IHTA 1984, s 4(1)*). As with other transfers of value, where the individual was domiciled in the UK immediately prior to death, the whole of his estate will be included.

Where he was non–UK domiciled, it will only be the UK assets which are included. In the 2015 Summer Budget, it was announced that from April 2017, UK residential property will be within the charge to IHT, even where it is held through offshore structures (such as an overseas company) where it is excluded property under current law.

The IHT liability on the estate at death will broadly depend on the identity of the legatees (eg whether they are chargeable or exempt), either in accordance with the deceased's will or under the law of intestacy (*AEA 1925, s 46*).

The table at the end of this chapter (**30.10**) explains how the deceased's estate will be distributed under the intestacy rules,.

> **Focus**
>
> Any transfers within the previous seven years need to be considered as this will affect the deceased's cumulative total and the death may mean that PETs are no longer exempt and CLTs are subject to additional tax (see **Chapter 29**).

Information on the IHT returns and payments due on a death can be found at **27.9–27.10**. HMRC publish the IHT400 series of forms and guidance on completing the forms on their website (www.gov.uk/government/publications/inheritance-tax-inheritance-tax-account-iht400).

Valuation of estate

30.2   The estate will consist of all property (other than excluded property, see **28.12**) to which the individual was beneficially entitled immediately prior to his death. Therefore it includes property owned personally (including his share of any jointly owned property) and any interests in settled property (*ss 5(1)*, *49(1)*).

Where an individual has powers which enable him to dispose of or charge money on any property (other than settled property), he is also treated as being beneficially entitled to that property.

The value of the individual's estate is computed as being the total price which the property comprised in that estate might reasonably be expected to fetch if sold on the open market immediately before his death.

The above rule refers to the value of the estate immediately before death; however, any changes which occur as a direct result of the death must be reflected, subject to the following exclusions:

- any life interests which terminate on death; and

- the passing of any interest by survivorship; and

- any decrease in the value of unquoted shares/securities in a close company due to an alteration in the shares/securities or rights attaching to them.

Example 30.1 – Changes on death

The most common example is life assurance, where the insured's death will usually greatly increase the value of the policy as it will now pay the death benefit. The provision also applies to any other benefit which arises on death, including under pension arrangements. The practice is to write such policies in trust so that the deceased would not receive the benefit. If the death results in property becoming vacant, this may also increase its value.

The value of shares in a close company may fall if a 'key man' dies, and in such cases that reduction would be taken into account. Many companies insure against this. If the fall in value arises because the rights attaching to shares fall away under the company's articles of association or other governing documents, the resulting fall in value is ignored.

Deductions

30.3   Certain liabilities are deductible from the value of the estate, such as those debts incurred by the deceased during his lifetime and either imposed by law or incurred for full consideration in money (or money's worth). This will include any tax liabilities even though no assessments had been made at the date of death. Where a liability is charged against a specific asset, it is normally deducted from the value of that asset.

However, *FA 2013, Sch 36* introduces provisions which mean that where the liability was incurred on acquiring or improving another asset, it is deducted from the value of that asset instead. The rules apply to transfers of value after 17 July 2013. Where the other asset is eligible for BPR or APR, the rule only applies to liabilities incurred after 5 April 2013 (*s 165B*). Where the other asset is excluded property, the rule applies whenever the liability was incurred (*s 165A*). The effect is to bring the charged asset back into IHT to the extent of the liability. *FA 2014, Sch 25* makes changes to ensure this rule catches foreign currency bank accounts.

Section 175A denies relief for certain liabilities which may not be settled.

Deductions are allowed for reasonable funeral expenses and any expenditure incurred in administering or realising property situated outside the UK, subject to an upper limit of 5% of the property's value.

Related property

30.4   There are special rules for valuing property that is included in an estate if there is other property that is 'related' to it. Related property is property that is:

- in the estate of a spouse or civil partner; or
- belongs to a charity or one of the political, national or public bodies to which exempt transfers may be made.

There are special rules for valuing related property (*s 161*).

The intention is to prevent assets, which may be worth less when broken down in smaller parts than they have as whole, from being divided between a couple (or an individual and an exempt body) to reduce IHT. The effect of the provisions is to consider the whole of the property for the purpose of valuation.

Examples of where this may apply are:

- shareholdings;
- sets of antique furniture;
- land and buildings;
- collections of paintings.

Where there is related property, the combined value of the related property is apportioned as follows:

$$\frac{\text{Value of Transferor's property}}{\text{Sum of the values of Transferor's and related property}} \times \text{Value of combined property}$$

Example 30.2 – Lease and reversionary interest

Pauline owns the freehold of her house. She grants her husband, Roger, a 25-year lease at £1 per annum. Pauline leaves the freehold reversion in her will to her children. It is established that the unencumbered freehold is worth £500,000, but the reversion is worth £150,000 and the lease £250,000.

The value of the reversion in Pauline's estate would be £187,500 for IHT purposes (ie £500,000 × £150,000/(£150,000 + £250,000). The lease would be valued at £312,500.

For shares of a single class, the apportionment is done on the basis of the number of shares. This also applies to other property divided into units.

If property in the estate is valued by the related property rule and is sold for a lower amount within three years of death, the taxpayer may be able to claim relief (*s 176*).

Focus

A side effect of the related property rules is that they apply in deciding whether spouses or civil partners have control of companies. If their combined interests in a company give them control, this applies in deciding whether BPR is available on the securities or any assets held personally, but used by the company.

Reliefs applying on or after death

30.5   The reliefs and exemptions which may be claimed on death include:

- inter-spouse/civil partner transfer exemption (**28.6**);

- gifts to charities/political parties or for national purposes (**28.7–28.9**);

- business property relief (**28.15**);

- agricultural property relief (**28.21**);

- woodlands relief (**28.28**);

- quick succession relief (**28.14**); and

- double tax relief (**27.11**).

The above have all been addressed in **Chapters 27** and **28**. In addition there are the following provisions that can affect the calculation of IHT on death:

- reduction in the value of the estate arising from the sale of shares within 12 months of death (*s 179*);

- reduction in the value of the estate arising from the sale of land within three years of death (*s 190*);

- instruments of variation within two years of death (*s 142*);

- complying with the testator's wishes within two years of death (*s 143*);

- distributions from property in trust within two years of death (*s 144*).

The first two are dealt with at **30.7.** The last three are dealt with in **Chapter 31**.

Free of tax legacies and partly exempt gifts

30.6   There are a number of complications caused by the interaction of exemptions and reliefs which can affect how an estate is divided up and therefore the amount of IHT payable.

If there are specific legacies in the will, these may require to be abated if the total value of the legacies exceeds the total value of the estate (*s 37*). Further, if there are gifts which are expressed to be free of tax, and there are also exempt gifts, the free of tax gifts need to be grossed up to determine the level of the exemption (*s 38*).

Example 30.3 – Free of tax legacy

Hilda dies leaving an estate of £700,000. She leaves a legacy of £400,000 free of tax to her son Peter and the balance of her estate to her husband Howard. She made no lifetime transfers.

Calculation of IHT on the estate	£
Gift to Peter	400,000
Less: NRB	325,000

Taxable net gift:	75,000
Grossed up tax – 60/40	£50,000
Reconciliation	
Estate	700,000
Less: residue to Howard (£700,000 less £400,000 to Peter and £50,000 tax)	(250,000)
	450,000
NRB	(325,000)
Taxable at 40%	125,000
Tax	50,000

A further complication arises where there are exempt gifts which would attract BPR or APR, and it is necessary to determine the appropriate share of the gifts which are exempt and other gifts which would be taxable (*s 39A*). This is a potential trap in that if the will is not drafted properly part of the BPR or APR will be set against exempt transfers and wasted, increasing the IHT payable on non-exempt gifts.

Example 30.4 – Interaction of BPR with exempt gifts

When George dies, his estate comprises shares in the family trading company worth £1,700,000, his house worth £600,000 and cash of £200,000. He leaves a legacy of £200,000 to his daughter and the rest of his estate equally between his wife and his son. There are no lifetime transfers to take into account.

Calculation of IHT on the estate	**£**
Total value of estate – *s 39A(4)(a)* – VE	2,500,000
Less BPR	(1,700,000)
Reduced value of estate – *s 39A(4)(b)* – RVE	800,000
Appropriate fraction – RVE/VE	32%
Reduced value of specific gift – £200,000 × 32%	64,000
Value of residue – RVE less reduced value of legacy	736,000
Exempt gift to widow – half	368,000
Taxable estate = RVE – exempt gift	432,000

NRB	(325,000)
Taxable at 40%	107,000
Tax	42,800

It might have appeared that property worth £1,150,000 (ie 50% × (£2,500,000 – £200,000)) would go to the widow and the rest would be covered by BPR, so no tax would be due. It may be possible to enter into an instrument of variation to rectify such a position by making specific gifts to non-exempt persons, perhaps a discretionary trust.

Finally there is the question of how the will should be interpreted where the residue is shared between exempt and non-exempt beneficiaries, for example where the will says 'to stand possessed of the residue as to one half for my children in equal shares absolutely and as to the remainder to my widow'. Following *Re Benhams Will Trust* [1995] STC 210, it was thought necessary to gross up the non-exempt beneficiaries' share in order to calculate IHT. However, in *Re Ratcliffe* [1999] STC 262, it was held that the non-exempt beneficiaries should receive their bequest without grossing up.

HMRC believe that a will along the lines of *Re Benham* is now unlikely.

Example 30.5 – IHT following wills in line with Re Radcliffe

Geraldine, who has never married, leaves her estate in equal shares to her sister and the Cats Protection League. The estate is worth £400,000. She has made significant gifts during her life and has used her nil rate band.

The tax on the estate will be £80,000 with her sister receiving £120,000 and the charity £200,000.

In some instances, it may be necessary to carry out double grossing-up.

A detailed examination of these provisions is beyond the scope of this book, although guidance from HMRC can be found at IHTM26000 onwards (www.hmrc.gov.uk/manuals/ihtmanual/IHTM26000.htm).

HMRC also publish grossing-up calculators at www.gov.uk/government/publications/inheritance-tax-grossing-up-calculators.

Sales of property following death

30.7   Where property is sold at a loss within a short period after death, some relief from IHT is available. One instance has been mentioned above in connection with related property (see **30.4**).

The provisions in *ss 178–189* apply to losses on sales of quoted shares or securities or units in authorised unit trusts made within 12 months of death. The claim is for the net loss in value of the estate, so that profits on other shares sold in that period will be set against the losses. There are rules to cover the effect of purchases, acquisitions of like investments, capital reorganisations and other changes which affect the holdings.

The provisions in *ss 190–198* apply to losses on sales of interests in land made within three years of death. The claim is to replace the value at death with the sale value. If a claim is made, the value of other interests sold in that period must also be replaced by their sale values. Again there are rules to cover the effect of purchases, sales of lesser interests, alterations and other changes which affect the land.

TRANSFERABLE NIL RATE BAND

30.8   Every individual's estate is subject to IHT at the nil rate to a certain threshold (£325,000 since 6 April 2009), referred to as the 'nil rate band'. Married couples and registered civil partners are also allowed to transfer assets between them during their lifetime or on death without having to pay IHT. There are no limits to this as long as the individual receiving the assets is domiciled in the UK. This is referred to as the spouse or civil partner exemption.

If an individual leaves everything to his surviving spouse or civil partner, his estate is exempt from IHT. However, this will mean that he has not used any of his own IHT nil rate band. When this happens, the unused part of the nil rate band can be transferred and used to increase the IHT threshold of the surviving spouse or civil partner when he dies (*s 8A*). This facility is available even if the survivor spouse has remarried or entered a civil partnership. In such cases, estates will not attract IHT if they are valued at up to £650,000 (for deaths after 5 April 2009) and larger estates only pay tax on the excess.

To transfer any unused threshold, the executors or personal representatives upon the death of the survivor spouse or civil partner need to send certain forms and supporting documents to HMRC. The claim to transfer unused nil rate band must be made by personal representatives within the 'permitted period', this being whichever ends later of:

- 24 months after the end of the month in which the second deceased died; or
- three months beginning with the date on which the personal representatives first acted as such.

An officer of HMRC has the discretion to extend that period where circumstances are appropriate (*s 8B(3)(a)*).

The transfer can only be made on the second death, which must have occurred on or after 9 October 2007 (the date these rules were introduced). There is no limit to the date that the first spouse or civil partner died, although if it was before 1975 the full nil rate band may not be available as the amount of spouse exemption was limited by earlier estate duty and capital transfer tax rules.

To determine the amount of nil rate band that can be claimed on the second death, it is not the unused amount of the first spouse or civil partner's nil rate band that determines how much can be transferred but the unused percentage. This percentage is then applied to the nil rate band in effect at the time of the second death (*s 8A(2)*).

A person has unused nil rate band where M is greater than VT.

M is the maximum that could be transferred on the first death at 0%. It is therefore:

- the nil rate band that applied at the first death;

- less the chargeable value of any lifetime transfers that use up the nil rate band first.

VT is the chargeable value of the transfer on death. This is the total of:

- the chargeable value of non-exempt or partially relievable legacies passing under the will or intestacy;

- assets passing by survivorship;

- gifts with reservation chargeable at death; and

- any assets held in trust which formed part of the deceased's estate.

Where M is greater than VT, the amount by which it is greater is expressed as a percentage of the nil rate band available on the first death. That percentage is the amount by which the nil rate band on the second death is increased. Where necessary, you should always take the percentage to four decimal places.

Example 30.6 – Transfer of nil rate band

Sydney gave his children £100,000 (after all exemptions) two years before he died in July 2004. He left the rest of his estate to his wife Teresa who died in March 2012.

Teresa's executors can claim an increased nil rate band, as follows:

Sydney's unused nil rate band at the date of his death is £163,000 (nil rate band at date of Sydney's death £263,000 less £100,000 lifetime transfers). This is 61.97% of the nil rate band at the date of Sydney's death.

Therefore on Teresa's death the executors have a nil rate band of £526,426 (£325,000 + 61.97% × £325,000) available.

Focus

The additional nil rate band is a proportion of the threshold at the second death (£325,000 in the example), not the earlier death (£263,000 in the example).

If the deceased has been 'widowed' more than once, then he may have more than one previous nil rate band to consider. However, no matter how much of his previous partners' bands remained unused, the maximum that can be claimed by a single individual is another full nil rate band, giving a maximum of twice the current nil rate band tax at the nil rate.

It might be thought that with this relief there would be little point in a married person using his nil rate band on the first death. However, on second marriages he may already be entitled to a second nil rate band. Also if the widow might remarry then there is the nil rate band for the new partner to consider (see **Example 31.2**).

If 100% of the unused threshold is being transferred and the value of the estate is less than twice the threshold when the second spouse or civil partner dies (£650,000 in 2015/16.), the estate may be classed as an 'excepted estate'.

Focus

In some cases, it may be necessary to decide whether the NRB should be used on the first death (is the surviving partner likely to remarry?) or preserved in the hope that the rate will increase (but the current NRB is to continue to 2020/21 as part of the measure to introduce the Residence Nil Rate Band).

The transferable nil rate band must be taken into account when interpreting (and drafting) nil rate band legacies in wills and undertaking inheritance tax planning.

In a decided case, *Loring v Woodland Trust* [2013] EWHC 4400 (Ch), the court concluded that the nil rate band legacy included the full amount of the nil rate band available to the deceased's estate of £650,000 (ie including the transferable nil rate band). The effect of this was a reduced residue available to a charity of £30,385, (as opposed to £355,385).

RESIDENCE NIL RATE BAND (RNRB)

30.9   The relief applies for relevant transfers on death on or after 6 April 2017. It will apply to reduce the tax payable by an estate on death; it will not apply to reduce the tax payable on lifetime transfers that are chargeable as a result of death.

It only applies where the deceased's interest in a residential property (which has at some time been his residence) is left to one or more direct descendants on death. Direct descendants include children, step-children, adopted children, foster children, grandchildren, great-grandchildren etc. It does not apply where the residence is left to parents, siblings, nephews, nieces or other relatives.

The relief will be limited to the lower of the maximum amount (see below) and the value of the property after any liabilities. Where there are several eligible properties in the estate, the executors can choose which to claim against. The deceased only has to have lived in the property at some time, it does not have to be their main residence. The relief can apply to a property that forms part of the deceased estate either because they owned it outright, were entitled to a qualifying interest in possession or the property is a gift with reservation (*s 8J(6)*).

The executors of a surviving spouse or civil partner will be able to claim any unused part of their partner's relief. The carried forward allowance is a percentage of the rate in force at the date of the partner's death, and this percentage is applied to the rate in force at the date of the second death.

Where a partner died prior to 5 April 2017, the 100% allowance will be available on the second death unless it is restricted because the estate of the first to die was over £2m.

Where the deceased has downsized (or ceased to own a residence) after 8 July 2015, the reduction in value will still be available provided that the deceased left assets of equivalent value, to direct descendants.

The relief is available where the residential property was held by a qualifying interest in possession trust, the deceased had an interest in possession and he had used the property as a residence. If the estate passes to a qualifying interest in possession trusts in which one or more direct descendants have an interest in possession, this is treated for the RNRB as if the descendant inherited it directly. The relief is not available if the trusts are relevant property.

The maximum amount will be phased in so that it is £100,000 for 2017/18, £125,000 for 2018/19, £150,000 for 2019/20, and £175,000 for 2020/21. It will then increase in line with CPI for subsequent years. Where the estate exceeds £2m then the relief is reduced by £1 for every £2 in excess of the £2m limit

---

Example 30.7 – Residence nil rate band

Robert dies on 31 December 2017 leaving assets worth £2.1m to his two sons including the family home. His wife had died in 2013 leaving everything to Robert. Robert will have a RNRB of £150,000 (2 x £100,000 less £100,000/2)

APPENDIX: DISTRIBUTION OF INTESTATE ESTATES

The following provisions relate to England and Wales only.

(*Administration of Estates Act 1925, s 46*)

30.10

(1) Spouse or civil partner and issue survive

Spouse or civil partner receives	*Issue receives*
● All personal chattels;	● One half of residue (if any) on statutory trusts.
● £250,000 absolutely (or the entire interest where this is less); and	
● One-half of residue (if any).	

(2) Spouse or civil partner survives without issue

Spouse or civil partner receives

● All personal chattels;
● The whole of the estate.

(3) No spouse or civil partner survives

Estate held in the following order with no class beneficiaries participating unless all those in a prior class have predeceased.

(a) issue of deceased;

(b)   parent(s);

(c)   brothers and sisters (or issue);

(d)   half-brothers and half-sisters (or issue);

(e)   grandparent(s);

(f)   uncles and aunts (or issue);

(g)   half-brothers and half-sisters of deceased's parents (or issue);

(h)   the Crown, the Duchy of Lancaster or the Duke of Cornwall.

Notes

1   *General* – The distribution of a deceased individual's estate, and the IHT liability in respect of the estate, can be affected if the individual died without having made a valid will.

2   *Civil partners* – The *Administration of Estates Act 1925* was extended (by the *Civil Partnership Act 2004, Sch 4, paras 7–12*) to include a surviving civil partner, who effectively acquires the same rights as a surviving spouse in cases of intestacy.

3   *Survivorship* – The above provisions in favour of the deceased's spouse or civil partner are subject to a 28-day survival period (*AEA 1925, s 46(2A)*).

4   *Further information* – See HMRC's IHT manual at IHTM12101 and the interactive tool at www.gov.uk/inherits-someone-dies-without-will. Further assistance can also be found at www.gov.uk/make-will.

31

IHT planning

SIGNPOSTS

- **General** – Planning to reduce IHT is generally a long-term project and will need to be updated as law, practice and the taxpayer's circumstances change (see **31.1**).

- **Lifetime planning overview** – In order to plan it is necessary to understand what the taxpayer will need during his life and what he is willing/able to dispose of before his death. Then steps should be taken as early as possible. If the individual has assets which are likely to grow in value, it may be easy to give away that growth without any significant tax cost (see **31.2–31.4**).

- **Business and agricultural property relief** – Putting assets eligible for these into trust may be effective, but the use of pilot trusts will no longer be effective after 9 December 2014 (**see 31.4**). Investing in assets eligible for APR/BPR will reduce the chargeable estate (see **31.5**).

- **Insurance** – Rather than avoiding IHT, provision can be made to pay the tax by insuring the cost in trust to keep the proceeds outside the estate. There are other insurance products which can mitigate IHT (see **31.6–31.7**).

- **Normal expenditure out of income** – An established pattern of gifts out of income can take substantial sums out of the IHT net (see **31.8**).

- **Wills and trusts** – Properly drafted wills are essential to minimise IHT. Consideration should be given to using them to create flexible trusts. This is particularly important if there is property eligible for APR or BPR (see **31.9**).

- **Post-death planning** – Even after death, savings can be made by using instruments of variation, disclaimers and distributions from discretionary trusts (see **31.10**).

- **Family home** – Planning around the family home is particularly troublesome, due to anti-avoidance provisions affecting IHT planning in this area. There are still some options, depending on whether the

> property is owned as 'joint tenants' or as 'tenants in common' (see **31.11–31.13**)
>
> - **The Residence Nil Rate Band (RNRB)** may mitigate the tax from April 2017 (see **31.14**), but this will be restricted for estate in excess of £2,000,000, so reducing the estate before death has additional benefits.
>
> - **Trust planning** – There are various methods of avoiding principal and exit charges for relevant property trusts by ensuring that the effective rate is nil (see **31.15**).

All references in this chapter are to IHTA 1984, unless otherwise stated.

INTRODUCTION

31.1 The first point to make about IHT planning is that it is a long-term consideration and the planner needs to take into account that the taxpayer's circumstances may change in the intervening period; in particular,

- their need for income or capital may change;

- the nature of their assets may change; and

- IHT law and practice may change.

What follows is an outline of some of the opportunities available, but a full analysis of the specific position should be undertaken, which is beyond the scope of this work.

LIFETIME PLANNING – OVERVIEW

31.2 The key feature of lifetime planning is to decide what assets the taxpayer is free to give away, taking into account his reliance on them (for income or capital) to maintain his lifestyle and how long that lifetime is likely to be. If the taxpayer wishes to continue to receive the income or capital from a gift, then the assets are likely to be caught by the rules for gifts with reservation (see **29.6**) or pre-owned assets (see **29.7**). This is particularly true in the case of the family home.

If the taxpayer's estate is over £2,000,000 this will reduce any **RNRB**. This can be mitigated by life time gifts and transfers to a spouse may help. (**31.14**).

If the taxpayer is the owner of a family company or business, there will also be questions concerning the control of that business or company going forward, which the taxpayer may be reluctant to give up.

If the taxpayer has surplus assets which can be given away without affecting his lifestyle, it is usually wiser to do this as early as possible as there would then be a greater chance of surviving for seven years so that the gifts fall out of the cumulative total. This will also use the lifetime allowances which would be lost otherwise. Where gifts are made, it is always worth discussing whether life assurance ought to be taken out to cover any tax which may arise if the donor dies within seven years. The younger and fitter the donor is, the cheaper this will be; but it can prove prohibitively expensive for an elderly or infirm donor.

If the donor does not wish to lose control of the assets, two possible strategies are available:

- using trusts; or

- where the assets are shares, share reorganisations.

It should be noted that, since 22 March 2006, where trusts are used these will usually be immediately chargeable transfers. Therefore, if the net value of the gift is more than the nil rate band (NRB) (currently £325,000), there would be an immediate charge to tax at 20%. It is important in planning for gifts, to consider the effects of other transfers within the previous seven years, because if the donor dies within seven years of the later gift, transfers up to 14 years before death could come into consideration.

Example 31.1 – Effect of cumulative transfers

Dorothy makes a chargeable transfer on 1 January 2010 of £325,000 by settling that amount on trust. She makes a potentially exempt transfer on 31 December 2016 by giving £200,000 to her favourite nephew. She dies on 1 December 2023.

As she died within seven years of the second gift, the earlier chargeable transfer will be taken into account in determining the tax on the failed PET on 31 December 2016, so that £16,000 will be due (40% × £200,000 less 80% taper relief).

If the second gift had been delayed until 1 January 2017, the first transfer would have fallen out of charge, so there would be no tax to pay on the failed PET, although it would use £200,000 of Dorothy's NRB.

Value freezing

31.3   For shares in companies which the donor controls, it may be possible to restructure the share capital of the company into different classes, giving the donor shares in the company which currently have a value equal to that of his current holding. Other shares, which have little value at the present time but which will grow if the company prospers, could be given away. Such a gift does not reduce his estate, but it would mean that the estate would not grow.

Pilot trusts

31.4 Prior to 10 December 2014 it was possible to create a number of separate pilot trusts on different days as a first step, and at a later date add property to each trust on the same day. Each trust would have its own nil rate band, because property added to other trusts on the same day would not have to be brought in account when calculating the rate of inheritance tax on an exit or ten year charge.

Changes were introduced from 6 April 2015 which will bring into account the value of additions to other trusts on the same day in determining the rate of tax. The changes apply from 6 April 2015 but trusts created before 10 December 2014 are protected provided the settlor has not made any "same day" additions since that date, subject to a de minimus of £5,000.

Transitional provisions apply for multiple transfers into trust on death. If a settlor's will was made before 10 December 2014 and they died before 5 April 2016 then the rules do not apply.

> **Focus**
>
> If the donor had a clear cumulative total, pilot trusts could each have an NRB very close to the full amount so a substantial sum could be shared across them free of IHT. The changes mean that pilot trusts will be less effective from 10 December 2014, but do not affect existing structures.

Maximising the use of BPR or APR

31.5 It is possible to mitigate the IHT charge on the estate by investing in assets qualifying for either business or agricultural property relief, but clearly this has to be done in sufficient time to meet the required periods of ownership/occupation. For BPR, this is a two-year period and therefore consideration might be given to acquisition of investments in trading companies listed on the Alternative Investment Market or by investing in shares eligible for Enterprise Investment Scheme relief. Such investments are inherently risky and this needs to be factored into the planning.

In order to attract APR, the planner will need to consider whether the investment is to be in land which is simply let to a farmer so that seven years are required to meet the ownership test, or whether arrangements can be made, such as contract farming, where the owner occupies the land for farming, and therefore only two years are required, although this needs more involvement in the business.

Where the taxpayer has borrowings, thought should be given to whether these can be structured so that they are charged on assets not eligible for the above reliefs rather than those which are. In the former case, the debts will be deducted from the ineligible assets in valuing the estate, thereby reducing the tax burden. The anti-avoidance rules in *ss 165A*, *165B* and *175A* restricting deductions for liabilities must be considered (see **30.3**).

Insurance

31.6   It is possible to take out insurance to cover the IHT charge, wither for the risk that a charge arises because the taxpayer dies within seven years, or to cover the whole or part of the expected bill. Such policies are normally written in trust so that they fall outside the estate of the person creating them. Although trusts created after 22 March 2006 will fall into the relevant property regime, it would be unusual for there to be a charge on creation because the initial value would be low. Also in most cases where the insured pays the premiums, these would be normal gifts out of income and exempt from IHT.

Discounted gift schemes

31.7   Another planning opportunity is to use a discounted gift scheme. Under these arrangements, a capital insurance policy is settled into trust, under which the settlor retains the right to take the 5% capital withdrawals from the trust each year, but the balance of the policy goes to other beneficiaries.

Depending on the age and health of the donor, the right to receive the withdrawals each year reduces the value of the gift which needs to be taken into account in determining the value transferred. The donor still benefits from these receipts. Such arrangements are considered to fall outside the gifts with reservation rules. When the donor dies, HMRC currently consider that the right to the unpaid withdrawals has no value.

> **Focus**
>
> The taxpayer will require financial services advice on whether this type of investment is appropriate to their circumstance.

Normal expenditure out of income

31.8   This exemption (see **28.4**) is often under-utilised but is potentially very valuable as it has no upper monetary limit.

It may be helpful to use the schedules in HMRC Form IHT403 to record gifts and other necessary information where this exemption is likely to be claimed (www.gov.uk/government/publications/inheritance-tax-gifts-and-other-transfers-of-value-iht403).

PLANNING ON DEATH – OVERVIEW

31.9   The first observation about planning for death is that it is important that the taxpayer creates a will. This gives considerably more flexibility than trying to resolve matters by an instrument of variation as an afterthought.

One structure which is very useful for wills is to create a flexible life interest for the surviving spouse or civil partner which would benefit from the spouse exemption, together with a flexible discretionary settlement to use up the nil rate band (NRB). It might be thought that this would be less necessary now that the NRB is transferrable (**30.8**), but it can still be useful. Where one or both of the couple has been widowed in the past, there is scope for additional NRB. The Residence Nil Rate Band will also need to be considered (see **30.9**).

Example 31.2 – Transferrable nil rate band on second marriage

Sheila was widowed some years ago and her husband George left his entire estate to her. She has remarried to Henry, whose estate is worth several million pounds. Henry's first wife, Julia, has also died, but on her death she made substantial bequests to her children so that her NRB was used up.

If Henry dies first, there is no point in preserving his NRB for use by Sheila, because she is already entitled to a full second NRB from George and cannot benefit any further.

Therefore it would be advisable for Henry to ensure that his will leaves sufficient assets to other beneficiaries to use his NRB. The beneficiaries of his will could vary it so that this effect is achieved.

If the estate includes property eligible for BPR or APR, transfers of such assets would either not be chargeable or be chargeable on a reduced amount, so do not as such benefit from the spouse exemption. Those assets could be left on discretionary trusts, so that the trustees can determine the best route way to distribute them, bearing in mind the needs of the beneficiaries at that stage.

If such assets have benefited from say BPR, it might be possible for the surviving spouse to purchase those assets from the trustees at market value. If he survives for the appropriate period, the value of his estate would also be reduced by BPR. In effect, relief would be given on the same assets twice.

Particularly in the case of second marriages, giving a surviving spouse an interest in possession in the family's assets ensures that those assets benefit from the spouse exemption, but are preserved to pass to the children. It is possible to include powers in such trusts to enable the trustees to appoint the life interest away from the surviving spouse, for example, should there be a further marriage. In this regard two points should be made:

- the exercise of the power by the trustees will result in a transfer of value by the surviving spouse, which will be a chargeable transfer if the assets remain in settlement, so they need to exercise some care;

- if the surviving spouse retains another interest in the property from which his interest in possession has been removed, this is deemed to be a gift (*FA 1986, s 102ZA*), and therefore the surviving spouse will be deemed to have reserved a benefit in that property, so it will remain in his estate.

Finally, if the taxpayer is philanthropic and has made gifts to charity in his will, are these gifts sufficient to ensure that the reduced rate will apply to the balance of the estate? Is it worth considering including a clause in the will to ensure that effect is achieved? If the taxpayer in question has died, can the same effect be achieved by an instrument of variation for the benefit of the non-charitable beneficiaries? (See **28.30.**)

POST-DEATH VARIATIONS

31.10 The position of an estate on death is not necessarily final; post-death arrangements are allowed in certain circumstances. An 'instrument of variation' can be executed and can bring about the desired changes, as long as it is completed within two years of a person's death (*s 142*).

Frequently an instrument of variation will be used to reallocate the property so as to minimise IHT and/or CGT liabilities but there are other potential reasons. For example:

- already wealthy beneficiaries who have children and may wish to pass any inheritance directly to those children so that their own IHT liability is minimised;

- to balance legacies between beneficiaries, eg siblings may receive different percentages but would prefer to have the same amounts;

- a way of balancing wealth, eg a wealthy child being left an equal share of the parent's estate might agree to alter the amounts so that a poorer sibling receives more.

A variation may be made in one of two ways:

- voluntarily by the recipients of the gifts; or

- by a court order under the *Inheritance (Provision for Family and Dependants) Act 1975, s 2.*

For the 'instrument of variation' to be effective for IHT purposes, the instrument must contain a statement setting out the changes to be made and specifying that the parties intend that *s 142(1)* is to apply. No further election is necessary.

An instrument of variation can only be used if:

- all of the beneficiaries who are adversely affected by the variation agree to it; and

- the parties receive no compensation for the changes (often referred to as 'reciprocation'), other than the making of variations or disclaimers of other bequests in the will.

Note that if the variation affects the rights of children (even unborn children), court approval will be necessary.

Focus

It is not possible to execute more than one instrument of variation over the same property for tax purposes. There can be a number of variations at different times within the two-year period over the same estate, provided each variation deals with separate distinct property.

When drafting any instruments, it is important to take this into account as a subsequent variation over the same asset will not be effective for IHT/CGT. It is preferable to deal with all variations in a single instrument.

Only the individual benefitting under the original dispositions needs to sign the instrument of variation and he can do so at any time within the two-year period. Contrary to popular belief there is no need for other beneficiaries of the will to sign.

Example 31.3 – Redirecting property to next generation

Wulfric leaves his estate equally to his three children, but his eldest son Halla has made a fortune designing climbing walls in Norway, and does not need the inheritance. He prepares a deed of variation leaving the property on trust for his own children.

Provided that this includes the declaration set out above, the transfer of value will be treated as if it been included in Wulfric's will, rather than being a gift by Halla.

Focus

Although the settlor of the trust is Wulfric for IHT purposes, it is Halla for income tax and capital gains tax, so Halla may be taxed on any income received by his children while they are minors.

The simplest form of variation is a disclaimer by a beneficiary of all/part of his entitlement under the will. The benefit given up will form part of the residue of the estate, so the person may 'recover' part of the property disclaimed if he is entitled to a share in residue (depending on how the disclaimer is expressed).

There is a corresponding relief for capital gains tax purposes in *TCGA 1992, s 62(6)*, but not for income tax.

Where property is distributed from a trust created under a will which would be a chargeable transfer, within two years of the death, the distribution is treated as if it had been made under the will (*s 144*). This allows the testator considerable flexibility, as he can leave property to trustees to distribute within that window and know that it will be dealt with as if it were a legacy for IHT.

These provisions can be used to ensure that any property eligible to BPR or APR is transferred to future generations, rather than the surviving spouse, while the spouse receives property which would otherwise be chargeable.

However, care should be taken as HMRC look out for arrangements where the variation is intended to secure the spouse exemption, without the spouse benefitting from the property.

For deaths before 10 December 2014, *s 144* generally did not apply for transfers within three months of death as there is no charge to IHT under the relevant property regime within the first quarter of the ten-year period, but *Finance (No 2) Act 2015* resolves this problem for deaths after 9 December 2014.

Example 31.4 – Variation to benefit from the spouse exemption

Zebulon leaves his estate to his children, as his wife Ariadne is well provided for. However, there is substantial IHT to pay, so the children vary the will so that Ariadne is entitled to an interest in possession in the property of the estate, but they have the power to terminate the interest at any time.

Two years and one day after Zebulon's death, the children as trustees terminate Ariadne's interest and get the property they would have inherited originally.

The original variation will create an IPDI, so the estate will benefit from the spouse exemption. However, HMRC are likely to argue that the combination of the instrument of variation and the trustees' action is pre-ordained tax avoidance which they can set aside.

THE FAMILY HOME

31.11   Over the last generation, property values have risen considerably, meaning that more and more people are likely to become subject to IHT due to the value of their property. As a result, as most estates will feature the family home as the main asset, it cannot be easily ignored where IHT mitigation is a priority.

Unfortunately, tax planning opportunities involving the family home are fairly limited, with legislation, case law and HMRC practice restricting the effectiveness of IHT schemes which seek to remove such property from the charge.

However, there are still opportunities for utilising the family home in IHT planning depending on whether it is owned as joint tenants or as tenants in common.

Joint tenants

31.12   The individuals own the whole of the property together, and each is deemed to have an equal half share. On the first death, the deceased's interest will pass automatically to the survivor. This interest cannot be bequeathed under the deceased's will. For IHT purposes, there will be a transfer of value of half the value of the property, although if they are married or in a civil partnership, the transfer will be exempt.

A joint tenancy may be terminated during their lifetime to create a tenancy in common (see below). Subject to the agreement of relevant beneficiaries, a joint tenancy can also be severed after death by an instrument of variation, for example to make use of the nil rate band on the first death.

Tenants in common

31.13 The individuals each hold a distinct share of the property, which may be in any ratio, for example to reflect each owner's contribution to the purchase price. Each tenant's share is a separate and distinct item of property and can be disposed of however he chooses during his lifetime or under the terms of his will. With this flexibility, tenancy in common is often the most suitable way for co-owners to hold property from an IHT planning perspective. In the absence of a will, the deceased's interest in the property will be dealt with under the laws of intestacy, which can produce undesirable results.

When a co-owner dies, the IHT value of the deceased's share in the property will be discounted by around 10–15% to reflect the restricted demand for part shares in property. However, this discount will not apply where the owners are spouses or civil partners as the related property rules will apply.

The deceased's share of the family home could be left to beneficiaries who are not exempt, such as the children. The surviving spouse could then agree to purchase that share of the property from those beneficiaries. This is often organised by creating a debt or charge over the house in favour of the children to be repaid by the surviving spouse's estate. (Note:, the debt will not be deductible from the surviving spouse's estate unless it can be shown that the property acquired in exchange for it did not arise from the first deceased. For example, if the husband provided all of the funds to buy the house, then the loan will not be deductible from the widow's estate because of the rules under *FA 1986, s 103* (*see Phizackerley v HMRC* [2007] STC (SCD) 328).)

Where the family home is occupied by people other than spouses or civil partners, it is possible to transfer a share in the ownership of the property from one occupier to another without falling foul of the gift with reservation (GWR) or pre-owned assets (POAT) rules (*FA 1986, s 102B; FA 2004, Sch 15 para 11(5)(c)*). The usual example is of a mother and daughter living together after the father has died, but might equally apply to other cases, such as sisters sharing a home. Provided that the donor and donee continue to occupy the property jointly, the share will not be treated as part of the donor's estate and there will be no POAT charge. The donor needs to pay his share of the running costs, as the relief does not apply if the donor receives a benefit from the gift. The original gift is a PET, so the donor needs to live for seven years to avoid any IHT completely.

There are two possible dangers. If the donee moves out, the property will no longer be protected from the GWR/POAT provisions, and it is likely that the gifted share will fall back into the donor's estate. If the donee dies first then his share will be taxable, which might mean that the property has to be sold to pay any tax.

> **Focus**
>
> It is certainly acceptable to gift a half share in this way, but the legislation places no limit on the donee's interest. However, HMRC might seek ways to challenge a transfer of, for example, 90%.

Residence Nil Rate Band

31.14   From 6 April 2017 additional relief will be available when the family home is passed to direct descendants (see **30.9**). Like the NRB, the allowance is 'transferable' to a spouse or civil partner. In addition, the relief will be preserved where the taxpayers have downsized. This will need to be factored into decisions about who is to benefit from the estate, any use of trusts. and post-death variations.

As the relief is tapered for estates with a value over £2 million, pre death planning can produce savings.

> **Example 31.4 – Reducing Estate before Death**
>
> Alfred is terminally ill and has an estate of £2,350,000. He has never married, but has a son by a former partner. His home is worth £200,000. He has made no previous gifts. If he dies after 5 April 2020, the IHT on his estate will be £810,000. If he makes a death bed cash gift of £350,000 to his son and leaves him his home, the IHT will be reduced to £730,000. His son will have £7,600 to pay on the failed PET. The overall saving will be £72,400.

Care needs to be taken before both deaths as the tapering may reduce the carry forward amount on the death of the first spouse.

In general transfers to a relevant property trust cannot benefit from the allowance

PLANNING FOR RELEVANT PROPERTY TRUSTS

31.15   There are a number of straightforward steps which may be considered for relevant property trusts to mitigate the charges applicable under that regime (see **35.13**).

If the trust will be liable to a significant principal charge on the next ten-year anniversary, but the rate on an exit before that date will be lower or nil, consider winding up the trust before the anniversary. However, care should be taken where the property attracts BPR and APR as this does not affect the rate of tax payable the first ten year anniversary.

If the trust has property which is eligible for BPR or APR and which is going to be sold consider:

* deferring the sale until after the anniversary;

* distributing the property before there is a binding contract for sale;

* acquiring replacement property to protect the relief until the anniversary.

Consideration will also need to be given to other taxes, in particular capital gains tax.

If the trust will be liable to tax on the next anniversary, is there sufficient time to acquire assets eligible for BPR so as to reduce the value of the assets for IHT? This may result in a nil rate for the next ten years.

Part 5
Trusts and Estates

32

Trusts and estates – outline

SIGNPOSTS

- **What is a trust?** – A trust is broadly an arrangement under which trustees have legal ownership of property for the benefit of beneficiaries. The expressions 'trust' and 'settlement' are often used interchangeably, but the latter can have a wider meaning to include arrangements that may not formally constitute a trust (see **32.1–32.2**).

- **Components of a trust** – A trust will have trustees, settlor, settled property and beneficiaries which will be defined in a trust deed (see **32.3–32.6**).

- **Types of trust** – The reason for setting up a trust will usually dictate its form but the varying tax treatments should be considered in the set-up process (see **32.7**).

- **Bare trust** – A bare trust is broadly a nominee arrangement where the beneficiary has an immediate and absolute right to both the capital and income held in the trust. It is commonly used to hold assets for minors (see **32.8**).

- **Common types of trust** – Many trusts will fall into one of three categories in practice, being life interest, discretionary or accumulation and maintenance trusts (see **32.9–32.11**).

- **Other categories of trust** – These include bereaved minor trusts, age 18 to 25 trusts and disabled persons trusts (see **32.12–32.19**).

- **Compliance** – Trusts fall under the self-assessment regime for income tax and capital gains tax. The trustees are responsible for filing self-assessment returns and for settling most tax liabilities (see **32.20–32.22**).

- **Trust records** – The trustees must keep appropriate records and may need to prepare trust accounts (see **32.24–32.25**).

- **IHT returns, etc** – The trustees are also responsible for preparing and filing IHT returns under the provisions for ten-year charges and exit charges (see **32.26–32.28**).

TRUSTS AND SETTLEMENTS

General

32.1   There is no legal definition of 'trust'. It is a legal arrangement where one or more 'trustees' are made legally responsible for holding assets. The assets are placed in trust by the 'settlor' for the benefit of one or more 'beneficiaries'. The assets are legally owned by the trustees but they must comply with the intentions of the settlor as set out in the trust deed and to deal with the trust property for the benefit of the beneficiaries.

> **Focus**
>
> For income tax purposes, the word 'settlement' has a wider meaning and includes certain arrangements that may not formally constitute a trust, such as a parent setting up a bank account for a minor child. For the purposes of this chapter the words are used as fully interchangeable, unless otherwise stated.

The treatment of trusts for tax purposes is the same throughout the United Kingdom. However, Scottish law on trusts and the terms used in relation to trusts in Scotland are different from those of England and Wales and Northern Ireland.

Tax legislation

32.2   From 6 April 2007, the income tax legislation relating to trustees and beneficiaries is in *ITA 2007, Pt 9 (ss 462–517)*.

For capital gains tax (CGT) purposes, *TCGA 1992, ss 68–98A* deals with settlements.

For inheritance tax (IHT) purposes *IHTA 1984, ss 43–93* deals with the treatment of settled property. Significant changes were introduced by *FA 2006* in respect of trusts for IHT purposes, with effect from 22 March 2006.

ITTOIA 2005, Pt 5, Ch 5 (ss 619–648) are anti-avoidance provisions. In appropriate circumstances they apply to all settlements, other than those set up by a will. For these purposes, the word settlement has a very wide meaning. It includes any disposition, trust, covenant, agreement, arrangement or transfer of assets.

Similar provisions apply for CGT, but since 2008/09 this is only relevant to certain offshore trusts.

Trustees

32.3   The trustees are responsible for:

- dealing with trust assets in line with the trust deed;

- managing the trust on a day-to-day basis and paying any tax due on the income or chargeable gains of the trust;

- deciding how to invest or use the trust's assets; and

- providing the beneficiaries with a statement when asked, showing how much trust income they received in a tax year and the tax paid on that income.

Trustees have a separate legal personality from the individuals making up the body of trustees. The trust can continue even though the trustees might change. Trustees have income tax, CGT and IHT liabilities arising from the income and assets held in the trust.

Most trusts have a minimum of two trustees, unless a corporate trustee is used. There is no legal reason why the settlor cannot be a trustee and this is often the case in many family trusts. This gives the settlor some say in the management and distribution of trust income and assets but it is important to keep the role of settlor and trustee separate as a failure to appreciate this can lead to actions for breach of trust and tax complications.

Settlor

32.4   A person is a settlor in relation to a trust if the settled property was put into the trust by that person. A trust may have more than one settlor but in most cases there will be just one. If a trust is added to at a later date, the person adding property will also be a settlor. The settlor's wishes for the trust are usually written down.

If created on the settlor's death it is referred to as a 'will trust'. Immediately before the death, that person must have been competent to dispose of the property to be comprised in the trust. If created during the settlor's lifetime, a legal document – 'trust deed' – is usual, but it is possible to place assets into trust without documentary support.

It is also possible to create a trust by reciprocal arrangement, for example a person settles property for the benefit of his sister's children and in return the sister settles property for the benefit of his children. In this case, each of them is treated as a settlor in relation to the settlement for their own children.

The tax legislation contains four definitions of settlor:

- a definition that applies for general income tax purposes in *ITA 2007, s 467*;

- a common definition of settlor for CGT purposes (*TCGA 1992, s 68A*);

- the 'settlements legislation' has its own, albeit similar, definition of settlor (*ITTOIA 2005, s 620*); and

- a definition for IHT purposes (*IHTA 1984, s 44*).

There are statutory rules for identifying the settlor where property is transferred between settlements, or if there is a variation of a will or intestacy.

Legislation at *ITA 2007, ss 470–471* applies for income tax purposes when property is transferred between settlements for less than full consideration. The corresponding CGT provision is *TCGA 1992, s 68B*.

For IHT purposes, *IHTA 1984, s 81* deals with property moving between relevant property trusts (see 35.5 for the definition of 'relevant property trust'). The property is treated as remaining in the first trust for the purposes of the IHT regime. This means that ten-year charges continue to arise on the property on the ten-year anniversary of the commencement of the original settlement and ensures that all of the originally settled property can have the benefit of only one IHT threshold. The transfer of property from one relevant property trust to another does not incur an exit charge, unless the powers of the new trust mean that the assets transferred are no longer relevant property.

There are income tax provisions (*ITA 2007, s 472–473*) which apply where there has been a variation of a will or intestacy. The corresponding CGT and IHT provisions are at TCGA *1992, s 68C* and *IHTA 1984, s 142* respectively.

A person ceases to be settlor when no property settled by him remains in the trust.

Settled property

32.5   Settled property is the assets held in a trust and can include any kind of property.

These assets are also called the trust 'capital' or 'fund'. The may produce income for the trust, such as interest, dividends or rent. The way this income is taxed will depend on the type of income and the type of trust.

Assets may also be sold, which might produce a capital gain for the trust.

ITA 2007, s 466 provides a definition of settled property for income tax purposes which mirrors the CGT definition in *TCGA 1992, s 68*. Settled property is any property held in trust by a person unless that person holds it as nominee; or bare trustee for another

This definition applies for general income tax purposes and for the application of CGT. It does not apply in respect of the 'settlements' legislation (*ITTOIA 2005, Pt 5, Ch 5*), which prevents trusts and settlements being used to gain tax advantages.

Beneficiaries

32.6   A beneficiary is anyone who benefits (or may benefit) from the assets held in the trust. There can be one or more beneficiaries, such as members of a family or the employees of a business. Each beneficiary may benefit from the trust in a different way (or not at all).

The beneficiaries are defined in the trust deed and are entitled to benefit from the trust income and/or assets. The precise beneficiary may be left to the discretion of the trustees but the trust deed will nominate a class of beneficiaries from which the trustees may choose.

For example, a beneficiary may benefit from:

- the income only – such as the income from letting a house held in a trust;

- the capital only – for example, they might get shares held on trust when they reach a certain age;

- both the income and capital of the trust – for example they might be entitled to the trust income and have a discretionary interest in trust capital.

Focus

Trustees (acting as such) may not benefit from the trust in terms of remuneration, although professional trustees are normally permitted to receive reasonable remuneration for their services. A Trustee can, however, be a beneficiary of the trust

---

If he settlor can benefit from a trust, the trust is 'settlor-interested'. Special tax rules then apply for income tax (see **33.14**), CGT (see **34.2**) and IHT (see **35.21**).

TYPES OF TRUST

Reasons for trusts

32.7   Trusts may be set up for a number of reasons, for example:

- to control and protect family assets, for example a trust created for a spouse that stipulates that on the spouse's death the trust assets pass directly to children or grandchildren;

- for someone too young or incapacitated to handle their own affairs;

- to pass on assets during the settlor's lifetime;

- to pass on assets on death;

- to conceal beneficial ownership (although new disclosure rules may limit this);

- under the rules of inheritance that apply when someone dies without leaving a valid will (England and Wales only);

- to create a pension scheme for employees;

- as a means of making charitable donations;

- for tax planning reasons, although the benefits have been reduced in recent years.

The reason for establishing a trust will dictate the type of trust used. The trust deed governs how the trustees should administer the trust assets and therefore it is essential that a copy of the original deed (and any supplementary documents) are obtained and fully understood before offering advice in respect of a trust.

Bare trusts

32.8   A bare trust (or 'simple trust') is an arrangement where the beneficiary has an immediate and absolute right to both the capital and income held in the trust. The trustee has no discretion over what income or capital to pass on to the beneficiary.

Once the trust has been set up, the beneficiaries cannot be changed.

Bare trusts are commonly used to transfer assets to minors as they cannot legally hold property. Typical examples are:

- a parent holding a bank account for a child;

- a bequest in a will to a minor but with direction that funds should not be paid to the child until he attains majority. If there are any other conditions that must be fulfilled before he becomes entitled, eg attaining a certain age, this would not be a bare trust.

The Trustee Act 1925, s 31 applies for UK trusts for minors (other than those set up or administered in Scotland). The trustees will have discretion over the use of income for the benefit of the minor and must accumulate the balance, unless the section is disapplied in the trust deed. Where the beneficiary's title to income and capital is indefeasible, HMRC will recognise the trust as a bare trust, despite the trustee having active duties to perform because of the beneficiary's incapacity (TSEM1563).

Trustees hold the assets on trust until the beneficiary is 18 in England and Wales, or 16 in Scotland. At this point, beneficiaries can demand that the trustees transfer the trust fund to them.

For income tax, CGT and IHT purposes, the beneficiaries are treated as if they owned the assets. Therefore, the beneficiaries of a bare trust would return any income and gains on their own personal tax returns and the trustees are not required to make a tax return. The trustees may pay the tax due to HMRC on behalf of a beneficiary, but it is the beneficiary who is chargeable to tax.

> **Focus**
>
> If there are conditions that must be met before the beneficiaries become entitled to the trust funds, it is probably not a bare trust and the trustees will have to return the income. If payment is merely deferred until the beneficiary reaches a particular age, it is probably a bare trust and the income should be returned as the beneficiaries'.
>
> Trustees should take legal advice if they are unsure whether they are dealing with a bare trust or not.

Interest in possession or life interest trusts

32.9   There is no definition of 'interest in possession' (IIP) in tax statutes. Following the case *Pearson v CIR* [1980] STC 318 it is recognised that the term means 'present right to enjoyment of income'. HMRC's Press Release of 12 February 1976 sets out its understanding that an IIP exists where the person with the interest has an immediate entitlement to any income produced by the trust. The trustees may have the power to terminate the beneficiary's right to future income, but this does not prevent the existence of a current IIP.

Under the terms of such a trust, the trustees must pay out the income of the trust to the named beneficiaries; the trustees have no power to accumulate income within the trust. If the trustees do have the power to accumulate income, there is no interest in possession.

The beneficiary is often called a 'life tenant' and is legally entitled to the net income of the trust, after taxes and expenses, each year. However, a beneficiary does not necessarily have the right to the income for the rest of his life – the right may be until a specified age or for a certain period of time.

An exclusive right to enjoy a trust asset is also an IIP, even if that asset does not produce any income, eg the right to occupy a house at less than full rent.

It is usual for the capital of the trust to pass to different beneficiaries at the end of the IIP. These beneficiaries are called the 'remaindermen' or 'reversionary beneficiaries'.

In many IIP trusts, the trustees will have flexible powers to distribute capital at their discretion. Therefore it is possible for a life tenant to receive a capital distribution or for a remainderman to receive trust capital before the IIP ends.

Finance Act 2006 made significant changes to the IHT treatment of IIP trusts created on or after 22 March 2006 (see **35.20**).

Discretionary trusts

32.10   When a settlor wishes assets to be used to benefit a group of beneficiaries but does not want to be too prescriptive as to how each will benefit, he would normally create a discretionary trust. The trustees are able to distribute the income and the capital of the trust within the discretion granted to them by the deed; the beneficiaries have no automatic right to receive either income or capital.

Discretionary trusts are sometimes set up to put capital aside for:

- a future need that may not be known yet, for example a grandchild that may require more financial assistance than other beneficiaries at some point in his life;

- beneficiaries who are not capable or responsible enough to deal with money by themselves.

Under the terms of the deed that creates the trust, there may be situations when the trustees are obliged to use income for the benefit of particular beneficiaries. However, they may still retain discretion about how and when to pay. The extent of the trustees' discretion depends on the terms of the trust deed.

Usually the trustees will have the power to accumulate income within the trust.

Accumulation and maintenance trusts

32.11   Accumulation and maintenance (A&M) trusts were form of settlement in which no interest in possession subsists and were the usual means by which property was settled for children. Prior to 22 March 2006 special tax applied, granting favourable treatment, provided that the trust fell with the rules laid down:

- any transfer to the trust was potentially exempt from IHT;

- capital appointments out of the trust were not chargeable (exit) IHT events; and

- there was never a periodic ten-year IHT charge (as the assets do not represent relevant property) (*s 71*).

This special rules applied to any settlement where:

- one or more persons would, on or before attaining a specified age not exceeding 25, become entitled to settled property or to an interest in possession in it (*s 71(1)*); and

- no interest in possession subsisted in the settled property and the income from it was to be accumulated in so far as it is not applied for the maintenance, education or benefit of such a person; and

- either:
  - ○ not more than 25 years have elapsed since the day on which the settlement was made or (if later) since the time when the settled property began to satisfy the above conditions; or

  - ○ all the persons who are, or have been, beneficiaries are, or were, grandchildren of a common grandparent (or are children, widows or widowers of such beneficiaries who died before becoming beneficially entitled) (*s 71(2)*).

Following the changes on 22 March 2006, the trustees of an A&M settlement had until 5 April 2008 to change the terms of the trust to ensure that either:

- the beneficiary/beneficiaries becomes/became absolutely entitled to the property in the trust on or before their 18th birthday, so the trust will/ would continue to be an A&M trust; or

- it met the conditions for a bereaved minors trust; or

- it met the conditions for an age 18 to 25 trust.

If nothing was done before 6 April 2008, the trust became a relevant property trust from that date.

Bereaved minor trusts

32.12 *Finance Act 2006* introduced 'trusts for bereaved minors'. Such trusts are available only under:

- the will (or intestacy) of a deceased parent (including where this is following a valid deed of variation); or

- the criminal injuries compensation scheme (*s 71A*).

A bereaved minor is someone, at least one of whose parents has died and is under the age of 18 (*s 71C*). 'Parent' includes any person who, immediately before their death, had parental responsibility for the minor. It is therefore possible for a trust of this sort to be set up under the intestacy of a grandparent, great grandparent, etc (*s 71H*).

For as long as the minor is under the age of 18 and alive:

- the settled property is only applied for the benefit of the minor (if at all) (*s 71A(3)(b), (c)*); and

- either he must be entitled to all income arising, or no such income may be applied for any other person.

At some point before (or on attaining) the age of 18, the minor must become entitled absolutely to the settled property and any income arising from it, along with any income that has been accumulated before that time (*s 71A(3)(a)*).

There will be no charge to IHT where:

- the minor receives absolute ownership on or before attaining the age of 18; or

- property is applied for the maintenance of the minor; or

- the minor dies before reaching 18.

However, a flat rate charge to IHT arises in any other circumstances where:

- *section 71A* ceases to apply to the settled property; or

- the trustees make any disposition which reduces the value of property held in the trust.

Where the conditions of *s 71A* apply to a trust which met the conditions of *s 71* before 22 March 2006 (A & M Trusts), *s 71A* takes precedence over *s 71* (*s 71(1B)*).

Age 18 to 25 trusts

32.13 Age 18 to 25 trusts were introduced in response to the protests about the abolition of the benefits available to A&M settlements, but they are more restrictive. To qualify:

- the trust property must be held for the benefit of someone under 25;

- a parent (or someone who had stood in that position) of that person has died;

- the trust arose under that parent's will or the criminal injuries compensation scheme;

- the beneficiary will become entitled to the income and capital (including accumulated income) on or before his 25th birthday; and

- the trust can never provide benefits to anyone else while the beneficiary is alive and under 25.

If the trust arises from converting an A&M trust, the second and third conditions do not need to be met.

Where these conditions are met, the fund will not suffer ten-year charges or exit charges while the beneficiary is under 18. If the beneficiary does not become entitled to the fund by his 18th birthday, there will be an exit charge based on a modified form of that for relevant property. This results in a maximum rate of 4.2% (6% × 28/40) where the fund vests at 25.

Disabled persons trusts

32.14 Following the changes to the IHT rules for trusts, there are now four types of trust for disabled people which attract special treatment. These are:

1   discretionary trusts qualifying under the old rules in *s 89*;

2   self-settled discretionary trusts created after 22 March 2006 meeting the rules in *s 89A*;

3   interest in possession trusts created after that date meeting the conditions in *s 89B*; and

4   self-settled interest in possession trusts created after that date meeting the conditions in *s 89B*.

In order to qualify, it is necessary to show that the beneficiary meets the disability condition either because he cannot manage his affairs as defined by the *Mental Health Act 1983* or by entitlement to certain state benefits (*s 89(4)*). For property transferred into trust after 7 April 2013, the definition of disabled person is found in *FA 2005, Sch 1A. FA 2014, s 291* extends the definition to further cases.

Types 2 and 4 above are aimed at cases where the beneficiary is at risk of becoming disabled and wishes to arrange his affairs before the disability strikes. A case where this might arise would be the onset of Alzheimer's disease. HMRC would expect to see evidence, such as a contemporaneous certificate from a medical practitioner that at the time of the settlement the settlor was suffering from a condition that could reasonably be expected to lead to their becoming disabled within *s 89(4)(a)–(c)*.

There are conditions to ensure that the trust property is applied for the benefit of the disabled person.

All four types are treated for IHT as qualifying IIP trusts and not relevant property trusts, even though types 1 and 2 above are discretionary. These are known collectively as 'disabled person's interests'. HMRC call these type 1, type 2, type 3 and type 4 trusts respectively.

Protective trust

32.15   Under a protective trust (within *IHTA 1984, s 88*), the right of the beneficiary is much the same as under an interest in possession, but that right will terminate if a particular event occurs, eg bankruptcy or an attempt to dispose of the life interest. Therefore, they are used where the settlor is not confident that the beneficiary will deal responsibly with the IIP.

On a termination of such a life interest, the trust property becomes settled into a discretionary trust for the benefit of the life tenant and his immediate family.

Trusts with vulnerable beneficiary

32.16   There is an opportunity for trustees to make a claim for special tax treatment for trusts with vulnerable beneficiaries.

Broadly, this protects the trust from the special trusts rate (see **33.5**) and the dividend trust rate by ensuring that the tax charged on the trustees' income and gains is no more than it would have been if the income and gains had been taxed on the vulnerable person (*FA 2005, ss 23–45*).

Charitable trust

32.17   Essentially, such trusts are discretionary trusts whose funds must be applied for charitable purposes.

Provided the trust is set up as a registered charity, it will be exempt from tax.

Mixed trusts

32.18   A mixed trust is one where there are distinct parts of the trust fund so that the income may be taxable on more than one basis. For example, a trust may be part discretionary and part IIP, or part settlor-interested and part not settlor-interested.

There may be distinct parts to the trust fund from the start so that the income is always held in different trusts. Or changes may occur due to alterations in the beneficiaries' circumstances as follows:

Example 32.1 – Trust becoming 'mixed'

Two children benefit from a trust. According to the terms of the trust deed, the beneficiaries are entitled to income received by the trust when they reach 18. Ben reaches 18 while Sam is still 13.

The part of the trust benefiting Ben becomes an IIP trust, while the part that benefits Sam remains a discretionary trust until he reaches 18. Therefore, when Ben reaches 18 the trust becomes a mixed trust.

Foreign trust

32.19   A foreign law trust is a trust that is governed by the laws of a country outside the United Kingdom.

TRUST TAX RETURNS AND PAYMENTS – INCOME TAX AND CGT

General

32.20   Trusts are subject to the self-assessment regime and the form used is a trust and estates tax return (SA900). Trustees who are responsible for managing a trust have joint responsibility for ensuring that tax is properly declared and paid.

Focus

There is no requirement to produce annual trust accounts but it is advisable to do so and really is essential for an IIP trust with more than one beneficiary or any trust with different funds. Specimen accounts are published by the Society of Trust and Estate Practitioners (STEP) in their book *STEP Accounting Guidelines*. There is also assistance with trust returns in the HMRC toolkit (www.gov.uk/government/publications/hmrc-trusts-and-estates-toolkit).

Where there is more than one trustee, one person – known as the 'principal acting trustee' – should be put forward to deal with HMRC. However, the actions of the principal acting trustee are treated as actions of all of the trustees, so if the principal acting trustee fails to fulfil the trustees' obligations, all of the trustees are treated as failing to meet their obligations.

All the trustees of a trust are jointly liable for any tax due, not just a share of it. As a result, HMRC can recover any tax or interest on tax from any trustee, if the principal acting trustee doesn't pay or pays late. Also, any trustee can be held liable for penalties or surcharges incurred during the period he was a trustee.

The trustees can appoint an agent to communicate with HMRC. On trust income tax and CGT matters, a Form 64-8 will need to be completed. On IHT issues, an entry of the relevant contact details should be made on Form IHT100. These forms can be found at www.gov.uk/government/collections/ trusts-and-estates-forms.

The trust tax return can be filed online or on paper. There are different deadlines for each and as with most tax filings HMRC encourage online filing wherever possible.

Notification of taxable income or gains

32.21   The principal acting trustee (hereafter referred to as 'the trustee') should notify HMRC by 5 October following the end of the tax year when:

- a new trust that will receive income or make chargeable capital gains has been set up; or

- a trust that has not been receiving income or making chargeable capital gains starts to do so.

The only exception to this is in the case of bare trusts, where the beneficiaries of the trust must declare any income or capital gains on their own personal tax returns.

The notification can be done using Form 41G (Trust) or by letter. This can be found at www.gov.uk/government/collections/trusts-and-estates-forms. The letter must contain all of the information that would have been included on Form 41G (Trust), including:

- the name of the trust;

- the names and addresses of all of the trustees;

- the contact details of any professional agent, or a trustee's telephone number if there is no professional agent;

- whether the trust is governed by UK law, Scots law or another country's law;

- whether the trust is employment related;

- whether the trust is for a vulnerable beneficiary;

- details of how the trust was created – for example this could be the deceased person's details if the trust is created by a will, or a settlor's details for a trust created during his lifetime;

- the date the trust started;

- whether the trust was created by a deed of variation or family arrangement; and

- details of all of the assets in the trust. For land or buildings, these details should include the full address. For shares, include the number and class of shares, and the company's registration number.

It is not necessary to send copies of trust deeds unless HMRC asks for them.

Self-assessment filing

32.22   The advice in **Chapter 1** on filing returns, paying tax, interest and penalties applies equally to trusts.

HMRC supplementary sheets and help sheets

32.23   In addition to the main body of the tax return (SA 900), the following supplementary pages should be used as appropriate:

- SA901 Trust and Estate Trade – to declare details of trades;

- SA901L Lloyd's Underwriters – to declare income from membership of Lloyd's Underwriters;

- SA902 Trust and Estate Partnership – to declare details of a partnership;

- SA903 Trust and Estate UK Property – to declare income from land and property;

- SA904 Trust and Estate Foreign – to declare income and capital gains received abroad;

- SA905 Trust and Estate Capital Gains – to declare capital gains;

- SA906 Trust and Estate Non-residence – to declare residence status;

- SA907 Trust and Estate Charities – to declare charity status;

- SA923 Estate Pension Charges, etc – to declare that an estate has received certain payments from registered pension schemes or from certain overseas pension schemes.

Record keeping – general

32.24   In all cases, source documents should be kept, for example:

- bank statements for current and deposit accounts (copies should be printed of online accounts);

- confirmation of interest paid on bank or building society accounts;

- national savings bonds or certificates;

- certificates issued by life assurance companies;

- dividend vouchers from companies and unit trusts;

- stockbroker reports and record of dividends;

- details of expenses paid by the trustees;

- details of all taxes paid by the trust;

- records of income payments to beneficiaries.

If the trust sells or buys assets during the year, the following will be needed:

- completion statements for property transactions;

- contract notes for stocks or shares;

- receipts for sale or purchase expenses – including estate agents' and solicitors' charges on the sale of property and details of any stamp duty paid.

If the trust owns property to let the following information will be needed:

- receipts for expenses connected with the property – including any mortgage interest;

- annual bills such as business or water rates;

- licence or rent agreements showing the rent payable.

If the trust has received additional assets, a record will be needed of:

- the amount or value of the asset received – the market value on the date of transfer into the trust;

- the date the additional money or asset was received;

- details of who made the payment or who put the asset into trust.

A record should also be kept of any important decisions made by the trustees, such as:

- minutes of meetings;

- deeds of appointment;

- any decisions that affect the distribution of capital or income.

Trustees need to keep records of any income payments made at their discretion to beneficiaries as this information is required as part of the trust and estate tax return for discretionary trusts.

Focus

Beneficiaries who receive income may ask the trustees to provide a statement showing how much income they've received and how much tax the trustees have deducted. The trustees may use Form R185 (Trust Income) (www.gov.uk/government/publications/trusts-and-estates-statement-of-income-from-trust-r185-trust-income) to do this. The beneficiary can then use the information on this form to prepare his own self-assessment tax return or claim a repayment of tax on Form R40 (Claim) for repayment of tax deducted from savings and investments (www.gov.uk/government/publications/income-tax-claim-for-repayment-of-tax-deducted-from-savings-and-investments-r40).

If the beneficiary is also the settlor and he – or his spouse or civil partner – has retained an interest in the trust, you should use Form R185 (Settlor) instead.

Trustees should keep copies of all the Forms R185 that they give to beneficiaries.

Record-keeping – time limits

32.25 The length of time records need to be kept varies with the circumstances:

- If the trust has business income (eg it owns property to let), business records must be kept for five more years after the normal filing deadline of 31 January provided the return was filed on time.

  For example, for a 2011/12 tax return submitted on or before 31 January 2013, the records must be kept until 31 January 2018.

- If the trust does not have business income and the tax return is sent in on or before 31 January, the records should be kept for one more year from 31 January.

  For example, for a 2011/12 tax return filed on or before 31 January 2013, you must keep your records until 31 January 2014.

If the return is submitted after 31 January because it was issued late or because it is submitted late, records should be kept until the latest of the following dates – 15 months after the date the return was submitted or five years after the normal 31 January filing deadline if there is business income.

If HMRC starts a check prior to the relevant date above, it will be necessary to keep the records until HMRC writes to confirm that they have finished the check.

If the records needed have been lost or destroyed, the trustees should try to obtain the missing information in other ways, such as requesting copy statements. Returns can be made using estimated figures pending receipt of the copy information. If it is not possible to obtain copy information, the missing information must be estimated. Tax returns including estimates should be flagged as such, being either:

- a provisional figure – one you want to use until you can confirm the actual amount (you must indicate when you expect to be able to provide the actual amount); or

- an estimate – a figure you want HMRC to accept as your final figure.

The 'additional information' section of the tax return should be used to say how the figures have been arrived at and why it is not possible to use actual figures.

It is possible to contact HMRC and give the correct figures within one year of the final date for filing the return, but if adjustments are made at a later date and tax has been underpaid there may be interest and penalties to pay.

IHT RETURNS AND PAYMENTS

Relevant property trusts and qualifying interest in possession trusts

32.26   Whenever a ten-year charge or an exit charge arises on a relevant property trust the trustees must submit a tax return, called an 'account', using a Form IHT100, and pay any tax due. They may also need to file an account and be liable for tax when an interest in possession terminates.

Legislation introduced in *FA 2014, Sch 25* means that where tax charges arise on or after 6 April 2014, trustees of relevant property settlements must deliver the IHT account six months after the end of the month in which the chargeable event occurs (*s 216(6)*) and pay the tax by the end of the same period (*s 226*).

For events before that date, the account must be delivered by the later of the following (*IHTA 1984, s 216*):

● 12 months after the end of the month in which the occasion of the charge took place; or

● the end of a three-month period beginning from the date on which the trustees became liable for tax.

The tax will become due (*IHTA 1984, s 226*):

● if the chargeable event takes place after 5 April but before 1 October, by 30 April of the following year; or

● if the chargeable event occurs after 30 September and before 6 April, by six months after the end of the month in which the event occurred.

On a ten-yearly charge, although the tax is payable by the trustees, no grossing up is necessary as the only asset leaving the trust is the cash being used to pay the IHT.

Tax on an exit charge may be paid either by the trustees or the beneficiary. If the trustees pay the tax, the rate must be grossed up. In some instances the value of the property attracting the tax may not be known at the due date. The trustees can either deposit money on account or buy a certificate of tax deposit.

When a qualifying interest in possession ends, this will be a transfer of value. A return may be required although the transfer may be a PET if the interest ends in the life tenant's lifetime. On the death of the life tenant, the return will often be dealt with by the personal representatives (PRs), although the trustees must file a return if no one else has (*IHTA 1984, s 216(5)*).

Payment of tax by instalments is allowed in certain instances specified in *IHTA 1984, ss 227–229*. The broad effect of *ss 227* and *228* is that on a chargeable transfer made on death, and in limited circumstances on other occasions of charge, the tax attributable to the value of specified qualifying property (which is not exactly the same on all occasions of charge) may be paid by ten equal annual instalments, if the person paying the tax gives notice in writing.

The right to pay by instalments ceases on sale of the qualifying property.

The instalment provisions are supplemented by *IHTA 1984, s 234* which provides some interest relief for instalments of tax on certain categories of qualifying property.

Interest and penalties

32.27 Interest is chargeable on IHT paid late and is not deductible for income tax (*IHTA 1984, s 233*). Repayment supplement is payable on any tax overpaid and interest will be paid on any certificate of tax deposit ultimately repaid; both are tax exempt.

A new penalty regime took effect from 1 April 2009 for deaths and other chargeable events occurring on or after that date, where the return is due to be filed on or after 1 April 2010 (*FA 2008, Sch 40* and *FA 2007, Sch 24*). The regime is the same as that for other taxes and is discussed at **53.8**. However, HMRC have previously acknowledged that, as IHT applies to a single event, certain concepts such as 'reasonable care' will be somewhat different than for taxes where returns are made on a more regular basis and that the position of personal representatives is different to trustees and individuals making a chargeable transfer.

Prior to 1 April 2009, an initial penalty of up to £100 was chargeable for failure to deliver an IHT account, with a further £100 becoming due if the return was more than six months late. However, the total of these penalties could not exceed the amount of tax payable. A daily penalty of up to £60 could also be charged from the date the failure to deliver was declared by a court or the Special Commissioners.

Notification of settlements

32.28 From April 2010, HMRC may use the powers granted by *FA 2008 Sch 36* to require third parties (for example, solicitors) to provide information or documents which they consider might relate to a taxpayer's IHT position, in the same way as those powers apply to other taxes (see **51.8**).

There is a further obligation which applies specifically to solicitors and other professional advisors (excluding barristers): if a UK-domiciled settlor makes a settlement with non-UK resident trustees, or gives the advisors cause to think such trustees will be appointed, the professional has an obligation to give notice to HMRC within three months (*IHTA 1984, s 218*).

33

Income tax and trusts

SIGNPOSTS

- **Scope** – The residence status of a trust is critical when quantifying the extent of its income tax liability. Income is categorised for trustees in the same way as for individuals (eg rental business income, trading income, etc) (see **33.1–33.2**).

- **Income tax rates** – The tax rates are determined by the type of trust rather than income levels, and therefore it is essential to determine what type of trust is in existence. It is also important to remember that different rules may apply to different elements within one trust (see **33.3–33.6**).

- **Trustee expenses** – A clear understanding is required of the treatment of trustee management expenses and in particular their interaction with income in determining the tax liability for the beneficiary and the trust (see **33.7**).

- **Capital or income?** – Certain capital receipts under trust law are specifically treated as income under tax law (see **33.8**).

- **Payments to beneficiaries** – Trustees must pay income to the beneficiaries of an interest in possession trust, or beneficiaries may be entitled to an annuity. If trustees of discretionary trusts decide to make payments to beneficiaries, the distributions are generally 'franked' by tax from the trust 'tax pool', and the beneficiary obtains a tax credit (see **33.9–33.13**).

- **Settlor-interested trusts** – Anti-avoidance provisions can apply to treat trust income as the settlor's income for tax purposes in certain circumstances. There are also provisions to deal with situations where capital payments are paid to or for the benefit of the settlor (see **33.14–33.17**).

- **Trusts for the vulnerable** – Special rules apply to reduce the tax liability for trusts set up for the benefit of a 'vulnerable person' (see **33.18**).

- **Dividend income** – New rates of income on dividends came into effect on 6 April 2016. These changes will also have consequences for trustees (see **33.19**).

- **Appendix: Trust income tax rates** – A table of trust income tax rates for 2016/17 and earlier years is included at the end of this chapter (see **33.20**).

TRUSTEE RESIDENCE

33.1   A body of trustees has a separate legal capacity and identity. The trustees are liable to income tax on income arising from trust property. Liability to income tax is determined by the residence of the trustees (*ITA 2007, ss 475–476*). A change in trustees will have no effect on the income tax treatment of the trust income unless it impacts on the trust's residence.

A UK resident trust is taxed on its worldwide income. A trust is UK resident at any time when either:

(a)   all the trustees are resident in the UK; or

(b)   at least one trustee is resident in the UK and at least one is not and there is a settlor who meets the appropriate condition:

- if the settlement arose on his death and immediately before his death he was resident, ordinarily resident or domiciled in the UK (see **Chapter 56**), the condition is met from the date of death until there is no property in the settlement provided by that settlor or derived from such property; or

- if the settlement did not arise on his death and, at the time when he made the settlement or was treated for tax purposes as making it, he was resident, ordinarily resident or domiciled in the UK, he meets the condition until there is no property in the settlement provided by him or derived from such property.

Where the settlement was made, or treated as made after 5 April 2013, the reference in the conditions to ordinarily resident does not apply (*FA 2013, Sch 46, para 57*).

A non-UK resident trust is taxed only on UK income.

Where the residence status changes during a tax year, the year is split.

LIABILITY OF TRUSTEES

33.2   The same categorisation rules apply to trustees as they do for individuals, ie rental profits are taxed under the rules for property businesses, bank interest is taxed under the interest rules, trades under the trading profits rules, etc. A trust can never be an employee and thus will never be liable to tax on employment income.

Where a trust arises under a will, there is normally no income tax liability on a trust until a distribution is made from the estate which is deemed to be an income distribution, or the estate's period of administration comes to an end whichever is the earlier. Until then the income is taxed under the rules for estates (see **Chapter 36**).

TRUST INCOME TAX CALCULATION

33.3   The rates applicable vary depending on the type of trust rather than the level of income.

Interest in possession trusts

33.4

- Up to 5 April 2016 dividend-type income (such as income from stocks and shares) is taxed at the 'dividend ordinary rate' of 10% covered by the underlying tax credit. From 6 April 2016 dividends are taxed at a rate of 7.5% with no underlying tax credit. Trustees are not eligible for the dividend allowance.

- All other income (rent, business income, savings, etc) is taxed at the 'basic rate', currently 20%.

- Certain capital transactions are taxed as income using the trust rate of tax which otherwise is only applicable to discretionary trusts (see **33.5**).

- There are no deductions for personal allowances, gift aid or pension contributions.

- Expenses incurred in managing the trust (trust management expenses – see below) are not deducted from the income subject to tax. However, such expenses are taken into account when calculating the income from the trust that is taxable on the beneficiaries.

- The beneficiaries are given credit for tax suffered by the trust.

- From 6 April 2016 tax will no longer be deducted from bank and building society interest. HMRC recognise that this measure may result in an additional administration burden and reporting requirements for those trusts that currently are not required to submit a tax return and they are monitoring the situation.

Example 33.1 – Calculation of tax for an interest in possession trust

Ben is the life tenant of an interest in possession trust. The income of the trust for 2016/17 is:

	£
Rental income	26,000
Bank interest	6,000
UK dividends	10,000
Expenses:	
Letting expenses	6,000
Trust management expenses	1,800

The trustees' tax charge is as follows:

	Non-savings	Savings	Dividends
	£	£	£
Rental profits (£26,000–£6,000)	20,000		
Bank interest		6,000	
UK dividends			10,000
Total income	20,000	6,000	10,000
Tax at 20%	4,000	1,200	
Tax at 7.5%			750
Less tax credit	–		
Tax due	4,000	1,200	750

Note that no relief has been taken for the trust management expenses as these are not deductible in calculating the trustees' income tax liability.

Discretionary trusts

33.5   The rate of income tax payable on trusts where the trustees have discretion over the distribution of income depends on the type of income and whether or not the income falls within the 'standard rate band'.

- The standard rate band available to a trust is £1,000 divided by the number of settlements created by the settlor. It cannot be reduced below a minimum, currently £200. If there is more than one settlor, the highest number of settlements made by any one of those settlors is used to restrict the standard rate band available (*ITA 2007, s 492*).

- Income within this band is taxed at 7.5% (10% before 6 April 2016) for dividends and similar income and 20% for other types of income.

- The standard rate band is applied first against non-savings income, then against non-dividend savings income and finally against dividend income (*ITA 2007, s 491*).

- Relief is given for trust management expenses in calculating income chargeable at the trust rate as these rates only apply to income that is available for distribution; income that has been used to meet these expenses is not available for distribution (*ITA 2007, s 484*). The order of set off is first against dividend income, then against savings income and finally against non-savings income. The income used to cover the trust expenses is still taxed but at the basic or dividend ordinary rate (depending on the type of income it is deducted from) rather than at the trust rates (see **33.7**).

- The remaining dividend income is taxed at the trust dividend rate (38.1% for 2016/2017 – *ITA 2007, s 479(3)*).

- All other income is taxed at the trust rate, currently 45% (*ITA 2007, s 479(4)*).

- The trustees must maintain a tax pool to ensure that the tax credits claimed by the beneficiaries do not exceed the tax paid by the trustees.

A table of trust income tax rates for 2016/17 and earlier years is included at the end of this chapter.

Example 33.2 – Discretionary trust: no trust management expenses

A discretionary trust has the following income in 2016/17:

	£
Rental profits net of expenses	800
Bank interest	600
UK dividends	2,000

The trustees' tax charge is as follows:

	Non-savings £	Savings £	Dividends £
Rental profits	800		
Bank interest		600	
UK dividends			2,000
Gross income	800	600	2,000
£1,000 × 20%	160	40	–
£400 × 45%	–	180	–
£2,000 × 38.1%	–	–	762
Less: tax credit	–		
Tax due	160	220	762

Example 33.3 – Discretionary trust: with trust management expenses

A discretionary trust has the following income in 2015/16:

	£
Rental profits net of expenses	30,000
Bank interest	20,000
UK dividends	10,000

Trust management expenses are £1850

The trustees' tax charge is as follows:

	Non-savings £	Savings £	Dividends £
Rental profits	30,000		
Bank interest		20,000	
UK dividends			10,000
Gross income	30,000	20,000	10,000
Less: expenses 1850 × 100/92.5			(2,000)
	30,000	20,000	8,000

Standard rate band:			
£1,000 taxed at 20%	200		
Income used to meet trust expenses: £2,000 taxed at 7.5%			150
Trust rates:			
£8,000 × 38.1%			3,048
£29,000 × 45%	13,050		
£20,000 × 45%		9,000	
Tax payable by trustees	13,250	9,000	3,198

Focus

Trust management expenses are deducted from gross trust income; therefore they must be grossed up at the tax rate suffered at source on the income, ie if they are being deducted from gross dividend income the expenses are grossed up by 100/92.5; if they are deducted from savings income they are grossed up at 100/80.

An income tax computation for a discretionary trust differs from that for an interest in possession trust in three main ways:

- A discretionary trust receives some relief for trust management expenses. The expenses are grossed up and deducted in order of priority from dividend income, then savings income and finally non-savings income.

- A discretionary trust pays tax at the basic or dividend rate on the first £1,000 of income and then at the trust rates of 45% on non-dividend income and 38.1% on dividend income.

- The income that has been used to pay trust expenses in a discretionary trust is taxable at the basic or dividend rate.

Mixed trusts

33.6 Special consideration is required where the trustees have discretion over only part of the trust income. An old style accumulation and maintenance (A&M) trust is a good example (see **32.11**). With effect from

22 March 2006, it is unlikely that new A&M trusts will be created as the IHT advantages are no longer available, but trusts in existence on that date will continue to run for income tax purposes until such time as the trust comes to an end. Therefore, it is necessary to know how to deal with such trusts for several years yet. The discussion which follows is also relevant more generally.

The main distinguishing feature of an A&M trust is that the beneficiary's entitlement under the terms of the trust will change at a specified age, which cannot exceed 25. If the trust deed does not specify the age, the *Trustee Act 1925, s 31* specifies that it shall be age 18.

There are no separate tax rules for income tax in respect of mixed trusts. The income over which a beneficiary has an interest in possession is taxed as such (see **33.4**) and the remainder is taxed as a discretionary trust (see **33.5**).

Example 33.4 – Calculation of tax for an A&M trust

For an A&M trust, under which the beneficiaries receive an interest in possession at age 25 and the capital at age 35, there are three beneficiaries (with equal entitlements), currently aged 23, 27 and 29. The income of the trust is as follows:

	£
Rental profits net of expenses	48,000
Bank interest	15,000
UK dividends	9,000
Expenses	2,775

The beneficiary aged 23 does not have an interest in possession in the fund, whereas the other two do. Therefore, one third of the trust income is taxed under the discretionary trust rules and will be chargeable at the rates applicable to trusts, with relief for the first slice of income falling into the standard rate band and for trust management expenses. Two thirds of the income will be charged to tax under the interest in possession rules at the basic and lower dividend rates, with no relief for trust management expenses.

The computation is prepared as if for a discretionary trust, out of which the interest in possession element is stripped:

	Non-savings £	Savings £	Dividends £
Rental profits	48,000		
Bank interest		15,000	
UK dividends			9,000
Less: income subject to interest in possession (two-thirds)	(32,000)	(10,000)	(6,000)
Discretionary income	16,000	5,000	3,000
Less expenses:			
2,775 × 100/92.5 × 1/3			(1,000)
Taxable income after expenses	16,000	5,000	2,000

The £23,000 total taxable income is taxed as follows:

	Non-savings £	Savings £	Dividends £
Standard rate band:			
£1,000 × 20%	200		
Income used to meet trust expenses:			
£1,000 × 7.5			75
At trust rates:			
£2,000 × 38.1%			762
£15,000 × 45%	6,750		
£5,000 × 45%		2,250	
Tax payable by trustees	6,950	2,250	837

With respect to the interest in possession income, the bank interest and rental income will suffer tax at 20% and dividends will suffer tax at 7.5%. Therefore the trustees' liability is £8,850, being the rental income of £32,000 at the basic rate of 20%, the bank interest of £10,000 at 20% and dividend income of £6,000 at 7.5%. The total tax liability of the trustees is £18,887 (ie £6,950 + £2,250 + 837 + £6,400 + 2000 + 450).

If a beneficiary takes an interest in possession part way through a tax year, the income is apportioned and taxed under the discretionary rules in the first part of the year and under the interest in possession rules in the second part. Apportionment is done on a time basis for rental income, trading income and trust expenses. Interest and dividends are allocated to the period in which they are received. The same applies if an interest in possession ends during the tax year.

Trust management expenses

33.7   Under general trust law, for trust management expenses (TMEs) to be chargeable to income they must be exclusively for the benefit of the income beneficiaries. This means those expenses:

- incurred in securing the income of the trust;

- in deciding how much to pay to income beneficiaries; and

- in distributing income to them.

(*Trustees of the Peter Clay Discretionary Trust v HMRC* CA 2008, 79 TC 473).

TMEs are expenses incurred by the trustees in managing the trust. Expenses that give a benefit to a beneficiary (eg the payment of a beneficiary's utility bill) are a distribution rather than a TME. If the trust carries on a trade or rental business then expenses in connection with these are not TMEs but are dealt with under the normal deduction rules for trades or rental businesses.

For discretionary and accumulation trusts the general trust law rules apply ahead of anything said in the trust deed. However, for an interest in possession settlement the trust deed may override the general law, so that it is possible for the deed to provide that certain capital expenses should be charged against income or that certain income expenses should be charged against capital.

If an expense applies to the trust in general, for example taking advice on whether to carry on a trust, to wind it up or in respect of which investments to make, this would not be properly chargeable against income and must be set against capital.

It is not permissible to apportion an expense which relates to the trust as a whole between income and capital, even though this might be thought to be appropriate in order to provide fairness between different classes of beneficiary. If a fee note covers a number of services and there is some reasonable method whereby it can be apportioned between time spent on purely income matters and time spent on purely capital matters, an apportionment can be made.

TMEs chargeable correctly against income are set off in the following order (*ITA 2007, s 486*):

1   dividend income, including stock dividends;

2   non-dividend savings income, eg interest; and

3   non-savings income.

TMEs are only taken into account for interest in possession trusts when calculating the income distributable to the beneficiaries, ie they have no impact on the amount of tax suffered on income. In a discretionary trust, tax relief is given at the trust rates for expenses properly chargeable against income but the income used to cover the expenses does still suffer some tax at the basic (20%) or dividend (10%) rate.

Focus

Prior to *ITA 2007*, HMRC took the view that relief was given for expenses in the period of payment but there was an argument that relief is available in the period in which expenses are incurred and properly accrued. This treatment is supported by the decision in *Peter Clay*. The legislation (*ITA 2007, s 484*) makes it clear that expenses are allowable when incurred.

If expenses exceed income then the excess can be carried forward for use in future years.

Capital transactions subject to income tax

33.8   The legislation does not define 'income' but certain receipts which are capital in trust law are deemed to be income for tax purposes (*ITA 2007, ss 481–482*) and from 6 April 2006 are subject to tax at the trust rates. This is because in most cases the trustees will treat such items as capital, so they will not be distributed to the beneficiaries.

The capital receipts which are to be treated as income are brought together in one list as follows (*ITA 2007, s 482*):

(i)   qualifying distributions by a company by way of redemption, repayment or purchase of its own shares or on the purchase of a right to acquire its own shares;

(ii)   accrued income profits treated as made by the trustees;

(iii)   offshore income treated as arising on the disposal of an asset;

(iv)   chargeable events in respect of employee share ownership trusts;

(v)   premiums under a short lease;

(vi)   profits from disposals of deeply discounted securities (including gilt strips) by UK trustees;

(vii)   gains on contracts for life assurance;

(viii) profit on transactions in deposit rights;

(ix)   profit on disposal of a future or option with guaranteed returns;

(x)   proceeds of sales of foreign dividend coupons;

(xi)   gains on artificial transactions in land.

These provisions do not apply to:

(a)   accumulation and discretionary settlements (in whose hands it is income by virtue of *ITA 2007, s 480*);

(b)   charitable trusts or unit trusts (*ITA 2007, s 481(1)*); or

(c)   income from property held by a superannuation fund relating to undertakings outside the UK (*ITA 2007, s 481(5), (6)*).

PAYMENTS TO BENEFICIARIES OF INTEREST IN POSSESSION TRUSTS

33.9   The beneficiary of an interest in possession trust is entitled to the net income of the trust and the trustees have no power to accumulate income. Therefore income less expenses and tax must flow through the trust and out to the life tenant.

The trust provides a Form R185 to a beneficiary to notify what income has been distributed and the associated tax credit. The form can be obtained from HMRC's website (www.gov.uk/government/publications/ trusts-and-estates-statement-of-income-from-trust-r185-trust-income).

Example 33.5 – Calculation of tax for an interest in possession trust

Using the figures in **Example 33.1**, the amount of income that can be distributed and should be shown on the R185 is:

	Dividend income £	Savings income £	Non savings income £
Gross trust income	10,000	6,000	20,000
Less: tax paid by trust	(750)	(1,200)	(4,000)
Less: allowable expenses	(1,800)	–	–
Distributable income	7,450	4,800	16,000
Tax credit thereon	604	1,200	4,000
Gross income to go on R185	8,054	6,000	20,000

The trust is transparent for the purposes of categorising the income in the beneficiary's hands, ie income deriving from dividends is shown as dividend income on the beneficiary's tax return, income deriving from interest is shown as savings income, etc.

If the trust had had insufficient dividend income to cover the expenses, the balance would have been offset against savings income and then non-savings income and the associated tax credit would be reduced accordingly.

If the trust income included foreign dividends, it would be grossed up for the UK tax and notional overseas tax credit.

Focus

The gross figures should be entered on the beneficiary's tax return. If he is a higher rate or additional rate taxpayer, he will have further tax to pay. If the beneficiary is a basic rate taxpayer no further tax will be due. If he has unused allowances or losses, these can be set against the trust income and tax credits might be refunded. Since 6 April 2016, the tax relating to the dividend is no longer notional and can be repaid. The beneficiary can keep any tax repaid on the above unless it relates to an annuity paid 'free of tax' (see below).

It is common practice for a life tenant to receive interim distributions during the year but tax is not addressed at this stage. Once the trust's accounts and tax return are drawn up, the total income distributed to the beneficiary is certified on the R185.

Annuities

33.10   A beneficiary may be entitled to an annuity (ie he has the right to receive a fixed sum from the trust each year, irrespective of the level of trust income in a particular year). Usually annuities are expressed as a gross amount but the payment is made to the beneficiary net of basic rate tax and the tax is paid over by the trustees on the normal due date for balancing payments under self-assessment. The trustees will provide the recipient with a certificate confirming basic rate tax has been withheld and the recipient will return the annuity on his tax return and pay higher rate tax thereon if it is due.

Annuities may be expressed 'free of tax' in order to guarantee the beneficiary the same amount each year whatever the basic rate of tax might be. The payment made is grossed up for the basic rate and the tax is paid over by the trustees as above. If the recipient can reclaim the tax on the free of tax annuity, it must be repaid to the trust.

In either case, it is the gross annuity that is treated as a deductible payment when calculating the taxable income of the trust. It is deducted first from non-savings income, then savings income and finally dividends.

PAYMENTS TO BENEFICIARIES OF DISCRETIONARY TRUSTS

33.11   Again, a Form R185 is provided to the beneficiary as notification of income distributed and the associated tax credit. Unlike interest in possession trusts, there is no transparency principle for discretionary trusts. Whatever the original source of the income, the distribution is simply certified as 'trust income' and is disclosed as non-savings income on the beneficiary's tax return. Any income distributed is deemed to have been paid net of tax at the trust rate, currently 45%, regardless of the underlying income tax position.

If the beneficiary is an additional rate taxpayer, no extra tax will be due on the trust income. If the beneficiary is liable to a lower rate of tax or not liable to tax, a repayment will be due. The beneficiary can reclaim and keep any tax overpaid on the distribution from the trust. The Form R185 is sent to HMRC in support of the claim.

A distribution by the trust must be franked by tax from the trust tax pool, ie the trustees must have actually paid tax to HMRC if the beneficiary is to get credit for it when calculating his tax position. The tax pool is a running total of tax paid by the trustees less any credits that have been taken out of the pool by the beneficiaries. A record of the tax pool is included on the trustees' tax return.

The following tax paid by the trustees is added to the tax pool each year:

- any tax paid at 20% or 7.5% on income (net of expenses) falling into the standard rate band;

- any tax paid on savings and non-savings income (net of expenses) at the trust rate of 45%; and

- any tax paid on dividends (after expenses) at the trust dividend rate of 38.1%

The following do not go into the tax pool:

- the tax on income that is used to pay expenses (even if it is taxed at 20% or 7.5%).

The tax credits on distributions to beneficiaries that are shown on a Form R185 will reduce the tax pool; these will always be calculated at the trust rate.

Focus

This creates practical problems for trusts where the main source of income is from dividends as these will have borne tax at the trust dividend rate, currently 38.1%. This can lead to the problem highlighted below.

Example 33.6 – Calculation of tax for a discretionary trust with shortfall in tax pool

	Trust income	Trust tax liability	Tax pool
	£	£	£
Dividend	880		
			nil
	880		
Tax thereon at 38.1%	(335)	335	
Income after tax	545		
Tax payable by trustees		335	335

	Trust income	Trust tax liability	Tax pool
	£	£	£
Trustees want to distribute the net income	545		
45% tax credit	445		(445)
Gross income of beneficiary	990		
Shortfall in tax pool			110

A similar problem will occur if the trust suffers significant trust management expenses chargeable against income.

If the tax pool has a negative balance at the end of a tax year, the trust must pay the deficit via its self-assessment return (*ITA 2007, s 496*). It will affect the payments on account calculation for the following year.

In a trust with only dividend income, distributions will need to be limited to 55% (50% before 6 April 2013) of the net dividends received in order to leave sufficient cash available to cover the shortfall in the pool.

If the tax pool has a positive balance at the end of the year, the credit is carried forward to the next year. The amount carried forward is not adjusted if the rate changes. Negative balances can never be carried forward as the tax will have been discharged by the trustees.

Annuities

33.12   If a fixed sum of income is paid to a beneficiary on an annual basis, this gives the annuitant an interest in possession in part of the fund. As with an interest in possession trust, the gross amount of the annuity can be treated as a deductible payment when calculating the trustees' tax liability.

The trustees must withhold tax at source at basic rate and this is paid over on the normal due date with the rest of the trustees' tax liability (*ITA 2007, s 449*).

Example 33.7 – Trust with management expenses and an annuity

A discretionary trust has the following income and expenses in 2016/2017

	£
Rental profits net of expenses	18,000
Bank interest	15,000

	£
UK dividends	3,000
An annuity payable to a beneficiary	5,000
Trust management expenses	3,500

The trustees' tax charge is as follows:

	Non savings £	Savings £	Dividends £
Rental profits	18,000		
Bank interest		15,000	
UK dividends			3,000
Less: deductible annuity	(5,000)		
Gross income	13,000	15,000	3,000
Less expenses:			
From dividends 2775 × 100/92.5			(3,000)
From interest 725 × 100/80		(906)	
Net taxable income	13,000	14,094	–

Taxed as follows:

	Non savings	Savings	Dividends
Standard rate band:			
£1,000 × 20%	200		
At trust rates:			
£nil taxed at 42.5%			–
£12,000 × 45%	5,400		
£14,094 × 45%		6342	
Income used to meet expenses:			
£3,000 × 10%			300
£906 × 20%		181	
Annuity:			
£5,000 × 20%	1,000		
Tax payable by trustees	6.600	6,523	300

PAYMENTS TO BENEFICIARIES OF MIXED TRUSTS

33.13   Any income distributed to a discretionary beneficiary follows the rules as for discretionary trusts above and any income the trustees are obliged to distribute under an interest in possession is subject to the rules for interest in possession trusts as above.

SETTLOR-INTERESTED TRUSTS

33.14   The legislation contains anti-avoidance provisions designed to prevent a person passing income, by means of a settlement, to another person who is not liable to tax or is liable at a lower rate (*ITTOIA 2005, Pt 5, Ch 5*). The arrangements dealt with here are:

(i)   a settlement where the settlor retains an interest;

(ii)   a settlement on an unmarried minor child of the settlor; and

(iii)   capital payments including loans to the settlor.

Retention of an interest by the settlor

33.15   Income of a trust is treated as belonging to the settlor if it arises during his lifetime and from property in which he has interest (*ITTOIA 2005, s 624*). He has an 'interest' in the trust property, or in any property derived from it, if it could be applied for his or his spouse's benefit (*ITTOIA 2005, s 625*).

The provisions are drawn in very wide terms, but are made subject to a number of exceptions. The settlor is taxed on the income arising in the trust but is given relief for any tax already paid by the trust. The ultimate effect is that the trust income is taxed at the rate it would bear if it formed the top slice of the settlor's income.

For these purposes 'settlement' has a very wide meaning: it includes 'any disposition, trust, covenant, agreement, arrangement or transfer of assets' (*ITTOIA 2005, s 620*). However, for the arrangement to be caught there must be an element of bounty (*IRC v Plummer* [1979] STC 793).

HMRC do not regard the rule as only applying to spouses and minor children but to any arrangement for income to be payable to a person where the settlor has an interest in the settlement and the arrangements are either:

●   bounteous;

●   not commercial;

- not at arms' length; or

- in the case of an outright gift to a spouse, wholly or substantially a right to income (TSEM4200).

There are similar, but not identical rules for IHT purposes (ie the 'gifts with reservation' provisions) and for CGT purposes prior to 6 April 2008 (*TCGA 1992, ss 77–79*).

The general rule is that income arising under a settlement during the life of the settlor is treated as income of the settlor, unless it derived from property in which he has no interest (*ITTOIA 2005, s 624*). A settlor is regarded as having an interest in property if there are any circumstances in which that property, or any related property, is or may become payable to the settlor, his spouse or his civil partner during the settlor's lifetime (*ITTOIA 2005, s 625(1)*). Therefore the rights of widows or civil partners after the settlor's death are not caught (NB references to spouse should be taken to include civil partner).

In addition to the obvious position where the settlor has an immediate interest in the trust property, these provisions apply if there are any circumstances where the settlor might benefit, such as:

- the funds revert to him under a revocable settlement;

- he is a discretionary beneficiary;

- he could be added in the future.

However, there is an exception if the settlor is not domiciled or not resident in the UK and the income would have been exempt from UK tax by virtue of his residence or domicile (*ITTOIA 2005, s 648(2)(3)*), for example non-UK source income of an offshore trust.

The income does not need to be paid to the settlor but it is taxed as if it were the highest part of his income. Trust management expenses cannot reduce the deemed income of the settlor. The settlor should enter the income on the trusts' supplementary pages of his tax return. This income retains its character in the hands of the settlor, as if it had arisen to him directly. Therefore he will be treated as receiving non-savings income, interest income or dividend income as appropriate (*ITTOIA 2005, s 619*) and he will be entitled to the same deductions and reliefs as if the income were actually his (*ITTOIA 2005, s 623*).

Where the income arises to trustees, they are liable to account for tax on the income as recipients (*ITTOIA 2005, s 646(8)*). Tax paid by the trustees in these circumstances is treated as paid on behalf of the settlor and is available to be used against the settlor's own tax liability. Where the income does not belong to the settlor (for example, it belongs to a spouse or civil partner as life tenant) the income is not taxable on the person entitled to it and the tax paid by the trustees is not available to that person.

As tax paid by the trustees on income attributable to the settlor under *s 624* is treated as paid on behalf of the settlor, it does not enter the tax pool. Discretionary payments made to other beneficiaries out of such trust income must also be returned on that beneficiary's tax return. The trustees will provide the beneficiary with a statement of income from trusts (Form R185), which will show the amount of income paid to the beneficiary and the associated tax credit at the trust rate, currently 45%. This means that the beneficiary will have no further tax to pay on the distribution but the tax credit is not repayable nor can it be set against any other income tax liability of the beneficiary (*ITTOIA 2005, s 685A(3)*).

Trustees of bare trusts are not generally required to make returns or pay income tax and therefore income arising is taxed directly on the settlor.

From 6 April 2010, settlors who receive tax repayments because their marginal tax rate is less than the trustees' rate are required to pass such repayments to the trustees. Any such payments will be disregarded for IHT purposes.

Focus

For a couple, it is sensible to hold some assets, such as bank accounts or shares, in joint names so that the personal allowances and the lower and basic rate bands of each of the spouses is fully utilised. This is sensible tax planning and is not attacked by HMRC under the anti-avoidance rules.

The settlements legislation was considered in *Garnett v Jones (re Arctic Systems Ltd)* HL 2007, 78 TC 597 (commonly known as the *Arctic Systems* case). The taxpayer and his wife each owned one share in a company which they had acquired from company formation agents and of which the taxpayer (Mr Jones) was the only director. The company earned profits by the taxpayer providing computer consultancy services to clients. The taxpayer's wife undertook all the book-keeping and administrative work for the company and was paid a salary commensurate with her duties. In the relevant year, the company's profits were distributed as dividends and the taxpayer and his wife each received half of them. The dividends paid were substantially greater than they would have been had the taxpayer drawn a salary commensurate with his earning power. The inspector issued a notice of amendment to the taxpayer's self-assessment on the basis that the taxpayer was liable to income tax on dividends paid to his wife.

The final decision went against HMRC and a Ministerial Statement was issued that legislation would be introduced on the treatment of income splitting between spouses. Draft legislation was issued in 2007 but it was widely criticised by professional bodies and in the 2008 Pre-Budget Report the Chancellor said that due to the 'current economic challenges' income-shifting legislation would not be included in *FA 2009*. There have been no proposals announced since to readdress the issue through a change in legislation. However the Tax Tribunal case (*DT Patmore v HMRC* [2010] UKFTT 334 (TC)) shows that HMRC have still been challenging cases where they think the existing legislation gives them a chance of success.

The main points to come out of the House of Lords' decision are as follows:

- The taxpayers had argued that there was no contract or mechanism in place at the outset either to agree the future income of the business or to decide on what might be done with any such income and therefore there was no settlement, but the House of Lords held that was an arrangement.

- If ordinary shares are the subject of an outright gift between husband and wife then the *s 626* let out will apply, given that an ordinary share cannot be substantially a right to income.

Therefore, if considering setting up a business in similar circumstances, fee earners should initially subscribe for all shares in a new company and then make a gift of some of their shares to their spouse.

TRUSTS FOR THE SETTLOR'S MINOR CHILDREN

33.16   A minor child is a child under 18 who has never been married or in a civil partnership. This includes a step-child (*ITTOIA 2005, s 629(7)*), an illegitimate child and an adopted child. Since 6 April 2006, discretionary income payments for the benefit of a vulnerable child are not caught by the settlement provisions in *s 629* (see **33.18**).

Parental trusts for minors are not a separate type of trust and so take any one of the forms detailed in the previous chapter. However, anti-avoidance rules apply to any trust set up by a parent for a minor child.

It should be noted that if the settlor (and spouse or civil partner) are not excluded from the trust then the rules for settlor interested trusts apply in precedence, - *s 629* is not a mirror image of *s 624*.

The effect of *s 629* is to tax income as that of the settlor. If the trustees have discretion to pay out or accumulate the income, it is only taxed on the settlor when it is distributed to the children. If the income is accumulated within the trust then it is simply taxed on the trustees (and the tax paid enters the tax pool) and is not attributed to the settlor. For bare trusts, the income belongs to the child, and is taxable on the settlor as it arises (TSEM4300).

There is limited relief in that if gross income distributed from all parental gifts in a tax year to any child is less than £100 (*s 629(3)*), the income is taxed in the hands of the child. If the gross income exceeds £100 then the whole amount is assessed on the settlor (Form SA107 Trusts, a supplementary page of the main SA100 tax return is used). The trustees will issue the R185 to the child beneficiary but there is no requirement to make any entry on the child's tax return.

Where *s 629* treats the child's income as that of the settlor and the settlor alone, the tax credit, as detailed on the R185, is available to the settlor to set off against the amount of tax he is due to pay (*ITA 2007, s 494*). If the trust rate applies and he is not an additional rate taxpayer, a tax refund can be claimed.

A payment of capital to a minor child can be treated as a distribution of income if the trustees have retained or accumulated income within the trust. This rule is there to prevent trustees making distributions of capital to such minor children in an attempt to avoid falling foul of *s 629* (*ITTOIA 2005, s 631(1)(b)*).

> **Focus**
>
> If the settlor is not the parent of the child then these settlement provisions do not apply, so trusts funded by grandparents can be advantageous from an income tax perspective.

Capital payments to the settlor

33.17 There are also special rules dealing with the situation where capital sums are paid to or for the benefit of the settlor (*ITTOIA 2005, ss 633–643*). Capital payments to the settlor or his spouse from the trust fund are matched with undistributed income of the fund and taxed as the settlor's income. The sum is grossed up at the trust rate of tax and the settlor is entitled to a tax credit to offset against his tax liability but not to any repayment.

If there is income within the trust available for distribution, such payments will be deemed to be income in the hands of the settlor in the year of receipt. If the capital sum exceeds the income then available for distribution, the excess capital sum will be treated as income for future years and taxed on the settlor in those years if income arises in the settlement in the following ten years (*ITTOIA 2005, s 634(4)*). Any part of the capital sum that has not been matched with available income after ten years cannot be treated as income of the settlor.

A 'capital sum' covers any sum paid by way of loan, even one made on commercial terms, a repayment of a loan and any sum paid otherwise than as income that is not paid for full consideration in money or money's worth (*ITTOIA 2005, s 634(1)*). A payment to a third party made at the direction of the settlor or as a result of his assignment is also caught (*ITTOIA 2005, s 634(5)*).

A potential trap for the unwary is that *s 633* catches situations where a loan made by a settlor to a trust is repaid. Such loans can arise inadvertently, for example when a settlor pays a trust tax liability because the trust did not have sufficient cash funds available at the due date.

The charge also applies to a capital sum received by the settlor from a body corporate connected with the settlement if the trustees have made an associated payment, directly or indirectly, to that body (*s 641*).The payment by the company is deemed to have been made to the settlor by the trustees. An 'associated payment' means any sum paid or asset transferred for less than full consideration in the five years before or after the date on which the company makes a payment to the settlor. If the payment to the settlor by the company is a loan or a repayment of a loan, it is excluded from these provisions if:

● it is repaid in full within 12 months; and

● in any period of five years there are no other loans outstanding for more than 12 months by the company to the settlor or by the settlor to the company.

TRUSTS FOR THE VULNERABLE

33.18   Special rules apply to reduce the tax liability for trusts set up for the benefit of a vulnerable person. This is either:

● a disabled person (*FA 2005, s 38*); or

● a relevant minor, meaning a person under the age of 18, at least one of whose parents has died (*FA 2005, s 39*).

They apply to discretionary and A&M trusts but not interest in possession trusts. The rules do not apply if the settlor has an interest in the trust.

There are six steps in calculating the income tax liability of this type of trust:

1   Calculate the income tax liability using the normal rules assuming the beneficiary is not vulnerable (*FA 2005, s 27*). This is called 'TQTI'.

2   Calculate the tax liability (including income and gains) of the vulnerable person assuming the trust income is his (*FA 2005, s 28(3)*). This is called 'TLV 1'.

3   Calculate the tax liability (income and gains) of the vulnerable person ignoring the trust income (*FA 2005, s 28(2)*). This is called 'TLV 2'. If any trust income is distributed to the beneficiary in the year it is ignored in this calculation.

4   Deduct TLV 1 from TLV 2 (*FA 2005, s 28(1)*). This is called VQTI.

5   Deduct TQTI from VQTI to calculate the trustees' tax relief (*FA 2005, s 26*).

6   Deduct the tax relief calculated at step 5 from the trustees' tax liability as calculated in step 1. The result is the revised trustees' tax liability.

Essentially, the aim of the above is to achieve a tax liability for the trustees as if the trust income had accrued directly to the vulnerable beneficiary, ie taking account of his personal allowances and any other reliefs available and reflecting a lower rate of tax if he is not an additional rate taxpayer.

Example 33.8 – Vulnerable beneficiary: tax calculations

The Isaac will trust was set up on 6 April 2011 on the death of Ester Isaac.

The trust is for the benefit of Ester's only son Nigel, who is 15. The trust is discretionary until Nigel reaches 25. The trust satisfies the conditions as being a trust with a vulnerable beneficiary.

The trust has the following income and expenses in 2016/2017

	£
Rental profits (net of expenses)	28,000
Bank interest	12,000
UK dividends	5,000
Trust management expenses	(1,350)

Nigel is still at school. His only income in 2016/2017 is as follows:

Wages from a part-time job at weekends/holidays	1,000
National Savings interest (gross)	400

This income is therefore wholly covered by personal allowances, so no liability arises.

We need to calculate the tax liability of the trustees.

Step (1) – Calculate trust tax liability using 'normal' rules

	Non-savings	**Interest**	**Dividends**
	£	**£**	**£**
Rental income	28,000		
Bank interest		12,000	
Dividends			5,000
Gross trust income	28,000	12,000	5,000
Less: expenses (£1,350 × 100/92.5)			(1,460)
Income after expenses	28,000	12,000	3,540

Tax

Basic rate:	£
£1,000 × 20%	200
Rates applicable to trusts (RAT):	
(£28,000 – £1,000) × 45%	12,150
£12,000 × 45%	5,400
£3540 × 38.1%	1,348
£1,460 × 7.5% (expenses)	110
	19,208

Less tax credits:

Tax payable by trustees ('TQTI')	19,208

Step (2) – Calculate Nigel's tax liability if the trust income was deemed to have accrued to him personally

	Non-savings	**Interest**	**Dividends**
	£	**£**	**£**
Earnings	1,000		
Trust rental income	28,000		
National Savings interest		400	
Trust bank interest		12,000	
Trust dividends			5,000
Net income	29,000	12,400	5,000
Less: personal allowance	(11,000)		
Taxable income	18,000	12,400	5,000

Tax

	£
£18,000 × 20%	3,600
£12,400 × 20%	2,480
£5,000 × 0%	0
Tax payable by Nigel ('TLV 1')	6,080

Step (3) – Calculate Nigel's tax liability ignoring trust income.

This is nil as all income is covered by personal allowances ('TLV 2')

Step (4) – 'TLV 1' minus 'TLV 2' = 'V'

	£
'TLV 1'	6,080
'TLV 2'	Nil
'VQTI'	6,080

Step (5) – 'TQTI' minus 'VQTI'

	£
'TQTI'	19,208
'VQTI'	6,080
Trustees' tax relief	13,128

Step (6) – Trustees' revised tax liability

	£
'TQTI' (from *Step 1*)	19,208
Less trustees' tax relief (from *Step 5*)	13,128
Revised trust liability	6,080

If the rules apply for only part of a year, eg a parent dies during a tax year or the beneficiary attains the age of 18 during the year, the trust income must be apportioned.

33.19 If the trust has beneficiaries that are vulnerable and some who are not, the trust income is apportioned between the beneficiaries and the rules applied to the income of the qualifying beneficiary.

There are two separate claims to consider:

- *The vulnerable person's election* (*FA 2005, s 37*) – This is a joint election by the trustees and the beneficiary (or his legal representative) to confirm that the trust is qualifying and that the beneficiary is vulnerable. The election must state the date from which it is effective and must be made by 31 January after the end of the tax year following that in which it first takes effect. HMRC do have the discretion to extend this deadline. It is irrevocable but will come to an end if the beneficiary ceases to be vulnerable, eg reaches 18, the trust ceases to qualify or it is wound up. The trustees are obliged to notify HMRC within 90 days of any of these events. The form to make the election can be obtained from the HMRC website (search2.hmrc.gov.uk/kb5/hmrc/forms/view.page?record=rvI1UsJ2vLE&formId=3299).

- *Claim for special tax treatment* (*FA 2005, s 25*) – The special tax rules do not apply automatically. The trustees must claim the relief. The claim is made annually via the self-assessment tax return of the trustees.

APPENDIX: TRUST RATES

(*ITA 2007, s 9*)

33.20

	Trust rate	**Dividend trust rate**
2016/17	**45%**	**38.1%**
2013/14 to 2015/16	45%	37.5%
2010/11 to 2012/13	50%	42.5%
2004/05 to 2009/10	40%	32.5%

Notes

1   A 'standard rate band' applies to the first £1,000 of taxable income arising in 2006/07 and later years (for 2005/06, the starting rate band was £500). Income within this band is not taxable at the above trust rates, but is generally taxable at the (non-trust) rates applicable to the particular source of income (eg 7.5% for dividend income, or 20% for other savings income or non-savings income (eg rental and business profits). In the case of trusts made by the same settlor, the standard rate band is divided by the number of such trusts, subject to a minimum starting rate band of £200 (*ITA 2007, ss 491, 492*).

2   The above trust rates broadly apply to accumulated or discretionary trust income (*ITA 2007, s 479*). Trustees of an interest in possession trust are generally liable to income tax (for 2010/11 to 2015/16) at 7.5% in respect of dividend income, or 20% on other savings income or non-savings income), although certain capital receipts for trust law purposes are liable at the above trust rates (*ITA 2007, ss 481, 482*).

34

Capital gains tax and trusts

SIGNPOSTS

- **Trustee residence issues** – The rules for determining residence changed from 6 April 2007. Beware of stringent anti-avoidance legislation affecting trustees and settlors in certain circumstances (see **34.1–34.2**).

- **Transferring assets into and out of the trust** – Each transfer is a disposal for CGT purposes. The mechanics for calculating a gain are usually the same as for a transaction between two individuals who are connected persons (see **34.3–34.5**).

- **Sub-fund elections** – It is important to understand why and how it may be preferable to run one trust as more than one settlement, and the tax consequences (see **34.6**).

- **Mitigating or deferring gains** – Many of the reliefs available to individuals will also be available to trustees. However, it is important to be aware of subtle differences in the rules (see **34.7–34.12**).

- **Adding to existing trusts** – Care must be taken to ensure that administrative burdens are not inadvertently created by additions to trusts that result in there being more than one settlor, or in partitioning a trust so that it falls into different tax regimes (see **34.13**).

All statutory references in this chapter are to TCGA 1992, unless otherwise stated.

TRUSTEE RESIDENCE

34.1   With effect from 6 April 2007, the rules for residence for CGT purposes were aligned with the income tax rules (see **33.1** and *TCGA 1992, s 69*) and liability to capital gains tax is determined by the residence of the trustees.

A UK-resident trust is taxed on its worldwide gains.

34.2 *Capital gains tax and trusts*

From 6 April 2015, disposals of UK property interests are taxable regardless of the residence position of the Trustees. Apart from these, a non-UK resident trust is not taxed on capital gains even if the asset is situated in the UK. However, gains can be attributed to the settlor or beneficiaries under anti-avoidance legislation:

- the 'settlor charge' in *s 86* taxes a UK resident and domiciled settlor on gains made by non-UK resident trustees of certain settlements made by him;

- the 'capital payments' charge in *s 87* taxes UK resident and domiciled beneficiaries on capital payments received by them to the extent of the gains made by an offshore trust.

Prior to 6 April 2013 these provisions also applied if the settlor or beneficiary was domiciled and ordinarily resident in the UK.

Trustees of a non-UK resident trust who own shares in a non-UK resident company can have chargeable gains realised by that company attributed to them under *s 13*.

Since 16 March 2005 it has not been possible to use a double tax treaty to argue that trustees are not resident in a particular year of disposal (*F(No 2) A 2005, s 33*).

For CGT purposes, if the trust is resident for any part of a tax year, gains arising at any time in the tax year are chargeable to capital gains tax. Where the trust becomes non-resident during the year there may be an exit charge.

The current legislative climate means that exporting a trust is no longer common practice. The trust deed must contain the power for a body of non-UK resident trustees to be appointed. The act of appointing non-UK trustees causes a deemed disposal and re-acquisition which results in a CGT liability payable by the retiring UK trustees *(s 80)*. In addition, any gains held over by the settlor on putting assets into the trust in the previous six years will become immediately assessable on the retiring UK trustees and, if not paid by them, on the settlor *(s 168)*. Once the trust has been exported it would be open to the settlor charge and the capital payments charge referred to above.

SETTLOR-INTERESTED TRUSTS

34.2

Focus

Gains of a settlor-interested UK resident trust ceased to be assessed on the settlor from 2008/09.

While from 2008/09, the gains of a settlor-interested trust are assessed on the trustees rather than the settlor, the concept remains as it is important for the purposes of holdover relief (see **34.8**).

For disposals before 6 April 2008, the settlor was treated as if the gains of the trustees were his gains (*s 77*), where:

- trust property or 'derived property' benefits, or may benefit, the settlor or his spouse. 'Derived property' means income from the property or any other property directly or indirectly representing the proceeds of the sale of that property; or

- there is a benefit for the settlor or his spouse that is derived directly or indirectly from the settlement property or derived property.

The rules are in line with those applied for income tax purposes (see **33.14**) and do not apply if the spouse can only benefit after the settlor has died.

DISPOSALS TO TRUSTEES

34.3   Unless the settlor settles only cash into the trust, the setting up of the trust is likely to give rise to a disposal by the settlor subject to CGT. The settlor and trustees are connected persons (*s 286(3)*) and all transactions between them are deemed to take place at market value (*s 17*). This will be the case even if the settlor is a beneficiary of the trust (*s 70*).

The trustees will be deemed to have acquired the asset with a base cost equal to the market value at the date of the settlement.

It may be possible to claim gift relief on the assets transferred into the trust, which will defer all or part of the capital gain (see **34.8**).

If IHT arises on the gift into trust, the IHT paid is an allowable deduction for the trustees for CGT purposes (*s 260(7)*), ie it is added to the trustees' base cost of the asset, but this cannot create a loss on a disposal of the asset by the trustees.

DISPOSALS BY TRUSTEES

34.4   If the trustees sell an asset that is subject to CGT at a profit, they will make a chargeable gain. The gain is reportable on the trustees' self-assessment return.

When a trust asset is appointed to a beneficiary there are CGT implications, as the trustees are deemed to dispose of the asset at market value (*s 71*). This could arise:

- from a discretionary distribution, under either the terms of the trust deed or under *TA 1925, s 32*. The beneficiary is deemed to have acquired the asset on the date of the appointment with a base cost equal to its market value;

- on the beneficiary becoming entitled to some or all of the trust capital under the terms of the trust, eg a life tenant may be entitled to the income arising from an asset until a specific age but on attaining that age the capital asset passes to the reversionary beneficiary, (the remainderman). Again, the beneficiary is deemed to have acquired the asset on the date of the appointment with a base cost equal to its market value;

- on the death of a beneficiary with an interest in possession in a trust that does not fall into the relevant property regime for IHT purposes. This is referred to as a 'qualifying interest in possession'. The trustees are deemed to have disposed of the entire trust capital at its market value on the date of death and immediately acquired it, but no chargeable gain accrues *(ss 72(1)(b)* and *73(1)(a))*. This rule applies if the capital passes to a remainderman or if another person receives an interest in possession. However, full exemption will not be available if a capital gain was deferred when the asset was originally put in to the trust *(s 74(1))*. In this instance, an amount equal to the gain held over will become chargeable;

- on the appointment of a 'divisible asset' or a full share of an 'indivisible asset' out of a mixed trust. A divisible asset is one that can be divided into tranches, for example shares. An indivisible asset is one that that cannot be divided, for example a property. Therefore, if a mixed trust holds shares and a property on behalf of two beneficiaries equally and one beneficiary reaches the age to become entitled to the trust capital, there will be a deemed disposal by the trustees of 50% of the shares but there will not be a deemed disposal of the property until the other beneficiary reaches the age at which he is entitled to his share *(Crowe v Appleby* [1975] STC 502).

The methodology for calculating CGT for UK trusts is virtually identical to that for UK individuals. However, the annual allowance is different (see **34.7**) and there is only one rate of tax applicable irrespective of the level of taxable income and gains. For 2016/2017 all trusts are subject to CGT at 20% on disposals and deemed disposals, except on residential property where the rate is 28%. (Prior to 2015/2016, the rate was 28% on all assets).

If IHT arises on an appointment from the trust to a beneficiary, the IHT paid is an allowable deduction for the beneficiary for CGT purposes *(s 260(7))*, ie it is added to the beneficiary's base cost of the asset but this cannot create a loss on a disposal of the asset by the beneficiary.

If the trustees make a loss on the sale of an asset, the normal loss rules apply (see **12.7**). In summary, losses must be offset against any gains in the same tax year, even if the effect is to waste the annual exemption. Excess losses are carried forward for use against future capital gains by the trustees (changes of trustees has no impact on the available loss). Capital losses cannot be carried back. A claim must be made for losses: from 2010/11 onwards the claim must be made within four years from the end of the year of realisation; prior to 2010/11 the claim period was five years and ten months. The claim is made by completing the capital gains self-assessment pages.

If a loss is made on a deemed disposal arising from an appointment to a beneficiary, the loss must be offset firstly against any trust gains arising in that tax year before the appointment. These are called 'pre-entitlement gains'. Any loss arising on a deemed disposal must be used in priority to any other trust losses arising in the year up to the date of appointment to determine the amount which can be transferred to the beneficiary. Any excess loss is transferred by the trustees to the beneficiary but that loss can only be used by the beneficiary against any gain arising on a future disposal of that particular asset (*s 71(2)*).

Prior to *6 April 2008*, gains arising in a settlor interested trust were charged on the settlor rather than the trustees. The only remaining CGT provision specific to settlor interested UK trusts is in respect of gift relief (see below). The settlor, or a relative of his, is a connected party to the trustees and therefore any loss arising on a disposal is ring-fenced under *s 18(3)*.

Focus

Remember to claim losses as they occur. Brought forward losses only need to be used to reduce gains down to the annual exemption threshold.

Disposal of an interest in possession

34.5   If a life tenant disposes of his interest in possession any gain is not chargeable to CGT (*s 76*) unless his interest was acquired for money or money's worth or the trust has been not resident in the UK. If the interest was bought for valuable consideration a capital gain would arise. A gain arises on the occasion on which the beneficiary becomes absolutely entitled to the settled property, when he will be treated as disposing of his interest in consideration for the assets to which he becomes absolutely entitled.

Anti-avoidance rules were introduced in *FA 2000* to block elaborate avoidance schemes that relied on *s 76*. Consequently, the exemption does not apply if the trust has ever been non-UK resident (*Sch 4A*).

THE SUB-FUND ELECTION

34.6   There may be situations where it may be desirable to run one trust as more than one fund. For example, a trust may be split between two or more sets of trustees with no trustees in common. This may arise where a will provided a life interest for the testator's widow, followed by trusts for each of the children. The property may be divided between separate funds relating to each child and, particularly if there is discretion over treatment of the capital, each branch of the family may prefer to have its own trustees. Privacy may also be a factor.

Where a single settlement has more than one sub-fund, the gains or losses of those sub-funds form part of the overall CGT computation of the main fund, even when there are separate trustees. However, *FA 2006* introduced the possibility for the trustees of the principal fund to elect to create sub-funds for CGT purposes (*Sch 4ZA*). The election is irrevocable. Thereafter, each sub-fund is treated as a separate settlement for CGT purposes but the annual exemption which would have been given to the principal settlement, but for the election, is divided equally between the principal settlement and the sub-fund settlement(s). Sub-funds can have beneficiaries and trustees in common but one of the conditions to be satisfied when the election is made is that a person cannot be a beneficiary of the sub-fund and the main fund.

The creation of the sub-fund will be a chargeable disposal by the trustees of the main fund at market value. There is no automatic holdover when a sub-fund is created but the usual gift relief claims are available if the conditions are met.

A valid election means that the sub-fund is treated as a separate settlement for all tax purposes with the exception of the annual exempt amount. The provisions for making an election and the consequences of doing so are in *Sch 4ZA*, which is given effect for income tax purposes by *ITA 2007, s 477* and for CGT purposes by *s 69A*. As far as trust law is concerned there remains just one trust.

REDUCING OR DEFERRING CGT

Annual exemption

34.7   The annual exemption for trustees for 2016/2017 is £5,550, – half of that available to an individual (*Sch 1, para 2(2)*). If the trust is for the disabled, the allowance is the same as that for an individual, currently £11,100.

To prevent the settlor setting up a number of trusts and claiming an annual exemption for each, the £5,550 exemption available is divided by the number of UK 'qualifying settlements' settled by the same settlor after 6 June 1978 (*Sch 1, para 2(4)*). The expression 'qualifying settlements' excludes charitable trusts, trusts for registered pension schemes and any overseas trusts (*Sch 1, para 2(7)*) but will cover all other settlements.

Gift holdover reliefs

34.8   Gift relief can be used to defer a gain under certain circumstances, under either *s 165* or *260*. The relief is not automatic; a claim must be made. If the transferor has capital losses to utilise or an annual allowance, these can be utilised in preference. A claim may be available when putting assets into a trust, on appointing an asset from the trust to a beneficiary or on a deemed disposal by the trustees.

A claim can be made under *s 165* if the gift is of business assets, which include:

(a)   assets used in a business (if the claim is made on an asset leaving the trust, the business can be carried on either by the trustee or by a beneficiary with an IIP);

(b)   shares in a personal trading company (minimum 5% voting rights);

(c)   any shares in an unlisted trading company;

(d)   land or buildings qualifying for agricultural property relief for IHT purposes.

The relief available under (b) is restricted if the company holds non-business assets (*Sch 7, para 7*). The amount of relief available is:

$$\text{Gain} \ \times \ \frac{\text{Chargeable business assets}}{\text{Chargeable assets}}$$

The restrictions also apply to a disposal under (c) above but only if the trustees had shares entitling them to 25% of the votes at any time in the 12 months prior to the disposal.

Alternatively a claim under *s 260* can be made if either:

●   the transfers are subject to IHT (even if the rate is nil), which will be the case in most transfers involving trusts after 22 March 2006; or

- the gain arises on a deemed disposal to the beneficiary of a trust which is for a bereaved minor on reaching age 18 (*s 260(2)(da)*) even though no IHT arises.

Holdover relief applies not only to gifts but also to transfers at undervalue.

Focus

It is not necessary for IHT to be payable on the transfer; but the transfer must just be chargeable to IHT. Therefore, if the transfer is covered by the settlor's nil rate band or a relief, such as business property relief, a claim can be made as the transfer is chargeable but the amount of tax is £nil.

However, no gift relief is available under *s 260* if an asset is appointed out of a trust within the first three months of the trust's creation or within three months of an IHT principal charge. This is because there is no transfer of value for IHT purposes and therefore no IHT exit charge on the appointment.

The effect of a claim under either *s 165* or *260* is that no immediate charge to CGT arises. The gain held over reduces the base cost of the asset to the transferee.

There are some restrictions to the availability of both of the gift reliefs for assets transferred on or after 10 December 2003:

- if the trust is settlor interested (*s 169B*); or

- the trust becomes settlor interested within six years after the end of the year of assessment in which the gift was made. This will result in a claw-back of any relief already given (*s 169C*).

The rules for deciding whether a trust is settlor-interested for CGT purposes are in *s 169F*. The rules used for income tax purposes do not apply. A settlor is treated as having an interest in a trust for CGT purposes if any of the following may benefit from the trust:

- a settlor;

- a settlor's spouse or civil partner; or

- an unmarried child/step child under the age of 18 of a settlor.

There is no requirement for the asset transferred to be formally valued if a gift relief claim is to be made which will eliminate the capital gain (*SP 8/92*). HMRC recognises that in practice it can be difficult obtaining values for assets such as land and unquoted shares. Therefore where no chargeable gain will arise, HMRC will simply require details of the assets transferred, the date of the gift and the base cost of the assets, as this information is sufficient to enable them to calculate the trustees' base cost. A valuation will be necessary if the gift is a chargeable transfer to a trust where IHT may be payable. The form to claim the relief can be obtained from the HMRC website (www.gov.uk/government/publications/relief-for-gifts-and-similar-transactions-hs295-self-assessment-helpsheet).

If both *s 165* and *s 260* are potentially available, *s 260* has priority (*s 165(3)(d)*).

In most instances a gift relief claim is made jointly by the donor and the donee (*s 165(1)(b)*) but when the donee is a trust, the claim is made by the transferor only; the consent of the trustees is not required (*s 260(1)(c)*).

A claim under either section must be made within four years after the end of the tax year in which the asset was transferred, ie for a gift in 2016/2017 a gift relief claim must be made by 5 April 2021 (*TMA 1970, s 43*).

It should be noted that a claim for gift relief under *s 260* precludes a later claim to principal private residence relief even if the property is used by a beneficiary as his only or main residence (*s 226A*).

Relief on replacement of business assets

34.9   This is known as 'rollover relief' and allows a trader to defer a CGT liability on the sale of a business asset by reinvesting the proceeds into the purchase of new assets for the business (*ss 151–158* – see **14.15**). The relief is available to trustees provided both the trade and the assets involved are owned by the trustees. The trustees can carry out the trade as sole traders or in partnership and, in the latter case, could be limited partners.

Enterprise Investment Scheme CGT deferral relief

34.10   The exemption from both income tax and CGT available to individuals in respect of Enterprise Investment Scheme (EIS) shares is not available to trustees. Only the deferral of CGT arising on an asset by rolling the gain into a qualifying subscription for EIS shares is available to certain trustees.

The rules for this relief are covered at **14.22**. The trustees to whom the deferral relief is available are:

- those of a discretionary trust where all the beneficiaries are individuals; and

- those of an interest in possession trust where at least one of the beneficiaries is an individual. However, if some of the beneficiaries are not individuals then relief is given in proportion to the interests of the individuals compared to the non-individuals.

The trustees must make both the gain being deferred and the qualifying EIS investment.

Principal private residence relief

34.11   If the trustees own a property and under the terms of the settlement they permit one or more beneficiaries to occupy the property as their only or main residence, then private residence relief is available on a disposal of the property (*s 225*). The case *Sansom & Another (Ridge Settlement Trustees) v Peay* Ch D 1976, 52 TC 1 confirmed availability of the relief to discretionary trusts.

Therefore where a trust property has been occupied by a beneficiary, the following periods of ownership will be exempt periods for the purposes of principal private residence (PPR) relief:

1   the period during which the property was occupied by the beneficiary;

2   the last 18 months of ownership irrespective of residence of the beneficiary (note – the previous period of 36 months no longer applies for any sale of property where contracts were exchanged on or after 6 April 2014 (*s 223*));

3   the 'deemed occupation' periods in *s 223(3)*, ie:

   (a)   periods of absence up to three years,

   (b)   periods of absence during which the beneficiary was abroad by reason of his employment,

   (c)   periods of absence up to four years where the beneficiary was required to work elsewhere.

   These deemed occupation periods can only apply to trust gains where the same beneficiary occupied the trust property both before and after the period of absence.

Where PPR relief is given on a trust gain, lettings relief will also be available in respect of periods during which the property was let to a third party tenant (*s 223 (4)*).

Example 34.1 – Calculating PPR relief

The Moon Family discretionary trust bought an investment property in Manchester for £150,000 in May 1998. The property was unoccupied for a year until May 1999 when the trustees permitted Ben, a beneficiary, to live in the property while he was at university in Manchester.

Ben moved out in May 2002 to take up employment in the south of England. The contract ended in May 2004 and Ben returned to Manchester to live in the trust property. The property had remained empty while Ben worked elsewhere.

Ben lived in the trust property for a further two years until he married and moved out in May 2006. The property was empty until May 2008 at which point another beneficiary, Sam, was permitted to occupy the property. Sam bought his own house in May 2010 and moved out.

The property then remained empty until it was sold in May 2014 for £810,000 (after expenses of disposal).

The gain made by the trustees will qualify for PPR relief as the property had been occupied by a beneficiary as a private residence under the terms of the settlement. We therefore need to determine periods of occupation and periods of absence over the 16 years of ownership:

The following periods qualify for PPR relief		Period (years)
May 1999 – May 2002		3
May 2002 – May 2004	(Note 1)	2
May 2004 – May 2006		2
May 2008 – May 2010	(Note 2)	2
Nov 2012 – May 2014	(Note 3)	1.5
Total		10.5

Notes

1   Ben occupied the property both before and after this two-year period of absence. And it will qualify as 'deemed occupation' under *s 223(3)*, either under the 'three-year rule' (*s 223(3)(a)*) or because Ben was required to work elsewhere (*s 223(3)(c)*).

2   Sam occupied the property and therefore the prior period May 2006 to May 2008 will not qualify under the three-year deemed occupation rule as a different beneficiary occupied the property after the absence.

3   As the property has been a PPR of a beneficiary and the contracts are
        exchanged after 6 April 2014, the last 18 months of ownership will
        qualify as deemed occupation (*s 223(2)(a)*).

The chargeable gain is calculated as follows:

	£
Proceeds	810,000
Less:	
Original cost	150,000
Gain	660,000
Less: PPR relief (660,000 × 10.5/16)	(433,125)
Chargeable gain	226,875

Where it is desirable to nominate which of two properties is the main residence,
a joint PPR election should be made by the trustees and beneficiary.

On any sales from 10 December 2003 onwards PPR relief will not be available
if gift relief under *s 260* has been claimed in respect of the property (*s 226A*).
This could occur in two instances:

(a)   if the settlor's capital gain was subject to a *s 260* gift relief claim and was
        therefore rolled against the trustees' base cost when the property was put
        into trust;

(b)   if the property is appointed to a beneficiary and the trustees obtain *s 260*
        gift relief on the deemed disposal. Therefore, if the beneficiary is likely
        to use the property as his only or main residence it may be preferable not
        to hold over the gain under *s 260*.

Transitional rules are in force where the property went into the trust before
10 December 2003 but is sold by the trustees after that date (*FA 2004,
Sch 22, para 8*): the period prior to 10 December 2003 will qualify for PPR.
This means that the usual relief for the last 18 months (36 months before
6 April 2014) of occupation will not be available on any sales after 9 December
2006 as those months fall in the period that is not eligible for PPR.

Entrepreneurs' relief

34.12   The rules apply in a similar way to a disposal by an individual but for
the relief to be available to the trustees, a beneficiary must have an interest in

possession in the trust. Therefore, entrepreneurs' relief (ER) is not available to wholly discretionary trusts. If the trustees are contemplating a sale, it may be worth appointing an interest in possession to a discretionary beneficiary but the time requirements in respect of share ownership must be borne in mind.

The trustees do not have their own lifetime allowance but they can utilise the allowance of the eligible beneficiary, ie a beneficiary with an interest in possession. Therefore, the beneficiary's lifetime allowance, currently £10 million, is reduced by any ER given to the trustees. Therefore, the claim for relief is a joint one between the trustees and the beneficiary (*s 169M*).

The disposal must be either of:

(a) business assets owned by the trustees but used in a business carried on by the beneficiary (either alone or in partnership). The business must have been carried on by the beneficiary for a period of 12 months ending within three years before the disposal and the beneficiary must have ceased to carry it on either at the time of the disposal or within the three years before; or

(b) shares in a qualifying company. The qualifying company must be:

- the beneficiary's personal company, ie he owns a minimum of 5% of the ordinary voting share capital;

- it must be a trading company or the holding company of a trading group;

- the beneficiary must be an employee or an officer of the company; and

these conditions must have applied for a 12-month period ending not more than three years prior to sale – the trustees have no minimum shareholding requirement.

Where a trust has more than one beneficiary with an entitlement to income, the gains eligible for entrepreneurs' relief are apportioned. The apportionment is by reference to the qualifying beneficiary's proportional entitlement to the trust income.

Focus

The government is concerned that the attractiveness of the lower rates of CGT encourages individuals to structure their affairs to benefit from lower tax rates and measures are being introduced in the *Finance Act 2016* to address this.

Example 34.2 – Trust gains and ER

Sarah Ross created a trust in 1990 which her twin sons, Ben and Sam, each has a right to 50% of the net trust income. Ben has worked for Able Ltd, an unlisted trading company, since leaving university in 2010. He holds 8.5% of the share capital. Sam works full time as a GP.

In 2016/2017, the trustees made the following capital disposals:

- an investment property, making a gain of £100,000;

- quoted shares, making a loss of £25,000;

- their 2.5% holding of shares in Able Ltd, making a gain of £125,000.

The CGT payable by the trustees for 2016/2017 is as follows:

	ER gains	Non-ER gains
	£	£
Investment property		100,000
Able Ltd shares (Note 1)	62,500	62,500
Less: loss on quoted shares (Note 2)		(25,000)
Chargeable gains	62,500	137,500
Less: annual exemption (Note 3)		(5,550)
Taxable gains	62,500	131,950
CGT @ 10%/20%	6,250	26,390

Total CGT payable £32,640

Notes

1   The trustees are eligible for ER in respect of part of their disposal of shares in Able Ltd because:

- Ben, a beneficiary with an interest in possession, has 5% or more of the shares in Able Ltd. The fact that the trustees have less than 5% of the shares is irrelevant;

- Ben works for the company;

- the company is trading; and

- Ben has held 5% of the shares;

- the last three conditions were satisfied for 12 months prior to the disposal;

- Ben will need to consent to the trustees' ER claim as it is his lifetime ceiling which is being utilised.

As Ben only has an interest in possession in 50% of the trust fund, only 50% of the trustees' gain on the disposal of the Able Ltd shares will be eligible for ER. Sam does not work for Able Ltd and does not have 5% or more of the shares and therefore is not eligible for ER.

2   The loss can be allocated against gains chargeable at the highest rate of tax.

3   It is assumed Sarah Ross has formed only the one trust. The AE can be allocated against the gains chargeable to the highest rate of tax.

ADDITIONS TO CAPITAL

34.13   HMRC need to keep a track of funds within a settlement and there is space on the self-assessment form (Question 12) to provide details of assets that have been gifted during the year. Sales of trust assets by the trustees are not relevant to this question.

It is possible to have more than one person settling assets into the same trust and it may be seen as a cheaper option than setting up and administering several trusts. However, this can lead to complications. For example, anti-avoidance rules for income tax purposes for settlor interested trusts (see **33.14**) and the reservation of benefit rules for IHT (see **29.6**), both require the trustees to identify which property was contributed by each settlor. Even with detailed record keeping, this becomes increasingly difficult with the passage of time as assets are sold and re-invested.

For IHT purposes, it is possible for part of a trust to fall within the relevant property regime and part not to, for instance if assets are added to a pre-22 March 2006 trust after that date.

From a CGT point of view, two trusts set up by two different individuals will have access to two annual exemptions (subject to the anti-fragmentation rules; see **34.7**), whereas only one annual exemption will apply to a single trust with one or more settlors.

Focus

Beware of the complications that can arise from contributing into a trust set up by someone else.

35

Inheritance tax and trusts

SIGNPOSTS

- **Scope** – The domicile of the settlor is a key factor for IHT purposes. The location of trust assets (ie UK or offshore) is also important in terms of establishing the scope of any IHT charge in respect of trust assets, subject to certain exceptions (see **35.1–35.2**).

- **Transfers into trust** – Most transfers into trust are (since 22 March 2006) chargeable lifetime transfers for IHT purposes (see **35.3**).

- **Relevant property trusts** – It is essential to establish whether a trust falls into the 'relevant property' regime as it will then be subject to the ten-year charges and exit charges applicable to such trusts (see **35.5–35.16**).

- **Simplifying relevant property trusts** – *Finance (No 2) Act 2015* introduced changes to simplify the tax computations of these trusts, but the changes reduce the advantages of pilot trusts as a planning tool (see **35.17**).

- **Interest in possession trusts** – The treatment varies for trusts created before 22 March 2006 and after that date. Transitional rules existed between 22 March 2006 and 5 April 2008 (see **35.18–35.20**).

- **Settlor-interested trusts** – The 'gift with reservation' (GWR) rules and the pre-owned assets income tax charge (POAT) must be considered if the settlor is capable of benefiting from the trust (see **35.21**).

- **Other trusts** – There are still some tax favoured trusts (eg 'bereaved minors' trusts – see **35.9** and trusts for disabled persons **35.11**) which are available for particular groups of beneficiary.

- **Other matters** – Compliance issues must be considered in relation to trusts, together with the possible reliefs, etc (see **35.22–35.23**).

All statutory references in this chapter are to IHTA 1984, unless otherwise stated.

INTRODUCTION

35.1   Prior to 22 March 2006, the IHT treatment of trusts turned on whether or not the trust was discretionary. Transfers to discretionary trusts were chargeable lifetime transfers (see **29.3**) and the trust property was subject to IHT ten-yearly charges (see **35.13**) and exit charges (see **35.15**). In contrast, transfers into interest in possession trusts and accumulation and maintenance trusts were usually potentially exempt transfers (see **29.2**) and did not incur ten-yearly charges or exit charges.

Finance Act 2006 introduced substantial changes to the taxation of trusts for IHT purposes. From 22 March 2006 most transfers into a trust will be chargeable lifetime transfers. The trustees must establish whether the trust is a 'relevant property trust' (see **35.5**) or a 'qualifying interest in possession trust'. Relevant property trusts are not comprised in the estate of the settlor or the beneficiary and are subject to exit and ten-year charges (previously only applicable to discretionary trusts). In contrast, qualifying interest in possession trusts are comprised in the estate of the beneficiary entitled to the income and are not subject to exit or ten-year charges.

Focus

It is important to understand the history of a trust and the law to determine the trust's current tax position. Lack of space prevents the history of the changes to trust law being fully explored in this work.

THE SCOPE OF THE IHT CHARGE

35.2

Focus

The scope of IHT is defined on the basis of domicile, and residence is not relevant. The domicile status of the trust follows that of the settlor when he set up the trust, ie if a non-UK domiciled individual sets up a trust, the trust is also treated as not UK domiciled. Neither the residence of the trust nor the residence or domicile of the beneficiaries is relevant for determining whether an IHT principal or exit charge arises. The trust will continue to be treated as non-UK domiciled even if the settlor later becomes domiciled in the UK, whether under general law or by being deemed domiciled under the 17-year residence rule (15 years from 6 April 2017 – see **27.3**).

Generally, subject to any overriding double tax treaty provisions, IHT will apply to the world-wide assets of a trust domiciled in the UK and the UK-situated assets of a non-UK domiciled trust.

If a non-domiciled trust holds foreign assets, or a holding in FOTRA ('free of tax to residents abroad') government securities, those assets are 'excluded property' and are not subject to ten-yearly charges and transfers of such assets will not give rise to an IHT exit charge (*ss 6, 48*). If a non-domiciled trust has a mixture of UK and foreign assets, the UK assets will be subject to ten-yearly and exit charges. However, in such cases it is possible to export assets, eg switch cash from a UK bank to an offshore bank account, just prior to an IHT charge arising either on a ten-year anniversary or on a distribution as this will avoid an IHT liability arising.

Example 35.1 – Non-UK domiciled individual and offshore trust

Mr Cook is resident in the UK but domiciled in Belize. He has lived in the UK since March 1991. In June 2002 he settled the following assets on to a discretionary trust for the benefit of his wider family, excluding himself:

	£
House in Belize	400,000
Cash in Belizean dollars (deposited into a Cayman Islands bank)	300,000
UK quoted shares	240,000
Total	940,000

In September 2010, the trustees made a capital distribution of BZ$100,000 (£50,000 sterling equivalent) to a UK beneficiary.

In June 2012, the trust assets were valued as follows:

	£
House in Belize	600,000
Cash in Belizean dollars (deposited into a Cayman Islands bank)	400,000
UK quoted shares	300,000
Total	1,300,000

The IHT implications of the above arrangements are as follows:

- In June 2002 when he set up the trust, Mr Cook was non-UK domiciled so would only have been liable to IHT in respect of transfers of UK assets (his foreign assets were excluded property). Therefore the chargeable transfer in 2002 was £240,000 being the UK shares only. This would have been covered by the nil rate band for 2002/03 leaving no tax payable.

- The trust is treated as if it was not UK domiciled. The fact that Mr Cook will have become deemed domiciled in 2007/08 as he had been resident in the UK for 17 years will not change the domicile status of the trust.

- The distribution of Belizean dollars to the UK beneficiary in September 2010 will not give rise to an exit charge as the Belizean bank account is excluded property. The fact that it is paid to a UK beneficiary is irrelevant.

- There will be a principal charge in 2012. The initial value of the non-relevant (overseas) property will be taken into account in calculating the tax rate to use but IHT will be charged on the UK assets only, being the UK quoted shares.

- There may be income tax and capital gains tax implications to consider.

Focus

The government has announce that from 6 April 2017 the law will be amended so that the value of residential property situated in the UK will be subject to IHT even if it is owned through a foreign company or other opaque overseas entity. This will reduce the scope for mitigating IHT on these assets.

The trustees of an offshore trust will be subject to IHT principal and exit charges, if either the settlor was UK domiciled or any of the assets are situated in the UK.

If the settlor of a trust created while he was not domiciled in the UK adds property to it after he acquires UK domicile (actual or deemed), the additional property is treated as if it was in a separate settlement. The additional property will be fully within the IHT regime, but the original assets are only chargeable if they are situated in the UK. This is not recommended as there may be problems determining which 'notional' trust particular assets belong to.

A reversionary interest is also 'excluded property' unless it was acquired for consideration or it arises in a settlor interested trust (*s 48*). A 'reversionary interest' is a future or contingent interest in trust property, for example the interest the remainderman will take when a qualifying interest in possession expires. Provided that the interest was not acquired for consideration, if the person with the reversionary interest dies before he becomes entitled to that interest, no part of the trust is included in his estate. Similarly, if he gives away his reversionary interest there is no transfer of value for IHT purposes.

HMRC's IHT manual (IHTM14396) makes it clear that the excluded property rules take precedence over the reservation of benefit regime (see **29.6**), so that foreign property in a trust established by an individual, who is not domiciled in the UK at the time of the gift, is not charged to IHT under the gift with reservation of benefit rules.

TRANSFERS INTO TRUST

35.3

	Before 22 March 2006	After 22 March 2006
Lifetime transfers		
Interest in possession trust	PET	CLT
A&M trust	PET	CLT
Discretionary trust	CLT	CLT

Before 22 March 2006, only transfers into discretionary trusts were immediately chargeable lifetime transfers (CLTs) to IHT and transfers into interest in possession (IIP) trusts and accumulation and maintenance (A&M) trusts were potentially exempt transfers (PETs). As from 22 March 2006, the creation of any lifetime non-charitable trust, other than a qualifying trust for a disabled person, is chargeable to IHT at half the death rates, currently 20%. Such trusts are within the 'relevant property' regime.

When calculating the IHT due on a lifetime transfer into a relevant property trust, the loss to the settlor's estate as a result of the transfer must be calculated. When carrying out this calculation, account needs to be taken of related property, eg similar assets held by the settlor's spouse.

If the settlor dies within seven years, there may be an additional tax re-calculation.

If two trusts are set up on the same day by the same settlor, they are called 'related settlements' (*s 62*), unless:

- either of the trusts is for charitable purposes; or

- the settlor's spouse has an immediate post-death interest in either of the settlements (*s 80*).

> **Focus**
>
> The effect of a related settlement is to eat into the nil rate band available when calculating the principal charge or the exit charge. Therefore, related settlements can increase the IHT payable on either of these events and should, if possible, be avoided during a settlor's lifetime. Trusts can be set up on consecutive days and will not fall within the definition of related settlements. However, where, on or after 10 December 2014, property is added to two or more settlements on the same day by the same transferor, the trusts will be aggregated to calculate the tax charges (*F(No 2)A 2015, Sch 1*) (see **35.17**).

Pilot trusts were used for tax planning to enable a settlor to avoid the related trust rules and enable access to multiple nil rate bands with a view to minimising exit and principal charges. Several pilot trusts would be set up with a nominal amount of cash (typically a £10 note attached to each trust deed). The pilot trusts would be set up during the settlor's lifetime and property could then either be added on his death or during his lifetime. Each trust would have had its own nil rate band and the notional transfer immediately after creation would only include the property added to that trust. The pilot trust route will no longer be effective as a result of the changes.

If a person sets up an interest in possession trust (IIP) for his spouse on death, this will not be treated as related to any other trusts set up under his will (*s 80*). If there are any continuing trusts after the IIP ends, such trusts are deemed to commence when that interest ends rather than on the settlor's death.

ACCUMULATION AND MAINTENANCE TRUSTS

35.4   Prior to 22 March 2006, accumulation and maintenance (A&M) trusts were a special form of settlement in which no interest in possession subsists and were the normal means by which property was settled on young children. Provided that the trust fell with the terms laid down, it was favourably treated (see 32.11)

RELEVANT PROPERTY TRUSTS AND NON-RELEVANT PROPERTY TRUSTS

35.5   Prior to 22 March 2006, where an interest in possession existed over settled property, that property was treated for IHT purposes as belonging to the person entitled to that interest.

Settled property without such an interest was not treated as part of any individual's estate. Such property is referred to as 'relevant property' and to prevent it escaping IHT a special ten-year charge (the 'principal charge') and exit charges ('proportionate' charges) are applied to relevant property. These charges are discussed below. The rest of this section sets out what property is outside the relevant property regime.

Focus

Changes introduced by *FA 2006* meant that from 22 March 2006 many more settlements are now treated as falling in the relevant property regime and therefore subject to the IHT rules that previously applied only to discretionary trusts.

However, there are still some trusts that fall outside this regime, referred to here as 'non-relevant property trusts' but they can also be called 'qualifying interest in possession trusts'. These include the following:

- interest in possession with 'immediate post-death interests' (*s 49A*);

- disabled person's interests (*s 89B*);

- transitional serial interests (*ss 49B, 49C, 49D, 49E*); and

- bereaved minors trusts (*ss 71A–71C*).

Immediate post-death interests (IPDI)

35.6   These arise where an individual becomes beneficially entitled to an IIP under a will or intestacy, unless the settled property falls within the definition of a trust for bereaved minors (s *71A*) or disabled person's interests.

Typically, this type of trust will arise if the deceased wants his spouse to receive income from or use the assets in his estate, but wishes to ensure that the assets pass to the next generation. The remaindermen in this instance would usually be the children or grandchildren.

Disabled person's interests (DPI)

35.7   There are four types of trust for disabled people which attract special treatment (see **35.11**).

Transitional serial interests (TSI)

35.8　　Once an IIP comes to an end after 21 March 2006, even if the trust continues, the *FA 2006* rules applying to trusts created after 21 March 2006 will apply unless a 'transitional serial interest' comes into effect between 22 March 2006 and 5 October 2008.

Provided the settled property does not fall within *s 71A* (trusts for bereaved minors) and the interest is not a disabled person's interest, there are three sets of circumstances where such an interest may arise:

●　Where there was an IIP in a trust created before 22 March 2006 and that IIP ceases before 6 October 2008 and is immediately followed by another IIP. The second IIP is treated as a qualifying IIP: therefore the trust assets are in the estate of the second beneficiary rather than being treated as relevant property (*s 49C*).

●　Where the life tenant of an IIP in a trust created before 22 March 2006 dies after 5 October 2008 and a succeeding IIP is taken by the spouse/ civil partner. The trust assets are treated as a qualifying IIP in the estate of the succeeding spouse (*s 49D*).

●　Where a person is beneficially entitled to an IIP in a trust created before 22 March 2006 and, on their becoming entitled to the interest, the settled property consisted of, or included, rights under a contract of life insurance (*s 49E*). Until 6 October 2008, the normal rules for TSI apply but thereafter, provided that successive IIPs arise on the death of each of the previous IIP beneficiaries, each interest is a TSI and the beneficiary will be treated as the absolute owner and it will form part of their estate for IHT purposes (*s 49(1)*). This treatment will continue until the settlement ceases to comprise rights under the pre-22 March 2006 life insurance contract.

The legislation (*s 49(1)*) attaches all of the value to the current interest in possession, and any interests in the future, called 'reversionary interests', are usually treated as excluded from an individual's estate on death, by virtue of *s 48*.

Example 35.2 – Interests in possession: IHT position

Sam is the life tenant of an IIP trust created by his father in 1998. The terms of the trust are that Sam will be entitled to income for life with a successive life interest to his brother, Ben, on his death. On Ben's death the trust assets pass to Ben's son, Isaac, as remainderman.

Sam died in May 2011.

The IHT implications are as follows:

- The initial gift to the trust by Sam's father in 1998 was a PET.

- As this is a pre-2006 IIP trust, the trust is a qualifying IIP.

- On Sam's death in 2011, the trust assets form part of his estate. The tax attributable to those assets is paid by the trustees.

- Ben has a successive life interest. This is not an immediate post-death interest under *s 49A* as he did not become entitled to an IIP on the death of the settlor.

- Ben's interest is not a TSI (under *s 49C*) as Sam's IIP did not cease before 6 October 2008. Therefore, Ben does not have a qualifying IIP. Instead, the IIP trust with Ben as life tenant will be treated as a relevant property trust and will be subject to exit and principal charges.

- Isaac's interest as remainderman is an excluded asset and the interest forms no part of his estate whilst any of the life tenants are still alive.

The answer would be different if Ben had been Sam's civil partner rather than his brother. In this case, the TSI rules under *s 49D* would apply and Ben's IIP would be treated as qualifying. Therefore on Ben's death, the trust assets would form part of his estate and there would be no exit or principal charges.

If the asset originally put into trust had been a life insurance contract on Isaac's life, the TSI rules (under *s 49E*) would apply and Ben's IIP would be treated as qualifying.

Bereaved minor's trust

35.9 These trusts were introduced by *FA 2006* to replace A&M trusts, but are far more restrictive in their application. The provisions governing them are found in *IHTA 1984, ss 71A–71D* (see **32.12**).

Bereaved minors trusts (BMTs) can only arise on the death of a parent and the minor must become entitled to the trust property at age 18. For income tax and CGT purposes, BMTs are taxed like discretionary trusts. For IHT purposes, they are not subject to exit charges or ten-year anniversary charges, provided certain conditions are complied with (*IHTA 1984, ss 71A, 71B*).

Age 18 to 25 trusts

35.10 Age 18 to 25 trusts were introduced in response to the protests about the abolition of the benefits available to A&M settlements, but they are more restrictive (see **32.13**).

Age 18 to 25 trusts can only arise on the death of a parent or by converting an existing A&M trust before 6 April 2008. The rules for creating an 18 to 25 trust on the death of a parent are slightly more restrictive than for BMTs as they can only arise under the will of the deceased parent, under the criminal injuries compensation scheme or under the victims of overseas terrorism compensation scheme (BMTs can arise under any of these, plus they can arise as statutory trusts following intestacy).

The beneficiary must become absolutely entitled to all the trust property by the age of 25 and up until then the settled property must be applied for his benefit and income arising must be applied for his benefit or accumulated.

Trusts for disabled persons

35.11   These trusts exist for the benefit of a disabled person and, whilst traditionally discretionary, are treated for IHT purposes as an IIP even though there might be a power to accumulate income provided the trust ensures that not less than half of the fund that is applied during the beneficiary's lifetime is applied for his benefit (*IHTA 1984, s 89*).

A qualifying disabled trust will not fall in to the relevant property regime provided one of four sets of conditions are satisfied at the outset; it is not sufficient that they come to be satisfied at a later stage (see **32.14**).

CHARGEABLE EVENTS FOR RELEVANT PROPERTY TRUSTS

35.12   There are two types of IHT charge for a trust falling into the relevant property regime:

- the ten-year charge, also known as the 'principal charge'; and

- the exit charge.

The trustees are required to report chargeable events on Form IHT100.

The ten-year ('principal') charge

35.13   The details here are for trusts set up from April 1974. The rules for calculating the principal charge are different for older trusts.

The principal charge first arises on the tenth anniversary of the date the settlement began (*s 61*) and every ten years thereafter as long as the trust continues to hold relevant property. If the trust was set up with a small initial amount, say £10, and the main trust assets were added later, it is the date on which the initial amount was settled that fixes the future ten-year anniversary dates (*s 60*). If a trust arises from a will or a deed of variation of a will, it is the date of death that dictates the commencement of the settlement. Even if a trust is not initially within the relevant property regime but later falls within it, the date that the trust was originally set up fixes the date of the ten-year anniversary rather than the date the trust came within the regime (*s 60*).

Where a trust is established under pension arrangements, the trust starts when the member joins the scheme which may be many years before any relevant property is held on trust. A similar issue arises when an A&M settlement falls into the relevant property regime on 6 April 2008 – a ten-year anniversary might arise shortly after that date.

Where property has not been in the relevant property regime for ten years at the date of charge, the charge is adjusted to reflect the number of quarters during which the regime applies.

If the trustees distribute all of the trust assets before the first ten-year anniversary, the trust will not suffer a principal charge but an exit charge may arise on the distribution.

When calculating the principal charge, the trustees are deemed to have made a transfer of value equal to the value of the trust property at the ten-year anniversary date. Therefore, the value of the property can be reduced by agricultural property relief (see **28.21**) or business property relief (see **28.15**), as appropriate. Contingent CGT liabilities are not valid deductions but liabilities secured on the trust property are (subject to the observations at **30.3**). The 'relevant property' has always included the capital and accumulated income of the trust, but from 6 April 2014 also includes any income that has remained undistributed for more than five years at the date of the charge (*s 64(1A)*).

The principal charge is calculated as follows (*s 66*):

Value of the relevant property at ten-year anniversary × Actual rate of tax

The 'actual rate of tax' is calculated by determining the 'effective rate of tax' and multiplying this by 30% (*s 66(1)*). Statute does not address the number of decimal places that should be used when calculating the effective and actual rates of tax, but rounding to three decimal places is accepted by HMRC.

The 'effective rate' is the rate of IHT which would be charged on a notional transfer (*s 66*). To calculate the effective rate, the IHT history of the settlor of the trust is used. It is assumed that the settlor had made a transfer of value equal to the relevant property in the trust at the ten-year anniversary. The initial value of any related settlements (as defined at **35.3**) is added to this notional transfer.

The initial value is the value at the date that the related trust was created, not the value at the date the principal charge arises.

Trusts created prior to 27 March 1974 were subject to estate duty rather than IHT. As such, the concept of cumulation was not applicable. The main difference in determining the principal charge will therefore be that chargeable transfers in the seven years prior to setting up the trust are not taken into account.

To calculate the notional tax, the IHT nil rate band at the date of the ten-year charge is used. Therefore for ten-year charges falling into 2016/17, the nil rate band used is £325,000. This nil rate band is reduced by:

- the settlor's cumulative chargeable transfers in the seven years prior to the creation of the trust, not the transfers made by the settlor in the seven years prior to the ten-year charge (*s 66(5)*). The position is different if the settlor adds property to the trust after it is formed – see below; and

- any distributions made by the trustees in the ten years immediately before the current anniversary. Therefore, any exit charges in the previous ten years of the trust will affect the principal charge.

The remaining nil rate band is used to calculate the tax on the notional transfer.

The following example acts as a pro forma for calculating the charge.

Example 35.3 – Calculating the ten-year charge

On 7 August 2001, Ben created a discretionary trust with £600,000 in cash. On the same day he created another discretionary trust with £100,000. He paid the IHT on the creation of the trusts. His chargeable transfers in the seven years prior to setting up the trust were £120,000.

On 15 December 2005, the trustees distributed £85,000 to a beneficiary. This gave rise to an IHT exit charge, which the beneficiary paid the tax on.

On 7 August 2011, the relevant property in the trust was worth £900,000. The principal charge that arises on the first ten-year anniversary is:

	£	£
Current value of relevant property at ten-year anniversary (net of liabilities and APR/BPR; see **28.15/28.21**) X1		900,000

Any property in the settlement which is not relevant property, valued at the date it was put into the settlement (this reflects any part of the fund that might be an interest in possession or have A&M powers, for example) – not applicable to events after 18/11/2015, see **35.17**	X2		0
Initial value of any related trust(s)	Y		100,000
	Z		1,000,000
Nil rate band at date of principal charge	NRB	(325,000)	
Less: settlor's chargeable transfers in seven years before creating the trust	CT	120,000	
Less: distributions by the trustees in last ten years (including IHT paid by trustees)	D	85,000	
Remaining nil rate band	RNRB		(120,000)
Taxable value	T		880,000
Notional tax (NT) thereon at 20%	T × 20%		176,000
Effective rate (ER) [(176,000/1,000,000) × 100]	NT/Z × 100%		17.600%
Actual tax rate (AR) (17.6% × 30%)	ER ×		5.280%
Principal charge (PC) (900,000 × 5.28%)	X1 × AR		£47,520

The principal charge is based on the value of relevant property in the trust at the anniversary date, and that value will include property added to the trust during the previous ten years. To allow for this it is necessary to calculate more than one 'actual tax rate': one as above, which is applicable to the current value of the original property and one for each addition, which is applied to the current value of that added property (*s 66(2)*). To calculate the latter the following is used:

$$\text{ER\%} \times 30\% \times \frac{(40 - \text{complete number of quarters between creation and addition})}{40}$$

This relates to property such as:

- added funds;

- accumulations of income;

- the end of an interest in possession; and

- trusts affected by the 2006 changes (eg A&M trusts) which were not modified to comply with the narrower definitions before 6 April 2008.

If property is added by a different settlor the trust is treated as two different settlements for tax purposes.

Additions by the same settlor may impact on the amount used as the settlor's total cumulative chargeable transfers in the calculation. Under normal circumstances the cumulative total includes the settlor's chargeable transfers in the seven years before the creation of the trust (CT in **Example 35.3**). However, where additions have been made, the settlor's chargeable transfers in the seven years before the addition to the trust are used instead of those in the seven years before the creation of the trust, if this creates a larger deduction. When calculating the chargeable transfers in the seven years before the addition, the transfers on the creation of the trust and on any related trusts are ignored (*s 67*).

The impact of this calculation should be considered before a settlor decides to add property to a trust. It may be preferable to set up a new trust, particularly if the date of a principal charge is approaching.

Where the settlor has made additions after 9 December 2014 to two or more settlements on the same day, the value of the property in the other settlements is also brought into account (see *ss 62A* and *62B*).

The exit (proportionate) charge

35.14   An exit charge arises when property in the trust ceases to be relevant property (*s 65*). The most common occurrence will be when the trustees make a capital distribution of relevant property to a beneficiary and the value of the trust property goes down. The amount of property leaving the trust is not necessarily the same as the value of the property being appointed to the beneficiary as the 'loss to the transferor' principle is used to calculate the reduction in value of the remaining trust property (*s 65(2)*).

There is no exit charge when the trustees pay costs or expenses attributable to the property (*s 65(5)(a)*) or if the distribution is of income (*s 65(5)(b)*).

The calculation depends on whether the exit takes place before or after the first principal charge.

Exit before the first principal charge

35.15   To calculate an exit charge before the first principal charge has occurred, both an effective rate of tax and an actual rate of tax must be calculated (*s 68*). The method is similar to when calculating the principal charge, in that the rate is affected by the settlor's cumulative chargeable transfers in the seven years before the trust was created and by any related trusts set up on the same day. However, there are a number of differences in the calculation:

- The initial value of both relevant property and non-relevant property when it was put into the trust is used rather than the values at the date of exit. The value of any property added to the trust by the same settlor after it was initially set up is included in the calculation. The initial values will be after any IHT paid by the trustees on the transfer(s) into the trust. (see **35.17** re changes)

- The initial value to the trust may be different from the transfer of value by the settlor for IHT purposes. For example, related property held by the settlor or his spouse is not relevant. APR or BPR will not be available (see **28.15, 28.21**), as even if the settlor was eligible for the relief on the transfer into the trust; the trustees cannot qualify until they have held the property for at least two years. If the exit charge arises after the trustees have held eligible assets for the qualifying period, the property distributed may qualify for APR or BPR which will reduce the transfer of value on which tax is charged (*ss 106, 117*).

- The nil rate band at the date of exit is used.

- Any previous distributions are ignored when determining how much of the nil rate band remains.

- The actual rate of tax depends on the number of complete quarters that have elapsed between the creation of the trust and the date of the exit charge (partial quarters are ignored). This means that the actual tax rate increases throughout the ten-year period.

The following example acts as a pro-forma for calculating the effective rate, the actual rate and the exit charge prior to the first ten-year anniversary. See **35.17** regarding changes to this calculation.

Example 35.4 – Calculation of exit charge

Sam set up a relevant property trust on 5 September 2004 by settling cash of £500,000 on discretionary trust. Sam paid the IHT on the transfer of the cash. He had made no other lifetime transfers. On the same day, Sam settled £120,000 in cash into an accumulation and maintenance trust for his grandchildren.

On 12 October 2011, the trustees of the discretionary trust appointed £80,000 in cash to a beneficiary, who agrees to pay the IHT liability.

As the asset concerned is cash, the reduction in value to the trust and the amount distributed are the same. There are 28 complete quarters between 5 September 2004 and 12 October 2011. The exit charge is calculated as follows:

		£	£
Initial value of relevant property when the trust was set up (net of liabilities and IHT paid by the trustees on the settlement)	X1		500,000
Initial value of non-relevant property	X2		0
Initial value of relevant property put into the trust since it was set up	X3		0
Initial value of any related trust(s)*	Y		120,000
Notional transfer	Z		620,000
Nil rate band at date of exit	NRB	(325,000)	
Less: settlor's chargeable transfers in seven years before creating the trust	CT	0	
Remaining nil rate band	RNRB		(325,000)
Taxable value	T		295,000
Notional tax (NT) thereon at 20%	T × 20%		59,000
Effective rate (ER) (59,000/620,000 × 100%)	NT/Z × 100%		9.516%
Complete quarters (n) – see below			28
Actual tax rate (AR) (9.516% × 30% × 28/40)	ER × 30 × n/40		1.998%
Distribution	D		80,000
Exit charge (80,000 × 1.998%)	D × AR		1,598

* If the changes made in *Finance (No 2) Act 2015* had been in force this would have been omitted as the assets in an A&M settlement would not have been relevant property at 5/09/04 (see **35.17**).

Note – The value of n depends on whether the asset leaving the trust was part of the original trust property or whether it is an addition after commencement. If it is original trust property n = the number of complete quarters between the date of commencement of the trust and date of exit. If it is a subsequent addition n as previously calculated is reduced by the number of complete quarters between the creation of the trust and the date the property was added.

If the addition to a trust cannot be separately identified from the original trust property because the property is the same, for example cash, the appointment is apportioned between the original and the added property on a just and reasonable basis, eg on a distribution from a trust set up with £400,000 cash to which £100,000 was added at a later date by the same settlor, 1/5 of the distribution will be treated as if it came from the added property and 4/5 from the original trust property.

Primary responsibility for paying the tax on an exit rests with the trustees, but they can delegate the responsibility to the beneficiary if they wish. If the trustees pay the tax on the exit, the actual tax rate must be grossed up. This recognises the fact that the loss to the trust is both the distribution and the IHT payable thereon.

To gross up use $\dfrac{AR\%}{100 - AR\%} \times 100$

If the trustees had paid the tax, the exit charge would have been £1,631, being $80,000 \times 2.039\%$ [$(1.998/(100 - 1.998)) \times 100\%$].

Exit after the first principal charge

35.16   To calculate tax on an exit after the first principal charge has occurred, an effective rate is calculated which is then turned into an actual rate that is used to calculate the IHT due, but in this instance the effective rate used is that which was in force at the date of the preceding principal charge (*s 69*). However, this effective rate must be adjusted if the IHT nil band has changed between the date of the principal charge and the date of the exit (*s 69(1)*).

Example 35.5 – Calculation of exit charge after the first ten-year charge

In the example of Ben (see **Example 35.3**), he set up a discretionary trust in August 2001 and IHT payable by the trustees on the principal charge on 7 August 2011 was calculated.

Let us assume that a distribution is made by the trustees in December 2016, when the nil rate band is £325,000.

On 21 December 2016, the trustees made a distribution of £120,000 to a beneficiary such that an exit charge will arise. The IHT on this exit is calculated as follows:

	£	£
Value of relevant property at last ten-year anniversary on 7 August 2011		900,000
Historic value of non-relevant property		0
Initial value of any related trust(s)		100,000
		1,000,000
Nil rate band at time of distribution	(325,000)	
Less: settlor's chargeable transfers in seven years before creating the trust	120,000	
Less: distributions by the trustees in last ten years	85,000	
Remaining nil rate band		(120,000)
Taxable value		880,000
Notional tax thereon at 20% (being the rate in force at 7 August 2011)		176,000
Effective rate [(176,000/1,000,000) × 100]		17.600%

As it is an exit charge that is being calculated, the revised effective rate at 7 August 2011 must not only be multiplied by 30% but also by n/40 where 'n' is the number of full quarters between the date of the last principal charge and the date of exit. In this case it is 21 quarters.

Actual tax rate (17.6% × 30% × 21/40)	2.770%
Exit charge (120,000 × 2.770%)	£3,326

It is necessary to adapt the calculation of the exit charge if the trust assets were not relevant property at the previous anniversary. Instead of using the value of the relevant property at the date of the last principal charge, the value when it became relevant property is used (*s 69(3)*). Again the quarters used in the calculation are reduced to reflect the period that the assets were not relevant property.

Further guidance and examples are available in the HMRC IHT manual at www.hmrc.gov.uk/manuals/ihtmanual/IHTM42000.htm.

Finance (No 2) Act 2015 **changes**

35.17   Following various consultations, the government has acted to simplify the calculation of the principal and exit charges. The main changes are:

- to leave non-relevant property out of the calculations;

- to take into account additions to other settlements where property is added to several settlements on the same day by the same settlor (*ss 62A, 62B, 62C, 66*).

The first change will simplify the calculations, but the other changes are likely to eliminate the benefit of pilot trusts (see **35.3**). The changes apply to chargeable events on or after 18 November 2015, but apply where same day additions were made on or after 10 December 2014.

The problem for trustees will be to identify and record additions to other settlements where they may not be the trustees.

INTEREST IN POSSESSION TRUSTS

35.18   Where a person is entitled to a trust's income, he is said to have an interest in possession (IIP) in the property of the trust (see **32.9**). In many cases the interest is for life and the person entitled to the interest is known as the life tenant. The person with that interest is referred to as the life tenant in the rest of this text, even where his interest is for a shorter duration.

Before 22 March 2006

35.19   Gifts into IIP trusts created during the lifetime of the settlor before March 2006 were usually potentially exempt transfers (PETs) (see **29.2**) and IHT was only chargeable if the settlor died within seven years of setting up the trust (*s 3A(1)*). There were a couple of exceptions to this rule:

- where the life tenant was the spouse of the settlor, the gift was exempt; and

- where the settlor himself was the life tenant, the transfer was ignored for IHT.

The life tenant of an IIP trust had a 'qualifying IIP'. The assets in a 'qualifying IIP' are treated as comprised in the estate of that beneficiary for IHT purposes and the trust assets form part of his estate on his death (*s 49*).

If the beneficiary only has an interest in part of the trust fund, that proportion of the assets in the trust is deemed to form part of his estate. Even though the life tenant may have only been entitled to the income of the trust during his lifetime, on his death he is treated as owning the capital assets of the qualifying IIP when calculating his estate for IHT purposes (*s 5(1)*).

Where a qualifying interest in possession terminates during a beneficiary's lifetime, he is then treated as having made a transfer of value. Before 22 March 2006, lifetime terminations are treated as PETs, where the recipient is:

* another individual; or

* another individual's IIP trust; or

* an A&M trust; or

* a trust for the disabled.

Focus

As 'qualifying IIPs' are already within the scope of IHT (as they are treated as assets of the life tenant), they are not subject to exit or ten-yearly charges.

After 22 March 2006

35.20   The creation of an IIP trust during the lifetime of the settlor on or after 22 March 2006 is a chargeable lifetime transfer for IHT purposes unless it is a gift into a disabled trust which remains a PET (*s 3A(1A)*).

Interests in possession created on or after 22 March 2006 are qualifying interests (*s 59(1)*) if they fall into one of these categories:

* a disabled person's interest (DPI) (**35.7**);

* an immediate post death interest (IPDI) (**35.6**); and

* a transitional serial interest (TSI) (**35.8**).

IPDIs and TSIs are treated in the same manner as IIP trusts created before 22 March 2006 (see **35.19**). IPDIs are considered at **35.6**. Where the trust terminates on or after 22 March 2006, this will only be a PET, if the transfer is to:

* another individual, unless the property was subject to the rules for bereaved minors and age 18 to 25 trusts; or

* an IPDI, TSI or DPI.

All other IIP trusts are treated for tax purposes as having 'relevant property' and the life tenants do not have a qualifying IIP. This means that the trust property is not comprised in the estate of either the settlor or the beneficiary and instead the relevant property is subject to IHT exit and ten-yearly charges.

Focus

The change in 2006 had some useful benefits:

- Where a trust had power to allow a beneficiary to occupy a trust property as his residence, that residence might be eligible for relief from CGT (*TCGA 1992, s 225*). Previously HMRC in some circumstances considered that this created an IIP so that an exit charge arose under the relevant property regime (*SP 10/79*). Since 22 March 2006, the creation of such an interest usually has no effect for IHT purposes.

- If they have power to do so, the trustees of a relevant property trust can create IIPs in favour of beneficiaries and terminate them without affecting the nature of the trust. Therefore there is no exit charge when an IIP is created and no charge when it is terminated. This can make distributing trust income easier and save tax where dividend income is receivable.

Following the death of the life tenant of a qualifying interest in possession, the capital value of the property (or his share of it, where appropriate) will be included in his chargeable estate on death. On death, any income of the IIP settlement must be split into accrued and apportioned income:

- 'Accrued income' is the income received by the trustees prior to the life tenant's death which had not yet been distributed and must be extracted from the value of the settled property. This amount must be included as part of the free estate, and not the settled property.

- 'Apportioned income' is any income received by the trustees following the life tenant's death, relating to a time before death. Apportionment is usually excluded under the terms of most trusts, so this income remains part of the settled property. Where it does apply, the trustees need to account to the estate for this income, in which case the amount must be included as part of the free estate, as above.

The trustees are liable for any IHT payable on the trust property.

SETTLOR-INTERESTED TRUSTS

35.21   If the trust is an IIP created before 22 March 2006, the life tenant is treated as being entitled to the underlying trust assets and on his death the value of the assets will be included in his estate. Therefore, if a settlor creates an IIP trust for himself he was not regarded as having made a transfer of value for IHT purposes as there has been no reduction to the value of his estate.

If the trust is a relevant property trust, ie an IIP created after 21 March 2006 or a discretionary trust, the trust assets are not treated as being owned by the beneficiary for IHT purposes and therefore the gift to the trust is a chargeable transfer and IHT may be due under *s 2* as there is a loss in value to the settlor's estate. Ten-yearly and exit charges will arise on the trust as normal.

If the gift into the relevant property trust was made on or after 18 March 1986 and the settlor has an interest, it will be caught by the gift with reservation of benefit rules (see **29.6**). This will be the case even if the settlor never receives any benefit from the trust; the possibility of benefiting is sufficient to trigger the rule. Therefore, on the settlor's death the trust assets will be deemed to form part of his estate at their then market value (*FA 1986, s 102(3)*). Any lifetime tax paid by the settlor or the trustees can be deducted from IHT payable by the executors of the estate. The rule does not apply to settlements that do, or may, benefit the settlor's spouse, but not the settlor, and are therefore narrower in scope than the settlor-interested rules for income tax and CGT.

If the reservation of benefit is released within seven years before the death of the settlor, he is treated as having made a PET at that time of release at its then value (*FA 1986, s 102(4)*).

If the settlor dies within seven years of creating a trust that is caught by the gift with reservation rules, a double tax charge arises as the trust assets will be taxable in his estate and there will be an additional charge on the lifetime transfer made within seven years of death. In this case, two sets of IHT calculations are prepared and whichever produces the highest amount of tax is the one applied (*SI 1987/1130*) (see **29.6**).

On 6 April 2005, a pre-owned assets (POA) income tax charge was introduced with the aim of deterring taxpayers from carrying out aggressive IHT planning by imposing an annual income tax charge (see **29.7**). The charge applies to arrangements made since 18 March 1986 and catches certain settlor-interested trusts (*FA 2004, Sch 15*). From 22 March 2006, further changes were introduced to stop reverter-to-settlor trusts being used to circumvent the POA charge (*FA 2006, s 80*).

Focus

In order to avoid falling into these penal traps, it is vital that a trust deed is drafted to ensure that neither the settlor nor his spouse can benefit from the trust under any circumstances. It is not sufficient to include a clause stating that they shall be excluded from benefiting from the trust. Consideration should also be given to ensure that none of the trust property can revert to them under unforeseen circumstances, for instance if the trust fails.

IHT RETURNS AND PAYMENTS

35.22   Relevant property trusts will have an IHT charge every ten years from the date of set up and on the exit of any trust property. When a chargeable event occurs, the trustees must submit an account on Form IHT100, which is the IHT equivalent of a tax return, and pay any tax due. Further details are provided at **27.9**, **27.10** and **32.26**.

These rules do not apply to:

- a pre-22 March 2006 IIP trust;

- a qualifying transitional series interest IIP trust; or

- an immediate post-death interest IIP trust.

RELIEFS

35.23   Agricultural property relief (see **28.21**) or business property relief (see **28.15**) may be available in the following circumstances:

- on the death of a life tenant with a qualifying interest in an IIP; or

- in respect of a discretionary trust when either the property enters the trust or on the ten-year anniversary or when there is an exit charge.

It is not possible to avoid a ten-year charge by simply swapping assets for relevant business or agricultural property immediately prior to a ten-year charge as the minimum ownership periods will not have been satisfied (*ss 106, 117*).

As detailed above, the benefit of BPR/APR cannot apply in calculating the rate used for the exit charge applied to appointments of assets during the first ten years (*s 68(5)(a)*). Therefore there could be an exit charge on assets which incurred no charge on entry into the trust unless the gross value of the assets falls within the nil rate band or the property attracts APR/BPR in the hands of the trustees.

There are clawback rules which need to be considered if the property was put into trust with the benefit of APR or BPR and the settlor dies within seven years. The trustees must continue to own the original property or qualifying replacement property at the date of the settlor's death and the property must still qualify for the APR or BPR in the hands of the trustees; otherwise there will be a withdrawal of the relief originally given (*ss 113A–113B; ss 124A–124B*). There is however a slight relaxation of the requirements in respect of shareholdings, as a change in business activity from trading to investment may not deny BPR.

36

Estates

SIGNPOSTS

- **Scope** – The personal representatives assume responsibility for the deceased's estate. This potentially includes submitting an IHT account to HMRC, although certain estates are excepted from this requirement (see **36.1–36.3**).

- **The deceased's tax position** – The personal representatives are also responsible for dealing with the deceased's tax returns up to the date of death (see **36.4**).

- **The personal representatives' tax position** – The personal representatives are liable for income tax and CGT arising in the estate during the administration period. It is therefore important to correctly determine the period of administration (see **36.5–36.7**).

- **The beneficiaries' tax position** – The taxation of beneficiaries of the estate depends on the nature of their interest in the estate (see **36.8–36.12**).

- **Instruments of variation** – Post-death variations of a will or intestacy can also change the CGT and IHT position, if certain conditions are satisfied. However, there is no similar provision for income tax purposes (see **36.13**).

PERSONAL REPRESENTATIVES

36.1   The role of personal representatives of a deceased person is to take control of that person's assets, realise those assets to discharge any liabilities of the deceased (including IHT), and then distribute the surplus between the eligible beneficiaries. The format for appointing personal representatives depends on whether the deceased made a will or not.

If the deceased made a will, then he will usually have named one or more people to act as his executors . However, executors are not obliged to act and in some cases may prefer to appoint a professional person to act instead.

If the deceased died without making a will (intestate) then close relatives such as a widow/widower or the children will usually apply for letters of administration. In this case, the personal representatives are called administrators. Again they may prefer to appoint a professional person to act as the intestacy rules are complex and, for example, the surviving spouse does not necessarily inherit the whole of the deceased's estate (see **30.10**).

The personal representatives (whether executors or administrators) will then gather together sufficient information to apply for probate and if necessary account for any IHT due, after which they will be able to gain control of the deceased's assets.

Where a will is made it will often include provision for a trust, and it is common in such cases to use the expression 'My Trustees' for the executors. Care is required to check the capacity under which a person is acting as the tax positions of executor and trustee are different.

> **Focus**
>
> In some circumstances it may be possible to deal with the deceased's estate without either letters of administration or probate. This is common where much of the property is held jointly and passes by survivorship, and the amounts held personally by the deceased in bank accounts and similar investments are below certain limits. However, even in this case, someone will have to take responsibility for determining the position and in particular finalising the deceased's tax liability and calculating whether any IHT is due or whether a return is required.

For small estates, HMRC operates informal payment procedures (see www. hmrc.gov.uk/manuals/tsemmanual/tsem7410.htm). HMRC have set up dedicated teams to deal with tax liabilities on bereavement (see www.hmrc. gov.uk/tools/bereavement).

There is helpful advice on the government website under 'What to do after someone dies' (www.gov.uk/after-a-death).

IHT – EXCEPTED ESTATES

36.2   The relevant IHT legislation (*IHTA 1984, s 216*) *starts* from the premise that personal representatives are required to submit an account of IHT in all cases. However, the *IHT (Delivery of Accounts (Excepted Estates))*

Regulations 2004, SI 2004/2543 limits this requirement in a number of cases. These fall under three heads:

- low value estates;

- exempt excepted estates; and

- foreign domiciliaries.

A 'low value estate' is one where the gross value of the estate including the deceased's share of any jointly owned assets plus any specified transfers and any specified exempt transfers (see below) does not exceed the IHT nil rate band (or twice that band where a claim for a transfer of the whole of a former spouse's nil rate band is available). If the death occurs before 6 August in a tax year, the nil rate band for the previous tax year applies for this purpose.

An 'exempt excepted estate' is one where the gross value of the estate, again including the share of jointly held assets plus any specified transfers and any specified exempt transfers, does not exceed £1 million, and the net chargeable value does not exceed the IHT nil rate band after deducting only liabilities, any spouse/civil partner exemption and any charity exemptions, but no other relief.

The estate of a foreign domiciliary is excepted if:

- the deceased is domiciled outside the UK at the date of death and has never been domiciled in the UK or deemed domiciled under *s 267*; and

- the value of the estate within the UK consists only of cash or quoted shares and securities where the gross value does not exceed £150,000.

Notwithstanding the above, an estate will not be an excepted estate if any of the following is in point:

- the deceased held an interest in possession in more than one settlement;

- a charge arises (under *ss 151A–151C*) on an alternatively secured pension fund;

- the deceased made a gift with reservation of benefit and that reservation still applied in the seven years before his death;

- the deceased elected to treat property as part of his estate where a pre-owned assets tax charge would apply, but for that election;

- where the deceased is regarded as deemed domiciled in the UK (under *s 267*);

- the estate includes assets held in trust where the gross value exceeds £150,000;

- the estate includes foreign assets with a gross value in excess of £100,000; or

- there have been specified transfers where the chargeable value exceeds £150,000 (see *SI 2004/2543, reg 4*).

'Specified transfers' are transfers within seven years of the deceased's death of cash, personal chattels, quoted shares or securities, and land (unless the 'gift with reservation' rules apply). 'Specified exempt transfers' are transfers within seven years of death exempt under the following headings (*reg 4(6)*):

- transfers between spouses;

- gifts to charities;

- gifts to political parties;

- gifts to housing associations;

- maintenance funds for historic buildings etc;

- employee trusts.

In determining whether the regulations avoid the need for a return, many normal lifetime exemptions are disregarded or scaled back. For example, if relief is to be claimed for normal gifts out of income, the relief must be restricted to £3,000 per annum in determining the limits. Also the exemptions for gifts to the deceased's spouse or civil partner, charities or political parties and a number of other heads are ignored in assessing whether the limits are breached. Therefore, careful enquiry will be necessary to determine whether the exemption is available.

There is also a complication in Scotland where the *Legitim Fund* might be claimed by the children of the deceased, even if left to another beneficiary.

Focus

Even if the estate is excepted under these rules, if letters of administration or a grant of probate are sought, an information return will be required by the Probate Registry before grant is issued. The relevant return for excepted estates is IHT205 or the equivalent forms for non-domiciliaries and Scottish estates.

IHT RETURNS

36.3   The principal IHT return for a deceased person is IHT400, which is supported by a number of supplementary forms to deal with particular types of property or exemption.

The forms and other relevant information can be found on the HMRC website at www.gov.uk/government/collections/inheritance-tax-forms.

As noted above, *s 216* requires the personal representatives to make a return, and this would cover not only the estate that the deceased was free to dispose of during his lifetime, but also covers:

- any property covered by a qualifying interest in possession from which the deceased benefited; and

- lifetime gifts, which may be brought into charge or subject to additional charges as a result of the deceased's death.

The time limit applying is 12 months from the end of the month during which the death occurred, or if later, three months after the personal representatives first acted as such. However, before probate or letters of administration are granted, the personal representatives must complete the appropriate IHT returns and pay the appropriate tax, so in many cases the time limit is controlled by the desire to deal with the estate expeditiously.

In addition, any person who is liable to tax as a result of the deceased's death, or would be if tax was actually chargeable on the value, is required to deliver an account in respect of the appropriate property. This is dealt with on Form IHT100. This covers failed potentially exempt transfers, gifts with reservation, terminations of interest in possession settlements, and various other occasions of charge where another person is liable, as well as the personal representatives, for the tax on the transfer value. However, if the person liable for tax is satisfied that the personal representatives have dealt with the matters for which they are liable, they are not required to make a return.

Where probate is sought for an excepted estate, an information return IHT205 (as already mentioned above) will be required.

For a discussion of the amount of tax arising, liability for and administration of IHT see **Part 4 – Inheritance Tax**.

INCOME TAX AND CAPITAL GAINS TAX OF THE DECEASED

36.4 The personal representatives are responsible for completing the tax returns of the deceased up to the date of death. Any tax repayment due for this period will be an asset of the estate and any liability will be deductible from it.

The position depends on whether the estate is a UK estate or a foreign estate. An estate is a UK estate (*ITTIOA 2005, s 651*) if:

A   all of the income has borne income tax at source or the personal representatives are directly assessable on that income (ignoring income within C); or

B   none of the aggregate income (ignoring income within C) escapes liability to UK tax because the personal representatives are non-resident; or

C   the aggregate income of the estate consists entirely of UK dividends and similar items (*ITTIOA 2005, s 680(3)*) or life assurance gains (*ITTIOA 2005, s 680(4)*).

Otherwise the estate is a foreign estate.

The personal representatives will need to contact the deceased's tax district and obtain the appropriate return, and in particular note on the return that it covers the period to the date of death. They may also be responsible for filing an earlier return if one is outstanding for a year of assessment which ended during the deceased's life.

For both income tax and capital gains tax, the period to the date of the deceased's death is treated as if it were a complete year for the purposes of personal allowances, the capital gains tax annual exempt amount and the tax rate bands, no matter how short that period. Therefore in many cases the deceased would be entitled to a tax repayment for that period.

If the deceased was trading as a sole proprietor, that business will cease at the date of his death and it will be necessary to draw up accounts to that date. On the assumption that the business is not going to be carried on by the personal representatives or any successor, thought should be given to any provision for liabilities which might arise from the operation of the trade prior to the deceased's death. If the business is to continue, some of these liabilities might be correctly apportioned to the successors.

The basis period for the year of death will follow normal principles and therefore run from the end of the basis period for the preceding year of assessment up to the date of death, and relief will be given for any overlap relief to which the deceased was entitled.

If the deceased was a partner in a firm, then it will be necessary to determine, according to the partnership's rules, his share of the profits for the period up to the date of death. Those profits will then be subject to tax in the same manner as if he had retired from the firm at the date of his death. The basis periods and overlap relief will be calculated as if he had a notional trade for his interest in the firm which ceased at the date of his death.

For employment income and pensions, the general rule is that the deceased will be taxable on the amount accruing to the date of death, which will be included in the tax return to that date (*ITEPA 2003, s 18(1), Rule 1; ss 571, 578*). However, occasionally, particularly if the deceased was a director of a company, he may become entitled to remuneration after the date of death, in which case this will be income of the personal representatives who would be taxable on that income (*ITEPA 2003, s 13(4), (4A)*).

Although it may be necessary in completing the IHT return to take account of any income which has accrued up to the date of the deceased's death under the *Apportionment Act 1870,* this does not apply for income tax (*IRC v Henderson's Executors* 1931, 16 TC 262). Therefore only investment income received or credited before death should be entered into the deceased's tax return and, for example, if the deceased owned gilt edged securities, it would not be necessary to apportion any part of an interest receipt paid after death to the period before their death: it would all be taxable on the personal representatives. Since April 1996 there is no deemed disposal for the purposes of the accrued income scheme.

On death, the assets in the deceased's estate are deemed to be disposed of at market value, but no capital gain arises (*TCGA 1992, s 62*). However, any disposal of assets prior to death must be brought into charge.

Focus

Prior to 1 April 2010, HMRC had three years from 31 January following the year of assessment in which the death occurs to raise the assessments. Since 1 April 2010, this has been extended to four years after the end of the tax year in which the death occurred. Where HMRC wish to recover lost tax, an assessment for making good tax due to careless or deliberate behaviour may only be made within those time limits, and only for any of the years ending not earlier than six years before the deceased's death. HMRC might attempt to seek a payment of lost tax from the personal representatives on a voluntary basis, but the personal representatives should not usually agree to such a request as this probably breaches their duty to the beneficiaries.

Although the provisions for payment of interest on overdue tax apply in these cases, under European law, penalties under the *Taxes Management Act 1970* are held to be criminal sanctions. Therefore HMRC cannot impose a penalty on the personal representatives in respect of tax arising for periods prior to the deceased's death.

INCOME TAX AND CAPITAL GAINS OF THE PERSONAL REPRESENTATIVES

36.5   The personal representatives are liable for income tax and capital gains tax arising in the estate during the period of administration.

The period of administration normally ends when the personal representatives have ascertained all the assets and liabilities of the estate and raised sufficient funds to meet any liabilities and any pecuniary legacies. The liabilities will include any tax liabilities of the deceased and any IHT due.

It is usually fairly straightforward to determine when the period of administration is ended. However, problems sometimes arise, for example where there is a dispute over how the estate should be distributed. HMRC will not usually dispute the date on which the personal representatives say the administration period has ended. However, they might argue for an earlier date if they consider the period is being extended artificially, for example where it is argued that liabilities have not been ascertained simply to delay the end of the period.

Determining the end of the period of administration is important because if the period has ended, even if the assets are still under the control of the personal representatives, the income and gains will be taxable on the beneficiaries or on any trusts arising under the will. For example, the personal representatives may claim that the estate is still in administration where a discretionary trust has arisen and the income would otherwise be liable to tax at the trust rate of 45%.

Further guidance can be found on the HMRC website in the 'Toolkit for Trusts & Estates' (www.gov.uk/government/publications/hmrc-trusts-and-estates-toolkit) and in their internal manual (www.hmrc.gov.uk/manuals/tsemmanual).

INCOME TAX AND ESTATES

36.6   The personal representatives of a UK estate are liable to tax on the whole of the income arising during the administration period. This income is taxed at the savings rate, the basic rate or the dividend ordinary rate, depending on the nature of the income. They are not entitled to any personal allowance or to claim any deductions except:

- interest relief for a loan taken out to pay IHT (*ITA 2007, ss 403, 404*). The relief only covers a loan to pay any IHT due on delivery of the Revenue account (IHT400) and only for the period of 12 months from the date of taking the loan;

- normal business expenses for any trade or property investment business carried on by the personal representatives.

Prior to 6 April 2016, the personal representatives would have no tax to pay on dividend income as it would be covered by the tax credit. As a result of the changes in *FA 2016*, from 6 April 2016, they will be liable to tax at 7.5%. They are not eligible for the dividend tax credit.

CAPITAL GAINS TAX AND ESTATES

36.7 The personal representatives will be deemed to have acquired the assets which passed to them on the death at their market value as agreed for probate. This does not give rise to a capital gain to the deceased because the transfer on death is not treated as a disposal.

Where the personal representatives pass an asset to a beneficiary as legatee, the beneficiary is deemed to acquire the asset at their value on the date of death (*TCGA 1992, s 62(4)*).

Where the personal representatives dispose of an asset while acting as such, a capital gain or loss arises in the normal way, based on the proceeds of disposal compared to the value at the date of death. Any incidental costs of disposal are allowed.

The personal representatives are entitled to the full annual exempt amount for the year of death and the following two years (*TCGA 1992, s 3(7)*). For gains made after 6 April 2016 the personal representatives are chargeable at 20%, except for residential property where the rate is 28%. For gains made after 23 June 2010 but before 5 April 2016, the personal representatives are chargeable at 28%. From 6 April 2008 until 23 June 2010, tax was charged at 18%. Prior to 6 April 2008, capital gains were charged at the trust rate.

Focus

In some cases it might be advantageous for a beneficiary rather than the personal representatives to be charged to tax on the disposal of an asset, for example where an asset is to be divided between multiple beneficiaries who would all benefit from the annual exempt amount. If the administration period has not ended, the personal representatives may assent to the asset being transferred to the beneficiary before the end of the period: in this case the disposal will be by the beneficiary rather than the personal representatives.

In contrast, the personal representatives might prefer to make disposals directly, for example where they have not used their annual exempt amount or have unused losses. In such cases HMRC might dispute that the period of administration is still running.

Where the personal representatives make a disposal, they may deduct certain costs in obtaining a valuation of the assets at the date of death, as set out in SP2/04. They may also be entitled to private residence relief on the sale of an asset which was occupied before the death by one or more individuals who were (together) entitled to at least 75% of the net proceeds of the disposal as legatee or have an interest in possession in those proceeds (*TCGA 1992, s 225A*).

TAXATION OF BENEFICIARIES

36.8   The taxation of beneficiaries of the estate depends on the nature of the benefit they take, which can be broken down into the following heads:

- *Interest arising on pecuniary legacies* – This will arise if payment of a monetary legacy is delayed and the personal representatives are obliged to add interest to the amount paid.

- *Specific legacies* – These relate to legacies of a specific asset, some of which may produce income such as shareholdings, while others such as jewellery would not.

- *Absolute interests in residue.*

- *Limited interests in residue.*

- *Discretionary interests in residue.*

Where interest arises on unpaid legacies, this is taxed in accordance with the normal rules for the taxation of interest, ie normally the date on which the beneficiary receives the interest payment.

Where income arises on specific legacies, the beneficiary is taxed on that income in the year in which it arises (*CIR v Hawley* KB 1927, 13 TC 327). However, in some cases the personal representatives may be entitled to use that income for some other purpose, and the beneficiary will not be taxed if he does not receive the income. Similarly if that income has borne tax, no repayment will be due to the beneficiary on any amount which the personal representatives have used for another purpose and not paid over.

The taxation of the various potential interests in residue is dealt with in detail below.

Interests in residue

36.9   The residue of the deceased's estate comprises the assets left over, once the personal representatives have determined the estate and paid any IHT and liabilities and dealt with any legacies or annuities arising under the estate.

A beneficiary has an absolute interest in that residue if he is entitled to both the capital and income in respect of a share of that residue. A beneficiary has a limited interest if he is entitled to the income arising from a share of residue but not the capital. A discretionary interest arises where the beneficiary is entitled to income from the estate at the discretion of the personal representatives.

Beneficiaries with an absolute interest

36.10

> **Focus**
>
> The effects of the following rules govern when the beneficiaries are taxed on their shares of estate income. Where significant sums are involved, the personal representatives should consider the time when any tax will be charged and whether the income should be spread to reduce the effective rate of tax.

The tax treatment of the beneficiaries is different in the final year of administration to those earlier in the period of administration.

For tax years before the year in which the administration is completed, the basic amount of estate income of the beneficiary is the lower of:

- the total of all sums paid in the tax year in respect of the beneficiary's interest; and

- the amount of that person's assumed income entitlement for the year in respect of it (*ITTOIA 2005, s 660(1)*).

For the final year of administration, the basic amount of the estate income is the person's assumed income entitlement for that year in respect of that interest.

The beneficiary's assumed income entitlement is the amount of the beneficiary's share of income for the period of administration to date, less tax on that income and any amounts which have been taxed on the beneficiary in previous years in respect of the absolute interest.

If the basic amount for the final year is a deficit, then the excess can be deducted from previous years' basic amounts, set against the most recent year first. Any necessary amendments to assessments are made to achieve this.

A point to note is that for this purpose, payments include not only payments of the income, but all value transferred to the beneficiary. For example, if the personal representatives transferred an asset to the beneficiary in settlement of part of the residue, the market value of the asset is a payment for this purpose. If the personal representatives are also beneficiaries and they appropriate an asset to themselves in satisfaction of their entitlement as beneficiaries, this is also a payment, even if there is no change in the title or situation of the asset.

The overall objective of these rules is to tax the beneficiaries on the income as they receive it, but on no more than they are entitled to.

In calculating the residuary income of the estate, the following deductions are allowed (*ITTOIA 2005, s 666*):

- any interest paid by the personal representatives in that capacity (apart from interest on IHT);

- any annual payments that are payable out of residue;

- payments of expenses of the personal representatives in that capacity in the management of the assets of the estate; and

- any deductions not taken in earlier years because there was insufficient income.

The basic amount and the assumed income entitlement are net payments, and need to be grossed up for income tax. Where income tax has been suffered by the personal representatives at different rates, the payment is first taken as coming out of income taxed at the basic rate, then the savings rate and then the dividend ordinary rate. This means that the effect of the personal representatives' expenses and interest payments is on those amounts of income which have suffered the least tax, ensuring that further tax suffered by the beneficiary is minimised or that he may recover the greatest repayment. To the extent that the grossing up is at the dividend ordinary rate, the effective tax credit on that amount is not recoverable by the beneficiary. From 6 April 2016 the underlying tax credit is abolished and the tax payable on dividend income by the personal representatives will be available for repayment (see **36.6**).

For a foreign estate, income is grossed up only where it is paid out of income within *ITTOIA 2005, s 680(3), (4)* (see **36.4**).

There are special provisions in *s 671* onwards to deal with cases where there are successive interests in the residue.

Example 36.1 – Beneficiary's estate income: absolute interest

Nick died in May 2012, leaving half of his estate to David absolutely and half to William for life and thereafter to George. The executors, Ed and Alan complete the administration in May 2015.

The executors receive the following income and make the following payments during the period of administration:

	2012/13	2013/14	2014/15	2015/16
	£	£	£	£
UK dividends	4,500	9,300	9,000	900
Interest received net of tax	8,000	8,000	4,000	2,000
Expenses	2,700	3,000	3,600	1,500
Payment to David		11,600	4,700	
Payment to William		8,000	4,700	3,000

As the only income is dividends and interest net of tax there is no further liability on the personal representatives. The residuary income of the estate is:

	2012/13	2013/14	2014/15	2015/16
	£	£	£	£
Dividends	4,500	9,300	9,000	900
Less: expenses	(2,700)	(3,000)	(3,600)	(900)
Net dividends	1,800	6,300	5,400	–
Tax credit	200	700	600	–
Gross dividend (a)	2,000	7,000	6,000	–
Interest	8,000	8,000	4,000	2,000
Less: expenses	–	–	–	(600)
Net interest	8,000	8,000	4,000	1,400
Tax deducted	2,000	2,000	1,000	350
Gross interest (b)	10,000	10,000	5,000	1,750
Residuary income (a) + (b)	12,000	17,000	11,000	1,750
The position of the beneficiary with the absolute interest is:				
David's share of net income[1]	4,900	7,150	4,700	700
Assumed income entitlement	4,900	12,050[2]	5,150[3]	1,150[3]
Amounts paid		11,600	4,700	
Basic amount of estate income[4]		11,600	4,700	1,150

	2012/13	**2013/14**	**2014/15**	**2015/16**
	£	**£**	**£**	**£**
Grossing up the basic amounts of the estate income gives:				
Interest income		8,000[5]	2,000[5]	700[5]
Tax deducted		2,000	500	175
Dividend income		3,600[6]	2,700[6]	450[6]
Tax credit		400	300	50
Total estate income (gross)		14,000	5,500	1,375

Notes

1 Half the net interest plus half the net dividends.

2 Total of David's share of net income to end of the current year.

3 Total of that income less basic amounts from previous years (ie in 2014/15 £4,900 + £7,150 + £4,700 – £11,600).

4 Lower of the assumed income entitlement and the amounts paid (except in the final year).

5 Share of net interest to date taken as top slice (less amounts already allocated) (ie in 2014/15 £4,000 + £4,000 + £2,000 – £8,000).

6 Balance taken from dividends.

It will be seen that if no payments are made until the administration is finalised the beneficiary may be charged at higher rates than necessary.

Income accrued at the date of death may be taken into account in determining liability for IHT, but also be included in the residuary income of the estate because it is received after the date of death. Relief is available (under *ITTOIA 2005, s 669*) to a beneficiary with an absolute interest in residue who would be liable for higher or additional rate tax on his share of that income,

At the time of writing there is no HMRC guidance on to how to complete a form R185E in the light of the changes to the taxation of dividends which came into force on 6 April 2016.

Tax position of limited interests

36.11 The basic amount is any sum paid in respect of the interest in the tax year in question. However, if the tax year is the final year in the administration period, it will include any sum which remains payable at the end of the administrative period. Similarly if the limited interest ends before the administration period, the income for the year it ends will include income paid in the later year before the end of the administration period or any amount which remains payable in respect of it at the end of that period (*ITTOIA 2005, ss 661, 654*).

Example 36.2 – Beneficiary's estate income: limited interest

Continuing the example above, in 2013/14 William's income is £8,000 grossed up at 20% to give £10,000 as it all comes out of interest.

In 2014/15 his income is:

	Net	Tax	Total
Interest	£2,000	£500	£2,500
Dividends	£2,700	£300	£3,000

Interest to date £10,000 (£20,000 × ½) less taxed in 2013/14 £8,000 = £2,000, balance taken from dividends.

In 2015/16, assuming that William is entitled to the balance of the residuary income his taxable income from the estate is (even if he receives it later):

Interest	£700	£175	£875
Dividends	£4,050	£450	£4,500

Interest to date £10,700 (£21,400 × ½) less taxed in 2013/14 and 2014/15 £10,000 = £700. Dividends to date £6,750 (£13,500 × ½) less taxed in 2014/15 £2,700 = £4,050.

Discretionary interests

36.12 If any payments are made at the discretion of the personal representatives, the taxable income is the amount of those payments as grossed up, again at the rates at which that income has borne tax, in the order specified at **36.10** above.

With regard to discretionary payments, it will often be the case that the will provides for the creation of a discretionary trust, and if the payments are made by the trustees rather than personal representatives, then the grossing up is required to be at the trust rate: 45% for the tax years 2013/14 to 2015/16; 50% for 2011/12 and 2012/13 and previously 40%.

Post-death variations

36.13 Frequently, the provisions made in the will of the deceased will have been overtaken by events after it was drawn up and the beneficiaries may wish to vary the bequests. Similarly, the beneficiaries of a person who died intestate may wish to deal with the property differently than the statutory rules would provide.

Without specific legislation, any such variation might be a transfer of value for IHT and give rise to a disposal for capital gains tax.

Example 36.3 – Effect of a variation

In his will, John leaves some shares in his company to his widow, but at the time of his death the company was preparing to float those shares on the stock exchange. This is finalised in the six months after his death. At the date of his death, HMRC agree that the value of the shares was £1 million, but following listing, those shares are now valued at £5 million. John's widow would prefer that those shares went to their children and she agrees to transfer them.

This would be a disposal of those shares by her on which holdover relief would not be available and would give rise to a taxable capital gain of £4 million. It would also be a transfer of value for IHT purposes on which business property relief is unlikely to be available.

However, provided that the transfer takes place within two years of John's death, the provisions of *TCGA 1992, s 62(6)* and *IHTA 1984, s 142* can be applied, provided that the appropriate declarations are made in the instrument of variation.

In this way, the children would be deemed to have acquired the shares as if they had been left to them under their father's will. There will be no disposal for capital gains tax by their mother and provided that the shares were eligible for business property relief at the date of their father's death, there will be no transfer chargeable to IHT.

It is no longer necessary to file the instrument of variation with HMRC (prior to 1 August 2002 a claim needed to be made to HMRC within six months of the variation for the provisions to apply). However, if the instrument affects the tax due HMRC will want to see it.

If an instrument of variation is to be made, it is important to ensure that care is taken to achieve the necessary changes at one go, because the rules only apply to a single variation in respect of the same assets or entitlement.

A similar effect can be achieved where the will creates a discretionary trust and the trustees exercise their discretion within two years of the death to transfer property to one or more beneficiaries. In this case the variation is read back into the will and deemed to be made as part of that will. This reading back is automatic and does not require any election. However, it is important that the distribution would fall to be an occasion of charge for IHT, so it must be made at least three months after the date of death to be effective (as there is no exit charge arising on a distribution from a trust in the first quarter).

Where the deceased died owning joint property, this will pass by survivorship to the other joint owners. It is possible to execute a deed of variation to sever that joint interest from before death, so that the deceased's share can be passed either under the terms of his will as part of the residue or to another specific beneficiary.

Focus

There is no similar provision to these variation rules for income tax purposes, so that if any income has been received by the beneficiary prior to the variation, it will remain his income for tax purposes. The current rules on the allocation of income to the beneficiaries of the estate mean that where the variation is effected to transfer the related income to the beneficiary taking the new interest in the deceased's property, that beneficiary will be taxed on the income if he receives it.

If the deed of variation creates a settlement, for income tax and capital gains tax purposes any beneficiary who has provided property as a result of that variation to the settlement will be a settlor, and if they can benefit from the settlement, they will be subject to the rules for settlor interested settlements detailed in **33.14** *et seq*.

Part 6
VAT

37

Value added tax – outline

SIGNPOSTS

- **Background** – VAT was introduced in 1973, and is the EU form of consumption tax. It has a legislative framework in the UK, which is subject to European law (see **37.1**).

- **Scope** – VAT is charged on supplies by a business. Inputs are goods and services supplied to the business, and outputs are goods and services supplied by the business (see **37.2**).

- **VAT rates** – There are basically three taxable VAT rates – 0% (zero rate), 5% (reduced rate) and 20% (standard rate). Alternatively, certain supplies are exempt from VAT (see **37.3–37.6**).

- **Tax point** – In order to decide when VAT has to be accounted for, it is necessary to determine the time of supply or tax point (see **37.7**).

- **Compliance** – VAT returns must normally be submitted quarterly and there are time limits for the returns and for making payments (see **37.8–37.9**).

- **Non-deductible VAT** – VAT cannot be reclaimed on certain purchases. This is known as 'blocked input tax' (see **37.10**).

- **HMRC powers, etc** – The law allows HMRC to carry out compliance checks and to levy penalties of up to 100% in appropriate cases (see **37.11–37.12**).

- **Appendix: VAT rates and fractions** – Tables of standard rates for earlier years and VAT fractions are included at the end of this chapter (see **37.13–37.14**).

'Beyond the everyday world, both counsel have explained to us, lies the world of value added tax (VAT), a kind of fiscal theme park in which factual and legal realities are suspended or inverted.'

(Sedley LJ in *Royal and Sun Alliance Insurance Group Limited v Customs and Excise Commissioners* [2001] STC 1476 at para 54.)

INTRODUCTION

37.1   Value added tax (VAT) was introduced into the United Kingdom in 1973, as a consequence of joining the European Economic Community (as it then was). The then Chancellor, Anthony Barber, described it as a 'simple straightforward tax'. VAT remains conceptually simple, but the application of detailed rules to individual situations has over the years become extremely complex. In particular, because VAT is a 'European tax', European law takes precedence over UK law, and the two are sometimes in conflict. This has led to a number of difficulties in interpretation. For example, European law does not sit easily with English or Scottish land law, and this type of anomaly leads to the problems being considered by Sedley LJ in the paragraph cited above. The impact of the result of the EU referendum on the UK VAT system is therefore more complex and uncertain than its impact on other UK taxes.

The basic legislative framework for UK VAT is contained in the *Value Added Tax Act 1994* (*VATA*), as amended from time to time. VATA is supplemented by a plethora of secondary legislation, of which the most important are the *Value Added Tax Regulations 1995, SI 1995/2518*.

HMRC publishes a wide range of VAT publications, including VAT Notices and Leaflets, to explain the treatment of different types of transactions, which can be found at the link below. The most important is VAT Notice 700: The VAT Guide (www.hmrc.gov.uk/thelibrary/vat.htm).

It should be noted that certain of the notices and leaflets have the force of law, in whole or in part. This is indicated in the relevant part of the leaflet, and generally relates to how certain computational matters should be addressed (for example, partial exemption or retail schemes).

HMRC also has VAT Manuals, which can be found in the library on its website, and which explain its interpretation of certain matters, and procedures, in the same way as the direct tax manuals.

> **Focus**
>
> HMRC VAT publications provide a useful guide to the rules. Where an approach has been based on such a publication, this should be noted to facilitate discussions with HMRC inspectors.

UK VAT legislation is required to conform to European Union law. If the two are in conflict, European law prevails. The main source of European law is *Council Directive 2006/112/EC*, of 28 November 2006.

INPUTS AND OUTPUTS

37.2 VAT is a tax on 'supplies', ie goods and services supplied by a business. For a business, outputs are the goods and services supplied by that business, and inputs are the goods and services supplied to it. Supplies can be either taxable, exempt, or outside the scope of VAT. Discounts, including discounts for prompt payment, reduce the value of the supply when the discount is taken up.

The VAT charged on standard and reduced rate sales is referred to as output tax and the VAT incurred on purchases (for business purposes) is input tax. A fully taxable business can, with certain minor exceptions (see **37.10**), reclaim all the VAT charged to it as this is attributable directly or indirectly to the taxable supplies which it makes. For a business which has exempt outputs, VAT incurred may not be recoverable and is therefore a cost to the business.

VAT RATES

37.3 Taxable supplies are those on which VAT is charged at zero rate, the reduced rate, or the standard rate of VAT. The current reduced rate of VAT is 5%. Zero rate supplies are those outlined at **37.4** below and reduced rate supplies are detailed at **37.5**.

The current standard rate of VAT is 20%. Up to 3 January 2011, the rate was 17.5% as it had been for a number of years, apart from the reduction to 15% as a temporary measure from 1 December 2008 to 31 December 2009, in order to aid economic recovery.

> **Focus**
>
> Determining the correct liability of supplies is crucial. Failure to do so may mean loss of competitiveness, or profit margins being eroded.

Zero-rated supplies

37.4 It is important to understand the distinction between a zero-rated supply and an exempt supply. A zero-rated supply is a taxable supply for VAT purposes (so that input tax on related costs can be recovered) but the tax is charged at a rate of nil. An exempt supply is one that is not subject to VAT, but attributable input tax cannot be recovered and is a cost to the business.

The VAT legislation contains a comprehensive list of zero-rated supplies as follows (*VATA 1994, Sch 8*):

Group 1	Food
Group 2	Water and sewerage
Group 3	Books and printed matter
Group 4	Talking books for the blind and handicapped and wireless sets for the blind
Group 5	Construction of new housing, etc
Group 6	Alterations to protected buildings for housing, etc (removed with effect from 1 October 2012), but zero-rating still available for disposals reconstructed from shell
Group 7	Work on goods for export and making of arrangements for the exportation of goods
Group 8	Aircraft, ships and associated services and passenger transport
Group 9	Supplies of residential caravans and houseboats
Group 10	Gold
Group 11	Issue of bank notes
Group 12	Certain medicines and aids for the handicapped, etc
Group 13	Imports and exports
Group 15	Certain supplies to and by charities
Group 16	Children's clothing
Group 17	Emissions Allowances – omitted from 1 November 2010
Group 18	Supplies of goods and services to an ERIC – effective from 1 January 2013

In all cases, there are likely to be exceptions to the zero-rating, and it is important to ensure that the product being sold falls precisely within the terms of zero-rating. An example of this is in relation to food, where zero-rating applies to cakes but not to biscuits wholly or partly covered with chocolate or a similar product. This prompted the famous tribunal case concerning whether a Jaffa Cake was in fact a cake (which would have attracted zero-rating) or a biscuit (which would be standard-rated). Following lengthy legal argument the tribunal decided that as Jaffa Cakes were moist and had the texture of a sponge cake, and sponge was a substantial part of the product in bulk and texture, rather than simply a base of jam and chocolate, a Jaffa Cake is indeed a cake (*United Biscuits (UK) Limited* (VTD6344)).

It should be noted that zero-rating is no longer permitted under EU legislation. The United Kingdom has a 'derogation' which allows it to keep existing zero rates, but not extend them.

Focus

Zero-rating is the most beneficial treatment, but all the groups above contain important restrictions and it is vital to ensure that 'zero-rated' supplies do not fall foul of these restrictions.

Reduced rate

37.5　　VAT at a reduced rate of 5% is charged on the following, which are detailed in *VATA 1994, Sch 7A*:

Group 1	Domestic fuel and power
Group 2	Installation of energy-saving materials in residential and charity buildings. The reduction for charitable buildings (those used by a charity for non-business use) has been withdrawn with effect from 1 August 2013
Group 3	Grant-funded installation of heating equipment, security goods (locks, bolts, etc), or connection of gas supply to the over 60s or persons in receipt of certain welfare benefits
Group 4	Women's sanitary products
Group 5	Children's car seats
Group 6	Residential conversions (this applies to the conversion of non-residential buildings, or parts of buildings to residential, or where the number of dwellings in a building is changed)
Group 7	Qualifying residential renovations (improvements to properties that have been empty for two years or more)
Group 8	Contraceptive products
Group 9	Welfare advice or information supplied by charities or state regulated private welfare institutions
Group 10	Installation of mobility aids for the elderly
Group 11	Smoking cessation products
Group 12	Static caravans not qualifying as residential (static holiday caravans) – effective from 6 April 2013
Group 13	Cable suspended passenger transport – effective from 1 April 2013

EXEMPT SUPPLIES

37.6 Both zero-rate and reduced-rate supplies discussed above allow the person selling such products and services to recover associated input VAT. Where a person makes exempt supplies, he cannot recover the input VAT attributable to those exempt supplies.

Exempt supplies are set out in groups to *VATA 1994, Sch 9*, as summarised briefly below.

Group 1   Land – this exemption applies to the grant of any interest in or right over land subject to a number of exceptions; some relating to the exploitation of the land (for example, fishing rights or admission to sporting events) rather than the land itself. Another notable exception is the use of property for holiday homes, including timeshare and other arrangements where the purchaser cannot occupy the property for the whole of the year. Freehold sales or long leasehold disposals of new residential property are zero-rated under *Sch 8, Group 5* and the freehold sale of new commercial buildings is standard rated.

Group 2   Insurance products – this relates to provision of insurance and making arrangements for it (intermediary services).

Group 3   Postal services – when provided by a universal service provider delivering throughout the UK. Because of the qualification this does not apply to business couriers (for example DHL) and the Post Office Business Service is also standard-rated, in order to provide a 'level playing field.' However, the 'universal postal service' (normal delivery of letters) remains exempt.

Group 4   Betting, gaming, dutiable machine games and lotteries.

Group 5   Finance – this heading includes banking services relating to any dealing with money, granting of credit, etc, but not advisory services.

Group 6   Education and vocational training provided by a school, university, college, etc on a not-for-profit basis. Private tuition and government-funded vocational training schemes.

Group 7   Provision of health and medical care by registered practitioners, including dentistry, together with certain ancillary items. It should be noted that this does not include 'alternative therapists' who are usually not required to be included on a statutory register. This group also provides for the exemption of welfare services when provided by a charity, public body or state regulated private welfare institution.

Group 8   Burial and cremation services.

Group 9   Subscriptions to trade unions, professional bodies and other public interest bodies.

Group 10   Sports services provided by non-profit making bodies.

Group 11   Works of art not subject to inheritance tax.

Group 12   Fundraising events by charities and similar bodies largely relating to admissions for events.

Group 13   Admissions to museums, galleries, art exhibitions, zoos, theatrical, musical or choreographic performances of a cultural nature, and where supplied by a public body or an 'eligible body' (basically a non-profit-making body).

Group 14   Supplies of goods where input tax cannot be recovered.

Group 15   Supplies of interests in investment gold.

Group 16   Cost sharing groups

Focus

Like zero-rating, exemption is subject to a number of exceptions, and the rules must be studied carefully in marginal cases.

Exempt supplies do not count as taxable supplies for the purposes of VAT registration. If a business only makes exempt supplies, it does not need to register.

The key issue for exempt supplies is that no VAT is chargeable on them, and the attributable input VAT cannot be recovered. This is different from zero-rated supplies which are taxable (although the VAT charged is nil).

TIME OF SUPPLY

37.7   The time of supply determines when VAT must be accounted for to HMRC. The basic 'tax point' for goods is the date the goods are actually removed or made available to the customer.

For services, the basic tax point is the date the services are performed (when all work except invoicing has been completed).

However, in relation to both goods and services an alternative 'actual tax point' can be created if:

● a tax invoice is issued or payment is received *before* the basic tax point; or

● the supplier issues a VAT invoice within 14 days *after* the basic tax point.

It is therefore possible to delay the basic tax point, provided a VAT invoice is issued within 14 days.

For an on-going operation which makes taxable supplies at the standard rate, the business will normally be paying money over to HMRC. In order to optimise cash flow, therefore, it is preferable for there to be as long a gap as possible between collecting VAT and paying it over to HMRC.

Much as we all might like to, we cannot control the rate at which our customers pay. However, if invoices are issued at the beginning of each VAT quarter, then this gives the best opportunity to retain the VAT for up to four months before having to pay it over.

If a trader is making mainly zero-rated supplies (see **37.4**), it may be more sensible to make monthly returns. However, this does involve increased requirements to make returns, with the associated increased possibility of errors and additional bureaucracy.

Where a business makes continuous supplies of services, a tax point is only created on receipt of payment or on the issue of an invoice. It may therefore be appropriate to use the so-called 'application for payment' system, where a document requesting payment is issued which does not contain all the detailed requirements for a tax invoice (for example, does not include the VAT number). The VAT invoice can then be issued when payment is received (which creates the actual tax point). This also avoids any problem with bad debts. The main disadvantage of this is the increase in paperwork required.

As an alternative, it may be suitable for qualifying businesses to use the cash accounting scheme. Under this, invoices issued and received are dealt with for VAT only when payment is made. Under this scheme it is beneficial in cash flow terms for purchase invoices to be paid towards the end of the VAT return period. The cash accounting scheme is discussed in more detail at **40.2**.

Focus

Cash flow is critical to any business. Keeping VAT for as long as possible before paying it over to HMRC clearly helps this.

Where appropriate, consider using cash accounting or applications for payment, to ensure VAT has been collected, before it is paid over to HMRC.

VAT RETURNS

37.8 VAT returns are generally made quarterly, although there are provisions in the VAT legislation to allow monthly returns (generally by persons who make zero-rated supplies and reclaim VAT on a regular basis) or annual returns in some cases (see **Chapter 40**).

From 1 April 2012, all VAT returns must be submitted online and must reach HMRC together with payment, by the relevant due date to avoid late payment surcharges. Payments are also required to be made by electronic means.

The VAT return must show the following:

• Box 1: VAT due in the period on sales and other outputs (including reverse charge services);

• Box 2: VAT due in the period on acquisitions from other EU member states;

• Box 3: The total VAT due (Box 1 *plus* Box 2);

• Box 4: The VAT reclaimed in the period on purchases and other inputs, including acquisitions / reverse charge;

• Box 5: Total VAT payable or reclaimable (Box 3 *minus* Box 4);

• Box 6: Tax exclusive value of outputs;

• Box 7: Tax exclusive value of inputs;

• Box 8: Tax exclusive value of all supplies of goods and related costs to other EU member states;

• Box 9: Tax exclusive value of all acquisitions of goods and related costs from other EU member states.

Note that there will be a direct correlation between the figure entered in Box 9 and the acquisition tax declared in Box 2 of the return if all the acquisitions are subject to VAT (no acquisition tax due on zero-rated purchases such as books).

The VAT return entries are different where the flat rate scheme is used, as set out at **40.3**.

The VAT return must be filed on or before 30 days from the end of the VAT return period, but this is extended by seven days where returns are submitted online and electronic payment is made.

VAT PAYMENTS

37.9 VAT payments must be made by electronic means from 1 April 2012 and as a result the due date for submission of the payment (and return) is extended by seven days (in addition to the normal 30-day period after the period end).

Where a trader discovers that he has made an error in his VAT return, which requires further payment, he should make a voluntary disclosure.

Focus

Ensure procedures are in place to confirm the VAT returns are submitted promptly, and tax paid, to avoid late payment surcharges.

In addition, ensure that errors are reported properly to HMRC when discovered.

NON-DEDUCTIBLE INPUT TAX

37.10 Input VAT on certain purchases cannot be claimed as input tax on a return. This is referred to as 'blocked' input tax.

The main items on which input tax is blocked are business entertainment and the purchase of motor cars (but not vans).

Entertainment includes hospitality of any kind, including food and drink, but not business promotion expenditure. However, meals for staff do not generally count as entertainment, unless they are part of an 'entertainment package'.

Example 37.1 – Non-deductible input VAT on entertainment

A salesman visits a client to take him out to lunch. This is part of an 'entertainment package' and no VAT is reclaimable. The main purpose of the visit is entertainment.

Example 37.2 – VAT on staff subsistence

A salesman visits a client away from the office to discuss an order. Following a lengthy (and successful) meeting, the salesman buys the client lunch.

The VAT on the salesman's lunch is treated as subsistence (recoverable). The client's lunch constitutes entertainment, so VAT is not recoverable.

Where a business leases motor cars, 50% of the input tax on the hire charge is disallowed (not the service element of the charge). The restrictions on input tax recovery do not extend to purchases or leases of cars which are used wholly for business purposes, such as cars for driving instructors, or private hire taxis, or cars for the disabled.

Where a motor dealer uses a car (e.g. a demonstrator car) for private use (allowing an employee to take it home overnight), no input tax restriction arises if the car is a 'qualifying car' (stock in trade of the dealer). Instead, the private use gives rise to an output tax charge.

As well as the general blocked items above, where a person constructing a new house (the sale of which is zero-rated) installs certain items in that house, input tax on these items is blocked. The items in question are:

- fitted furniture, other than kitchen furniture, or materials for the construction of such furniture;

- electrical or gas appliances other than for heating space or water, ventilation or air purification, door entry system, systems for waste disposal or compacting in multiple dwellings, burglar or fire alarms, fire safety equipment, systems solely for summoning aid in an emergency;

- carpets or carpeting material;

- any items not ordinarily installed by builders as fixtures (this might include landscaping work in show homes, for example).

Focus

Correct coding will ensure input tax is not recovered on blocked items.

HMRC POWERS

37.11 HMRC adopts a risk-based approach to compliance. Traders, all of whose supplies are taxable and do not operate in businesses identified as 'high risk' by HMRC, will generally not be subject to onerous compliance visits. However, HMRC does have power to visit any business premises and to satisfy themselves that businesses are operating VAT correctly.

Risk is assessed on a number of factors, including compliance, tax throughput, complex liability, etc. Where HMRC has identified the business as being high risk, HMRC is likely to visit more frequently, particularly if they perceive that there are problems, either in terms of an aggressive attitude towards VAT planning, or a 'careless' approach towards VAT compliance.

Visits will normally be arranged by appointment and agreement; however, there are instances where HMRC can make unannounced visits to business premises, for example to check till readings at a cash business. Unannounced visits must however be authorised and made at a reasonable time and the inspecting officer must provide a notice in writing to the business owner or any other person who appears to be in charge.

VAT penalty regime

37.12 The VAT civil penalty regime was broadly aligned with that for direct taxes with effect from 1 April 2008. Existing penalties for dishonest conduct can still apply but only in limited situations. Most penalties will result from two possible situations:

- *Giving HMRC an incorrect document* – This term is very wide, and includes communicating information to HMRC in any form. This can include telephone, e-mail, statements or in documents. It is therefore vital that the flow of information to HMRC is properly controlled.

- *Failure to notify HMRC of any under-assessment.*

The degree of penalty to be levied is a percentage of the amount of tax lost, and the percentage depends on the culpability of the person which has led to a loss of tax. The 'culpability levels' are:

- *Loss of tax despite the taxpayer taking reasonable care*: no penalty.

- *Loss of tax caused by the taxpayer failing to take reasonable care*: 30% penalty (this can be reduced to nil by an unprompted disclosure, or 15% by a disclosure prompted by the possibility of a visit from HMRC).

- *Deliberate understatement (not amounting to criminal behaviour)*: 70% penalty (reduced to 20% for unprompted disclosure and 35% for prompted).

- *Deliberate and concealed understatement (not amounting to criminal behaviour)*: 100% penalty (reduced to 30% for unprompted disclosure and 50% for prompted).

HMRC has a range of sanctions in relation to suspected criminal activity, which are beyond the scope of this book.

> **Focus**
>
> HMRC are more likely to visit businesses with poor compliance records. Therefore ensuring proper compliance is likely to lead to lower costs in the long run.

APPENDIX: VAT RATES AND FRACTIONS

VAT rates

(VATA 1994, s 2(1))

37.13

Effective date	Standard rate
	%
04.01.11	20.0
01.01.10	17.5
01.12.08 – 31.12.09	15.0
01.04.91	17.5

Notes

1   *Reduced rate* – Set at 5% for certain supplies made, and acquisitions taking place, after 31 October 2001 (*VATA 1994, s 29A, Sch 7A*).

2   *Standard rate* – This rate of VAT was increased from 17.5% to 20% in relation to any supply made from 4 January 2011, and any acquisition or importation taking place from that date (*F(No 2)A 2010, s 3*). Anti-avoidance provisions introduce a supplementary VAT charge of 2.5% on certain supplies that span the date of the change in VAT rate (*F(No 2)A 2010, Sch 2*).

VAT fraction

37.14

VAT percentage	VAT fraction
%	
20.0	1/6
17.5	7/47
15.0	3/23
5.0	1/21

Note – The VAT fraction is used to calculate the VAT element of VAT-inclusive goods and services at the appropriate rate.

38

VAT – registration and deregistration

SIGNPOSTS

- **Registration** – For UK businesses, there is a requirement to register for VAT if taxable turnover exceeds a registration threshold, and it is important for traders to keep the position under review. The artificial splitting of a business into separate elements to remain below the registration threshold is likely to be challenged by HMRC (see **38.1**).

  From 1 December 2012, non-established taxable persons making taxable supplies in the UK are required to register, irrespective of the value of the taxable supplies made.

- **Procedure** – Registering involves completing the necessary forms, normally VAT1 but possibly other forms as well, such as in relation to groups or partnerships (see **38.2–38.3**).

- **Deregistration** – If taxable turnover falls below a threshold, it is possible to apply to deregister for VAT. Alternatively, it is possible for a business to be deregistered compulsorily in some cases (see **38.4–38.5**).

- **Appendix: Registration limits** – A table of current and previous VAT registration thresholds is included at the end of this chapter (see **38.6**).

REQUIREMENT TO REGISTER

38.1   A person is required to register if their taxable turnover is above the registration threshold, which is £83,000 for 2016/17.

Taxable turnover can comprise:

- taxable supplies made in the UK;

- supplies to UK non-business customers made by persons outside the UK (known as 'distance sales');

- acquisitions (purchases of goods from within the EU);

- standard-rated disposals of land;

- the value of 'reverse charge services' received from abroad.

A taxable person is anyone carrying on a business (defined in EU law as an 'economic activity') and for a supply to exist for VAT purposes there must be consideration.

A 'taxable person' for VAT purposes includes a sole trader, a partnership, a limited company, a trust (for example, a charitable trust) which supplies services, and central and local government and many others.

As noted above, the registration threshold is £83,000 and a taxable person is required to be registered if either their turnover in the past 12 months has exceeded this threshold, or the anticipated turnover in the next 30 days will exceed £83,000. This could, for example, occur if a property is to be sold. A trader making taxable supplies below the registration threshold, or an intending trader, can apply to register voluntarily, to reclaim input tax.

If a person intends to acquire a business from another person as a going concern, and that business is required to be registered, the acquirer must register for VAT with effect from a date on or before the transfer date, for the transfer to be treated as not a supply for VAT purposes (ie outside the scope of VAT). In order to achieve this, it is vital that the intended acquiring company has applied to be registered for VAT with effect from a date on or before the transfer date.

If an elected (for VAT to be charged) property is to be transferred as part of a transfer of a going concern, the transferee must elect to charge VAT on the property ('Opt to Tax') with effect from a date on or before the transfer date for the transfer to be treated as a transfer of a going concern. The acquirer must also confirm that their VAT election will not be disapplied under the anti-avoidance rules.

Focus

A trader needs to monitor monthly turnover to avoid potential penalties for failing to register on time.

Where you are acquiring a business as a going concern, ensure all VAT registration matters and any option to tax issues are properly dealt with before the acquisition date.

Example 38.1 – Monitoring turnover for registration

KP starts trading in January providing consultancy services. His turnover is erratic, because he depends on a few large contracts. His monthly turnover is as set out below:

	Monthly £	Cumulative £
Jan	10,000	10,000
Feb	2,000	12,000
Mar	23,000	35,000
Apr	nil	35,000
May	22,000	57,000
June	10,000	67,000
July	25,000	92,000
Aug	10,000	102,000
Sep	2,000	104,000
Oct	31,000	135,000
Nov	15,000	150,000
Dec	28,000	178,000

KP's turnover exceeds the registration threshold (£83,000) on 31 July and he must apply to register by 31 August. He will then be registered from 1 September. If he does not apply in time, all supplies he makes from 1 September will be treated as VAT inclusive. For example, if he applied to register at the end of December, all supplies during September to December (£76,000) are treated as VAT inclusive. At 20% VAT, HMRC would require £12,666.67, to be declared as output tax on the first return, plus a penalty for late notification will be levied based on the net liability for that period (output tax less input tax).

More information on registration can be found on HMRC's website (www. hmrc.gov.uk/vat/start/register/index.htm).

A person who only makes zero-rated supplies can apply for exception from registration, but would not then be able to reclaim input tax.

When a person registers for VAT, he can reclaim VAT on certain goods and services purchased before registration, subject to certain conditions. Full details can be found at www.hmrc.gov.uk/vat/start/register/purchases-before. htm.

For goods, the conditions are, briefly:

- the goods must have been bought by the entity now registered within four years before registration;

- the goods are to be used for making taxable supplies;

- the goods are still held at date of registration, or have been used to make other goods still held at registration;

- the person must keep records showing the dates and quantities of purchased goods, when any goods were used to make other goods, and when the goods were disposed of after registration.

For services, the conditions are, briefly:

- the services must have been bought by the registered entity within six months before registration;

- they must relate to taxable supplies made by the registered entity after the registration date (not used prior to registration, e.g. work on goods that have been sold prior to the registration date);

- the entity must keep records showing the dates the services were supplied, the cost and the VAT paid, and be able to demonstrate the use they were put to.

If any form of disaggregation is being considered to avoid the need to register on all or part of a business (by splitting the business into two or more discrete elements, one or more of which is below the VAT registration threshold and therefore not registered) then considerable care must be taken to ensure that both the legal and the practical operation supports the view taken.

HMRC will normally examine financial, economic and organisational links of closely associated activities in depth, to ensure there really are discrete businesses. If HMRC consider that there is artificial separation, then they will direct that the activities should be treated as one business for VAT purposes. When HMRC invoke the measures, the liability to be registered as a single business will take effect from the date of the direction.

Focus

HMRC regard business splitting (to avoid the need to register one or both businesses) as avoidance and will seek to counteract it.

It is therefore vital that businesses seeking to do this ensure their paperwork is in order and that the contractual rules laid down are strictly adhered to.

THE REGISTRATION PROCESS

38.2　As noted above, a person is required to be registered if his taxable turnover in the past 12 months, or in the following 30 days, will exceed £83,000.

Even if a person does not register, he qualifies as a taxable person, and must account to HMRC for VAT on any supplies made whilst he is required to be registered. This could involve paying substantial amounts of tax to HMRC if the person registers belatedly.

An application for registration is made by the submission of Form VAT1, although there may in many circumstances be other prescribed forms. For example, a partnership is required to complete Form VAT2 giving details of the partners. If a group registration is required, the representative member of that group registration (the person in whose name the registration was made) must complete Form VAT50, and all other companies in the group must complete Form VAT51.

Where the business is involved in property related transactions, Form VAT5L must also be completed and accompany the VAT1.

Focus

When registering a business, review HMRC's VAT registration website to ensure you have completed all the forms relevant to your registration.

Otherwise, the application may be rejected, but will certainly be delayed.

Group registration is possible where companies are within a group (51% control) or under common ownership. It is in some circumstances possible to register UK branches of foreign companies as a group with UK subsidiary companies. A detailed discussion of group VAT registration is beyond the scope of this work, but the broad effect is to treat all the members of the group as a single entity for VAT purposes, and to ignore supplies between the companies within the VAT group. However, all companies within the group are joint and severally liable for the VAT payable.

VAT REGISTRATION – PRACTICAL ISSUES

38.3   Where a person is required to be registered, the registration takes place with effect from the date of that requirement. However, the person cannot actually add VAT until he has a VAT registration number. He should add an amount equivalent to the VAT and note on the invoices that a VAT registration number has been applied for. Tax invoices can then be issued once he has received his VAT registration number.

From 1 August 2012, all VAT registration applications can be made online, but HMRC are still accepting paper applications at this time. The benefit of an online application is that receipt is acknowledged electronically and a reference given, so that it is easier to query the progress of the application with HMRC.

It is important to note that it is the entity, not the business, which is being registered.

Example 38.2 – Trader with more than one business

If a sole trader accountant turns over £70,000 per annum, he is not required to be registered. However, if he also makes other taxable supplies, amounting to more than £13,000 (therefore exceeding the registration threshold) he will be obliged to register. It should also be noted for these purposes that the accountant's turnover will include any recharged expenses involved in his work.

If, on the other hand, the accountant is registered, and also owns some residential property which is let (an exempt supply) he will need to consider carefully whether any part of the input tax attributable to his business generally will need to be disallowed as relating to exempt supplies.

Returns must be completed for three-monthly periods ending on the dates notified in the certificate of registration. In order to spread the flow of returns over the year, taxable persons are allocated to one of the three groups of VAT periods, and it is possible to request one that will coincide with the business' accounting period.

DEREGISTRATION

38.4   If the taxable turnover of a UK business reduces to £81,000 or less, the taxpayer can deregister for VAT. For a retail business (or anyone supplying customers that cannot recover VAT) this can be beneficial.

If at the date of deregistration the business has stock and assets on hand on which VAT has been recovered, the business needs to account for this VAT to HMRC on a final return. This is subject to a de minimis limit of £1,000.

There is no deregistration threshold for businesses not established in the UK who are making taxable supplies here.

How to cancel your VAT registration

38.5   In order to cancel VAT registration, Form VAT7 should be completed and sent to HMRC. This is normally sent to:

HMRC Grimsby Deregistration Unit,
Imperial House,
77 Victoria Street,
Grimsby
DN31 1DB.

A business may also request deregistration via their online account.

A business can either be deregistered compulsorily (normally when it has ceased to make taxable supplies), when its legal status changes or in certain other limited circumstances.

HMRC may seek further information about the business' intention before agreeing to deregister.

More details can be found at www.hmrc.gov.uk/vat/managing/change/cancel. htm.

> **Focus**
>
> If a business' taxable turnover reduces below the £81,000 threshold, and is likely to stay that way, consider deregistering, particularly if most customers cannot reclaim VAT.

APPENDIX: REGISTRATION LIMITS

UK-taxable supplies

(*VATA 1994, Sch 1, para 1*; Supplement to Notices 700/1 and 700/11)

38.6

Effective date	Turnover: (a) Past year exceeded; or (b) Next 30 days will exceed:	Exception: Turnover for next year will not exceed:
	£	£
01.04.16	83,000	81,000
01.04.15	82,000	80,000
01.04.14	81,000	79,000
01.04.13	79,000	77,000
01.04.12	77,000	75,000
01.04.11	73,000	71,000
01.04.10	70,000	68,000
01.05.09	68,000	66,000
01.04.08	67,000	65,000
01.04.07	64,000	62,000

Notes

1 *Taxable supplies* – Turnover includes zero-rated and reduced rate sales, but not exempt, non-business or outside the scope supplies. Supplies of capital assets (excluding any supplies of land on which the option to tax has been exercised) do not count towards the turnover limit. The same applies to any taxable supplies which would not be taxable supplies apart from *VATA 1994, s 7(4)* (ie in connection with 'distance selling'). Any supplies or acquisitions to which *VATA 1994, s 18B(4)* (last acquisition or supply of goods before removal from fiscal warehousing) applies, and supplies treated as made by him under *s 18C(3)* (self-supply of services on removal of goods from warehousing), are also disregarded (*VATA 1994, Sch 1, para 1(7)–(9)*).

2 *Compulsory registration* – A person who makes taxable supplies but is not registered under *VATA 1994* becomes liable to be registered if: (a) the one-year, or (b) 30-day turnover limits above are exceeded (*Sch 1, para 1*). However, the one-year turnover test in (a) above is subject to an exception (see Note 4 below).

3   *Going concern* – If all or part of a business carried on by a taxable person
     is transferred to another person as a going concern, and the transferee
     is not registered under *VATA 1994* at the time of transfer, the transferee
     becomes liable to be registered if: (a) the one-year, or (b) 30-day limits
     above are exceeded (*Sch 1, para 2*). However, the one-year turnover test
     in (a) above is subject to an exception (see Note 4 below).

4   *Exception* – A person does not become liable to be registered under the
     mandatory (see Note 2) or going concern (see Note 3) provisions under
     the one-year turnover test in (a) above if HMRC are satisfied that the
     value of his taxable supplies in the one-year period beginning when
     he would otherwise become liable to be registered does not exceed the
     exception limits in the table above (*Sch 1, para 3*).

5   *Non-UK established businesses* – From 1 December 2012, businesses
     without a UK establishment (non-established businesses) who make any
     UK taxable supplies must register for UK VAT regardless of the value of
     taxable supplies they make in the UK (*Sch 1A*).

39

VAT – place of supply

SIGNPOSTS

- **Supply of goods** – If a business supplies goods to customers in other countries, it is necessary to consider the rules which determine whether VAT has to be charged at the standard rate or at 0% (see **39.2**).

- **Supply of services** – Supplies of services to overseas customers may be standard rated, zero-rated or subject to the reverse charge rules (see **39.3–39.4**).

- **Foreign transactions** – Businesses subject to the reverse charge rules need to consider their VAT position with regard to registration and VAT returns (see **39.5**).

- **Compliance** – Businesses selling goods or services to the EC are required to complete an EC sales list and may be instructed to complete intrastat returns (see **39.6–39.7**).

INTRODUCTION

39.1   If UK VAT was added to charges for goods and services supplied to people in other countries, either this would form an absolute cost to them, or they would need to go through a procedure to reclaim the VAT. Rules have therefore been devised to ensure that the VAT system works smoothly when dealing with supplies of goods and services to overseas customers.

There are four basic rules, depending on whether the supplies in question are goods or services, and whether or not the recipient is established in an EU member state. The position also depends, for EU supplies of goods, on whether the recipient is carrying on a business and for services, there are a number of types of service which do not fall within the general rule.

GOODS

39.2   Where goods are exported to a place outside the European Union by the supplier, these goods can be zero rated. Evidence of export should be retained, to satisfy HMRC on review that the goods have been properly exported. This will normally take the form of shipping documentation.

> **Focus**
>
> Ensure all shipping documentation is retained to justify the zero rating of exports of goods.

Where the customer is established in the EU, the VAT treatment depends on whether the customer is a business customer or a private individual.

Where the customer is a business customer, and the supplier obtains evidence of such, (usually the VAT number), he can zero rate the supply. The purchaser then accounts for 'acquisition tax' in his home territory, as an output tax declaration (Box 2 on the UK VAT return). Recovery of the related input tax depends on the overall use to which the goods are put.

> **Focus**
>
> Where charging business customers in another EU member state, it is vital to get the other party's VAT number.
>
> Evidence of shipment to the customer should also be retained.

> **Example 39.1 – Goods imported for a business**
>
> Harry runs a business. He strips the walls of his business premises, and spends £100,000 on importing tiles for his premises from a supplier in Italy. The agreed percentage VAT recovery for Harry's business is 80%. The Italian supplier does not charge VAT on the invoice as Harry has supplied his UK VAT registration number to him.
>
> Harry must include output tax (at 20%) of £20,000 in Box 2 of his return. The recoverable input tax is 80% of £20,000, i.e. £16,000, which is included in Box 4.

Where the purchaser is a private individual, they cannot, of course, account for the VAT. Supplies of goods by an EU business to private individuals in a different EU country are therefore chargeable to VAT in the country of supply. This gives rise to a danger of 'VAT rate shopping' or goods escaping the VAT net altogether (low value consignments from outside the EU).

In order to prevent this, the distance selling regulations were introduced, and they apply to any goods sold to private individuals in the United Kingdom (or elsewhere in the EU) by a non-established supplier. The supplier must register if the value of their distance sales is over the registration limit for that particular country.

BUSINESS TO BUSINESS SERVICES ('B2B')

39.3   The place of supply rules for services were significantly altered with effect from 1 January 2010. The general rule is that the place of supply of services which are supplied business to business ('B2B') is where the customer belongs. The recipient is required to account for VAT under local rules, using the 'reverse charge' mechanism.

This requires the recipient to account for input and output VAT locally (in the EU country of receipt), paying over the output VAT, and reclaiming input tax in accordance with its normal recovery percentage. For a fully taxable business (one which only makes taxable supplies) this should not result in any cost. The UK procedure is set out at the end of this chapter (see **39.5**).

There are, however, specific exceptions to this general rule. Travel related services, such as hotel and restaurant services, and admissions to events are taxed in the country of consumption. There is a procedure available (under the Eighth EU VAT Directive) to reclaim these costs from the VAT authorities in the country where they were incurred, provided that a local trader would have been able to reclaim the same input tax. The refund application is submitted to HMRC online and the details are passed to the refunding country who will make contact directly via e-mail about the progress of the application.

The place of supply of land-related services is where the land is situated and for passenger transport services is where the transport takes place. This could require VAT registrations in other EU countries; for example, an estate agent who supplies services relating to properties in Spain (by selling them) should register for Spanish VAT.

The general place of supply rules are also modified in relation to the hiring of goods, telecoms, broadcasting and electronically supplied services, where the place of supply is subject to the 'use and enjoyment' provisions in certain cases. These provisions would come in to play where, for example, a UK business supplies a business outside the EU, but the services are used and enjoyed in the UK. Under the general rule, the place of supply would be outside the EU, but under the use and enjoyment provisions, the supplies are deemed to be supplied in the UK and UK VAT is charged.

Focus

Check whether services you are supplying fall within any of the exception categories before deciding not to add VAT. For services supplied to businesses in other EU countries, you also need to obtain evidence that your customer is registered for VAT.

BUSINESS TO CONSUMER SERVICES ('B2C')

39.4   Where a business supplies services to a person in a private capacity located in another EU country, the place of supply is deemed to be where the supplier belongs and VAT charged accordingly. However, the place of supply of most intangible services continues to be where the customer belongs when provided to non-business customers outside the EU.

From 1 January 2015, where a telecom, broadcasting and e-services business located in an EU member state supplies a consumer in another EU member state, the supply is treated as supplied where the consumer belongs. To avoid the need for companies to set up multiple registrations in different member states, a 'mini one stop shop' allows businesses to register only in the UK and account for the different countries' VAT on a single return.

The effect of these changes is that purchasers of, for example, e-books, will have to pay VAT at the rate in their home country, not that of the retailer. Retailers such as Amazon who currently account for VAT at a lower rate in Luxembourg will need to account for UK VAT at 20%, which will remove some of the price advantage of being based outside the UK.

Focus

When supplying services to private individuals ensure the recipient is outside the EU before deciding not to charge VAT.

VAT ACCOUNTING IN RELATION TO FOREIGN TRANSACTIONS

39.5   A person purchasing services from overseas which are required to be accounted for under the reverse charge mechanism, accounts for these as an output tax declaration in Box 1 of the VAT return (assuming that the service is actually standard rated under UK rules). The business may be able to reclaim this reverse charge VAT as input tax, depending on what activity the cost is attributable to. If related wholly to taxable activities, the value of the reverse charge output tax is included as input tax on the return.

> **Focus**
>
> Exempt businesses buying services from abroad need to bear in mind the possible need to register for VAT by virtue of the VAT to be accounted for under the reverse charge procedure.

It should be noted that the value of reverse charge services received counts towards the VAT registration limit.

For example, a person who has otherwise made taxable supplies of £60,000 in the past year must register for UK VAT if the value of services received from abroad (together with the £60,000) exceeds the registration threshold. This means that largely exempt businesses buying services from abroad may be required to register and account for VAT on these supplies (the related input tax being wholly or mainly irrecoverable).

With regard to the recovery of input tax, where a UK supplier makes supplies outside the United Kingdom (many international services) the general approach is to consider whether such supplies would have been taxable if made in the United Kingdom. If they would have been taxable if made in the UK, then input tax relating to them is treated as recoverable (in effect they are treated the same way as zero-rated supplies), but if the supplies would have been exempt if made in the United Kingdom, the input tax attributable is generally not recoverable. However, where the supplies are of a finance or insurance nature, and are made outside the European Union, the input tax attributable to such supplies is recoverable.

EC SALES LIST

39.6   A business which sells goods or services to businesses in other EC countries is required to complete an EC sales list (ESL). An ESL is completed calendar quarterly with details of both the value of goods and services (Boxes 8 and 9 of the VAT return are goods only). Full details of the ESL procedure can be found on the HMRC website (www.hmrc.gov.uk/vat/managing/international/esl/reporting-esl.htm#1).

These returns are used by the VAT authorities in the destination country to monitor compliance with VAT rules. Where completion of an EC Sales List is required, these can also be submitted online.

INTRASTAT RETURNS

39.7   Where a business conducts substantial business with the rest of the EU, consisting of trade in goods, it must complete further statistical returns for acquisitions or dispatches. HMRC will notify traders who are required to complete Intrastat returns. This is done electronically, within 21 days of the end of the return period in question. Returns are required where dispatches (sales to other EU countries) exceed £250,000, or arrivals (purchases from other EU countries) exceed £1,500,000. Full details can be found on the HMRC website.

HMRC monitor dispatches and arrivals using Boxes 8 and 9 of the VAT Return, and will write to any business whose trade levels are close to the limits to remind them of the need to submit Intrastat returns.

Focus

Businesses required to complete EC sales lists and Intrastat returns should ensure they register online and have arrangements in place for prompt completion, in order to avoid penalties.

40

VAT – simplification schemes for small business

SIGNPOSTS

- **Annual accounting scheme** – Under this arrangement a business pays an estimate of its VAT liability monthly, and then has to pay any balance due when it submits an annual return (see **40.1**).

- **Cash accounting scheme** – Some businesses can choose to account for VAT on the basis of cash accounting which can be advantageous if their debtors are slow to pay (see **40.2**).

- **Flat rate scheme** – Under a flat rate scheme the business accounts for VAT on the basis of a multiple of turnover but does not recover any input tax. In addition, a farmers' flat rate scheme provides an alternative to VAT registration for farmers (see **40.3–40.4**).

- **Appendix: Cash accounting scheme** – Further information on the cash accounting scheme is included at the end of this chapter (see **40.5**).

ANNUAL ACCOUNTING

40.1   Under the annual accounting scheme, a business pays its VAT liability on a monthly or quarterly basis, based on the previous year's returns, but submits only one VAT return per annum.

The main disadvantage of this (at least for accountants and other advisers) is that it does not require a business to keep its records up to date. In addition, the balancing payment made when the return is submitted may result in a substantial loss of cash flow when the business is expanding.

A company can join the annual accounting scheme if its taxable turnover (excluding VAT) is not more than £1,350,000 per annum. The normal payment method is that nine equal monthly payments are made, each amounting to 10% of the total VAT paid in the previous year. These payments are made on the last working day of each of the 4th to 12th months of the accounting year. As an alternative, 25% of the previous year's liability can be paid in the 4th, 7th and 10th months.

The return is then submitted within two months after the end of the 12th month of the VAT year. It is possible to use both the annual accounting scheme and the VAT flat rate scheme together, provided that the business qualifies for both (see **40.3–40.4** for details of the flat rate scheme).

Further details on the operation of the annual accounting scheme, including how to apply, can be found on HMRC's website (www.hmrc.gov.uk/vat/start/schemes/annual.htm).

Forms VAT 600 AA (application to join the scheme) and VAT 600 AA/FRS (to join both this and the flat rate scheme) can be found using links on this page.

> **Focus**
>
> The annual accounting scheme is intended as a simplification measure, and may benefit the cash flow of an expanding business.

CASH ACCOUNTING SCHEME

40.2 A business can use the cash accounting scheme if its turnover does not exceed £1,350,000 on an annual basis. It does not need to apply to HMRC to operate this. The scheme is very useful for businesses which give their customers extended credit (willingly or unwillingly!).

The business issues its VAT invoices as normal, but only pays over the VAT once it has received the cash from its customers. This clearly gives the business a cash flow advantage and also provides it with automatic bad debt relief, since VAT is only paid when the cash is actually received.

The corollary of this is that input tax cannot be claimed until the invoices are actually paid. The scheme is therefore most useful to a business which has relatively low input tax and fully taxable outputs which it invoices on a credit basis.

The other main disadvantage of using the scheme is that it does require additional accounting records to be kept, to ensure that VAT is paid over when cash is received and reclaimed when invoices are paid.

The following points about the scheme should be noted:

- A business can use the scheme if it has reasonable grounds for believing that its taxable supplies in the next 12 months will not exceed £1,350,000.

- It is up to date with its returns, or it has agreed a basis for settling any outstanding amounts and the business has not been convicted of any form of VAT offence or assessed for a penalty for dishonest contact.

- Zero-rated supplies count towards the turnover limit (which is taxable supplies) and exempt ones do not count.

- A business does not need to inform HMRC before using this scheme.

- The scheme can be used from the beginning of a VAT year but the cash accounting scheme does not cover lease or hire purchase agreements, credit sales or conditional sale agreements or supplies where full payment is not due within six months, or advance payments.

- A business must leave the scheme if its taxable supplies have exceeded £1.6 million in the previous four VAT quarters. If, however, the business can show that this increase was exceptional and that the value of its supplies will go back down below £1.6 million, it can stay within the scheme. For example, if a business sells its (opted) property for £800,000 plus VAT, and its normal level of taxable supplies is £1 million, the property sale will cause the value of the supplies to exceed £1.6 million. However, it should be possible in those circumstances to agree with HMRC that the business should continue within the scheme.

The scheme may not be suitable for a new business, since it usually purchases the necessary equipment to set itself up on credit. However, once the business is up and running, if it supplies services and therefore has low input tax, the cash accounting scheme may be very suitable.

If the business decides to join the cash accounting scheme (at the start of the VAT year), it must be very careful to differentiate between invoices accounted for under the 'normal scheme' and invoices accounted for under cash accounting, to avoid accounting for any VAT twice.

The business will need to keep a cash book summarising payments received and made, with a separate column for the VAT, or some other form of VAT account, to demonstrate how the VAT return figures are arrived at.

Focus

Consider cash accounting if the business allows customers credit, or has disputed bills.

THE FLAT RATE SCHEME

40.3   The flat rate scheme is a VAT simplification measure, under which a business accounts for VAT by applying a specified percentage to its turnover, without claiming input VAT in the normal way. It is normally unsuitable for businesses which recover more input tax than its output tax on a regular basis, since the input tax will not be recoverable.

It should be noted that the key purpose of this scheme is simplification, and businesses may pay more net VAT to HMRC as a result of using the scheme, rather than less.

VAT is calculated at the appropriate percentage (depending on the company's trading activity) of the 'scheme turnover'. This includes zero-rated and exempt sales as well as taxable sales (including VAT), and businesses which make such supplies should check very carefully whether there is any benefit in using the scheme. Flat rate traders still issue VAT invoices as normal.

The scheme is only available to very small businesses, being those where the expected taxable turnover in the next 12 months will not exceed £150,000 (net of VAT) and cannot be used in conjunction with the cash accounting scheme.

The VAT return liability is therefore calculated by applying the appropriate flat rate percentage to relevant turnover and declared as follows on the VAT return:

- Box 1: VAT due under the flat rate scheme plus any other output tax (usually from sales of capital assets on which input tax has been recovered).

- Box 2: VAT due in the period on acquisitions from other EU member states.

- Box 3: the sum of Boxes 1 and 2.

- Box 4: normally nil unless there is a claim in respect of purchases of capital items exceeding £2,000 or stocks and assets on registration.

- Box 5: total VAT payable or reclaimable (Box 3 *minus* Box 4).

- Box 6: the value of turnover including VAT to which the flat rate scheme percentage is applied, plus the value of any supplies accounted for outside the scheme, such as supplies of capital assets.

- Box 7: normally nil (unless including capital purchases outside the scheme or EU acquisitions).

- Boxes 8 and 9: as normal.

A flat rate trader ceases to be eligible for the scheme if, at the anniversary of the start date, the total value of the turnover is more than £230,000, or there is reason to assume that the total value of the income during the 30 days beginning on that date will exceed £230,000, or he becomes a tour operator, or intends to acquire, construct or otherwise obtain an item falling within the capital goods scheme.

More information on the VAT flat rate scheme can be found on HMRC's website (www.hmrc.gov.uk/vat/start/schemes/flat-rate.htm).

This includes a link to Form VAT 600 FRS, the application to join the flat rate scheme.

The flat rate to be used depends on the type of business, and there is an extensive menu of rates on the website above. The 'base' rate is 12%, but this is amended for various businesses, including (this list is a small sample, and *not* comprehensive, and the reader is referred to the list on the HMRC website):

- Accountancy and bookkeeping   14.5%*
- Catering services   12.5%
- General building services   9.5%
- Labour only building services   14.5%
- Food manufacture   9%
- Post offices   5%
- Sport or recreation   8.5%

*The 14.5% rate also applies to a number of other professional services.

Newly registered businesses can take advantage of a 1% discount on the relevant rate for a period of one year from the date of registration, after which they revert to the full rate.

Focus

It is important to check whether using the flat rate scheme will actually benefit the business before deciding to use it.

FARMERS' FLAT RATE SCHEME

40.4   The farmers' flat rate scheme is an alternative to VAT registration for farmers, ie it provides a method for small farms and other agricultural businesses to avoid the need to complete VAT returns and allows them to recover a small amount of VAT.

The farmers' scheme works by a farmer adding the flat rate addition of 4% of his sales to VAT registered customers only. This addition applies even where the goods would be zero-rated. For example, sales to a supermarket would attract the 4% addition, but sales to private individuals (for example, on 'pick your own' schemes) would not. The purchaser can reclaim this 'addition' as if it was input tax, and the farmer retains the amount charged.

Designated activities that can be included in the scheme are: most agricultural production activities, including general agricultural, stock farming, poultry, rabbit farming, bee-keeping and similar; forestry; and freshwater fish farming. Production and processing is covered when it is essentially processing of products derived from the agricultural production.

Activities such as dealing in animals, training animals, breeding pets or processing farm produce do not normally qualify to be included in the scheme.

APPENDIX: CASH ACCOUNTING SCHEME

(VAT Regulations 1995 (SI 1995/2518), regs 58, 60; HMRC Notice 731)

40.5

Effective date	Joining threshold (Column 1)	Leaving threshold (Column 2)
	£	£
1.4.07	1,350,000	1,600,000
1.4.04	660,000	825,000
1.4.01	600,000	750,000

Notes

1   *Joining threshold* – A business can use the scheme if estimated taxable supplies in the next year is not expected to exceed the above joining threshold, and subject to certain other criteria (see *SI 1995/2518, reg 58* and VAT Notice 731, para 2.1).

2   *Leaving threshold* – A business must leave the scheme if the value of taxable supplies for a 12-month period (ending at the end of a tax period) has exceeded the above leaving threshold (*SI 1995/2518, reg 60*; see also VAT Notice 731, para 6.2).

3   *'One-off' sales increases* – A business may remain on cash accounting where it exceeds the amount in column 2 above because of a one-off increase in sales resulting from a genuine commercial activity, provided there are reasonable grounds for believing that the value of its taxable supplies in the next 12 months will be below the amount in column 1 (see VAT Notice 731, para 2.6).

41

VAT – special schemes and partial exemption

SIGNPOSTS

- **Retail schemes** – These provide a means of arriving at the VAT due for businesses such as shops that do not usually issue invoices (see **41.2**).

- **Second hand goods schemes** – Dealers in second hand goods such as cars can use a special scheme under which they only account for VAT on the margin (see **41.3**).

- **Tour operator's margin scheme** – This scheme applies mainly to package holidays of travel and accommodation, and allows the business to account for VAT on the margin rather than having to try to reclaim non-UK VAT (see **41.4**).

- **Partial exemption** – Businesses that have taxable supplies and exempt supplies are partially exempt, and can only recover a proportion of their input VAT (see **41.5–41.6**).

- **Capital goods scheme** – This scheme applies to the recovery of VAT on expenditure on land and buildings, computer equipment, aircraft and boats but adjustments are only required for businesses where VAT recovery on costs is restricted (see **41.7**).

- **Appendix: Partial exemption** – A table of partial exemption *de minimis* limits is included at the end of the chapter (see **41.8**).

INTRODUCTION

41.1   VAT is intended as a tax on the final consumers, but one which is collected by businesses. It applies on an EU-wide basis, but each EU member state has its own VAT system. There are a number of special schemes available to facilitate VAT accounting:

- retail schemes;
- tour operators' margin schemes (TOMS);
- second hand goods schemes.

RETAIL SCHEMES

41.2   Where one business supplies goods to another, it is required to issue a VAT invoice, which contains specific details and allows the recipient to reclaim the input VAT. It is recognised that businesses dealing directly with the public (primarily shopkeepers) would find it difficult to keep records of every sale and the retail schemes are therefore methods to arrive at a value for the VAT due and determine what percentage of sales are subject to VAT at the different rates.

For larger businesses, approximation methods have largely been superseded by electronic point of sales systems, which can precisely identify the amount of VAT charged from bar codes.

The various retail schemes are set out in detail in VAT Notice 727/2 and this Notice has the force of law. It is important to consider carefully which retail scheme is best used, since HMRC will not allow retrospective changes from one scheme to another.

It is also important to bear in mind that the amount of VAT paid by any retail business effectively constitutes a cost to that business, and the adviser will seek to minimise this legitimately wherever possible. The choice of which retail scheme to use is therefore an important consideration for the profitability of the business.

> **Focus**
>
> The choice of an appropriate and correct retail scheme could improve business profitability.

Briefly the schemes are as follows:

Point of sale scheme	Available when all sales are at one rate of VAT (VAT fraction applied), or where supplies are made at two or more rates and liability identified at point of sale. Turnover limit £130 million.
Apportionment scheme 1	Sales split to tax rates in the same proportion as goods purchased for resale. Turnover limit £1 million.
Apportionment scheme 2	Sales at different rates determined by calculating expected selling prices (ESPs) of standard rate and reduced rate goods purchased. Turnover limit £130 million.

Direct Calculation   ESPs of minority goods only calculated.
scheme 1   Turnover limit £1 million.

Direct Calculation   As above but with an annual stock adjustment.
scheme 2   Turnover limit £130 million.

Where the £130 million threshold is exceeded a business must agree a bespoke scheme with HMRC.

Further details are available on HMRC's website (www.hmrc.gov.uk/vat/start/ schemes/retail.htm).

SECOND HAND GOODS SCHEMES

41.3 Such a scheme applies to goods that are sold back by private individuals or non VAT registered businesses to dealers who will then sell them on again. The most obvious example is cars, but this also applies to washing machines and other domestic appliances and furniture.

In such cases, the dealer may use a second hand goods scheme and only account for VAT on the margin.

The scheme is not compulsory and goods eligible for the scheme can still be sold in the normal way (VAT accounted for on the full selling price). VAT margin schemes are discussed in detail in HMRC Notice 718, which can be accessed on HMRC's website.

More detail can be found at www.hmrc.gov.uk/vat/start/schemes/margin.htm.

Example 41.1 – Second hand goods scheme for a garage

A garage buys a used car from a customer for £5,000. After servicing and any necessary repairs and refurbishment, the garage sells it for £7,400.

The VAT inclusive margin is then £2,400, of which £400 (1/6th) is accounted for as VAT. Any input tax incurred on the refurbishment (for example, on parts) can be deducted as normal in box 4 of the VAT return.

The margin scheme covers virtually all second hand goods and is available in countries throughout the EU. There are a number of conditions and record keeping requirements outlined in the Notice and if these are not adhered to, HMRC can insist that VAT is accounted for on the full selling price.

> **Focus**
>
> If the business wants to operate a margin scheme, ensure that all record keeping and invoicing requirements are adhered to, in order to avoid a challenge by HMRC.

TOUR OPERATOR'S MARGIN SCHEME

41.4 The tour operator's margin scheme (TOMS) is a special scheme for businesses that buy in and sell packages of travel, accommodation, etc. It is an EU-wide provision to enable VAT to be accounted for on travel supplies without the business needing to register in different EU countries, ie it can be used to deal with the issue arising from package holidays which are sold in one country (for example, the United Kingdom) by a tour operator and enjoyed in another (for example, Spain). Naturally, the Spanish hotelier would need to charge Spanish VAT and there are problems with the UK VAT operator reclaiming this.

The overall principle is that VAT is only accounted for on the margin between the VAT inclusive purchase price of the individual margin scheme supplies (no VAT recoverable) and the selling price of the package and although intended as a simplification measure it can be extremely complex to operate. For further details see VAT Notice 709/5 which has force of law. This can be found on the HMRC website.

When margin scheme supplies are made in the UK, the margin is standard rated when the supplies are enjoyed in the EU and zero-rated when enjoyed outside the EU.

TOMS does not only apply to normal 'tour operators', but can also apply to packages of bus travel and event tickets, for example, organised solely within the UK.

> **Focus**
>
> TOMS may apply to anyone who organises 'package' trips.

PARTIAL EXEMPTION – INTRODUCTION

41.5 The following should be borne in mind:

- every business situation is different;
- irrecoverable VAT is a cost to the business.

Some businesses make supplies that are wholly taxable, or wholly exempt. They can recover respectively all or none of the input VAT attributable to those supplies. However, many businesses make a mixture of both taxable and exempt supplies. Still other businesses will make supplies that are taxable and also have non-business income (for example, they may receive grants where no supplies are made to the funder in return for the consideration). Such businesses can recover an 'appropriate proportion' of the VAT they incur, to the extent that it is attributable to taxable supplies.

This principle of attribution underlies the whole of partial exemption and non-business apportionment. VAT incurred that is attributable to non-business activities is irrecoverable (unless allowable under a special refund scheme for public bodies etc). Input tax incurred that is attributable to exempt activities can only be recovered if within the de minimis limits.

Where a business makes certain incidental supplies (for example, a manufacturing company places money on deposit and earns interest, which is an exempt supply) the input tax attributable to this interest is ignored, on the basis that it would be minimal. The true business of the company is manufacturing, and that is what the input tax incurred is attributable to.

Where exempt supplies are not 'incidental' however, there needs to be a fair and reasonable apportionment of overhead input tax to those supplies. For example, a sole practitioner accountant will often be registered for VAT, because his turnover exceeds the threshold. If the accountant also owns residential investment property, in his sole name and receives exempt rental income, then he is partially exempt for VAT purposes; having outputs which are both taxable (accountancy services) and exempt (rental). The accountant is required, in principle, to directly attribute his input tax to those activities and apportion any overhead (residual) VAT between the two.

The partial exemption calculation comprises a two stage process. The first stage is to attribute those inputs which are used wholly for either taxable or exempt supplies. Using **Example 38.2** above, repairs to one of the houses would be wholly attributable to exempt supplies, so the input VAT would, in principle, be lost. On the other hand, if the accountant has an office (not used to manage the property letting side of the business), the heating bills for that office would be wholly attributable to taxable supplies, and therefore recoverable in full.

This will leave a 'pot' of residual input tax which cannot be attributable directly either to taxable, or to exempt, supplies. For example, the accountant's tax return (assuming that he pays someone to do this for him) will include both his practice income and his property income. The question is how much of this can be reclaimed.

The standard method of partial exemption apportions residual input tax in the ratio of taxable outputs to total outputs for the period concerned. For example, if a business has residual input tax of £10,000 and total income of £100,000 of which £80,000 is taxable (80%), the taxable portion that is recoverable would be £8,000.

This leaves £2,000 irrecoverable 'exempt input tax' on overheads in addition to any VAT that is wholly related to his exempt supplies.

It is reasonable to suggest that the amount of effort expended in earning £1,000 of accounting income is greater than that involved in earning £1,000 of rental income. For this reason, it is likely that an apportionment based on turnover might be unfair to the accountant and an alternative 'special method' can be agreed. In practice however, unless the directly attributable exempt input tax is particularly high (due to refurbishment, for example), for businesses of this kind, exempt input tax is likely to be within the *de minimis* limit (£7,500 per annum and less than 50% of total input tax incurred) and will be fully recoverable.

In all cases, the key issue is to adopt a method which appears fair to both the taxpayer and HMRC (since HMRC will need to agree any special method) and present the case, arguing forcefully for the chosen method.

Where the amounts of input tax are relatively small, so that the total exempt input tax (input directly or indirectly attributed to exempt supplies) is less than both £7,500 per annum and 50% of total input tax, all input tax can be reclaimed.

Where returns are made quarterly, the initial calculation is done on a quarterly basis (with an 'exempt' input tax de minimis limit of £1,875). Where returns are done monthly, the monthly limit is £625. An annual calculation is performed at the partial exemption tax year end (March, April or May) and appropriate adjustments made.

Example 41.2 – Input tax: de minimis limit

Romney's exempt input tax (wholly attributable and a percentage of residual) is as follows:

Quarter to	Exempt input tax
30.6	£1,300
30.9	£2,000
31.12	£1,500
31.3	£1,700

In all cases, Romney's total input tax is £20,000 per quarter, so the exempt input tax is less than half the total.

Romney reclaims all his input tax in the quarters to 30 June, 31 December and 31 March, but disallows £2,000 in his September return.

Romney's total exempt input tax for the year to 31 March is £6,500, within the annual *de minimis* limit (£7,500). So he can reclaim the £2,000 in his June return that year.

Focus

Partial exemption is a complex issue, which depends on the facts in each case. The business case for any special method proposed should be made carefully, as HMRC will only approve alternatives to the standard (turnover-based) method if they consider that the alternative gives a fair and reasonable result.

The standard method does not require HMRC approval, however, where this does not give a fair and reasonable result, a standard method override calculation must be undertaken. The requirement for a standard method override (based on use) might suggest that a special method is required for the future.

Partially exempt businesses are those which make significant exempt supplies. Exempt supplies are listed at **37.6**. The following businesses are likely to be partially exempt (the list is not comprehensive):

- banks and building societies;

- insurance companies and brokers;

- retailers of 'big ticket' items, where a substantial proportion of income is generated from finance or insurance commission;

- post offices;

- businesses which sell or let land;

- schools and educational establishments.

NON-BUSINESS METHODS

41.6   Similar considerations apply where, for example, a charity has both business and non-business income. A supply is anything done for consideration in the course of a business. VAT incurred is not recoverable if it relates to something which is not a supply (for example, a grant, provision of services not for consideration, or other goods and services provided free of charge or below cost by a charity).

The procedure for apportioning VAT incurred may be similar to that for partial exemption. In fact, for charities, there may well be a two stage process, because many charitable supplies are themselves exempt. The first stage is to attribute the VAT incurred between non business (attributable to 'non-supplies') and business, and then apportion the resulting business input tax between that attributable to taxable and exempt supplies. HMRC may allow a combined non-business and partial exemption method if required. VAT attributable to non-business activities is, however, wholly irrecoverable (not subject to de minimis limits).

CAPITAL GOODS SCHEME (CGS)

41.7   If a business incurs VAT bearing capital expenditure of more than £50,000 (net) on computer equipment or an aircraft or boat or more than £250,000 (net) on the taxable purchase, construction, extension or refurbishment of land and buildings, the capital goods scheme provisions come into play. The input tax initially recovered is adjusted over a five-year period for computer equipment, an aircraft, boat or other vessel, or a ten-year period for land and buildings to take account of any changes in the ratio of taxable to total use.

For fully taxable businesses there are not likely to be any change of use adjustments. However, for partially exempt businesses and those with non-business income, the capital goods scheme can work to the advantage, as well as the disadvantage, of the taxpayer.

Example 41.3 – Capital goods scheme adjustments

Grant incurs VAT of £100,000 on the construction of a building he initially uses for a business which is 60% taxable and 40% exempt as determined in his partial exemption calculation. Grant will initially recover VAT of £60,000 and first use/completion determines the start of the first capital goods scheme year (referred to as an interval). The first interval ends at the same time as the partial exemption tax year.

If, after two years, the building is no longer used for the business, but let, the VAT recovered will need to be adjusted over the remaining capital goods scheme intervals.

Each year for the remaining intervals of the capital goods scheme, 1/10th of the input tax incurred is adjusted by the relevant change in use percentage. In the above example, if the rental income is exempt, the adjustment calculation would be:

100,000/10 × −60% = −£6,000 repayable to HMRC each remaining CGS interval.

Alternatively, if the business opts to tax the property so that the rental income is taxable, then there will be 100% taxable use and the calculation in each remaining interval will be:

100,000/10 × 40% = £4,000 to be claimed from HMRC each remaining CGS interval.

Focus

Where CGS applies, ensure the required adjustments are made, and consider whether actions such as opting to tax property can increase recovery.

APPENDIX: PARTIAL EXEMPTION *DE MINIMIS* LIMITS

(*VAT Regulations, SI 1995/2518, regs 106, 107*; HMRC Notice 706)

41.8   Exempt input tax not exceeding:

- £625 per month on average; and

- 50% of total input tax for the period concerned.

Notes

1   *De-minimis threshold* – Businesses which have both taxable and exempt income can treat all their exempt input tax as taxable input tax and recover it all, provided the exempt input tax is below the *de minimis* limit. The input tax claimed in each tax period is provisional until any under or over recovery of input tax is accounted for in an annual adjustment.

2   *New tests* – For VAT periods starting on or after 1 April 2010, two optional simplified *de minimis* tests are available, and also the opportunity for a business to treat itself as *de minimis* throughout a tax year if it was *de minimis* in the previous tax year – but still subject to an annual adjustment at the end of the tax year, which could make the business partly exempt and subject to an input tax payback (see *SI 1995/2518, reg 107*; VAT Information Sheet 04/10).

42

VAT – land and property

SIGNPOSTS

- **Zero-rating** – This applies to some transactions in land and property, in particular to house building (see **42.1–42.2**).

- **Reduced rate** – A 5% rate of VAT applies to conversion work if it converts a commercial building into a residential one or there is a changed number of dwellings conversion (see **42.3**). It also applies to refurbishments where the residential property has been empty for at least two years.

- **DIY housebuilders' scheme** – This puts individuals building a house for themselves or their family in the same position as a commercial house builder (see **42.4**).

- **Commercial property** – Sales of such property can be standard-rated if a new construction, or exempt (subject in most cases to an option to tax) (see **42.5**).

- **Option to tax** – This allows businesses to tax rent on commercial property, which would otherwise be exempt so that input tax on costs can be recovered, if certain requirements are met and the option is properly notified to HMRC (see **42.6**).

INTRODUCTION

42.1   VAT legislation relating to land and property is highly complex, and there are generally large sums of money at stake.

Supplies relating to land and property, including construction services, can be:

- zero-rated;
- charged at the reduced rate (5%);
- standard-rated (20%); or
- exempt.

It is also important to note that in certain circumstances the VAT position may impact on the stamp duty land tax position of the purchaser, and this can often be a factor in negotiations between vendor and purchaser in cases where the transfer of a going concern (TOGC) provisions could apply and the transaction is ignored for VAT purposes.

> **Focus**
>
> It is vitally important to ensure that the VAT issues are carefully considered before undertaking land-related transactions.

ZERO-RATING

42.2   The first grant of a major interest (freehold sale or long (more than 21 years) lease) in new dwellings (built or partially built) and new 'relevant residential' or 'relevant charitable' buildings is zero-rated, when made by the person constructing.

Similarly, construction services relating to dwellings are zero-rated (with certain exceptions relating to furniture, white goods and similar 'non-integral' items).

The zero-rating for construction services for new dwellings applies to main contractors and subcontractors. Construction services for 'relevant residential' or 'relevant charitable' purpose buildings are zero-rated by certificate when supplied to the person who is going to use that building. It follows therefore that subcontract services do not qualify for zero-rating in relation to certificated buildings.

For zero-rating to apply to the disposal of new dwellings the grant must be made by the person constructing. If the house sale relates to an existing renovated property, construction services are reduced or standard-rated, and the sale is exempt, so the VAT is a cost.

The only exception is where an existing dwelling has been empty for ten years and it is then refurbished and sold. In such cases, the dwelling loses its original 'residential status' and after renovation (at the reduced rate) the disposal can be zero-rated if made by the person converting.

A dwelling for this purpose comprises self-contained living accommodation. 'Relevant residential' accommodation is accommodation where people live but it does not contain all the facilities required for living in individual flats or houses, for example kitchens and/or bathrooms may be shared. This could include student accommodation or homes for persons in need of care by reason of physical or mental disabilities.

The definition of a 'relevant charitable' purpose building, is a building for use by a charity for non-business purposes otherwise than for use as an office.

As previously stated, where a building is for a 'relevant residential' or 'relevant charitable' purpose, the user of the building must give the builder a certificate stating that the building is to be used for such a purpose. Without this certificate, zero-rating is not allowed.

If residential property is constructed and is to be used for an exempt purpose (for example, short term lets) then it makes sense to appoint a contractor under a design and build contract. The main contractor will engage all sub-contractors, including architects and other professionals and recover any VAT charged as relating to his onward supply (zero-rate). These professional services businesses would otherwise have to standard-rate their services to the property investor, which would be an additional cost to the project.

Zero-rating can only apply to the construction and disposal of new residential property. An existing residential property only ceases to exist when it is demolished completely to ground level or if one wall remains on an existing building, as a result of planning requirements. If further parts of an existing building remain, then HMRC will resist any claim that the building is 'new'. There are numerous VAT tribunal cases on this point.

CONVERSION WORK

42.3   Where an existing commercial building is converted to become a residential building, or the project involves changing the number of dwellings in a property, then these construction services are charged at the reduced rate of VAT.

In relation to the liability on the onward sale of converted properties, the first grant of a major interest in a property that has been converted from commercial to residential will qualify for zero-rating (same as new dwellings).

The disposal of property that has always been residential (changed number of dwellings conversion) will, however, be exempt (unless previously empty for ten years – see **42.2** above), with a consequent restriction on recovery of the VAT incurred on costs. The 5% VAT rate for conversion services clearly has a beneficial effect on profit margins for such work – see the following example.

Example 42.1 – Refurbishment or conversion

Bob buys a large house in a derelict state for £200,000. He decides to refurbish the house for sale at an estimated value of £500,000. Excluding VAT, the refurbishment will cost £100,000. Bob's profit and loss account will be as follows (stamp duty land tax is ignored):

	£	£
Sale proceeds (exempt)		500,000
Acquisition costs (exempt)	200,000	
Construction costs	100,000	
VAT on construction costs – irrecoverable	20,000	
Total costs		(320,000)
Profit		180,000

However, if Bob decides to convert the existing house into four flats, each of which sells for £125,000. Bob's profit and loss account is then as follows:

	£	£
Sale proceeds (4 × 125,000, all exempt)		500,000
Acquisition costs (exempt)	200,000	
Construction costs	100,000	
VAT on construction costs @ 5%	5,000	
Total costs		(305,000)
Profit		195,000

It should be noted that there are a number of very detailed issues on the use of the reduced rate of VAT during conversion, and these need to be studied carefully in any particular instance. The above is the most usual example in practice.

Focus

Ensure the VAT consequences are properly understood and costed into the project where appropriate, before undertaking any major house building project.

DIY HOUSEBUILDERS

42.4   The 'do-it-yourself' housebuilders scheme enables private individuals to claim a refund of VAT incurred on the construction of a house that is to be used as the main residence of that individual or a member of his family.

The purpose of this is to put the 'DIY' housebuilder on all fours with a developer who can recover the VAT on any costs as they relate to an onward zero-rate sale. The refund claim must be made within three months of practical completion.

Further details on the HMRC requirements can be found on HMRC's website (www.hmrc.gov.uk/vat/sectors/consumers/new-home.htm).

> **Focus**
>
> If you are a DIY housebuilder, ensure you keep all receipts to make a refund claim.

COMMERCIAL BUILDINGS

42.5   The VAT rules on commercial buildings came into force in 1989, in response to a European Court judgment. From that date:

- sales of new (less than three years old) or partly completed commercial buildings are standard-rated;
- all other sales and leases of commercial buildings are exempt, subject in almost all cases to an 'option to tax';
- all construction services in relation to commercial property are standard-rated.

The option to tax

42.6   It is often the case in the UK that professional property investors will acquire land, develop a commercial building on that land, and let it to an end user. Following the changes in 1989, all such construction work became standard-rated. Therefore, without the option to tax, all such construction costs will be attributable to an exempt output (rent) and therefore irrecoverable.

The 'option to tax' provisions allow a person to tax certain supplies which would otherwise be exempt. Where an option to tax has been exercised, all supplies made in relation to the commercial land and property will become taxable, with a consequence that the VAT on costs is recoverable.

By exercising an option to tax, a commercial property developer can recover the VAT costs on the development. VAT must then be charged on any rental charges or disposal proceeds.

An option to tax must be notified to HMRC in writing and constrains the opter to charge VAT on all of its outputs relating to that building (including rental and sales). There are complex rules as to what constitutes a building for the purpose of opting to tax, but essentially, where there are a number of letting units within the same development, this will normally count as a single building for the purposes of the option.

> **Example 42.2 – Effect of an option to tax**
>
> A shopping centre may contain supermarkets, clothes shops and other 'normal' retailers plus banks and a post office.
>
> If the lessor has opted to tax, the VAT is likely to be, at least in whole or in part, a cost to the post office and the banks.

The legislation (in particular, the anti-avoidance rules) for the option to tax is complex. It can be found in *VATA 1994, Sch 10*. In particular, where an exempt business has financed the construction of a building, and leases that building, or a connected partly exempt business leases the building, from a landlord, the option to tax may not always be permitted.

Options to tax are notified to HMRC on Form 1614A, which can be downloaded from the HMRC website.

Where property has been opted, Stamp Duty Land Tax is chargeable on the VAT inclusive price.

There are a number of related forms, which deal with specific issues. These are also listed on the HMRC website.

Whilst a developer will almost invariably give detailed consideration to opting to tax a property, in order to reclaim input tax, the option can only be revoked after 20 years, and opting to tax is likely to restrict the letting market in certain geographical areas where there is a high concentration of exempt financial businesses (for example, the City of London).

Focus

Owners of land and buildings should always give careful consideration before opting to tax them, particularly where some or all of the tenants may make exempt supplies (so not be able to recover all their input tax).

An option to tax cannot apply to residential or charitable buildings.

In addition, an option to tax has no effect in relation to any grant to a relevant housing association, if the association certifies that the land is to be used for the construction of dwellings.

Part 7
National Insurance Contributions

43

National Insurance – employers and employees

SIGNPOSTS

- **Scope** – National Insurance contributions (NICs) fund certain state benefits, and are payable by individuals between age 16 and state retirement pension age. A National Insurance number is issued to every person in the UK about to reach the age of 16 (see **43.1–43.3**).

- **Classes of NIC** – There are currently six different classes of NIC. Classes 1, 1A and 1B apply to income and benefits from employment. Classes 2 and 4 are paid by the self-employed, and Class 3 NICs are voluntary contributions. The law dealing with NICs can be found in primary and secondary legislation (see **43.4–43.5**).

- **Class 1 NICs** – These are due on 'earnings' which can include some benefits and expenses, and comprise primary contributions (payable by the employee) and secondary contributions (payable by the employer) (see **43.6–43.10**).

- **Earnings periods** – The calculation of NICs can be affected by irregular payment of earnings, and it is therefore important to establish the correct earnings period (see **43.11–43.15**).

- **Company directors** – The calculation of NICs for company directors is subject to special rules, with contributions assessed on an annual earnings period (see **43.16–43.17**).

- **NIC rates and thresholds** – There are standard rates and thresholds for primary and secondary NICs, with some special rules and reduced rates in certain circumstances (see **43.18–43.26**).

- **Returns, payments, etc** – Primary and secondary contributions are collected via the PAYE system, and employers are required to file certain returns with HMRC. Interest and penalties can be imposed for non-compliance (see **43.27–43.31**).

- **Class 1A NICs** – These are paid by employers only, on Annual Return Form P11D benefits (see **43.32–43.36**).

- **Class 1B NICs** – Special contributions are payable by employers who enter into a PAYE Settlement Agreement (PSA) (see **43.37**).

- **Appendix: Primary and Secondary NICs** – A Table of Class 1 NIC rates and thresholds is included at the end of this chapter (see **43.38–43.39**).

INTRODUCTION

43.1   The National Insurance system was first set up by the *National Insurance Act 1911*. The aim of the system was to provide basic social security for the working population. Employees and their employers paid contributions towards a weekly 'stamp', which entitled the employees to certain benefits when required.

To a certain extent this principle continues today, with National Insurance contributions (NICs) maintaining the Treasury's National Insurance Fund, which provides state benefits for individuals, such as the state pension, bereavement benefits and the employment and support allowance. These are known as 'contributory benefits', since they are linked to an individual's NIC.

'Non-contributory' benefits, such as health care (provided by the National Health Service), personal independence payments (which have replaced various disability allowances) and the universal credit (see **6.15**) are not *specifically* linked to NIC, but are funded out of general taxation (although payments *towards* the cost of the NHS are taken from the NIC system under the *Social Security Administration Act 1992*).

However, the NIC system is increasingly seen and treated as another form of taxation with the government appointing the Office of Tax Simplification to report on the closer alignment of income tax and NIC (issued on 7 March 2016).

Who pays NICs?

43.2   Individuals pay NICs (as long as they earn more than a certain level), if they are aged 16 or over, employed or self-employed and stop paying when they reach state pension age.

Some individuals elect to pay voluntary NICs (explained in more detail below).

The collection of NICs is administered by the National Insurance Contributions Office (NICO) currently based at Longbenton, Newcastle upon Tyne, which is an executive office of HMRC. However, most of the actual NIC collection is in fact made by HMRC either through the PAYE system, or via self-assessment.

National Insurance number

43.3 The National Insurance number (NINO) is important, since it is used by HMRC to record and collect contributions and by the Department for Work and Pensions (DWP) for paying out benefits.

The NINO consists of three letters and six numbers in the format: AA123456A. The final letter is always A, B, C, or D.

A NINO is issued to every person in the UK who is about to reach the age of 16.

- Employees must inform their employer of their NINO, since employers are required to record it on their payroll records.

- Overseas workers coming to the UK are required to register for a NINO immediately they incur a UK NIC liability.

Employers may ask prospective employees to produce a NINO to prevent charges of illegal working under the *Asylum and Immigration Act 1996, s 8*.

A NINO can now be checked using payroll software under Real Time Information (RTI) to send a National Insurance number verification request (NVR).

DIFFERENT CLASSES OF NIC

43.4 There are currently six classes of NICs. These can be summarised as follows:

- *Class 1* – Payable in respect of *employed earners*. **Employees** pay *primary* contributions and **employers** pay *secondary* contributions.

- *Class 1A* – Paid by **employers** *only*, on P11D benefits.

- *Class 1B* – Paid by **employers** who enter into a PAYE Settlement Agreement (PSA).

- *Class 2* – Flat rate contributions paid by the **self-employed**.

- *Class 3* – **Voluntary** contributions paid by those not liable for other contributions.

- *Class 4* – Paid by the **self-employed** on their earnings falling within a band (in addition to Class 2).

Classes 1, 1A and 1B are dealt with in the remainder of this chapter from **43.6** onwards. Classes 2 and 4 are dealt with in **Chapter 44**, and Class 3 in **Chapter 45**.

LEGISLATION

43.5 The main provisions for NICs are found as follows:

- *Social Security Contributions and Benefits Act 1992 (SSCBA 1992)*, with much of the detail being contained in:

- *Social Security (Contributions) Regulations 2001 (SI 2001/1004)*. Supplementary legislation on the current system is also contained in the following statutes:

- *Social Security Administration Act 1992 (SSAA 1992)*.

- *Social Security Act 1998 (SSA 1998)*.

- *National Insurance Contributions Act 2002 (NICA 2002)*.

Amendments to the above (such as increases in NIC rates) are found in subsequent NICs Acts.

CLASS 1 NICs – OUTLINE

43.6 Liability to Class 1 NICs arises in relation to 'employed earners'. Both the employee (primary) and employer (secondary) are required to pay Class 1 NICs on the employee's 'earnings', unless they are exempt.

An employed earner is any person who is gainfully employed in Great Britain either:

- under a contract of service, or

- in an office (including an elective office),

where the 'earnings' therefrom are chargeable to income tax as employment income *(SSCBA 1992, s 2(1)(a))*.

There is no liability for Class 1 NICs (both *primary* and *secondary*) on certain employed earners as follows *(SSCBA 1992, s 6(1))*:

- individuals under 16 years of age;

- individuals whose earnings are below the lower earnings limit (LEL) (£5,824 pa, £112 per week for 2016/17);

- individuals employed by a close relative for non-business purposes in the home where they both live;

- spouse/civil partner employed by their spouse/civil partner for non-business purposes;

- individuals employed for the purposes of elections or a referendum, such as returning and counting officers and any person employed by them;

- individuals (not resident in the UK) of visiting armed forces or employed with certain international organisations (*Social Security (Categorisation of Earners) Regulations 1978, SI 1978/1689*).

No Class 1 *primary* contribution is due for employed earners who have reached pensionable age. However, the *secondary employer's* contribution remains payable (*SSCBA 1992, s 6(3)*).

Certain individuals will always be categorised as 'employed earners' for Class 1 NICs purposes, such as vicars. Certain lecturers used to be treated the same, although there was a change of view by HMRC which took effect from 6 April 2012 and their status for tax and PAYE will be determined by the usual case law considerations for employment/self-employment (www.hmrc.gov.uk/manuals/esmmanual/esm4503.htm).

Following the decision in *ITV Services Ltd v Revenue & Customs Commissioners* [2010] UKFTT 586 (TC) the *Social Security (Categorisation of Earners) Regulations 1978, SI 1978/1689* has been repealed in respect of *entertainers*, with effect from 6 April 2014, so that entertainers pay Class 2 and Class 4 NICs on their earnings (instead of Class 1 NICs) (*SI 2014/635, reg. 2(2)(b)*). (See also www.hmrc.gov.uk/briefs/national-insurance/brief 3513.htm.)

It has also been announced that from 6th April 2017 sporting testimonials will be subject to tax and NIC, although this will be subject to a £50,000 exemption as long as the testimonial is not a contractual right. These rules will apply to testimonials granted on or after 25th Nov 2015.

Earnings for NICs

43.7

> **Focus**
>
> Earnings for Class 1 NICs purposes include any remuneration or profit derived from an employment. Basically this largely comprises gross pay, but also includes certain benefits and expenses (see below).

Tips paid directly by the customer to an employee are not liable to NICs but, if there is any involvement of the employer (in the distribution of the tips) then Class 1 NICs are due.

Currently, termination payments (on cessation of employment) that are contractual are liable to Class 1 NICs, but no NICs are due if the payment is for 'damages' such as compensation for loss of office. It is proposed that legislation will be introduced with effect from April 2018 abolish the current income tax distinction between contractual and non-contractual payments in lieu of notice (PILONs) and to treat certain damages payments as taxable (see **2.60**) At the same time there will also be an alignment of the income tax and NIC provisions in this area.

Most statutory payments, such as statutory sick pay (SSP) and statutory maternity pay (SMP) are treated as earnings for NIC purposes (*SSCBA 1992, s 3*).

Since Class 1 NICs are calculated on gross pay, no deduction is made for employees' contributions to registered pension schemes, or for charitable donations under the payroll giving scheme.

Certain benefits and expenses

43.8   Payments of benefits in the form of readily convertible assets (*ITEPA 2003, s 702*) such as stocks and shares and gold bullion, are specifically included in gross pay and are therefore subject to Class 1 NICs via the PAYE system.

Also, Class 1 NICs are specifically imposed on the benefit of most non-cash vouchers, with some exceptions, being broadly those exempt from income tax – see HMRC's National Insurance Manual at NIM02416 (www.hmrc.gov.uk/manuals/nimmanual/NIM02416.htm).

Meeting an employee's pecuniary liability, ie paying his personal bill or meeting his liability to another, is not regarded as a payment in kind, but as earnings and is therefore liable to Class 1 NICs. Whilst these payments are reported on the P11D at the tax year end for income tax purposes, Class 1 NICs are payable *at the time* of payment and accounted for directly through the payroll (*SSCBA 1992, s 4*).

However, most taxable P11D benefits escape the charge to Class 1 NIC, since the benefit is provided *directly* by the employer and therefore regarded as a payment in kind and chargeable to Class 1A NICs, payable *only* by the employer (see **43.32** below) (*SI 2001/1004, Sch 3*).

HMRC dispensations, (which allowed certain expense payments to be disregarded for tax and NIC purposes), have been replaced from 6 April 2016 with new exemptions which remove the charge to tax and NIC on deductible expenses and benefits.

The tax exemptions for incidental personal expenses (such as those incurred when an employee is working away from home overnight) also apply to NICs, as does the tax exemption for meeting the cost of directors' liability insurance or professional indemnity insurance.

More guidance about NIC on benefits and expenses can be found in the following HMRC booklets:

- CWG5 (2016) *Class 1A NICs on Benefits in Kind* (www.hmrc.gov.uk/guidance/cwg5.pdf); and

- Chapter 5 of CWG2 (2016) *Employer Further Guide to PAYE and NICs* (www.hmrc.gov.uk/guidance/cwg2.pdf).

See also **Chapter 2** of this book.

Focus

Class 1 NICs are *not* payable on most benefits in kind.

Therefore, NIC savings can be made for employees earning *less* than the upper earnings limit, currently £43,000 pa, if they receive certain benefits *instead* of pay.

Business expenses

43.9   Expenses payments made to employees are not regarded as earnings to the extent that there is a *business purpose*. So, for example, an employee can be reimbursed for business travel or staying in a hotel on the employer's business, without the payment normally being treated as earnings.

However, care should be taken where an employee is reimbursed for his home telephone bill, since the reimbursed cost of private (ie non-business) telephone calls and all reimbursed line rental is treated as earnings. It is important therefore that comprehensive records and receipts are kept of all genuine business expenses, so that employers can reduce the liability to Class 1 NICs (and income tax).

Where an employer reimburses an employee using his own car for business mileage, any identifiable profit element is earnings for NIC purposes. This is calculated as the excess of the mileage rate paid over the authorised mileage rates for the first 10,000 miles (currently 45 pence per mile). This applies, regardless of whether the business miles travelled exceed 10,000 miles.

So, the amount reimbursed in the period is compared with the 'NIC free' amount (of 45 pence per mile) for the *total* business miles travelled and Class 1 NIC is payable on the excess (and note that, unlike income tax, if an employee is paid less than the 'NIC free' amount, they cannot claim any relief for the balance).

This approach may be subject to challenge following the case of *Cheshire Employer and Skills Development Limited (formerly Total People Limited) v HMRC* [2012] EWCA Civ 1429) where it was held in the Court of Appeal that on the facts of that case the car allowance was not earnings for NIC purposes. But HMRC are known to see this case as being specific to the facts as presented and not setting a precedent.

The 'NIC-free' rate for carrying a fellow employee as a passenger on business journeys is the same as for tax (currently 5 pence per mile per passenger) and no relief is given if an allowance is not paid.

For motor cycles (24 pence per mile) and cycles (20 pence per mile) the 'NIC free' rates are the same as for tax.

See also **Chapter 2**.

Directors' personal bills

43.10   If a company pays a director's personal bill and then charges the amount to the director's account with the company, the payment is *not* treated as pay (and therefore liable to Class 1 NICs), *unless*:

- the payment results in the account becoming overdrawn (or more overdrawn); and

- it is normal practice for the company to make such a payment in anticipation of the director's earnings (for example, bonuses).

In such circumstances, HMRC regard the payment as amounting to drawings on account of future earnings and NICs (and tax) are payable on the overdrawn amount.

If on the other hand, the debit is cleared by the credit of dividends, no NICs are due.

EARNINGS PERIODS FOR NICs

43.11　The liability to Class 1 NICs for an employed earner arises when the *payment* of his earnings is *received*, which is broadly based on the earnings basis for income tax (*ITEPA 2003, ss 15, 18*).

In general, earnings are treated as being paid when a sum (representing those earnings) is placed *unconditionally* at the disposal of the employee, eg when salary is credited to a bank account.

If a loan is made to an employee in anticipation of earnings, the Class 1 NIC liability does not arise unless and until, the employee is released from his obligation to repay the loan. However the anti-avoidance rules governing disguised remuneration need to be considered, which may in some circumstances advance the NIC point.

In the case of directors, the rules are more complicated (see **43.16**), but generally the liability to Class 1 NICs arises at the time when the director has an *unencumbered* right to draw on sums put at his disposal.

The earnings paid (in respect of NIC) then need to be assessed over an 'earnings period'.

The rules for identifying this earnings period are outlined below and are found in *SI 2001/1004, reg 3* onwards.

More detailed guidance can also be found in HMRC booklet CWG2 (2016) *Employer Further Guide to PAYE and NICs.*

Earnings periods – basic rule

43.12   The basic rule is that an earnings period is based on the frequency of payment of earnings to an employed earner. It is the *timing* of the period of payment that is important. The period in respect of which the earnings are deemed to be earned is irrelevant.

So, where an employee is paid at regular intervals, the earnings period will generally match the payment interval, eg weekly, four-weekly, monthly, quarterly or annually. This is subject to the earnings period being a minimum of at least seven days (subject to the minor exception below).

The first earnings period always begins on the first day of that tax year. Unlike income tax, Class 1 NICs for employees are calculated on a non-cumulative basis. This means that only the earnings in the earnings period are taken into account for Class 1 NIC purposes (with the end of regular weekly or monthly earnings periods coinciding with the end of the tax week or month of the PAYE system).

Example 43.1 – Determining earnings periods

Molly is paid weekly and therefore her earnings period for NIC purposes is deemed to be weekly and her earnings are subject to the weekly NIC limits (see **43.21**).

Geoff is paid monthly, so his earnings period is monthly and his earnings are subject to the monthly limits.

Molly is paid £160 on 15 April 2016. The first weekly earnings period for 2016/17 starts on 6 April and runs until 12 April 2016 and the second period runs from 13 April until 19 April 2016. The payment to Molly on 15 April is therefore assessed to NIC in the second weekly earnings period of 2016/17.

Geoff is paid £800 on 30 June 2016. This falls within the third monthly earnings period of 2016/17, which runs from 6 June to 5 July 2016.

Where an employee has a weekly earnings period, then there will always be an earnings period shorter than seven days at the end of each tax year. This will comprise one day in a 365 day year, two days in a leap year. However, this is an exception to the rule that an earnings period must be a minimum of seven days.

Where the first pay day falls on 6 April (in normal years, 7 April in leap years), then an employee paid on a weekly earnings basis may be paid 53 lots of weekly wages in a year. In this case, week 53 is treated as a full week, even though the employee would benefit from a total NIC free band (53 × primary earnings threshold), which would be more than the annual limit.

Conversely, if an employee is paid at a frequency of four weeks (instead of monthly), then in one calendar year they may end up paying Class 1 NICs for 56 weeks, (based on four-weekly earnings periods) instead of 52. In this instance, no refund of the excess over 53 weeks is made.

Where an employee has two or more regular pay intervals, (eg monthly salary plus annual bonus), the shortest pay interval will form the basis of the earnings period, unless this rule is used as a means of avoiding contributions (see also directors' earning periods at **43.16**).

If on the other hand, more than half the earnings are paid at longer intervals (and it is likely to continue), then the employee or employer may request HMRC to issue a formal notice to direct the employer to use the longer payment interval instead.

Example 43.2 – Earnings period: payments made annually or six-monthly

Neil is a sales manager, who receives a monthly salary, a six-monthly performance bonus and a year end (annual) bonus, as follows:

21 April 2016	Monthly salary for April =	£2,000
28 April 2016	Six-monthly performance bonus =	£1,000
3 May 2016	Annual bonus (re year ended 31 March 2016) =	£3,500

The earnings period for NIC purposes is monthly, so all of the above amounts fall within the same monthly earnings period, being PAYE month 1, which runs from 6 April – 5 May 2016.

So NIC contributions (both primary and secondary) for 'month 1' would be based on Neil's total earnings in that month of £6,500.

Earnings periods – payments derived from past employment

43.13   Where payments are made in respect of an employment which has ended (and where earnings were paid regularly) and the payment is an addition to a payment made before the employment ended and/or is not a payment in respect of a regular interval (eg ad hoc bonus) then the earnings period shall be deemed to be the week in which the payment is made (*SI 2001/1004, reg 3(5)*).

Earnings periods – irregular pay intervals

43.14 Special rules apply to determine the earnings period where earnings are paid at irregular intervals (and would not otherwise be treated as being paid regularly) (*SI 2001/1004, reg 4*).

- The basic rule is that the earnings period is set by the length of the period for which the payment is made, subject to a minimum of a week.

- Where this is not reasonably practicable to determine, the earnings period is based on the length of the period (ie number of days) since the last payment (or the start of the employment, if the first payment).

- Payments made before the employment begins or after it ends, are based on a weekly earnings period.

Earnings periods – deemed earnings

43.15 Where payments are deemed to be earnings under employment protection legislation (*SSCBA 1992, s 112*), the earnings period is the length of the protected period, or that part of it in respect of which the earnings are paid, subject to a minimum of a week.

If the earnings period (in respect of the above) crosses a tax year end, or falls wholly in two or more tax years other than the tax year in which they are paid, the employee can request that the contributions be treated as being paid proportionally to the tax year or years in which the earnings period fell (*SI 2001/1004, reg 5*).

EARNINGS PERIODS – COMPANY DIRECTORS

43.16 Since Class 1 NICs are calculated on the earnings period basis which is not cumulative like PAYE income tax, this can result in lower Class 1 NICs being due on earnings which are paid irregularly throughout the year.

As directors are often paid irregular amounts at irregular intervals and are more likely to be in a position to control the regularity of those payments, they are therefore assessed on an annual earnings period coinciding with the tax year (regardless of whether they are paid at regular intervals or not) (*SI 2001/1004, reg 8*).

Where a person is a director at the beginning of the tax year, his earnings period is the tax year, even if he ceases to be a director during the year.

Where a director is first appointed during a tax year, the earnings period is the number of tax weeks from the week in which he is appointed, until the end of the tax year.

When calculating NICs for directors therefore, you should look at the *cumulative* earnings in the annual earnings period (or from the start of appointment if later) and compare the total earnings to date with the annual limits shown below at **43.21** (or with a pro rata limit for directors appointed during the year, by scaling down the annual limits, as appropriate).

Class 1 NICs (both primary and secondary) are then calculated accordingly and NICs already paid in the tax year are deducted, to leave Class 1 NICs due in respect of the payment in question.

No Class 1 NIC is therefore due on a director's earnings unless they reach the annual (or pro rata) primary earnings threshold of £8,060 (for 2016/17) – see below. (Note that although there are strictly 53 tax weeks in a tax year, you should use 52 weeks when calculating the pro rata period. However, if a director is appointed in tax week 53, the earnings period is always at least one week.)

Where directors are paid at regular intervals (for example, monthly), the above cumulative calculation (over an annual earnings period) causes a distortion in their NIC liability, depending upon the amount they are *regularly* paid.

This may mean they pay little or no NICs in the first few months of the year, if their earnings for the year to date are below the annual primary earnings threshold, but then play 'catch-up' for the remainder of the tax year with higher NIC payments.

Moreover, those who are paid large regular monthly salaries may find that high amounts of employee Class 1 NICs at 12% need to be paid in the first few months of the year, with later months' employee NICs being paid at 2% (as soon as their year to date earnings exceeds the annual upper earnings limit).

This may cause unnecessary financial hardship to those directors concerned. So, to alleviate this, they can be assessed on the *actual* pay intervals, as if the special rules for directors did not apply. This is known as the 'alternative arrangements'.

Focus

When the last payment of the tax year is made (normally tax month 12), a *cumulative* calculation must be carried out based on the annual earnings period, in order to reassess the director's total annual liability.

The *reassessed* annual NICs are then compared to those already paid over to HMRC (for the director) and any adjustment made to the final NIC payment due in the tax year. (This reassessment is carried out so that those who may seek to gain advantage, by only using the 'normal' rules, are thus prevented from doing so.) See examples below and in HMRC guidance booklet CA44 (2016) (www.hmrc.gov.uk/nitables/ca44.pdf).

Example 43.3 – Calculating director's NICs: one-off bonus

Ceri is a director of Bramble Electronics Limited. She has been a director for the whole of the tax year.

On 30 September 2016, she receives the following payments:

- gross monthly pay of £4,000; and

- a one-off £10,000 gross bonus.

Her cumulative earnings to date therefore, up to tax month 6 (September), are £4,000 per month × 6, plus the bonus of £10,000 which equals £34,000.

Using the annual limits and Class 1 NIC rates for 2016/17 (see also **43.21**), her *primary* Class 1 NIC liability *only*, would be as follows:

Applicable Annual NIC Limits for 2016/17:		**£**
Annual lower earnings limit	LEL	5,824
Annual secondary earnings threshold (not applicable in this example)	ST	8,112
Annual primary earnings threshold	PT	8,060
(NIC charged at 12% on earnings between PT and UEL)		
Annual upper earnings limit (NIC charged at 2% on earnings above UEL)	UEL	43,000

First, her earnings to date of £34,000 easily exceed the annual primary earnings threshold (PT) of £8,060, but come under the annual upper earnings limit (UEL) of £43,000.

So her *cumulative* Class 1 NIC liability for the tax year to date would be:		34,000	
Less	PT	(8,060)	
	12%	25,940	3,112.80

Class 1 NIC liability already paid in the tax year (ie up to tax month 5)		(1,432.80)
Class 1 NIC liability due for September (tax month 6 (effectively (£4,000 + £10,000) × 12%).)		1,680.00

Alternatively, since Ceri is paid at regular intervals (ie monthly), her company could request that her pay is assessed to NIC under the 'alternative arrangements' as mentioned above.

This would mean her Class 1 NIC liability for the tax year would be calculated on a monthly earnings basis using the 'normal rules' as follows:

Applicable Monthly NIC Limits for 2016/17

Monthly	LEL	486
Monthly	PT	672

(NIC charged at 12% on earnings between PT and UEL)

Monthly	UEL	3,583

(NIC charged at 2% on earnings above UEL)

First, based on the monthly NIC limits her normal NIC each month would be:

	UEL	3,583	
Less	PT	(672)	
	12%	2,911	349.32
Plus		4,000	
Less	UEL	(3,583)	
	2%	417	8.34
Total primary Class 1 NIC each month would be a *regular* payment of			357.66

For month 6 (September) when she received the bonus payment of £10,000, her NIC liability that month would be:

NI as above	12%		349.32
NI on	4,000 + 10,000	14,000	
	UEL	(3,583)	
	2%	10,417	208.34
Total for month 6			557.66

693

By tax month 11, her total NIC paid is 10 months at		357.66	3,576.60
1 month at			557.66
			4,134.26

At tax month 12 (with the final payment of earnings in the tax year), Ceri's NIC would be *reassessed* under the 'alternative arrangements' rules, by reference to an **annual** earnings period as follows:

Total earnings for tax year	(£4,000 × 12 + £10,000)		58,000
So NIC is	UEL	43,000	
	PT	(8,060)	
	12%	34,940	4,192.80
Plus		58,000	
	UEL	(43,000)	
	2%	15,000	300.00
Total NIC *reassessed* for tax year			4,492.80
Already paid			(4,134.26)
Total final payment due			358.54

Since Ceri's regular monthly salary of £4,000 already exceeds the monthly upper earnings limit of £3,583, she is already being charged to NICs at 12% on the majority of her monthly salary, which falls below that limit.

We would therefore expect any one-off additional earnings in a month, such as her bonus, to be charged to NICs at the rate of 2% (for earnings above the UEL).

Any 'irregular' payments made to Ceri during the tax year, although *reassessed* on the annual earnings period in month 12, do not therefore disproportionately affect her final NIC payment due, ie:

Final NIC payment = £358.54, compared with regular monthly NICs of £357.66 (with the 88p difference being due to rounding of the annual limits within the legislation).

Example 43.4 – Directors: NICs on a bonus with lower monthly salary

If, on the other hand, Ceri's regular monthly salary had been £2,000, the effect of having her NICs on her bonus and salary *reassessed* in month 12 would be as follows:

	£	£
First, her earnings would be assessed under the 'normal rules'. Again using the *monthly* NIC limits, her normal NIC each month would be:		
Monthly salary	2,000	
Less PT	(672)	
12%	1,328	159.36

For month 6 (September) when she received the bonus payment of £10,000, her NIC liability that month would be:

		£	£
	UEL	3,583	
Less	PT	(672)	
	12%	2,911	349.32
plus	£2,000 + £10,000	12,000	
	UEL	(3,583)	
	2%	8,417	168.34
so total for month 6			517.66

		£
By tax month 11, her total NICs paid are:	10 months at £159.36	1,593.60
	+ 1 month at	517.66
		2,111.26

As before, at tax month 12, Ceri's NIC would be *reassessed* under the 'alternative arrangements' rules, by reference to an **annual** earnings period as follows:

		£	£
Total earnings for tax year	(£2,000 × 12 + £10,000)	34,000	
Less	PT	(8,060)	
Total NICs for tax year	12%	25,940	3,112.80
less NICs already paid of			(2,111.26)
total final payment due of			1,001.54

The additional NICs due at the end of the tax year in month 12 of £822 can be explained as follows:

Her £10,000 bonus plus £24,000 annual salary = £34,000, which falls *below* the annual UEL of £43,000.

Expected rate of NICs on her 'irregular' bonus payment for the annual earnings period would be:

	12%	10,000	1,200.00

In month 6, her bonus along with her salary was assessed on a normal monthly basis, so NICs due on the bonus *only* would have been:

	UEL	3,583	
	Salary	(2,000)	
	12%	1,583	189.96
Bonus		10,000	
Less above		(1,583)	
	2%	8,417	168.34

Therefore, her NICs paid on the bonus *only*, assessed on a monthly basis under the 'normal rules'	358.30
But, her *actual* NICs due on the bonus, as assessed over the *annual* earnings period (as calculated above)	1,200.00
Less paid	(358.30)
Additional NICs due in month 12 (rounded)	842

As we have seen in **Example 43.4**, waiting until the final payment of the tax year to carry out the reassessment of Class 1 NICs could lead to a disproportionate amount of primary Class 1 NICs becoming due at the end of the tax year.

In these circumstances, the company can request to carry out the final reassessment at the time the bonus or irregular payment is paid. However, the director's earnings must then be assessed under the annual earnings period rules for the *remainder* of the tax year.

Where a director is appointed part way through the tax year, he would be assessed to Class 1 NICs under the pro rata annual earnings period rules as follows:

Example 43.5 – NICs for a director appointed part-way through the tax year

Ray is first appointed a director of Bramble Electronics Limited on 12 September 2016, which falls in tax week 23, meaning the number of tax weeks (including the tax week of appointment), until the end of the tax year on 5 April 2016 is 30. Therefore, Ray's earnings period for the tax year 2016/17 is 30 weeks.

His pro rata NIC limits (by using multiples of the weekly limits or by scaling down the annual limits as appropriate) would be:

		£
Lower earnings limit (LEL)	30 × 112	3,360
Secondary earnings threshold (ST) (not used in this example)	8,112 / 52 × 30	4,680
Primary earnings threshold (PT) *(NICs charged at 12% on earnings between PT and UEL)*	8,060 / 52 × 30	4,650
Upper earnings limit (UEL) *(NICs charged at 2% on earnings above UEL)*	43,000 / 52 × 30	24,808

(**Note** – See also the useful 'Quick Guide' in HMRC booklet CA44 (2016), for working out pro rata annual earnings periods and pro rata NIC limits.)

On the 31 October 2016, Ray is paid a gross monthly salary of £6,000 and also a £9,000 gross bonus.

		£	£
His cumulative earnings to date from when he was *first appointed a director are:*	6,000 per month × 2 (September and October's monthly gross pay),		12,000
	plus the bonus paid in October		9,000
Earnings to date	Total		21,000

Earnings to date exceed the pro rata annual primary earnings threshold (PT) of £4,650, but fall below the pro rata annual upper earnings limit (UEL) of £24,808.

Cumulative Class 1 NIC liability for the pro rata annual earnings period to date would be:

Earnings to date		21,000	
Less PT		(4,650)	
	12%	16,350	1,962
Class 1 liability already paid in his pro rata earnings period since he was appointed a director was:	September gross pay	6,000	
Less PT		(4,650)	
	12%	1,350	(162)
Primary Class 1 NIC liability for October (month 7) (effectively £(6,000 + 9,000) × 12%)			1,800

As with the examples above, since Ray is paid at regular *monthly* intervals, his earnings could be assessed to NICs under the 'alternative arrangements' as outlined above.

So his Class 1 NIC liability for the remainder of the tax year would be calculated on a *monthly* earnings basis using the 'normal rules', but his NIC liability would still need to be *reassessed* with the final payment of the tax year using his **30-week** pro rata earnings period, established above.

In all the above examples, the company would also be liable to pay secondary (employer) Class 1 NICs at a rate of 13.8% on their directors' earnings over the secondary earnings threshold (ST).

This would be assessed under the same basis as their directors' primary NICs, using the annual ST of £8,112, (or pro rata ST of £4,680, as calculated above) as applicable.

Special rules also apply for directors in certain situations, for example:

- directors with more than one job with the same company;

- directors earning from both non-contracted-out and contracted-out jobs (but see **43.22**);

- directors also acting as professional advisors; and

- directors reaching state pension age.

Further guidance is available in HMRC booklet CA44 (2016) *National Insurance for Company Directors*.

Earnings periods – company directors: timing of receipt

43.17   As noted at **43.11**, it is the timing of the *receipt* of payment which is important, so that the liability to Class 1 NICs arises in the tax year the earnings are *received*, rather than for the tax year to which they are deemed to relate.

Focus

In the case of directors, the timing of the receipt can be summarised as being the *earliest* of the following times (*ITEPA 2003, s 18*):

- when payment is *made* of, or on account of, earnings;

- when an individual becomes *entitled* to payment of, or on account of, earnings;

- when sums on account of earnings are *credited* to the director's current, or loan account;

- where the amount of earnings for a period is determined *before* the period ends, the time when the period *ends*;

- where the amount of earnings for a period is not known until the amount is determined *after* the period has ended, the time when the amount is *determined*.

So, broadly speaking, in a typical company, if a director's loan account is in credit, since he has built up a balance from undrawn earnings (fees, etc), which have been credited to his account, the Class 1 NIC liability will have arisen at the time the earnings have been *credited* to his account.

Therefore when the director makes drawings against this credit balance, there is no further liability to Class 1 NICs, (since the director is merely reducing the balance of his loan account).

If a director's loan account is *overdrawn*, through the debiting of drawings from the account in *anticipation* of future earnings (eg fees, bonus), then the liability to Class 1 NICs will have arisen when the items have been debited to the account.

So, when the future earnings in question are eventually credited to the account, there will be no further Class 1 NIC liability, to the extent that these items are simply bringing the account back into credit, by being allocated against those debit items which created the overdraft in the first place and which have already been assessed for NIC purposes.

Note that where a debit has been made to the director's loan account in anticipation of future payments, such as *dividends*, which are not *earnings*, then no Class 1 NIC liability arises.

Care should be taken however, to ensure that the payment in respect of dividends has been correctly treated by the company (such as noted in the AGM minutes) and is not merely a waiver of a loan to the director (on which Class 1 NICs would be due) (*Stewart Fraser Ltd v Revenue & Customs Commissioners* [2011] UKFTT 46 (TC) (TC00923)).

See also HMRC booklet CA44 (2016) *National Insurance for Company Directors*.

CONTRIBUTION RATES AND THRESHOLDS

Primary contributions

43.18 As we have seen at the beginning of this chapter, employed earners are liable to pay *primary* Class 1 NICs on their earnings in the 'earnings period', which exceed the primary earnings threshold.

There are two rates of *primary* Class 1 NICs:

• the main primary percentage of 12% on earnings which exceed the primary threshold (PT) and up to the upper earnings limit (UEL) (see below);

• the additional primary percentage of 2% on earnings exceeding the UEL.

Contributions – deemed primary contributions

43.19 Employed earners are *deemed* to have paid primary contributions when their earnings are not less than the lower earnings limit (LEL), and do not exceed the primary threshold (PT).

No contributions are actually payable, but a notional Class 1 NIC is deemed to have been paid, in order to protect contributory benefit entitlement for low earners (*SSCBA 1992, s 6A*).

Contributions – secondary contributions

43.20 The secondary contributor in the case of an employed earner under a contract of service is the employer.

Where an employed earner is an office holder with general earnings, the secondary contributor is deemed to be either:

- such a person as prescribed in the regulations;

- or the government department, public authority or body of persons responsible for paying the office holder's 'general earnings' (*SSCBA 1992, s 7*).

There are exceptions to the basic secondary contributor rule, such as:

- where a 'host employer' is appointed as the secondary contributor in place of a 'foreign employer' (ie one who does not fulfil the conditions as to residence or presence as prescribed in the regulations);

- where a person who has the 'general control and management of an employee' rather than his immediate employer is deemed to be the 'secondary contributor' as opposed to the employer (*Social Security (Categorisation of Earners) Regulations 1978, SI 1978/1969, reg 5, Sch 3*).

The secondary contributor is required to pay *secondary* Class 1 NICs at the secondary percentage rate of 13.8% on earnings above the secondary threshold (ST), but unlike primary contributions, there is *no upper limit* for secondary contributions (*SSCBA 1992, s 9*).

The secondary contribution is an allowable expense in computing the employer's trading profits.

Focus

From 6 April 2016, employers with apprentices under the age of 25 are no longer required to pay secondary Class 1 NICs on earnings paid up to the AUST (Apprentice Upper Secondary Threshold) and this continues (from 6 April 2015), for employees under the age of 21, where no Employer's NIC is payable up to the UST (Upper Secondary Threshold)

The AUST and UST are the same as the UEL (£43,000) for 2016/17.

Contribution rates and thresholds tables

43.21   The Class 1 NIC rates and (weekly) thresholds are shown at **43.38**, but for ease of reference, they are replicated below, together with the daily, monthly and annual limits.

43.21 *National Insurance – employers and employees*

The thresholds and limits are expressed in *weekly* terms in the legislation, but are adjusted when payment of earnings is made other than at weekly intervals, as follows (*SI 2001/1004, regs 10, 11*, as amended).

	Day £	Week £	Month £	Annual £	NIC Rate
LEL (lower earnings limit)	16.00	112	486	5,824	Nil
PT (primary threshold)	22.14	155	672	8,060	Earnings above PT up to UEL: 12%
UEL (upper earnings limit)	118.14	827	3,583	43,000	Earnings above limit: 2%
ST (secondary threshold)	22.29	156	676	8,112	Earnings above threshold: 13.8%

Focus

The *National Insurance Contributions (Rate Ceilings) Act 2015* sets a ceiling on the rates for Class 1, Class 1A and Class 1B NIC (based on the current rates) and the UEL (based on the higher rate threshold for income tax) which cannot be exceeded for the duration of the current Parliament.

Example 43.6 – Calculating primary and secondary NICs

The gross pay for the employees of Blackberry Conserves Limited for the month ending 30 June 2016 is as follows:

- Steve – £500

- Judith – £460

- Callum – £2,000

- Geraint – £5,000

Class 1 NICs (primary and secondary) are due as follows:

- No Class 1 NICs – primary or secondary – are due on Steve's monthly pay, since his pay received for the month of £500 is below *both* the monthly PT and ST.

- However, Steve's pay is over the monthly LEL of £486, so he is deemed to have paid *notional* Class 1 primary contributions to protect his entitlement to benefits, such as the state pension.

702

- Judith's monthly salary of £460 will be under the monthly LEL of £486, so no NICs will be paid on her salary and she will not retain her entitlement to benefits (via this employment).

- Callum's monthly pay of £2,000 for this month is liable to both Class 1 primary and secondary contributions as follows:

  Class 1 NICs primary (payable by employee):

  (£2,000 − £672) × 12% = £159.36 for the month.

  Class 1 NICs secondary, payable by his employer:

  (£2,000 − £676) × 13.8% = £182.71 for the month.

- Geraint's pay for the month of June would be liable to Class 1 NICs as follows:

  Class 1 NICs primary (payable by employee):

  (£3,583 − £672) × 12% = £349.32 *plus*

  (£5,000 − £3,583) × 2% = £28.34, total employee NIC = £377.66.

  Class 1 NICs secondary, payable by his employer:

  (£5,000 − £676) × 13.8% = £596.71 (no upper limit for employer's NIC).

Contributions – contracting out

43.22 Previously employees (and their employers) could elect to be contracted out of the state second pension (S2P) in favour of their own approved pension scheme.

As a result, both employee and employer were given a discount on the full NIC rates in return for the employee giving up their right to the 'earnings-related' S2P.

This discount was known as the 'contracted-out rebate' and the rates were 1.4% for employees and 3.4% for employers, on earnings between the LEL and the upper accrual point (£770 per week for 2015/16).

Contracting out ceased for money purchase occupational pension schemes and similar private pension plans from 6 April 2012. Thereafter, contracting out was only available to salary related occupational pension schemes (ie final salary pension schemes).

All contracting out has now ceased from 6 April 2016, with the introduction of the flat rate state pension.

Contributions – reduced rate

43.23   Women who were married or widowed as at 6 April 1977, could elect (before 12 May 1977) to pay Class 1 primary contributions at a reduced rate.

If they still hold a valid reduced rate certificate of election, then NICs are due at a flat rate of 5.85% for 2016/17 on earnings between the primary threshold of £155 per week and the upper earnings limit (UEL) of £827 per week. They still pay NICs at 2% on earnings above the UEL.

There is no reduced rate of NICs for employers' secondary contributions, which remain payable at the full rate.

Women who pay reduced-rate contributions however, do not have any entitlement to contributory state benefits (apart from statutory maternity or adoption pay and statutory sick pay). However, they may be entitled to the basic state pension and bereavement benefits based on their husband's or civil partner's NIC record.

An election can be cancelled (if the woman no longer qualifies under the regulations, eg after divorce), or revoked.

In some cases a revocation of the election may be of advantage, for example where a woman earns between the LEL and PT, since she would become entitled to contributory benefits, even though no contributions were payable (*SI 2001/1004, regs 126–139*).

See also HMRC's National Insurance Manual from NIM30000 onwards (www.hmrc.gov.uk/manuals/nimmanual/nim30000.htm).

Contributions – category letters

43.24   As we have seen previously, different types of employee can pay Class 1 NICs at different rates.

In order that the correct amount of Class 1 NICs can be deducted from an employee's pay, HMRC provide category letter tables, which denote the different categories of employee for Class 1 NIC purposes.

The relevant category letter is then applied via the payroll software, or employers using manual systems can refer to the HMRC tables which correspond to each category letter and which show the NIC due on an employee's earnings (see also **43.25**).

The 'category letters' below, apply to the most common types of employee:

Employees – Category Letters

Category letter	Applies to
A	All employees apart from those in the groups listed below in this table.
B	Married women and widows entitled to pay reduced-rate Class 1 NICs.
C	Employees over the state pension age (re secondary contributions).
J	Employees entitled to defer full rate payment of Class 1 NICs, (because they are already paying full rate NIC in another job).
H	Apprentice under 25.
M	Employees under 21.
Z	Employees under 21 who can defer Class 1 NICs, (because they are already paying it in another job).

Employers use category letter 'X' for employees who don't have to pay Class 1 NICs, eg because they are under 16.

Contracted-out money purchase schemes ended in April 2012, but some employees may still be part of one (and pay Class 1 NIC at the full rate). For these category letters, please refer to www.gov.uk/national-insurance-rates-letters/category-letters or Tax Guide 2012/13.

Contributions – calculation

43.25   Once the earnings and earnings period have been established and the rates and thresholds are known for the tax year, the employer can carry out the calculation of contributions by using either of the following methods:

● *Exact percentage method* – Where calculations are rounded to the nearest penny (0.5 pence being rounded down).

● *Tables method* – The tables are linked to the category letters listed at **43.24** so, for example, Table A is used for 'standard rate contribution' employees.

Since the introduction of Real Time Information (RTI) for reporting PAYE/NIC, the tables produced by HMRC are incorporated in the payroll software used by employers.

However, the tables are still published each tax year by HMRC and are downloadable from the HMRC website, for those employers who are exempt from filing or are unable to file payroll information online and use manual systems.

The employer chooses the appropriate table and looks up the contributions due dependent upon each employee's earnings. Both weekly and monthly tables are published with 'additional gross pay' tables to deal with earnings in excess of the UEL.

See links to downloadable NIC tables under 'Useful References and Links' at **46.15**.

Contributions – aggregation

43.26 As we have seen in previous sections of this chapter, no NICs are due on earnings up to the primary threshold.

If an employee has more than one job with different employers, then his NIC liability is calculated separately for each job. So, this may result in the employee quite legitimately paying no NICs in total if each lot of earnings from his separate employments comes to below the primary threshold.

To prevent NIC manipulation by dividing up a single employment between several associated businesses, the legislation provides for aggregating earnings where an employed earner (*SI 2001/1004, reg 15*):

- has different jobs with different employers, but who are carrying on business in association with each other;

- has different jobs with different employers, but only one of whom is deemed to be the 'secondary contributor';

- has different jobs with different persons, and some other person is deemed by the legislation to be the 'secondary contributor'.

According to the guidance published in HMRC booklet CWG2 (2016) *Employer Further Guide to PAYE and NICs*, employers are considered to be carrying on business in association with each other if:

- their respective businesses serve a common purpose; and

- to a significant degree, they share such things as accommodation, personnel, equipment or customers.

If an employed earner has more than one job with the same employer at the same time, the general rule is that all the earnings must be aggregated together and the NIC liability worked out on the total earnings.

However, if the earnings from each job are separately calculated, the employer does not have to aggregate the earnings from the separate jobs together if it is '*not reasonably practicable*' to do so (*SI 2001/1004, reg 14*).

The example given in CWG2 (2016) is of a computerised payroll system which is unable to perform the separate calculation and the employer would then have to do it manually, thus incurring more running costs within the business.

The guidance goes on to point out that 'there is no definition of the phrase "not reasonably practicable" in National Insurance law and that the onus is on the employer to show that aggregation is 'not reasonably practicable'.

See also HMRC's National Insurance Manual at NIM10009 for HMRC's views on 'not reasonably practicable' (www.hmrc.gov.uk/manuals/nimmanual/nim10009.htm).

Further guidance on aggregation can be found in the above mentioned guide – CWG2 (2016) *Employer Further Guide to PAYE and NICs* and HMRC's National Insurance Manual from NIM10000 onwards (www.hmrc.gov.uk/manuals/nimmanual/NIM10000.htm).

CLASS 1 NICs – RECORDS, RETURNS, PAYMENT AND PENALTIES

43.27   See also **Chapter 2** regarding the operation of PAYE.

Records and collection

43.28   Both primary and secondary Class 1 contributions are collected via the PAYE system (along with income tax) and are thereby governed by the PAYE regulations, namely *ITEPA 2003, s 684*, with further legislation specific to NICs found under *SI 2001/1004, regs 66–69*.

The secondary contributor (normally the employer) is responsible for the accounting and payment of Class 1 NICs. He must retain records of monthly (or quarterly) payments of both the employees' (primary) and employer's (secondary) Class 1 NICs, net of any recovery of NICs relating to any statutory payments.

Since the introduction of RTI for the operation of PAYE from 6 April 2013, HMRC require that employers report the payment details of all employees they pay, including even those earning below the LEL (£112 for 2016/17). RTI basically requires employers to report the payroll deductions of tax and NIC electronically, at the same time as they pay their employees, rather than waiting until the tax year end (as with the previous PAYE system).

As almost all employers (with few exceptions) are now required to operate their payroll via RTI, PAYE records can be maintained using the 'Basic PAYE Tools' software (downloadable from HMRC's website), or alternatively by using one of the commercial software packages available, or the services of a payroll bureau or agent.

PAYE records are required to be kept for the current tax year and the previous three tax years.

Returns

43.29   As noted above, almost all employers are now required to report payments made to their employees through PAYE, using RTI payroll software, simultaneously as they pay their employees.

This removes the requirement for PAYE end of year returns on Forms P14 and P35 and also the reporting of starter/leaver information (for the employer) using Forms P46/P45.

As in previous years, where expenses/benefits subject to Class 1 NICs (such as reimbursement of an employee's private bill) are required to be declared on Form P11D, then these must be returned by the 6 July (after the tax year end). Copies of the appropriate form should also be given (by 6 July) to employees who were in employment at the end of the tax year (see also Class 1A NICs at **43.32**).

For the small number of employers who for PAYE purposes are exempt from online filing (for example, on religious grounds) and for those few who are required to file on paper only (namely employers/employees with direct collection arrangements with HMRC), see www.hmrc.gov.uk/payerti/reporting/paper-filing.htm and also **Chapter 2**.

For those required to file online, there are several electronic methods available. As mentioned above, these are namely:

- the Basic PAYE Tools software (downloadable from the HMRC website);
- a commercial payroll software package;
- using the services of a (PAYE online registered) payroll bureau or agent;

plus

- HMRC's free online PAYE service for returns and forms; or
- electronic data interchange (EDI) (more suitable for large companies).

Employers can use a combination of the above methods, if so desired. (See www.hmrc.gov.uk/payerti/index.htm and Chapter 2 for further guidance.)

As with PAYE, Forms P60 (showing NICs/PAYE tax deducted) are still required to be provided to all *current* employees by the 31 May (after the tax year end).

Payment

43.30   Payments of Class 1 NICs (and PAYE tax) should be recorded on Form P32, or in the P30BC (yellow) payslip booklet issued by HMRC to employers, for those currently making payments by cheque.

The payment date (see below) is extended for electronic payments and in any case, large employers (with 250 or more employees) are required to make electronic payments of PAYE.

Each tax month ends on the 5th of the month, so payments of NIC/PAYE are required to be made by the 19th of the month (ie 14 days later). Electronic payments can be made by the 22nd of the month (or the previous working day when the 22nd falls on a bank holiday or weekend).

Employers can make *quarterly* payments if their *net* PAYE is expected to average less than £1,500 *per month*.

HMRC's computer system can struggle to allocate payments made early correctly and late payment notices are sometimes issued in error.

In order to stop payment reminders, employers must let HMRC know if they have no PAYE/NICs payment to make for a month, quarter or previous year. Notification should be made using payroll software under RTI.

Basically an employer payment summary (EPS) should be sent to HMRC by the 19th of the month following the end of the tax month in which no employees were paid for that particular pay period.

The EPS can also be used to tell HMRC that there will be no payments to be made for future months (up to 12 tax months at a time). Employers exempt from filing online, can return a signed payslip Form P30B, from their PAYE (yellow) booklet, for the appropriate month marked 'Nil due', or by calling HMRC's Payment Helpline on 0300 200 3401, quoting their Accounts Office reference number and giving details of the month(s) where no payment is due.

If there is agreement between the employer and employee, the employer is permitted to transfer their secondary Class 1 NICs liability to their employee, under *SI 2001/1004, reg 69*.

Focus

From 6 April 2016, the employment allowance has been increased to £3,000 per tax year for employers to set against their Class 1 NIC. This continues to be available for most private sector employers (including employers of carers) and charities.

The allowance can be claimed by ticking a box on the first EPS submitted for the tax year.

Companies where a director is the *only* employee who is paid earnings above the secondary threshold will no longer be able to claim the employment allowance with effect from 6 April 2016 *(SI 2016/344 - The Employment Allowance (Excluded Companies) Regulations 2016)*.

It was announced at the Budget 2016 that changes will be brought in to withdraw this allowance for one year if an employer receives a civil penalty from the Home Office for hiring an illegal worker. The first period to be assessed will be 2017/18 with the exclusion coming into force in 2018/19.

You can check eligibility and the main conditions at www.gov.uk/employment-allowance.

Interest and penalties

43.31   Interest is charged on a daily basis (currently at 2.75%, since 23 August 2016) if Class 1 NICs (and/or PAYE) are paid late *(SI 2001/1004, reg 67A)*.

Penalties apply to the late payment of NIC / PAYE whether the PAYE periods are monthly, quarterly or annually. The penalties start at 1% increasing to 4%, with further penalties of 5% becoming due for persistent late payment (ie over six months late). The first late payment does not count as a default so there is no penalty if there are no further late payments in the tax year *(FA 2009, s 107, Sch 56)*.

Under RTI, employers need to make a full payment submission (FPS) each time they pay their employees and late filing penalties will be issued for late submission. The size of these penalties will depend on the number of employees within the PAYE scheme, starting at £100 for one to nine employees, rising to £400 for 250 employees or more. The penalties will be charged on a monthly basis, but notified via a quarterly filing penalty notice, normally in July, October, January and April.

Where submissions are made more than three months late, a further penalty may be charged at 5% of the PAYE tax/NIC that should have been declared on the late return.

For the late filing of Form P11D, penalties of up to £300 per form (plus £60 per day for persistent failure to file) can be raised.

Penalties for inaccurate PAYE returns are based on the amount of tax lost, ranging from a 'statutory maximum' of 30% for 'careless behaviour' to 100% for 'deliberate and concealed'. Penalties can be reduced dependent upon the amount of disclosure and co-operation by the PAYE employer.

It should be noted that company directors can also be held liable by HMRC for the employer company's failure to pay over Class 1 NIC (see *Stephen Roberts & Alan Martin v Revenue & Customs Commissioners* [2011] UKFTT 268 (TC)).

CLASS 1A NICs

43.32   Class 1A NICs are payable by employers (and other secondary contributors) only at the flat rate of 13.8% on the taxable value of virtually all *benefits in kind* provided to their directors, or employees.

Class 1A carries no benefit entitlement and employees do not pay Class 1A NICs.

Scope of Class 1A NICs

43.33   The basic rule is that liability to Class 1A NICs arises where a director or employee (or a member of their family) receives general earnings from employment and all or part of those earnings are *not* already chargeable to Class 1 NICs (such as non-cash vouchers).

'General earnings' and the 'relevant employment' are as defined for income tax purposes under *ITEPA 2003*. The effect of this rule is to *exclude* those benefits (from Class 1A):

● which are already exempt for income tax purposes (such as mobile phones, or workplace parking facilities); and

● any amounts included within a PSA and therefore liable to Class 1B NICs (see **43.37** below);

Note that from 2016/17 the concept of a 'P11D' and 'P9D' employee was abolished and all employees were brought into the charge to tax and NIC for benefits and expenses. Before this time, employees earning less than £8,500 were exempt from be assessed on many benefits in kind.

See also HMRC booklet 480 (2016) *Expenses and Benefits – A Tax Guide* (www.hmrc.gov.uk/guidance/480.pdf).

For overseas issues with Class 1A NICs, see **46.7**.

Computation of Class 1A NICs

43.34 The Class 1A NIC liability is calculated at the secondary percentage rate of 13.8% (for 2016/17) on the amount of benefit as computed for income tax purposes.

This is the amount taken from the relevant box on the annual Form P11D (see **43.35**) but firstly taking account of the following:

- Any amounts made good by the employee or director which reduce the total amount liable to Class 1A NICs.

- Any amount fully offset by a matching deduction for tax purposes (such as a reimbursed business travel expense), which then effectively reduces the P11D amount to nil and Class 1A NICs are not payable.

However, benefits or expenses which are only *partially* deductible for tax purposes (under *ITEPA 2003*), namely where there is both a business and private element, are liable to Class 1A NICs on the *full* amount of benefit or expense.

Example 43.7 – Amount liable to Class 1A NICs

If an employee obtains a discounted air ticket for a business journey but the employer reimburses him for the full price ticket, then Class 1A NICs would be payable on the full amount reimbursed.

This is the case, even though the employee can make a claim for tax purposes to deduct the business element of his expense from his general taxable earnings.

Although the employee can claim back a tax deduction, the employer is effectively suffering the cost of paying 13.8% on a business expense (although this can be reduced by the tax relief received on the expense on the employer's own income or corporation tax return) (*SSCBA 1992, s 10*).

Example 43.8 – Calculation of Class 1A NICs

Lucy is an employee with an annual salary of £30,000, who received the following benefits and expenses during the tax year 2016/17 (as calculated for earnings purposes):

	£
Car benefit	2,700
Car fuel benefit	3,978
Private medical insurance	900
Local gym club membership	350
Fashion chain store vouchers	100
Professional subscription	275
Business travel expenses	500

- The professional subscription and business travel expenditure are allowable in *full* as deductions for tax purposes and therefore no Class 1A NICs are payable on these.

- The store vouchers would be subject to Class 1 NICs at the primary and secondary rates prevailing *at the time* they were provided, which in practice would be charged through the payroll (and not at the tax year end, unlike the income tax due).

Therefore the Class 1A NIC liability for 2016/17 would be as follows:

	£
Car benefit	2,700
Car fuel benefit	3,978
Private medical insurance	900
Local gym club membership	350
Total benefits liable to Class 1A NIC:	7,928

Class 1A NIC liability = £7,928 × 13.8% = £1,094.06

The Class 1A NIC rate applied is that for the tax year in which the benefit is *provided* (not the tax year in which the Class 1A NICs are actually paid) and is not affected by reduced-rate (for certain married women) elections.

Class 1A NICs – returns and records

43.35   As mentioned above, the amounts liable to Class 1A NICs are reported on Form P11D at the end of the tax year. The relevant boxes are colour-coded brown and marked '1A'.

The amounts from the P11D 1A boxes are totalled up and entered on Form P11D(b) and then the *secondary percentage* rate of 13.8% (for 2016/17) applied to the total. The P11D(b) form is a combined return, in that it shows the simple calculation of Class 1A NICs due and is also a declaration of whether Forms P11D are attached, or are not due.

Both the P11D(b) and P11D are required to be submitted by 6 July after the end of the tax year (these can be filed online or on paper). Payment is due by the 19 July (see below).

Copies of Forms P11D are required to be sent (by 6 July), to those who were in employment at the end of the tax year.

Not all items to be reported on the P11D are liable to Class 1A NICs since, as mentioned earlier, some items have already been charged (via the payroll) to Class 1 NICs.

Examples of such items include:

- non-cash vouchers (eg for high street stores);
- settlement of an employee's personal bills by the employer (eg private telephone bills);
- mileage allowances paid above HMRC's approved mileage rates (AMAPs).

See also HMRC Guide CWG5 (2016), Appendix 1 for a list of 'Common Expenses and Benefits' and their National Insurance treatment and Appendix 2 for an example of Form P11D (www.hmrc.gov.uk/guidance/cwg5.pdf).

The P11D records must be kept for at least three years and employers must be able to substantiate the totals returned and charged to Class 1A. No other records are required to be kept for Class 1A NIC purposes.

Class 1A NICs – payment

43.36   Payment of Class 1A NICs (as calculated on the P11D(b)) is required by the 19 July after the tax year end, or 22 July for electronic payments (compulsory for 'large employers').

As with Class 1 NIC, there are penalties for both the late filing of the P11D(b) form and late payment of Class 1A NIC.

The Class 1A NICs are payable by the employer or 'secondary contributor'. This is the person who is liable to pay the Class 1 secondary contribution on the employee's ('employed earner's') general earnings. This will include a 'host employer' or 'deemed secondary contributor' (*SSCBA 1992, s 10*).

If the benefit liable to Class 1A NICs is provided by a person other than the employer, ie a third party, then the liability falls on them and Class 1A NICs should be accounted for and paid in the normal way.

Non-cash vouchers provided by third parties are also liable to Class 1A NICs and not Class 1.

If the employer is involved in arranging the provision of the 'third party benefit or non-cash voucher', then the responsibility falls on the employer to account for the Class 1A NIC, instead (*SSCBA 1992, ss 10ZA, 10ZB*).

Where a business changes hands, the liability for Class 1A NICs continues with the new employer for those employees retained.

For any employee not staying on with the new employer, the previous employer must meet their Class 1A liabilities within 14 days after the end of the month, in which the last payment of employment earnings is made.

Similarly if a business ceases to trade, all Class 1A NICs are due within 14 days after the end of the final month.

CLASS 1B NICs

43.37   Class 1B NICs are a special class of contribution, which employers pay on items (and income tax thereon) covered by a PAYE settlement agreement (PSA).

Generally, employers enter into a PSA with HMRC in order to pay the income tax and NIC liability on behalf of their employees on minor or irregular employee provided benefits.

This avoids having to account and report for such items separately on the Form P11D, or to account for them on the payroll through RTI.

Employers pay Class 1B NICs on:

- the value of the items covered by the PSA, which would normally give rise to a Class 1 or Class 1A liability; and

- the total amount of tax payable by the employer under the PSA.

In effect, the items included in the PSA are grossed up at the appropriate income tax rate to reflect the tax borne by the employer. Class 1B is then charged on both the value of the taxable benefit and the tax borne.

Class 1B NICs are charged at the fixed percentage rate of the Class 1 NIC secondary contribution, which as with Class 1A is 13.8% (for 2016/17) (*SSCBA 1992, s 10A*).

Example 43.9 – Calculation of Class 1B NICs

Toffee Finance Limited employs 500 staff.

- 300 employees are chargeable to basic rate tax on minor benefits valued at £30 each.

- 200 employees are chargeable to higher rate tax on benefits valued at £50 each.

Toffee Finance Limited's tax and Class 1A NICs payable under their PSA for the tax year 2016/17 would be calculated as follows:

	£
Value of benefits provided to 'basic rate' (20%) employees	9,000.00
Grossed up at 100/80 to include tax borne by employer	11,250.00
Tax borne by employer (£11,250 × 20%)	2,250.00
Value of benefits provided to 'higher rate' (40%) employees	10,000.00
Grossed up at 100/60 to include tax borne by employer	16,666.67
Tax borne by employer (£16,666.67 × 40%)	6,666.67
Total value of items liable to Class 1B NIC:	19,000.00
Total tax due (£2,250 + £6,666.67):	8,916.67
Total Class 1B NIC due: (£8,916.67 + £19,000) × 13.8%	3,852.50

The Class 1B NICs and the tax due under the PSA are both payable at the same time and are due by the 19 October following the tax year end (or 22 October for electronic payments).

Once a PSA has been agreed with the relevant PAYE tax office (on Form P626) for a particular tax year, the tax inspector will agree the amounts payable with the employer after 6 July (following the tax year end).

The details are then confirmed on a Notice to Pay (Form P630), together with a payslip, in time for the employer to make the appropriate payments due by the deadline date shown above.

No formal records need to be kept specifically for Class 1B NIC purposes. However, employers need to keep those records which, in general, are required for tax purposes, so that they can identify any items given to employees and be able to substantiate the amounts payable under a PSA. Records must be kept for a minimum of three years (see also HMRC's National Insurance Manual from NIM18000–19000, www.hmrc.gov.uk/manuals/nimmanual/nim18000. htm).

Employers who operate taxed award schemes (TAS) may find it preferable to enter into a PSA instead. See HMRC's Employment Income Manual at EIM11235 and EIM11270.

For residence issues in connection with the liability to Class 1B NICs, see **46.7**.

APPENDIX: PRIMARY AND SECONDARY NICs

Class 1 Primary (employee) contributions

(SSCBA 1992, ss 5(1), 8, 19(4); SI 2001/1004, regs 10, 131; Pension Schemes Act 1993, ss 41, 42A; SI 2006/1009, art 3)

43.38

Class 1 NIC rates and thresholds	2016/17	2015/16	2014/15	2013/14	2012/13
Lower earnings limit (LEL)	£112 per week £486 per month £5,824 per year	£112 per week £486 per month £5,824 per year	£111 per week £481 per month £5,772 per year	£109 per week £473 per month £5,668 per year	£107 per week £464 per month £5,564 per year
Primary threshold (PT)	£155 per week £672 per month £8,060 per year	£155 per week £672 per month £8,060 per year	£153 per week £663 per month £7,956 per year	£149 per week £646 per month £7,755 per year	£146 per week £634 per month £7,605 per year
Upper accrual point (UAP) (see Note 2 below)	Abolished	£770 per week £3,337 per month £40,040 per year	£770 per week £3,337 per month £40,040 per year	£770 per week £3,337 per month £40,040 per year	£770 per week £3,337 per month £40,040 per year
Upper earnings limit (UEL)	£827 per week £3,583 per month £43,000 per year	£815 per week £3,532 per month £42,385 per year	£805 per week £3,489 per month £41,865 per year	£797 per week £3,454 per month £41,450 per year	£817 per week £3,540 per month £42,475 per year
Not contracted out	12% on earnings between PT and UEL 2% on excess over UEL	12% on earnings between PT and UEL 2% on excess over UEL	12% on earnings between PT and UEL 2% on excess over UEL	12% on earnings between PT and UEL 2% on excess over UEL	12% on earnings between PT and UEL 2% on excess over UEL

Contracted out (see Note 3 below)	Abolished	10.6% on earnings between PT and UAP 12% on earnings between UAP and UEL 2% on excess over UEL	10.6% on earnings between PT and UAP 12% on earnings between UAP and UEL 2% on excess over UEL	10.6% on earnings between PT and UAP 12% on earnings between UAP and UEL 2% on excess over UEL
Contracted out rebate – flat rate (see Note 3 below)	Abolished	1.4%	1.4%	1.4%
Reduced rate (see Note 4 below)	5.85% on earnings between PT and UEL 2% on excess over UEL	5.85% on earnings between PT and UEL 2% on excess over UEL	5.85% on earnings between PT and UEL 2% on excess over UEL	5.85% on earnings between PT and UEL 2% on excess over UEL

(Additional column: 10.6% on earnings between PT and UAP; 12% on earnings between UAP and UEL; 2% on excess over UEL / 1.4% / 5.85% on earnings between PT and UEL; 2% on excess over UEL)

Notes

1 *Nil band* – No Class 1 contributions are payable on earnings between the lower earnings limit and primary threshold, but the employee is treated as having paid such contributions for the purposes of establishing or protecting entitlement to certain state benefits (*SSCBA 1992, s 6A*).

2 *'Upper accrual point' (UAP)* – This broadly represented the point at which entitlement to contributory related benefits ceased to accrue. This was only relevant before 6 April 2016 (see note 3 below).

3 *Contracting out* – This was abolished for defined contribution (money purchase) pension schemes from 6 April 2012 and for defined benefit (final salary) pension schemes from 6 April 2016 when the single tier state pension was introduced.

4 *Reduced rate* – This applies to women married before 6 April 1977 who have elected to pay a reduced rate of Class 1 contributions.

719

Class 1 Secondary (employer) contributions

(SSCBA 1992, ss 6(1)(b), 9; SI 2001/1004, reg 10; Pension Schemes Act 1993, ss 41, 42A; SI 2006/1009, arts 2, 3)

43.39

Class 1 NIC rates and thresholds	2016/17	2015/16	2014/15	2013/14	2012/13
Secondary threshold (ST)	£156 per week £676 per month £8,112 per year	£156 per week £676 per month £8,112 per year	£153 per week £663 per month £7,956 per year	£148 per week £641 per month £7,696 per year	£144 per week £624 per month £7,488 per year
Upper secondary threshold (UST) (Under 21) (see Note 2 below)	£827 per week £3,583 per month £43,000 per year	£815 per week £3,532 per month £42,385 per year	N/A	N/A	N/A
Apprentice upper secondary threshold (AUST) (see Note 3 below)	£827 per week £3,583 per month £43,000 per year	N/A	N/A	N/A	N/A
Not contracted out rate	13.8% on earnings above ST	13.8% on earnings above ST	13.8% on earnings above ST	13.8% on earnings above ST	13.8% on earnings above ST
Contracted out rates					
Salary related (COSR) (see Note 4 below)	Abolished	10.4%	10.4%	10.4%	10.4%

Money purchase (COMP) (see Note 4 below)	Abolished	Abolished	Abolished	Abolished	Abolished	Abolished
Contracted out rebate rates						
Salary related (COSR) (see Note 4 below)	Abolished	3.4%	3.4%	3.4%	3.4%	3.4%
Money purchase (COMP) (see Note 4 below)	Abolished	Abolished	Abolished	Abolished	Abolished	Abolished

Notes

1. *Age Limits* – Class 1 contributions are not payable in respect of individuals under the age of 16 at the time of payment of the earnings. An employee who is at or over state pension age (SPA) at the time of payment is not liable to pay primary Class 1 contributions, but employers must continue to pay secondary Class 1 contributions for employees over their SPA (*SSCBA 1992, s 6(3)*) (see NIM1001).

2. *Under 21* – From 6 April 2015, employers' Class 1 NIC will not be payable on earnings up to the upper secondary threshold (UST), in respect of employees aged under 21 (*NICA 2014, s 9*).

3. *Under 25* – From 6 April 2016, employers' Class 1 NIC will not be payable on earnings up to the apprentice upper secondary threshold (AUST), in respect of apprentices aged under 25 (*NICA 2015, s 1*).

4. *Contracting out* – This was abolished for defined contributions (money purchase) pension schemes from 6 April 2012 and for defined benefit (final salary) schemes from 6 April 2016 when the single tier state pension was introduced.

5. *Disguised remuneration* – Class 1 employee and employer contributions can arise on certain 'disguised remuneration' from Employee Benefit Trusts (EBTs), unapproved pension schemes (EFRBS) and other third party intermediaries where such income would not otherwise be within the charge to NICs (see *ITEPA 2003, ss 554A–554Z20; SI 2001/1004* as amended by *SI 2011/2700*).

44

National Insurance – self-employed

SIGNPOSTS

- **Scope** – Self-employed earners are currently liable to pay Class 2 and Class 4 National Insurance contributions (NICs), subject to certain exceptions (see **44.1**).

- **Class 2 NICs** – Contributions are liable at a flat rate, unless the small profits threshold applies. Class 2 NICs will be abolished from April 2018 and absorbed into Class 4 NICs (see **44.2–44.3**).

- **Class 4 NICs** – Contributions are earnings-related contributions paid by self-employed earners through the self-assessment system. The Class 4 NIC rates are currently 9% (main rate) and 2% (additional rate) (see **44.4–44.5**).

- **Appendix: NIC rates** – A table of rates for Class 2 NICs and Class 4 NICs is included at the end of this chapter (see **44.6–44.7**).

INTRODUCTION

44.1　　Class 2 NICs and Class 4 NICs are payable in general (and unless specifically exempted) by self-employed persons over the age of 16.

Broadly speaking:

- *Class 2 NICs* are liable at a flat weekly rate (depending upon 'earnings') (*SSCBA 1992, s 11*); and

- *Class 4 NICs* are payable under the tax self-assessment regime on taxable trading profits (over a specified limit) (*SSCBA 1992, s 15*).

Class 2 NICs give entitlement to certain statutory benefits, such as the state pension and maternity allowance (*SSCBA 1992, s 21*).

Class 4 NICs carry no entitlement to any contributory benefits (although they are paid into the National Insurance Fund to help spread the cost of benefits for the self-employed).

CLASS 2 NICs

44.2 Currently Class 2 NICs are liable at the flat rate of £2.80 per week (2016/17), by 'self-employed earners', ie those who are 'gainfully employed' (in the UK) otherwise than as employees.

As with Class 1 and Class 1A NIC, liability is limited to those who meet the required conditions as to 'residence or presence in Great Britain'. However, see **46.7** for special rules that apply for those working abroad.

Certain persons are exempt from paying Class 2 NICs, such as:

- those aged under 16;

- those who are over pensionable age;

- married women (or widows) who are in possession of a 'reduced rate election' certificate; and

- those earners who have profits below the small profits threshold of £5,965 (2016/17) as detailed below.

More details can be found in HMRC's National Insurance Manual at NIM20775 (www.hmrc.gov.uk/manuals/nimmanual/nim20775.htm).

Special rates of Class 2 NICs apply to 'share fishermen' (£3.45 per week for 2016/17) and 'volunteer development workers' (£5.60 per week for 2016/17) (*SSCBA 1992, s 117(1); SI 2001/1004, regs 125, 152(b)*).

Class 2 NICs – notification and payment

44.3 A person must notify HMRC as soon as he becomes a 'self-employed earner' and indeed when he ceases self-employment (see www.gov.uk/set-up-sole-trader/register).

From April 2015, the liability to pay Class 2 NICs no longer arises on a weekly basis. Although the amount of Class 2 NICs due continues to be calculated based on the number of weeks of self-employment in the year, it is determined when the individual completes their self-assessment return and is paid alongside their income tax and Class 4 NICs on 31 January following the end of the tax year. The payment requests for Class 2 NICs now form part of the self-assessment statements.

Class 2 NICs collected through the self-assessment system is subject to the penalties and appeals regime which currently exists within the *Taxes Management Act 1970* (*TMA 1970*) for income tax and Class 4 NICs.

Where a person has no profits (chargeable to tax under the *Income Tax (Trading and Other Income) Act 2005, Pt. 2, Ch 2*) or profits below the small profits threshold of £5,965 for 2016/17, they no longer have to apply in advance for an exception from paying Class 2 NICs and therefore the small earnings exception certificate ceased to be applicable from April 2015.

Those individuals who do not need to report income through self-assessment, have the option to voluntarily pay Class 2 NICs at the end of the tax year, in order to maintain their entitlement to contribution-based benefits, such as maternity allowance and the state pension.

Those that are self-employed and also have Class 1 NICs to consider (ie they are within PAYE and self-employed) no longer have to apply for deferment of their Class 2 NICs as liability for Class 2 is not assessed until after the end of the relevant tax year.

Also, those individuals with more than one self-employment are only liable to one lot of weekly Class 2 NICs, even though they may have several self-employments.

See, however, **Chapter 46** for 'annual maxima' provisions where the taxpayer is also employed.

(*SSCBA 1992; SI 2001/1004*, as amended by *NICA 2015, Sch 1 – Reform of Class 2 Contributions*)

Focus

Class 2 NICs are to be abolished from April 2018 and changes are expected to be made to the legislation of Class 4 NICs so that self-employed individuals can continue to build entitlement to contributory benefits such as the state pension.

CLASS 4 NICs

44.4   Class 4 NICs are also payable by self-employed earners (in addition to Class 2 contributions).

However, Class 4 is an earnings-related contribution and, as such, is subject to the tax self-assessment regime and payable on taxable profits (see below).

As with Class 2 NICs, there are certain people who are exempted from paying Class 4 NICs, such as the following:

- those aged under 16;

- those who are over pensionable age;

- those who are treated for income tax purposes as not resident in the UK; and

- self-employed earners who, under special rules, are liable to Class 1 NICs on their trading income (*SI 2001/1004, regs 91–94A*).

See HMRC's National Insurance Manual at NIM24510 (www.hmrc.gov.uk/manuals/nimmanual/NIM24510.htm) for more details.

For partnerships, in addition to Class 2 NICs, each partner (or member of an LLP) is liable to Class 4 NICs on their own share of the profits of the trade or profession carried on by the partnership (*SSCBA 1992, s 15, Sch 2, para 4*).

Class 4 NICs – payment

44.5   Class 4 NICs are payable at the main percentage rate of 9% (for 2016/17) on trading profits between the lower profits limit of £8,060 per year and the upper profits limit of £43,000 per year (for 2016/17).

An additional rate of 2% is charged on profits above the upper profits limit.

The profits are broadly defined for Class 4 NIC purposes as follows:

- they must be immediately derived from the trade(s);

- they must be profits chargeable to income tax under *ITTOIA 2005*; and

- not profits of a trade, profession or vocation carried on wholly outside the UK.

In general, the trading profits are calculated along the same principles as the income tax rules (under *ITTOIA 2005*) with the Class 4 liability based on profits for the tax year in which the accounting year ended.

Focus

For Class 4 NIC purposes, trading losses (allowed under *ITA 2007, ss 64, 72*) are only set against other trading income (and not non-trading income as for income tax purposes). This ensures that relief for Class 4 NIC is able to be obtained on all trading losses.

Any unused trading losses for Class 4 purposes are carried forward to be set against future trading profits. In addition, relief can be claimed for certain interest which qualifies for tax relief under *ITA 2007, s 383* (*SSCBA 1992, Sch 2, para 3(5)(b)*).

Profits from multiple trades or professions are aggregated together in calculating the Class 4 NIC liability.

As mentioned previously, Class 4 NICs are assessed with income tax under the self-assessment provisions. They are therefore collected at the same time as the income tax liability, with payments on account becoming due on the 31 January and 31 July.

In effect, each payment on account will include an amount equal to half of the previous year's Class 4 NICs, with any adjustments made with the balancing payment on the 31 January following.

As with income tax, late payment interest and penalties apply (with repayment interest due for any refunded Class 4 NICs) (*SSCBA 1992, ss 15–17, Sch 2*).

For further information, see HMRC's National Insurance Manual at NIM24001 onwards (www.hmrc.gov.uk/manuals/nimmanual/NIM24001.htm).

See also **46.1** for the 'annual maxima' provisions which may apply to reduce the payment of Class 4 NICs.

Example 44.1 – Calculation of Class 4 NICs

Charlotte and Lee are in partnership sharing profits 60:40. The tax-adjusted partnership profits assessable for the tax year 2016/17 are £80,000.

Lee had only become a partner from 6 April 2016, so had no partnership profits to declare for previous years.

They also receive rental income of £12,000 each per year.

Lee also runs a separate business and has assessable profits for the tax year 2016/17 of £15,000. In the previous tax year (2015/16), he had made a qualifying trading loss of £10,000.

Class 4 NICs only for 2016/17 (rounded for example purposes) would be payable as follows:

Charlotte	£
Assessable partnership profits: £80,000 × 60%	48,000
Class 4 NICs due at 9% on (£43,000 – 8,060)	3,145
Class 4 NICs due at 2% on (£48,000 – 43,000)	100
Total Class 4 NICs due for 2016/17	3,245

Lee	£
Assessable partnership profits £80,000 × 40%	32,000
Own business profits	15,000
Total profits assessable for self-employments	47,000
Less: trading loss b/fwd from 2015/16	(10,000)
Total trading profits assessable to Class 4 NICs	37,000
Class 4 NICs due at 9% on (£37,000 – 8,060)	2,604

Notes

1   Lee's trading loss of £10,000 for the tax year 2015/16 was allowable under *ITA 2007, s64* and for income tax purposes was claimed in full against his other (non-trading) income of that year, ie the rental income of £12,000. However, for Class 4 NIC purposes the trading loss can only be set against trading profits. He had no other trading income in 2015/16, so the trading loss of £10,000 is carried forward to reduce the trading profits assessable under Class 4 NIC in 2016/17.

2   Class 2 NIC would also be payable by both Charlotte and Lee and calculated at the weekly rate of £2.80.

APPENDIX: NIC RATES

Class 2 contributions

(*SSCBA 1992, ss 11, 12*)

Rates (weekly)

(*SSCBA 1992, ss 11(1), 117(1); SI 2001/1004, regs 125(c), 152(b)*)

44.6

Tax year	Flat rate	Share fishermen	Volunteer development workers
	£	£	£
2016/17	2.80	3.45	5.60
2015/16	2.80	3.45	5.60

Tax year	Flat rate	Share fishermen	Volunteer development workers
	£	£	£
2014/15	2.75	3.40	5.55
2013/14	2.70	3.35	5.45
2012/13	2.65	3.30	5.35
2011/12	2.50	3.15	5.10

Notes

1   *Age limits* – Class 2 contributions are payable by self-employed persons over the age of 16, but are not payable in respect of any period after the earner has reached state pension age.

2   *Collection* – Class 2 is payable on 31 January 2018 for the tax year 2016/17.

Class 4 contributions

(SSCBA 1992, s 15)

Class 4 NIC rates

(SSCBA 1992, s 15(3ZA))

44.7

Tax year	Main Class 4 percentage	Additional Class 4 percentage	Lower profits limit	Upper profits limit
	%	%	£	£
2016/17	9	2	8,060	43,000
2015/16	9	2	8,060	42,385
2014/15	9	2	7,956	41,865
2013/14	9	2	7,755	41,450
2012/13	9	2	7,605	42,475
2011/12	9	2	7,225	42,475

Notes

1   *General* – Class 4 contributions are payable on profits from UK trades, professions or vocations, which are chargeable to income tax under *ITTOIA 2005, Pt 2, Ch 2*.

2   *Exceptions* – Individuals who are over state pension age, or aged under 16 at the beginning of the relevant tax year, are exempt from paying Class 4 NICs if they obtain a certificate of exception from HMRC (*SI 2001/1004, regs 91, 93*).

3   *Due on* – Class 4 contributions are payable at the main rate on profits between the lower and upper profits limits, and at the additional rate on profits above the upper profits limit.

4   *Annual maximum* – Class 4 contributions are subject to an annual maximum, calculated in accordance with *SI 2001/1004, reg 100*. The liability for contributions at the main rate is broadly limited to a maximum of 53 times the appropriate weekly amount of Class 2 NICs, plus the maximum amount of Class 4 contributions payable at the main rate, less any Class 2 NICs and any Class 1 NICs paid at the main rate. However, Class 4 NICs remain payable at the additional rate. An application to HMRC for a refund of Class 4 NICs (if appropriate) can be made on Form CA5610 (see www.hmrc.gov.uk/forms/ca5610.pdf).

45

Class 3 NICs

SIGNPOSTS

- **Scope** – Class 3 National Insurance contributions (NICs) are voluntary for those individuals eligible to pay them (see **45.1**).

- **Eligibility** – Only individuals over 16 and below state pension age can be eligible to make Class 3 contributions at a fixed weekly rate (see **45.2–45.3**).

- **Why pay Class 3 NICs?** – Normally, individuals will only want to make voluntary payments to secure their state pension (see **45.4**).

- **Payment** – There are rules about when Class 3 contributions can be made and payment methods (see **45.5**).

- **Appendix: NIC rates** – A table of Class 3 NIC rates for current and earlier years is included at the end of this chapter (see **45.6**).

INTRODUCTION

45.1   Class 3 NICs are voluntary contributions. To be eligible to pay them, individuals must be over 16 years of age and satisfy the conditions of residence or presence in the UK (see HMRC's National Insurance Manual at NIM25002 (www.hmrc.gov.uk/manuals/nimmanual/NIM25002.htm)).

They must also comply with HMRC's conditions as to methods of payment and time limits (see below) (*SSCBA 1992, ss 13–14*).

ELIGIBILITY

45.2   Certain people are not eligible to pay Class 3 voluntary contributions, such as married women with a reduced rate NIC election, or individuals who have already reached state pension age in the relevant tax year (but see Class 3A NICs below).

Voluntary Class 3 contributions are made in order to maintain (or create) entitlement to a limited number of benefits, most notably the state pension, where the individual's other contributions would not create such entitlement, or during unemployment or absence abroad (see **46.7–46.9**).

Class 3A NICs – From 12 October 2015 a new class of voluntary NICs was introduced to give those who reached state pension age before 6 April 2016, an opportunity to top up the weekly amount of the state pension they are due to receive by between £1 and £25 per week, by making a lump sum payment before the 5 April 2017.

The cost varies according to age (and decreases as you get older), for example, an extra £1 per week of pension for a 66 year old man would cost £871, so the cost of the maximum 'top up' of £25 per week for that same person would be £21,775.

It may however, be more cost effective to make voluntary contributions before making a state pension top up, where an individual has gaps in their NIC record (see below).

RATE

45.3   The rate for Class 3 NICs for 2016/17 is £14.10 per week.

BACKGROUND TO VOLUNTARY PAYMENTS

45.4   The main reason for making voluntary Class 3 contributions is to maintain entitlement to the full basic state pension where an individual has not achieved the required number of contribution years.

Focus

An individual can check his contribution record directly with NICO by requesting a 'state pension statement', or by using the gov.uk website link (www.gov.uk/state-pension-statement).

However, HMRC will normally notify people annually (between September and January) whether there is a gap in their contribution record and how they can make up any shortfall, if they wish to do so.

Since the number of qualifying years required for a full new state pension has recently reduced to ten qualifying years (with effect from 6 April 2016), most people will now not need to top up their contribution record (but see **45.2** above regarding Class 3A NICs).

It should be noted however, that the number of qualifying years for entitlement to bereavement benefits remains at 39 for a woman and up to 44 for a man.

PAYMENT

45.5   Class 3 contributions can normally be paid up to six years after the tax year to which they relate.

Payments made after the end of the tax year following that for which contributions are payable may have to be made at a higher rate than that in force for the year to which they relate.

In some cases, you can pay for gaps from more than six years ago.

If you were entitled to receive the (old) state pension before the 6 April 2016, you have six years *after* you have reached the state pension age to make voluntary contributions.

For example, if you reached state pension age on 1 February 2015, you will have until 31 January 2021 to pay voluntary contributions.

For those eligible to receive the new state pension (from 6 April 2016), HMRC have extended the time limit for paying voluntary contributions until 5 April 2023, to make up for gaps between April 2006 and April 2016. These contributions can be paid at different rates if paid by 5 April 2019.

See www.gov.uk/voluntary-national-insurance-contributions/deadlines.

Payment of Class 3 NICs can be made by various methods (see www.gov. uk/pay-voluntary-class-3-national-insurance). Regular payments of Class 3 NICs may be paid by monthly direct debit or a request can be made for HMRC to issue quarterly 'payment requests' in arrears.

Further guidance and application to pay Class 3 NICs is provided with HMRC Helpsheet CA5603 (available from the HMRC website at www.hmrc.gov.uk/ nic/ca5603.pdf) (*Social Security (Contributions) Regulations, SI 2001/1004, reg 89*).

Focus

If the individual is self-employed, it would currently be preferable to pay voluntary Class 2 NICs, if eligible, since they are lower (£2.80 per week for 2016/17) and grant entitlement to a wider range of benefits (see **44.3**).

APPENDIX: CLASS 3 CONTRIBUTIONS

(*SSCBA 1992, s 13*)

45.6

Tax year	Weekly rate
	£
2016/17	14.10
2015/16	14.10
2014/15	13.90
2013/14	13.55
2012/13	13.25
2011/12	12.60

Notes

1   *Eligibility* – Individuals wishing to pay Class 3 contributions in order to meet the conditions for entitlement to certain benefits must be over the age of 16 and satisfy conditions as to residence in Great Britain or Northern Ireland in the relevant tax year (*SSCBA 1992, s 1(6)(b)*; *SI 2001/1004, regs 48(1), 145(1)(e)*).

2   *Earnings factor* – An individual is entitled to pay Class 3 contributions if his earnings factor (EF) derived from Class 1, 2 and/or 3 NICs is less than the qualifying earnings factor for the relevant tax year, subject to certain restrictions on the right to pay. A qualifying earnings factor is an amount equal to 52 times that year's lower earnings limit for Class 1 contributions (*SSCBA 1992, s 14*; *SI 1979/676, Sch 1, Pt 2*) (see NIM25001).

46

NIC planning

SIGNPOSTS

- **Multiple earnings** – Individuals who have more than one employment or who are self-employed as well as employed could be subject to multiple NIC liabilities without the provisions for annual maximum contributions and deferment of contributions (see **46.1–46.5**).

- **Salary sacrifice** – Individuals may enter into arrangements with their employer for additional contributions to be made to their pension scheme in lieu of salary; this can be efficient if dealt with properly (see **46.6**).

- **Working in the UK and abroad** – The NIC rules which apply to individuals leaving the UK to work abroad and the reverse position where individuals come to work in the UK are complex (see **46.7–46.13**).

- **Anti-avoidance** – There are provisions dealing with abnormal pay practices, and practices which avoid or reduce liability for contributions (see **46.14**).

- **Further information** – There are a number of useful sources of further information on NIC and links to these are shown (see **46.15–46.16**).

ANNUAL MAXIMA AND DEFERMENT – MULTIPLE EMPLOYMENTS

46.1 Without specific provisions in the legislation, persons with more than one job would be liable to pay National Insurance contributions (NICs) for *each* of those employments.

For example, a person with just one employment may have the same *total* income as another person, who is both employed and self-employed. However, because of the way NICs work, the one who is in single employment may pay substantially less NICs than the one with two or more employments or self-employment.

The legislation therefore provides for 'annual maxima' to prevent such anomalies. There are different rules and methods of calculation for each 'annual maximum', which are set out in the sections below and can also be found in the legislation and/or HMRC's National Insurance Manual, as noted for each case.

If the particular annual maximum is exceeded, then the 'earner' (whether employed or self-employed) can claim a refund (subject to a minimum level). However, they are *initially* liable for the full amount of NICs payable and the refund is made after the tax year in question (see www.gov.uk/claim-national-insurance-refund).

In certain circumstances, deferment can be applied for if it is evident that the annual maximum is to be exceeded in any case (either year on year or for one particular tax year).

This is covered further in **46.5** below.

> **Focus**
>
> There is no annual maximum for employers' secondary contributions (currently payable at 13.8%).

Class 1 and 2 – annual maximum

46.2 The Class 1 and 2 NIC annual maximum is set for persons who are engaged in more than one employment or, in addition to being employed, are also self-employed (and paying Class 2 NICs only).

It should be noted (as set out at **43.26**) that in certain circumstances, such as when a person has several employments with the same employer, his earnings are aggregated into a *single* employment. No 'annual maximum' applies in these cases.

For the purposes of the annual maximum only, earners who would normally pay Class 1 primary NICs at a reduced rate, such as married women with a reduced rate election certificate, are treated as if they were liable to pay Class 1 NICs at the full 'standard' rate of 12%.

Where the annual maximum is applicable and a refund is payable, this must be greater than 1/15th of the weekly Class 1 NICs due on earnings, at the standard 12% rate, ie (£827 – £155) × 12% × 1/15 = £5.38 (for 2016/17).

46.2 *NIC planning*

The 'annual maxima' for Classes 1 and 2 NIC purposes is calculated as follows (*Social Security (Contributions) Regulations, SI 2001/1004, reg 21* (as amended):

Step 1

Calculate $53 \times (UEL - PT)$

where UEL is the weekly upper earnings limit (£827 for 2016/17) and PT is the weekly primary threshold (£155 for 2016/17).

Step 2

Multiply *Step 1* by 12%

Step 3

Add together for all employments the amount of earnings, which in each employment is greater than the PT, but does not exceed the UEL (ie using either the weekly, monthly or annual UEL / PT limits as appropriate, so the maximum for an annual salary would be £43,000 – £8,060 for each employment for 2016/17).

Step 4

Subtract *Step 1* from *Step 3*

Step 5

If *Step 4* = positive then multiply it by 2%

If *Step 4* = nil or is negative, then treat the answer as nil for *Step 8*

Step 6

Add together in all employments, the amount of earnings in each employment which exceeds the UEL

Step 7

Multiply *Step 6* by 2%

Step 8

Add together *Steps 2, 5* and *7*

This gives the individual his personalised annual maximum, as prescribed by the legislation (see **Example 46.1** below).

For further guidance, calculation and examples see HMRC's National Insurance Manual at NIM01160 onwards (www.hmrc.gov.uk/manuals/nimmanual/nim01160.htm).

Example 46.1 – Calculating the annual maximum: Class 1 and 2 NICs

Jamie has two employments, earning £10,000 pa in one and £44,000 pa in the other. He also runs his own small business in which he earned £6,500 for the tax year 2016/17.

Jamie's NIC paid for the tax year 2016/17 would be:

	£
Class 1 (employment 1):	
(£10,000 – £8,060) × 12%	232.80
Class 1 (employment 2):	
(£43,000 – £8,060) × 12%	4,192.80
(£44,000 – £43,000) × 2%	20.00
Class 2: 52 × £2.80	145.60
Total NIC paid for 2016/17:	4,591.20

His Class 1 and 2 NIC annual maximum for 2016/17 would be:

	£
Step 1: 53 × (£827 – £155)	35,616.00
Step 2: £35,616 × 12%	4,273.92
Step 3: (£10,000 – £8,060) + (£43,000 – £8,060)	36,880.00
Step 4: £36,880 – £35,616	1,264.00
Step 5: £1,264 × 2%	25.28
Step 6: £44,000 – £43,000	1,000.00
Step 7: £1,000 × 2%	20.00
Step 8: add together Steps 2, 5 and 7:	
£4,273.92 + £25.28 + £20.00	4,319.20

This is Jamie's maximum Class 1 and 2 NICs payable for the year.

A refund will therefore be due from NICO as follows:

	£
Jamie's annual maximum (as calculated above):	4,319.20
Less: NIC actually paid:	(4,591.20)
Refund due:	(272.00)

Points to note:

- Jamie should claim a refund from NICO at www.gov.uk/claim-national-insurance-refund (see **46.1**).

- The refund of NIC in this case mainly comprises of the Class 1 NICs paid on Jamie's employments at 12%, which effectively have been paid twice.

- That is, NIC due at 12% on the earnings of 'employment one' has already been covered by the NIC paid on the earnings of 'employment two' (which exceeded the UEL).

- However, the annual maximum provides for these 'additional' earnings to be assessed to Class 1 NIC at the lower rate of 2% (this is the overall purpose of Step 5).

- So, Class 1 NICs on 'employment one', payable as per the annual maximum, would be (£10,000 – £8,060) = £1,940 × 2% = £38.80.

- If we deduct from this the Class 1 NICs already paid of £232.80, a refund of £194.00 becomes due, which is effectively 10% (12% – 2%) × £1,940.

- The annual maximum is further adjusted (at Steps 4 and 5) to give an additional one week's relief at the Class 1 NIC 2% rate of:

  (£34,940 – £35,616) × 2% = (£13.52).

  ie the maximum amount of annual earnings between the UEL and PT of £43,000 – £8,060, *less* the maximum set at 53 weeks by the legislation.

- However, the Class 1 and 2 NIC annual maximum is set (at Steps 1 and 2) so as to *limit* the Class 1 and Class 2 NIC refund by the following amount:

  (£35,616 – £34,940) × 12% = £81.12.

  being the maximum set at 53 weeks, *less* the maximum amount of annual earnings between the UEL and PT of £43,000 – £8,060.

- The net effect of this means, that the week 53 limit within the annual maximum, is restricted to 10% of the weekly earnings between the UEL and PT, ie £672 × (12% – 2%) = £67.20.

- In the above example, the Class 2 NICs paid of £145.60 (ie £2.80 × 52 weeks) is also refundable.

- So the total refund due, as shown above is: (£194 + £13.52 + £145.60) = (£353.12), reduced by £81.12 = (£272.00).

Class 4 NICs – annual maximum

46.3   The Class 4 NICs annual maximum is set for both employed and self-employed persons, who in addition to paying both Class 1 and 2 NICs may also be liable to pay Class 4 NICs.

The purpose of the legislation is to give relief from Class 4 NICs at 9%, where earnings from employment have *also* been subject to primary Class 1 NICs at 12%. The 'annual maximum', however, ensures that at least the 2% rate of NIC is charged on profits above the annual Class 4 lower profits limit.

As with the Class 1 and Class 2 annual maximum (see **46.2**), earners paying Class 1 NICs at a reduced rate will be deemed, for these purposes, to be liable at the full primary Class 1 NIC rate of 12%.

As mentioned at **46.2**, the amount to be refunded must exceed 1/15th of the weekly Class 1 NIC due on earnings, at the standard 12% rate, ie £5.38 (for 2016/17).

The annual maximum for Class 4 NIC purposes is calculated as follows (*SI 2001/1004, reg 100,* as amended):

Step 1

Upper profits limit – lower profits limit (ie £43,000 – £8,060 for 2016/17)

Step 2

Multiply *Step 1* by 9%

Step 3

Add *Step 2* + (53 × weekly Class 2 contribution), ie £2.80 for 2016/17

Step 4

Step 3 – (Class 2 contributions paid + Class 1 contributions paid at 12%), ie the main primary percentage

The answer to *Step 4* is divided into three cases:

- If Case 1 applies, then *Steps 5–9* do not apply and the annual maximum is the result of *Step 4*.

- If Case 2 or Case 3 applies, then *Steps 5–9* apply and the annual maximum is calculated by adding together *Steps 4, 8* and *9*.

Case 1 – If *Step 4* is positive and exceeds the *total* of:

(a) Class 1 contributions payable at the main primary percentage (12%),

(b) Class 2 contributions payable, and

(c) Class 4 contributions payable at the main Class 4 percentage (9%),

in respect of the earner's earnings, profits and gains for the year, then this Step is the maximum amount of all Class 4 contributions payable.

Case 2 – If *Step 4* is positive but does not exceed the total calculated in Case 1, then this is the maximum Class 4 NIC payable at the main Class 4 percentage rate (9%).

Case 3 – If *Step 4* is negative, the maximum amount of Class 4 NICs payable at the main Class 4 percentage is *nil* and the result of *Step 4* is treated as nil.

The following steps apply for Cases 2 and 3:

Step 5

Step 4 × 100/9

Step 6

Subtract the lower profits limit from the lesser of the upper profits limit and the amount of profits for the year

Step 7

Step 6 – *Step 5*. If the result is negative, treat as nil.

Step 8

Step 7 × 2%

Step 9

Multiply by 2% the amount by which the profits and gains for the year exceed the upper profits limit for the tax year.

Then to calculate the Class 4 annual maximum, add together *Steps 4, 8* and *9*.

Where the annual maximum is exceeded, Class 4 contributions are refunded (subject to a minimum level) up to the amount of the excess.

Class 1 NICs (at 12%) and Class 2 NICs are payable in the normal way, whether there is a Class 4 refund or not, but are limited to those amounts already paid, as calculated at *Step 4*.

For further guidance, calculation and examples, see HMRC's National Insurance Manual at NIM24170 onwards (www.hmrc.gov.uk/manuals/nimmanual/NIM24170.htm).

Example 46.2 – Calculating the annual maximum: Class 4 NICs

Rhian is employed earning an annual salary of £45,000. She also runs her own business which has assessable profits of £25,000 for 2016/17.

Rhian's Class 4 NICs paid for the tax year 2016/17 would be:

	£
Class 1:	
(£43,000 – £8,060) × 12%	4,192.80
(£45,000 – £43,000) × 2%	40.00
Class 2: 52 × £2.80	145.60
Class 4:	
(£25,000 – £8,060) × 9%	1,524.60
Total NIC paid for 2016/17:	5,903.00

Her Class 4 NICs annual maximum for 2016/17 would be:

	£
Step 1: (£43,000 – £8,060)	34,940.00
Step 2: £34,940 × 9%	3,144.60
Step 3: £3,144.60 + (53 × £2.80)	3,293.00
Step 4: £3,293.00 – (£145.60 + £4,192.80)	(1,045.40)

Result is negative therefore Case 3 applies, so the maximum Class 4 NICs payable at the main Class 4 percentage rate is nil and *Step 4* = nil

Step 5: nil × 100/9	nil
Step 6: £25,000 – £8,060	16,940.00
Step 7: £16,940 – nil	16,940.00
Step 8: £16,940 × 2%	338.80
Step 9: 2% × profits above upper profits limit	nil

To calculate the annual maximum:

Add together *Steps 4, 8* and *9*:

(nil + £338.80 + nil) =	338.80
A refund will therefore be due from NICO as follows:	£
Rhian's annual maximum (as calculated above)	338.80
Less: Class 4 NICs Actually paid	(1,524.60)
Refund due	(1,185.80)

Rhian's Class 4 NICs liability is therefore restricted to Class 4 at the additional percentage rate of 2%, on her assessable profits between the lower profits limit and the upper profits limit, ie £16,940 × 2%.

In effect, her Class 4 NICs refund due, amounts to 7% of her assessable profits, ie £16,940 × (9% – 2%).

Refunds for Class 4 NICs can be claimed online or by filling in Form CA5610 (available from the HMRC website) and sending it off to the Deferment Services at NICO.

Class 2 and 4 NICs – annual maximum

46.4   For earners who are self-employed *only*, there is no 'official' annual maximum set out in the legislation, since the earner's maximum liability to Class 2 and Class 4 NICs would in any case be based on his *actual* liability as calculated along normal procedures.

It should be remembered at this point that multiple self-employments are treated as one single 'self-employment' (since an individual is deemed to have only one 'self' by whom he may be employed!).

This is in contrast to a person with several employments, who would be liable to NICs on each separate employment (as shown at **46.2**).

The calculation method, therefore, for determining a person's actual Class 2 and Class 4 NICs payable, would be as follows:

Step 1

Multiply the amount of profits (aggregating all self-employments together) falling between the lower profits limit (£8,060 for 2016/17) and the upper profits limit (£43,000 for 2016/17) by the main Class 4 NICs percentage rate (9%).

Step 2

Multiply the amount of profits that exceed the upper profits limit by the additional Class 4 NICs percentage rate (2%), again ensuring that all self-employments are aggregated.

Step 3

Multiply the relevant Class 2 NIC weekly rate by the number of actual weeks of self-employment in the tax year.

Step 4

Add together the results of *Steps 1, 2* and *3*, to find the actual amount of Class 2 and Class 4 NICs payable by an earner who is self-employed only.

Example 46.3 – Calculating the annual maximum: Class 2 and 4 NICs

Katie started up her new business part way through 2016/17, which amounted to 40 weeks of self-employment for that tax year. She made assessable profits of £30,000 for the year (she was previously unemployed).

Half way through the year, she started up another business (whilst continuing with her first business), earning £15,000 profits assessable for the tax year.

Her maximum actual Class 2 and Class 4 NIC liability for 2016/17 would be calculated as follows:

	£
Class 4:	
Profits assessable = (£30,000 + £15,000)	45,000.00
Class 4 NIC:	
(£43,000 – £8,060) × 9%	3,144.60

	£
(£45,000 – £43,000) × 2%	40.00
Class 2: 40 × £2.80	112.00
Total Class 2 and Class 4 NIC payable for 2016/17	3,296.60

Points to note

- Even though Katie started up another business half way through the tax year, she is only required to pay one lot of the Class 2 NIC weekly rate for her 'self-employments' as a 'single entity'.

- She is assessable from when she first registered as self-employed until the end of the tax year, ie her actual weeks of self-employment amounted to 40 in the tax year 2016/17.

Since there is no requirement for an annual maximum for Class 2 and Class 4 only, there is as such no automatic refund procedure carried out by NICO. However, in circumstances where a person believes he may have overpaid Class 4 or Class 2 NIC, he may apply to NICO for a refund (see www.gov.uk/claim-national-insurance-refund).

Further guidance and the basic calculation method required, together with some examples, are provided in HMRC's National Insurance Manual at NIM24152 onwards (www.hmrc.gov.uk/manuals/nimmanual/NIM24152.htm).

Class 1, 2 and 4 NICs – deferment

46.5　As we have seen previously, employees with more than one employment are liable to pay Class 1 NICs on each of those employments at the main primary percentage rate (ie 12%). Their liability however, is subject to the annual maximum (as detailed at **46.2**) and the earner is permitted to claim a refund of any overpaid NICs.

To avoid having to make initial overpayments of NICs and then claim a refund at a later date, an employee may apply to NICO for deferment of some of his contributions, providing certain conditions are met.

The basic condition is that the employee will pay primary Class 1 NICs (12%) on at least one of his employments at the upper earnings limit (UEL), throughout the tax year. (So for 2016/17, he would be paying the full Class 1 primary percentage of 12% on £43,000, in at least one job, ie 'the main employment'.)

There are guidance notes which accompany the deferment application, which explain further the conditions that must be met for deferment to be granted. Application for the deferment of Class 1 NICs should be made on Form CA72A (which can be obtained at www.gov.uk/defer-national-insurance).

If deferment is granted, the employee will be required to pay Class 1 NICs at the additional percentage rate of 2% on all his earnings in the 'deferred employments' above the primary threshold (PT) (ie 2% on £155 per week or £8,060 pa for 2016/17).

At the end of the tax year, NICO check to see if the maximum contributions (at Class 1 primary) have been paid throughout the year. If so, then the earnings from 'deferred employment' are formally excepted from liability at the primary percentage rate.

If there is a shortfall of maximum contributions, then this is collected directly from the employee.

Focus

Confirmation of deferment is notified to the employee and the (deferring) employer will be sent a deferment certificate.

Strictly speaking, the grant of deferment only applies for one particular tax year and the employee is required to apply for a new deferment for each subsequent tax year.

In practice however, once deferment is granted for the first year, employees are invited to re-apply for deferment for the coming tax year. (Forms are required to be returned by 14 February during the tax year in question.)

Employer Class 1 secondary contributions (payable at 13.8%) are unaffected by deferment.

If an earner is both employed and self-employed and expects to pay Class 1 primary (employee) contributions as well as Class 2 and/or Class 4 NICs, then due to the reforms in the collection of Class 2 NIC, from 6 April 2015 HMRC no longer require individuals to apply or re-apply for Class 2 and/or Class 4 deferment.

Instead, HMRC will use the information they already hold along with the information provided in the individual's tax return to let them know about any

Class 2 and Class 4 NICs they may need to pay. Details of the amounts to be paid will be shown on their self-assessment calculation.

In effect, if a person is both employed and self-employed with employment earnings exceeding the UEL, then this is likely to result in no Class 2 NICs being payable and Class 4 NICs payable at 2% only.

> **Focus**
>
> In the above cases, applying for deferment is preferable to overpaying NICs throughout the tax year and then awaiting a refund of NICs later.

SALARY SACRIFICE ARRANGEMENTS

46.6   A salary sacrifice arrangement is a contractual agreement, whereby an employee gives up the right to receive part of his salary, normally in return for his employer agreeing to provide some form of non-cash benefit.

Since currently no Class 1 NICs are payable (either primary or secondary) on employer's contributions paid into an employee's personal pension plan, it may be beneficial to enter into such an arrangement for an employee.

The arrangement would work by the employee agreeing to take *less* salary, in return for the employer making a pension contribution plus the employer's NIC saving.

This would result in a higher pension contribution being paid than would normally result from just the employee's payment.

Employers must ensure that such arrangements are effective and that the contractual entitlement of the employee must be that they are to receive a lower cash salary plus a (non-taxable) benefit.

Guidance regarding salary sacrifice arrangements is provided by HMRC at www.gov.uk/guidance/salary-sacrifice-and-the-effects-on-paye.

> **Focus**
>
> The government is to consider limiting the range of benefits that attract income tax and NICs advantages when provided as part of a salary sacrifice arrangement. However it is intended that pension savings, childcare and health-related benefits (such as cycle to work schemes) will continue to benefit from income tax and NICs relief when provided this way.

Example 46.4 – Salary sacrifice and employer pension contributions

Tom earns a basic salary of £30,000 per year (after allowances) and makes net personal pension contributions of £1,600 (£2,000 gross) in 2016/17.

The amount of gross salary required to cover his pension contribution would be:

	£
Salary	2,352
Less:	
Tax at 20%	(470)
NIC at 12%	(282)
Net salary to cover personal pension contribution	1,600

The following salary sacrifice arrangement could instead be made:

	£
Salary: £30,000 – £2,352 = new agreed salary of	27,648
Non-taxable benefit:	
Employer's pension contribution of	2,352
Plus: NIC saving of 13.8% × £2,352	324
Total non-taxable benefit to be paid as pension contribution	2,676

Thus, Tom's *net* pay would have been reduced by £1,600 (£2,352 – (470 + 282)), which would leave him in the same position as before, when he paid the pension contribution himself.

The gross pension contribution, however, will have been increased by £676 (£2,676 – £2,000).

OVERSEAS ISSUES

46.7   The statutory residence test (see **Chapter 56**) does not generally apply to NIC. Therefore the rules that applied to income tax up to 5 April 2013 (ie before the introduction of the statutory residence test) are still relevant for the purpose of NIC after that date. These were covered in **Chapter 57** of *Bloomsbury Professional Tax Guide 2012/13* (The TACS Partnership)).

Under these rules, for a person to be liable to pay Class 1, 1A, 1B or Class 2 NICs:

- they must be UK resident (or ordinarily resident); or

- present in Great Britain (this does not include Northern Ireland, but each country's social security system is linked under the 'UK scheme').

'Present' in the UK is determined by the facts of each case and has a less stringent meaning than 'resident' (*SSCBA 1992, s 1(6)(a); SI 2001/1004, regs 145, 146*).

As the liability to Class 4 NICs is linked to the income tax rules, where a person is treated for income tax purposes as not resident in the UK, Class 4 NICs are not payable.

Leaving or coming to the UK

46.8   The rules relating to persons leaving or coming to the UK are complex, particularly in relation to European Union (EU) legislation, which currently is directly applicable to UK NIC. However, there is clearly the potential for the result of the EU referendum to impact upon this in the future.

What follows, is a summary of the basic rules and further guidance should be sought by either writing to the NICO – International Caseworker Centre (at the address in the 'NIC References' section) or by phoning 0300 200 3506. There is also some guidance on the international aspects of NICs in CWG2, HMRC's National Insurance Manual, NI38 (see below) and on HMRC's website at www.gov.uk/national-insurance-if-you-go-abroad.

In general, the rules depend on whether or not the person is going to, or has come from, a country within the European Economic Area (EEA), or with which the UK has a reciprocal social security agreement (such as Jersey, Guernsey or the USA – see list provided in NI38).

The UK is linked with the EEA countries (and Switzerland) under the EU social security rules to ensure that reciprocal arrangements for NICs apply in each country. Similar arrangements apply for NICs in those countries outside the EEA, with whom the UK has reciprocal agreements.

Broadly speaking, the arrangements relate to the payment of Class 1 NICs and their purpose is to ensure that workers only pay NICs in the country in which they are actually employed.

Employees in these countries will therefore be covered by that country's social security laws and may be entitled to benefits there.

For employees temporarily sent to work in those countries covered by the EU social security rules, it is possible to remain in their home country scheme if a certificate of continuing liability (Form A1) is obtained. This will normally apply only to secondments for less than two years.

Leaving the UK

46.9   Normally if an employee works outside the UK or the EEA and not in one of those countries with a reciprocal agreement with the UK, his earnings will be outside the scope for Class 1 NICs. However,

- if the employee remains on the UK payroll, ie:

    ○   his employer has a place of business in the UK, and

    ○   the employee was UK resident prior to moving overseas, and

    ○   the employee is 'ordinarily resident' in the UK,

    then a liability for both Class 1 primary and secondary contributions will continue for the first 52 weeks abroad;

If a person is self-employed abroad, then there is not normally a requirement to pay Class 2 NICs. However, a person may wish to continue to pay Class 2 contributions whilst abroad, in order to protect entitlement to certain benefits (see below).

Details as to eligibility for paying Class 2 (or Class 3) contributions whilst abroad, together with useful guidance on employees working overseas, are provided in HMRC's booklet NI38 – *Social Security Abroad* (www.hmrc.gov. uk/pdfs/nico/ni38.pdf).

Voluntary contributions

46.10   If a UK earner wishes to maintain his entitlement to certain statutory benefits, such as the state pension, whilst abroad, he may wish to pay voluntary contributions.

This is most likely to be the case when an employee has finished paying the first 52 weeks contributions, or where they are employed in a country covered by the EU social security provisions, as noted above.

There are certain conditions to be met for eligibility to pay voluntary contributions whilst employed (or self-employed) abroad, which are set out in detail in HMRC booklet NI38 (see above).

The basic condition, however, for the entitlement to pay Class 2 voluntary contributions abroad, is that you must first be employed or self-employed abroad and no longer liable to pay Class 1 NIC.

Payment of Class 2 NICs whilst abroad is preferable to paying Class 3 NICs, since it gives entitlement to a wider range of benefits and is much cheaper at £2.80 per week (for 2016/17), although as noted in Chapter 44, Class 2 NICs are to be abolished from April 2018.

If a person is not eligible to pay Class 2 NICs whilst abroad, he may consider paying Class 3 voluntary contributions, which will at least maintain entitlement to the state pension, whilst overseas.

Class 3 contributions can be paid whether a person is working abroad or not, but like Class 2, cannot be paid whilst the worker is still liable to Class 1 NICs. Class 3 NICs are payable at the weekly rate of £14.10 (for 2016/17).

Coming to the UK

46.11   If an employee comes to the UK from a country outside the EEA and which does not have a reciprocal agreement with the UK, then Class 1 NICs are payable, except for the first 52 weeks where the employee:

- is temporarily seconded to the UK by an overseas employer; or
- is a student from outside the UK working on holiday.

Once the first 52 weeks are up, Class 1 primary and secondary contributions become payable, with liability resting on the 'host employer', or secondary contributor (where 'resident', 'present' and /or 'place of business conditions' are met - but see **46.12** below).

For self-employed persons coming to the UK, they are required to pay Class 2 NICs if they are ordinarily resident in the UK, or have been resident for 26 weeks or more out of the last 52.

Note for employers

46.12   In general, the basic rule provides for employers to pay UK NICs if their employees are subject to UK NIC.

However, HMRC did not normally enforce this rule prior to the new EU regulations coming into being (1 May 2010), if the employer was not resident or present or did not have a place of business in the UK.

The EU regulations introduced an 'equality of treatment' meaning that an employer present or resident in one EU member state (or EEA country) has the same obligations and duties as an employer in another member state (or EEA country).

This means that an employer based in those countries covered by the EU regulations, who sends an employee to work in the UK will be responsible for collecting both employee primary and employer secondary contributions and meeting filing obligations, as if they had a place of business in the UK.

The regulations are of course reciprocal and so UK employers will have similar obligations for their UK employees subject to EU social security legislation in another country.

> **Focus**
>
> EU Regulations are in force compelling employers from other EU (or EEA) countries to be responsible for the collection and reporting of UK NICs in respect of their UK-based employee's primary and employer's secondary contributions.

ANTI-AVOIDANCE

46.14   There are very few anti-avoidance provisions currently within the NIC legislation, just two regulations, which are dealt with briefly below.

However, legislation in the *National Insurance Contributions Act 2014* brought NICs within the scope of the General Anti-Abuse Rule (GAAR) which came into effect in relation to tax arrangements entered into on or after 13 March 2014.

Previously, the main reason for this apparent lack of anti-avoidance measures was that NICs had been gradually broadened over the years to counter each loophole in the legislation, or 'avoidance scheme' that came along.

This was initially achieved by increasing the scope of Class 1 NICs to catch 'quasi-cash schemes', such as paying bonuses in non-cash form.

Then from 6 April 2000, Class 1A contributions were widened to include virtually all benefits in kind.

46.15 *NIC planning*

The two anti-avoidance regulations that still exist are as follows:

1 *Abnormal pay practices*

This is aimed at practices in the payment of earnings which are deemed to be 'abnormal' in respect of the relevant employment and as a result reduce or avoid Class 1 NICs.

The regulation basically empowers HMRC to determine the Class 1 NIC liability as if the 'abnormal pay practice' did not apply (*SI 2001/1004, reg 30*).

2 *Practices avoiding or reducing liability for contributions*

This is basically aimed at incidences where there are irregular or unequal payments of earnings and, as a result, Class 1 NICs are either reduced or avoided.

In this instance, HMRC can direct that Class 1 NICs would be payable as if the practice had not been followed in the first case (*SI 2001/1004, reg 31*).

USEFUL REFERENCES AND LINKS

46.15   National Insurance Contributions Office address:

National Insurance Contributions and Employer Office
HM Revenue and Customs
BX9 1AN
United Kingdom

Further guidance on National Insurance can be found at the gov.uk website:
www.gov.uk/national-insurance

Current NIC Rates and Allowances:
www.gov.uk/government/publications/rates-and-allowances-national-insurance-contributions

CWG2 Employer Further Guide to PAYE and NICs:
www.gov.uk/government/publications/cwg2-further-guide-to-paye-and-national-insurance-contributions

HMRC NIC Toolkit (*only* covering Class 1, 1A and 1B):
www.gov.uk/government/publications/hmrc-national-insurance-contributions-and-statutory-payments-toolkit

CA44 National Insurance for Company Directors:
www.gov.uk/government/publications/ca44-national-insurance-for-company-directors

CWG5 Class 1A NIC on Benefits in Kind:
www.gov.uk/government/publications/cwg5-class-1a-national-insurance-contributions-on-benefits-in-kind

NIC Voluntary Contributions - General Guidance:
www.gov.uk/voluntary-national-insurance-contributions/who-can-pay-voluntary-contributions#top

Application/Guidance to pay Class 3 NIC:
www.gov.uk/government/publications/national-insurance-application-to-pay-voluntary-national-insurance-contributions-ca5603

NI38 - Social Security Abroad:
www.gov.uk/government/publications/social-security-abroad-ni38

Gov.UK website (for state pension advice including a state pension statement):
www.gov.uk/state-pension

Useful links to NIC Tables:

CA38 National Insurance Contributions –Tables A, H, J, M and Z:
www.gov.uk/government/publications/ca38-national-insurance-contributions-tables-a-and-j

CA41 National Insurance Contributions –Tables B and C:
www.gov.uk/government/publications/ca41-national-insurance-contributions-tables-b-and-c

There are also links to NIC Tables for less common types of employee as follows:

CA40 National Insurance Contributions – Employee only contributions for employers and employees authorised to pay their own contributions:
www.gov.uk/government/publications/ca40-employees-allowed-to-pay-their-own-national-insurance

CA42 National Insurance Contributions – Foreign-going mariners and deep sea fisherman's contributions for employers:
www.gov.uk/government/publications/ca42-foreign-going-mariners-and-deep-sea-fishermen

Other useful website links, forms and guidance from HMRC

46.16   Guidance for operating PAYE:
www.gov.uk/topic/business-tax/paye

Guidance for employers exempt from online filing (PAYE):
www.gov.uk/find-out-which-employers-are-exempt-from-online-payroll-reporting

Guidance on PAYE and NIC payments:
HMRC's Employer PAYE and NIC Payment Enquiry Helpline: 0300 200 3401.

Part 8
Stamp Duties

47

Stamp duty land tax

INTRODUCTION

47.1 Stamp duty land tax (SDLT) is a tax on land transactions. It replaced stamp duty on land transactions with effect from 1 December 2003. There are still transitional provisions dealing with transactions undertaken before that date but which were not stamped (for whatever reason). Stamp duty (see **Chapter 48**) is a charge on documents, whereas SDLT is a tax on transactions. Thus, whenever land is transferred for consideration, that consideration is chargeable to SDLT, which is levied on the buyer.

> **Focus**
>
> SDLT is an additional cost of acquiring land.

SDLT was introduced by *Finance Act 2003*, and most of the provisions dealing with the tax can be found in that legislation (as amended). Guidance on HMRC's interpretation can be found in the SDLT Manual, and the SDLT section of the HMRC website (www.hmrc.gov.uk/sdlt/index.htm).

RATES OF TAX

Residential

47.2 SDLT is charged on the chargeable consideration for the transaction. The rules changed significantly on 4 December 2014 to move from a 'flat rate' system to a 'band' system, and purchasers who had exchanged before that date, but completed afterwards, could choose which method to use.

For purchases, the chargeable consideration is usually the purchase price. Where the relevant property is wholly residential, SDLT rates under the old flat rate system were as follows, with the applicable rate being charged on the whole of the consideration:

Relevant consideration	%
Less than £125,000	0
Over £125,000 but less than £250,000	1
Over £250,000 but less than £500,000	3
Over £500,000 but less than £1 million	4
Over £1 million but less than £2 million	5
Over £2 million	7

Under the new rules, tax is charged on each slice of the consideration that falls into the relevant band, at the following rates:

Relevant consideration	Standard rate %	Additional property rate %
Up to £125,000	0	3
£125,001–£250,000 (£125,000 band)	2	5
£250,001–£925,000 (£675,000 band)	5	8
£925,001–£1,500,000 (£575,000 band)	10	13
Over £1,500,001	12	15

The higher rate is charged on "additional" residential properties costing more than £40,000 where completion occurs on or after 1 April 2016 (subject to limited exemptions for contracts entered into before 26 November 2015). This new rate will broadly apply where, at the end of the day of the transaction, the purchaser owns more than one residential property, although a limited exemption applies for certain purchasers of dwellings with self-contained annexes or outbuildings that are, themselves, dwellings. Where the second property was acquired to replace the purchaser's main home, but the property it was replacing had not been sold by that time, the higher rate will apply to the transaction although a refund can be claimed if the previous main home is sold within 36 months.

For houses costing less than £937,500, the tax under the new rules is less than that under the old rules. The calculations are illustrated in the following examples:

Consideration for house	SDLT: Old Rules	SDLT: New Rules (not additional)
£300,000	3% × £300,000 = £9,000	2% × £125,000 + 5% × £50,000 = £5,000
£600,000	4% × £600,000 = £24,000	2% × £125,000 + 5% × £350,000 = £20,000
£1,250,000	5% × £1,250,000 = £62,500	2% × £125,000 + 5% × £675,000 + 10% × £325,000 = £68,750

SDLT no longer applies in Scotland. Instead, purchasers pay a similar tax, called Land and Buildings Transaction Tax (LBTT). LBTT is similar in principle to the new band system of SDLT, but with different bands.

Where residential property costing over £500,000 (£2 million before 20 March 2014) is transferred to a corporate body or similar purchaser, the SDLT higher rate of 15% may be charged in certain cases. Broadly, these are where the property is let to, or otherwise used by, a person connected with the owner. Where the 15% rate applies, the Annual Tax on Enveloped Dwellings (see **8.20**) will also normally apply.

Non-residential

47.3   The equivalent rates for non-residential properties for transactions which completed before 17 March 2016 were as follows, with the applicable rate being charged on the whole of the consideration:

Relevant consideration	%
Not more than £150,000	0
Over £150,000 but less than £250,000	1
Over £250,000 but less than £500,000	3
Over £500,000	4

For transactions completing on or after 17 March 2016, these rates have been changed to a band system and tax is now charged on each slice of the consideration at the following rates:

Relevant consideration	%
Up to £150,000	0
£150,000 to £250,000	2
Over £250,000	5

The new rates give a lower SDLT cost for transactions under £1,050,000.

In a similar way to how the change was introduced for residential properties, purchasers who exchanged contracts before 17 March 2016, but complete afterwards, can choose which rules to use (subject to certain exceptions).

Where a building comprises a mixture of residential and non-residential property, the tax is levied under the non-residential rates.

CONSIDERATION

47.4   SDLT on leases is dealt with at **47.7**. It is important to note that, where the property is commercial and the option to tax has been exercised to charge VAT on rents and sales of the property, the consideration includes any VAT chargeable. This can have a dramatic effect, and in such cases you should carefully consider whether the option to tax applies. This is illustrated in the example below.

Example 47.1 – SDLT on a property subject to an option to tax

Mick agrees to sell Keith a commercial property known as Stone House. The purchase consideration is agreed at £450,000 but Mick has opted to tax the property.

If the property is not let and HMRC will not accept a transfer of the business as a going concern for VAT purposes, the SDLT consideration is treated as £450,000 plus £90,000 of VAT, in other words £540,000.

Under the old rules, SDLT at 3% on £450,000 was £13,500, but SDLT at 4% on £540,000 was £21,600. The additional SDLT by reason of the VAT charged was therefore £8,100.

The new rules reduce this "unfair" result as the VAT element of the consideration is taxed at the highest rate without bringing all of the consideration into charge at that rate. SDLT on £540,000 is £16,500 compared with £12,000 on £450,000.

Focus

When considering opting to tax land for VAT purposes, bear in mind the SDLT consequences.

Consideration includes anything given for the acquisition of the land. In particular, if the land is subject to a debt (such as a mortgage) and the consideration includes the assignment or extinguishing of that debt, the amount of the debt is part of the consideration.

Similarly, where property is exchanged (where A sells property A to B in exchange for B selling property B to A), SDLT is in principle chargeable on both transactions. Relief is available where a person buys a house from a developer, and sells his house in part exchange. In such cases, SDLT is only charged on the greater value.

Focus

Consideration is not always in money. Where it is in kind, the market value is the consideration.

Where a property is sold to a connected company, the consideration for SDLT purposes is usually the market value of the property. This is dealt with in more detail at **47.12**.

SDLT RELIEFS AND EXEMPTIONS

Exemptions

47.5 There are a number of transactions which are regarded as exempt from SDLT, summarised as follows:

- A transaction for no chargeable consideration (in other words, a gift). However, if an individual transfers a property to a connected company, the general market value rule for such transfers applies (see **47.12**).

- The grant of a lease by a registered social landlord (normally a housing association).

- Transfers on incorporation of a limited liability partnership.

- Transfers between spouses on separation or divorce or in connection with the dissolution of civil partnerships.

- Assents and appropriations by personal representatives (on death of an individual).

- Variations of dispositions in wills.

- Where the purchaser is a public office or a department of the Crown or government, no payment of SDLT is required if that payment would be borne by the Crown. This exemption includes ministers acting as such, but not local authorities or similar bodies and it does not apply to the acquisition of private property for the Queen.

Reliefs

47.6 There are the following reliefs from SDLT:

- Sales and leaseback or surrender and re-grant of a lease – effectively only the net consideration is taken into account for SDLT purposes.

- Acquisitions of residential properties by builders in exchange for sales of new properties. Only the more expensive property is subject to SDLT.

- Certain acquisitions of more than one dwelling by the same purchaser (multiple dwellings relief) – this allows the purchaser to calculate SDLT at the rate for the average value of the property acquisitions, rather than on the aggregate consideration. See also **47.13** on linked transactions.

- First acquisitions of zero-carbon homes.

- A dwelling acquired from an employee being relocated, in order to facilitate that relocation.

- Property acquired under a compulsory purchase order to facilitate development.

- Purchases by public authorities in connection with planning agreements.

- Certain group, reconstruction and acquisition reliefs (dealt with at **47.8**).

- Transfers on demutualisation of an insurance company or building society.

- Transfers between public bodies on reorganisation, including transfers to NHS foundation trusts.

- Transfers arising out of the reorganisation of parliamentary constituencies.

- Acquisitions by charities.

- Acquisitions by certain bodies established for national purposes.

- Right to buy and shared ownership transactions.

- Certain acquisitions by registered social landlords (housing associations).

- Acquisitions by alternative property finance (Islamic finance) which involves the lender taking an interest in the property.

- Collective enfranchisement by leaseholders (following *FA 2009, s 80* this no longer needs to be via a company).

- Crofting community right to buy legislation.

- Sub-sale relief – note this relief has been restricted due to the use of sub-sale arrangements for a number of tax avoidance schemes.

It should be noted that all the reliefs listed above are subject in certain cases to restrictions under the rules in *FA 2003, s 75A*, which contains a general anti-avoidance rule for SDLT purposes. This should be borne in mind when considering all schemes for SDLT mitigation, to which these rules may apply.

> **Focus**
> Do not forget to review the possible application of SDLT reliefs when considering the other tax implications of transactions.

SDLT ON LEASES

47.7 SDLT is charged on premiums paid on the grant of a lease, and also on a rent.

Premiums are charged at the rates set out for transfers, but SDLT on rent is calculated in accordance with a special formula. Essentially, the net present value of the rent payable over the term of the lease is calculated by applying the formula set out in *FA 2003, Sch 5(3)* as follows:

$$V = \sum_{i=1}^{n} \frac{r_i}{(1+T)^i}$$

where:

V is the net present value;

r_i is the rent payable in respect of the year i;

i is the particular year in which the calculation is to be performed (and the calculation is required for each year);

n is the period of the lease in years; and

T is the time discount rate (currently at 3.5%).

In the legislation, the net present value of the rent (V above) is referred to as the relevant rental value. SDLT is then charged as a percentage of so much of the value as falls within each rate band in the table below.

Relevant rental value – residential

Up to £125,000	0%
Over £125,000	1%

Relevant rental value – non-residential / mixed

Up to £150,000	0%
£150,000 to £5,000,000	1%
Over £5,000,000 (see note)	2%

Note: the rate of 2% applicable to non-residential or mixed use properties where the relevant rental value exceeds £5,000,000 was introduced in respect of transactions with an effective date falling on or after 17 March 2016. Where the transaction straddles that date, the lessee can choose which rules to use (subject to certain exceptions).

Before 17 March 2016, any premium paid for the grant of a lease of non-residential property could not benefit from the 0% SDLT rate where the relevant rent (not the NPV) on the lease was more than £1,000. This rule has now been removed from that date.

There is a SDLT lease calculator tool on the HMRC website which provides details of duty chargeable in any case (www.hmrc.gov.uk/sdlt/calculate/calculators.htm#2).

Example 47.2 – Rent: calculation

Roger rents a house to Pete for a period of 25 years. The net present value of the lease is calculated as £200,000.

Pete must pay SDLT at 1% on £75,000 (ie £200,000 less £125,000) which equals £750.

It should be noted there is a difference between a lease of land and a licence to utilise or occupy land. The latter does not attract SDLT. From a legal standpoint, the main difference is that a lease of land confers exclusive occupation rights, whereas a licence does not.

Focus

Check that what is being granted/assigned is a chargeable interest and use the lease calculator where appropriate.

GROUPS OF COMPANIES

47.8 If two companies are members of the same group, transfers between them are exempt from SDLT (*FA 2003, Sch 7(1)*).

If the transferee company leaves the group within three years of the transfer, still owning the property, or there are arrangements within that period in place for this to happen, the group relief is clawed back (*FA 2003, Sch 7(3)*).

Group relief is denied if there are arrangements for the transferee company to leave the group at the date of transfer (*FA 2003, Sch 7(2)*).

There are a number of exceptions to the clawback, which have been published in HMRC's SDLT Manual at SDLT23080.

Group relief is claimed on the SDLT Return.

> **Example 47.3 – Transfers within a group**
>
> Dave Limited has two subsidiary companies, George Limited and Nick Limited. George Limited sells a property worth £1 million to Nick Limited.
>
> Two years later, Dave Limited decides that it wants to dispose of Nick Limited, and sells the shares in Nick Limited outside the group.
>
> On the transfer by George Limited to Nick Limited, group relief was claimed, and no SDLT was paid.
>
> However, the group relief will be withdrawn on the sale of Nick Limited, if that takes place within three years of the transfer.

RECONSTRUCTION AND ACQUISITION RELIEFS

Reconstruction relief

47.9   Reconstruction relief applies where a company (Company A) acquires the whole or part of the trade or undertaking of another company (Company B) in pursuance of a scheme for the reconstruction of Company B and three further conditions are met. Any land transactions entered into in connection with that reconstruction are exempt from SDLT.

The three conditions are:

1   The consideration for the acquisition consists wholly or partly of the issue of non-redeemable shares in the acquiring company to all the shareholders of the target company. Where the consideration is not wholly in the form of non-redeemable shares, the remaining consideration comprises only the assumption or discharge by Company A of the liabilities of Company B.

2   After the acquisition, the shareholdings of each of the companies are mirrored.

3   The acquisition is effected for bona fide commercial reasons and does not form part of a scheme or arrangement of which the main purpose, or one of the main purposes, is the avoidance of liability to tax. This can normally be demonstrated by providing to HMRC a copy of the tax clearance obtained (assuming this has been applied for) in connection with the reorganisation (see **26.6**).

Acquisition relief

47.10   Where Company A acquires the whole or part of the undertaking of Company B and certain conditions are fulfilled, the rate of SDLT is limited to 0.5%. This is known as acquisition relief. The conditions are:

1   The consideration for the acquisition consists wholly or partly of the issue of non-redeemable shares in Company A to Company B, or some or all of its shareholders. Where the consideration consists partly of the issue of non-redeemable shares, the remainder of the consideration must consist wholly of cash, not exceeding 10% of the nominal value of the non-redeemable shares so issued, and/or the assumption or discharge by Company A of the liabilities of Company B.

2   Company A is not associated with another company who is party to arrangements with Company B relating to shares of Company B. Broadly, this means that there should not be arrangements by a third party to acquire the shares of Company B.

3   The part of the business acquired by Company A must be a trade and must not consist wholly or mainly of dealing in land interests.

4   The transaction must be effected for bona fide commercial reasons and does not form part of arrangements of which the main purpose, or one of the main purposes, is the avoidance of liability to tax. As before, it is sensible to include a copy of any clearance application or clearance receipt (see **26.6**) from HMRC in connection with the transaction.

Acquisition or reconstruction relief can be withdrawn if a third party acquires control of Company A within a three-year period after acquisition, or in connection with an arrangement entered into within that three-year period.

Reconstruction and acquisition reliefs are claimed on the SDLT return.

> **Focus**
>
> It is vital that the conditions for reconstruction or acquisition relief are fully complied with before claiming.
>
> In particular, HMRC will normally want to see copies of the share register.

PARTNERSHIPS

47.11 The SDLT regime for partnerships is governed by *Finance Act 2003, Sch 15*. This schedule has been described by a leading tax barrister as 'the worst drafted piece of tax legislation in the statute book'. Whilst there are other contenders for this dubious 'honour', these comments are well founded. The overall intention of the legislation appears to be to tax that element of the property which changes hands.

The legislation is notoriously complex, and can give rise to capricious results. The relevant detailed provisions of *Sch 15* should be examined in detail when an issue may arise. Essentially, however, where real property is brought into, or leaves, a partnership, or the partners change (for a property investment partnership), the 'relevant proportion' of the value of the property is deemed to change hands for SDLT purposes. This is demonstrated in **Examples 47.4** and **47.5** below.

It should be noted that the profit-sharing ratios referred to are income-sharing ratios, and not, where different, capital-sharing ratios.

It should also be noted that a 'property investment partnership' for SDLT purposes includes any partnership whose objects are investing or dealing in chargeable land interests. This is wider than 'property investment' for income tax purposes.

The SDLT is calculated first by preparing a calculation known as the 'sum of the lower proportions'. This is essentially the interest retained by continuing persons in the partnership.

Where the partnership is not a property investment partnership, the continuing persons can include connected persons. The rules apply in similar ways (at least most of the time) to limited liability partnerships.

Example 47.4 – Property transferred into a partnership

Dave, George and Nick are in partnership, sharing profits and losses in the ratio 50:40:10. Dave owns the property used by the partnership. This property is worth £600,000. Dave decides to introduce the property into the partnership.

The stamp duty land tax payable by the partnership is calculated by reference to the interests effectively transferred to George and Nick, namely 50%. 50% of £600,000 is £300,000, so the SDLT payable is £4,500 (ie £150,000 at 0% plus £100,000 at 2% plus £50,000 at 5%).

Example 47.5 – SDLT on partner leaving

Nick subsequently decides to leave the partnership after five years.

Effectively, he is regarded as selling his share of the property to the partnership. 10% of £600,000 is £60,000, so no SDLT is payable.

Focus

SDLT on partnership transactions is complex, and the rules need to be studied carefully to ascertain how they apply to any specific situation.

CONNECTED PERSONS

47.12   It should be noted that where the purchaser is a company connected with the vendor (for example, an individual transfers land and buildings to a company owned by him) the consideration is treated as the market value (*FA 2003, s 53*), except where:

- the company holds the property as trustee in the course of its business as a trustee management company;

- the company holds the property as trustee, and the trustees of the trust are participators in the company;

- the vendor is a company and the transaction is part of the distribution of the assets of that company (in connection with its winding up or otherwise) and the land has not previously been the subject of an intra-group transfer by the transferor in the past three years (*FA 2003, s 54*).

LINKED TRANSACTIONS

47.13   The rules on linked transactions are essentially an anti-avoidance device. Where two or more transactions are 'linked', being between the same purchaser and vendor, or persons connected with them, the transactions can be aggregated for SDLT purposes, which can result in a higher SDLT rate being applied to the transactions (*FA 2003, s 55(4)*).

Example 47.6 – Linked transactions

Ed and his wife, Yvette, decide to buy a house valued at £900,000. They split the transaction up, so that Ed buys the house for £495,000 and Yvette buys the garden for £405,000.

Without the 'linked transaction' rules, the transactions would be subject to total tax of £25,000

However, the transactions in this case are regarded as linked, because Ed and Yvette are connected, and the entire transaction is taxed on the basis of consideration of £900,000, on which the tax is £35,000.

Where a property investor decides to buy a number of properties off plan from an unconnected developer, and the transactions are not 'obviously' linked (for example there is no significant discount for bulk buying) the linked transaction rules will not apply. However, the multiple dwellings relief rules will apply.

Example 47.7 – Bulk purchase off plan

Grant is a developer who has built a block of flats and is selling each of the flats for £200,000.

Andrew decides to buy four flats 'off plan' (at a discount because of the upfront payment) to let to nurses, for £180,000 each. Andrew claims multiple dwellings relief, allowing for the SDLT liability to be calculated on the average price of each property separately, rather than the total consideration paid for all four properties. As Andrew owns his own home, the additional rates apply.

Andrew pays SDLT as follows:

$4 \times (3\% \times £125,000 + 5\% \times £55,000) = £26,000$

This compares to the liability of £47,600 (on the total consideration of £720,000) which would apply if multiple dwellings relief was not claimed (ie $3\% \times £125,000 + 5\% \times £125,000 + 8\% \times £470,000$).

Focus

Consider the application of the linked transactions and multiple dwellings rules whenever connected parties buy two or more parcels of land or buildings.

ADMINISTRATION AND ENFORCEMENT

Submission of returns

47.14 A purchaser of land or property or the lessee of such land usually needs to notify HMRC of the transaction by completing the SDLT Return. This is also referred to as a land transaction return. This can be done online or on a paper form.

The return must be sent in within 30 days of the effective date of the transaction. The 'effective date' is the earlier of the date of completion, or the date the contract is 'substantially performed'. The SDLT payable in respect of a land transaction must generally be paid not later than the filing date for the land transaction return (*FA 2003, s 86*).

Substantial performance occurs at the earliest of the following:

- when the bulk of the purchase price (generally 90%) is paid;

- when the purchaser is entitled to possession of the property; or

- when the first payment of rent is made.

The land transaction return is normally prepared by the solicitor dealing with the paperwork, since he has the documentation to accompany the return.

Once the land transaction return is accepted, Form SDLT 5 is issued which the Land Registry requires before registering the new title.

Where the purchaser wishes to claim any relief, this is claimed in the return.

The procedure in Scotland is slightly different. It is possible to register land simultaneously when dealing with LBTT matters by using the 'automated registration title to land' (ARTL) service.

Review of returns

47.15 Once a return is submitted, HMRC generally has nine months from the date of submission to enquire into that return.

There are penalties for late or incorrect SDLT returns and these have been aligned with the general tax penalty regime.

Focus

Compliance with the return timetable is vital to avoid penalties.

48

Stamp duty and stamp duty reserve tax

INTRODUCTION

48.1   Stamp duty is one of the oldest taxes, being largely still governed by the *Stamp Act 1891*.

Originally, the scope of stamp duty was much wider than it is today, applying to land and goodwill. With effect from 1 December 2003, stamp duty was effectively replaced by stamp duty land tax for land transactions, and stamp duty on goodwill was later abolished.

Stamp duty now largely only applies to transfers of chargeable securities, at a rate of 0.5%.

Chargeable securities

48.2   Chargeable securities are:

- stocks, shares or loan capital;

- interests in, or in dividends or other rights arising out of stocks, shares or loan capital;

- rights to allotments of or to subscribe for, or options to acquire, stocks, shares or loan capital; and

- units under a unit trust scheme.

> **Focus**
>
> Consider the stamp duty implications whenever shares, securities or related assets are acquired.

Situs of transaction

48.3   For stamp duty to be chargeable, the transaction must have a UK situs. That is, the register must be kept in the UK (other than for unit trusts, or, in the second or third cases, in **48.2** above, shares paired with UK registered shares, such as Eurotunnel shares).

If the share transaction takes place outside the UK, it does not need to be stamped (unless it is intended to produce the documents in a court). However, there may be an equivalent capital duty in the country where the register is situated.

A tax on documents

48.4   Stamp duty is a tax on documents, rather than on transactions. Therefore, if there is no document (such as a stock transfer form), then there is nothing to stamp and therefore no duty. In this sense, stamp duty can be described as a 'voluntary' tax although unstamped documents may not be accepted as evidence in a court of law.

It should be noted, however, that a contract to transfer an equitable interest in shares (such as a beneficial interest under a trust) is subject to ad valorem duty.

Stamp duty rates

48.5   There are two types of duty:

- ad valorem (charged on a percentage of the value); and

- fixed.

There are also a number of documents which are treated as exempt from duty. These are largely transfers for nil consideration and a full list is provided below. Stamp duty is not chargeable where a land transfer has already been subject to stamp duty land tax.

EXEMPTIONS

48.6   The following documents are exempt from duty:

- The transfer of a trust property on a change of trustees, being the appointment of a new trustee, or continuing trustees on the retirement of one of them.

- The transfer of a property which is the subject of a specific devise or legacy to the beneficiary named in the will (or to his nominee).

- The transfer of property which forms part of the intestate person's estate to the person entitled on his intestacy or his nominee.

- The appropriation of a property in satisfaction of a general legacy of money or in satisfaction of an interest of a surviving spouse, or in Scotland, any interest of issue.

- The conveyance or transfer of property which forms part of the residuary estate to a beneficiary or his nominee to satisfy an entitlement under the will.

- The conveyance or transfer of property to satisfy the interest of a beneficiary, where that interest was not acquired for money or money's worth, which is a distribution of property in accordance with the provisions of the settlement.

- The transfer of property only in consideration of marriage to a party to the marriage or to trustees to be held under the terms of a settlement made only in consideration of that marriage.

- The conveyance or transfer of property in connection with divorce.

- The conveyance or transfer of a property by a liquidator, where that property formed part of the assets of a company in liquidation to a shareholder of that company or his nominee in satisfaction of the shareholder's rights on the winding up.

- The conveyance or transfer of a property as a voluntary disposition between living persons for no consideration in money or money's worth, nor any consideration taking the form of a release or satisfaction of a debt.

- The conveyance or transfer of property varying dispositions on death.

- Declarations of trust within life assurance policies.

Stock transfer forms used to include a form of certificate that the transfer fell within the exempt instruments regulations (*Stamp Duty (Exempt Instruments) Regulations 1981, SI 1987/516*), but this has been revised with effect from 6 April 2012.

Where the transfer is a gift or the consideration is less than £1,000 the transfer is exempt. Although gifts do not normally now require adjudication, transfers with a value of less than £1,000 will require certification that they do not form part of a series of transactions with a greater value.

FIXED AND *AD VALOREM* DUTIES

Fixed duties

48.7   Certain other instruments carry a fixed £5 duty, although the scope of these has been much reduced by *Finance Act 2008*.

The only remaining fixed duties relate to instruments effecting a pre-SDLT land transaction.

Focus

Review the exemptions where there is a transaction not involving the payment of monies.

Ad valorem duties

48.8   Ad valorem duties originally covered a wide range of instruments, including shares and land, and interests in land. Most of these duties have been abolished (or replaced, for example by SDLT).

The main remaining duty is chargeable on transfers of chargeable securities (including shares), but not the issue of shares. The rate of duty is 0.5% (rounded up to the nearest £5) and the document must be adjudicated in order to file share transfers at Companies House.

Adjudication here refers to the process by which documents are sent to HMRC for stamping.

CORPORATE REORGANISATIONS

48.9   Where companies are members of a 75% group (ie 75% of the issued share capital, and rights to income and capital held directly or indirectly) transfers between members of that group are exempt from stamp duty (*FA 1930, s 42*). This exemption must be adjudicated by the Commissioners. The exemption will not apply if any part of the consideration is provided directly or indirectly by a third party, or if there are any arrangements whereby the transferor and transferee were to become no longer associated.

Where a company acquires the whole or part of an undertaking of another company (the 'target company') under a scheme of reconstruction of the target company, acquisition relief may be available (*FA 1986, s 75*). For this relief to apply a number of conditions must be met, including:

- the consideration payable for the acquisition of shares must consist of the issue of new shares in the acquiring company to all of the shareholders in the target company and can include nothing else but the assumption or discharge of liabilities of the target company by the acquiring company; and

- the percentages and nature of the new shares in the acquiring company after the acquisition must be identical to those of the old shares in the target company (in other words, the new holdings must be a 'mirror image' of the old holdings).

Acquisition relief may also be available where a company acquires the whole of the share capital of another company (the 'target company') where the transaction is not part of a scheme of reconstruction (*FA 1986, s 77*) – this could be the case where a new holding company is inserted. Similar (although not identical) conditions to that required for *s 75* relief apply for the purpose of *s 77*.

The conditions for relief under either of these provisions are very detailed and not able to be covered fully in this chapter – they must be reviewed carefully to ensure that the transaction can benefit from the relief. Where it does, no stamp duty will be payable.

Both these reliefs have to be claimed and there is an official form to complete and send to the Commissioners which deal with this. In both cases, the relief depends on there being no tax avoidance motive for the transaction. Tax clearance under *TCGA 1992, s 138* will normally be applied for to confirm HMRC agree this to be the case (see **26.6**), and a copy of the application and clearance should be sent to the stamp office to demonstrate that this condition is satisfied.

A late amendment to the *Finance Act 2016* saw the introduction of *FA 1986, s 77A*, a new anti-avoidance measure which can restrict the availability of relief under *s 77* where there are arrangements to secure a change of ownership of the company (*FA 2016, s 137*). This clearly has the potential to prevent the relief from applying where a new holding company is inserted before a transaction, although it is understood that this is not the intended target of the new provisions. At the time of writing, further guidance is awaited from HMRC and therefore care must be taken in considering pre-transaction planning of this nature.

Focus

Ensure that formal application is made for relief where it is sought.

CONSIDERATION

48.10 Stamp duty is chargeable on the full consideration payable for the transaction, including money's worth given. Where the consideration is subject to VAT, the amount stampable includes VAT (this will not usually be the case with shares).

It should also be noted that, where the consideration is uncertain, stamp duty is chargeable under the contingency principle, which works as follows:

- where the consideration is fixed, that consideration;

- where a maximum consideration is specified, or can be calculated, that maximum;

- where a minimum, but no maximum, consideration is specified, that minimum; and

- where neither is specified but there is a fixed consideration, that fixed consideration.

STAMP DUTY RESERVE TAX

48.11   As noted above, stamp duty is a charge on documents. Where shares and securities are regularly traded, for example on a stock exchange, there is generally no stock transfer form produced for transactions within a stock exchange period of account. Thus, a number of transfers would escape duty altogether. Stamp duty reserve tax (SDRT) was introduced to deal with this problem.

Example 48.1 – Calculation of SDRT and stamp duty

Ginger sells 10,000 shares to Jack for £10,000. Jack immediately sells 7,500 of the shares to Eric for £7,500.

In documentary terms, Ginger transfers 2,500 shares to Jack and 7,500 shares to Eric.

Jack is treated as if he had made two agreements. The first relates to the 2,500 shares transferred to him by Ginger, on which he will pay stamp duty on £2,500 (£12.50). The second relates to the 7,500 shares which Jack has sub-sold to Eric, and on which Jack will pay SDRT of £37.50, and Eric will pay stamp duty of £37.50 on the transfer of the 7,500 shares direct from Ginger.

Rate of SDRT

48.12   Like stamp duty, SDRT is charged at 0.5% on the value of the consideration of a transfer on sale, but like stamp duty land tax, it applies to an agreement to transfer. The charge arises on the purchaser.

If shares are issued or transferred to a clearance service, or depositary receipt service, so interests in them can be transferred without incurring a charge to stamp duty or SDRT, the initial issue or transfer attracts a 1.5% duty.

Where the service is EU based, following a 2009 European Court judgment (in *HSBC Holdings plc and Vidacos Nominees Ltd v HMRC* Case C–569/07), SDRT should not be levied.

Interaction with stamp duty

48.13 It is quite possible for stamp duty and SDRT to become payable on the same transaction, for example if a sale (subject to SDRT) is completed by a stock transfer form (on which stamp duty is chargeable).

In such circumstances, the SDRT charge is cancelled and repaid if a stamped transfer form is produced within six years.

SDRT applies in particular to stock exchange transactions, where shares are traded very frequently, and transfers during a stock exchange period of account (normally a fortnight) are not recorded on stock transfer forms.

Exemption

48.14 Where stock is sold and repurchased (repos), or lent and returned, such transactions do not attract SDRT, provided that:

* the same number of the same type of securities are sold/lent as are returned;

* at least one of the parties is authorised by an authority in an EEA member state to carry on such business; and

* the shares in question are of a kind regularly traded on a recognised exchange.

Responsibility and accounting

48.15 Where shares are bought through a broker, the buying broker will normally be the person responsible for accounting for SDRT, although the client is liable for the tax.

When an investor buys shares or securities direct from a stock exchange member firm, the person liable is the investor, but under the regulations the stock exchange member firm is responsible for notifying HMRC of the charge and accounting for the tax (unless the SDRT is explicitly added to the price charged).

APPENDIX: SDRT RATES

(FA 1986, Pt IV; FA 1999, Sch 19, Pt II)

48.16

Charge	Rate
General share transactions *(FA 1986, s 87)*	0.5%
Transfer of securities into depository receipt schemes and clearance services *(FA 1986, ss 93, 96)*	1.5%
Charge in respect of units in unit trusts and shares in open-ended investment companies *(FA 1999, Sch 19, para 3)*	0.5%

Notes

1   *Rounding* – The above charges are rounded to the nearest penny, taking any ½p as nearest to the next whole penny above *(FA 1986, s 99(13))*.

Part 9
HMRC Powers, Penalties, etc

49

HMRC powers and penalties, etc – an overview

SIGNPOSTS

- **Background** – The tax administration system in the UK has a long history, which dates back to the land taxes of the 17th century (see **49.1**).

- **Taxpayer's charter** – This charter (referred to by HMRC as 'Your charter') sets out the rights and responsibilities of HMRC and taxpayers (see **49.2**).

- **HMRC guidance, etc** – The main sources of additional information are the manuals on HMRC's website (see **49.3**).

THE UK TAX ADMINISTRATION SYSTEM – AN OVERVIEW

49.1　Whilst it is beyond the scope of this book (and certainly beyond the patience of this author) to give a full history of the development of the UK tax administration system, the changing regulations and approaches to how our taxes are collected and how the public revenue is secured can be seen as reflecting our political and social history.

Whilst sexual intercourse might have started in 1963 (at least according to Philip Larkin), tax professionals have been getting excited by tax regulations for many years before that. Land taxes of the 17th and 18th century and duties on pleasurable/anti-social items such as alcohol were joined in 1798 by the introduction of a tax on income. This income tax was viewed as a temporary expedient, raising funds to pay for the military adventures of the age, but it became a permanent feature of state money-raising in 1842. The scope of what is to be taxed has been added to (but seldom reduced) since then.

From the earliest days, the state has acted to protect revenue from those citizens who did not share an overwhelming desire to pay over funds to the exchequer. From the early excise men (whose methods of dealing with smugglers, and others seeking to avoid payment of duties, could include shooting them) through to the modern day officers of HMRC (whose powers do not, at the time of writing, extend to the use of lethal weapons!) the role of the state's tax enforcers has been governed by a mixture of law and practice.

In some ways the changing role of the taxman reflects the differing views taxpayers take about taxation. If all taxpayers took the view of Oliver Wendell Holmes who said:

'I like to pay taxes. It is purchasing civilisation'

then perhaps the taxman's role would be easier. But often the taxman will be faced by people more sympathetic to the views of the American property tycoon, Leona Helmsley, who said:

'We don't pay taxes. Only the little people pay taxes'

(although this was before she was jailed for 19 months for tax evasion …).

The taxman has also to work within the interpretations of the law set out in the courts, which have varied over the years. In the 1930s a judge concluded that;

'Any one may so arrange his affairs that his taxes shall be as low as possible; he is not bound to choose that pattern which will best pay the Treasury; there is not even a patriotic duty to increase one's taxes.' (Judge Learned Hand, *Helvering v Gregory* 69 F 2d 809, 810-11 (2d Cir 1934))

By the 1990s the world had changed and (in this context at least) the judiciary had moved on as well so we get pronouncements such as:

'In common with my predecessors I regard tax avoidance schemes of the kind invented and implemented in the present case as no better than attempts to cheat the Revenue.' (Lord Templeman, *IRC v Fitzwilliam* [1993] 67 TC 756)

The climate has changed still further in the last few years with the introduction of a General Anti-Abuse Rule and the paying of tax being claimed by some politicians to have a moral dimension (although the involvement of some politicians themselves in offshore arrangements might remind the reader of Molière who said "One should examine oneself for a very long time before thinking of condemning others").

The following chapters set out the rules of the game as established by current legislation and the way in which HMRC interpret these rules. By definition, these chapters only give a general overview of the main rules impacting on tax enquiries and if faced with any of these matters in practice, taxpayers and their agents should seek specialist advice. Dealing with these issues requires a mixture of 'art and science' and only the brave or foolish would enter into combat with HMRC armed only with the outline contained below.

Finally, the author recommends that if anyone's blood pressure rises whilst considering what follows, a final quote from Edmund Burke might help:

'To tax and to please, no more than to love and to be wise, is not given to men.'

TAXPAYER'S CHARTER

49.2   HMRC publish a 'Taxpayers charter' (referred to by HMRC as 'Your charter'), which sets out their view of the rights and responsibilities of HMRC and the taxpayer. This is required under *Commissioners for Revenue and Customs Act 2005, s 16A* (as amended).

Under this, the commissioners must prepare a charter which 'must include standards of behaviour and values to which HMRC will aspire when dealing with people in the exercise of their functions'.

A new Charter was published in January 2016 which can be accessed via the HMRC website www.gov.uk/government/publications/your-charter.

This sets out a set of mutual responsibilities for the taxpayer and HMRC, as follows:

What the taxpayer can expect from HMRC:	**What HMRC expect from the taxpayer:**
Respect you and treat you as honest	Be honest and respect our staff
Provide a helpful, efficient and effective service	Work with us to get things right
Be professional and act with integrity	Find out what you need to do and keep us informed
Protect your information and respect your privacy	Keep accurate records and protect your information
Accept that someone else can represent you	Know what your representative does on your behalf
Deal with complaints quickly and fairly	Respond in good time
Tackle those who bend or break the rules	Take reasonable care to avoid mistakes

Each of these responsibilities is expanded on in the full charter. It might be thought that some of these responsibilities are not entirely matched (for example a taxpayer must "Respond in good time" whilst HMRC have to "Deal with complaints quickly and fairly" – which begs the question what they do with questions, as opposed to complaints, and what "quickly" means).

It is also noted that the promise in earlier versions of the charter that "You will be treated in the same way as other taxpayers in similar circumstances" has quietly been dropped.....

A new "Charter Oversite Committee" has been established with representatives of HMRC, advisers and taxpayers. It seems that the committee has been tasked to ensure that the charter is communicated properly and applied fairly, rather than considering the scope of the charter. In any event we are likely to see modifications to the charter during the coming years.

> **Focus**
>
> It is important to ensure that HMRC are reminded of their commitments under the charter in any case where the approach to the taxpayer appears to fall short of these charter commitments.

In the tribunal decision in *Dovey v HMRC* [2012] UKFTT 190 (TC) (which concerned an appeal regarding the late payment of income tax), the tribunal judge, Anne Redston, noted that the charter does not set out statutory obligations but rather 'aspirations'. She commented:

> 'taxpayers do not have a right of appeal to this Tribunal if HMRC fail to live up to those aspirations'.

So formal appeals based on the failure of HMRC to live up to their own stated standards are doomed to failure. But ensuring that HMRC are kept to their promises in their dealings with the taxpayer can be helpful in the overall enquiry process.

FURTHER INFORMATION

49.3   The following chapters give an overview of the statutory regime governing HMRC enquiry work, the interest and penalty regimes that apply and the key factors to consider when confronted with an HMRC review.

More details can be found via the HMRC website (www.hmrc.gov.uk/), and in particular in the published HMRC Manuals such as the Compliance Handbook and Enquiry Manual.

For a fuller explanation of all these issues please refer to *HMRC Investigations and Enquiries* (Bloomsbury Professional).

Focus

Dealing with HMRC is a mixture of art and science, requiring a knowledge of the legislation but also an understanding of the demands on and approach of the HMRC personnel who are running any inquiry.

50

Filing returns and paying tax

SIGNPOSTS

- **Scope** – There are statutory requirements to notify HMRC of taxable activity, to make returns and to pay any tax due. Failure to comply with these rules will normally attract penalties. Rules will vary according to the category of tax concerned (see **50.1**).

- **Individuals** – Paper returns must generally be submitted by 31 October following the tax year; for online returns the time limit is 31 January following the tax year. For individuals, there are two key dates for paying tax – 31 January when outstanding tax from the prior year must be paid along with the first instalment of tax for the current year, and 31 July, when the second instalment of tax for the year just ended must be paid. Proposals have been tabled which will see the end of the annual tax return, being replaced with a 'real time' online tax account (see **50.2–50.3**).

- **Companies** – Returns for companies must be filed online within 12 months of the end of the accounting period, together with accounts in iXBRL format. Smaller companies must pay their corporation tax by nine months after the end of the accounting period; larger companies must generally pay their corporation tax in four quarterly instalments, two before the end of the period. For companies with taxable profits of over £20m it is proposed that the instalment payments will be advanced by three months from April 2019 (see **50.4–50.5**).

- **Trustees** – They are governed by the same rules as individuals (see **50.6**).

- **VAT** – Quarterly VAT returns are due one month after the end of the quarter and virtually all returns must now be made online; VAT must be paid by the same date with an additional seven days allowed if the return is made online (see **50.7**).

- **PAYE** – Deductions under the PAYE system must be paid by the 19th of the month following the end of the period to which they relate; payments made electronically have a three-day extension (see **50.8**).

- **Direct recovery of debts** – Since 18 November 2015 HMRC has been able to access taxpayers' bank accounts directly to recover unpaid tax debts of over £1,000 (see **50.9**).

REQUIREMENTS TO SUBMIT RETURNS AND PAY TAX

50.1   All taxpayers (whether individuals, companies, trustees, etc) are obliged to make a return of taxable income and gains as set down in legislation. These returns are to be made in a designated format and by a designated date, and penalties exist for:

(a)   those taxpayers who submit incorrect returns; and

(b)   those taxpayers who fail to submit required returns on time.

There are also rules which require taxpayers to notify HMRC of new sources of income and gains, and requirements to pay over tax due. Again failure to comply with these rules will attract penalties.

INDIVIDUAL TAXPAYERS

Requirements regarding returns etc

50.2   A tax return must be completed and submitted if HMRC ask for one. Even where no such request is made it is the taxpayer's responsibility to notify HMRC of any new source of taxable income or gain by 5 October following the end of the tax year (*FA 2009, Sch 55*).

Failure to do this will result in a penalty being charged, the magnitude of which will be based on the reasons why the taxpayer failed to comply with the requirement and the amount of tax unpaid because of the failure (see **Chapter 53**) (*FA 2008, Sch 41*).

There is guidance on HMRC's website about registering for self-assessment online: see www.hmrc.gov.uk/online/new.htm#2.

Tax returns must be sent to HMRC by certain deadlines. These are:

- 31 October following the end of the tax year if the return is submitted on paper.

  (**Note** – If HMRC do not issue a request for an individual to file a tax return until after 31 July following the tax year in question, then the submission date is extended to three months following the date that the request is received by the taxpayer.)

- 31 January following the end of the tax year if the return is submitted online.

  (**Note** – If HMRC do not issue a request for an individual to file a tax return until after 31 October following the tax year in question, then the submission date is extended to three months following the date that the request is received by the taxpayer.)

In all cases, the return must be submitted to HMRC by midnight on the above dates for the deadlines to be met.

Proposals have been tabled that will replace the annual tax return with a real-time online tax account for all individuals by 2020. This will be phased in over that time, with the first stage (digital tax accounts for all individuals and small businesses) being available from April 2016 (see **1.12**).

> **Focus**
>
> Care needs to be taken if paper returns are being submitted on or near the deadline date. If returns are posted then it is the taxpayer's responsibility to ensure they arrive by the deadline date; the act of posting the return is not enough.
>
> Receipts are not issued by HMRC and so robust delivery records should be kept as evidence. This could include date-stamped delivery lists of all returns submitted by hand on or near the deadline date.

If an individual misses a deadline for the submission of a tax return, penalties may apply (see **Chapter 53** regarding penalties).

It should be noted that there is a separate requirement to file a partnership return (*TMA 1970, s 12AA*).

Payment of income tax

50.3   Where tax is due payment must be made within a statutory time frame, and there are two key dates during each year:

31 January

This is the date by which all tax from the previous tax year must be paid – this final payment is called the balancing payment. So, for example, for the tax year ended 5 April 2015 the balancing payment must be paid by 31 January 2016.

Unless otherwise requested by the taxpayer, HMRC will automatically collect any balancing payment under the self-assessment system through the PAYE system where:

- the tax due is less than £3,000;

- the taxpayer already pays tax through PAYE (eg they are an employee or receive a company pension); and

- they filled a paper return by 31 October or an online return by 30 December following the tax year.

Any amounts collected via the PAYE system are subject to the normal overriding limit, whereby the amount of tax collected must not exceed 50% of the relevant payment. Furthermore, HMRC will not collect amount in this way where the amount due exceeds the individuals expected liability for the year in which it will be collected (ie where the taxpayer would end up paying more than twice as much tax as they would normally).

In addition to the balancing payment, a first payment on account (POA) may be needed on this date in respect of tax of the 'current year'. POAs are part payments towards a taxpayer's total tax bill, so on 31 January 2016 a payment may be required of part of the estimated tax bill for the tax year to 5 April 2016 (ie 2015/16).

31 July

This is the deadline for making a second POA in respect of the tax year ended on the previous 5 April. So, for example on 31 July 2016 a second POA in respect of the tax due for 2015/16 may be due.

Normally, HMRC will issue statements confirming what is due (based on information sent to them by the taxpayer and, for example, their employers), but even if statements are not issued the payments of tax must be made on time. Failure to pay on time will result in interest being charged and can give rise to penalties (see **Chapter 53**).

POAs are based on the actual tax liability of the previous year (excluding capital gains), half this sum being due by 31 January and half by 31 July as above. If the prior year tax was less than £1,000 or over 80% of the prior year tax was accounted for by deduction at source (eg through the PAYE system) then no payments on account will be required.

The proposed replacement of the annual tax return by a real-time online tax account may also see changes to the tax payment system.

> **Focus**
>
> If circumstances change, a taxpayer can apply to have payments on account reduced. For example, a source of income might have ceased. But interest will be charged if tax does eventually fall due and penalties may be charged if the reduction is claimed without the taxpayer taking proper care.

COMPANIES

Requirements regarding returns etc

50.4   HMRC are automatically notified when a company is set up at Companies House, and they will issue a unique tax reference to the registered office of the company shortly after that time. This number can be used to access the corporation tax online service to enable the company to register for corporation tax.

When a company starts a trade or business, HMRC must be notified within three months. This notification can be made as part of the registration process at Companies House (if the intention is to commence trade or business immediately), or otherwise through the corporation tax online service or by notifying HMRC by letter.

The previous procedure of using Form CT41G has ceased for all but unincorporated clubs, societies, voluntary associations or other similar bodies who carry on a business and will be subject to corporation tax.

Companies must file their corporation tax returns within 12 months of the end of the company's corporation tax accounting period. This is known as the 'statutory filing date'.

Since April 2011, all returns for companies have had to be made online and must be submitted in inline eXtensible Business Reporting Language (iXBRL) format.

Returns filed late will give rise to an automatic penalty, even where no corporation tax is owed.

> **Focus**
>
> It is important to check whether HMRC have issued a notice requiring a return from companies which are dormant as omitting to submit the return will incur a penalty.

Payment of corporation tax

50.5 Subject to the quarterly instalment payment (QIP) provisions described below for 'large' companies, companies are required to settle their corporation tax liability by the normal due date, which is nine months and one day after the end of the relevant corporation tax accounting period (CTAP). For example, if a company's CTAP ends on 31 May, its corporation tax payment is due on or before 1 March the following year.

A company is considered to be 'large' if its corporation tax profits are more than £1.5 million, with this limit rateably reduced where the CTAP is less than 12 months and where there are related 51% group companies (measured by reference to the last day of the preceding CTAP).

If a company falls within the QIP regime its tax liability needs to be settled in instalments of three monthly intervals, starting six months and 13 days from the start of the CTAP and ending three months and 14 days after the end of the CTAP. Where a company has a 12 month CTAP the payments will fall as follows:

- six months and 13 days from the start of the CTAP;

- nine months and 13 days from the start of the CTAP (ie three months after the first instalment);

- 14 days after the end of the CTAP (ie three months after the second instalment);

- three months and 14 days after the end of the CTAP.

Where a company has a CTAP of less than 12 months the first, second and third instalments are only required to the extent that their due dates fall before the due date of the final instalment.

The amount of each instalment is calculated as $3/n \times CTL$ where:

- CTL is the total corporation tax liability

- n is the number of whole calendar months falling within the CTAP

Care should be taken where the CTAP is less than 12 months to ensure that the final payment is adjusted so that the total amount paid does not exceed the actual tax liability for the CTAP.

Example 50.1 – Payment by instalments

Warne Spinners Limited has a 12 month accounting period ending of 31 December 2016. The instalment payment dates are:

- first payment 14 July 2016;

- second payment 14 October 2016;

- third payment 14 January 2017;

- final payment 14 April 2017.

Focus

It is necessary to monitor carefully whether a company is required to make instalment payments.

It is proposed that for accounting periods commencing on or after 1 April 2019, the instalment dates for companies with annual taxable profits exceeding £20m (defined as 'very large companies') will be brought forward three months so that they fall due in the third, sixth, ninth and twelfth month of their accounting period.

TRUSTS – REQUIREMENTS REGARDING RETURNS, ETC

50.6   Trustees should tell HMRC as soon as the trust is created if the trust expects to receive income or make chargeable capital gains (profits) within the next tax year. If an existing trust starts receiving income or making chargeable gains, HMRC need to be notified by 5 October following the end of the tax year.

HMRC will issue Tax Return Form SA900 (Trust and estate tax return) to all trusts that they have been notified about.

Note that in cases of a bare trust the tax responsibility lies with the beneficiaries and therefore the tax issues must all be dealt with by those beneficiaries through their own tax returns.

The tax return and payment deadlines are as for individual taxpayers, as set out in **50.2** and **50.3** above.

VAT

50.7 Since April 2012, virtually all VAT-registered businesses have had to submit online VAT returns and pay electronically.

The normal due date for making a return and payment is one calendar month after the end of the VAT period, or two calendar months after the end of the VAT period if the annual accounting scheme is used.

But for online returns and payment an extra seven calendar days are allowed, unless:

● the VAT Annual Accounting Scheme is being used; or

● payments on account are being made (unless monthly returns are being made).

HMRC provide a VAT deadline calculator at www.gov.uk/vat-payment-deadlines.

PAYE

50.8 See **2.13** for details of the main PAYE return requirements and deadlines.

PAYE must be paid to HMRC by the 19th of the month following the end of the tax month or quarter to which it relates. However, if the payment is made 'electronically', eg by bank transfer, etc, then the payment must reach HMRC's bank account no later than the 22nd of the month following the end of the tax month or quarter to which it relates.

If the PAYE due will be on average less than £1,500 per month, quarterly payments can be agreed.

> **Focus**
>
> Complying with these requirements will not only avoid the possibility of penalty action but will also demonstrate the acceptable 'behaviour' that HMRC are now keen to see.

DIRECT RECOVERY OF DEBTS

50.9 Since 18 November 2015 HMRC have had the right to directly access bank accounts to recover funds from taxpayers who had failed to pay their tax.

Such recovery will be permissible where:

- the debt is over £1,000;

- the 'normal' channels of persuading the taxpayer to account for tax have been exhausted;

- the taxpayer has more than £5,000 in his bank accounts.

The tax debts targeted will be the debts owed by individuals and self-employed businesses either under legislation or through contract settlement with HMRC.

HMRC have proposed a number of 'safeguards' which are aimed at ensuring that mistakes are avoided and any action does not result in hardship. It is perhaps unsurprising that these proposals have been greeted with a degree of scepticism from taxpayers and agents alike, who have had experience of HMRC's somewhat mixed track record in getting things right under their existing procedures. Banks and other financial Institutions will be required to give details of the accounts and sums held by the taxpayer and to transfer funds to HMRC. Any administrative cost will be charged to the account holder.

The taxpayer can appeal to the county court against this action.

51

HMRC enquiries

SIGNPOSTS

- **Scope** – The self-assessment system operates on a 'process now, check later' basis. HMRC generally have 12 months from the date the return is received to raise an enquiry, but this is subject to certain exceptions, such as if the return is filed late (see **51.1–51.3**).

- **Type of enquiry** – HMRC can make 'random' enquiries if they wish. In addition, an enquiry may concern one or more specific issues (an 'aspect' enquiry), or cover the return in general (a 'full' enquiry) (**51.4–51.6**).

- **Information and inspection powers** – HMRC have statutory powers to require the provision of information and documents, including the power to inspect business premises, subject to certain restrictions (see **51.7–51.8**).

- **The enquiry process** – HMRC can assess earlier years outside the 12-month limit if they make a 'discovery'. In the most serious cases, they can go back 20 years (see **51.9–51.11**).

- **How are enquiries settled?** – Most enquiries conclude with a contract settlement and payment of a global sum to cover tax, penalties, etc. A certificate of full disclosure and statement of assets and liabilities may also be completed (see **51.12**).

- **Code of Practice 9** – HMRC will consider criminal prosecution in the most serious cases. Alternatively, HMRC may use a stringent investigation approach, as set out in its Code of Practice 9 (see **51.13**).

BACKGROUND

51.1 The introduction of the self-assessment regime for individual taxpayers and companies changed the relationship between the taxman and the taxpayer.

Before these changes, the role of HMRC was largely checking returns on submission and assessing if they were correct and complete. This gave a degree of certainty to the process which gave the taxpayer the comfort that a return had been accepted and would not be reopened unless some material additional facts were 'discovered' by HMRC.

Now the system works on a 'process now, check later' approach which means that submitted returns are normally processed based on the taxpayer figures. HMRC then has a period of time in which to enquire into the return. Only once that time period has elapsed can the taxpayer have comfort that the figures submitted are accepted, subject to any new facts being 'discovered' at a later date.

Enquiry or correction?

51.2   HMRC have the power to make corrections to returns where there is:

● an obvious error or omission, such as an arithmetical error; or

● anything else that HMRC has reason to believe is incorrect based on information already held and where no more information is needed.

Such corrections must be made within nine months of receiving a return and they do not fall to be treated as an enquiry. Such corrections cannot be formally 'appealed', but there is a right of rejection of the correction. If HMRC disagree with such a rejection, this can lead to an enquiry.

Time limits

51.3   For individuals the enquiry window runs for 12 months following the date that the return is received by HMRC. The only changes to this are:

● Where the return is made late, in which case the enquiry window is extended until the quarter day (that is 31 January, 30 April, 31 July and 31 October) following the 12-month anniversary of the date the return was made. The same extension will apply to cases where a return had been amended, but the extended time limit will only apply to the item that has been amended, not to the whole of the return.

● Where a return has been requested later than normal so that the return filing deadline is after the normal 31 January date (see **50.2**). In such cases the enquiry window will always run for 12 months after this revised filing date.

For companies, the position is a little more complicated. Since 2008, different rules have applied depending on the size of the company:

● For:

(a)   single companies, or

    (b)   companies in small groups (as measured by *Companies Act 2006, s 383*),

where a return is received on or before the statutory filing date, the enquiry time limit is 12 months from the date of receipt of the return.

- For companies in a group that is not 'small' where a return is received on or before the statutory filing date, the time limit is 12 months from the statutory filing date.

If any company, whatever its size, delivers a return late, the enquiry window runs up to and including the quarter date (31 January, 30 April, 31 July or 31 October) next following the first anniversary of the day on which the return was delivered.

> **Focus**
>
> It should be noted that HMRC must deliver a notice of enquiry before the expiry of the time limit, ie it must be received by the taxpayer by that date. Notices sent through the post (and they will almost always be delivered in this way) are deemed to be delivered within four working days if sent by second class post and two working days if delivered by first class post.
>
> This time limit only applies where there is no discovery of an error leading to an enquiry, see **51.10** below.

TYPE OF ENQUIRY, ETC

HMRC notices of enquiry

51.4   HMRC is allowed to open enquiries under the following statute:

Nature of enquiry	Legislative reference
Returns	*TMA 1970, s 9A* – individuals and trusts
	TMA 1970, s 12AC – partnership
	FA 1998, Sch 18, para 24 – companies
Amendments to a return	*TMA 1970, s 9A(5)* – individuals and trusts
	TMA 1970, s 12AC(5) – partnerships
	FA 1998, Sch 18, para 25(2) – companies
Claims	*TMA 1970, Sch 1A, para 5*

HMRC guidance (see HMRC's Enquiry Manual at EM1503 (www.gov.uk/hmrc-internal-manuals/enquiry-manual/em1503)) sets out the formal 'rules of the game' that they should follow in launching enquires. These include:

- They should be neutral in opening an enquiry – not assuming a problem.

- They should be open-minded – even where they hold information suggesting a potential problem. That information might be wrong or capable of an explanation.

- No distinction should be made between a random enquiry and a targeted enquiry and generally no reasons for the enquiry should be given at the opening.

- They should be aware of errors in both HMRC's and the taxpayer's favour.

- The enquiry opening should simply seek the evidence on which an objective judgement on the accuracy of the return can be reached.

The author will be excused for a degree of cynicism as to whether this guidance is in practice always followed by each and every HMRC officer.

Random or targeted enquiry?

51.5   The working assumption should be that an enquiry will be launched because HMRC believe there is a 'problem' with a return.

However, a very small number of cases are taken up on a random basis, where cases are selected centrally by HMRC. Reading the guidance on these procedures at EM0093 might lead one to conclude that such random enquires are undertaken for statistical purposes only, which may come as little comfort to a taxpayer who has to deal with the inconvenience and cost of dealing with such an enquiry.

Full or 'aspect' enquiry?

51.6   An enquiry might be raised either because of concerns over some specific issue or issues on a return (an aspect enquiry) or some wider concerns over the return in general (a full enquiry).

The sort of enquiry should be clearly stated in HMRC's opening letter and will inform the taxpayer and his advisor on the approach being adopted by HMRC. In particular, if an aspect enquiry is opened HMRC should confine their interest to the terms of the enquiry and should not pursue a wider agenda without making it clear that they are actually reclassifying the enquiry as 'full'.

HMRC requests for information

51.7   An enquiry will open with HMRC requesting a voluntary disclosure of information. If such a voluntary disclosure is not made, HMRC have powers to force information from the taxpayer.

These formal powers have been radically overhauled in recent years. This publication covers the rules that have applied since 1 April 2010.

Information and inspection powers

51.8   *FA 2008, Sch 36* introduced a new framework of information and inspection powers for HMRC. The key features of these powers are as follows:

- HMRC can give written notice to a taxpayer requiring the provision of information and documents. HMRC can also demand this information from third parties (eg a bank or a customer of the taxpayer).

- HMRC can only take this route if the information or documents are 'reasonably required' for the purpose of checking a tax position.

- Anyone getting such a notice can appeal against it to an independent tribunal, unless what is requested:

  ○ forms part of a taxpayer's statutory records; or

  ○ forms any person's records that relate to the supply of goods and services, the acquisition of goods from another European Union (EU) member state, or the importation of goods from outside the EU by a business.

HMRC cannot require:

- information relating to the conduct of appeals against HMRC decisions;

- legally privileged information;

- advice from auditors or tax advisers to a client about that client's tax affairs;

- information about a person's medical or spiritual welfare; or

- journalistic material.

In addition there are time constraints:

- information over six years old can only be included in a notice issued by or with the approval of an authorised officer; and

- HMRC cannot give a notice in respect of the tax position of a deceased person more than four years after the person's death.

ENQUIRY PROCESS

Meetings with HMRC

51.9 Following the initial notice of enquiry and information requests, HMRC will review the information provided to establish the accuracy and 'trustworthiness' of the records.

If they wish to continue with their enquiry, HMRC will almost always then ask for a meeting with the taxpayer. This gives the taxpayer the opportunity to deal with any misunderstandings that HMRC might have and to disclose any matters which need to be addressed in bringing matters up to date. HMRC will wish to clarify their understanding of the taxpayer's affairs, the nature and scope of the records kept and the overall 'wealth' position of the taxpayer.

> **Focus**
>
> There is no ultimate compulsion for a taxpayer to attend a meeting but, in the view of the author, they do provide an opportunity both to agree the scope of HMRC's enquiries and to demonstrate cooperation which can have a beneficial impact on the penalty position at the conclusion of an enquiry.

Meeting with HMRC can be traumatic for taxpayers, even in cases where there is 'nothing to hide'. Whilst cost implications must always be considered, it is almost always better for the taxpayer to have professional representation at a meeting, ensuring that HMRC play by the 'rules of the game' and that the taxpayer's case is firmly but politely stated.

The meeting will be followed by the gathering of further information and a conclusion on the scope and quantum of any additional tax due.

Adjusting earlier years

51.10 As set out in **51.3** above, there is a 'normal' 12-month time limit for enquiries. However, if it is 'discovered' that tax has been under-assessed or underpaid HMRC can go back into earlier years.

To make a discovery assessment HMRC must establish that a tax liability has been understated or undeclared, or tax relief has been overstated in cases where full, complete and accurate details were not provided due to either:

- insufficient information being provided to HMRC; or

- an error arising deliberately or due to the carelessness of the taxpayer or agent.

There is a requirement that an HMRC officer completing an enquiry could not have reasonably been expected to have been aware of the loss of tax, etc based on the information provided and that the original position was not in accordance with the prevailing practice at the time of the original return.

Once all these tests are passed (and in the writer's experience HMRC do not always double check that all these requirements have been met) assessments can be made, but only within strict time limits.

From 1 April 2010, the main extended time limits are as follows:

Income tax

● Where there has been no careless or deliberate behaviour by the taxpayer – four years from the end of the year of assessment.

● Where there has been careless behaviour by the taxpayer – six years from the end of the year of assessment.

● Where there has been deliberate behaviour by the taxpayer – 20 years from the end of the year of assessment.

Corporation tax

● Where there has been no careless or deliberate behaviour by the company or agent – four years from the end of the accounting period.

● Where there has been careless behaviour by the company or agent – six years from the end of the accounting period.

● Where there has been deliberate behaviour by the company or agent – 20 years from the end of the accounting period.

> **Example 51.1 – Time limit for discovery assessment**
>
> Jeremy runs a manufacturing business and in 2015, he claimed full relief for several 'business' trips around the country, despite these being meetings with his brothers to discuss trust issues. This was only discovered on a review of his tax affairs several years later.
>
> HMRC are able to raise a discovery assessment to recover the additional tax due, despite the fact that this is beyond the normal enquiry window.

Claims by the taxpayer

51.11 A similar time limit regime applies to claims to Overpayment Relief made by a taxpayer, with a four-year time limit applying. *TMA 1970, Schedule 1AB*.

SETTLING ENQUIRIES

51.12   At the end of an enquiry, HMRC will seek to recover any tax lost, interest on that tax (accruing from the date the tax should have originally been paid to the date that the tax is actually paid) and a penalty (see **Chapter 53**).

Whilst HMRC have powers to formally assess and recover each of these items, most cases conclude with a 'contract settlement' between the taxpayer and HMRC, under which a global sum is paid by the taxpayer on the basis that HMRC agree not to issue formal assessments to recover the sums due.

At the end of an enquiry, HMRC may also ask the taxpayer to complete both a statement of assets and liabilities and a certificate of full disclosure, asking the taxpayer to confirm that all matters relevant to the taxpayer's affairs have been disclosed. False statements signed by the taxpayer can have serious consequences, with HMRC considering criminal prosecution in the most serious cases.

Often the contract settlement will be agreed at a final meeting with HMRC, which again will almost always see the taxpayer professionally represented.

The end of an enquiry will be marked by the issuing of a closure notice.

HMRC will issue a separate closure notice in respect of each return or claim that has been subject to an enquiry.

A notice will be issued either when:

- HMRC considers the enquiries are complete (whether the position has been agreed with the taxpayer or not); or

- when the tribunal directs that a closure notice should be issued, for example when a taxpayer successfully requests such a direction.

HMRC will set out in the closure notice their view of the tax position on the conclusion of the enquiry and will make any appropriate amendments.

A taxpayer usually has rights of appeal against both HMRC conclusions and any amendments made but a company can only appeal against the amendments. Any appeal must be made and received by HMRC within 30 days of the issue of the closure notice.

On the appeal the taxpayer may request that decisions in the closure notice are reviewed by HMRC. This is an internal review by HMRC by an officer who will normally be outside the direct line management chain of the original decision maker who issued the closure notice and was not involved in making that decision.

The stated aim of the review system is to provide an additional opportunity to resolve the tax dispute without the need for a tribunal hearing, and HMRC say that the review provides a fresh viewpoint ensuring both that the decision has been properly made and that, in HMRC's view, it is legally correct and one which they would defend at tribunal. The fact that this is an internal HMRC review might lead some taxpayers to question if this is a truly impartial review forum, although the review process does allow the taxpayer to make further representations to the reviewing officer to ensure there are no 'misunderstandings'.

HMRC will inform the taxpayer of the outcome of the review and the taxpayer has the right to appeal against the review decision to the tax tribunal.

An Alternative Dispute Resolution (ADR) approach to resolving tax disputes, for individuals and small and medium-sized enterprises is also available. This mirrors the concept of mediation that has successfully been adopted as a method of resolving legal disputes. Going forward this may form the basis of a revised approach to dealing with cases which have become 'bogged down' in a morass of 'yes it is, no it isn't' argument between HMRC and the taxpayer or, more usually, his agent.

Details of how this system operates can be found at www.gov.uk/guidance/tax-disputes-alternative-dispute-resolution-adr#.

Focus

Settling a dispute through negotiation is almost always commercially a better decision than taking a case to the tax tribunal, although taxpayers need to 'stand their ground' against any approach from HMRC which is ill-conceived.

SERIOUS CASES OF FRAUD

51.13   In the most serious cases HMRC will consider criminal prosecution.

An alternative, more stringent investigation procedure may be adopted as set out in HMRC's *Code of Practice 9* (COP9). In such cases the taxpayer will be invited to make a full disclosure of the tax 'mischief' that has occurred and to commission a report from a professional adviser on the taxpayer's behalf which sets out in detail the disclosure and the tax lost. These reports are costly and time consuming but will protect the taxpayer from further action by HMRC. The report is then used as the basis of a contract settlement as at **51.12**.

Whilst traditionally used in cases with substantial tax at stake, since 31 January 2012 the COP9 procedure has applied to any case with no *de minimis* limit. In this context see the HMRC publications regarding the contractual disclosure facility process at www.gov.uk/guidance/admitting-tax-fraud-the-contractual-disclosure-facility-cdf.

Focus

Dealing with an HMRC enquiry can be time consuming, expensive and emotionally draining. HMRC often have little real appreciation of the impact of such enquiries on the taxpayer.

It is strongly recommended that any taxpayer faced with an enquiry will benefit from expert assistance. This is seldom an area where a 'DIY' approach is appropriate.

52

Payment of tax

SIGNPOSTS

- **Scope** – HMRC will accept payment of tax through a number of routes, including credit card, BACS and Bank Giro. Post-dated cheques will only be accepted by HMRC in certain circumstances (see **52.1–52.8**).

- **Problems paying tax** – These should be addressed as soon as possible, to avoid additional penalties and enforcement action. HMRC may agree 'time to pay' arrangements in some cases of genuine inability to pay in full and on time. However, there is no guarantee that HMRC will agree to this, and there is no right of appeal if HMRC decides not to allow time to pay (see **52.9**).

- **Collection and recovery of tax paid late** – If payment is not made and no time to pay agreement has been reached, HMRC will take legal proceedings to recover what is owed plus costs, where appropriate (see **52.10–52.14**).

INTRODUCTION

52.1   Details of the time limits for paying tax are shown in **Chapter 50**. The mechanics of payment have altered in recent years with facilities being available to pay tax by:

- direct debit;

- debit or credit card (via internet);

- bank transfer via internet or telephone banking using Faster Payment Service (FPS) BACS or CHAPS;

- Bank Giro;

- at the Post Office;

- by post; or

- by an agreed budget payment plan or by coding out tax due – subject to restrictions.

What follows is an outline of the main methods of payment. Full details can be found at www.gov.uk/topic/dealing-with-hmrc/paying-hmrc.

It is important that when any payment is made, the correct reference for the taxpayer / tax is used so that the payment is allocated to the right place, for example:

- personal tax self-assessment payments - include the taxpayers 10-digit unique tax reference followed by a 'K'.

- corporation tax self-assessment payments – include the 17-character reference included on the payslip for that period (the first 10 characters will be the company's 10-digit unique tax reference while the remaining characters specify the accounting period to which the payment relates).

- PAYE payments – include the 13-character accounts office reference issued upon registration.

- VAT payments – include the 9-digit VAT registration number.

DIRECT DEBIT PAYMENTS

52.2   HMRC have two direct debit systems, one for paying VAT and one for paying other taxes. Details of both of these systems can be found on HMRC's website as above.

As with all direct debit arrangements this system benefits from the protection under the direct debit guarantee scheme, which importantly includes the following commitment:

'If an error is made in the payment of your direct debit by HMRC or your bank or building society, you are entitled to a full and immediate refund of the amount paid from your bank or building society.'

PAYING BY DEBIT OR CREDIT CARDS

52.3   Taxpayers can pay their liability online using a debit or credit card, although a fee will be charged for payments by credit card.

From 1 April 2016, payments made by personal credit cards will attract a fee of between 0.374% to 0.606% while for corporate credit cards the fee is between 1.508% to 2.406%. Before this time, a flat rate of 1.5% applied to all payments by credit card. The actual rate charged depends on the type of card used (VISA or MasterCard) with different rates applying to different variations of each.

HMRC will record the payment on the date it is made rather than the date it reaches their account – including on bank holidays and weekends.

The previous facility to make payments using the BillPay system run by Santander has been withdrawn.

Full details on this service can be found at: www.gov.uk/pay-tax-debit-credit-card.

From 1 January 2016, HMRC have limited the number of times a credit or debit card can be used within a certain time to pay tax. There is not a set limit – it depends on HMRC's view of what's reasonable based on payment card industry standards and guidance. These rules apply to multiple card payments against the same tax – multiple payments can be made if they relate to different taxes, eg corporation tax and employers' PAYE.

PAYMENT USING FPS, BACS OR CHAPS

52.4   Tax payments can be made by transfer from a bank account by FPS (faster payments service), BACS (bankers automated clearing services) or CHAPS (clearing house automated payment system).

Payments by FPS (online or telephone banking) usually reach HMRC on the same or next day, including weekends and bank holidays.

BACS payments normally take three working days to reach HMRC.

CHAPS will usually reach HMRC the same working day if they are paid within the bank's processing times (usually between 9.00 am and 3.00 pm) however they are more expensive than other payment methods and so are generally only used for very large payments.

You must obviously ensure that the correct bank details for HMRC are used, and these can vary depending upon the tax liability which you are settling. You should therefore use the details included on the payslip issued in respect of that liability, or otherwise refer to HMRC's website.

PAYMENT AT A BANK OR BUILDING SOCIETY

52.5 Taxpayers can make payments at their bank or building society (others may refuse to accept it or may make a charge) by cheque or cash if the taxpayer:

- still gets paper statements from HMRC, and

- has a paying-in slip from HMRC

Cheques should be made payable to 'HM Revenue and Customs only' followed by the correct reference number.

For personal tax self-assessment payments, HMRC will accept the payment as being made on the working day it was paid (or if paid on a weekend, the next working day) and not the date it reaches their account. However, other payments will be treated as being received when they reach HMRC's bank account, which could take up to three working days.

PAYMENT AT THE POST OFFICE

52.6 Tax payments can be made at the Post Office by debit card, cash or cheque (made payable to 'Post Office Ltd') if the taxpayer:

- still gets paper statements from HMRC, and

- has a paying-in slip from HMRC.

The maximum payment that can be made in this way is £10,000. The timing of the receipt of payments by HMRC is the same as that for bank or building society payments (see **52.5**).

PAYMENT BY POST

52.7 Some taxes are not payable by post.

Since 1 April 2011, corporation tax and related payments have had to be made electronically while since 1 April 2012, virtually all VAT-registered traders have had to pay electronically.

If postal payments are used, cheques must be payable to 'HM Revenue & Customs only' (followed by the relevant reference number), must be accompanied by the relevant payslip and must be sent either using the pre-addressed envelope or addressed to:

HMRC

Direct

BX5 5BD

HMRC's system, in common with others, does not like folded cheques, paper clips or staples.

At least three working days should be allowed for the payment to reach HMRC and there have been numerous cases where the lack of proof of posting has led to disputes as to whether payments have been received on time.

POST-DATED CHEQUES

52.8

> **Focus**
>
> HMRC will generally only accept a post-dated cheque if the cheque is for the full amount due and it arrives by and is dated on or before the due date for payment.

The only other occasion where such cheques might be accepted is where a prior arrangement has been made with HMRC to settle a liability in this way.

HMRC systems will not pick up the fact that a cheque is post-dated unless there is a covering letter explaining the position.

PROBLEMS IN PAYING TAX

52.9   Failure to pay taxes on time can not only result in interest and penalties but also in formal recovery proceedings. The approach taken by HMRC will depend on the action taken by the taxpayer in these circumstances.

If a taxpayer identifies a problem *before* a payment demand has been sent by HMRC, they should call either the:

- Business payment support service helpline on 0300 200 3835, or
- Self-assessment payment helpline on 0300 200 3822.

52.9 *Payment of tax*

The taxpayer will be asked for the following:

- a tax reference number;
- the name of the taxpayer or business;
- the address including the postcode;
- a contact telephone number;
- details of the tax that the taxpayer will have difficulty paying; and
- details of any tax repayments the taxpayer is receiving or may receive from HMRC in the future.

The taxpayer will need to explain:

- why he is unable to pay in full and on time;
- what has been done to try and raise the money to pay the debt;
- how much can be paid immediately; and
- how long is needed to pay the rest.

HMRC are likely to probe further to establish the taxpayer's ability to clear this debt and make future payments. This will involve HMRC establishing details of the taxpayer's income, expenditure and assets and to look at changes being made that might allow the taxpayer to meet future payments on time.

If a taxpayer has had any previous time to pay arrangements, deeper questioning may follow, and HMRC may ask for documentary evidence before agreeing to allow further time to pay. The taxpayer will be charged interest on the late payment even when agreed with HMRC, but surcharges and penalties can be avoided if the agreement is struck before the relevant surcharge date and the taxpayer sticks to the terms of this agreement.

HMRC will only agree time to pay in cases where there is a genuine inability to pay in full and on time. If time to pay is agreed, HMRC will request that payments are made by direct debit. If the taxpayer fails to pay the agreed sums under the time to pay agreement or fails to keep his tax affairs up to date, HMRC will cancel the arrangement and take legal action to recover the outstanding amount.

HMRC can legally set off any tax repayments falling due against the debt covered by the arrangement.

If a taxpayer deals with a payment problem *after* receiving a payment demand notice or letter warning of legal action, the taxpayer must immediately contact HMRC using the contact details on the relevant letter or demand. Failure to make contact with HMRC may lead to the case being handed to a private debt collection firm.

When the taxpayer contacts HMRC, he will need to explain the reason behind the problem and will be questioned as set out above. HMRC will look to establish if the taxpayer is able to pay immediately (pressing the taxpayer to make a payment over the phone by debit/credit card or setting up a standing order).

If it is established that the taxpayer cannot pay immediately, HMRC will try to establish if the taxpayer can pay off the debt whilst keeping on top of ongoing liabilities. The procedure is similar to that which is set out above, but contact made after the issue of demands or letters preceding legal action removes the protection for the taxpayer from penalties and surcharges for late payment.

> **Focus**
>
> There is no right of appeal against an HMRC decision not to allow time to pay.

RECOVERY PROCEEDINGS

HMRC enforcement

52.10   In cases where no payment has been made and no time to pay agreement has been made, HMRC will take action to recover the sums due.

As mentioned above, HMRC use private debt collection firms to recover money owed to them, and may also take legal action to recover the debt and costs.

If HMRC considers a taxpayer insolvent they may start bankruptcy action or winding up proceedings.

For taxpayers who are in employment or who receive a pension, debts can be collected through the their PAYE tax code. Since April 2015, the maximum debt which can be collected in this way has been £17,000 however the actual amount is dependent upon the earnings of the taxpayer, with this maximum only applying where the taxpayer has earnings in excess of £90,000.

Distraint proceedings

52.11   In other cases, HMRC may commence distraint proceedings where a taxpayer's possessions can be taken and auctioned to pay the debt and additional costs.

The procedure starts with HMRC visiting the taxpayer to ask them to pay the debt. If they do not pay, the officer will make a list of possessions that could be sold to cover both the debt and the costs of selling them, eg fees for auctioneers or advertising.

These possessions can then either be:

- taken immediately by the officer; or
- left with the taxpayer under a 'controlled goods agreement'.

These items can then be sold if payment is not made within 7 days of the visit. If they sell for more than the tax liability, the difference will be paid back to the taxpayer. If the items sell for less, the taxpayer will be liable for the difference.

Further details of the fees can be found online at www.gov.uk/if-you-dont-pay-your-tax-bill/taking-control-of-goods.

Magistrates' court proceedings

52.12   HMRC can start magistrates' court proceedings against a taxpayer in cases where they have separate debts of £2,000 each or less, and the money has been outstanding for under a year. Taxpayers will be summoned to appear at court, and will be told in writing how much is owed. A taxpayer can avoid court action by paying what is owed.

If there is a dispute on the amount owed, the taxpayer must contact HMRC to establish the correct position as the magistrates will not be able to rule on the size of the bill. What they can do is order the taxpayer to pay the bill plus costs and if such an order is ignored they can send bailiffs to seize the taxpayer's possessions.

Further details can be found online at www.gov.uk/if-you-dont-pay-your-tax-bill/court-action.

County court

52.13   Action may also be taken in the county court (in England and Wales) under which an order will be made obliging the taxpayer to pay what is owed, together with additional court fees and HMRC costs. The taxpayer's details will be put on a register of judgments, orders and fines, which will impact on the taxpayer's credit history. But a taxpayer who pays within one month of the judgment can ask to have such an entry removed.

In Scotland similar proceedings can be undertaken through the sheriff's court.

Further details can be found online at www.gov.uk/if-you-dont-pay-your-tax-bill/court-action.

Direct recovery of debts

52.14   The *Finance (No 2) Act 2015* introduced direct recovery of debts from taxpayers' bank accounts (see **50.9**).

> **Focus**
>
> HMRC will actively pursue tax due to them and will aggressively chase debt, particularly in cases where there is no contact made by the taxpayer.
>
> It is always better to talk to HMRC ahead of any problems rather than after the event.

53

Interest and penalties

SIGNPOSTS

- **Scope** – The current penalty regime was introduced in *FA 2008* and *FA 2009*. Different levels of penalty apply, depending on the nature of the offence and the reason for the offence.

- **Failure to notify** – Penalties for failure to notify tax liability can range between 0% and 100% of the lost tax, and for offshore matters can be doubled (see **53.1–53.2**).

- **Late filing** – There are penalties for missing the deadline for submitting a tax return which start from £100, even if the return is only one day late (see **53.3–53.4**).

- **Late payment** – There are also penalties for paying tax late, with different rules for self-assessment tax, PAYE and VAT (see **53.5–53.7**).

- **Errors** – Penalties for inaccuracies in returns or other documents can range between 0% and 100% (or double, in cases involving offshore matters) and depend on a number of factors including whether the disclosure was unprompted or not. The level of penalty will be determined by the behaviour of the taxpayer (see **53.8–53.13**).

- **Interest** – interest is charged on all tax paid late (see **53.14**).

- **General Anti-Abuse Rule** – The *Finance Act 2016* introduces a new penalty regime for abusive tax avoidance arrangements falling within the GAAR (see **53.15**).

- **Appendix: Errors in returns, etc** – A table of penalties for errors in returns, etc is included at the end of this chapter (see **53.16–20**).

PENALTIES FOR INDIVIDUALS WHO FAIL TO NOTIFY TAX LIABILITY

53.1   The requirement to notify HMRC of tax liability is set out at **50.2**. The penalty regime is governed by legislation at *FA 2008, Sch 41*.

The level of penalties is linked to the reasons for the failure. These can be seen by reference to the following chart, but note that penalties can be doubled where offshore matters are involved.

Reason for failure to notify	How the problem was disclosed	Minimum penalty	Maximum penalty
Reasonable excuse		No penalty	No penalty
Not deliberate	Unprompted	0% if disclosure is made within 12 months of tax being due, otherwise 10%	30%
Not deliberate	Prompted	10% if disclosure is made within 12 months of tax being due, otherwise 20%	30%
Deliberate	Unprompted	20%	70%
Deliberate	Prompted	35%	70%
Deliberate and concealed	Unprompted	30%	100%
Deliberate and concealed	Prompted	50%	100%

PENALTIES FOR COMPANIES WHO FAIL TO NOTIFY LIABILITY TO CORPORATION TAX

53.2   The requirement to notify HMRC of tax liability is set out at **50.4**. The penalty regime is governed by legislation at *FA 2008, Sch 41*.

The level of penalties relate to the reasons for the failure. These can be seen by reference to the following chart.

Type of failure	Maximum penalty payable
Reasonable excuse	No penalty
Non-deliberate	30% of the potential lost revenue
Deliberate but not concealed	70% of the potential lost revenue
Deliberate and concealed	100% of the potential lost revenue

PENALTIES FOR INDIVIDUALS MISSING A TAX RETURN DEADLINE

53.3 The penalty regime is governed by legislation at *FA 2009, Sch 55*.

Note that penalties can be doubled where offshore matters are involved, and may be reduced where there is a reasonable excuse or a special circumstance.

Delay	Penalty
1 day late	£100
3 months late	The £100 one day late penalty + £10 for each day late up to a maximum of £900
6 months late	The £100 one day late penalty + £10 for each day late up to a maximum of £900 + the higher of £300 or 5% of the tax due
12 months late	Up to 100% of the tax due

An estimate of the penalties and interest for late self-assessment tax returns and payments can be made at www.gov.uk/estimate-self-assessment-penalties.

PENALTIES FOR COMPANIES MISSING A RETURN DEADLINE

53.4 The penalty regime is governed by legislation at *FA 2009, Sch 55*.

Note that penalties may be reduced where there is a reasonable excuse for a late delivery (*FA 1998, Sch 18, para 19*).

Date of return	Penalty
1st and 2nd late returns – up to three months late	£100
3rd consecutive late return – up to three months late	£500
1st and 2nd late returns – three to six months late	£200
3rd consecutive late return – three to six months late	£1,000
Returns filed between 18 months and 24 months after the end of company's accounting period	10% of tax outstanding
Return not filed 24 months after the end of the accounting period	20% of tax outstanding

PENALTIES FOR PAYING TAX LATE – SELF-ASSESSMENT

53.5 **Chapter 50** above gives some background to the payment requirements, and the legislation governing these penalties can be found at *FA 2009, Sch 56*.

These rules replaced the old surcharge regime from 2010/11. An appeal process is available and penalties can be reduced or suspended if there are special circumstances explaining the late payment.

Time tax paid	Penalty
30 days late	5% of the tax unpaid at that date
Six months late	5% of the tax unpaid at that date (in addition to the 5% above)
12 months late	5% of the tax unpaid at that date (in addition to the two 5% penalties above)

An estimate of penalties and interest for late self-assessment tax returns and payments can be made at www.gov.uk/estimate-self-assessment-penalties.

PENALTIES FOR LATE PAYE/NICs PAYMENTS

53.6 **Chapter 50** includes commentary on the payment regime. From 6 April 2010, the legislation at *FA 2009, Sch 56* applies as set out below. There are provisions for appeals, reductions and suspensions of the penalty and in particular the penalties can be suspended if there is a time to pay arrangement agreed (*FA 2009, Sch 56, para 10*).

Focus

Penalties will be charged by reference to each PAYE scheme run.

There will be no penalty if only one PAYE amount is late in a tax year – unless that payment is over six months late.

If a penalty position arises the amount will depend on how late the payment is and how many times payments have been late in a tax year.

Number of late payments in a tax year	Penalty percentage	Amount to which penalty percentages apply
1	No penalty (as long as the payment is less than six months late)	Total amount of tax paid late in the tax year (ignoring the first late payment in that year)
2–4	1%	
5–7	2%	
8–10	3%	
11 or more	4%	

If tax remains unpaid after six months a further penalty of 5% may arise.

If tax remains unpaid after 12 months an additional penalty of 5% may be charged.

PENALTIES FOR MISSING A VAT DEADLINE

53.7   These penalties are governed by *VATA 1994, ss 59–59B* and HMRC notice 700/50.

Businesses with a turnover of less than £150,000 will be 'in default' if by the due date HMRC has not received a VAT return and payment has not been made.

In those cases HMRC send a 'help and support' letter. If there is a second default within 12 months HMRC will issue a 'surcharge liability notice' explaining what will happen if another deadline is missed during the following 12 months. This is defined as a 'surcharge period'.

If a default occurs during a surcharge period, a 'default surcharge' may be raised based on a percentage of the unpaid VAT. For each additional late VAT return or payment, the surcharge percentage will increase and the surcharge period will be extended for a further 12 months.

These rules can be summarised as follows:

Defaults	Surcharge	Surcharge period
First default	No surcharge. Help letter issued.	None
Second default	No surcharge. Surcharge liability notice issued.	12 months

Defaults	Surcharge	Surcharge period
Third default in a surcharge period	2% (unless it is less than £400)	12 months from the date of the most recent default
Fourth default in a surcharge period	5% (unless it is less than £400)	12 months from the date of the most recent default
Fifth default in a surcharge period	10% or £30 (whichever is more)	12 months from the date of the most recent default
Sixth and subsequent defaults in a surcharge period	15% or £30 (whichever is more)	12 months from the date of the most recent default

For businesses with a turnover of more than £150,000 similar rules apply, but there is no 'second chance' and the surcharge regime kicks in on second default. The following sets out the position for those companies:

Defaults	Surcharge	Surcharge period
First default	No surcharge. Surcharge liability notice issued.	12 months
Second default in a surcharge period	2% (unless it is less than £400)	12 months from the date of the most recent default
Third default in a surcharge period	5% (unless it is less than £400)	12 months from the date of the most recent default
Fourth default in a surcharge period	10% or £30 (whichever is more)	12 months from the date of the most recent default
Fifth and subsequent defaults in a surcharge period	15% or £30 (whichever is more)	12 months from the date of the most recent default

PENALTIES FOR INACCURACIES

53.8   *FA 2007, s 97, Sch 24* introduced new penalties for inaccuracies in returns or other documents which were due to be filed on or after 1 April 2009 relating to a tax period beginning on or after 1 April 2008. Where offshore matters are in point the penalty as set out below can be doubled.

Reductions or suspensions of a penalty may be available in special circumstances and an appeal can be made against a penalty decision.

Further details can be found in the HMRC compliance handbook at: www.gov. uk/hmrc-internal-manuals/compliance-handbook/ch80000.

The penalty regime applies to 'persons' which includes:

* individuals;
* companies;
* partners and partnerships;
* representative members of a VAT group;
* personal representatives;
* trustees; and
* pension scheme administrators.

The penalty will apply where:

1   a person gives HMRC an inaccurate document (including but not limited to a tax return);

and:

2   this leads to:

     (a)   an understatement of tax liability; or

     (b)   a false or inflated tax loss or claim; and

3   the inaccuracy was either:

     (a)   careless; or

     (b)   deliberate.

It should be noted that in cases of a deliberate act or failure by a company, HMRC can levy the whole or part of a penalty on an officer of the company who was responsible (*FA 2008, Sch 41, para 22*).

LEVEL OF PENALTY FOR INACCURACY

53.9

Nature of the inaccuracy	How the problem was disclosed	Minimum penalty	Maximum penalty
Reasonable care taken		No penalty	No penalty
Careless	Unprompted	0%	30%
Careless	Prompted	15%	30%
Deliberate	Unprompted	20%	70%
Deliberate	Prompted	35%	70%
Deliberate and concealed	Unprompted	30%	100%
Deliberate and concealed	Prompted	50%	100%

A more comprehensive table of penalties for inaccuracies is included at the end of this chapter.

REASONABLE CARE

53.10

Focus

This is a subjective judgement, but in deciding if a taxpayer has taken 'reasonable care', HMRC will look at evidence such as whether accurate records have been kept, if attention has been paid to filling in the return from those records and if advice has been taken in any case where the taxpayer is in doubt. This test will be applied in light of the taxpayer's knowledge and experience.

Example 53.1 – Penalty for inaccuracy: omitted income

John Smith is a 24-year old plumber who sends in his tax return on time. In addition to his trade income he has dividends of £200 from some shares left to him by his aunt. He assumes that he has no further tax to pay on these dividends because of the tax credit, and rings HMRC to check this. After looking at his file and seeing him as a basic rate taxpayer they confirm that 'there is no further tax to pay on dividends'.

However, in the tax year his income takes him into the higher rate bands. He misses the dividends off his return on the basis he thinks he has no further tax to pay.

HMRC agree that in these circumstances he has taken reasonable care and charge him no penalty.

Example 53.2 – Penalty for inaccuracy: understated profits

Susan Chambers is the finance director of a large company with several branches across the UK. Under pressure of work she signs off the tax return not noticing that figures used were picked up from an early draft document setting out the company profit which has subsequently been altered. By doing this, profits had been understated by £10,000.

The problem is spotted by HMRC and, when asked, Susan sees immediately what has happened. As clearly there has been a failure to take reasonable care when completing the return, a penalty will be charged.

NATURE OF INACCURACY

53.11 A 'careless' error is one where reasonable care has not been taken.

A 'deliberate' inaccuracy is one where a taxpayer knowingly sent an incorrect document to HMRC.

A 'deliberate and concealed' inaccuracy is where a taxpayer knowingly sends in an incorrect document and then takes steps to try and hide that inaccuracy.

Example 53.3 – Deliberate inaccuracy

Greg Davies runs a small shop. When completing his tax return, he adds up his sales for the year but realises that he will struggle to pay the tax on the level of profit that gives. He therefore decides to transfer the final two months of sales through to next year's tax return.

HMRC pick up the problem on a VAT visit and Greg admits to what he has done. His actions are classified by HMRC as deliberate and a penalty is charged accordingly.

Example 53.4 – Deliberate and concealed inaccuracy

Vernon Smith is a freelance journalist. In calculating his taxable profit for the year he 'estimates' his expenditure which gives rise to a significant drop in the taxable profit for the year. When asked about the way he has worked out his expenses he tells HMRC that they were based on diary entries and receipts that he has lost. He produces a spreadsheet which adds up to the figure used in his return.

When questioned, he admits that he didn't actually keep any receipts, that some of the expenses on the spreadsheet were 'really just made up' and that the figures used were wrong.

He is charged a penalty on the basis that the inaccuracy was deliberate and concealed.

BEHAVIOURS WHICH INFLUENCE THE LEVEL OF PENALTY

53.12   Once the nature of the penalty is established, the actual penalty charged within the range set out will be influenced by the way in which the taxpayer deals with the enquiry. In particular HMRC will look at:

- How the taxpayer told HMRC about the inaccuracy, considering when they were told, whether what they were told was full and clear so that the full scope of the problem is identified along with the reasons for the problem arising.

- How the taxpayer has helped HMRC quantify the tax downside, where they will look for positive assistance (as opposed to passive acceptance or obstruction), active engagement in the work to quantify the problem and the volunteering of information related to the issue.

- What access the taxpayer gives HMRC to the relevant papers.

Example 53.5 – Penalty reduction for cooperation

Andy and Rebekah run a news agency. Acting on information received, HMRC challenge their personal tax returns and in both cases it is established that they have submitted returns in which they deliberately entered items which they knew to be wrong. On this basis, the penalty range to be considered is between 35% and 70% of the tax lost.

Rebekah arranges to see HMRC with her advisors and delivers a full explanation of what the problem was and how it arose. HMRC challenge some of these explanations and establish that some changes need to be made. Rebekah instructs her advisors to work with HMRC to agree the tax lost and gives access to her files. At the end of the investigation, HMRC agree a penalty of 40% of the tax lost, given the approach taken by Rebekah.

Andy denies any wrongdoing when challenged by HMRC and only reluctantly finally agrees that there might be an 'issue to answer'. He does not agree to a meeting with HMRC but asks his advisors to try and look for any 'legal loopholes' which will make the allegations go away. He does not respond promptly to questions and HMRC have to dig through a mass of documents they had to obtain through formal channels to try and work out what tax has been lost. At the end of the enquiry, HMRC charge a penalty of 70% of the tax lost, given Andy's lack of cooperation.

Focus

Increasingly, HMRC's approach to enquiry work is guided by the approach taken by the taxpayer both before and during the enquiry process.

This does not mean that the taxpayer must agree with everything HMRC say, but it does mean that clear, prompt and comprehensive responses should be given to any challenge.

AGENTS

53.13 A taxpayer cannot get rid of his responsibility for his return by appointing an agent.

If an agent makes a mistake on a return the error is still the responsibility of the taxpayer (who may, of course, consider taking action against the advisor to recover any loss the taxpayer suffers due to the actions, or inactions of the adviser).

Having said that, the Tax Tribunal has decided in a number of cases that where the issue concerned is complex, the taxpayer should not be penalised for an agent's error. See, for example, *The Research & Development Partnership Ltd* TC 00271 and *Rich v HMRC* [2011] UKFTT 533 (TC). But other cases have been decided against the taxpayer where it was held that the taxpayer could and should have ensured the matter was dealt with. See, for example, *Huntley Solutions Ltd* TC 00272 and *Mr M R Brookes* TC 00423.

To put forward an argument that the taxpayer should not be penalised because of the errors of his agent, it would need to be shown that the tax issues concerned were complex, and the taxpayer was not in a position himself to apply specialist knowledge, and it would have been reasonable for any such taxpayer facing those issues to obtain specialist help. The taxpayer may also be able to establish that he has taken every reasonable step he could to provide the adviser with information, but the delay or error lies entirely with the adviser.

Similar arguments could apply where the adviser makes an error due to misleading advice provided by HMRC, but note that for VAT purposes there is a specific exclusion which prevents reliance on 'any other person' or third party from being a reasonable excuse for VAT purposes (*Value Added Tax Act 1994, s 71*).

INTEREST

53.14   Interest is charged on all taxes (final balances and instalments) paid late. The current rates charged in respect of the main taxes are:

- late payment interest rate – 2.7%;

- repayment interest rate (for overpaid tax) – 0.5% (with effect from 29 September 2009)

For underpaid corporation tax instalments the interest rate is currently 1.25% (with effect from 15 August 2016) and for overpaid instalments the rate is 0.5% (with effect from 21 September 2009).

A full list of current and historic rate can be found on HMRC's website at www.gov.uk/government/publications/rates-and-allowances-hmrc-interest-rates-for-late-and-early-payments/rates-and-allowances-hmrc-interest-rates.

Interest paid by companies is allowable for corporation tax purposes and interest received is liable to corporation tax.

GENERAL ANTI-ABUSE RULE (GAAR)

53.15   The *Finance Act 2016* introduces a new penalty regime for the GAAR which will be triggered when a taxpayer submits to HMRC a return, claim or document that includes arrangements which are later found to come within the scope of the GAAR. The intention of this is to strengthen and deterrent effect of the GAAR, although at the time of writing, no cases have actually been brought before the GAAR advisory panel so you may conclude that the GAAR itself is a sufficient deterrent.

A penalty of 60% of any tax advantage counteracted under the GAAR will be charged and this must be paid within 30 days. There are special rules to calculate the tax advantage where the arrangements result in an unused loss or a deferral of tax due.

The GAAR penalty regime will sit alongside the existing penalty regime however, in situations where a penalty is charged under both, the GAAR penalty will be capped so as to ensure that the combined penalties do not exceed 100% of the amount of tax at stake. Where the arrangements are in relation to offshore matters, the cap is increased to ensure that the maximum penalty under the existing penalty regime can apply (which can be up to 200% of the amount of tax at stake).

The GAAR penalty will apply to transactions entered into on or after 15 September 2016, the date that the *Finance Act 2016* received Royal Assent.

APPENDIX: ERRORS IN RETURNS, ETC

(FA 2007, s 97, Sch 24)

53.16   The position at the time of writing is that where there is a tax offence involving an offshore territory the penalty levels are determined by the category into which the territory falls. This is explained at HMRC compliance handbook manual CH403145 which confirms that the categorisation depends on how readily the offshore jurisdiction shares information with HMRC.

FA 2015 introduced changes to these rules which are expected to be effective from April 2016, and the new rules are covered below.

Category 1 territories are those which have agreed to exchange tax information automatically with the UK. This category includes the UK itself.

Category 2 territories are those which have agreed to exchange tax information with the UK on request.

Category 3 territories are those which have not agreed to share any tax information with the UK.

A list of countries in Category 1 and 3 is set out at HMRC manual CH403147. Any country not on those lists is taken as a Category 2 territory.

The following tables show the penalty regime applying to each category.

Category 1 Territory

53.17

Behaviour	Unprompted disclosure		Prompted disclosure	
	Maximum penalty	**Minimum penalty**	**Maximum penalty**	**Minimum penalty**
Careless	30%	0%	30%	15%
Deliberate but not concealed	70%	20%	70%	35%
Deliberate and concealed	100%	30%	100%	50%

Note

Category 1 information – This is information involving:

(a)   A UK domestic matter; or

(b)   An offshore matter, where the territory is in Category 1 or it is information which would enable or assist HMRC to assess a tax other than income tax or CGT.

Category 2 Territory

53.18

Behaviour	Unprompted disclosure		Prompted disclosure	
	Maximum penalty	**Minimum penalty**	**Maximum penalty**	**Minimum penalty**
Careless	45%	0%	45%	22.5%
Deliberate but not concealed	105%	30%	105%	52.5%
Deliberate and concealed	150%	45%	150%	75%

Note

Category 2 information – This is information involving an offshore matter, in a *Category 2* territory, which would enable or assist HMRC to assess an income tax or CGT liability.

Category 3 Territory

53.19

Behaviour	Unprompted disclosure		Prompted disclosure	
	Maximum penalty	Minimum penalty	Maximum penalty	Minimum penalty
Careless	60%	0%	60%	30%
Deliberate but not concealed	140%	40%	140%	70%
Deliberate and concealed	200%	60%	200%	100%

Note

Category 3 information – This is information involving an offshore matter, in a Category *3* territory, which would enable or assist HMRC to assess an income tax or CGT liability.

Changes to offshore penalties regime

53.20   *FA 2015, ss 120* and *121* introduced changes to the offshore penalties regime, which built on the results of a consultation process. A new Category 0 was introduced which will have the same level of penalty as the current Category 1 territories shown above. Category 0 will apply to those countries deemed to have transparent tax regimes which have adopted the global Common Reporting Standard set out by the OECD.

The detailed changes include:

- raising the maximum penalty levels for Category 1 territories to 125% of the new Category 0 levels;

- introducing a new 'aggravated penalty' of moving the proceeds of tax evasion in order to escape tax transparency, which may increase any penalty charged by 50%. This new power can apply to the movement of funds after 27 March 2015;

- the offshore penalty regime was also extended to include inheritance tax and will cover events where the proceeds of non-compliance are hidden offshore.

These new rules will (apart from the aggravated penalty rule above) take effect from April 2016.

The Summer Budget of 2015 also launched a series of additional consultations which include looking at enhanced civil and criminal penalties for offshore avoidance and evasion. No doubt the results of these consultations will form the basis of further legislation that may be introduced in the coming years.

54

Reporting tax 'schemes'

SIGNPOSTS

- **Disclosure of tax avoidance schemes (DOTAS)** – Taxpayers and agents are required to report tax avoidance schemes to HMRC under the DOTAS provisions. These provisions identify the occasions when a report is required and, although different rules apply to different taxes, the test is based in most cases on whether the arrangement has certain 'hallmarks'. Penalties exist where there is a failure to report a scheme or quote a scheme reference number (see **54.1–54.4**).

- **The General Anti-Abuse Rules (GAAR)** – *Finance Act 2013* introduced the GAAR which radically changed the environment in which taxpayers and their advisors have to work (see **54.5**).

- **Upfront payment of tax** – *Finance Act 2014* introduced the right for HMRC to issue notices requiring upfront payment of tax from any taxpayer who has participated in a scheme notified under DOTAS, rejected by HMRC under the GAAR or which has failed in the courts. In effect, this will require any taxpayer involved in such schemes to pay tax upfront whilst the scheme is being challenged (see **54.6–54.8**).

DISCLOSURE OF TAX AVOIDANCE SCHEMES (DOTAS)

54.1   The DOTAS rules require notification (or disclosure) to be given to HMRC of arrangements (including any scheme, transaction or series of transactions) that will or are intended to provide the user with a tax and/or national insurance advantage when compared to adopting a different course of action.

Any taxpayer who designs and implements their own scheme must disclose it to HMRC within 30 days of it being implemented while promoters of such schemes must disclose them to HMRC within 5 days of certain 'trigger events' which include, for example, making the scheme available for implementation by another person.

There are certain case where, even though the user of the scheme is not responsible for its design, they are themselves responsible for disclosing it to

HMRC. This is the case where, for example, the scheme promotor is based outside of the UK or they are a lawyer and their legal professional privilege prevents them from providing such information required to HMRC.

Where disclosure is required, HMRC must be provided with details of the scheme including what tax advantage is being achieved. This must be provided in the format set out by HMRC, either online or via the completion of the relevant form.

Each scheme so notified will receive a unique eight-digit 'scheme reference number' or 'SRN' which must be provided to any user of the scheme and quoted on their tax return.

The promotor must also provide HMRC with a periodic list of any person to whom they have been required to provide an SRN.

Since this regime was first introduced, many changes have been made to strengthen it and widen its scope, in particular, Schedule 17 to FA 2015 introduced additional rules including:

- requiring employers to notify their employees of involvement in avoidance schemes;

- giving HMRC powers to identify users of undisclosed schemes;

- increasing the penalties for users who do not comply with the DOTAS reporting requirements;

- giving protection to those who volunteer information to HMRC about failures to comply with the DOTAS rules;

- requiring promotors of schemes to notify changes to a disclosed scheme to HMRC; and

- giving HMRC the power to publish information about promotors and schemes.

Penalties of up to £1 million exist in cases where there is a failure to notify a scheme, although separate rules apply for VAT schemes. There are also penalties for failure by the user to quote a SRN on their relevant tax return, these being:

- £100 per scheme for a first occasion;

- £500 per scheme on the second occasion within three years (whether or not it relates to the same scheme); and

- £1,000 per scheme on the third and subsequent occasions (whether or not the failure relates to schemes involved in a previous occasion).

> **Focus**
> Remember that the penalties for users of these schemes are just for failing to write a number on a form!

The DOTAS provisions are wide ranging, complex and somewhat of a moving beast. As such, it is only possible to provide a very brief overview of them within this book and reference should always be made to the relevant legislation (see **54.2**) and the guidance issued by HMRC (see **54.4**).

Legislation

54.2   The primary legislation governing this regime can be found at:

- FA 2004, Pt 7 (as amended);

- TMA 1970, s 98C;

- SSAA 1992, s 132A;

- VATA 1994, Sch 11A.

Although this legislation governs the overriding structure of the provision, details of the types of arrangements which fall within the scope of the regime are set out in secondary legislation, and there are a raft of statutory instruments in this respect.

When the DOTAS regime applies

54.3   All of the major taxes are covered by this regime, although different rules are applied to different taxes, and these are highlighted below. It should be noted though that where arrangements are outside the scope of the DOTAS provisions in respect of one tax, it does not prevent them being brought into the scope of the provisions in relation to another.

Income tax, corporation tax, capital gains tax and national insurance

For these taxes, a tax arrangement must be disclosed when:

- the arrangement enables a person to obtain a tax advantage;

- the tax advantage is at least one of the main benefits of the arrangement; and

- the tax arrangement falls within one of the 'hallmarks'.

The hallmarks looked for in any such arrangement are:

○   the desire to keep the arrangements confidential from competitors;

○   the desire to keep the arrangements confidential from HMRC;

○   the arrangements are ones for which a premium fee could reasonably be charged;

○   the arrangements are 'standardised' or packaged tax products;

○   the arrangements create losses;

○   the arrangements involve certain leasing arrangements;

○   the arrangements are aimed at preventing a charge under the disguised remuneration provisions;

○   the arrangement include a financial product which are directly linked to the tax advantage.

These hallmarks have been amended and extended on a regular basis to ensure that any ambiguity is eliminated and any perceived loopholes are closed. For example, changes made with effect from 23 February 2016 ensure that the standardised product hallmark now looks at the substance of the arrangement (rather than just their legal form) and removes the previous grandfathering provisions in this area (which prevented the need to disclose schemes that were 'substantially the same' as arrangement used before the introduction of this hallmark).

●   *Annual tax on enveloped dwellings (ATED)*

The disclosure regime applies to ATED cases where:

○   there are arrangements to enable an ATED related advantage to be obtained;

○   the advantage is a main benefit of the transaction;

○   the arrangements alter the ownership or value of the property in order that it would fall outside of the scope of the ATED provisions; and

○   the arrangements are not excluded.

Excluded arrangements for this purpose include the transfer of property on commercial terms, between certain companies in the same group or by way of a distribution in certain cases.

●   *Stamp duty land tax (SDLT)*

The disclosure regime relating to SDLT applies in cases where:

○   there are arrangements to enable an SDLT advantage to be obtained; and

○   the advantage is a main benefit of the transaction.

Where the arrangements comprise certain steps or certain combinations of those steps, there is no need to disclose. This sets out an effective 'white list' of SDLT arrangements that are outside the scope of the regime.

There are also grandfathering provisions, which exclude certain transactions being brought into account, where they are 'substantially the same' as arrangements that were available before 1 April 2010 (although a number of arrangements are 'carved out' from this exclusion).

● *Inheritance tax (IHT)*

An IHT scheme will be disclosable in cases where:

○   the scheme results in property becoming 'relevant property' as defined under *IHTA 1984, s 58(1)*; and

○   the reduction, deferral or avoidance of an IHT entry charge is the main benefit of the scheme.

As such, arrangements where the aim is to avoid or reduce the IHT entry charge when transferring property into trust will be within the scope of the regime.

Schemes which are the same or substantially the same as arrangements made available before 6 April 2011 are currently exempted from disclosure under what are known as the grandfathering provisions. However, as part of a wider consultation of the DOTAS regime in 2015, significant changes were proposed to the provisions relating to IHT including the removal of the these grandfathering provisions.

There was significant concern within the profession that the proposals put forward in that consultation would bring many aspects of 'normal' IHT planning into the regime and that, although some safeguards were proposed, these were not robust enough. As a result, the majority of the changes proposed have been deferred (subject to a further consultation during 2016) but with effect from 23 February 2016 the confidentiality and premium fee hallmarks (as applicable to income tax etc) will apply for the purpose of IHT too.

● *Value added tax*

VAT scheme disclosure must be made where a taxable person is a party to a scheme which results in a 'relevant event', their turnover exceeds a minimum threshold and either:

○   the scheme is a listed scheme, or

○   the scheme is not a listed scheme but contains one or more hallmarks and has a main purpose of obtaining a tax advantage.

Relevant events for this purpose occur where:

○ a VAT return is submitted which reflects different figures than those that would have been used;

○ a VAT claim is made on figures higher than would have been claimed;

○ at any time where less non-deductible VAT arises than would have done had the scheme not taken place.

A listed scheme is one that involves:

○ the first grant of a major interest in a building;

○ payment handling services;

○ value shifting;

○ leaseback agreements;

○ extended approval periods;

○ groups and third party suppliers;

○ education and training by a non-profit making body;

○ education and training by a non-eligible body;

○ cross-border face-value vouchers;

○ a surrender of a relevant lease.

The hallmarks for the purpose of VAT are:

○ confidentiality agreements;

○ agreements to share a tax advantage;

○ contingent fee agreements;

○ prepayments between connected parties;

○ funding by loans, share subscriptions or subscriptions in securities;

○ off-shore loops;

○ property transactions between connected persons;

○ issue of face-value vouchers.

Guidance and forms

54.4 HMRC produce a full guidance note to these issues which can be found on the HMRC website at: www.gov.uk/government/publications/disclosure-of-tax-avoidance-schemes-guidance.

Separate guidance is provided for the disclosure of VAT schemes at: www.gov.uk/government/publications/vat-notice-7008-disclosure-of-vat-avoidance-schemes/vat-notice-7008-disclosure-of-vat-avoidance-schemes#the-listed-schemes.

Details of the forms on which disclosure can be made can be found at: www.gov.uk/guidance/forms-to-disclose-tax-avoidance-schemes.

THE GENERAL ANTI-ABUSE RULE (GAAR)

54.5   The *Finance Act 2013, ss 206–215* introduced a GAAR which applies to the following taxes with effect to any arrangement entered into on or after 17 July 2013:

- income tax;

- capital gains tax;

- inheritance tax;

- corporation tax (including any sum charged as if it was corporation tax, such as CFC, bank levy, tonnage tax);

- diverted profit tax;

- petroleum revenue tax;

- SDLT; and

- ATED.

Separate legislation is contained in the *National Insurance Contributions Act 2014* to extend the GAAR to national insurance contributions with effect from March 2014.

The GAAR is based on the premise that all taxpayers must pay their 'fair' contribution. It rejects the notion (expressed in a number of past court judgements) that a taxpayer can use whatever legal stratagems they wish to reduce their tax bill, even if the tax outcome was at odds with the economic reality.

This was expressed in HMRC's guidance note to these rules which states that:

'Taxation is not to be treated as a game where taxpayers can indulge in any ingenious scheme in order to eliminate or reduce their tax liability.'

Links to the guidance notes can be found at www.gov.uk/government/publications/tax-avoidance-general-anti-abuse-rules.

The stated aim of the GAAR is to act as a deterrent to taxpayers entering into (and promoters promoting) abusive tax schemes. If a taxpayer is not deterred and goes ahead with an abusive tax scheme the GAAR provides for counteraction steps to be taken which prevents the tax advantage being sought.

It is important to understand that the GAAR does not replace the existing tax law but it does have precedence over all the taxes it applies to, and applies to 'tax arrangements' that are 'abusive'.

Tax arrangements are defined to mean any arrangement which has at its main purpose (or one of its main purposes) obtaining a tax advantage.

An abusive arrangement is one where:

- the outcome gives a favourable tax position which Parliament did not anticipate when the tax rules were introduced; and

- the arrangements could not 'reasonably be regarded as reasonable'.

It is clear that these rules contain a mixture of objective and subjective tests, which is always difficult ground for the taxpayer and advisor to work through.

For the GAAR to apply the onus will be on HMRC to show that the arrangements fall within the rules, not on the taxpayer to show that the rules do not apply.

Tax advantage in the GAAR is defined to include

- relief (or increased relief) from tax;

- repayment (or increased repayment of) tax;

- avoidance (or a reduction) of a charge to tax or an assessment to tax;

- avoidance of a possible assessment to tax;

- a deferral of a payment of tax or an advancement of a repayment of tax; and

- avoidance of an obligation to deduct or account for tax.

This is not an exhaustive list and the definition is deliberately widely written.

'Arrangements' includes any:

- agreement;

- understanding;

- scheme; or

- transaction or series of transactions;

whether or not legally enforceable.

Again this definition is deliberately widely written, and can catch not just 'transactions' but also any element of a wider set of actions that as a whole might be presented (one might say 'dressed up') as having a commercial purpose.

To decide if an arrangement is abusive a number of questions will be considered:

- Was this a reasonable course of action in relation to the relevant tax provisions?

- How do the substantive results of arrangements compare with the principles on which the relevant tax provisions are based?

- Did the means of achieving the results involve contrived or abnormal steps?

- Did the arrangements intend to exploit any shortcomings in the relevant tax provisions?

- Do the arrangements pass the 'double reasonableness' test – whether the arrangements 'cannot reasonably be regarded as a reasonable course of action'.

Examples of the initial HMRC thinking on how these questions will be considered are contained in the guidance notes. The legislation sets out some indicators of what is, and what is not, an abusive arrangement.

Abusive arrangements might be indicated by arrangements resulting in:

- an amount of income, profits or gains for tax purposes that is significantly less than the amount for economic purposes;

- deductions or losses of an amount for tax purposes significantly greater than the amount for economic purposes; or

- a claim for the repayment or crediting of tax (including foreign tax) that has not been, and is unlikely to be, paid.

However, where the arrangements are:

- in line with established practice; or

- HMRC had (at the time when the arrangements were entered into) indicated its acceptance of that practice;

then that would be indicative that the arrangements were not abusive.

If, after applying the above tests, HMRC conclude that:

- there has been an arrangement that gives rise to a tax advantage;
- the tax advantage relates to a tax covered by the GAAR;
- it is reasonable to conclude that obtaining the tax advantage was the main purpose (or one of the main purposes) of the arrangement;

then that would be indicative that the arrangement was abusive.

Then an adjustment can be made to counteract the tax advantage in a 'just and reasonable' way. This is aimed to ensure that the counteraction gives rise to the most likely tax outcome had the abusive arrangement not been entered into, rather than to maximise the tax yield of HMRC. The reader might share the author's concern that the application of this principle will run counter to some of HMRC's actions in investigation cases in the past.

The counteraction can take the form of making or modifying assessments, amending or disallowing claims but is not limited to these approaches.

For a counteraction to be successful HMRC must apply to the Advisory Panel all of whom will be independent of HMRC itself who will give a view on whether such an approach is appropriate, based on the facts as presented by HMRC and responded to by the taxpayer.

If, following the Advisory Panel guidance, HMRC continue with the counteraction the case could proceed to tribunal or court, but in such cases it will be for HMRC to show that the GAAR applies, not for the taxpayer to show that it does not apply. This is a reversal of the rules normally governing appeals against HMRC assessments, etc.

Focus

HMRC attack what they see as abusive planning schemes and taxpayers need to be aware of both the legal and practical consequences of entering into such planning devices.

It is neither illegal nor inappropriate for anyone to manage their financial affairs to mitigate their tax burden. But, where the result is far removed from might be regarded as 'commercial common sense', there should be no surprise when HMRC robustly challenge such arrangements.

The *Finance Act 2016* introduced changes to allow for HMRC to make provisional counteractions under the GAAR and to allow for an opinion of the GAAR Advisory Panel to be applied to counteract equivalent arrangements by other users. Furthermore, a new GAAR penalty was also introduced (see **53.15**).

ACCELERATED PAYMENTS OF TAX

54.6   Legislation was introduced in *Pt 4* of *FA 2014* and the *National Insurance Contributions Act 2015 (s 4* and *Sch 2) to* enable HMRC to collect tax 'upfront' in cases where tax avoidance schemes are being used.

Finance Act 2015 extended the law to situations involving a loss or other amount which has been claimed or surrendered as group relief.

The legislation allows HMRC to use Follower Notices and Accelerated Payment Notices to overturn the tax advantage claimed through the use of a tax avoidance scheme and recover the tax.

Issue of a 'Follower Notice'

54.7   This notice will state that HMRC believe that the taxpayer has taken advantage of a scheme which has been defeated in the courts.

HMRC cannot issue a Follower Notice unless:

* for tax – either an enquiry has been opened into a return or an appeal has been made against a closure notice, assessment, or determination;

* for NICs – either a relevant contributions dispute is in progress or an appeal has been made against a NICs decision.

The taxpayer should, therefore, already be aware that their arrangements are being challenged by HMRC.

In addition, it must be shown that the return being enquired into, or subject to appeal, involves the use of a tax avoidance arrangement, there is a judicial ruling which applies to those arrangements and no previous Follower Notice related to this matter has been issued.

The Follower Notice must be issued within 12 months of the later of the date of the return or appeal or the applicable judicial ruling. The taxpayer will have 90 days from the issue of the notice to take corrective action to amend the return or claim to counteract the impact of the savings claimed.

Representations can be made against the Follower Notice within those 90 days but there is no right of appeal against the notice to the tribunal. HMRC will either withdraw the notice or confirm it. In such cases the deadline for taking corrective action is extended to 30 days from the date of HMRC's confirmation of the notice or any other date set by that confirmation letter.

If corrective action is not taken then a penalty of up to 50% will be imposed based on the 'denied advantage', effectively the tax advantage originally claimed which is being challenged.

Accelerated Payment Notices (APNs)

54.8   If corrective action is taken after a Follower Notice then the taxpayer will be required to pay the tax admitted in the normal way. Failure to take corrective action will lead to HMRC issuing an APN.

These notices can be given either where the taxpayer:

- has been given a Follower Notice;
- has used a DOTAS notifiable arrangement;
- is subject to a GAAR counteraction notice.

Again, these notices can only be used where there is an open enquiry or appeal and a tax advantage has arisen from the arrangements being challenged.

On receipt of an APN the taxpayer must pay the sum demanded within 90 days of the notice.

As with Follower Notices, representations can be made to HMRC against the APN but there is no right of appeal. If representations are made, the due date for payment is the later of the original 90 days or 30 days from the date HMRC issues its decision on the representation (unless, of course, HMRC withdraw the APN, which in practice is highly unlikely).

Full guidance on Follower Notices and APNs is issued by HMRC at www.gov.uk/government/publications/follower-notices-and-accelerated-payments/follower-notices-and-accelerated-payments.

55

Record keeping

SIGNPOSTS

- **Scope** – There are legal requirements to keep records and for tax purposes these requirements will depend on the specific rules of the taxes involved (see **55.1–55.2**).

- **What records must be kept?** – The particular legislative requirement to keep records varies according to the tax, etc concerned. The tax requirements are in addition to any other regulatory requirements, such as those relating to the *Companies Act 2006* (see **55.3–55.6**).

- **Penalties** – Failure to keep records will lead to problems in complying with the wider tax requirement to make accurate and timely returns. Penalties exist for failure to keep records (see **55.7**).

INTRODUCTION

55.1   Whilst there is no statutory requirement regarding the form in which business records are kept, there are legislative requirements that documents should be retained which support the tax returns, etc which a taxpayer must make.

Whatever record method is chosen, the taxpayer needs to be in a position to provide information to HMRC to support entries on tax returns and to answer any legitimate queries raised. Appropriate and contemporaneous original documentation must be kept for the required time.

Over and above any legal requirements, it is good practice to have documentary evidence available to deal with any enquiries, as without evidence HMRC may argue for interpretations of the facts which can lead to a higher tax bill.

Legislation

55.2   *FA 2008, Sch 37* amended the existing record-keeping legislation (in particular *TMA 1970, s 12B, Sch 1A, para 2A*) in a move to align the record-keeping requirements across a number of taxes. The *FA 2008* changes took effect from 1 April 2009 and impacted on:

- income tax;
- capital gains tax;
- corporation tax;
- direct taxes claims not included in a return; and
- VAT.

Further changes made by *FA 2009, Sch 50* took effect from 1 April 2010 and made similar amendments to:

- insurance premium tax;
- stamp duty land tax;
- aggregates levy;
- climate change levy; and
- landfill tax.

In addition, record keeping requirements apply to:

- bank payroll tax from 8 April 2010; and
- excise duties from 1 April 2011.

Quality of records

55.3   As mentioned above, the precise format of the records kept is a decision for the taxpayer, but whatever records are kept must be up to date and contain sufficient detail to allow correct and complete returns to be made, allow a correct calculation of tax to be paid or claimed, and allow HMRC to check the figures.

For limited companies, the requirements of *Companies Act 2006, s 386* must also be considered.

What records must be kept – legal requirements

55.4   As mentioned at **55.2**, there are legislative requirements to keep records. The details vary according to the tax concerned, as the following brief outline sets out:

- *Income tax, capital gains tax and corporation tax*

The taxes are all covered by the general rule requiring that records must allow the delivery of a correct and complete tax return – this applies to personal tax returns, partnership tax returns and trust tax returns (*TMA 1970, s 12B(1)*) as well as corporation tax returns (*FA 1998, Sch 18, para 21(1)*).

For taxpayers carrying on a trade, profession or business (including that of property letting), whether alone or in partnership, there are specific requirements to maintain records of all receipts and expenses in the course of the trade, profession or business, or company activities, detailing the matters covered by those receipts and expenses and recording sales and purchases made 'in the course of any trade involving dealing in goods' (*TMA 1970, s 12B(3)*).

Similar provisions apply to companies (*FA 1998, Sch 18, para 21(5)*).

● *Direct taxes claims not included in a return*

These rules cover claims made by a taxpayer and the general rule is that records must be kept to allow a correct and complete claim to be made (*TMA 1970, Sch 1A, para 2A*).

● *VAT*

Taxpayers must keep the records HMRC specify in regulations. Some VAT special schemes have detailed accounting requirements, and if a VAT-registered person wants or is required to use a special scheme then they must keep the records laid down for that scheme.

The VAT regulations require that the following records must be kept (*VATA 1994, Sch 11, para 6; SI 1995/2518, regs 31, 31A, 31B, 168*):

○ business and accounting records;

○ a VAT account;

○ a refunds for bad debts account;

○ copies of all VAT invoices issued or received;

○ acquisitions of goods from other EU member states and supplies of goods or services where those acquisitions or supplies are either zero-rated or treated as taking place outside the UK;

○ documentation received relating to acquisitions of goods from other EU member states;

○ copy documentation issued or received relating to the transfer, dispatch or transportation of goods to other EU member states;

○ documentation relating to imports and exports;

  o credit notes, debit notes, or other documents that are received or issued which show an increase or decrease in consideration;

  o any self-billing agreement to which they are a party including the name, address and VAT registration number of each supplier with whom they have entered into any self-billing agreement.

• *Insurance premium tax*

A taxpayer carrying on insurance business will need to keep specific records for insurance premium tax purposes including (*FA 2009, Sch 50, para 1; SI 1994/1774*):

  o business and accounting records;

  o copies of all invoices, renewal notices, etc;

  o policy documents, cover notes, endorsements, etc (or copies of those documents);

  o credit and debit notes (or any other documents) which show an increase or decrease in the amount of any premiums due (or copies of such documents); and

  o for businesses which are taxable intermediaries, records relating to any fees charged.

• *Stamp duty land tax*

Legislation requires that a purchaser must keep records to enable them to make and deliver a correct and complete return. This will require the retention of documents relating to the transaction, including contracts or conveyances, supporting maps, plans or similar documents as well as records of payments, receipts, etc (*FA 2003, Sch 10, para 9; FA 2009, Sch 50, para 5*).

• *Aggregates levy, climate change levy and landfill tax*

Legislation sets out the detailed requirements for records that should be kept in respect of these taxes (*FA 2001, Sch 7, paras 2, 3; FA 2000, Sch 6, para 125; FA 1996, Sch 5, para 2; FA 2009, Sch 50, paras 15–21*).

How should records be kept?

55.5 A taxpayer can meet his obligations by either keeping the original records or by preserving the information contained in them.

But some original records must be kept, and these are:

• any written statement showing the value of a qualifying distribution and the associated tax credit;

- any written statement showing income tax deducted from a payment;

- any written statement showing a payment under a construction contract, detailing the gross and net sums received; and

- records required to make an accurate claim for tax paid under non-UK law (or the tax that would have been paid had the tax not been covered by a double tax agreement).

For other records, the preservation of the information in the form of photocopied, computerised or electronic versions is acceptable as long this captures the information needed to make a correct and complete return, and the information can be reproduced in a legible form (*TMA 1970, s 12B, Sch 1A, para 2A; FA 1998, Sch 18, para 22; VATA 1994, Sch 11, paras 6, 6A; FA 2008, s 114; FA 2010, Sch 1, para 34; CEMA 1979, s 118A*).

How long do records need to be retained?

55.6   The rules will vary depending on the taxes to which the records relate. The rules are as follows:

Income tax and capital gains tax:

Where a taxpayer carries on a trade, profession or business, records must be retained until the latest of the following (*TMA 1970, s 12B*):

- where the return is for a tax year, the fifth anniversary of the 31 January next following the year of assessment;

- where the return is for a period that is not a tax year, the sixth anniversary of the end of the period;

- the completion of an enquiry into the return; and

- the day on which the enquiry window for that return closes without an enquiry being opened.

Where a taxpayer does not carry on a trade etc, records must be retained until the latest of:

- the first anniversary of 31 January next following the year of assessment;

- the completion of an enquiry into the return; and

- the day on which the enquiry window for that return closes without an enquiry being opened.

55.6 *Record keeping*

Corporation tax

For companies and unincorporated associations, records must be retained until the latest of the following (*FA 1998, Sch 18, para 21; CA 2006, s 388*):

- the sixth anniversary of the end of the accounting period;
- the date any enquiry into the return is completed; and
- the day on which the enquiry window for the return closes without an enquiry being opened.

Direct taxes claims not included in a return

Records to support a claim must be retained until the later of the following (*TMA 1970, Sch 1A, para 2A*):

- the date any enquiry into the claim or amended claim is completed; and
- the day after the enquiry window closes without an enquiry being opened.

PAYE and construction industry scheme

For employers or those who make payments under the construction industry scheme, records must be kept for three years after the end of the tax year to which they relate.

However, note that if these records are also required to make a return of business profits, the longer period for holding records as set out above must be complied with (*SI 2003/2682, reg 97(1); SI 2005/2045, 51(10)*).

Insurance premium tax (IPT)

IPT records must be kept for six years although HMRC may agree a shorter record keeping period (*FA 1994, Schs 6, 6A, 7; SI 1994/1774; FA 2009, Sch 50, para 5*).

Stamp duty land tax

A purchaser must keep relevant records until the later of the following (*FA 2003, Sch 10, para 9, Sch 11A, para 3; FA 2009, Sch 50, para 5*);

- the sixth anniversary of the effective date of the transaction (or an earlier date if specified by HMRC); and
- the date an enquiry into the return is completed, or the date on which HMRC no longer has the power to enquire into the return.

Aggregates levy, climate change levy and landfill tax

These records must be kept for six years, although HMRC may agree a shorter record-keeping period (*FA 2001, Sch 7, paras 2, 3; FA 2000, Sch 6, para 125; FA 1996, Sch 5, para 2; FA 2009, Sch 50, paras 15–21*).

VAT

There is a required six–year retention period for VAT records (*VATA 1994, Sch 11, paras 6, 6A*) such as:

- Documents that record individual events should be retained for six years from the date of issue.

- Documents that summarise matters (eg a set of accounts) should be retained for six years from the date they are prepared.

- Documents which record a series of transactions (such as a ledger book) should normally be retained for six years from the date of the last entry.

Excise duties

Records must be kept for six years, although HMRC may agree a shorter record-keeping period (*CEMA 1979, s 118A*).

PENALTIES FOR FAILURE TO KEEP RECORDS

55.7

Focus

Legislation provides for a penalty of up to £3,000 for each failure to keep or to preserve adequate records in support of a tax return (*TMA 1970, s 12B(5)*).

Traditionally these penalties (and others related to failure to keep records) have only been imposed in the most serious cases and have often been superseded by the penalties related to the failures (for example, to make accurate and timely returns) that stem from the failure to keep such records.

Part 10
Leaving or Arriving in the UK

Residence and domicile

SIGNPOSTS

- **Scope** – Residence and domicile of an individual are key factors in determining liability to UK tax. Individuals who are UK resident and domiciled are normally subject to UK tax on worldwide income and gains, whether remitted to the UK or not (see **56.1–56.2**).

- **The statutory residence test** – From April 2013, there are a series of tests that must be worked through in order to determine the residence status of an individual (see **56.3–56.5**); previously the position was determined largely from case law.

- **Domicile** – This is a concept of general law which has relevance for income tax, capital gains tax and inheritance tax, the latter having an extended definition (ie 'deemed' domicile). Your domicile is not fixed and may change. Major changes are proposed from 6 April 2017 which extend the concept of deemed domicile to all taxes (see **56.6**).

- **Compliance issues** – The determination of an individual's status is now part of the self-assessment regime and a claim for not UK resident or domiciled status is made by completing supplementary pages to the self-assessment return (see **56.7**).

RESIDENCE AND DOMICILE – OUTLINE OF TERMS

56.1   Unlike many other countries which use a relatively straightforward arithmetic test for residence, the UK did not have a single statutory definition of residence and the position was determined by looking at HMRC practice and decided cases, and was set out in HMRC6 which is available on the HMRC website (www.gov.uk/government/publications/hmrc6). It was also covered in detail in Chapter 58 of *Bloomsbury Professional Tax Guide 2012/13* (The TACS Partnership).

The potential problems caused by relying on HMRC practice was illustrated by a number of high profile tax cases where individuals believed that they had achieved non-resident status based on HMRC6 but were eventually held to be resident by the courts (eg *Robert Gaines-Cooper v HMRC* [2011] UKSC 47).

Proposals for a Statutory Residence Test were released in June 2011 and were enacted with effect from 6 April 2013 (*FA 2013, s 215, Sch 45*). The rules are by no means simple as *Sch 45* stretches to over 50 pages and includes a number of new concepts. There was a lot of criticism of the new rules in the professional press, mainly for the complexity and length of the provisions but also for the subjective concepts introduced, such as 'home'. In some simple cases, it is possible to apply the rules and determine residence status quite quickly; unfortunately for many individuals with more complicated lifestyles, the position will be far from clear.

HMRC have issued a Guidance Note on the provisions with a number of useful examples (www.gov.uk/government/publications/rdr3-statutory-residence-test-srt).

The Statutory Residence Test determines an individual's residence status for income tax and capital gains tax but not National Insurance contributions.

Residence usually requires an individual to be physically present in the UK, and if he is in the UK for 183 days or more in a tax year, he is classed as a resident in the UK.

Up to 6 April 2013 *ordinary residence* was also relevant for tax purposes, but that is no longer the case (*FA 2013, s 219, Sch 46*).

Domicile is a matter of general law, not tax law, and an individual is normally domiciled in the country where he has his permanent home.

> **Focus**
>
> Since different countries have different rules on residence, it is possible to be tax resident in more than one country at the same time under their respective domestic provisions.

LIABILITY TO UK TAX – OUTLINE

56.2   A UK resident individual is normally liable to income tax on his worldwide income. Special deductions apply to the earned income of seafarers who work abroad for a 'qualifying period', and to overseas pensions.

Normally, worldwide income includes foreign income arising irrespective of whether the income is brought into the UK. However, individuals who are UK resident but not UK domiciled may be taxed on the remittance basis, ie only on foreign income which is remitted to the UK (see **Chapter 57**).

Individuals who are UK resident and UK domiciled are liable to capital gains tax on worldwide gains as they arise. Individuals who are UK resident but not UK domiciled may be taxed on gains on the remittance basis (see **Chapter 57**).

Liability to inheritance tax is determined on the basis of domicile so that a UK domiciled individual is subject to UK inheritance tax on their worldwide assets, whereas an individual domiciled elsewhere is only charged on UK property. An extended definition of domicile applies for inheritance tax which takes account of residence in the UK over a period (*IHTA 1984, s 267*) (see **27.3**).

THE NEW STATUTORY RESIDENCE TEST

56.3   The new rules require an individual to work methodically through a series of tests:

- *The automatic overseas tests* – An individual is automatically non-resident for a tax year if he meets any one of these tests (*FA 2013, Sch 45, paras 11–16*).

- *The automatic residence tests* – An individual is automatically resident in the UK for a tax year if he meets any one of these tests (*FA 2013, Sch 45, paras 6–10*).

- *The sufficient ties test* – If an individual's status has not been decided by the previous tests then this is used to determine the position (*FA 2013, Sch 45, paras 17–20*).

Most people will not have to use the sufficient ties tests as their status will be determined as being either resident or non-resident from the automatic overseas or residence tests.

It is not anticipated that the new rules will change the status of a large number of individuals. Most people will retain their status under the old rules, either resident or non-resident, unless there is a change in their circumstances.

Automatic overseas test

56.4   The rules are set out below in the form of a decision tree.

The automatic overseas tests

Test 1 – you are resident in the UK for one or more of the previous three tax years and spend fewer than 16 days in the UK in the tax year	YES	Non-resident
Test 2 – you are non-resident for the whole of the three previous tax years and spend fewer than 46 days in the UK in the tax year	YES	Non resident
Test 3 – you work full-time overseas in the tax year without any significant breaks (31 days or more when not working for at least three hours per day) and spend fewer than 91 days in the UK in the tax year and the number of days in the tax year when more than three hours are spent working in the UK are fewer than 31	YES	Non resident

If the answer is NO to the above three tests continue

The automatic residence tests

Test 1 – you spend 183 days or more on the UK in the tax year	YES	Resident
Test 2 – there is a period of 91 consecutive days (at least 30 days in the tax year) when you have a home in the UK in which you spend at least 30 days during the tax year and either you have no overseas home, or have one or more homes overseas in none of which you spend more than 30 days in the tax year	YES	Resident
Test 3 – you work full-time in the UK for 365 days or more with no significant break from UK work and all or part of that work period falls within the tax year, and on more than 75% of that 365 day period you perform more than three hours of work in the UK and at least one day in the tax year is a day when you work for more than three hours in the UK	YES	Resident

If the answer is NO to the above three tests continue

The sufficient ties tests

Family tie – UK resident family

Accommodation tie – accessible accommodation in the UK used for at least one night

Work tie – works in the UK for at least 40 days in the tax year

90-day tie – spent more than 90 days in the UK in either of the previous two tax years

Country tie – present in the UK for at least as many days as in any other single country (only relevant for residents leaving the UK)

Count how many of the ties are satisfied and how many days are spent in the UK and apply the tables below

Days in UK	Number of ties Individual coming to the UK	Number of ties Individual leaving the UK
<16	Always non-resident	Always non-resident
16–45	Always non-resident	Resident if 4 or more ties
46–90	Resident if 4 or more ties	Resident if 3 or more ties
91–120	Resident if 3 or more ties	Resident if 2 or more ties
121–182	Resident if 2 or more ties	Resident if 1 or more ties
>183	Always resident	Always resident

In the above table, the sufficient ties test distinguishes between 'arrivers' and 'leavers' and it is harder for 'leavers' to become non-resident as they have to meet a more stringent day count.

Accessible accommodation in the sufficient ties test does not have to be property owned by the individual, for example' it could be owned by a close relative or be holiday accommodation. There are provisions which can apply if accommodation is regularly let out for periods with the intention of ensuring that it is not available for use.

The HMRC website has a useful Tax Residence indicator tool which can be found at tools.hmrc.gov.uk/rift/screen/SRT+-+Combined/en-GB/ summary?user=guest.

Focus

Days spent in the UK are key to many of the tests, therefore it is important for an individual to keep records of visits to the UK including supporting evidence such as flight tickets and boarding cards. A detailed diary, showing dates spent in each country, where he is staying and whether he is working and for what hours, may also be helpful including other evidence, such as visa applications. Invoices for accommodation costs should also be retained as well as correspondence with other agencies such as insurance companies and local authorities.

Normally, a person is considered to have spent a day in the UK if he is here at the end of the day. However, for the purpose of the sufficient ties test, in some circumstances, it is necessary to count days when he is deemed to be in the UK, ie where he has left before the end of the day.

The following examples show the use of the Automatic Overseas, Automatic Residence and Sufficient Ties Tests.

Example 56.1 – The automatic overseas tests

Rudy has lived in Russia all his life. In July 2015 he comes to the UK for a holiday, spending a month in the UK (31 days). He decides to move to the UK permanently in 2016/17.

Rudy will be non-resident for 2015/16 based on Test 2. His status for 2016/17 will have to be checked when the information is available. His intention to move to the UK is irrelevant.

Example 56.2 – The automatic residence tests

Charles has lived on Merseyside all his life and his home is there. He decides to spend some time travelling around the world before he goes to university.

During 2015/16 he visits a number of different countries but does not establish a home overseas. Between trips he returns briefly to Merseyside and is present there on 41 days in tax year 2015/16.

Charles is present in his UK home on at least 30 days during tax year 2015/16 (Test 2) and does not meet any of the automatic overseas tests. He is therefore UK resident for 2015/16.

Example 56.3 – The sufficient ties tests

Alex and his wife Catherine both spend 140 days in the UK in a tax year.

Neither of them was resident in any of the three previous tax years.

They have a house in the UK and a villa in Spain and do not work. They have no close family members who are resident in the UK.

They are not conclusively non-resident based on the automatic non-residence test because they have spent more than 46 days in the UK.

They are not conclusively resident based on the automatic residence test as they have a home overseas.

As individuals coming to the UK they only have one obvious tie – accessible accommodation in the UK which they used.

Based on this, they would both be non-resident as with 140 days in the UK they would each need two ties to be resident.

Their family tie to each other in determining their residence status can be ignored.

OTHER PROVISIONS IN THE NEW RULES

56.5   There are special rules which are beyond the scope of this book to deal with 'international transportation workers' such as pilots, aircrew and lorry drivers.

There are also special rules for determining the status of individuals who die in the year.

Normally an individual is either resident or non-resident for a tax year but, as in the old rules, there are provisions for splitting the year into a period of residence and a period of non-residence if an individual leaves the UK to live or work abroad, or comes to the UK to live or work or joins his partner who is working abroad. The rules are complicated but the following example is a simple illustration of how they work.

Example 56.4 – Split year treatment

Christopher has lived in the UK for the whole of his life to date. Now he has graduated, he has decided to work abroad for a charity and gets a job in Africa on a three-year contract. He leaves the UK on 1 September 2015.

He returns to visit his family at Christmas for two weeks for a holiday.

In 2016/17, he works in Africa for the whole of the year except a two-week Christmas holiday.

In 2015/16 he qualifies for split-year treatment because he was UK resident in 2014/15 and 2015/16 but non-resident for 2016/17 (based on the automatic tests above).

From 1 September 2015 until 5 April 2016 he does not work in the UK at all and only spends 14 days in the UK.

He will be UK resident in 2015/16 until 1 September 2015 and non-resident after that date.

There are special rules for children who are being educated in the UK. Whilst they may be UK resident, in some circumstances, their presence in the UK is not a family tie for their parents.

When counting up the number of days spent in the UK for the various tests mentioned above, it may be possible to ignore some days if presence in the UK is due to exceptional circumstances beyond your control. Examples of such circumstances might be emergencies, such as civil unrest, natural disasters, war or a sudden serious illness or injury to the individual or his spouse or partner.

The new rules apply only from 2013/14 onwards, however, in applying some of the tests it is necessary to know your residence status in earlier years. Normally that would be determined based on the rules applying in those years but the individual can elect to use the new rules for the earlier years when considering his status for 2013/14–2015/16 only. This does not change the actual residence status for years before 2013/14 which is still based on the old rules.

Focus

The new rules are in some ways more generous than the previous position as it may be possible to become non-resident without having to demonstrate a definite break from the UK.

DETERMINING DOMICILE STATUS

56.6   An individual's domicile is the country where he has his permanent home.

At birth a child normally acquires a *domicile of origin* which is the domicile of the child's father and may not be the country where the child was born.

Until an individual has the legal capacity to change it, his domicile is determined as a *domicile of dependency* which means that he takes the domicile of the person he is legally dependent upon. Up to 1974, this rule also applied to married women who automatically took the domicile of their husband.

Once over the age of 16, an individual can acquire a *domicile of choice* by settling in another country indefinitely or permanently.

Example 56.5 – Acquiring a domicile of choice

Sam's father is an Australian domiciled individual, who was working in the UK when Sam was born.

Sam's *domicile of origin* will be Australia.

When he retired, Sam's father left the UK. However, Sam remained here and made the UK his permanent home, but visited his parents occasionally.

Sam has established a *domicile of choice* in the UK.

The current rules for determining domicile status and the tax advantages available to a non-UK domiciliary has been criticised in the press for some time. In particular, the press has highlighted the position of high profile wealthy individuals who appear to benefit from being non-UK domiciled despite them having been in the UK for many years.

In response to this, the government is proposing three main changes which have been consulted on and will be included in *Finance Bill 2017* to take effect from 6 April 2017:

- **The deemed domicile rule for long term residents**

    Individuals who have been UK resident for more than 15 of the past 20 years but who are not UK domiciled under general law will be deemed to be UK domiciled for all UK tax purposes. This means that it will no longer be possible to claim non-domiciled status for an indefinite period of time. It has not been decided whether split years of UK residence count towards the 15 years.

The actual and deemed domicile status of children is looked at independently; at birth they take their father's domicile and will be deemed UK domiciled if the rule for long term residents applies but they do not become UK domiciled just because their parents are deemed UK domiciled.

- **The returning UK domiciliary rule**

  Individuals who are born in the UK with UK domicile will keep that UK domicile for tax purposes whenever they are UK resident even if under general law they have acquired a domicile in another country.

- **A special rule for UK residential property**

  UK residential property owned directly or indirectly by non-domiciled individuals will be subject to UK inheritance tax.

COMPLIANCE AND ADMINISTRATION

56.7   The determination of an individual's status is dealt with under the self-assessment regime. A supplementary page (SA109) has to be completed by an individual who claims to be not resident or not domiciled in the UK, or dual resident in the UK and another country. This form asks for information regarding the facts of the individual's UK stay (in particular the number of days spent in the UK in the current and previous three years) and regarding the individual's future intentions.

As a result of the self-assessment regime, HMRC no longer give residence rulings.

If an individual leaves the UK part of the way through the tax year and thinks that he may be due a tax refund, it is possible to complete a Form P85, which requires information on the individual's circumstances and details of his income after leaving the UK to enable residence status to be considered. This form is available from the HMRC website (www.gov.uk/government/publications/income-tax-leaving-the-uk-getting-your-tax-right-p85).

57

Taxation of individuals not resident in the UK, or not domiciled in the UK

SIGNPOSTS

- **Income tax** – Individuals who are not UK resident may still be liable to UK income tax if they work in the UK or have UK source income (see **57.1**).

- **Capital gains tax** – Non-UK resident individuals may be liable to UK tax under the ATED rules or the charges on sales of UK residential property (see **57.2**).

- **Remittance basis** – The remittance basis is an alternative basis of taxation to the 'arising basis', which otherwise generally applies (see **57.3**).

- **Who qualifies for the remittance basis?** – The remittance basis is generally available to individuals who are UK resident but not UK domiciled (see **57.4**).

- **What qualifies for the remittance basis?** – It broadly applies to foreign income, and gains on foreign assets (see **57.5**).

- **Remittance basis charge** – There is a £30,000, £60,000 or £90,000 'entry fee' (called the 'remittance basis charge') if an individual wishes to be taxed under the remittance basis, although not everyone has to pay (see **57.6**).

- **Calculation and payment of tax** – The mechanics of the remittance basis are not straightforward, as the rules require income or gains to be nominated as deemed remittances to result in tax due of £30,000 (or £60,000 or £90,000) (see **57.7**).

- **Compliance** – Claims for the remittance basis and payment of the remittance basis charge are in general dealt with through the self-assessment system (see **57.8**).

INCOME TAX

57.1   A person who is resident in the UK is in general liable to UK tax under the 'arising basis' so that he pays tax on all his income as it arises, whether from UK or overseas sources, subject to specific exemptions for certain classes of income.

Individuals who are not UK resident (whether or not they are UK domiciled) may still be liable to UK income tax on some of their income as follows:

*   employment income from duties performed in the UK;

*   profits of a trade or profession carried on wholly or partly in the UK;

*   UK pensions;

*   investment income with a UK source.

However, effectively, the UK income tax liability of a non-resident is limited to tax on income from a trade or profession in the UK, a UK property business and tax deducted at source from investment income. This is achieved by taking out of charge 'disregarded' investment income, such as bank interest and dividends (*ITA 2007, ss 811–814*). Although UK dividends no longer carry a tax credit from 6 April 2016, they will continue to be treated as disregarded income for non-UK residents and so there should still be no additional UK income tax liability in respect of the UK dividends received by non-residents.

Example 57.1 – Disregarded income

Victoria and David are non-UK resident throughout 2015/16, but they are each entitled to a basic UK personal allowance. Their UK income tax calculation would normally be as follows, based on their UK income:

	%	Victoria £	David £
Rental income (after expenses) received gross		12,500	18,835
Bank interest received gross		12,060	2,160
Dividends		3,240	
Tax credit on dividend		360	
Total UK income		28,160	20,995
Less: Personal allowance		(10,600)	(10,600)
Taxable UK income		17,560	10,395

Income tax:			
Starting rate for savings £5,000	0	0	0
Basic rate on £8,960/5,395	20	1,792	1,079
Dividend ordinary rate £3,600	10	360	
		2,152	1,079
Less: Dividend tax credit		(360)	
Tax on all UK source income		1,792	1,079
Tax on non-disregarded income – property income		12,500	18,835
At basic rate	20	2,500	3,767
So they pay the lower of the two figures, ie		1,792	1,079

Certain individuals can claim to be taxed under the 'remittance basis' on their foreign source income so that it is taxed in the UK only to the extent that it is remitted to the UK. This claim is available for individuals who are resident in the UK but not domiciled in the UK. This is dealt with in more detail in **57.4** below.

There are also specific rules to tax 'temporary non-residents' on certain income. These rules mirror to some extent the capital gains tax provisions which were introduced in 1998 to tax gains realised by short-term non-residents (see **57.2**), however, only certain types of income are caught. The main aim is to stop people becoming non-UK resident for a relatively short time during which they crystallise income which is not taxable in the UK. The types of income caught by these rules are ones where the taxpayer can influence the date of receipt such as dividends from close companies. The rules basically apply to individuals who have been UK resident in four of the seven years prior to departure and are non-resident for five years or less (*FA 2013, Sch 45, para 109 et seq*).

CAPITAL GAINS TAX

57.2   An individual who is UK resident is in general subject to UK capital gains tax on an arising basis on all gains wherever in the world they arise (*TCGA 1992, s 2(1)*).

Strictly, even if only resident for a part of a year of assessment, then a charge to UK CGT applies for the whole of the year. However, where the conditions of *FA 2013*, *Sch 45*, *para 39* onwards are satisfied, the year can be split so that gains arising when not resident are not subject to UK tax.

Historically, the UK has not charged non-UK residents UK capital gains tax on UK assets, even UK properties. *FA 2013* introduced a CGT charge on high value residential property owned by non-resident, non-natural persons with effect from April 2013 (see **8.20**). Following on from this, a new capital gains charge on non-residents disposing of UK residential property was introduced with effect from 6 April 2015 (*TCGA 1992, ss 14B-14H*).

The rules are complex but in essence they apply to *all* non-resident persons (including companies, trusts, partnerships and personal representatives of non-resident deceased individuals) and tax the profits on UK residential property accruing after 5 April 2015. Properties owned before 5 April 2015 are effectively rebased. (It should be noted that the ATED charge mentioned above has a different rebasing point.) Residential property is a building suitable for use as a dwelling but there are exclusions including boarding schools, hospitals and care homes, hotels and some student accommodation.

There are three different methods of dealing with the rebasing and the taxpayer can choose the one that gives the best result. The alternatives are:

- Using a valuation at April 2015;

- Time-apportioning the gain over the whole ownership period; or

- Taxing the gain/loss over the whole period of ownership.

Focus

The third option is only likely to be attractive if there is a pre-April 2015 loss or an overall loss. However it should be noted that any loss from this calculation can only be used against future gains on UK residential property realised by the same person. If you become UK resident at a later time, any unused losses will be able to be set against any future gain.

The vendor must notify HMRC of a property disposal within 30 days from the day after the conveyance in all cases. If the vendor is covered by self-assessment or ATED, any liability will be dealt with in the normal filing process otherwise a special return is required and the tax must be paid within 30 days. (The form is available on-line at https://online.hmrc.gov.uk/shortforms/form/ NRCGT_Return?dept-name=&sub-dept-name=&location=43&origin=http:// www.hmrc.gov.uk)

The above provisions do not seek to tax property development which is taxed as trading income, although new anti-avoidance provisions were introduced with effect from 16 March 2016 which prevent the use of offshore structures to avoid UK tax on profits from dealing in or developing UK land (see **24.7**). It is possible to claim to be taxed on the remittance basis on foreign gains only if an individual is resident in the UK but not domiciled in the UK (see **57.4**).

For CGT only, a concept of short-term non-residence was introduced in 1998 to prevent individuals from arranging their affairs so that they moved abroad for a relatively short period (but more than a tax year) and became not UK resident or ordinary resident and during the period of non-residence crystallised a significant capital gain outside the UK tax net.

If the individual was a short-term non-resident, ie the period of non-UK residence was less than five full tax years, then on resumption of UK residence, any capital gains in the period of residence abroad were charged to CGT (*TCGA 1992, s 10A*).

These provisions were amended in *Finance Act 2013* to bring them in line with the rules for the income of temporary non-residents (see **57.1**) from 5 April 2013.

> **Focus**
>
> If an individual hopes to escape paying UK income and capital gains tax by becoming non-UK resident, he may have to be prepared to move abroad for more than five tax years.

INTRODUCTION TO THE REMITTANCE BASIS

57.3   The remittance basis is an alternative basis of taxation to the arising basis, in that foreign income and gains are subject to UK tax only when remitted to the UK. By contrast, under the arising basis, which generally applies to UK residents, income and gains are taxed as they arise whether in the UK or elsewhere.

The main legislation on the remittance basis can be found in *ITA 2007, ss 809A–809Z10.*

Additional information about the remittance basis can also be found on the HMRC website in the residence domicile and remittance basis manual at RDRM30000 onwards.

REMITTANCE BASIS – WHO QUALIFIES, AND WHEN?

57.4   The remittance basis generally applies to an individual who is resident but not domiciled in the UK.

Currently, a claim must be made for each year in which that individual wants this basis to apply (*ITA 2007, s 809B*). The Autumn Statement in December 2014 contained a consultation on making the election to pay the charge apply for a minimum of three years but this has not been enacted in view of the other proposals to domicile status in **56.6**. The consequences of making a claim are loss of personal allowances and loss of the capital gains tax annual exempt amount (*ITA 2007, s 809G*).

There are some circumstances where a claim is not necessary (see **57.6** below), and in these cases there is no loss of personal allowances or the annual exempt amount.

> **Focus**
>
> The current government belief is that long term UK resident non-domiciliaries should pay UK tax on their personal worldwide income and gains, regardless of whether the amounts are received in the UK or overseas. Effectively they are hoping to reduce the use of the remittance basis dramatically.

What qualifies?

57.5   For capital gains tax purposes, the remittance basis only applies to an individual who is not domiciled in the UK in respect of his gains on the disposal of foreign assets (*TCGA 1992, s 12*). A foreign asset is one that is situated outside the UK.

There are special rules to determine where an asset is situated (*TCGA 1992, s 275*). For example, shares in a company incorporated in the UK are located in the UK (no matter where the shares are physically held, as used to be the case with bearer shares), foreign currency in a foreign bank account is located outside the UK, and an interest in a foreign property is situated where the property is located.

As noted at **56.6**, it is proposed that, from 6 April 2017, long-term non-domiciled individuals (ie who have been UK resident for more that 15 of the past 20 years) will be deemed to be UK domiciled for all UK tax purposes. The 2016 Budget makes clear that a deemed domiciled individual is only subject to UK CGT on gains after April 2017 so their offshore assets will be automatically rebased at that date.

Paying the remittance basis charge

57.6   Anyone over the age of 18 who is eligible to use the remittance basis, who makes a claim, and who has been UK tax resident for at least seven out of the last nine years ('the 7-year test') preceding the year in question has to make an annual payment of £30,000. For longer term residents, there are higher charges (see below).

The remittance basis charge is in addition to the tax payable on actual remittances. However, a calculated amount of foreign income and foreign gains is taxed on the arising basis so as to give a tax liability of £30,000. The taxpayer has to 'nominate' which income and gains this applies to. If the amount nominated is insufficient, the balance is deemed to be out of foreign income whether or not there is in fact sufficient foreign income to cover it.

Consequently, when nominated income or gains are (deemed to be) remitted to the UK no further tax is payable. However, there are special rules for determining what income or gains are deemed to have been remitted if any nominated income is in fact remitted and any remittance basis income or gains for periods from 6 April 2008 when the remittance basis applied remains unremitted (*ITA 2007, ss 809I–809J*). This has the effect of treating the £30,000 remittance basis charge as only being available to frank the final remittance of income and gains and so maximises the tax payable. As a result the rules are, in HMRC's words, 'very complex' and require quite detailed records to be kept to identify (inter alia) the source of funds, what assets have been purchased out of these funds, what assets have been derived from these assets, and transfers to relevant persons.

'Relevant persons' include spouses, civil partners, cohabitees, children and grandchildren under the age of 18, closely held companies, and trusts in which they or another relevant person is a beneficiary (*ITA 2007, s 809M*).

If there are mixed funds there are special rules for deciding the order in which amounts are deemed to have been withdrawn (*ITA 2007, s 809Q*). Having initially applied these rules to decide whether nominated income has been paid out, the different ordering rules in *s 809I–J* take over if nominated income has been paid out. If it turns out that what has been remitted is capital then the mixed fund rules continue to operate. Perhaps the best policy is to remit nominated income and gains only if and when all other foreign income and gains have been remitted, if at all possible.

Money that is paid directly from abroad to HMRC to settle the £30,000 remittance basis charge will not be treated as a remittance (*ITA 2007, s 809V*). However, if this is refunded for any reason, possibly because a remittance basis claim is not made for that year, it will be treated as a remittance and be taxed accordingly (*ITA 2007, s 809V(2)*). This may be relieved by provisions in *FA 2013, s 21* if the conditions are met.

From 2012/13 to 2014/15 the charge increased to £50,000 for individuals who have been resident in the UK for at least 12 out of the last 14 years ('the 12-year test') (*ITA 2007, s 809C*).

From 2015/16 onwards, the charge is imposed at one of three rates:

- £90,000 for those who have been resident in at least 17 of the 20 immediately preceding tax years ('the 17-year test');

- £60,000 for those who meet the 12-year test but not the 17-year test for the year; and

- £30,000 for those who meet the 7-year test and who do not meet the 17-year and 12-year tests for the year.

The £90,000 charge will become redundant after 6 April 2017 if the provisions in **56.6** are enacted since individuals who have been resident for more than 15 years will no longer be able to benefit from the remittance basis as they will be deemed UK domiciled.

However, a form of relief for remittances used to make business investments was introduced in *FA 2012*. The effect is that the remittance basis charge does not apply to remittances for the purposes of specified commercial investment (ie such amounts are treated as not remitted to the UK), if certain conditions are satisfied (*ITA 2007, ss 809VA–809VO*).

There are two exceptions to the remittance basis charge. One is that minors (people aged below 18) do not have the pay the charge (although they would lose their allowances if they claim to use the remittance basis).

The other exception to this is individuals with unremitted foreign income and/ or gains in the tax year less than £2,000 who can use the remittance basis without having to make a claim (*ITA 2007, s 809D*). They are automatically taxed on the remittance basis and continue to have a UK personal tax allowance and an annual exemption for CGT purposes. In addition, they do not have to pay the remittance basis charge.

In addition there is an exemption intended to cover itinerant workers with relatively low income who would only have a minimal UK tax liability. The conditions for the exemption are:

- You must be UK resident but not UK domiciled;

- You are employed wholly or partly in the UK;

- Your income from overseas employment is less than £10,000 and is all subject to foreign tax;

- Your overseas bank interest is less than £100 and is subject to foreign tax;

- You have no other overseas income or gains;

- Based on worldwide income and gains you are a basic rate or starting rate taxpayer.

If you meet these conditions you are automatically taxed on the arising basis but you are not liable to UK tax on your foreign income either when it arises or when it is brought into the UK and you do not have to claim the remittance basis. *(ITA 2007, s828A-C)*

Focus

The £30,000/£60,000/£90,000 remittance basis charge (which if due is payable in addition to income tax and CGT on remitted income) together with the loss of the personal allowance and CGT annual exemption mean that claiming the remittance basis is only likely to be advantageous in a limited number of cases.

If an individual is eligible to use the remittance basis *and* chooses to use it for a particular tax year, they will still be subject to UK tax on all UK income and gains as they arise in that year. They will only be liable to UK tax on foreign income and gains if and when they bring/remit them to the UK.

Even if an individual qualifies for the remittance basis, he does not *have* to use it and can continue to be taxed on all income and gains on the arising basis. It is necessary to calculate the effect of claiming the remittance basis for a tax year as it will not always save tax when the effect of the loss of allowances and payment of the remittance basis charge are taken into account.

Focus

Effectively, the remittance basis has been withdrawn from all but the very wealthy and individuals with very little overseas income.

Example 57.2 – Whether to claim the remittance basis

Mr P has been resident in the UK a number of years, and is a 40% taxpayer.

He has income arising in the BVI of £3,500 in 2016/17 which has not suffered foreign tax and has not been remitted to the UK.

Tax on the BVI income on the arising basis would be 40% of £3,500, ie £1,400.

The loss of personal allowance in 2016/17 would increase his tax liability by 40% of £11,000 = £4,400.

It is therefore not advantageous for Mr P to claim the remittance basis in that year, whether or not he has to pay the remittance basis charge.

It is also important to note that there are special rules that apply in this context to decide when income or gains have been 'remitted' as it would be relatively easy to arrange to remit funds indirectly, for example by using foreign income to buy assets abroad and then bringing the assets into the UK (*ITA 2007, s 809L*).

A remittance is money or other property deriving from foreign income or gains which is brought directly or indirectly into the UK for an individual's benefit or for the benefit of a 'relevant person'.

Focus

Remittance does not just mean cash sent to the UK, as the scope of 'remittance' was significantly widened so that property, services, debts and gifts may have to be considered.

CALCULATION AND PAYMENT OF TAX ON THE REMITTANCE BASIS

57.7   Where any nominated income has been remitted the rules in *ITA 2007, ss 809I–809J* come into play to determine the order in which remittances are deemed to be made.

Income and gains from a later tax year are deemed to be remitted before those of an earlier tax year ('last in first out' or LIFO) (*ITA 2007, s 809J(1)*).

There are also 'mixed fund' rules which require amounts transferred out of a mixed fund to be identified in a specified order (*ITA 2007, s 809Q* but subject to *s 809J* taking precedence).

> **Focus**
>
> Very careful record keeping is required for anyone who may wish to claim the remittance basis at some stage as some individuals may move between the remittance basis and the arising basis.

TAX RETURNS AND PAYMENTS

57.8   In general, in order to claim to be taxed under the remittance basis, it is necessary to complete a self-assessment tax return including the supplementary pages SA109 ('Residence, remittance basis, etc'). If an individual is not domiciled in the UK and wishes to use the remittance basis for foreign gains, the supplementary pages SA108 ('Capital gains summary') must be completed.

However, if unremitted foreign income and/or gains are less than £2,000 it is not necessary to complete a self-assessment return in order to claim to be taxed on the remittance basis. There may, however, be other reasons why the taxpayer needs to complete a return, and in general it is necessary to complete any return which is issued by HMRC.

The liability to pay the remittance basis charge (see **57.6**) is generated by completion of the relevant pages of the self-assessment return and is treated as a tax payment due on the normal due dates for tax.

To the extent that the remittance basis charge is based on nominated income, it is treated as income tax payable for that particular tax year and will be taken into account in arriving at the payments on account for the following year.

If the remittance basis charge is based on nominated gains, it is charged as CGT which is not taken into account in arriving at payments on account for the following year.

58

Double taxation relief

SIGNPOSTS

- **Scope** – When income and gains are taxed twice, this is referred to as 'double taxation' and most often happens when a person has foreign income, which is taxed in his home country and in the foreign territory (see **58.1**).

- **What relief is available?** – Most developed countries are party to a number of double taxation agreements, which seek to determine who has the right to tax the income or gains. If no agreement exists, 'unilateral' or 'credit relief' may be claimed (see **58.2**).

- **Income tax** – The income tax on foreign dividends received by an individual is generally calculated by imputing a tax credit, as was the case for a UK dividend up to 2015/16 (see **58.3**).

- **Capital gains** – The capital gains tax charged in two jurisdictions can be relieved in a similar way to income tax, but there can be complications if the gain is charged on different taxpayers, or in different periods (see **58.4**).

- **Companies** – Corporation tax is not normally charged on foreign dividends received by a company as they are usually exempt (see **58.5**).

- **Tax on death, lifetime gifts, etc** – Inheritance tax and similar foreign wealth and transfer taxes can usually be relieved under treaty or unilaterally (see **58.6**).

- **Administration** – Double tax relief must normally be claimed (see **58.7**).

INTRODUCTION

58.1   Countries can tax their subjects on their worldwide income, and can tax non-residents on income arising from within their territory. An individual who has income arising in a foreign territory may therefore be subject to tax in that territory and also in the country in which he lives.

Relief is therefore generally available, either to exempt income that has already suffered tax elsewhere, or to give credit for that tax against the home country's tax. The UK tends to favour the latter approach over the exemption approach, although this is not now always the case, as will be seen later.

TYPES OF DOUBLE TAX RELIEF

58.2   Relief can be given as follows:

- under the terms of a tax treaty between the UK and the other country;

- in the absence of a treaty, unilateral relief can be used to eliminate or at least mitigate the effects of double taxation. Unilateral relief will give credit for the foreign tax up to the amount of UK tax on that income. Excess foreign tax is lost;

- alternatively, the foreign tax can be deducted from that income, which might be more beneficial where, for example, losses might be available to eliminate any UK tax on that income.

A tax treaty will generally provide a list of rules to decide on the residence of a person where he would otherwise be dual resident and whether an activity carried on in one country by a resident in the other country is sufficient to establish a taxable base, known as a permanent establishment, in that country. A treaty may reduce the rate of foreign withholding tax on dividends, interest, royalties and technical assistance fees.

Treaties generally have a 'non-discrimination clause', which provides that a resident of a contracting state is not to be taxed more harshly in the other state than a resident of that other state.

If one country gives a tax holiday to encourage particular enterprises to set up there, the treaty may allow relief for the tax that would have been suffered in the absence of the tax holiday. This is known as tax sparing relief.

Focus

There are common features to most tax treaties, as they are usually based on an OECD Model Agreement.

However, it is crucial to read the relevant tax treaty you are relying on, as there may be specific rules which can allow or restrict relief.

A treaty cannot impose a tax liability where one would not otherwise exist. Nor can domestic law override a treaty, but this does not stop governments from trying to do so from time to time.

The UK has an extensive network of tax treaties and these are the first port of call when establishing what reliefs are available. Details of current treaties can be obtained from the HMRC website (www.hmrc.gov.uk/taxtreaties/index.htm).

Relief is available only for foreign taxes that are calculated by reference to income or gains arising or accruing in that territory and not for taxes on capital or levied on turnover.

INCOME TAX

58.3   Prior to 6th April 2016 Individuals who received dividends from non-resident companies were treated as if the dividend came with a tax credit of 1/9 of the dividend which satisfied a basic rate taxpayer's liability as it would have for a UK dividend (*ITTOIA 2005, s 397A*). The tax credit was abolished from 6 April 2016.

If the dividend had a withholding tax levied, this might have been set off against any dividend higher or additional rate tax but would have been lost to a basic rate taxpayer for periods up to 5 April 2016 before the new rules for dividends start.

There are special rules for dealing with foreign tax suffered on profits that form the basis of assessment for more than one tax year such as the opening years of a new partnership, the so-called overlap profits (*TIOPA 2010, s 22*).

However, a word of caution as the following example shows, whether double tax relief is available may not always be an easy question to answer.

Example 58.1 – No relief available

Mr Anson was a member of a Delaware LLC which was treated for US tax purposes as a partnership and he was taxed in the US accordingly on his share of the profits.

However, for UK tax purposes the LLC was treated as 'opaque' and his income from it was effectively treated as a dividend and taxed accordingly in the UK. No double tax relief was available because the income was

---

held by the Upper-tier Tribunal to be from a different source. The Court of Appeal upheld the decision but, in a landmark ruling on 1 July 2015, the Supreme Court found that his share of profits did belong to him and allowed his claim to double tax relief because the LLC was not 'opaque'.

Example 58.1 is based on the case of *Anson v Commissioners for Her Majesty's Revenue and Customs* [2015] UKSC 44.

Focus

Be careful that the income in respect of which you are claiming double tax relief is from the same source.

Example 58.2 – Tax credit on foreign company dividend

Ms Buxton received a dividend of £25,000 in 2003/04 from a Guernsey company. She claimed relief for the 20% corporate tax that the company had suffered on its profits by grossing up the dividend received to £31,250 and claiming double tax relief on the underlying tax of £6,250.

This claim failed because relief is not available to an individual for underlying tax and it was not a withholding tax. At the time that she received the dividend, the legislation in force only allowed a dividend from a UK company to be treated as coming with a 1/9 credit, but her advisors argued that this was contrary to Article 56 of the European Community Treaty (freedom of movement of capital).

Unfortunately for her, the tribunal held that a proper claim had not been made within the time limit. The claim should have been quantified and made in her tax return which could have been altered by a supplementary claim if an error or mistake had been made (*TMA 1970, s 42(2), (9)*). The time limit for this is now four years after the end of the period of assessment to which it relates (*TMA 1970, s 43*). For 2008/09 and subsequent years, the legislation now provides for claims of a 1/9th credit from overseas dividends (*ITTOIA 2005, s 397A*) up to 5 April 2016.

Example 58.2 is based on the case of *Vanessa Buxton* [2012] UKFTT 506(TC).

CAPITAL GAINS TAX

58.4   Foreign tax charged in the country where the asset is located is allowable against the UK capital gains tax on its disposal.

Tax treaties may limit the scope of one of the countries to charge tax. Problems can arise where the gain is taxed on a different person in each of the jurisdictions and in these circumstances Statement of Practice SP6/88 can be of assistance. It helpfully points out that there is no requirement that the gain should arise at the same time and to the same person.

CORPORATION TAX

58.5   Dividends received by a company from foreign companies are generally exempt from corporation tax (*CTA 2009, Pt 9A*). For a small company, dividends from a company resident in a country which has a non-discrimination article will generally be exempt. Tax havens do not usually have such treaties, so dividends from them may not be exempt.

Where the recipient is a large company, distributions from its subsidiaries, from non-redeemable shares, and from portfolio holdings (less than 10% of the share capital) are generally exempt.

Where exceptionally the dividends are taxable, relief can be available for any withholding tax suffered together with underlying tax. Underlying tax is the tax suffered by the overseas company on the profits out of which the dividend was paid. Under most tax treaties the recipient has to hold 10% or more of the share capital to obtain relief for the underlying tax. Where there is no treaty the recipient or its parent company has to control at least 10% of the voting power in the overseas company before it can make a claim for unilateral relief (*TIOPA 2010, s 12*).

It is possible to elect for foreign dividends to be taxable, which will mean that relief can be obtained for withholding tax (*CTA 2009, s 931R*).

Focus

An individual recipient of a foreign dividend cannot benefit from the exemption for dividends from foreign companies, and he cannot usually claim treaty relief for underlying tax.

It may therefore be more tax-efficient for investments in foreign companies to be held in a UK company.

Profits from an overseas permanent establishment of a UK company are generally chargeable to tax in the territory of the permanent establishment and in the UK, subject to double tax relief. Such profits are not chargeable to corporation tax if an election is made (*CTA 2009, s 18A*). The election takes effect for the next and subsequent accounting periods, and once the next accounting period starts it is irrevocable. The relief also prevents losses from that permanent establishment being brought into account for UK tax purposes and is subject to an array of anti-avoidance rules.

INHERITANCE TAX

58.6   Treaty relief and unilateral relief are available for foreign tax suffered by reference to death or on gifts which is similar in nature to inheritance tax (*IHTA 1984, ss 158–159*).

HOW TO CLAIM DOUBLE TAX RELIEF

58.7   A claim is required for double tax relief for income tax, corporation tax and capital gains tax (*TIOPA 2010, s 6(6)*).

The claim must be made within four years following the end of the tax year in which the income is taxed (*TMA 1970, s 43*). However, where an adjustment subsequently becomes necessary to the amount of the foreign tax that is allowable, this can be made within six years from the time when all material determinations have been made (*TIOPA 2010, s 79*).

Where interest or royalties are payable abroad and there is an obligation to deduct income tax (*ITA 2007 ss 874, 906*) the amount of tax may be reduced or eliminated under the terms of a double tax treaty where a claim is made (see www.gov.uk/guidance/double-taxation-relief-for-companies).

Overseas lenders can register under the double taxation treaty passport (DTTP) scheme to simplify this process (see www.gov.uk/guidance/double-taxation-treaty-passport-scheme). A consultation was launched on 26 May 2016 to consider renewing and extending the scope of the DTTP scheme.

> **Focus**
>
> This claim process can be quite time consuming, so it is possible for a company to pay a royalty overseas deducting only the reduced rate of tax under the DTA without prior clearance (*ITA 2007, s 911*; see CTM35270).

Part 11
Financial Reporting

59

Financial reporting

SIGNPOSTS

- **General** – For tax purposes, profits normally have to be calculated using generally accepted accounting practice (GAAP), subject to any adjustment required or authorised by law (see **59.1**).

- **What accounting bases are GAAP?** – There are several bases which are accepted as being GAAP, and there are rules for dealing with adjustments that arise when changing from one accounting basis to another (see **59.2–59.3**).

- **Accruals basis** – The accruals basis is an accepted part of GAAP (see **59.4**).

- **Shareholder loans** – The introduction of FRS 102 changes the way in which interest free loans are accounted for, which may impact upon the way in which they are taxed (see **59.5**).

- **Bad debts, provisions, etc** – Provisions for bad and doubtful debts are made in respect of the impairment of trade debtors and so are a valuation matter. For other types of provision a liability must exist at the balance sheet date for them to be allowable (see **59.6–59.7**).

- **Work in progress** – There is specific guidance on when revenue should be recognised in respect of work-in-progress (see **59.8**).

- **Post-balance sheet events** – These may be 'adjusting events' or 'non-adjusting events' (see **59.9**).

- **Finance leases** – These provide a route for acquiring assets using borrowed money. Legal ownership remains with the lessor, but the assets are shown in the lessee's accounts to reflect the economic position (see **59.10**).

- **Research and development** – Such expenditure may be written off as incurred or capitalised. The tax treatment (capital or revenue) will not necessarily follow the accounting treatment (see **59.12**).

- **Pension contributions** – Whether made to a defined contribution or defined benefit scheme, these are only allowed for tax purposes when paid, although the accounting treatment will be different and adjustments will be required (see **59.15**).

- **Mergers and acquisitions** – Accounting for corporate acquisitions can be by acquisition or merger accounting. This does not have any particular tax implication, but can affect the ability to pay dividends out of pre-acquisition profits (see **59.17**).

- **Other matters** – Accounting standards exist for foreign currency (**59.11**), intangible assets (**59.13**), depreciation (**59.14**), deferred tax (**59.16**), government grants (**59.19**), VAT (**59.20**), transfers from current assets to fixed assets (**59.21**) and lease incentives (**59.22**). A 'compulsory common consolidated tax base' may be introduced in the future for companies operating in Europe (**59.18**).

FINANCIAL REPORTING

59.1   For income tax and corporation tax purposes, business profits have to be calculated using generally accepted accounting practice (GAAP), but this is subject to any adjustment required or authorised by law (*ITTOIA 2005, s 25* for income tax and *CTA 2009, s 46* for corporation tax).

There is a limited exception to this rule which allows barristers to draw up their accounts on a cash basis for the first seven years from starting their practice and there are special rules for Lloyds Underwriters. From 2013/14 onwards a new cash basis came into force for small businesses whose income is not more than the VAT registration threshold, currently £83,000. Barristers already using the cash basis can continue until the end of the seven-year period. The cash basis is dealt with in more detail in **Chapter 3** on self-employment (see **3.13**).

If accounts do not comply with GAAP or are not drawn up at all, then GAAP compliant accounts have to be prepared and used as the basis for taxation (*CTA 2009, s 599*). If in a group of companies one company prepares accounts under international accounting standards (IAS) and another company under UK GAAP and there are transactions between them that exploit the difference in bases, then both have to use UK GAAP (*CTA 2010, s 996*).

However, the fact that an amount is shown as income in a set of accounts does not determine whether it is taxable. In *Pertemps Recruitment Partnership Ltd v Revenue and Customs* [2010] UKFTT 218 (TC), the tribunal said:

'We note that [*CTA 2009, s 46*] applies for the purposes of *Sch D, Case I* to compute the amount of profits. However, the first step is to determine the nature of the receipt – does it fall within *Case I* in the first place? Only if it does, is [*s 46*] brought into action to determine the amount that is brought into account as profits.'

ACCOUNTING BASES

What bases are GAAP?

59.2   GAAP is defined as UK accounting practice that is intended to give a true and fair view and also accounts prepared in accordance with international accounting standards (*CTA 2010*, *s 1127* for corporation tax, and identically *ITA 2007*, *s 997* for income tax).

The following bases are generally accepted accounting practices:

(a)   *UK GAAP*

Accounts prepared under UK GAAP had to comply with accounting standards which came in a variety of forms from SSAPs to FRSs and UITFs.

However, for accounting periods that start on or after 1 January 2015, these have been replaced by FRS 102 for unlisted companies. FRS 102 is based on IFRS but essentially only differs from the previous UK GAAP in presentation in accounts, treatment of investment properties, financial instruments, business combinations, deferred tax, defined benefit pension schemes and accounting for associates and joint ventures.

(b)   *Financial Reporting Standard for Small and Micro-Entities*

For accounting periods starting on or after 1 January 2016 the FRSSE can no longer be used. Small companies can use FRS 102 Section 1A and micro-entities can choose between FRS 102 Section 1A or FRS 105. A micro-entity has to satisfy 2 of the following: turnover £632,000 or less, balance sheet total £316,000 or less, and not more than 10 employees. Companies that are members of groups may be ineligible to be treated as micro-entities but LLP's and partnerships with corporate partners can be so treated.

(c)   *International Financial Reporting Standards (IFRS)*

Companies whose securities are admitted to trading on a regulated market of any EU member state must produce their consolidated accounts using international accounting standards known as IAS (*Regulation EC 1606/2002*). For accounting periods that start on or after 1 January 2015, FRS 101 reduces the disclosure requirements for certain companies, such as subsidiaries of listed companies that are required to use IFRS.

Some accounting standards which are most often relevant for tax purposes are listed below, with cross-references to the commentary:

- FRS 102 Section 1A and FRS 105 (financial reporting standards for small and micro-entities);

- FRS 102, Section 10 (accounting policies, estimates and errors);

- FRS 102, Section 24 (accounting for government grants) (see **59.19**);

- FRS 102, Section 29 (accounting for VAT) (see **59.20**);

- FRS 102, Sections 13 (inventories) and 23 (revenue) (see **59.8**);

- FRS102, Section 32 (events after the end of the reporting period) (see **59.9**);

- FRS 102, Section 30 (foreign currency translation) (see **59.11**);

- FRS 102, Section 20 (accounting for leases and HP contracts) (see **59.10**);

- FRS 102, Section 28 (accounting for pension costs) (see **59.15**);

- FRS 102, Section 12 (other financial instruments issues) (see **Example 59.1**);

- FRS 102, Section 18 (intangible assets other than goodwill) (see **59.12–59.13**);

- FRS 102, Sections 19 (business combinations and goodwill) (see **59.13**);

- FRS 102, Section 11 shareholder loans on non-arm's length terms (see **59.5**);

- FRS 102, Section 21 (provisions, contingent liabilities and contingent assets) (see **59.7**);

- FRS 102, Sections 11 and 12 (accruals basis, bad debts, financial instruments) (see **59.4**, **59.5** and **59.6**);

- FRS 102, Sections 16 and 17 (transfers from current assets to fixed assets) (see **59.21**);

- FRS 102, Sections 20.15A and 20.25A (lessee accounting for reverse premiums and similar incentives) (see **59.22**);

- FRS 102, Section 2.6 (materiality).

HMRC's view on the relationship between accounting and tax is set out in their Business Income Manual at BIM31000.

For FRS 101 and 102, see www.gov.uk/government/publications/accounting-standards-the-uk-tax-implications-of-new-uk-gaap.

Example 59.1 – Non-GAAP compliant accounts

The case of *Greene King plc v HMRC* [2014] UKUT 178 (TCC) illustrates that if it is held that the accounts do not comply with GAAP, the tax outcome may be the opposite of what was intended.

The tax planning arrangements involved a loan from the parent company to a subsidiary (GKBR) followed by the assignment of the right to receive interest to another subsidiary (GKA) in exchange for the issue of preference shares.

The tribunal held that [FRS 102 Section 12] required the value of the loan to be reduced immediately after the assignment and then written up over the life of the loan with that write up being taxable. GKBR obtained tax deductions for the interest it paid and GKA was taxed on the receipt although it argued that most of it was not taxable because it was transferred to its share premium account.

The taxpayer's claim that this was unfair because it led to double taxation was dismissed because it had endeavoured to obtain a tax deduction with no corresponding tax on the interest receipt.

However, see the case of *GDF Suez Teesside Ltd* [2015] UKFTT 413 (TC) in which the GAAP compliant accounts were overridden because they did not fairly reflect profits arising on assignments of contingent assets as part of a tax avoidance scheme.

ADJUSTMENT INCOME

59.3   Where there is a change from one valid basis to another and the difference gives rise to a prior year adjustment (*ITTOIA 2005, s 227* for income tax and *CTA 2009, s 180* for corporation tax), the adjustment is taxed/ deductible as if it arose on the last day of the accounting period in which the new basis is adopted (*ITTOIA 2005, s 233* and *CTA 2009, s 181*). However, where it relates to trading stock or work in progress the adjustment is made in the period in which the relevant asset is realised or written off (*ITTOIA 2005, s 235* and *CTA 2009, s 184*).

On a change from an invalid basis to a valid basis, the invalid basis needs to be corrected in the year in which it first occurred and the following periods restated. If the adjustments are outside the time limits for amending the tax return then no tax can be reclaimed or collected, unless of course a discovery can be made by HMRC. This treatment applies to material errors but not to non-material errors or changes in estimates which are adjusted in the period in which they come to light or the estimate is changed.

For loan relationships there are different rules. In the case of non-basic financial instruments, these have to be accounted for under FRS 102, Section 12 at fair value. Where there is a change in accounting from the former UK GAAP to FRS 102, the difference between the closing value in the previous period and the opening value under FRS 102 is brought into account in full but spread over ten years (FRS 102, Section 12, *CTA 2009, ss 315–319* and *SI 2004/3271*).

ACCRUALS BASIS

59.4   Accounts are required to be prepared on an accruals basis (FRS 102, Section 2.36).

A summary of the accruals basis is given in the following quote taken from the case of *Craig v Revenue & Customs* [2012] UKFTT 90 decided in January 2012 by the First-tier Tribunal:

'50. The principle of generally accepted accounting practice with which we are concerned is the accruals basis of accounting. Mr Orrock [the HMRC reporting accountant]'s report records, and it was not challenged, that the accruals basis for accounting requires the non-cash effects of transactions and other events to be reflected, as far as possible, in the financial statements for the accounting period in which they occur, and not in the period in which any cash involved is received or paid.

51. There was some discussion in the evidence about trade creditors in contrast with accruals. According to Mr Orrock's evidence and report, which we accept, trade creditors are liabilities to pay for goods or services received or supplied which have been formally agreed with the supplier. Accruals are liabilities to pay for goods or services received or supplied which have not been paid, invoiced or formally agreed with the supplier.

52. Applying these principles to the Appellant means that any services received by him from WB [the Appellant's limited company] should be accounted for in accordance with the accruals concept. These services should be treated as expenses in the periods to which they relate and this should be, as far as possible, in the periods when the services were received. Furthermore, any services paid or invoiced in advance of them being provided should be treated as a pre-payment (in the balance sheet), if paid, and carried forward to the appropriate accounting period when they are provided.'

SHAREHOLDER LOANS

59.5   FRS 102, Section 11.13 requires interest free loans to be discounted by the interest forgone and the discount taken into account over the period of the loan such that by the repayment date the loan is shown as the full amount due – this has the potential to effect many shareholder loans. The accounting entries for this potentially gave rise to asymmetry in their tax treatment so that relief would have been available for the interest expense but that the corresponding credit, being treated as a capital contribution, might be exempt from tax. In such cases tax relief will not be available on the notional interest expense (*CTA 2009, s 446A* introduced by *Finance Act 2016* with effect from 1 April 2016).

HMRC issued some draft (although still useful) guidance on loans of this nature in October 2015 www.gov.uk/government/publications/corporation-tax-treatment-of-interest-free-loans-and-other-non-market-loans.

Loans that are repayable on demand or those issued on arm's length terms continue to be shown at the amount borrowed. Also where FRS 105 applies, Section 9 requires interest free loans whether repayable on demand or not to be shown as the amount borrowed.

Where under FRS 102, Section 11.13 loans to shareholders are shown at less than the amount lent, because for example they are interest free, the full amount is still taxed under CTA 2010, Section 455 (see **18.4** and www.gov.uk/government/publications/hmrc-directors-loan-accounts-toolkit-2013-to-2014).

BAD DEBTS

59.6   Under FRS 102, Section 11.14(a) trade debtors are required to be valued on an amortised cost basis. The value is written down for any impairment or uncollectibility and there are detailed rules for recognition and measurement of the impairment (Sections 11.21–11.26).

The tax relief for provisions for bad and doubtful debts for unincorporated entities is governed by *ITTOIA 2005, s 35*. This specifically states that relief can only be given for a debt that is bad or that is estimated to be bad. Thus general provisions would not be allowed.

PROVISIONS

59.7   A provision is a liability that is of uncertain timing or amount, to be settled by the transfer of economic benefits (FRS 102 Section 21). It follows that Section 21 has no application to bad debt provisions or stock provisions which are concerned with the valuation of the assets to which they relate and not to liabilities (BIM46510). The liability must exist at the balance sheet date for a provision to be made. Costs that need to be incurred to operate in the future but were not liabilities at the balance sheet date must not be provided for. It must be possible to make a reliable estimate of the liability. If no reliable estimate is possible it should be noted as a contingent liability but not provided for (FRS 102, 21.4 and 21.12).

The standard says that "An entity shall measure a provision at the best estimate of the amount required to settle the obligation at the reporting date. The best estimate is the amount an entity would rationally pay to settle the obligation at the end of the reporting period or to transfer it to a third party at that time" (FRS 102 21.7).

The standard does not apply to executory contracts, ie contracts where each side has performed its obligations to an equal extent or not at all, unless the contracts are onerous.

The standard allows provisions to be discounted to reflect the passage of time and to show the related movements as interest. However, as this 'interest' does not derive from loan relationships it is just a movement in the provision.

Future operating losses should not be recognised but present obligations under onerous contracts should be.

Provisions are allowable for tax purposes if they comply with FRS 102 Section 21, are not capital and are not specifically disallowed.

HMRC say that provisions must be estimated with sufficient accuracy to be allowable (BIM 46555), however, as we have seen above the standard uses the phrases 'best estimate' and 'reliable estimate'. The House of Lords in the case of case of *Owen v Southern Railway of Peru Ltd* HL 1956, 36 TC 602 used the phrases 'fair estimate' and 'reliable enough [for the purposes of adequately stating the profits]'. In that case a statutory provision for compensation payments to the employees when they ceased to be employed was disallowed because it had not been calculated with sufficient accuracy, but there was otherwise no rule of law that would have prevented its deduction. Because the compensation payments would not be made for 30 or 40 years the Lords held that the provision was a serious overprovision and should have been discounted to reflect this. This case was heard some years before FRS 102 section 21 and its predecessor FRS 12 applied, but on the same facts now the provision would probably not comply with Section 21 because it had not been discounted and so would still be disallowable.

A provision for rent payable on empty properties, if calculated accurately and discounted if appropriate, is allowable (*Herbert Smith v Honour* [1999] STC 173).

Reliable estimates of warranty provisions should similarly be allowable.

The tax treatment of provisions for future repairs of plant and machinery depends on whether the plant is owned or leased. FRS 102 does not permit a future repairs provision on owned assets whereas it does for leased assets where the lessee has an obligation to repair the asset.

WORK IN PROGRESS

59.8   FRS 102, Section 13 (inventories) deals with stock and work in progress but not construction contracts or the rendering of services which are dealt with in Section 23 (revenue). There is no practical difference between the old and new bases and the normal rule for valuing stock and work in progress is that it should be valued at the lower of cost or net realisable value. Uncompleted professional work in progress should be valued in accordance with FRS 102 Section 23.14.

Revenue associated with the rendering of services should only be brought into account when:

(a)   the amount of revenue can be measured reliably;

(b)   it is probable that the economic benefits associated with the transaction will flow to the entity;

(c)   the stage of completion of the transaction at the end of the reporting period can be measured reliably; and

(d)   the costs incurred for the transaction and the costs to complete the transaction can be measured reliably.

See also HMRC Manual at BIM 33165.

POST-BALANCE SHEET EVENTS

59.9   If at the balance sheet date a liability exists or is likely to exist as a result of a past event then the best estimate of this liability has to be provided for.

However, there may be events that occur after the balance sheet date which might shed light on conditions at the balance sheet date and these should be taken into account in estimating this liability. These are known as adjusting events. Non-adjusting events are those which relate to conditions which happened after the balance sheet date.

For example, a provision for building repairs after damage to a factory wall after the balance sheet date would be a non-adjusting event as would stock destroyed in a fire after the balance sheet date (FRS 102, Section 32).

FINANCE LEASES

59.10   Finance leases are used by a business to enable it to acquire equipment using borrowed money. The equipment is owned by the finance company, the lessor, but its economic ownership is with the business which uses it in its activities, the lessee. The lessee pays rent to the lessor and when the lease comes to an end the lessor sells the asset to a third party and most of the proceeds are given back to the lessee as a rebate of rentals. A finance lease differs from a hire purchase agreement which has an option for the lessee of the asset to acquire the asset at some future date. The existence of such an option would allow the lessee rather than the lessor to claim capital allowances (*CAA 2001, s 67*), and this would prevent it from being a long funding lease (*CAA 2001, s 70J(3)*) which is discussed below.

The accounting treatment under IAS 17 and FRS 102, Section 20 aims to reflect the economic reality. It treats the lessor as providing finance and the lessee as owning the asset by showing it as a fixed asset with a corresponding liability for the capital element of the future rental payments. However, the tax treatment does not follow the accounting treatment and there are special rules for equipment leases.

How finance leases are treated for tax depends on whether they are long funding leases, which essentially are leases that exist for more than five years or more than seven years in certain cases. Leases of more than five years but less than seven are not long funding leases if:

(a)   they are finance leases under GAAP; and

(b)   the residual value of the equipment is expected to be 5%, or less, of its market value at the beginning of the lease; and

(c)   the profile of the rentals does not increase or increases less than 10% from year 2 to the final year and the second year is not more than 10% higher than the first year. Variations because of changes in interest base rate are excluded (*CAA 2001, s 70I*).

The lessor in a long funding lease is only taxed on the interest that he earns over the period of the lease and the lessee is generally entitled to claim capital allowances on the capital element of the lease rentals. The lessee will obtain a tax deduction for the hire element of the lease rentals. In other types of leases that are not long funding leases, the lessor claims the capital allowances and the lessee obtains tax relief on the rental payments.

FOREIGN CURRENCY

59.11   IAS 21 and FRS 102, Section 30 govern the accounting treatment of foreign exchange. However, for corporation tax the basic rule is that the income and chargeable gains of a company must be calculated and expressed in sterling (*CTA 2010, s 5*).

Where accounts are prepared in a foreign currency and the functional currency is sterling, for example because they are being consolidated with an overseas parent, then it is required to calculate its profits or losses in sterling as if the accounts had been prepared in sterling (*CTA 2010, s 6*).

However, where the functional currency is not sterling and the accounts are prepared in foreign currency then the profits or losses are calculated in the foreign currency and then converted to sterling (*CTA 2010, ss 7, 8*) using the average rate for the year or the spot rate for single transactions (*CTA 2010, s 11*). In such cases, losses which are being carried forward or back are not converted into sterling for the accounting period in which they arise.

Exchange gains and losses can only arise if the assets and liabilities computed for tax purposes are in a different currency from that used to prepare the accounts.

RESEARCH AND DEVELOPMENT

59.12   The accounting treatment of research and development (R&D) is governed by FRS 102, Section 18.

The general rule is that R&D expenditure incurred on pure and applied research is written off as incurred because it is part of a company's continuing operations required to maintain its competitive position and no one particular period benefits over another period.

R&D that relates to product development may be, but does not have to be, capitalised and written off as part of the cost of the final product. For the capitalisation treatment it has to relate to a clearly defined project whose outcome is technically feasible, commercially viable and there must be adequate resources to complete the project.

However, capitalising R&D in the accounts does not establish that it is capital for tax purposes so that, as a claim for R&D tax relief can only be made for revenue expenditure, the accounting treatment is not relevant. HMRC make the following comment in their corporate intangibles research and development manual (at CIRD81700):

'This is particularly in point when R&D tax relief is claimed by SMEs in the pre-trading stage, or prior to a development in the trade. For that reason, while the principles of capital expenditure still need to be considered, we would not normally wish HMRC officers to pursue arguments in grey areas where the facts do not clearly support a characterisation of expenditure as capital.'

In such cases, R&D expenditure is allowable when it is incurred not when it is written off in the accounts. But note that the definition of R&D for tax purposes is not the same as for accounting purposes (see **25.8**).

INTANGIBLE ASSETS

59.13   The accounts treatment of intangible assets is governed by FRS 102, Sections 18 and 19. It claims that 'its objective is to ensure that purchased goodwill and intangible assets are charged in the profit and loss account in the periods in which they are depleted.'

Purchased goodwill, but not internally generated goodwill, has to be capitalised and written off through the profit and loss account usually over a period of up to 20 years and subject to impairment reviews. Under FRS 102, if a reliable estimate of the assets' life cannot be made they must be written off over not more than five years. Other internally generated intangible assets can be capitalised if they have a market value that can be readily ascertained.

For details of the tax treatment of goodwill see **25.7**.

DEPRECIATION

59.14   Depreciation on fixed assets charged in the profit and loss account is not allowable in computing the taxable profits (*CTA 2009, s 53*). This also applies to the loss (or profit) on sale of fixed assets which represents additional (a reduction in) depreciation. However, FRS 102, Section 13.8 requires that the costs of producing stock should include production overheads and this includes the depreciation of assets used in production. This element of the depreciation is charged to the profit and loss account in the periods when the stock is sold and it is only this part that is added back. This treatment follows the House of Lords decision in the 2007 cases of *HMRC v William Grant & Sons Distillers Ltd* HL 2007, 78 TC 442 and *Small (HMIT) v Mars UK Ltd* HL 2007, 78 TC 442, and is a departure from HMRC's previous practice.

PENSIONS

59.15   FRS 102, Section 28 deals with the accounts treatment of retirement benefits. There are different accounting rules for defined contribution schemes and for defined benefit schemes. Defined contribution schemes have fixed regular contributions and the employer has no further liability to fund the scheme. In contrast, defined benefit schemes provide benefits which are not directly related to the assets in the scheme.

However, in both cases it is only the amounts paid in the period that are allowable for tax purposes. This assumes that the payments are wholly and exclusively incurred for the purposes of earning profits in the trade and do not need to be spread and that the schemes are registered schemes (see **19.8** for details on the spreading provisions). It is assumed in what follows that the payment is allowable and does not need to be spread.

For defined contribution schemes, the cost shown in the accounts is equal to the contributions payable for the period and so the only adjustment necessary to calculate the taxable profit is to substitute the amount paid.

For defined benefit schemes, the rules are complicated. The fair value of the scheme assets and the actuarial value of the scheme liabilities are compared and, after taking into account deferred tax, the resultant net pension asset or liability is shown on the balance sheet. The movement during the year is split between employee costs, a theoretical interest cost or interest income, and an actuarial gain or loss. The employee expense and interest are shown in the profit and loss account and the actuarial gain or loss net of deferred tax is shown in the statement of comprehensive income. For accounts prepared under IAS this is the statement of recognised income and expense (known as the SORIE). None of these items, including the interest (which is not real interest as the loan is only in the minds of the standard setters) are allowable for tax and must be eliminated in the tax computation. There may be contributions not yet paid over to the scheme in creditors in the balance sheet. Where these relate to employer contributions they will need to be taken into account in determining the amounts actually paid.

DEFERRED TAX

59.16 The objective of deferred tax is to even out timing differences arising from items being allowed or charged to tax in different periods from those in which they are recorded in the accounts. It is covered in FRS 102 Section 29 and confusingly headed Income Tax.

The following are common examples of timing differences. Tax relief for machinery or plant is given by the capital allowance system but machinery or plant is written down in the accounts annually by a depreciation charge. A provision for future losses may not become tax allowable until the losses materialise and the provision is utilised. Actual losses that are being carried forward from an earlier period may be utilised in a later period. A provision for employer payments into a registered pension scheme will not be allowable until it is paid. A bonus accrued in the accounts but not paid within nine months of the year end will not be allowed until the period in which it is paid.

The applicable rate of tax for calculating the deferred tax liability, or asset, is that which has been enacted or substantially enacted. For example, if the balance sheet date falls after the final reading of a Finance Bill in the House of Commons but before the Bill becomes an Act then the rates proposed in the Bill are used (see FRS 102, Appendix 1: Glossary).

Deferred tax assets may be recognised to the extent that they are more likely than not to be recovered. Deferred tax was not previously allowed to be provided on the revaluation of an asset which was not being sold or on the roll-over of a gain into another asset. However, under FRS 102 there is no such prohibition and deferred tax is required to be provided by Section 29.16 on investment properties that are measured at fair value under FRS 102, Section 16. This includes properties let to other group entities. The movements in fair value are not of course taxable until the assets are sold or otherwise disposed of. Deferred tax in not allowed to be provided under FRS 105.

ACQUISITION AND MERGER ACCOUNTING

59.17   Where one company acquires another, the accounting treatment depends upon whether acquisition accounting or merger accounting is used. Merger accounting can only be used when:

- the acquiring company acquires at least 90% of the target company for the issue of shares to the members of the target company;

- the acquiring company can also pay cash but this must not be more than 10% of the nominal value of the shares it issued for the target company;

- adoption of the merger method of accounting accords with FRS 102 Section 19.27.

(*Small Companies and Groups (Accounts and Directors' Reports) Regulations 2008, SI 2008/409, Sch 6, para 10* and the *Large and Medium Companies and Groups (Accounts and Reports) Regulations 2008, SI 2008/410, Sch 6, para 10*)

Acquisition accounting requires that:

- the identifiable assets and liabilities of the undertaking acquired must be included in the consolidated balance sheet at their fair value as at the date of acquisition;

- the income and expenditure of the undertaking acquired must be brought into the group accounts only as from the date of the acquisition;

- there must be set off against the acquisition cost of the interest in the shares of the undertaking, the interest of the parent company in the adjusted capital and reserves of the undertaking acquired;

- the resulting amount if positive must be treated as goodwill, and if negative as a negative consolidation difference.

(*Small Companies and Groups (Accounts and Directors' Reports) Regulations 2008, SI 2008/409, Sch 6, para 9* and the *Large and Medium Companies and Groups (Accounts and Reports) Regulations 2008, SI 2008/410, Sch 6, para 9*)

Merger accounting requires that:

- the assets and liabilities of the undertaking acquired must be brought into the group accounts at the figures at which they stand in the undertaking's accounts;

- the income and expenditure of the undertaking acquired must be included in the group accounts for the entire financial year, including the period before the acquisition;

- there must be set off against the aggregate of:

  o the appropriate amount in respect of qualifying shares issued by the parent company in consideration for the acquisition of shares in the undertaking acquired, and

  o the fair value of any other consideration for the acquisition of shares in the undertaking acquired, determined as at the date when those shares were acquired,

  the nominal value of the issued share capital of the undertaking acquired;

- the resulting amount must be shown as an adjustment to the consolidated reserves.

(*Small Companies and Groups (Accounts and Directors' Reports) Regulations 2008, SI 2008/409, Sch 6, para 11* and the *Large and Medium Companies and Groups (Accounts and Reports) Regulations 2008, SI 2008/410, Sch 6, para 11*)

Shares in a limited company must each have a fixed nominal value (*CA 2006, s 542*). If a company issues shares for more than par it is required to transfer the difference to a share premium account (*CA 2006, s 610*).

However, if the acquirer acquires shares in the target in exchange for consideration that includes a new issue of equity shares and the acquirer owns at least 90% of each class of the target company's equity share capital, then merger relief will apply and a share premium does not need to be recognised in respect of those consideration shares (*CA 2006, s 612*).

Similarly a wholly owned subsidiary company issuing shares to its parent does not need to recognise any premium under group reconstruction relief (*CA 2006, s 611*).

Dividends may be paid up from a subsidiary to its parent company out of its profits, including pre acquisition profits, in the normal way. Whether the parent company can pay them on to its shareholders will depend on whether it has to write down the carrying value of its subsidiary to reflect any reduction in its market value caused by the payment of the dividends and thereby reduce its distributable reserves.

If merger accounting and merger relief apply, the parent company's balance sheet will show the nominal value of the new shares issued and the carrying value of the subsidiary at the same amount. Consequently the payment of a dividend out of pre-acquisition profits should not affect the ability of the parent company to pay the dividend on to its shareholders.

However, if acquisition accounting has to be used there may well be a restriction on what can be paid out.

EUROPEAN COMPULSORY COMMON CONSOLIDATED CORPORATE TAX BASE

59.18 On 19 April 2012, the European Parliament voted in favour of a compulsory common consolidated tax base (CCCTB) for companies operating in Europe. Marianne Thyssen MEP said:

'This harmonised system for calculating the tax base makes it possible for companies to consolidate the results of their individual branches, which allows them to compensate for any losses a group member might have. This makes it easier for companies to have and keep branches in different Member States and it reduces red tape. In addition, the system ensures that economic and social aspects are more important than purely fiscal reasons when companies choose their locations.'

It would apply only to those countries that agreed to adopt CCCTB. For the first five years, it would apply to European cooperative societies, and then to large companies. Small and medium-sized enterprises (SMEs) would have the option to use the CCCTB.

There would be a single set of rules for calculating taxable profits but it would not impose a common tax rate.

A consultation on the proposed directive ended on 8 January 2016 although the result of the EU-referendum will obviously bring into question the impact of this upon the UK.

FRS 102, SECTION 24 ACCOUNTING FOR GOVERNMENT GRANTS

59.19   Government grants are given to support capital projects or to plug a hole in income. Grants that are made as a contribution towards specific fixed assets should be recognised over the useful economic lives of the assets to which they relate. Income grants should be recognised in the profit and loss account to match them with the expenditure. Where they are for immediate financial support or to cover costs previously incurred they should be recognised in the profit and loss account in the period in which they are receivable. However, recognition should not be before the conditions for eligibility for the grant are satisfied.

Grants to buy assets are taken into account in reducing the capital allowances on the assets. Income grants are taxable in the same way as the income to which they relate is taxed.

For further information on the tax treatment of grants see HMRC's Business Income Manual (BIM40451–40475).

FRS 102, SECTION 29 ACCOUNTING FOR VAT

59.20   This standard requires that VAT should not be included in income or expenditure unless the VAT is irrecoverable. This is because the business is a collector of the tax where it is fully recoverable. Where it is irrecoverable, it should be included in the cost of the items reported in the financial statements. The tax treatment follows the accounting treatment.

FRS 102, SECTIONS 16 & 17 TRANSFERS FROM CURRENT ASSETS TO FIXED ASSETS

59.21   The accounting treatment for an asset that is transferred from current assets to fixed assets or investment properties is dealt with under Sections 16 and 17 of FRS 102. Section 16 requires such assets to be restated at their fair value if this can be measured reliably but if not then cost is used and Section 17 applies.

For investment properties dealt with under Section 16 any increase in value is credited to the profit and loss account *(FRS 102, Section 16.7)*.

For investment properties dealt with under Section 17 revaluations are dealt with in other comprehensive income unless it reverses a revaluation decrease recognised previously in the profit and loss account *(FRS 102 Section17.15E)*.

This differs from the previous standard which required the lower of cost and net realisable value to be used.

The tax treatment of such a transfer follows the accounting treatment (*TCGA 1992, s 161(2)*). However, transfers from fixed assets to trading stock have to be done at market value unless an election is made to give a no gain no loss disposal (*TCGA 1992, s 161 (1), (3)*).

FRS 102, SECTIONS 20.15A AND 20.25A OPERATING LEASE INCENTIVES

59.22   The benefits of lease incentives should be recognised over the period of the lease or for the period up to the next rent review on a straight line basis unless another systematic basis is more representative of the timing of the benefit. Benefits include reverse premiums to encourage a prospective tenant to enter into a lease and fitting out costs where these do not increase the property's value as they are specific to the lessee's business. Where expenditure that is being reimbursed enhances the value of the property, that is not an inducement to enter into the lease and should not be treated as an incentive. The renewal of the lifts in a building for example would not be an incentive if reimbursed.

The tax treatment of the reverse premium in the hands of the tenant follows the accounting treatment, subject to an anti-avoidance provision, if the payment or benefit is paid or provided by the landlord, or someone connected with him, as an inducement for the tenant, or someone connected with him, entering into a lease or interest in land (*CTA 2009, s 96* or *ITTOIA 2005, s 99*). The payer of the reverse premium will obtain tax relief, if at all, under general principles. For a property developer it will be an expense of his trade but for a landlord the payment may be capital for which no relief will be available.

However, where the parties are connected and the arrangements are not at arm's length, the whole of the reverse premium is brought into account for tax purposes in the period in which the transaction is entered into or, where the transaction is for the purposes of a trade which has not yet started, in the period when the trade starts (*CTA 2009, s 99* or *ITTOIA 2005, s 102*).

> **Example 59.2 – Reverse premium**
>
> A property development company is a member of a group of companies and grants a 99-year lease to a group trading company. It also pays the trading company a reverse premium of £1 million. The trading company spreads the reverse premium over the period of the lease in its accounts and the payer writes off the payment in the year of payment. The property developer

obtains an immediate tax deduction for the £1 million but because this is not an arm's length arrangement the lessee has to bring into its corporation tax computation the full amount of the reverse premium in the accounting period in which it was made instead of spreading the receipt over 99 years at just over £10,000 per annum.

A reverse premium that is a contribution to fitting out costs that qualify for capital allowances in the tenant's hands and so reduces his qualifying expenditure is not taxed as a reverse premium (*CAA 2001, s 532* and *CTA 2009, s 97* or *ITTOIA 2005, s 100*).

Index

[all references are to paragraph number]

933